A Writer's Reader

A WRITER'S READER

SIXTH EDITION

Donald Hall

D. L. Emblen
Santa Rosa Junior College

HarperCollins*Publishers*

Sponsoring Editor: Patricia Rossi
Project Editor: Shuli Traub
Design and Cover Coordinator: Mary Archondes
Cover Design: CIRCA 86
Cover Art: Helen Frankenthaler. *Flood*. 1967. Synthetic polymer on canvas.
124 × 140 inches (315 cm × 355.6 cm). Collection of Whitney Museum of
American Art. Purchase, with funds from the Friends of Whitney Museum
of American Art. 68.12
Director of Production: Jeanie Berke
Production Administrator: Beth Maglione
Compositor: TCSystems
Printer/Binder: The Maple-Vail Book Manufacturing Group
Cover Printer: New England Book Components, Inc.

A WRITER'S READER, Sixth Edition
Copyright © 1991 by HarperCollins Publishers Inc.

ISBN   0–673–52120–6 (student edition)
ISBN   0–673–49992–8 (teacher edition)

Library of Congress Cataloging-in-Publication Data

A Writer's reader / [edited by] Donald Hall, D. L. Emblen.—6th ed.
    p.   cm.
    ISBN 0–673–52120–6
    1. College readers. 2. English language—Rhetoric. I. Hall,
Donald, 1928–   . II. Emblen, D. L. (Donald Lewis), 1918–   .
PE1417.W67   1990
808'.0427—dc20   90–42267
                                                      CIP

92 93 9 8 7 6 5 4 3

For William R. Booth

Contents

Preface

Reading well precedes writing well. Of all the ancestors claimed by a fine piece of prose, the most important is the prose from which the writer learned his craft. Writers learn craft, not by memorizing rules about restrictive clauses, but by striving to equal a standard formed from reading.

A composition course, then, must be two courses: one in reading, another in writing. If students lack practice in writing, they are usually unpracticed readers as well. Most students lack quality of reading as well as quantity; and if we assert that good models help us, we admit that bad models hurt us. People who read bad prose twelve hours a week—newspapers, popular fiction, textbooks—are as ill served as people who read nothing at all. Surely most textbooks, from freshman handbooks through the text for Psych 101, encourage the illusion that words merely stand in for ideas, or carry information on their backs—that words exist for the convenience of thinking much as turnpikes exist for the sake of automobiles.

This barbarism underlies the vogue of speed reading, which urges us to scan lines for comprehension, ignoring syntax and metaphor, ignoring image and feeling and sound. If we are to grow and to learn—and surely if we are to write well—we must learn to read slowly and intimately, and to read good writing. We must learn to read actively, even aggressively, without the passivity derived from watching television. The active reader questions as he reads, subjects each author's ideas to skeptical scrutiny, and engages the writer in dialogue as part of the reading process.

For language embodies the human psyche. Learning to read—that privilege so recently extended to the ancestors of most of us—allows us to enter human history. In books we perceive the gesture, the pulse, the heartbeat, the pallor, the eye movement, the pitch, and the tone of people who lived before us, or who live now in other places, in other skins, in other habits, customs, beliefs, and ideas.

Language *embodies* the human psyche, which includes ideas and the feelings that properly accompany ideas. There is no sleight-of-mind by which the idea may be separated from its body and remain alive. The body of good writing is rhythm and image, metaphor and syntax, order of phrase and order of paragraph.

A NOTE TO LATER EDITIONS

Many teachers have helped us prepare the many editions of *A Writer's Reader*—in letters, in conversations at colleges all over the country, in responses to the publisher's survey of users. We thank more people than we can list.

We have added considerable material, and we are pleased with the result. We believe that we have made a representative sampling of good prose. We like some pieces more than others, heaven knows, but we believe that all of them provide something to learn from. We have included a wide variety of prose, mostly contemporary but also historical. We hope that young Americans will attach themselves to the body of our history by immersion in its significant utterances.

We have numbered paragraphs for ease of reference. Although *A Writer's Reader* is a collection of essays, we have again violated coherence by including fiction, feeling that the contrast afforded by a few short stories among the essays was useful and refreshing. We have also included several poems, for the same reason. Perhaps we should make an argument for including poems—but let us just say that we enjoy them, and we hope you do too. To satisfy students' curiosity, we have included headnotes to the poems; but we have stopped short of suggesting questions after them, lest we seem to surround a landscape garden with a hundred-foot-high concrete wall.

We have chosen to arrange our essays, stories, and poems alphabetically by author. This arrangement makes for random juxtaposition, irrational sequence, and no sense at all—which is why we chose it. We expect no one to teach these pieces in alphabetical order. We expect teachers to find their own order—which they would do whatever order we attempted to impose. In our first edition we struggled to make a stylistic organization, listing some essays as examples of "Sentences," others as examples of "Paragraphs." For the editors themselves, a year after deciding on our organization, it was no longer clear why essay X was to be studied for its sentences, essay Y for its paragraphs. With a rhetorical organization, one runs into another sort of problem. Although an essay may contain Division, or Process Analysis, or an example of Example, the same essay is likely to use three or four other patterns as well. No piece of real prose is ever so pure as our systems of classification. Thematic organizations, which have their attractions, have similar flaws; is E. B. White's theme in "Once More to the Lake" Mortality? Aging? Youth and Age? or, How I Spent My Summer Vacation?

Our arrangement is more arbitrary than an arrangement by style or rhetoric or theme, and presents itself only to be ignored. At the same time, there are dozens of ways in which these essays (and poems and stories) can be used together. Our Instructor's Manual suggests several combinations. Our Rhetorical Index, printed as an appendix to the text itself, lists single-paragraph examples of rhetorical patterns as well as longer units. We hope that students will find the Rhetorical Index useful. Freshmen who return to their rooms from class, set to write a paper using Comparison and Contrast, sometimes find themselves in need of a concrete example of the assigned pattern to imitate. We have also added a Thematic Index.

Thus, we have tried to supply some useful maps to go with our arbitrary arrangement. Following suggestions from several teachers, we have chosen to represent a few authors by small clusters of their work. We have expanded our representation of writing by scientists. In response to many suggestions, we have looked for short, complete essays in exposition and argument on a variety of topics.

If you miss essays or authors that we eliminated in this edition, please let us know. If there are authors we overlook, whom you would recommend, we solicit your help. Although we intend to remain alert to good prose and to the needs of the classroom, we need help from the outside.

ACKNOWLEDGMENTS

We thank the following users of the first, second, third, fourth, and fifth editions for their helpful comments: Louise Ackley, Maureen Andrews, Tony Ardizzone, Jo Ann Asbury, Ann Avery, Tom Barnwell, Conrad S. Bayley, Jane Berk, Meredith Berman, Dennis Berthold, Barbara Blaha, C. Bogarad, Linda Schafer Bulinski, Charles E. Bolton, Charles Bressler, Patrick Broderick, Otis Bronson, Laurel Broughton, Ingrid Brunner, Ed Buckley, Linda Bulinski, Sandra Burns, Jon Burton, Ann Cameron, Suzanne Carlson, Marti Carpenter, Richard Cloyed, Edythe Colello, Randy Conine, Steven Connelly, Roger Conner, Rebecca Coogan, Charles L. Cornwell, Valecia Crisafulli, Garber Davidson, Virginia de Araujo, Loretta Denner, Salli and Robert Duxbury, Ida Egli, Cirre Emblen, Lee Engdahl, Elizabeth Failla, Ralph Farve, Gala Fitzgerald, Frances B. Foreman, Susan Forrest, David S. Gadziola, Peggy Gledhill, Ronald Gurney, Barbara Hamilton, Bill Harby, Walter Harrison, Carol T. Hayes, Peter Heitkamp, Allan Hirsh, Samuel G. Hornsby, Jr., Nancy Hunt, John Huntington, C. S. Joyce, Donald Kansch, Gregory Keeler, Jeff Kluewer, Deborah Lambert, John Larner, Karen LeFerre, Kennedy P. Leisch, Richard H. Lerner, Opal A. Lovett, Neillie McCrory, Sherry McGuire, Andrew Makarushka, Steven J. Masello, Richard Maxwell, Deanne Milan, Molly Moore-Kehler, Harriet Napierkowski, Wayne Neel, Jean O'Donnell, Barbara Olive, Stephen O'Neil, Patrick Pacheco, Beverly Palmer, John V. Pastoor, Ray Peterson, Muriel Rada, Martha Rainbolt, Shari Rambo, Dennison G. Rice, James Rosen, Harriet Susskind Rosenblum, Robert Schwegler, Terry Shelton, Marvin and Helen Sherak, James Shokoff, Donald K. Skiles, Thomas Skmetzo, Marilyn Smith, Arnold Solkov, Andrew Solomon, Richard Speakes, David A. Spurr, Helen Stauffer, Art Suchoki, Bernard Sugarman, Kathleen Sullivan, Ron Taylor, Jane Bamblin Thomas, Richard Tubbs, E. Guy Turcotte, Darlene Unrue, Peter Valenti, Sara Varhus, Craig Watson, Richard Webster, Joyce Welch, Dorothy Wells, Joseph F. Whelan, Roberta White, Shirley and Russell White, Edith Wiard, Richard A. Widmayer, Gary Williams, Suzanne Wilson, George Wymer, B. Yu, and Robert Lee Zimmerman.

Donald Hall
D. L. Emblen

*Henry Adams (1838–1918) entertained notions of a political
career, in keeping with family traditions, but never ran for
office. For a time, he taught history at Harvard and edited the*
North American Review. *He wrote political journalism and
essays on geology, economics, and history; he wrote two novels
that he published anonymously. In middle life he undertook and
completed the massive* History of the United States During the
Administrations of Jefferson and Madison, *recently reissued in
two volumes by the Library of America. Later he wrote the
books by which he is most remembered,* Mont St. Michel and
Chartres *(1904) and his autobiography—written in the third
person and called* The Education of Henry Adams *(1907)—from
which we take this fragment of reminiscence.*

*Hundreds of American writers have recollected visits to
grandfather's house; none other was grandson to one president
and great-grandson to another. Adams's contrasts of style—
eighteenth century with nineteenth, Boston with the small town
of Quincy, the Brooks grandfather with the Adams grandfather
—culminate in an anecdote that illuminates the fundamental
contrast of private and public.*

1

HENRY ADAMS
Winter and Summer

Boys are wild animals, rich in the treasures of sense, but the New
England boy had a wider range of emotions than boys of more equable
climates. He felt his nature crudely, as it was meant. To the boy Henry
Adams, summer was drunken. Among senses, smell was the strongest—smell of hot pine-woods and sweet-fern in the scorching summer
noon; of new-mown hay; of ploughed earth; of box hedges; of peaches,
lilacs, syringas; of stables, barns, cow-yards; of salt water and low tide
on the marshes; nothing came amiss. Next to smell came taste, and the
children knew the taste of everything they saw or touched, from penny-
royal and flagroot to the shell of a pignut and the letters of a spelling
book—the taste of A-B, AB, suddenly revived on the boy's tongue sixty

years afterwards. Light, line, and color as sensual pleasures, came later and were as crude as the rest. The New England light is glare, and the atmosphere harshens color. The boy was a full man before he ever knew what was meant by atmosphere; his idea of pleasure in light was the blaze of a New England sun. His idea of color was a peony, with the dew of early morning on its petals. The intense blue of the sea, as he saw it a mile or two away, from the Quincy hills; the cumuli in a June afternoon sky; the strong reds and greens and purples of colored prints and children's picture-books, as the American colors then ran; these were ideals. The opposites or antipathies, were the cold grays of November evenings, and the thick, muddy thaws of Boston winter. With such standards, the Bostonian could not but develop a double nature. Life was a double thing. After a January blizzard, the boy who could look with pleasure into the violent snow-glare of the cold white sunshine, with its intense light and shade, scarcely knew what was meant by tone. He could reach it only by education.

2   Winter and summer, then, were two hostile lives, and bred two separate natures. Winter was always the effort to live; summer was tropical license. Whether the children rolled in the grass, or waded in the brook, or swam in the salt ocean, or sailed in the bay, or fished for smelts in the creeks, or netted minnows in the salt-marshes, or took to the pine-woods and the granite quarries, or chased muskrats and hunted snapping-turtles in the swamps, or mushrooms or nuts on the autumn hills, summer and country were always sensual living, while winter was always compulsory learning. Summer was the multiplicity of nature; winter was school.

3   The bearing of the two seasons on the education of Henry Adams was no fancy; it was the most decisive force he ever knew; it ran through life, and made the division between its perplexing, warring, irreconcilable problems, irreducible opposites, with growing emphasis to the last year of study. From earliest childhood the boy was accustomed to feel that, for him, life was double. Winter and summer, town and country, law and liberty, were hostile, and the man who pretended they were not, was in his eyes a schoolmaster—that is, a man employed to tell lies to little boys. Though Quincy was but two hours' walk from Beacon Hill, it belonged in a different world. For two hundred years, every Adams, from father to son, had lived within sight of State Street, and sometimes had lived in it, yet none had ever taken kindly to the town, or been taken kindly by it. The boy inherited his double nature. He knew as yet nothing about his great-grandfather, who had died a dozen years before his own birth: he took for granted that any great-

grandfather of his must have always been good, and his enemies wicked; but he divined his great-grandfather's character from his own. Never for a moment did he connect the two ideas of Boston and John Adams; they were separate and antagonistic; the idea of John Adams went with Quincy. He knew his grandfather John Quincy Adams only as an old man of seventy-five or eighty who was friendly and gentle with him, but except that he heard his grandfather always called "the President," and his grandmother "the Madam," he had no reason to suppose that his Adams grandfather differed in character from his Brooks grandfather who was equally kind and benevolent. He liked the Adams side best, but for no other reason than that it reminded him of the country, the summer, and the absence of restraint. Yet he felt also that Quincy was in a way inferior to Boston, and that socially Boston looked down on Quincy. The reason was clear enough even to a five-year-old child. Quincy had no Boston style. Little enough style had either; a simpler manner of life and thought could hardly exist, short of cave-dwelling. The flint-and-steel with which his grandfather Adams used to light his own fires in the early morning was still on the mantelpiece of his study. The idea of a livery or even a dress for servants, or of an evening toilette, was next to blasphemy. Bathrooms, water-supplies, lighting, heating, and the whole array of domestic comforts, were unknown at Quincy. Boston had already a bathroom, a water-supply, a furnace, and gas. The superiority of Boston was evident, but a child liked it no better for that.

The magnificence of his grandfather Brooks's house in Pearl Street 4 or South Street has long ago disappeared, but perhaps his country house at Medford may still remain to show what impressed the mind of a boy in 1845 with the idea of city splendor. The President's place at Quincy was the larger and older and far the more interesting of the two; but a boy felt at once its inferiority in fashion. It showed plainly enough its want of wealth. It smacked of colonial age, but not of Boston style or plush curtains. To the end of his life he never quite overcame the prejudice thus drawn in with his childish breath. He never could compel himself to care for nineteenth-century style. He was never able to adopt it, any more than his father or grandfather or great-grandfather had done. Not that he felt it as particularly hostile, for he reconciled himself to much that was worse; but because, for some remote reason, he was born an eighteenth-century child. The old house at Quincy was eighteenth-century. What style it had was in its Queen Anne mahogany panels and its Louis Seize chairs and sofas. The panels belonged to an old colonial vassal who built the house; the furniture had been brought back from Paris in 1789 or 1801 or 1817, along with porcelain and books and much else of old diplomatic remnants: and neither of the two eighteenth-century styles—neither English Queen Anne nor French Louis Seize—was comfortable for a boy, or for anyone else. The dark mahogany had been painted white to suit daily life in the winter gloom. Nothing seemed to favor, for a child's objects, the older forms. On the contrary, most boys, as well as grown-up people, preferred the new, with good reason, and the child felt himself distinctly at a disadvantage for the taste.

5   Nor had personal preference any share in his bias. The Brooks grandfather was as amiable and as sympathetic as the Adams grandfather. Both were born in 1767, and both died in 1848. Both were kind to children, and both belonged rather to the eighteenth than to the nineteenth centuries. The child knew no difference between them except that one was associated with winter and the other with summer; one with Boston, the other with Quincy. Even with Medford, the association was hardly easier. Once as a very young boy he was taken to pass a few days with his grandfather Brooks under charge of his aunt, but became so violently homesick that within twenty-four hours he was brought back in disgrace. Yet he could not remember ever being seriously homesick again.

6   The attachment to Quincy was not altogether sentimental or wholly sympathetic. Quincy was not a bed of thornless roses. Even there the curse of Cain set its mark. There as elsewhere a cruel universe combined to crush a child. As though three or four vigorous brothers and sisters, with the best will, were not enough to crush any child, everyone else conspired towards an education which he hated. From cradle to grave this problem of running order through chaos, direction through space, discipline through freedom, unity through multiplicity, has always been, and must always be, the task of education, as it is the moral of religion, philosophy, science, art, politics, and economy: but a boy's will is his life, and he dies when it is broken, as the colt dies in harness, taking a new nature in becoming tame. Rarely has the boy felt kindly towards his tamers. Between him and his master has always been war. Henry Adams never knew a boy of his generation to like a master, and the task of remaining on friendly terms with one's own family, in such a relation, was never easy.

7   All the more singular it seemed afterwards to him that his first serious contact with the President should have been a struggle of will, in which the old man almost necessarily defeated the boy, but instead of leaving, as usual in such defeats, a lifelong sting, left rather an impression of as fair treatment as could be expected from a natural enemy. The

boy met seldom with such restraint. He could not have been much more than six years old at the time—seven at the utmost—and his mother had taken him to Quincy for a long stay with the President during the summer. What became of the rest of the family he quite forgot; but he distinctly remembered standing at the house door one summer morning in a passionate outburst of rebellion against going to school. Naturally his mother was the immediate victim of his rage; that is what mothers are for, and boys also; but in this case the boy had his mother at unfair disadvantage, for she was a guest, and had no means of enforcing obedience. Henry showed a certain tactical ability by refusing to start, and he met all efforts at compulsion by successful, though too vehement protest. He was in fair way to win, and was holding his own, with sufficient energy, at the bottom of the long staircase which led up to the door of the President's library, when the door opened, and the old man slowly came down. Putting on his hat, he took the boy's hand without a word, and walked with him, paralyzed by awe, up the road to the town. After the first moments of consternation at this interference in a domestic dispute, the boy reflected that an old gentleman close on eighty would never trouble himself to walk near a mile on a hot summer morning over a shadeless road to take a boy to school, and that it would be strange if a lad imbued with the passion of freedom could not find a corner to dodge around, somewhere before reaching the school door. Then and always, the boy insisted that this reasoning justified his apparent submission; but the old man did not stop, and the boy saw all his strategical points turned, one after another, until he found himself seated inside the school, and obviously the centre of curious if not malevolent criticism. Not till then did the President release his hand and depart.

The point was that this act, contrary to the inalienable rights of 8 boys, and nullifying the social compact, ought to have made him dislike his grandfather for life. He could not recall that it had this effect even for a moment. With a certain maturity of mind, the child must have recognized that the President, though a tool of tyranny, had done his disreputable work with a certain intelligence. He had shown no temper, no irritation, no personal feeling, and had made no display of force. Above all, he had held his tongue. During their long walk he had said nothing; he had uttered no syllable of revolting cant about the duty of obedience and the wickedness of resistance to law; he had shown no concern in the matter; hardly even a consciousness of the boy's existence. Probably his mind at that moment was actually troubling itself little about his grandson's iniquities, and much about the iniquities of

President Polk, but the boy could scarcely at that age feel the whole satisfaction of thinking that President Polk was to be the vicarious victim of his own sins, and he gave his grandfather credit for intelligent silence. For this forbearance he felt instinctive respect. He admitted force as a form of right; he admitted even temper, under protest; but the seeds of moral education would at that moment have fallen on the stoniest soil in Quincy, which is, as everyone knows, the stoniest glacial and tidal drift known in any Puritan land.

___ CONSIDERATIONS _____

1. Earlier in his autobiography, Adams gives the reader some idea of how the young Henry, because of the peculiar nature of his family and its position, was burdened with expectations arising from the family's deep involvement in American history and politics. In the present excerpt, study his vocabulary and look for words that express his constant awareness of that involvement.

2. Adams chose an unusual point of view for an autobiography—the third person. Change a given paragraph to the first person point of view to see what difference the author's decision on that technical matter can make.

3. What illustrations does Adams use to help the reader understand what is meant by "He felt his nature crudely . . ."?

4. Adams's essay might fairly be said to be built upon a system of opposites. List several of these opposites to understand how a series of contrasts can serve as an organizing principle of an essay.

5. In paragraph 6, Adams sets forth clearly and firmly his conviction about what education must be. Judging from your educational experience, to what extent can you agree with him?

6. What allowed the boy to respect his grandfather, even as the old man was disciplining him?

James Agee (1909–1955) was a journalist, critic, poet, and novelist. He was an early and most influential film critic, and wrote the script for The African Queen, *among other movies. A heart attack killed him at forty-five, before he had finished his novel,* A Death in the Family. *Editors assembled the final manuscript and included as a prologue the essay reprinted here. The novel was awarded the Pulitzer Prize in 1958. Agee's prose evokes lost time; detail is described with intimate precision, landscape rendered exactly, with a wash of nostalgia.*

2

JAMES AGEE
Knoxville: Summer 1915

We are talking now of summer evenings in Knoxville, Tennessee 1
in the time that I lived there so successfully disguised to myself as a
child. It was a little bit mixed sort of block, fairly solidly lower middle
class, with one or two juts apiece on either side of that. The houses
corresponded: middle-sized gracefully fretted wood houses built in the
late nineties and early nineteen hundreds, with small front and side and
more spacious back yards, and trees in the yards, and porches. These
were soft-wooded trees, poplars, tulip trees, cottonwoods. There were
fences around one or two of the houses, but mainly the yards ran into
each other with only now and then a low hedge that wasn't doing very
well. There were few good friends among the grown people, and they
were not poor enough for the other sort of intimate acquaintance, but
everyone nodded and spoke, and even might talk short times, trivially,
and at the two extremes of the general or the particular, and ordinarily
nextdoor neighbors talked quite a bit when they happened to run into
each other, and never paid calls. The men were mostly small businessmen, one or two very modestly executives, one or two worked with

their hands, most of them clerical, and most of them between thirty and forty-five.

2   But it is of these evenings, I speak.

3   Supper was at six and was over by half past. There was still daylight, shining softly and with a tarnish, like the lining of a shell; and the carbon lamps lifted at the corners were on in the light, and the locusts were started, and the fire flies were out, and a few frogs were flopping in the dewy grass, by the time the fathers and the children came out. The children ran out first hell bent and yelling those names by which they were known; then the fathers sank out leisurely in crossed suspenders, their collars removed and their necks looking tall and shy. The mothers stayed back in the kitchen washing and drying, putting things away, recrossing their traceless footsteps like the lifetime journey of bees, measuring out the dry cocoa for breakfast. When they came out they had taken off their aprons and their skirts were dampened and they sat in rockers on their porches quietly.

4   It is not of the games children played in the evening that I want to speak now, it is of a contemporaneous atmosphere that has little to do with them: that of the fathers of families, each in his space of lawn, his shirt fishlike pale in the unnatural light and his face nearly anonymous, hosing their lawns. The hoses were attached at spigots that stood out of the brick foundations of the houses. The nozzles were variously set but usually so there was a long sweet stream of spray, the nozzle wet in the hand, the water trickling the right forearm and the peeled-back cuff, and the water whishing out a long loose and low-curved cone, and so gentle a sound. First an insane noise of violence in the nozzle, then the still irregular sound of adjustment, then the smoothing into steadiness and a pitch as accurately tuned to the size and style of stream as any violin. So many qualities of sound out of one hose: so many choral differences out of those several hoses that were in earshot. Out of any one hose, the almost dead silence of the release, and the short still arch of the separate big drops, silent as a held breath, and the only noise the flattering noise on leaves and the slapped grass at the fall of each big drop. That, and the intense hiss with the intense stream; that, and that same intensity not growing less but growing more quiet and delicate with the turn of the nozzle, up to that extreme tender whisper when the water was just a wide bell of film. Chiefly, though, the hoses were set much alike, in a compromise between distance and tenderness of spray (and quite surely a sense of art behind this compromise, and a quiet deep joy, too real to recognize itself), and the sounds therefore were pitched much alike; pointed by the snorting start of a new hose; decorated by some man

playful with the nozzle; left empty, like God by the sparrow's fall, when any single one of them desists; and all, though near alike, of various pitch; and in this unison. These sweet pale streamings in the light lift out their pallors and their voices all together, mothers hushing their children, the hushing unnaturally prolonged, the men gentle and silent and each snail-like withdrawn into the quietude of what he singly is doing, the urination of huge children stood loosely military against an invisible wall, and gentle happy and peaceful, tasting the mean goodness of their living like the last of their suppers in their mouths, while the locusts carry on this noise of hoses on their much higher and sharper key. The noise of the locust is dry, and it seems not to be rasped or vibrated but urged from him as if through a small orifice by breath that can never give out. Also there is never one locust but an illusion of at least a thousand. The noise of each locust is pitched in some classic locust range out of which none of them varies more than two full tones: and yet you seem to hear each locust discrete from all the rest, and there is a long, slow pulse in their noise, like the scarcely defined arch of a long and high set bridge. They are all around in every tree, so that the noise seems to come from nowhere and everywhere at once, from the whole shell heaven, shivering in your flesh and teasing your eardrums, the boldest of all the sounds of night. And yet it is habitual to summer nights, and is of the great order of noises, like the noises of the sea and of the blood her precocious grandchild, which you realize you are hearing only when you catch yourself listening. Meantime from low in the dark, just outside the swaying horizons of the hoses, conveying always grass in the damp of dew and its strong green-black smear of smell, the regular yet spaced noises of the crickets, each a sweet cold silver noise threenoted, like the slipping each time of three matched links of a small chain.

But the men by now, one by one, have silenced their hoses and 5 drained and coiled them. Now only two, and now only one, is left, and you see only the ghostlike shirt with the sleeve garters, and sober mystery of his mild face like the lifted face of large cattle enquiring of your presence in a pitchdark pool of meadow; and now he too is gone; and it has become that time of evening when people sit on their porches, rocking gently and talking gently and watching the street and the standing up into their sphere of possession of the trees, of bird-hung havens, hangars. People go by; things go by. A horse, drawing a buggy, breaking his hollow iron music on the asphalt; a loud auto; a quiet auto; people in pairs, not in a hurry, scuffling, switching their weight of aestival body, talking casually, the taste hovering over them of vanilla, strawberry, pasteboard and starched milk, the image upon them of lovers and horsemen, squared with clowns in hueless amber. A street car raising its iron moan; stopping, belling and starting; stertorous; rousing and raising again its iron increasing moan and swimming its gold windows and straw seats on past and past and past, the bleak spark crackling and cursing above it like a small malignant spirit set to dog its tracks; the iron whine rises on rising speed; still risen, faints; halts, the faint stinging bell; rises again, still fainter; fainting, lifting, lifts, faints forgone: forgotten. Now is the night one blue dew.

> Now is the night one blue dew, my father has drained, he has
>   coiled the hose.
> Low on the length of lawns, a frailing of fire who breathes.
> Content, silver, like peeps of light, each cricket makes his com-
>   ment over and over in the drowned grass.
> A cold toad thumpily flounders.
> Within the edges of damp shadows of side yards are hovering
>   children nearly sick with joy of fear, who watch the unguard-
>   ing of a telephone pole.
> Around white carbon corner lamps bugs of all sizes are lifted
>   elliptic, solar systems. Big hardshells bruise themselves, as-
>   sailant: he is fallen on his back, legs squiggling.
> Parents on porches: rock and rock: From damp strings morning
>   glories: hang their ancient faces.
> The dry and exalted noise of the locusts from all the air at once
>   enchants my eardrums.

6   On the rough wet grass of the back yard my father and mother have spread quilts. We all lie there, my mother, my father, my uncle, my aunt, and I too am lying there. First we were sitting up, then one of us lay down, and then we all lay down, on our stomachs, or on our sides, or on our backs, and they have kept on talking. They are not talking much, and the talk is quiet, of nothing in particular, of nothing at all in particular, of nothing at all. The stars are wide and alive, they seem each like a smile of great sweetness, and they seem very near. All my people are larger bodies than mine, quiet, with voices gentle and meaningless like the voices of sleeping birds. One is an artist, he is living at home. One is a musician, she is living at home. One is my mother who is good to me. One is my father who is good to me. By some chance, here they are, all on this earth; and who shall ever tell the sorrow of being on their earth, lying, on quilts, on the grass, in a summer evening, among the sounds of the night. May God bless my people, my uncle, my aunt, my

mother, my good father, oh, remember them kindly in their time of trouble; and in the hour of their taking away.

After a little I am taken in and put to bed. Sleep, soft smiling, draws me unto her: and those receive me, who quietly treat me, as one familiar and well beloved in that home: but will not, oh, will not, not now, not ever; but will not ever tell me who I am.   7

⸺ CONSIDERATIONS ⸺

1. Agee is famous for his close attention to the senses. In this piece, which one—seeing, hearing, smelling, tasting, touching—is exercised the most?

2. What do you make of Agee's paragraph sense? Compare, for example, paragraph 2 with paragraph 4. Would you recommend breaking the latter into smaller units? Where? Why, or why not?

3. The first sentence of paragraph 1 offers an opportunity for experimentation. Copy it out *without* the following words or phrases: "so successfully," "disguised," and "to myself." Then replace the phrases, one at a time, considering how each addition changes the dimension, the direction, or the depth of the story. Which of the three works the greatest change? Why?

4. How does the opening sentence embody a theme important to the whole story? Where else is that theme sounded in the story?

5. Agee's evocation of a summer evening might seem strange to an apartment-dweller in Knoxville in 1991. Would it be possible to write so serenely about a summer evening in the Knoxville—or Detroit, or Minneapolis, or San Francisco—of today?

6. Agee's attempt to recapture and thus understand his childhood—or at least a moment of it—relates to the efforts of several other writers in this book. Compare and contrast "Knoxville: Summer 1915" with the selections of: Henry Adams, Frank Conroy, Lillian Hellman, Langston Hughes, or E. B. White.

Woody Allen (b. 1935) is a universal genius, best known for acting in, writing, and directing movies. His films range from What's New, Pussycat? *(1964) through* Love and Death *(1975) and* Annie Hall *(1977) to* Hannah and Her Sisters *(1986) and* Crimes and Misdemeanors *(1989). He has also published short fiction in* Playboy *and the* New Yorker. *In 1978 he won an O. Henry Award for the best American short story of the previous year. His prose is collected in three volumes:* Getting Even *(1972),* Without Feathers *(1975), and* Side Effects *(1980).*

Allen began his career as a comedy writer for television shows, then became a comedian himself. His first great successes were the Broadway plays Don't Drink the Water *(1966) and* Play It Again, Sam *(1969). This playlet comes from* Getting Even.

3

WOODY ALLEN
Death Knocks

1 *(The play takes place in the bedroom of the Nat Ackermans' two-story house, somewhere in Kew Gardens. The carpeting is wall-to-wall. There is a big double bed and a large vanity. The room is elaborately furnished and curtained, and on the walls there are several paintings and a not really attractive barometer. Soft theme music as the curtain rises. Nat Ackerman, a bald, paunchy fifty-seven-year-old dress manufacturer, is lying on the bed finishing off tomorrow's* Daily News. *He wears a bathrobe and slippers, and reads by a bed light clipped to the white headboard of the bed. The time is near midnight. Suddenly we hear a noise, and Nat sits up and looks at the window.)*

NAT: What the hell is that?

(Climbing awkwardly through the window is a sombre, caped figure. The intruder wears a black hood and skintight black clothes.

The hood covers his head but not his face, which is middle-aged and stark white. He is something like Nat in appearance. He huffs audibly and then trips over the windowsill and falls into the room.)

DEATH *(for it is no one else):* Jesus Christ. I nearly broke my neck.

NAT *(watching with bewilderment):* Who are You?

DEATH: Death.

NAT: Who?

DEATH: Death. Listen—can I sit down? I nearly broke my neck. I'm shaking like a leaf.

NAT: Who *are* you?

DEATH: *Death.* You got a glass of water?

NAT: Death? What do you mean, Death?

DEATH: What is wrong with you? You see the black costume and the whitened face?

NAT: Yeah.

DEATH: Is it Halloween?

NAT: No.

DEATH: Then I'm Death. Now can I get a glass of water—or a Fresca?

NAT: If this is some joke—

DEATH: What kind of joke? You're fifty-seven? Nat Ackerman? One eighteen Pacific Street? Unless I blew it—where's that call sheet? *(He fumbles through pocket, finally producing a card with an address on it. It seems to check.)*

NAT: What do you want with me?

DEATH: What do I want? What do you think I want?

NAT: You must be kidding. I'm in perfect health.

DEATH *(unimpressed):* Uh-huh. *(Looking around)* This is a nice place. You do it yourself?

NAT: We had a decorator, but we worked with her.

DEATH *(looking at the picture on the wall):* I love those kids with the big eyes.

NAT: I don't want to go yet.

DEATH: *You* don't want to go? Please don't start in. As it is, I'm nauseous from the climb.

NAT: What climb?

DEATH: I climbed up the drainpipe. I was trying to make a dramatic entrance. I see the big windows and you're awake reading. I figure it's worth a shot. I'll climb up and enter with a little—you know . . . *(Snaps fingers)* Meanwhile, I get my heel caught on some vines, the drainpipe breaks, and I'm hanging by a thread. Then my cape begins to tear. Look, let's just go. It's been a rough night.

NAT: You broke my drainpipe?

30 DEATH: Broke. It didn't break. It's a little bent. Didn't you hear anything? I slammed into the ground.

NAT: I was reading.

DEATH: You must have really been engrossed. *(Lifting newspaper Nat was reading)* "NAB COEDS IN POT ORGY." Can I borrow this?

NAT: I'm not finished.

DEATH: Er—I don't know how to put this to you, pal . . .

35 NAT: Why didn't you just ring downstairs?

DEATH: I'm telling you, I could have, but how does it look? This way I get a little drama going. Something. Did you read *Faust?*

NAT: What?

DEATH: And what if you had company? You're sitting there with important people. I'm Death—I should ring the bell and traipse right in the front? Where's your thinking?

NAT: Listen, Mister, it's very late.

40 DEATH: Yeah. Well, you want to go?

NAT: Go where?

DEATH: Death. It. The Thing. The Happy Hunting Grounds. *(Looking at his own knee)* Y'know, that's a pretty bad cut. My first job, I'm liable to get gangrene yet.

NAT: Now, wait a minute. I need time. I'm not ready to go.

DEATH: I'm sorry. I can't help you. I'd like to, but it's the moment.

45 NAT: How can it be the moment? I just merged with Modiste Originals.

DEATH: What's the difference, a couple of bucks more or less.

NAT: Sure, what do you care? You guys probably have all your expenses paid.

DEATH: You want to come along now?

NAT *(studying him):* I'm sorry, but I cannot believe you're Death.

50 DEATH: Why? What'd you expect—Rock Hudson?

NAT: No, it's not that.

DEATH: I'm sorry if I disappointed you.

NAT: Don't get upset. I don't know, I always thought you'd be . . . uh . . . taller.

DEATH: I'm five seven. It's average for my weight.

55 NAT: You look a little like me.

DEATH: Who should I look like? I'm your death.

NAT: Give me some time. Another day.

DEATH: I can't. What do you want me to say?

NAT: One more day. Twenty-four hours.

DEATH: What do you need it for? The radio said rain tomorrow. 60

NAT: Can't we work out something?

DEATH: Like what?

NAT: You play chess?

DEATH: No, I don't.

NAT: I once saw a picture of you playing chess. 65

DEATH: Couldn't be me, because I don't play chess. Gin rummy, maybe.

NAT: You play gin rummy?

DEATH: Do I play gin rummy? Is Paris a city?

NAT: You're good, huh?

DEATH: Very good. 70

NAT: I'll tell you what I'll do—

DEATH: Don't make any deals with me.

NAT: I'll play you gin rummy. If you win, I'll go immediately. If I win, give me some more time. A little bit—one more day.

DEATH: Who's got time to play gin rummy?

NAT: Come on. If you're so good. 75

DEATH: Although I feel like a game . . .

NAT: Come on. Be a sport. We'll shoot for a half hour.

DEATH: I really shouldn't.

NAT: I got the cards right here. Don't make a production.

DEATH: All right, come on. We'll play a little. It'll relax me. 80

NAT *(getting cards, pad, and pencil):* You won't regret this.

DEATH: Don't give me a sales talk. Get the cards and give me a Fresca and put out something. For God's sake, a stranger drops in, you don't have potato chips or pretzels.

NAT: There's M&M's downstairs in a dish.

DEATH: M&M's. What if the President came? He'd get M&M's too?

NAT: You're not the President. 85

DEATH: Deal.

(Nat deals, turns up a five.)

NAT: You want to play a tenth of a cent a point to make it interesting?

DEATH: It's not interesting enough for you?

NAT: I play better when money's at stake. 90

DEATH: Whatever you say, Newt.

NAT: Nat. Nat Ackerman. You don't know my name?

DEATH: Newt, Nat—I got such a headache.

NAT: You want that five?

95   DEATH: No.

NAT: So pick.

DEATH *(surveying his hand as he picks):* Jesus, I got nothing here.

NAT: What's it like?

DEATH: What's what like?

100   *(Throughout the following, they pick and discard.)*

NAT: Death.

DEATH: What should it be like? You lay there.

NAT: Is there anything after?

DEATH: Aha, you're saving twos.

105   NAT: I'm asking. Is there anything after?

DEATH *(absently):* You'll see.

NAT: Oh, then I will actually see something?

DEATH: Well, maybe I shouldn't have put it that way. Throw.

NAT: To get an answer from you is a big deal.

110   DEATH: I'm playing cards.

NAT: All right, play, play.

DEATH: Meanwhile, I'm giving you one card after another.

NAT: Don't look through the discards.

DEATH: I'm not looking. I'm straightening them up. What was the knock card?

115   NAT: Four. You ready to knock already?

DEATH: Who said I'm ready to knock? All I asked was what was the knock card.

NAT: And all I asked was is there anything for me to look forward to.

DEATH: Play.

NAT: Can't you tell me anything? Where do we go?

120   DEATH: We? To tell you the truth, *you* fall in a crumpled heap on the floor.

NAT: Oh, I can't wait for that! Is it going to hurt?

DEATH: Be over in a second.

NAT: Terrific. *(Sighs.)* I needed this. A man merges with Modiste Originals . . .

DEATH: How's four points?

125   NAT: You're knocking?

DEATH: Four points is good?

NAT: No, I got two.

DEATH: You're kidding.

NAT: No, you lose.

DEATH: Holy Christ, and I thought you were saving sixes. 130

NAT: No. Your deal. Twenty points and two boxes. Shoot. *(Death deals.)* I must fall on the floor, eh? I can't be standing over the sofa when it happens?

DEATH: No. Play.

NAT: Why not?

DEATH: Because you fall on the floor! Leave me alone. I'm trying to concentrate.

NAT: Why must it be on the floor? That's all I'm saying! Why 135
can't the whole thing happen and I'll stand next to the sofa?

DEATH: I'll try my best. Now can we play?

NAT: That's all I'm saying. You remind me of Moe Lefkowitz. He's also stubborn.

DEATH: I remind him of Moe Lefkowitz. I'm one of the most terrifying figures you could possibly imagine, and him I remind of Moe Lefkowitz. What is he, a furrier?

NAT: You should be such a furrier. He's good for eighty thousand a year. Passementeries. He's got his own factory. Two points.

DEATH: What? 140

NAT: Two points. I'm knocking. What have you got?

DEATH: My hand is like a basketball score.

NAT: And it's spades.

DEATH: If you didn't talk so much.

(They redeal and play on.) 145

NAT: What'd you mean before when you said this was your first job?

DEATH: What does it sound like?

NAT: What are you telling me—that nobody ever went before?

DEATH: Sure they went. But I didn't take them.

NAT: So who did? 150

DEATH: Others.

NAT: There's others?

DEATH: Sure. Each one has his own personal way of going.

NAT: I never knew that.

DEATH: Why should you know? Who are you? 155

NAT: What do you mean who am I? Why—I'm nothing?

DEATH: Not nothing. You're a dress manufacturer. Where do you come to knowledge of the eternal mysteries?

NAT: What are you talking about? I make a beautiful dollar. I sent two kids through college. One is in advertising, the other's married. I got my own home. I drive a Chrysler. My wife has whatever she wants. Maids, mink coat, vacations. Right now she's at the Eden Roc. Fifty dollars a day because she wants to be near her sister. I'm supposed to join her next week, so what do you think I am—some guy off the street?

DEATH: All right. Don't be so touchy.

160   NAT: Who's touchy?

DEATH: How would you like it if I got insulted quickly?

NAT: Did I insult you?

DEATH: You didn't say you were disappointed in me?

NAT: What do you expect? You want me to throw you a block party?

165   DEATH: I'm not talking about that. I mean me personally. I'm too short, I'm this, I'm that.

NAT: I said you looked like me. It's a reflection.

DEATH: All right, deal, deal.

(They continue to play as music steals in and the lights dim until all is in total darkness. The lights slowly come up again, and now it is later and their game is over. Nat tallies.)

NAT: Sixty-eight . . . one-fifty . . . Well, you lose.

170   DEATH *(dejectedly looking through the deck):* I knew I shouldn't have thrown that nine. Damn it.

NAT: So I'll see you tomorrow.

DEATH: What do you mean you'll see me tomorrow?

NAT: I won the extra day. Leave me alone.

DEATH: You were serious?

175   NAT: We made a deal.

DEATH: Yeah, but—

NAT: Don't "but" me. I won twenty-four hours. Come back tomorrow.

DEATH: I didn't know we were actually playing for time.

NAT: That's too bad about you. You should pay attention.

180   DEATH: Where am I going to go for twenty-four hours?

NAT: What's the difference? The main thing is I won an extra day.

DEATH: What do you want me to do—walk the streets?

NAT: Check into a hotel and go to a movie. Take a *schvitz.* Don't make a federal case.

DEATH: Add the score again.

185   NAT: Plus you owe me twenty-eight dollars.

DEATH: *What!*

NAT: That's right, Buster. Here it is—read it.

DEATH: *(going through pockets):* I have a few singles—not twenty-eight dollars.

NAT: I'll take a check.

DEATH: From what account?   190

NAT: Look who I'm dealing with.

DEATH: Sue me. Where do I keep my checking account?

NAT: All right, gimme what you got and we'll call it square.

DEATH: Listen, I need that money.

NAT: Why should you need money?   195

DEATH: What are you talking about? You're going to the Beyond.

NAT: So?

DEATH: So—you know how far that is?

NAT: So?

DEATH: So where's gas? Where's tolls?   200

NAT: We're going by car!

DEATH: You'll find out. *(Agitatedly)* Look—I'll be back tomorrow, and you'll give me a chance to win the money back. Otherwise I'm in definite trouble.

NAT: Anything you want. Double or nothing we'll play. I'm liable to win an extra week or a month. The way you play, maybe years.

DEATH: Meantime I'm stranded.

NAT: See you tomorrow.   205

DEATH *(being edged to the doorway):* Where's a good hotel? What am I talking about hotel, I got no money. I'll go sit in Bickford's. *(He picks up the* News.)

NAT: Out. Out. That's my paper. *(He takes it back.)*

DEATH *(exiting):* I couldn't just take him and go. I had to get involved in rummy.

NAT *(calling after him):* And be careful going downstairs. On one of the steps the rug is loose.

(And, on cue, we hear a terrific crash. Nat sighs, then crosses to   210
the bedside table and makes a phone call.)

NAT: Hello, Moe? Me. Listen, I don't know if somebody's playing a joke, or what, but Death was just here. We played a little gin . . . No, *Death.* In person. Or somebody who claims to be Death. But, Moe, he's such a *schlep!*

CURTAIN

_____ **CONSIDERATIONS** _____

1. Death is a subject most people avoid discussing; instead, they fall back on euphemisms. Make a list of euphemisms for death and dying and write an essay on the subject.

2. Nat is insulted by the suggestion that he doesn't know anything about death. "I make a beautiful dollar," he protests. "I sent two kids through college. . . ." What do you think of the logic of his reply?

3. Obviously, dialogue is everything in a play. Study how some of the other writers in this book make use of dialogue in essays and stories. Try using dialogue in a forthcoming essay.

4. NAT: You want to play a tenth of a cent a point to make it interesting?
   DEATH: It's not interesting enough for you?
What does this exchange suggest about habitual or superficial versus real or essential values? Are the same ideas suggested by the hackneyed expression, "The condemned man ate a hearty breakfast"?

5. The Kew Gardens mentioned in the stage-setting for "Death Knocks" is not the site of the Royal Botanical Gardens in London, but a predominantly Jewish middle- and upper-middle-class neighborhood of Queens in New York City. As you *listen* to the lines of the play, do you hear any clues that the characters are New Yorkers, not Londoners? Can you find other authors in this book who make use of voice in their work?

6. Woody Allen's playlet presents a somewhat unusual example of personification. What are some more common personifications of death—in essays, stories, poems, cartoons, movies? Many other authors in this book use this literary device. Study their examples, then try your hand at personification.

Maya Angelou (b. 1928) told an interviewer, "One would say of my life—born loser—had to be; from a broken family, raped at eight, unwed mother at sixteen . . . it's a fact, but it's not the truth."

When she grew up, Maya Angelou became an actress, a singer, a dancer, a songwriter, a teacher, an editor, and a poet. She sang and danced professionally in Porgy and Bess *with a company that traveled through twenty-two countries of Europe and Asia. She wrote for the* Ghana Times *and she taught modern dance in Rome and in Tel Aviv. Her recent books are* All God's Children Need Travelling Shoes *(1986) and* Poems *(1986).*

In 1969 she began her autobiography, I Know Why the Caged Bird Sings, *which was an immediate success. As she says, "I speak to the black experience, but I am always talking about the human condition." The book recounts her early life, with realism and with joy. This section describes a masterful black con man, skillful at turning white bigotry into black profits.*

4

MAYA ANGELOU
Mr. Red Leg

Our house was a fourteen-room typical San Franciscan post-Earthquake affair. We had a succession of roomers, bringing and taking their different accents, and personalities and foods. Shipyard workers clanked up the stairs (we all slept on the second floor except Mother and Daddy Clidell) in their steel-tipped boots and metal hats, and gave way to much-powdered prostitutes, who giggled through their makeup and hung their wigs on the door-knobs. One couple (they were college graduates) held long adult conversations with me in the big kitchen downstairs, until the husband went off to war. Then the wife who had been so charming and ready to smile changed into a silent shadow that played infrequently along the walls. An older couple lived with us for a year or so. They owned a restaurant and had no personality to enchant or interest a teenager, except that the husband was called Uncle Jim, and the wife Aunt Boy. I never figured that out.

2   The quality of strength lined with tenderness is an unbeatable combination, as are intelligence and necessity when unblunted by formal education. I was prepared to accept Daddy Clidell as one more faceless name added to Mother's roster of conquests. I had trained myself so successfully through the years to display interest, or at least attention, while my mind skipped free on other subjects that I could have lived in his house without ever seeing him and without his becoming the wiser. But his character beckoned and elicited admiration. He was a simple man who had no inferiority complex about his lack of education and, even more amazing, no superiority complex because he had succeeded despite that lack. He would say often, "I had been to school three years in my life. In Slaten, Texas, times was hard, and I had to help my daddy on the farm."

3   No recriminations lay hidden under the plain statement, nor was there boasting when he said, "If I'm living a litter better now, it's because I treats everybody right."

4   He owned apartment buildings and, later, pool halls, and was famous for being that rarity, "a man of honor." He didn't suffer, as many "honest men" do, from the detestable righteousness that diminishes their virtue. He knew cards and men's hearts. So during the age when Mother was exposing us to certain facts of life, like personal hygiene, proper posture, table manners, good restaurants and tipping practices, Daddy Clidell taught me to play poker, blackjack, tonk and high, low, Jick, Jack and the Game. He wore expensive tailored suits and a large yellow diamond stickpin. Except for the jewelry, he was a conservative dresser and carried himself with the unconscious pomp of a man of secure means. Unexpectedly, I resembled him, and when he, Mother and I walked down the street his friends often said, "Clidell, that's sure your daughter. Ain't no way you can deny her."

5   Proud laughter followed those declarations, for he had never had children. Because of his late-arriving but intense paternal sense, I was introduced to the most colorful characters in the Black underground. One afternoon, I was invited into our smoke-filled dining room to make the acquaintance of Stonewall Jimmy, Just Black, Cool Clyde, Tight Coat and Red Leg. Daddy Clidell explained to me that they were the most successful con men in the world, and they were going to tell me about some games so that I would never be "anybody's mark."

6   To begin, one man warned me, "There ain't never been a mark yet

that didn't want something for nothing." Then they took turns showing me their tricks, how they chose their victims (marks) from the wealthy bigoted whites and in every case how they used the victims' prejudice against them.

Some of the tales were funny, a few were pathetic, but all were amusing or gratifying to me, for the Black man, the con man who could act the most stupid, won out every time over the powerful, arrogant white.   7

I remember Mr. Red Leg's story like a favorite melody.   8

"Anything that works against you can also work for you once you understand the Principle of Reverse.   9

"There was a cracker in Tulsa who bilked so many Negroes he could set up a Negro Bilking Company. Naturally he got to thinking, Black Skin means Damn Fool. Just Black and I went to Tulsa to check him out. Come to find out, he's a perfect mark. His momma must have been scared in an Indian massacre in Africa. He hated Negroes only a little more than he despised Indians. And he was greedy.   10

"Black and I studied him and decided he was worth setting up against the store. That means we were ready to put out a few thousand dollars in preparation. We pulled in a white boy from New York, a good con artist, and had him open an office in Tulsa. He was supposed to be a Northern real estate agent trying to buy up valuable land in Oklahoma. We investigated a piece of land near Tulsa that had a toll bridge crossing it. It used to be part of an Indian reservation but had been taken over by the state.   11

"Just Black was laid out as the decoy, and I was going to be the fool. After our friend from New York hired a secretary and had his cards printed, Black approached the mark with a proposition. He told him that he had heard that our mark was the only white man colored people could trust. He named some of the poor fools that had been taken by that crook. It just goes to show you how white folks can be deceived by their own deception. The mark believed Black.   12

"Black told him about his friend who was half Indian and half colored and how some Northern white real estate agent had found out that he was the sole owner of a piece of valuable land and the Northerner wanted to buy it. At first the man acted like he smelled a rat, but from the way he gobbled up the proposition, turns out what he thought he smelled was some nigger money on his top lip.   13

"He asked the whereabouts of the land but Black put him off. He told this cracker that he just wanted to make sure that he would be interested. The mark allowed how he was being interested, so Black   14 said he would tell his friend and they'd get in touch with him. Black met the mark for about three weeks in cars and in alleys and kept putting him off until the white man was almost crazy with anxiety and greed and then accidentally it seemed Black let drop the name of the Northern real estate agent who wanted the property. From that moment on we knew we had the big fish on the line and all we had to do was to pull him in.

15   "We expected him to try to contact our store, which he did. That cracker went to our setup and counted on his whiteness to ally him with Spots, our white boy, but Spots refused to talk about the deal except to say the land had been thoroughly investigated by the biggest real estate concern in the South and that if our mark did not go around raising dust he would make sure that there would be a nice piece of money in it for him. Any obvious inquiries as to the rightful ownership of the land could alert the state and they would surely push through a law prohibiting the sale. Spots told the mark he would keep in touch with him. The mark went back to the store three or four times but to no avail, then just before we knew he would crack, Black brought me to see him. That fool was as happy as a sissy in a C.C.C. camp. You would have thought my neck was in a noose and he was about to light the fire under my feet. I never enjoyed taking anybody so much.

16   "Anyhow, I played scary at first but Just Black told me that this was one white man that our people could trust. I said I did not trust no white man because all they wanted was to get a chance to kill a Black man legally and get his wife in the bed. (I'm sorry, Clidell.) The mark assured me that he was the only white man who did not feel like that. Some of his best friends were colored people. In fact, if I didn't know it, the woman who raised him was a colored woman and he still sees her to this day. I let myself be convinced and then the mark began to drag the Northern whites. He told me that they made Negroes sleep in the street in the North and that they had to clean out toilets with their hands in the North and even things worse than that. I was shocked and said, 'Then I don't want to sell my land to that white man who offered seventy-five thousand dollars for it.' Just Black said, 'I wouldn't know what to do with that kind of money,' and I said that all I wanted was to have enough money to buy a home for my old mom, to buy a business and to make one trip to Harlem. The mark asked how much would that cost and I said I reckoned I could do it on fifty thousand dollars.

17   "The mark told me no Negro was safe with that kind of money. That white folks would take it from him. I said I knew it but I had to have at least forty thousand dollars. He agreed. We shook hands. I said it

would do my heart good to see the mean Yankee go down on some of 'our land.' We met the next morning and I signed the deed in his car and he gave me the cash.

"Black and I had kept most of our things in a hotel over in Hot 18 Springs, Arkansas. When the deal was closed we walked to our car, drove across the state line and on to Hot Springs.

"That's all there was to it." 19

When he finished, more triumphant stories rainbowed around the 20 room riding the shoulders of laughter. By all accounts those storytell- ers, born Black and male before the turn of the twentieth century, should have been ground into useless dust. Instead they used their intelligence to pry open the door of rejection and not only became wealthy but got some revenge in the bargain.

It wasn't possible for me to regard them as criminals or be any- 21 thing but proud of their achievements.

The needs of a society determine its ethics, and in the Black 22 American ghettos the hero is that man who is offered only the crumbs from his country's table but by ingenuity and courage is able to take for himself a Lucullan feast. Hence the janitor who lives in one room but sports a robin's-egg-blue Cadillac is not laughed at but admired, and the domestic who buys forty-dollar shoes is not criticized but is ap- preciated. We know that they have put to use their full mental and physical powers. Each single gain feeds into the gains of the body collective.

Stories of law violations are weighed on a different set of scales in 23 the Black mind than in the white. Petty crimes embarrass the commu- nity and many people wistfully wonder why Negroes don't rob more banks, embezzle more funds and employ graft in the unions. "We are the victims of the world's most comprehensive robbery. Life demands a balance. It's all right if we do a little robbing now." This belief appeals particularly to one who is unable to compete legally with his fellow citizens.

My education and that of my Black associates were quite different 24 from the education of our white schoolmates. In the classroom we all learned past participles, but in the streets and in our homes the Blacks learned to drop *s*'s from plurals and suffixes from past-tense verbs. We were alert to the gap separating the written word from the colloquial. We learned to slide out of one language and into another without being conscious of the effort. At school, in a given situation, we might re- spond with "That's not unusual." But in the street, meeting the same situation, we easily said, "It be's like that sometimes."

CONSIDERATIONS

1. Most of Angelou's essay is devoted to Mr. Red Leg telling a story. Notice how close to pure narration that story is. Compare it with the selections in this book by Carol Bly, George Orwell, or Richard Wright, and contrast the amount of description and narration in Mr. Red Leg's story to that in one of the others.

2. Compare Angelou's essay with that of Frank Conroy, who also emphasizes memorable characters. How do the two authors differ in their reasons for devoting so much space to Mr. Red Leg and to Ramos and Ricardo, respectively?

3. At the end of her essay, Angelou sets out an important linguistic principle. Paraphrase that idea and provide examples from your own experience or research.

4. "Stories of law violations are weighed on a different set of scales in the Black mind than in the white." Does a similar difference occur in the minds of two generations? Discuss relative justice versus absolute law.

5. Angelou demonstrates her versatility as a writer throughout this essay by managing two voices. Find examples and discuss.

6. From what you learn of Angelou's upbringing in the essay, compile a *negative report* by a social worker on Angelou's childhood. Are there positive details in the essay that would allow you to refute a negative report?

Barbara Lazear Ascher (b. 1946) graduated from Bennington College in 1968 and currently lives in New York City. After marrying and having a daughter she attended law school, practiced law for two years, then gave it up to become a writer. Ascher's essays appear in the New York Times, Vogue, Redbook, McCalls, Newsday, *and the* Yale Review. *This piece comes from her collection* Playing After Dark *(1986), essays that are personal and that work toward the universal. In 1989 she published another collection,* The Habit of Loving.

5

BARBARA LAZEAR ASCHER
On the Road
with the College Applicant

My sixteen-year-old daughter slumped against the doorway of the college admissions office. "It happened," she groaned. "I had a stress interview." 1

She exhaled as though she'd been holding her breath for the previous forty-five minutes, and sank to the ground, risking grass stains on the carefully selected, conservative interview skirt that must appear the next day on the next campus. "The minute I walked into his office," she explained, "he demanded, 'So! What can you do for this college?'" The tone she captured sounded like that of a police interrogator—"Were-you-or-were-you-not-at-the-scene-of-the-crime-the-night-of-the crime?"—a tone that tempts one to admit guilt in order to be free of the questioning. "Then it turned into a game show. If I responded the way he wanted me to, he'd say, 'Good answer! Good answer!'" She looked at me with astonishment, "And *then* he said, 'There's an invisible box on my desk with things in it that describe you. What's in the box?'" 2

3   "What did you say? What did you do?" I asked anxiously, the beats of my heart quickly catching up to the race of her own. Did she black out? Did she excuse herself and go to the bathroom? Was the course of her future determined by five minutes of silence?

4   "I went on automatic pilot," my daughter responded, adding, "In a stress interview, you separate your mouth from your brain and hope it works."

5   Later the adults in her life become witty, bright and piercingly intelligent over the food and wine of a family dinner. With a safe distance between ourselves and the Ivy League interrogation chamber, with a safe distance between ourselves and our own tremulous youth, we sound like Bartlett's Familiar Quotations. We are not struggling to describe ourselves with objects that could fit inside an invisible box. There are no cold sweats, stutters, blushes or stammers here.

6   Her grandfather says, "When he asked what she could do for the college, she should have said, 'What can your college do for me?'" Another diner suggests, "She should have looked him in the eye and said, 'If the point of an interview is to become acquainted with the applicant, why are you determined to make me ill at ease?'" A wise guy notes, "When he asked what was in the box, she should have said, 'Your head!' and walked out."

7   Easy for us to say. Smug as we are with degrees under our belts. She, on the other hand, can't afford the luxury of brashness nor the time to change the system. Chances are she'll even apply to and pray for acceptance at the source of the stress interview. It's a seller's market. College-bound high school seniors can rattle off admissions statistics the way they once might have memorized batting averages. Numbers culled from college catalogues march through their brains: "In 1984 approximately 12,636 applications were reviewed for 1,360 places in the freshman class." SAT scores, CEEB scores, AP scores and grade point averages join the parade. It keeps them up nights.

8   Lack of sleep and fear of rejection take their toll. My daughter has become crazed. Every high school senior I know has become crazed. One of them told me that she thought it was a trick question when her interviewer asked her one balmy August morning, "It's such a lovely day, would you like to meet outside?" Another became so nervous that he lost all sense of spatial relations, and after pulling up a chair across from the interviewer's desk, he promptly sat on the floor. When it was time to leave, he walked into the closet rather than out the door. My daughter tells me that she is certain, "When the interviewer asks you where you want to sit, your choice MEANS something." Even success-

ful interviews are belittled in the general mood of overwhelming pessimism that the students adopt, in part to protect themselves from what they perceive as inevitable disappointment.

There's perversion at work here. Applicants begin to assume that   9
the harder it is to get into a college, the better that college. And they, who happen to be at the age of least self-confidence, feel they couldn't possibly be "good" enough to be acceptable. Admissions committees aggravate this sense of insecurity by flaunting the number of applications they receive, statistics of which they are justly proud—statistics that reduce sixteen- and seventeen-year-olds to a sense of barely tolerable inadequacy.

I watched an applicant walk onto the campus of one of the "hard-   10
est to get into" universities, look around at what appeared to me to be no more than the normal sampling of collegiate scruffiness, and remark fearfully, "Look at all those geniuses!"

"It's hard not to feel victimized," my daughter tells me. "Even   11
when it's not a stress interview, these are strangers probing into your life, and you didn't invite them there." Some interviewers are sensitive to the intrusive nature of their jobs and the vulnerability of their "victims." At one of the most competitive colleges an admissions officer, upon shaking my daughter's hand and finding it cold said, "Let me make some coffee to warm you up." If an applicant is in a position to decide, decisions have been based on less than that.

They're also based on the personality of the tour guide and some   12
sort of Rorschach reaction to the appearance of students and campus. While admissions officers are seated in the position of power, they are not alone in the seat of judgment. Applications come equipped with the ruthlessly critical eye of adolescence. I have heard hundreds of years of academic glory dismissed in a sentence:

College A "is full of preps."   13

College B "is like Coca-Cola, they spend more money on their   14
image than the product."

At College C, "The students are refugees from Westchester going   15
native in L. L. Bean boots."

College D "has gone commercial with the quota system. They   16
make certain to show you a specific number of jocks, brains, wimps and weirdos."

College E "was great! The guy who interviewed me was a Mets   17
fan."

Chance encounters also make an impression. My daughter and I   18
were having a pre-interview lunch in College F's cafeteria when a

student walked in with a Steiff bunny rabbit puppet on her hand. She spoke exclusively through the rabbit. When another student asked, "How are you?" the bunny's head bobbed up and down to the lilt of a Walt Disney cartoon voice, "Just fine, thank you." I promptly addressed the tuna fish sandwich at hand, but caught a glimpse of my companion rolling her eyes.

19   It doesn't look good for College F.

20   However, in spite of the stress, the defenses, the critical eye, there are moments of love at first sight. Such events are unpredictable except that they hardly ever happen on rainy days and rarely on Saturdays when one senses the interviewer's annoyance at having to work weekends. For my own daughter, these moments occurred when an interviewer lost track of time and talked with her for two hours, when she met with a Classics professor who had the tenderness and wisdom of Catullus behind his eyes, and when she dined with a professor who shared her passion for Shelley and Keats.

21   And that is supposed to be the point of all this—passion. The goal of higher education is to seduce students into a love of learning, to nurture and encourage a lifelong love affair. The root of the word "education" comes from the Latin *educo*—to bring out or lead forth. It seems that both applicants and admissions personnel lose sight of this in a system that has become rife with stress, statistics, slick catalogues and superficial encounters, that has created a kind of painful endurance test for parents and children. I wonder if colleges are even aware that admissions procedures have placed intimidation and interviewers' invisible boxes before their gates? And that many will stumble there, many who should be brought in, in order to be "brought out."

_____ CONSIDERATIONS _____

1. If an interviewer in the admissions office of your school asked, "What can you do for this college?", what would you say? Is this an effective question?

2. Suppose you, as an applicant, had the chance to visit three or four colleges you had heard might be desirable choices. Ignoring the possibility of interviews for the moment, what would you look for on each campus to help you make a judgment? For that matter, why did you choose your school?

3. Ascher says that "The goal of higher education is to seduce students into a love of learning." Read Caroline Bird's "Where College Fails Us" and discuss how the two writers' ideas differ.

4. Is the attempt to select and enter a school as stressful an experience for everyone as it was for Ascher's daughter, or is that experience limited to a relatively small group? If necessary, ask several of your classmates before explaining your answer.

5. How might Nancy Mairs (in "The Unmaking of a Scientist") advise Ascher's daughter in her quest for the right college?

Margaret Atwood (b. 1939) is a Canadian novelist and poet. Born in Ottawa, she now lives in Toronto with her daughter and husband. Her novels include The Edible Woman *(1969),* Surfacing *(1972),* Lady Oracle *(1976),* Life Before Man *(1979),* Bodily Harm *(1982),* The Handmaid's Tale *(1986), and* Cat's Eye *(1988). Her original* Selected Poems *came out in 1976, a second volume in 1987. In 1978 she issued a collection of short stories,* Dancing Girls, *and in 1986 published* Bluebeard's Egg and Other Stories.*

She wrote of "Homelanding" that it "purports to be a speech made by an alien being to a group of other alien beings in an attempt to describe its place of origin."

6

MARGARET ATWOOD
Homelanding

1   Where should I begin? After all, you have never been there, or, if you have, you may not have understood the significance of what you saw or thought you saw. A window is a window, but there is looking out and looking in. The native you glimpsed, disappearing behind the curtain or into the bushes or down a manhole of the main street—my people are shy—may have been only your reflection in the glass. My country specializes in such illusions.

2   Let me propose myself as typical. I walk upright on two legs and have in addition two arms with ten appendages—that is to say, five at the end of each. On the top of my head, but not on the front, there is an odd growth, like a species of seaweed. Some think this is a kind of fur; others consider it modified feathers, evolved perhaps from scales like those of lizards. It serves no functional purpose and is probably decorative.

3   My eyes are situated in my head, which also possesses two small holes for the entrance and exit of air, the invisible fluid we swim in, and one larger hole equipped with bony protuberances called teeth, by

Reprinted by permission of the author.

means of which I destroy and assimilate certain parts of my surroundings and change them into myself. This is called eating. The things I eat
include roots, berries, nuts, fruit, leaves, and the muscle tissues of
various animals and fish. Sometimes I eat their brains and glands as
well. I do not as a rule eat insects, grubs, eyeballs, or the snouts of
pigs—though these are eaten with relish in other countries.

Some of my people have a pointed but boneless external appendage   4
in the front, below the naval or mid-point. Others do not. Debate about
whether the possession of such a thing is an advantage or a disadvantage
is still going on. If this item is lacking and in its place is a pocket or
inner cavern in which fresh members of our country are grown, it is
considered impolite to mention it openly to strangers. I tell you this
because it is the breech of etiquette most commonly made by tourists.

In some of our more private gatherings, the absence of cavern or   5
prong is politely overlooked, like clubfeet or blindness. But sometimes
a prong and a cavern will collaborate in a dance or illusion using mirrors
and water, which is always absorbing to the performers but frequently
grotesque for the observers. I notice you have similar customs.

Whole conventions and a great deal of time have recently been   6
devoted to discussions of this state of affairs. The prong people tell the
cavern people that the latter are not people at all and are in reality more
akin to dogs or potatoes, and the cavern people abuse the prong people
for their obsession with images of poking, thrusting, probing, and stabbing. Any long object with a hole at the end, out of which various
projectiles can be shot, delights them.

I myself—I am a cavern person—find it a relief not to have to   7
worry about climbing over barbed wire fences or getting caught in
zippers. But that is enough about our bodily form.

As for the country itself, let me begin with the sunsets, which are   8
long and red, resonant, splendid, and melancholy—symphonic, you
might almost say—as opposed to the short, boring sunsets of other
countries, no more interesting than a light switch. We pride ourselves
on our sunsets. "Come and see the sunset," we say to one another. This
causes everyone to rush outdoors or over to a window. Our country is
large in extent, small in population, which accounts for our fear of large
empty spaces and also our need for them. Much of it is covered in water,
which accounts for our interest in reflections, sudden vanishings, the
dissolution of one thing into another. Much of it, however, is rock,
which accounts for our belief in fate.

In summer we lie about in the blazing sun, almost naked, covering   9
our skin with fat and attempting to turn red. But when the sun is low in

the sky and faint, even at noon, the water we are so fond of changes to something hard and white and cold and covers up the ground. Then we cocoon ourselves, become lethargic, and spend much of our time hiding in crevices. Our mouths shrink, and we say little.

10   Before this happens, the leaves on many of our trees turn blood red or lurid yellow, much brighter and more exotic than the interminable green of jungles. We find this change beautiful. "Come and see the leaves," we say and jump into our moving vehicles and drive up and down past the forests and sanguinary trees, pressing our eyes to the glass.

11   We are a nation of metamorphs. Anything red compels us.

12   Sometimes we lie still and do not move. If air is still going in and out of our breathing holes, this is called sleep. If not, this is called death. When a person has achieved death, a kind of picnic is held, with music, flowers, and food. The person so honored, if in one piece and not, for instance, in shreds or falling apart, as one is if exploded or a long time drowned, is dressed in becoming clothes and lowered into a hole in the ground or else burnt up.

13   These customs are among the most difficult to explain to strangers. Some of our visitors, especially the young ones, have never heard of death and are bewildered. They think that death is simply one more of our illusions—our mirror tricks; they cannot understand why, with so much food and music, the people are sad.

14   But you will understand. You, too, must have death among you. I can see it in your eyes.

15   I can see it in your eyes. If it weren't for this, I would have stopped trying long ago to communicate with you in this half-way language which is so difficult for both of us, which exhausts the throat and fills the mouth with sand. If it weren't for this, I would have gone away, gone back. It's this knowledge of death which we share, where we overlap. Death is our common ground. Together on it we can walk forward.

16   By now you must have guessed: I come from another planet. But I will never say to you, "Take me to your leaders." Even I, unused to your ways though I am, would never make that mistake. We ourselves have such beings among us—made of cogs, pieces of paper, small disks of shiny metal, scraps of colored cloth. I do not need to encounter more of them.

17   Instead, I will say, "Take me to your trees. Take me to your breakfasts, your sunsets, your bad dreams, your shoes, your nouns. Take me to your fingers; take me to your deaths."

18   These are worth it; these are what I have come for.

—— CONSIDERATIONS ———————————————————

1. If you had made a "homelanding" on another planet and were trying to help the beings there understand humankind, how would you go about it? Study Margaret Atwood's way of explaining eating (paragraph 3), or getting a tan (paragraph 9), or the difference between sleep and death (paragraph 12). Forcing yourself to be as specific yet as concise as Atwood, try your hand at describing walking or writing or bathing or listening to music.

2. How does Atwood support her generalization in paragraph 11 that "Anything red compels us"?

3. What, according to Atwood, is the one thing that humans share with the beings she addresses on another planet?

4. Most readers would identify "Homelanding" as a satire. What qualities here support such an identification? If "Homelanding" is a satire, what is its target or targets?

5. What idea lies beneath Atwood's choice of alternates to "leaders" (paragraphs 16 and 17)? What principle of writing does she demonstrate by expressing that choice as trees, breakfasts, sunsets, bad dreams, shoes, nouns, fingers, deaths?

Although she is largely known for her novels, Margaret Atwood has published much nonfiction, including literary criticism as well as topical essays like this one.

7

MARGARET ATWOOD
Pornography

1   When I was in Finland a few years ago for an international writers' conference, I had occasion to say a few paragraphs in public on the subject of pornography. The context was a discussion of political repression, and I was suggesting the possibility of a link between the two. The immediate result was that a male journalist took several large bites out of me. Prudery and pornography are two halves of the same coin, said he, and I was clearly a prude. What could you expect from an Anglo-Canadian? Afterward, a couple of pleasant Scandinavian men asked me what I had been so worked up about. All "pornography" means, they said, is graphic depictions of whores, and what was the harm in that?

2   Not until then did it strike me that the male journalist and I had two entirely different things in mind. By "pornography," he meant naked bodies and sex. I, on the other hand, had recently been doing the research for my novel *Bodily Harm,* and was still in a state of shock from some of the material I had seen, including the Ontario Board of Film Censors' "outtakes." By "pornography," I meant women getting their nipples snipped off with garden shears, having meat hooks stuck into their vaginas, being disemboweled; little girls being raped; men (yes, there are some men) being smashed to a pulp and forcibly sodomized. The cutting edge of pornography, as far as I could see, was no longer simple old copulation, hanging from the chandelier or otherwise: it was death, messy, explicit and highly sadistic. I explained this to the nice Scandinavian men. "Oh, but that's just the United States," they

said. "Everyone knows they're sick." In their country, they said, violent "pornography" of that kind was not permitted on television or in movies; indeed, excessive violence of any kind was not permitted. They had drawn a clear line between erotica, which earlier studies had shown did not incite men to more aggressive and brutal behavior toward women, and violence, which later studies indicated did.

Some time after that I was in Saskatchewan, where, because of the scenes in *Bodily Harm*, I found myself on an open-line radio show answering questions about "pornography." Almost no one who phoned in was in favor of it, but again they weren't talking about the same stuff I was, because they hadn't seen it. Some of them were all set to stamp out bathing suits and negligees, and, if possible, any depictions of the female body whatsoever. God, it was implied, did not approve of female bodies, and sex of any kind, including that practised by bumblebees, should be shoved back into the dark, where it belonged. I had more than a suspicion that *Lady Chatterley's Lover*, Margaret Laurence's *The Diviners*, and indeed most books by most serious modern authors would have ended up as confetti if left in the hands of these callers.

For me, these two experiences illustrate the two poles of the emotionally heated debate that is now thundering around this issue. They also underline the desirability and even the necessity of defining the terms. "Pornography" is now one of those catchalls, like "Marxism" and "feminism," that have become so broad they can mean almost anything, ranging from certain verses in the Bible, ads for skin lotion and sex texts for children to the contents of *Penthouse*, Naughty '90s postcards and films with titles containing the word *Nazi* that show vicious scenes of torture and killing. It's easy to say that sensible people can tell the difference. Unfortunately, opinions on what constitutes a sensible person vary.

But even sensible people tend to lose their cool when they start talking about this subject. They soon stop talking and start yelling, and the name-calling begins. Those in favor of censorship (which may include groups not noticeably in agreement on other issues, such as some feminists and religious fundamentalists) accuse the others of exploiting women through the use of degrading images, contributing to the corruption of children, and adding to the general climate of violence and threat in which both women and children live in this society; or, though they may not give much of a hoot about actual women and children, they invoke moral standards and God's supposed aversion to "filth," "smut" and deviated *preversion*, which may mean ankles.

The camp in favor of total "freedom of expression" often comes out howling as loud as the Romans would have if told they could no longer have innocent fun watching the lions eat up Christians. It too may include segments of the population who are not natural bed-fellows: those who proclaim their God-given right to freedom, including the freedom to tote guns, drive when drunk, drool over chicken porn and get off on videotapes of women being raped and beaten, may be waving the same anticensorship banner as responsible liberals who fear the return of Mrs. Grundy, or gay groups for whom sexual emancipation involves the concept of "sexual theater." *Whatever turns you on* is a handy motto, as is *A man's home is his castle* (and if it includes a dungeon with beautiful maidens strung up in chains and bleeding from every pore, that's his business).

7   Meanwhile, theoreticians theorize and speculators speculate. Is today's pornography yet another indication of the hatred of the body, the deep mind–body split, which is supposed to pervade Western Christian society? Is it a backlash against the women's movement by men who are threatened by uppity female behavior in real life, so like to fantasize about women done up like outsize parcels, being turned into hamburger, kneeling at their feet in slavelike adoration or sucking off guns? Is it a sign of collective impotence, of a generation of men who can't relate to real women at all but have to make do with bits of celluloid and paper? Is the current flood just a result of smart marketing and aggressive promotion by the money men in what has now become a multibillion-dollar industry? If they were selling movies about men getting their testicles stuck full of knitting needles by women with swastikas on their sleeves, would they do as well, or is this penchant somehow peculiarly male? If so, why? Is pornography a power trip rather than a sex one? Some say that those ropes, chains, muzzles and other restraining devices are an argument for the immense power female sexuality still wields in the male imagination: you don't put these things on dogs unless you're afraid of them. Others, more literary, wonder about the shift from the 19th-century Magic Woman or Femme Fatale image to the lollipop-licker, airhead or turkey-carcass treatment of women in porn today. The proporners don't care much about theory: they merely demand product. The antiporners don't care about it in the final analysis either: there's dirt on the street, and they want it cleaned up, now.

8   It seems to me that this conversation, with its *You're-a-prude/You're-a-pervert* dialectic, will never get anywhere as long as we continue to think of this material as just "entertainment." Possibly we're deluded by the packaging, the format: magazine, book, movie, theatri-

cal presentation. We're used to thinking of these things as part of the "entertainment industry," and we're used to thinking of ourselves as free adult people who ought to be able to see any kind of "entertainment" we want to. That was what the First Choice pay-TV debate was all about. After all, it's only entertainment, right? Entertainment means fun, and only a killjoy would be antifun. What's the harm?

This is obviously the central question: *What's the harm?* If there   9
isn't any real harm to any real people, then the antiporners can tsk-tsk and/or throw up as much as they like, but they can't rightfully expect more legal controls or sanctions. However, the no-harm position is far from being proven.

(For instance, there's a clear-cut case for banning—as the federal   10
government has proposed—movies, photos and videos that depict children engaging in sex with adults: real children are used to make the movies, and hardly anybody thinks this is ethical. The possibilities for coercion are too great.)

To shift the viewpoint, I'd like to suggest three other models for   11
looking at "pornography"—and here I mean the violent kind.

Those who find the idea of regulating pornographic materials   12
repugnant because they think it's Fascist or Communist or otherwise not in accordance with the principles of an open democratic society should consider that Canada has made it illegal to disseminate material that may lead to hatred toward any group because of race or religion. I suggest that if pornography of the violent kind depicted these acts being done predominantly to Chinese, to blacks, to Catholics, it would be off the market immediately, under the present laws. Why is hate literature illegal? Because whoever made the law thought that such material might incite real people to do real awful things to other real people. The human brain is to a certain extent a computer: garbage in, garbage out. We only hear about the extreme cases (like that of American multimurderer Ted Bundy) in which pornography has contributed to the death and/or mutilation of women and/or men. Although pornography is not the only factor involved in the creation of such deviance, it certainly has upped the ante by suggesting both a variety of techniques and the social acceptability of such actions. Nobody knows yet what effect this stuff is having on the less psychotic.

Studies have shown that a large part of the market for all kinds of   13
porn, soft and hard, is drawn from the 16-to-21-year-old population of young men. Boys used to learn about sex on the street, or (in Italy, according to Fellini movies) from friendly whores, or, in more genteel surroundings, from girls, their parents, or, once upon a time, in school,

more or less. Now porn has been added, and sex education in the schools is rapidly being phased out. The buck has been passed, and boys are being taught that all women secretly like to be raped and that real men get high on scooping out women's digestive tracts.

14   Boys learn their concept of masculinity from other men: is this what most men want them to be learning? If word gets around that rapists are "normal" and even admirable men, will boys feel that in order to be normal, admirable and masculine they will have to be rapists? Human beings are enormously flexible, and how they turn out depends a lot on how they're educated, by the society in which they're immersed as well as by their teachers. In a society that advertises and glorifies rape or even implicitly condones it, more women get raped. It becomes socially acceptable. And at a time when men and the traditional male role have taken a lot of flak and men are confused and casting around for an acceptable way of being male (and, in some cases, not getting much comfort from women on that score), this must be at times a pleasing thought.

15   It would be naïve to think of violent pornography as just harmless entertainment. It's also an educational tool and a powerful propaganda device. What happens when boy educated on porn meets girl brought up on Harlequin romances? The clash of expectations can be heard around the block. She wants him to get down on his knees with a ring, he wants her to get down on all fours with a ring in her nose. Can this marriage be saved?

16   Pornography has certain things in common with such addictive substances as alcohol and drugs: for some, though by no means for all, it induces chemical changes in the body, which the user finds exciting and pleasurable. It also appears to attract a "hard core" of habitual users and a penumbra of those who use it occasionally but aren't dependent on it in any way. There are also significant numbers of men who aren't much interested in it, not because they're undersexed but because real life is satisfying their needs, which may not require as many appliances as those of users.

17   For the "hard core," pornography may function as alcohol does for the alcoholic: tolerance develops, and a little is no longer enough. This may account for the short viewing time and fast turnover in porn theatres. Mary Brown, chairwoman of the Ontario Board of Film Censors, estimates that for every one mainstream movie requesting entrance to Ontario, there is one porno flick. Not only the quantity consumed but the quality of explicitness must escalate, which may

account for the growing violence: once the big deal was breasts, then it was genitals, then copulation, then that was no longer enough and the hard users had to have more. The ultimate kick is death, and after that, as the Marquis de Sade so boringly demonstrated, multiple death.

The existence of alcoholism has not led us to ban social drinking. On the other hand, we do have laws about drinking and driving, excessive drunkenness and other abuses of alcohol that may result in injury or death to others.   18

This leads us back to the key question: what's the harm? Nobody knows, but this society should find out fast, before the saturation point is reached. The Scandinavian studies that showed a connection between depictions of sexual violence and increased impulse toward it on the part of male viewers would be a starting point, but many more questions remain to be raised as well as answered. What, for instance, is the crucial difference between men who are users and men who are not? Does using affect a man's relationship with actual women, and, if so, adversely? Is there a clear line between erotica and violent pornography, or are they on an escalating continuum? Is this a "men versus women" issue, with all men secretly siding with the proporners and all women secretly siding against? (I think not; there *are* lots of men who don't think that running their true love through the Cuisinart is the best way they can think of to spend a Saturday night, and they're just as nauseated by films of someone else doing it as women are.) Is pornography merely an expression of the sexual confusion of this age or an active contributor to it?   19

Nobody wants to go back to the age of official repression, when even piano legs were referred to as "limbs" and had to wear pantaloons to be decent. Neither do we want to end up in George Orwell's *1984*, in which pornography is turned out by the State to keep the proles in a state of torpor, sex itself is considered dirty and the approved practice it only for reproduction. But Rome under the emperors isn't such a good model either.   20

If all men and women respected each other, if sex were considered joyful and life-enhancing instead of a wallow in germ-filled glop, if everyone were in love all the time, if, in other words, many people's lives were more satisfactory for them than they appear to be now, pornography might just go away on its own. But since this is obviously not happening, we as a society are going to have to make some informed and responsible decisions about how to deal with it.   21

——— CONSIDERATIONS ———

1. In explaining that "pornography" means different things to different people, Atwood separates "erotica" from *her* definition of "pornography." How does she make that distinction and, more important, why?

2. Paragraph 7 consists largely of questions. Are they real questions or rhetorical questions? Explain the difference.

3. According to Atwood, what is the central question in the debate about pornography?

4. What is Atwood's strategy as demonstrated in paragraph 11? What does she hope to accomplish using it?

5. In paragraph 6, Atwood refers to "the return of Mrs. Grundy." Who was Mrs. Grundy, and why does her name pop up in many discussions of pornography, sexual values, and the like? You will find references to Mrs. Grundy in a literary handbook (e.g., *The Reader's Encyclopedia*, edited by William Rose Benet, or *The Oxford Companion to English Literature*, edited by Margaret Drabble).

6. Why do many people, including judges and lawyers, continue to disagree on a definition of "pornography"? Think of issues that pose the same problem. Note Atwood's wisdom in clarifying early in her essay what *she* means by the word. Discuss your own views of pornography.

Wendell Berry (b. 1934), essayist, novelist, and poet, was born and educated in Kentucky. He left home to teach in New York and California, and eventually returned to his "native hill." In 1986 his collection of short stories, The Wild Birds, *was published by the North Point Press, which has also reissued his earlier novels,* A Place on Earth *and* Nathan Coulter. *Among his many volumes of poetry are* Collected Poems: 1957–1982 *and* Sabbaths *(1987). His essay collections include* Recollected Essays, The Gift of Good Land *(both 1982), and* Standing By Words *(1984).*

Wendell Berry writes an essay—or a novel or a short story or a poem—in the same spirit with which he plows a field.

8

WENDELL BERRY
A Native Hill

I start down from one of the heights of the upland, the town of Port   1
Royal at my back. It is a winter day, overcast and still, and the town is
closed in itself, humming and muttering a little, like a winter beehive.

The dog runs ahead, prancing and looking back, knowing the way   2
we are about to go. This is a walk well established with us—a route in
our minds as well as on the ground. There is a sort of mystery in the
establishment of these ways. Any time one crosses a given stretch of
country with some frequency, no matter how wanderingly one begins,
the tendency is always toward habit. By the third or fourth trip, without
realizing it, one is following a fixed path, going the way one went before.
After that, one may still wander, but only by deliberation, and when
there is reason to hurry, or when the mind wanders rather than the feet,
one returns to the old route. Familiarity has begun. One has made a
relationship with the landscape, and the form and the symbol and the
enactment of the relationship is the path. These paths of mine are
seldom worn on the ground. They are habits of mind, directions, and

turns. They are as personal as old shoes. My feet are comfortable in them.

3   From the height I can see far out over the country, the long open ridges of the farmland, the wooded notches of the streams, the valley of the river opening beyond, and then more ridges and hollows of the same kind.

4   Underlying this country, nine hundred feet below the highest ridgetops, more than four hundred feet below the surface of the river, is sea level. We seldom think of it here; we are a long way from the coast and the sea is alien to us. And yet the attraction of sea level dwells in this country as an ideal dwells in a man's mind. All our rains go in search of it and, departing, they have carved the land in a shape that is fluent and falling. The streams branch like vines, and between the branches the land rises steeply and then rounds and gentles into the long narrowing fingers of ridgeland. Near the heads of the streams even the steepest land was not too long ago farmed and kept cleared. But now it has been given up and the woods is returning. The wild is flowing back like a tide. The arable ridgetops reach out above the gathered trees like headlands into the sea, bearing their human burdens of fences and houses and barns, crops and roads.

5   Looking out over the country, one gets a sense of the whole of it: the ridges and hollows, the clustered buildings of the farms, the open fields, the woods, the stock ponds set like coins into the slopes. But this is a surface sense, an exterior sense, such as you get from looking down on the roof of a house. The height is a threshold from which to step down into the wooded folds of the land, the interior, under the trees and along the branching streams.

6   I pass through a pasture gate on a deep-worn path that grows shallow a little way beyond and then disappears altogether into the grass. The gate has gathered thousands of passings to and fro, that have divided like the slats of a fan on either side of it. It is like a fist holding together the strands of a net.

7   Beyond the gate the land leans always more steeply toward the branch. I follow it down, and then bear left along the crease at the bottom of the slope. I have entered the downflow of the land. The way I am going is the way the water goes. There is something comfortable and fit-feeling in this, something free in this yielding to gravity and taking the shortest way down. The mind moves through the watershed as the water moves.

8   As the hollow deepens into the hill, before it has yet entered the woods, the grassy crease becomes a raw gulley, and along the steepening

slopes on either side I can see the old scars of erosion, places where the earth is gone clear to the rock. My people's errors have become the features of my country.

It occurs to me that it is no longer possible to imagine how this country looked in the beginning, before the white people drove their plows into it. It is not possible to know what was the shape of the land here in this hollow when it was first cleared. Too much of it is gone, loosened by the plows and washed away by the rain. I am walking the route of the departure of the virgin soil of the hill. I am not looking at the same land the first-comers saw. The original surface of the hill is as extinct as the passenger pigeon. The pristine America that the first white men saw is a lost continent, sunk like Atlantis in the sea. The thought of what was here once and is gone forever will not leave me as long as I live. It is as though I walk knee-deep in its absence. 9

The slopes along the hollow steepen still more and I go in under the trees. I pass beneath the surface. I am enclosed, and my sense, my interior sense, of the country becomes intricate. There is no longer the possibility of seeing very far. The distances are closed off by the trees and the steepening walls of the hollow. One cannot grow familiar here by sitting and looking as one can up in the open on the ridge. Here the eyes become dependent on the feet. To see the woods from the inside one must look and move and look again. It is inexhaustible in its standpoints. A lifetime will not be enough to experience it all. 10

Not far from the beginning of the woods, and set deep in the earth in the bottom of the hollow, is a rock-walled pool not a lot bigger than a bathtub. The wall is still nearly as straight and tight as when it was built. It makes a neatly turned narrow horseshoe, the open end downstream. This is a historical ruin, dug here either to catch and hold the water of the little branch, or to collect the water of a spring whose vein broke to the surface here—it is probably no longer possible to know which. The pool is filled with earth now, and grass grows in it. And the branch bends around it, cut down to the bare rock, a torrent after heavy rain, other times bone dry. All that is certain is that when the pool was dug and walled there was deep topsoil on the hill to gather and hold the water. And this high up, at least, the bottom of the hollow, instead of the present raw notch of the streambed, wore the same mantle of soil as the slopes, and the stream was a steady seep or trickle, running most or all of the year. This tiny pool no doubt once furnished water for a considerable number of stock through the hot summers. And now it is only a lost souvenir, archaic and useless, except for the bitter intelligence there is in it. It is one of the monuments to what is lost. 11

12   Like the pasture gates, the streams are great collectors of comings and goings. The streams go down, and paths always go down beside the streams. For a while I walk along an old wagon road that is buried in leaves—a fragment, beginningless and endless as the middle of a sentence on some scrap of papyrus. There is a cedar whose branches reach over this road, and under the branches I find the leavings of two kills of some bird of prey. The most recent is a pile of blue jay feathers. The other has been rained on and is not identifiable. How little we know. How little of this was intended or expected by any man. The road that has become the grave of men's passages has led to the life of the woods.

> And I say to myself: Here is your road
> without beginning or end, appearing
> out of the earth and ending in it, bearing
> no load but the hawk's kill, and the leaves
> building earth on it, something more
> to be borne. Tracks fill with earth
> and return to absence. The road was worn
> by men bearing earth along it. They have come
> to endlessness. In their passing
> they could not stay in, trees have risen
> and stand still. It is leading to the dark,
> to morning where you are not. Here
> is your road, beginningless and endless as God.

13   Now I have come down within the sound of the water. The winter has been rainy, and the hill is full of dark seeps and trickles, gathering finally, along these creases, into flowing streams. The sound of them is one of the elements, and defines a zone. When their voices return to the hill after their absence during summer and autumn, it is a better place to be. A thirst in the mind is quenched.

14   I have already passed the place where water began to flow in the little stream bed I am following. It broke into the light from beneath a rock ledge, a thin glittering stream. It lies beside me as I walk, overtaking me and going by, yet not moving, a thread of light and sound. And now from below comes the steady tumble and rush of the water of Camp Branch—whose nameless camp was it named for?—and gradually as I descend the sound of the smaller stream is lost in the sound of the larger.

15   The two hollows join, the line of the meeting of the two spaces obscured even in winter by the trees. But the two streams meet precisely as two roads. That is, the stream *beds* do; the one ends in the other. As for the meeting of the waters, there is no looking at that. The

one flow does not end in the other, but continues in it, one with it, two clarities merged without a shadow.

All waters are one. This is a reach of the sea, flung like a net over 16 the hill, and now drawn back to the sea. And as the sea is never raised in the earthly nets of fishermen, so the hill is never caught and pulled down by the watery net of the sea. But always a little of it is. Each of the gathering strands of the net carries back some of the hill melted in it. Sometimes, as now, it carries so little that the water seems to flow clear, sometimes it carries a lot and is brown and heavy with it. Whenever greedy or thoughtless men have lived on it, the hill has literally flowed out of their tracks into the bottom of the sea.

There appears to be a law that when creatures have reached the 17 level of consciousness, as men have, they must become conscious of the creation; they must learn how they fit into it and what its needs are and what it requires of them, or else pay a terrible penalty: the spirit of the creation will go out of them, and they will become destructive. The very earth will depart from them and go where they cannot follow.

My mind is never empty or idle at the joinings of streams. Here is 18 the work of the world going on. The creation is felt, alive, and intent on its materials, in such places. In the angle of the meeting of the two streams stands the steep wooded point of the ridge, like the prow of an upturned boat—finished, as it was a thousand years ago, as it will be in a thousand years. Its becoming is only incidental to its being. It will be because it is. It has no aim or end except to be. By being it is growing and wearing into what it will be. The fork of the stream lies at the foot of the slope like hammer and chisel laid down at the foot of a finished sculpture. But the stream is no dead tool; it is alive, it is still at its work. Put your hand to it to learn the health of this part of the world. It is the wrist of the hill.

Perhaps it is to prepare to hear some day the music of the spheres 19 that I am always turning my ears to the music of streams. There is indeed a music in streams, but it is not for the hurried. It has to be loitered by and imagined. Or imagined *toward*, for it is hardly for men at all. Nature has a patient ear. To her the slowest funeral march sounds like a jig. She is satisfied to have the notes drawn out to the lengths of days or weeks or months. Small variations are acceptable to her, modulations as leisurely as the opening of a flower.

The stream is full of stops and gates. Here it has piled up rocks in 20 its path, and pours over them into a tiny pool it has scooped at the foot of its fall. Here it has been dammed by a mat of leaves caught behind a fallen limb. Here it must force a narrow passage, here a wider one.

Tomorrow the flow may increase or slacken, and the tone will shift. In an hour or a week that rock may give way, and the composition will advance by another note. Some idea of it may be got by walking slowly along and noting the changes as one passes from one little fall or rapid to another. But this is a highly simplified and diluted version of the real thing, which is too complex and widespread ever to be actually heard by us. The ear must imagine an impossible patience in order to grasp even the unimaginableness of such music.

21   But the creation is musical, and this is a part of its music, as birdsong is, or the words of poets. The music of the streams is the music of the shaping of the earth, by which the rocks are pushed and shifted downward toward the level of the sea.

22   And now I find lying in the path an empty beer can. This is the track of the ubiquitous man Friday of all our woods. In my walks I never fail to discover some sign that he has preceded me. I find his empty shotgun shells, his empty cans and bottles, his sandwich wrappings. In wooded places along roadsides one is apt to find, as well, his over-travelled bedsprings, his outcast refrigerator, and heaps of the imperishable refuse of his modern kitchen. A year ago, almost in this same place where I have found his beer can, I found a possum that he had shot dead and left lying, in celebration of his manhood. He is the true American pioneer, perfectly at rest in his assumption that he is the first and the last whose inheritance and fate this place will ever be. Going forth, as he may think, to sow, he only broadcasts his effects.

23   As I go on down the path alongside Camp Branch, I walk by the edge of croplands abandoned only within my own lifetime. On my left are south slopes where the woods are old, long undisturbed. On my right, the more fertile north slopes are covered with patches of briars and sumacs and a lot of young walnut trees. Tobacco of an extraordinary quality was once grown here, and then the soil wore thin, and these places were given up for the more accessible ridges that were not so steep, where row-cropping made better sense anyway. But now, under the thicket growth, a mat of bluegrass has grown to testify to the good nature of this ground. It was fine dirt that lay here once, and I am far from being able to say that I could have resisted the temptation to plow it. My understanding of what is best for it is the tragic understanding of hindsight, the awareness that I have been taught what was here to be lost by the loss of it.

24   We have lived by the assumption that what was good for us would be good for the world. And this has been based on the even flimsier assumption that we could know with any certainty what was good even

for us. We have fulfilled the danger of this by making our personal pride and greed the standard of our behavior toward the world—to the incalculable disadvantage of the world and every living thing in it. And now, perhaps very close to too late, our great error has become clear. It is not only our own creativity—our own capacity for life—that is stifled by our arrogant assumption; the creation itself is stifled.

We have been wrong. We must change our lives, so that it will be possible to live by the contrary assumption that what is good for the world will be good for us. And that requires that we make the effort to *know* the world and to learn what is good for it. We must learn to cooperate in its processes, and to yield to its limits. But even more important, we must learn to acknowledge that the creation is full of mystery; we will never entirely understand it. We must abandon arrogance and stand in awe. We must recover the sense of the majesty of creation, and the ability to be worshipful in its presence. For I do not doubt that it is only on the condition of humility and reverence before the world that our species will be able to remain in it. 25

Standing in the presence of these worn and abandoned fields, where the creation has begun its healing without the hindrance or the help of man, with the voice of the stream in the air and the woods standing in silence on all the slopes around me, I am deep in the interior not only of my place in the world, but of my own life, its sources and searches and concerns. I first came into these places following the men to work when I was a child. I knew the men who took their lives from such fields as these, and their lives to a considerable extent made my life what it is. In what came to me from them there was both wealth and poverty, and I have been a long time discovering which was which. 26

It was in the woods here along Camp Branch that Bill White, my grandfather's hired hand, taught me to hunt squirrels. Bill lived in a little tin-roofed house on up nearer the head of the hollow. And this was, I suppose more than any other place, his hunting ground. It was the place of his freedom, where he could move without subservience, without considering who he was or who anybody else was. On late summer mornings, when it was too wet to work, I would follow him into the woods. As soon as we stepped in under the trees he would become silent, and absolutely attentive to the life of the place. He was a good teacher and an exacting one. The rule seemed to be that if I wanted to stay with him, I had to make it possible for him to forget I was there. I was to make no noise. If I did he would look back and make a downward emphatic gesture with his hand, as explicit as writing: Be quiet, or go home. He would see a squirrel crouched in a fork or lying along the top 27 of a branch, and indicate with a grin and a small jerk of his head where I should look; and then wait, while I, conscious of being watched and demanded upon, searched it out for myself. He taught me to look and to listen and to be quiet. I wonder if he knew the value of such teaching or the rarity of such a teacher.

28   In the years that followed I hunted often here alone. And later in these same woods I experienced my first obscure dissatisfactions with hunting. Though I could not have put it into words then, the sense had come to me that hunting as I knew it—the eagerness to kill something I did not need to eat—was an artificial relation to the place, when what I was beginning to need, just as inarticulately then, was a relation that would be deeply natural and meaningful. That was a time of great uneasiness and restlessness for me. It would be the fall of the year, the leaves would be turning, and ahead of me would be another year of school. There would be confusions about girls and ambitions, the wordless hurried feeling that time and events and my own nature were pushing me toward what I was going to be—and I had no notion what it was, or how to prepare.

29   And then there were years when I did not come here at all—when these places and their history were in my mind, and part of me, in places thousands of miles away. And now I am here again, changed from what I was, and still changing. The future is no more certain to me now than it ever was, though its risks are clearer, and so are my own desires. I am the father of two young children whose lives are hostages given to the future. Because of them and because of events in the world, life seems more fearful and difficult to me now than ever before; but it is also more inviting, and I am constantly aware of its nearness to joy. Much of the interest and excitement that I have in my life now has come from the deepening, in the years since my return here, of my relation to this countryside that is my native place. For in spite of all that has happened to me in other places, the great change and the great possibility of change in my life has been in my sense of this place. The major difference is perhaps only that I have grown able to be wholeheartedly present here. I am able to sit and be quiet at the foot of some tree here in this woods along Camp Branch, and feel a deep peace, both in the place and in my awareness of it, that not too long ago I was not conscious of the possibility of. This peace is partly in being free of the suspicion that pursued me for most of my life, no matter where I was, that there was perhaps another place I *should* be, or would be happier or better in; it is partly in the increasingly articulate consciousness of being here, and of the significance and importance of being here.

After more than thirty years I have at last arrived at the candor   30
necessary to stand on this part of the earth that is so full of my own
history and so much damaged by it, and ask: What *is* this place? What is
in it? What is its nature? How should men live in it? What must I do?

I have not found the answers, though I believe that in partial and   31
fragmentary ways they have begun to come to me. But the questions are
more important than their answers. In the final sense they *have* no
answers. They are like the questions—they are perhaps the same
questions—that were the discipline of Job. They are part of the necessary enactment of humility, teaching a man what his importance is,
what his responsibility is, and what his place is, both on the earth and in
the order of things. And though the answers must always come ob-
scurely and in fragments, the questions must be persistently asked.
They are fertile questions. In their implications and effects, they are
moral and esthetic and, in the best and fullest sense, practical. They
promise a relationship to the world that is decent and preserving.

They are also, both in origin and effect, religious. I am uneasy with   32
the term, for such religion as has been openly practiced in this part of
the world has promoted and fed upon a destructive schism between
body and soul, heaven and earth. It has encouraged people to believe
that the world is of no importance, and that their only obligation in it is
to submit to certain churchly formulas in order to get to heaven. And so
the people who might have been expected to care most selflessly for the
world have had their minds turned elsewhere—to a pursuit of "salvation" that was really only another form of gluttony and self-love, the
desire to perpetuate their own small lives beyond the life of the world.
The heaven-bent have abused the earth thoughtlessly, by inattention,
and their negligence has permitted and encouraged others to abuse it
deliberately. Once the creator was removed from the creation, divinity
became only a remote abstraction, a social weapon in the hands of the
religious institutions. This split in public values produced or was accompanied by, as it was bound to be, an equally artificial and ugly
division in people's lives, so that a man, while pursuing heaven with the
sublime appetite he thought of as his soul, could turn his heart against
his neighbors and his hands against the world. For these reasons, though
I know that my questions *are* religious, I dislike having to *say* that
they are.

But when I ask them my aim is not primarily to get to heaven.   33
Though heaven is certainly more important than the earth if all they
say about it is true, it is still morally incidental to it and dependent on
it, and I can only imagine it and desire it in terms of which I know of the

earth. And so my questions do not aspire beyond the earth. They aspire *toward* it and *into* it. Perhaps they aspire *through* it. They are religious because they are asked at the limit of what I know; they acknowledge mystery and honor its presence in the creation; they are spoken in reverence for the order and grace that I see, and that I trust beyond my power to see.

34   The stream has led me down to an old barn built deep in the hollow to house the tobacco once grown on those abandoned fields. Now it is surrounded by the trees that have come back on every side—a relic, a fragment of another time, strayed out of its meaning. This is the last of my historical landmarks. To here, my walk has had insistent overtones of memory and history. It has been a movement of consciousness through knowledge, eroding and shaping, adding and wearing away. I have descended like the water of the stream through what I know of myself, and now that I have there is a little more to know. But here at the barn, the old roads and the cow paths—the formal connections with civilization—come to an end.

35   I stoop between the strands of a barbed wire fence, and in that movement I go out of time into timelessness. I come into a wild place. I walk along the foot of a slope that was once cut bare of trees, like all the slopes of this part of the country—but long ago; and now the woods is established again, the ground healed, the trees grown big, their trunks rising clean, free of undergrowth. The place has a serenity and dignity that one feels immediately; the creation is whole in it and unobstructed. It is free of the strivings and dissatisfactions, the partialities and imperfections of places under the mechanical dominance of men. Here, what to a housekeeper's eye might seem disorderly is nonetheless orderly and within order; what might seem arbitrary or accidental is included in the design of the whole as if by intention; what might seem evil or violent is a comfortable member of the household. Where the creation is whole nothing is extraneous. The presence of the creation here makes this a holy place, and it is as a pilgrim that I have come—to give the homage of awe and love, to submit to mystification. It is the creation that has attracted me, its perfect interfusion of life and design. I have made myself its follower and its apprentice.

36   One early morning last spring, I came and found the woods floor strewn with bluebells. In the cool sunlight and the lacy shadows of the spring woods the blueness of those flowers, their elegant shape, their delicate fresh scent kept me standing and looking. I found a rich delight in them that I cannot describe and that I will never forget. Though I had been familiar for years with most of the spring woods flowers, I had never seen these and had not known they grew here. Looking at them, I

felt a strange feeling of loss and sorrow that I had never seen them before. But I was also exultant that I saw them now—that they were here.

For me, in the thought of them will always be the sense of the joyful surprise with which I found them—the sense that came suddenly to me then that the world is blessed beyond my understanding, more abundantly than I will ever know. What lives are still ahead of me here to be discovered and exulted in, tomorrow, or in twenty years? What wonder will be found here on the morning after my death? Though as a man I inherit great evils and the possibility of great loss and suffering, I know that my life is blessed and graced by the yearly flowering of the bluebells. How perfect they are! In their presence I am humble and joyful. If I were given all the learning and all the methods of my race I could not make one of them, or even imagine one. Solomon in all his glory was not arrayed like one of these. It is the privilege and the labor of the apprentice of creation to come with his imagination into the unimaginable, and with his speech into the unspeakable. 37

—— **CONSIDERATIONS** ————————————————————

1. To think of habits as paths worn in the mind is no very original metaphor. How does Berry distinguish this image as he works it into the essay?

2. Berry's essay, like the walk he is reporting, is a leisurely experience that should be taken in an unhurried manner. Much of this easy pace is due to his style: he makes an observation, then pauses to reflect on it and related things, then moves along to another observation, and another reflective pause, and so on. The result is a pleasing, thoughtful mix of the factual and the insightful. Try writing a short, descriptive essay in this style.

3. "Nature has a patient ear," writes Berry in paragraph 19, using a literary technique called personification. Look for examples of personification in the works of other writers, or make up several yourself (e.g., "the blindness of the night," "the laughter of the wind," "the soul of the abandoned house"). Then explain the meaning of personification and its value to a writer like Berry.

4. Assuming paragraph 30 is an explicit pronouncement of his thesis, what varied means does Berry use to embody these ideas?

5. On his walk, Berry follows the downward course of streams and slopes and gulleys. In what way does his essay also follow downward, converging courses to lead you to his conclusion?

6. Throughout his essay, Berry works to evoke a sense of place—that hill where he grew up and to which he now returns. Yet he also thinks on a wider scale—the state of the nation, and even the world. Is he successful in fusing the various planes? If so, how does he manage it? If not, why not?

Ambrose Bierce (1842–1914?) was born in a log cabin on Horse Cave Creek in Ohio. He educated himself by reading the books in his father's small library, and as a young man served in the army during the Civil War. Starting as a journalist in California, he made himself an elegant writer of short stories, which were often supernatural or macabre in theme. Because he was writing in the primitive West, in a country still generally primitive, his serious work went largely unrecognized. Melancholy deepened into misanthropy. The definitions in The Devil's Dictionary *(1906) are funny indeed—but the humor is serious, and the wit is bitter.*

In 1913, Bierce put his affairs in order and went to Mexico, which was in the midst of a civil war. He wrote a friend as he left, ". . . if you hear of my being stood up against a Mexican stone wall and shot to rags please know that I think it a pretty good way to depart this life. It beats old age, disease, or falling down a flight of stairs." He was never heard from again.

9

AMBROSE BIERCE
Some Devil's Definitions

1   *Belladonna, n.* In Italian a beautiful lady; in English a deadly poison. A striking example of the essential identity of the two tongues.

2   *Bigot, n.* One who is obstinately and zealously attached to an opinion that you do not entertain.

3   *Bore, n.* A person who talks when you wish him to listen.

4   *Brute, n. See* HUSBAND.

5   *Cabbage, n.* A familiar kitchen-garden vegetable about as large and wise as a man's head.

6   *Calamity, n.* A more than commonly plain and unmistakable reminder that the affairs of this life are not of our own ordering. Calamities are of two kinds: misfortune to ourselves, and good fortune to others.

Cannibal, n. A gastronome of the old school who preserves the 7
simple tastes and adheres to the natural diet of the pre-pork period.

Cannon, n. An instrument employed in the rectification of na- 8
tional boundaries.

Cat, n. A soft, indestructible automaton provided by nature to be 9
kicked when things go wrong in the domestic circle.

Christian, n. One who believes that the New Testament is a 10
divinely inspired book admirably suited to the spiritual needs of his
neighbor. One who follows the teachings of Christ in so far as they are
not inconsistent with a life of sin.

Clairvoyant, n. A person, commonly a woman, who has the power 11
of seeing that which is invisible to her patron—namely, that he is a
blockhead.

Commerce, n. A kind of transaction in which A plunders from B 12
the goods of C, and for compensation B picks the pocket of D of money
belonging to E.

Compromise, n. Such an adjustment of conflicting interests as 13
gives each adversary the satisfaction of thinking he has got what he ought
not to have, and is deprived of nothing except what was justly his due.

Compulsion, n. The eloquence of power. 14

Congratulation, n. The civility of envy. 15

Conservative, n. A statesman who is enamored of existing evils, as 16
distinguished from the Liberal, who wishes to replace them with
others.

Consul, n. In American politics, a person who having failed to 17
secure an office from the people is given one by the Administration on
condition that he leave the country.

Consult, v.t. To seek another's approval of a course already de- 18
cided on.

Corsair, n. A politician of the seas. 19

Coward, n. One who in a perilous emergency thinks with his legs. 20

Curiosity, n. An objectionable quality of the female mind. The 21
desire to know whether or not a woman is cursed with curiosity is one
of the most active and insatiable passions of the masculine soul.

Cynic, n. A blackguard whose faulty vision sees things as they are, 22
not as they ought to be. Hence the custom among the Scythians of
plucking out a cynic's eyes to improve his vision.

Dance, v.i. To leap about to the sound of tittering music, prefera- 23
bly with arms about your neighbor's wife or daughter. There are many
kinds of dances, but all those requiring the participation of the two

sexes have two characteristics in common: they are conspicuously innocent, and warmly loved by the vicious.

24   *Debauchee, n.* One who has so earnestly pursued pleasure that he has had the misfortune to overtake it.

25   *Decalogue, n.* A series of commandments, ten in number—just enough to permit an intelligent selection for observance, but not enough to embarrass the choice.

26   *Defame, v.t.* To lie about another. To tell the truth about another.

27   *Dentist, n.* A prestidigitator who, putting metal in your mouth, pulls coins out of your pocket.

28   *Die, n.* The singular of "dice." We seldom hear the word, because there is a prohibitory proverb, "Never say die."

29   *Discussion, n.* A method of confirming others in their errors.

30   *Distance, n.* The only thing that the rich are willing for the poor to call theirs, and keep.

31   *Duel, n.* A formal ceremony preliminary to the reconciliation of two enemies. Great skill is necessary to its satisfactory observance; if awkwardly performed the most unexpected and deplorable consequences sometimes ensue. A long time ago a man lost his life in a duel.

32   *Eccentricity, n.* A method of distinction so cheap that fools employ it to accentuate their incapacity.

33   *Edible, adj.* Good to eat, and wholesome to digest, as a worm to a toad, a toad to a snake, a snake to a pig, a pig to a man, and a man to a worm.

34   *Education, n.* That which discloses to the wise and disguises from the foolish their lack of understanding.

35   *Effect, n.* The second of two phenomena which always occur together in the same order. The first, called a Cause, is said to generate the other—which is no more sensible than it would be for one who has never seen a dog except in pursuit of a rabbit to declare the rabbit the cause of the dog.

36   *Egotist, n.* A person of low taste, more interested in himself than in me.

37   *Erudition, n.* Dust shaken out of a book into an empty skull.

38   *Eulogy, n.* Praise of a person who has either the advantages of wealth and power, or the consideration to be dead.

39   *Female, n.* One of the opposing, or unfair, sex.

40   *Fib, n.* A lie that has not cut its teeth. A habitual liar's nearest approach to truth: the perigee of his eccentric orbit.

Fiddle, n. An instrument to tickle human ears by friction of a   41
horse's tail on the entrails of a cat.

Friendship, n. A ship big enough to carry two in fair weather, but   42
only one in foul.

Garter, n. An elastic band intended to keep a woman from coming   43
out of her stockings and desolating the country.

Ghost, n. The outward and visible sign of an inward fear.   44

Glutton, n. A person who escapes the evils of moderation by   45
committing dyspepsia.

Gout, n. A physician's name for the rheumatism of a rich patient.   46

Grammar, n. A system of pitfalls thoughtfully prepared for the   47
feet of the self-made man, along the path by which he advances to
distinction.

Guillotine, n. A machine which makes a Frenchman shrug his   48
shoulders with good reason.

CONSIDERATIONS

1. To appreciate the humor in some of Bierce's definitions, you may have
to look up in your dictionary some of the words found here, such as "gastronome," "zealously," "adversary," "civility," "insatiable," "prestidigitator,"
"perigee," "dyspepsia." How do you add words to your working vocabulary?

2. *The Devil's Dictionary* was first published in 1906. Judging from the
definitions here, would you say that Bierce's book is dated? Which items strike
you as most relevant to our times? Which are least relevant? Why?

3. Do you find a consistent tone or attitude in Bierce's dictionary? Explain and provide ample evidence.

4. George Orwell, in "Politics and the English Language," is critical of
euphemisms. Would Bierce agree with Orwell?

5. Who among these authors would most appreciate Bierce's brand of
humor: Margaret Atwood ("Homelanding"), Frederick Douglass ("Plantation
Life"), Flannery O'Connor ("A Good Man Is Hard to Find"), or George Orwell
("A Hanging")? Explain, making comparisons.

6. Compose a page of definitions for your own Devil's Dictionary, perhaps concentrating on words currently popular.

Caroline Bird (b. 1915) was born in New York City, taught at Vassar, and now divides her time between Manhattan and Poughkeepsie. She has been an editor and a teacher and is the author of Born Female *(1968),* The Case Against College *(1975),* What Women Want *(1979),* The Two-Paycheck Marriage *(1982), and* The Good Years: Your Life in the 21st Century *(1983). Here she argues the case against college with a clear vigor and a committed pugnacity; only a skilled debater with a good college education could dispute her.*

10

CAROLINE BIRD
Where College Fails Us

1   The case *for* college has been accepted without question for more than a generation. All high school graduates ought to go, says Conventional Wisdom and statistical evidence, because college will help them earn more money, become "better" people, and learn to be more responsible citizens than those who don't go.

2   But college has never been able to work its magic for everyone. And now that close to half our high school graduates are attending, those who don't fit the pattern are becoming more numerous, and more obvious. College graduates are selling shoes and driving taxis; college students sabotage each other's experiments and forge letters of recommendation in the intense competition for admission to graduate school. Others find no stimulation in their studies, and drop out—often encouraged by college administrators.

3   Some observers say the fault is with the young people themselves—they are spoiled, stoned, overindulged, and expecting too much. But that's mass character assassination, and doesn't explain

all campus unhappiness. Others blame the state of the world, and they are partly right. We've been told that young people have to go to college because our economy can't absorb an army of untrained eighteen-year-olds. But disillusioned graduates are learning that it can no longer absorb an army of trained twenty-two-year-olds, either.

Some adventuresome educators and campus watchers have 4 openly begun to suggest that college may not be the best, the proper, the only place for every young person after the completion of high school. We may have been looking at all those surveys and statistics upside down, it seems, and through the rosy glow of our own remembered college experiences. Perhaps college doesn't make people intelligent, ambitious, happy, liberal, or quick to learn new things—maybe it's just the other way around, and intelligent, ambitious, happy, liberal, and quick-learning people are merely the ones who have been attracted to college in the first place. And perhaps all those successful college graduates would have been successful whether they had gone to college or not. This is heresy to those of us who have been brought up to believe that if a little schooling is good, more has to be much better. But contrary evidence is beginning to mount up.

The unhappiness and discontent of young people is nothing new, 5 and problems of adolescence are always painfully intense. But while traveling around the country, speaking at colleges, and interviewing students at all kinds of schools—large and small, public and private—I was overwhelmed by the prevailing sadness. It was as visible on campuses in California as in Nebraska and Massachusetts. Too many young people are in college reluctantly, because everyone told them they ought to go, and there didn't seem to be anything better to do. Their elders sell them college because it's good for them. Some never learn to like it, and talk about their time in school as if it were a sentence to be served.

Students tell us the same thing college counselors tell us—they go 6 because of pressure from parents and teachers, and stay because it seems to be an alternative to a far worse fate. It's "better" than the Army or a dead-end job, and it has to be pretty bad before it's any worse than staying at home.

College graduates say that they don't want to work "just" for 7 the money: They want work that matters. They want to help people and save the world. But the numbers are stacked against them. Not only are there not enough jobs in world-saving fields, but in the current slowdown it has become evident that there never were, and probably never will be, enough jobs requiring higher education to go around.[1]

8   Students who tell their advisers they want to help people, for example, are often directed to psychology. This year the Department of Labor estimates that there will be 4,300 new jobs for psychologists, while colleges will award 58,430 bachelor's degrees in psychology.

9   Sociology has become a favorite major on socially conscious campuses, but graduates find that social reform is hardly a paying occupation. Male sociologists from the University of Wisconsin reported as gainfully employed a year after graduation included a legal assistant, sports editor, truck unloader, Peace Corps worker, publications director, and a stockboy—but no sociologist per se. The highest paid worked for the post office.

10   Publishing, writing, and journalism are presumably the vocational goal of a large proportion of the 104,000 majors in Communications and Letters expected to graduate in 1975. The outlook for them is grim. All of the daily newspapers in the country combined are expected to hire a total of 2,600 reporters this year. Radio and television stations may hire a total of 500 announcers, most of them in local radio stations. Non-publishing organizations will need 1,100 technical writers, and public-relations activities another 4,400. Even if new graduates could get all these jobs (they can't, of course), over 90,000 of them will have to find something less glamorous to do.

11   Other fields most popular with college graduates are also pathetically small. Only 1,900 foresters a year will be needed during this decade, although schools of forestry are expected to continue graduating twice that many. Some will get sub-professional jobs as forestry aides. Schools of architecture are expected to turn out twice as many [architects] as will be needed, and while all sorts of people want to design things, the Department of Labor forecasts that there will be jobs for only 400 new industrial designers a year. As for anthropologists, only 400 will be needed every year in the 1970s to take care of all the college courses, public-health research, community surveys, museums, and all the archaeological digs on every continent. (For these jobs graduate work in anthropology is required.)

12   Many popular occupations may seem to be growing fast without necessarily offering employment to very many. "Recreation work" is

[1] [Editors' Note: Ms. Bird's article appeared in 1975.] According to the Department of Labor Bureau of Statistics, 20.8 million college graduates will enter the work force from 1982 to 1995; the bureau predicts only 16.9 million job openings in traditional jobs for college graduates during that period.

always cited as an expanding field, but it will need relatively few workers who require more special training than life guards. "Urban planning" has exploded in the media, so the U.S. Department of Labor doubled its estimate of the number of jobs to be filled every year in the 1970s—to a big, fat 800. A mere 200 oceanographers a year will be able to do all the exploring of "inner space"—and all that exciting underwater diving you see demonstrated on television—for the entire decade of the 1970s.

Whatever college graduates *want* to do, most of them are going to wind up doing what *there is* to do. During the next few years, according to the Labor Department, the biggest demand will be for stenographers and secretaries, followed by retail-trade salesworkers, hospital attendants, bookkeepers, building custodians, registered nurses, foremen, kindergarten and elementary-school teachers, receptionists, cooks, cosmetologists, private-household workers, manufacturing inspectors, and industrial machinery repairmen. These are the jobs that will eventually absorb the surplus archaeologists, urban planners, oceanographers, sociologists, editors, and college professors.   13

Vocationalism is the new look on campus because of the discouraging job market faced by the generalists. Students have been opting for medicine and law in droves. If all those who check "doctor" as their career goal succeed in getting their MDs, we'll immediately have ten times the target ratio of doctors for the population of the United States. Law schools are already graduating twice as many new lawyers every year as the Department of Labor thinks we will need, and the oversupply grows annually.   14

Specialists often find themselves at the mercy of shifts in demand, and the narrower the vocational training, the more risky the long-term prospects. Engineers are the classic example of the "Yo-Yo" effect in supply and demand. Today's shortage is apt to produce a big crop of engineering graduates after the need has crested, and teachers face the same squeeze.   15

Worse than that, when the specialists turn up for work, they often find that they have learned a lot of things in classrooms that they will never use, that they will have to learn a lot of things on the job that they were never taught, and that most of what they have learned is less likely to "come in handy later" than to fade from memory. One disillusioned architecture student, who had already designed and built houses, said, "It's the degree you need, not everything you learn getting it."   16

A diploma saves the employer the cost of screening candidates and gives him a predictable product: He can assume that those who have   17 survived the four-year ordeal have learned how to manage themselves. They have learned how to budget their time, meet deadlines, set priorities, cope with impersonal authority, follow instructions, and stick with a task that may be tiresome without direct supervision.

18   The employer is also betting that it will be cheaper and easier to train the college graduate because he has demonstrated his ability to learn. But if the diploma serves only to identify those who are talented in the art of schoolwork, it becomes, in the words of Harvard's Christopher Jencks, "a hell of an expensive aptitude test." It is unfair to the candidates because they themselves must bear the cost of the screening—the cost of college. Candidates without the funds, the academic temperament, or the patience for the four-year obstacle race are ruled out, no matter how well they may perform on the job. But if "everyone" has a diploma, employers will have to find another way to choose employees, and it will become an empty credential.

19   (Screening by diploma may in fact already be illegal. The 1971 ruling of the Supreme Court in *Griggs* v. *Duke Power Co.* contended that an employer cannot demand a qualification which systematically excludes an entire class of applicants, unless that qualification reliably predicts success on the job. The requiring of a high school diploma was outlawed in the *Griggs* case, and this could extend to a college diploma.)

20   The bill for four years at an Ivy League college is currently climbing toward $70,000; at a state university, a degree will cost the student and his family about $10,000 (with taxpayers making up the difference).

21   Not many families can afford these sums, and when they look for financial aid, they discover that someone else will decide how much they will actually have to pay. The College Scholarship Service, which establishes a family's degree of need for most colleges, is guided by noble principles: uniformity of sacrifice, need rather than merit. But families vary in their willingness to "sacrifice" as much as the bureaucracy of the CSS thinks they ought to. This is particularly true of middle-income parents, whose children account for the bulk of the country's college students. Some have begun to rebel against this attempt to enforce the same values and priorities on all. "In some families, a college education competes with a second car, a color television, or a trip to Europe—and it's possible that college may lose," one financial-aid officer recently told me.

22   Quite so. College is worth more to some middle-income families than to others. It is chilling to consider the undercurrent of resentment that families who "give up everything" must feel toward their college-

age children, or the burden of guilt children must bear every time they goof off or receive less than top grades in their courses.

The decline in return for a college degree within the last genera-   23
tion has been substantial. In the 1950s, a Princeton student could pay his expenses for the school year—eating club and all—on less than $3,000. When he graduated, he entered a job market which provided a comfortable margin over the earnings of his agemates who had not been to college. To be precise, a freshman entering Princeton in 1956, the earliest year for which the Census has attempted to project lifetime earnings, could expect to realize a 12.5 percent return on his invest-ment. A freshman entering in 1972, with the cost nearing $6,000 annu-ally, could expect to realize only 9.3 percent, less than might be avail-able in the money market. This calculation was made with the help of a banker and his computer, comparing college as an investment in future earnings with other investments available in the booming money mar-ket of 1974, and concluded that in strictly financial terms, college is not always the best investment a young person can make.

I postulated a young man in 1974 (the figures are different with a   24
young woman, but the principle is the same) whose rich uncle would give him, in cash, the total cost of four years at Princeton—$34,181. (The total includes what the young man would earn if he went to work instead of to college right after high school.) If he did not spend the money on Princeton, but put it in the savings bank at 7.5 percent interest compounded daily, he would have, at retirement age sixty-four, more than five times as much as the $199,000 extra he could expect to earn between twenty-two and sixty as a college man rather than a mere high school graduate. And with all that money accumulating in the bank, he could invest in something with a higher return than a diploma. At age twenty-eight, when his nest egg had reached $73,113, he could buy a liquor store, which would return him well over 20 percent on his investment, as long as he was willing to mind the store. He might get a bit fidgety sitting there, but he'd have to be dim-witted to lose money on a liquor store, and right now we're talking only about dol-lars.

If the young man went to a public college rather than Princeton,   25
the investment would be lower, and the payoff higher, of course, be-cause other people—the taxpayers—put up part of the capital for him. But the difference in return between an investment in public and pri-vate colleges is minimized because the biggest part of the investment in either case is the money a student might earn if he went to work, not to

college—in economic terms, his "foregone income." That he bears himself.

26   Rates of return and dollar signs on education are a fascinating brain teaser, and, obviously, there is a certain unreality to the game. But the same unreality extends to the traditional calculations that have always been used to convince taxpayers that college is a worthwhile investment.

27   The ultimate defense of college has always been that while it may not teach you anything vocationally useful, it will somehow make you a better person, able to do anything better, and those who make it through the process are initiated into the "fellowship of educated men and women." In a study intended to probe what graduates seven years out of college thought their colleges should have done for them, the Carnegie Commission found that most alumni expected the "development of my abilities to think and express myself." But if such respected educational psychologists as Bruner and Piaget are right, specific learning skills have to be acquired very early in life, perhaps even before formal schooling begins.

28   So, when pressed, liberal-arts defenders speak instead about something more encompassing, and more elusive. "College changed me inside," one graduate told us fervently. The authors of a Carnegie Commission report, who obviously struggled for a definition, concluded that one of the common threads in the perceptions of a liberal education is that it provides "an integrated view of the world which can serve as an inner guide." More simply, alumni say that college should have "helped me to formulate the values and goals of my life."

29   In theory, a student is taught to develop these values and goals himself, but in practice, it doesn't work quite that way. All but the wayward and the saintly take their sense of the good, the true, and the beautiful from the people around them. When we speak of students acquiring "values" in college, we often mean that they will acquire the values—and sometimes that means only the tastes—of their professors. The values of professors may be "higher" than many students will encounter elsewhere, but they may not be relevant to situations in which students find themselves in college and later.

30   Of all the forms in which ideas are disseminated, the college professor lecturing a class is the slowest and most expensive. You don't have to go to college to read the great books or learn about the great ideas of Western Man. Today you can find them everywhere—in paperbacks, in the public libraries, in museums, in public lectures, in adult-education courses, in abridged, summarized, or adapted form in maga-

zines, films, and television. The problem is no longer one of access to broadening ideas; the problem is the other way around: how to choose among the many courses of action proposed to us, how to edit the stimulations that pour into our eyes and ears every waking hour. A college experience that piles option on option and stimulation on stimulation merely adds to the contemporary nightmare.

What students and graduates say that they did learn on campus   31 comes under the heading of personal, rather than intellectual, development. Again and again I was told that the real value of college is learning to get along with others, to practice social skills, to "sort out my head," and these have nothing to do with curriculum.

For whatever impact the academic experience used to have on   32 college students, the sheer size of many undergraduate classes in the 1970s dilutes faculty–student dialogue, and, more often than not, they are taught by teachers who were hired when colleges were faced with a shortage of qualified instructors, during their years of expansion and when the big rise in academic pay attracted the mediocre and the less than dedicated.

On the social side, colleges are withdrawing from responsibility   33 for feeding, housing, policing, and protecting students at a time when the environment of college may be the most important service it could render. College officials are reluctant to "intervene" in the personal lives of the students. They no longer expect to take over from parents, but often insist that students—who have, most often, never lived away from home before—take full adult responsibility for their plans, achievements, and behavior.

Most college students do not live in the plush, comfortable   34 country-clublike surroundings their parents envisage, or, in some cases, remember. Open dorms, particularly when they are coeducational, are noisy, usually overcrowded, and often messy. Some students desert the institutional "zoos" (their own word for dorms) and move into run-down, overpriced apartments. Bulletin boards in student centers are littered with notices of apartments to share and the drift of conversation suggests that a lot of money is dissipated in scrounging for food and shelter.

Taxpayers now provide more than half of the astronomical sums   35 that are spent on higher education. But less than half of today's high school graduates go on, raising a new question of equity: Is it fair to make all the taxpayers pay for the minority who actually go to college? We decided long ago that it is fair for childless adults to pay school taxes because everyone, parents and nonparents alike, profits by a literate population. Does the same reasoning hold true for state-supported higher education? There is no conclusive evidence on either side.

36   Young people cannot be expected to go to college for the general good of mankind. They may be more altruistic than their elders, but no great numbers are going to spend four years at hard intellectual labor, let alone tens of thousands of family dollars, for "the advancement of human capability in society at large," one of the many purposes invoked by the Carnegie Commission report. Nor do any considerable number of them want to go to college to beat the Russians to Jupiter, improve the national defense, increase the Gross National Product, lower the crime rate, improve automobile safety, or create a market for the arts—all of which have been suggested at one time or other as benefits taxpayers get for supporting higher education.

37   One sociologist said that you don't have to have a reason for going to college because it's an institution. His definition of an institution is something everyone subscribes to without question. The burden of proof is not on why you should go to college, but why anyone thinks there might be a reason for not going. The implication—and some educators express it quite frankly—is that an eighteen-year-old high school graduate is still too young and confused to know what he wants to do, let alone what is good for him.

38   Mother knows best, in other words.

39   It had always been comfortable for students to believe that authorities, like Mother, or outside specialists, like educators, could determine what was best for them. However, specialists and authorities no longer enjoy the credibility former generations accorded them. Patients talk back to doctors and are not struck suddenly dead. Clients question the lawyer's bills and sometimes get them reduced. It is no longer self-evident that all adolescents must study a fixed curriculum that was constructed at a time when all educated men could agree on precisely what it was that made them educated.

40   The same with college. If high school graduates don't want to continue their education, or don't want to continue it right away, they may perceive more clearly than their elders that college is not for them.

41   College is an ideal place for those young adults who love learning for its own sake, who would rather read than eat, and who like nothing better than writing research papers. But they are a minority, even at the prestigious colleges, which recruit and attract the intellectually oriented.

42   The rest of our high school graduates need to look at college more closely and critically, to examine it as a consumer product, and decide if

the cost in dollars, in time, in continued dependency, and in future returns, is worth the very large investment each student—and his family—must make.

_____ **CONSIDERATIONS** _____

1. To what extent is Bird's essay an attack on the conviction that universal education is the surest way to cure the ills and injustices of the world?

2. In her first paragraph, the author states three popular justifications for a college education. Examine her essay to see how closely it is organized around those three reasons.

3. In her final paragraph, Bird urges high school graduates to examine college "as a consumer product." Is this possible? Explain. Read about Richard Wright's struggle to educate himself ("The Library Card") and try to imagine him examining that experience as "a consumer product."

4. Bird makes extensive use of statistics to prove her first proposition: that college is a poor investment. Does she cite the sources of her figures? Does she use the figures fairly? How can you tell?

5. How many of your college friends have clear ideas of their vocational or educational goals? Do you? What about friends who are not in college?

6. Bird points out, rightly enough, that "you don't have to go to college to read the great books or learn about the great ideas of Western Man." Judging from your experience with self-directed reading programs, how effective is Bird's statement as an argument?

7. What would Barbara Lazear Ascher, Nancy Mairs, and Lynne V. Cheney think of Bird's emphasis on college as a vocational prep school?

*Roy Blount, Jr. (b. 1941) was born in Georgia and currently
lives in Massachusetts. His work appears frequently in the*
Atlantic, Sports Illustrated, *and* Esquire. *He also has written and
performed for the popular radio program "A Prairie Home
Companion." Among Blount's earlier books is a meditation on
the Pittsburgh Steelers called* Three Bricks Shy of a Load *(1981).
His essay collections include* What Men Don't Tell Women
(1984) and One Fell Swoop *(1982), as well as* Not Exactly What I
Had in Mind *(1985), from which we take this account of the
making of a football player. Most recently he has collected*
Soupsongs and Webster's Ark *(1987).*

11

ROY BLOUNT, JR.

How to Raise Your Boy to Play Pro Ball

1   Since I have done a good deal of work in the sportswriting field,
people ask me, "Where did you get that unusual tan?" (I go to a nearby
tannery every spring, lay out twenty-eight dollars and a little something
for the attendant, and have myself dipped.) "What is the right grip for
squash?" (Grasp the squash firmly by the neck with your left hand, then
take a knife with the right hand and bring it down in short, crisp strokes
on the part of the squash not covered by the left hand.) But most of all
they ask me, "How do I raise my boy to be a professional football
player?" This last question I answer by saying, "Set an example. Lay and
finish nine sets of steps in one day."

2   And then I speak of concrete grit, pride of workmanship, and what
Ray Mansfield's father, the man who laid the steps, called "that preservation meanness."

3   Mansfield still sells his millions of insurance in Pittsburgh, but he
has finished out his career on the gridiron, where, he once told me, he

felt like a knight in armor. For over a decade, through 1976, he was the Steeler's starting center, emergency placekicker, and stalwart of beer and stories. The Old Ranger, they called him. Still call him, actually. His father, Owen Mansfield, was proof that you can be legendary in your work even if your work isn't something glamorous like bowling people over so that somebody can run a leather-covered bladder past them.

In '75 I went with Ray to visit Owen in Kennewick, Washington. 4 Owen was a tall, well-preserved-looking man of sixty-five who had finally given up heavy labor because of his heart. He puttered around his small house, picked and sang Jimmie Rodgers songs, and reminisced about working and fighting.

Owen grew up on an Arkansas farm. When he was no more than a 5 sprout himself, he was "putting sprouts in the new ground. Start plowing and the plow would hit me in the stomach. Plow'd run into a root right under the ground, the mules would stop, the end of the plow would come around and hit me in the shin." But he had the example of *his* father before him. "My dad. That was the workingest old man you ever saw. And he was a Christian, believed in living right. I remember one day my dad was getting the best of Uncle Port, and Uncle Port's dog run up and bit him. He turned around and held Uncle Port and hollered, 'Somebody kill that god-d . . . that dog.' He thought better of himself, you see. Uncle Port was the meanest man that ever hit that country down there."

Since he couldn't be the meanest or the most industrious man in 6 Arkansas, in the late twenties Owen rode the rails west. He'd stop off and scratch around for work or live off the land. "I remember if somebody had eaten a lot of bananas, I'd pick up them banana peelings and eat 'em. They was good. I could eat a tree, I believe." He dodged the railroad cops. "Texas Slim. He lined up forty of us one time and said, 'All right. First one that catches the train, I'm going to shoot him.' He wore a nice suit, a big white hat, two guns. He was a *nice*-looking guy. But a *mean* son of a gun. I just patted my hands when I heard he was killed. I wish I'd been a fast draw, *I'*d a killed him.

"I was 'Slim,' too, all my life nearly, working. Had the longest 7 neck of anybody in the country."

His first job as a married man was splitting logs for rails. He and 8 Mrs. Mansfield eventually had nine kids. When Ray was born, the family was living in a tent in a farm labor camp outside Bakersfield, California, and Owen was in the hospital with a rattlesnake bite. "They gave me a shot of some stuff and I started trembling all over, got quivery all through my body. I said, 'Dag burn it, I guess I'm going to die in this little old place.'

9   "Then, when I got well, our first daughter, Merelene, got pneumonia. They took Merelene to the same room I'd been in. Wasn't long till she died. I tell you, it was hard times. She was seven and a half. Merelene. A name I studied out myself, to get something there wasn't anything like."

10   "We all took Merelene back to Missouri," Ray says. "Like the marines never leave their dead behind, my parents didn't want to leave their child out there in California on the road. This was in 'forty-one. Dad put Merelene and all the rest of us except Gene, my oldest brother, on the train, and then he put a mattress on the back seat of the car and put Gene on it and just took off. I don't know whether he got to Missouri before the train or just after it. Driving a broken-down 1929 Chevy. Mother said she saw my dad the whole day, off and on, when the road came close to the tracks."

11   Owen told me, "The car broke down once and I was fixing it and that train passed. Made me so lonesome I couldn't sit still."

12   When they got Merelene buried back home, they headed back out looking for a place to settle. A few years later, living in Arizona, Owen flipped a coin to decide whether to go just to Joplin, Missouri, or all the way to the state of Washington. And Washington won. That's where Ray grew up, in Kennewick, where Owen got into concrete. "One of the hardest jobs in America," Ray says.

13   "Dad was always top hand on the job," says Ray's younger brother Bill, who played football at Washington State and now is back in Kennewick, in concrete himself. "It's a good thing he's not working today. It'd kill him to see the way people work these days. He wasn't any college professor, but he was as good as there was at what he did. Guys like him are gone forever. We'd lay a floor, I'd think it was finished—it would be, today—and he'd say, 'Son, we can't leave until you can dance on it.'

14   "You talk to Dad's old foreman and he says, 'That Owen was the finest-working man I ever knew.' When we'd work with him, he'd grab a shovel and all you'd see was sand. A forty-eight-year-old man outworking our ass. When he was fifty-nine years old, he was going full speed. My brother Gene kept saying, 'Dad, cool it a little bit.' He'd say, 'Ah, let's get the job done.' Now it's: make money and get by if you can. He never learned. . . .''

15   Ray says, "We grew up expecting to work. It came with breathing air. He hired us out when I was in the second or third grade. Me and my sister and older brother, we'd be out at four in the morning cutting asparagus until eight, go right from work to school.

"When I got older, I'd sell papers on the streets. I just loved being   16
on the streets. Even though there wasn't but one main street in Kennewick. I was afraid I would miss something.

"I worked all one morning to get fifteen cents to go to the movie. I   17
ran all the way to the movie and found out it was twenty cents. I ran all
the way home, pissed off, kicking things. I told my father what was
wrong. (He was home in between his work in concrete. He had to lay it
in the morning, wait for it to set, and then go back late to finish it up.)
He reached in his pocket, pulled out a handful of sand, and came up
with a nickel. His fingers all dry and split open from the concrete. He
gave me the nickel. It was probably the only nickel in the house. I ran all
the way back to the movie: James Mason as Rommel in *The Desert Fox.*

"When I came home, my father was back at work. I lay awake   18
until one in the morning, when he came home. I sneaked downstairs
and watched him get undressed and go to bed. I never thanked him. I
just wanted to look at him and think what kind of dad I had.

"There was so much warmth around the house," Ray says. "We   19
didn't have any mean kids in our family. Everybody was loving of each
other and tolerant of other people. I got into a lot of fights, but I didn't
like it especially. If you ever want to get a Mansfield mad, pick on
another Mansfield. We've got almost too much family pride. I remember there was a big kid around Campbell's Cabins, where we lived for a
while. I did everything I could to avoid him. But he picked on my little
brother Odie, and I went after him and nearly coldcocked him. I had no
fear when one of my brothers was being picked on. But even after I
whipped that big kid, I was still scared of him."

Bill tells an old family story: "This guy, thirty-five, got into an   20
altercation with our grandfather, Pa, when Pa was sixty-five years old.
Our Uncle Granville was seventeen, and he goes flying through the air,
kicks the guy's ass through the dusty streets till the guy whimpers like
a dog and gets out of there. My dad's eyes gleam when he tells about it.
That's why it was good having Moynihan in the U.N. You can't take too
much shit."

Ray and Bill Mansfield and I were drinking and getting profound in   21
this place in Kennewick, and Bill said to Ray, "Remember when we
were working out—I was just getting ready to go to Washington State—
and you said, 'Bill, don't ever, ever accept getting beat. Don't ever let a
guy beat you and walk away and say, 'Well, he beat me.' You have to
fight and scratch and bite. If you're bleeding and crying and scratching
and shitting, keep on fighting and that guy will quit. As long as *you*
don't.' "

22   Not many occupations today bring together fighting and working the way football does. But working was a kind of fighting for Owen. And both working and fighting were kinds of sports. "I'd get a kick out of troweling cement with other trowelers," he said. "Out of staying about the length of this table ahead of the other fella. That would tickle me to death." The story about their father that made Ray's and Bill's eyes light up the brightest—Bill almost boiled up out of his chair telling it—was the one about the steps.

23   "He laid and finished *nine sets of steps in one day.* Did a Cool Hand Luke shot. Then two thousand, three thousand square feet of concrete. It was superhuman. How it happened: It was a Monday, and the man told him it had to be done by Wednesday. My dad said, 'Don't worry.' The man said, 'Well, you better get it done.'

24   "That made my dad mad. So he said, 'I'll show you.' And he did it all in eight hours. Edged it, everything. He was running the whole time, and he was forty-five. When he finished, there was smoke coming off his body, but there were the nine sets of steps. All those assholes were scratching their heads and saying, How did he do it? It's still a legend around here."

25   Right after Ray's last season, Owen was talking to Gene and Odie, and they told him he'd better do something about his hair—he'd let it grow awfully long. "I'm not going to get a haircut," Owen said. "I'm going to buy a dress." And he rocked back laughing and suddenly died.

26   Afterward, Ray's brother told him Owen had been glad that Ray was retiring from football. Owen had said he'd always thought of Ray as a boy, of course, but that Ray was getting too old to play a kid's game.

CONSIDERATIONS

1. One of the attractive features of Blount's essay is the way he captures the voice of Owen Mansfield. Make a small collection of words and phrases that distinguish his voice, and compare it with Studs Terkel's rendering of "Phil Stallings, Spot Welder," or with the voices of characters in short stories.

2. How did the father's hard-working life spill over into the son's, and what does that have to do with how to raise your boy to be a professional football player?

3. Is there anything negative about the competitiveness that kept Owen Mansfield ahead of other concrete workers?

4. Was the father's "preservation meanness" tempered by a sense of humor? Is humor at work in the closing sentence of the essay, or is it simply an expression of the man's values? Find support for your answer elsewhere in the essay.

5. There is a gap between paragraphs 20 and 21. What is the function of that extra space?

Carol Bly (b. 1930) was born in Minnesota and graduated from Wellesley College. Now living in Minnesota, she lectures, writes, and teaches—in the Spring of 1990 as the Benedict Distinguished Visiting Professor of English at Carleton College. Her short stories from the New Yorker *and the* American Review, *among other magazines, are collected in* Backbone *(1985). This essay was originally published in* Preview, *magazine of Minnesota Public Radio, and collected in her 1981 book,* Letters from the Country.

12

CAROL BLY
Getting Tired

1 The men have left a gigantic 6600 combine a few yards from our grove, at the edge of the stubble. For days it was working around the farm; we heard it on the east, later on the west, and finally we could see it grinding back and forth over the windrows on the south. But now it has been simply squatting at the field's edge, huge, tremendously still, very professional, slightly dangerous.

2 We all have the correct feelings about this new combine: this isn't the good old farming where man and soil are dusted together all day; this isn't farming a poor man can afford, either, and therefore it further threatens his hold on the American "family farm" operation. We have been sneering at this machine for days, as its transistor radio, amplified well over the engine roar, has been grinding up our silence, spreading a kind of shrill ghetto evening all over the farm.

3 But now it is parked, and after a while I walk over to it and climb up its neat little John-Deere-green ladder on the left. Entering the big cab up there is like coming up into a large ship's bridge on visitors' day—heady stuff to see the inside workings of a huge operation like the Queen Elizabeth II. On the other hand I feel left out, being only a

dumbfounded passenger. The combine cab has huge windows flaring wider at the top; they lean forward over the ground, and the driver sits so high behind the glass in its rubber moldings, it is like a movie-set spaceship. He has obviously come to dominate the field, whether he farms it or not.

The value of the 66 is that it can do anything, and to change it from   4 a combine into a cornpicker takes one man about half an hour, whereas most machine conversions on farms take several men a half day. It frees its owner from a lot of monkeying.

Monkeying, in city life, is what little boys do to clocks so they   5 never run again. In farming it has two quite different meanings. The first is small side projects. You monkey with poultry, unless you're a major egg handler. Or you monkey with ducks or geese. If you have a very small milk herd, and finally decide that prices plus state regulations don't make your few Holsteins worthwhile, you "quit monkeying with them." There is a hidden dignity in this word: it precludes mention of money. It lets the wife of a very marginal farmer have a conversation with a woman who may be helping her husband run fifteen hundred acres. "How you coming with those geese?" "Oh, we've been real disgusted. We're thinking of quitting monkeying with them." It saves her having to say, "We lost our shirts on those darn geese."

The other meaning of monkeying is wrestling with and maintaining machinery, such as changing heads from combining to cornpicking.   6 Farmers who cornpick the old way, in which the corn isn't shelled automatically during picking in the field but must be elevated to the top of a pile by belt and then shelled, put up with some monkeying.

Still, cornpicking and plowing is a marvelous time of the year on   7 farms; one of the best autumns I've had recently had a few days of fieldwork in it. We were outside all day, from six in the morning to eight at night—coming in only for noon dinner. We ate our lunches on a messy truck flatbed. (For city people who don't know it: *lunch* isn't a noon meal; it is what you eat out of a black lunch pail at 9 A.M. and 3 P.M. If you offer a farmer a cup of coffee at 3:30 P.M. he or she is likely to say, "No thanks, I've already had lunch.") There were four of us hired to help—a couple to plow, Celia (a skilled farmhand who worked steady for our boss), and me. Lunch was always two sandwiches of white commercial bread with luncheon meat, and one very generous piece of cake-mix cake carefully wrapped in Saran Wrap. (I never found anyone around here self-conscious about using Saran Wrap when the Dow Chemical Company was also making napalm.)

It was very pleasant on the flatbed, squinting out over the yellow   8 picked cornstalks—each time we stopped for lunch, a larger part of the field had been plowed back. We fell into the easy psychic habit of farmworkers: admiration of the boss. "Ja, I see he's buying one of those big 4010s," someone would say. We always perked up at inside information like that. Or "Ja," as the woman hired steady told us, "he's going to plow the home fields first this time, instead of the other way round." We temporary help were impressed by that, too. Then, with real flair, she brushed a crumb of luncheon meat off her jeans, the way you would make sure to flick a gnat off spotless tennis whites. It is the true feminine touch to brush a crumb off pants that are encrusted with Minnesota Profile A heavy loam, many swipes of SAE 40 oil, and grain dust.

9   All those days, we never tired of exchanging information on how *he* was making out, what *he* was buying, whom *he* was going to let drive the new tractor, and so on. There is always something to talk about with the other hands, because farming is genuinely absorbing. It has the best quality of work: nothing else seems real. And everyone doing it, even the cheapest helpers like me, can see the layout of the whole— from spring work, to cultivating, to small grain harvest, to cornpicking, to fall plowing.

10   The second day I was promoted from elevating corncobs at the corn pile to actual plowing. Hour after hour I sat up there on the old Alice, as she was called (an Allis-Chalmers WC that looked rusted from the Flood). You have to sit twisted part way around, checking that the plowshares are scouring clean, turning over and dropping the dead crop and soil, not clogging. For the first two hours I was very political. I thought about what would be good for American farming—stronger marketing organizations, or maybe a law like the Norwegian Odal law, preventing the breaking up of small farms or selling them to business interests. Then the sun got high, and each time I reached the headlands area at the field's end I dumped off something else, now my cap, next my jacket, finally my sweater.

11   Since the headlands are the last to be plowed, they serve as a field road until the very end. There are usually things parked there—a pickup or a corn trailer—and things dumped—my warmer clothing, our afternoon lunch pails, a broken furrow wheel someone picked up.

12   By noon I'd dropped all political interest, and was thinking only: how unlike this all is to Keats's picture of autumn, a "season of mists and mellow fruitfulness." This gigantic expanse of horizon, with everywhere the easy growl of tractors, was simply teeming with extrovert energy. It wouldn't calm down for another week, when whoever was

lowest on the totem pole would be sent out to check a field for dropped parts or to drive away the last machines left around.

The worst hours for all common labor are the hours after noon   13
dinner. Nothing is inspiring then. That is when people wonder how they ever got stuck in the line of work they've chosen for life. Or they wonder where the cool Indian smoke of secrets and messages began to vanish from their marriage. Instead of plugging along like a cheerful beast working for me, the Allis now smelled particularly gassy. To stay awake I froze my eyes onto an indented circle in the hood around the gas cap. Someone had apparently knocked the screw cap fitting down into the hood, so there was a moat around it. In this moat some overflow gas leapt in tiny waves. Sometimes the gas cap was a castle, this was the moat; sometimes it was a nuclear-fission plant, this was the horrible hot-water waste. Sometimes it was just the gas cap on the old Alice with the spilt gas bouncing on the hot metal.

Row after row. I was stupefied. But then around 2:30 the shadows   14
appeared again, and the light, which had been dazing and white, grew fragile. The whole prairie began to gather itself for the cool evening. All of a sudden it was wonderful to be plowing again, and when I came to the field end, the filthy jackets and the busted furrow wheel were just benign mistakes: that is, if it chose to, the jacket could be a church robe, and the old wheel could be something with some pride to it, like a helm. And I felt the same about myself: instead of being someone with a half interest in literature and a half interest in farming doing a half-decent job plowing, I could have been someone desperately needed in Washington or Zurich. I drank my three o'clock coffee joyously, and traded the other plowman a Super-Valu cake-mix lemon cake slice for a Holsum baloney sandwich because it had garlic in it.

By seven at night we had been plowing with headlights for an hour.   15
I tried to make up games to keep going, on my second wind, on my third wind, but labor is labor after the whole day of it; the mind refuses to think of ancestors. It refuses to pretend the stalks marching up to the right wheel in the spooky light are men-at-arms, or to imagine a new generation coming along. It doesn't care. Now the Republicans could have announced a local meeting in which they would propose a new farm program whereby every farmer owning less than five hundred acres must take half price for his crop, and every farmer owning more than a thousand acres shall receive triple price for his crop, and I was so tired I wouldn't have shown up to protest.

A million hours later we sit around in a daze at the dining-room   16
table, and nobody says anything. In low, courteous mutters we ask for

the macaroni hotdish down this way, please. Then we get up in ones and twos and go home. Now the farm help are all so tired we *are* a little like the various things left out on the headlands—some tools, a jacket, someone's thermos top—used up for that day. Thoughts won't even stick to us any more.

17   Such tiredness must be part of farmers' wanting huge machinery like the Deere 6600. That tiredness that feels so good to the occasional laborer and the athlete is disturbing to a man destined to it eight months of every year. But there is a more hidden psychology in the issue of enclosed combines versus open tractors. It is this: one gets too many impressions on the open tractor. A thousand impressions enter as you work up and down the rows: nature's beauty or nature's stubbornness, politics, exhaustion, but mainly the feeling that all this repetition—last year's cornpicking, this year's cornpicking, next year's cornpicking—is taking up your lifetime. The mere repetition reveals your eventual death.

18   When you sit inside a modern combine, on the other hand, you are so isolated from field, sky, all the real world, that the brain is dulled. You are not sensitized to your own mortality. You aren't sensitive to anything at all.

19   This must be a common choice of our mechanical era: to hide from life inside our machinery. If we can hide from life in there, some idiotic part of the psyche reasons, we can hide from death in there as well.

_____ CONSIDERATIONS _____

1. In paragraphs 5 and 6, Carol Bly clarifies the slang term "monkeying." Hers is not a conventional definition; does she make the term understandable to someone who had never heard it before? What are the requirements of a definition? Have you read essays built as extended definitions? See Daniel Boorstin's "The Pseudo-Event" and Consideration 6 following that essay.

2. Compare paragraphs 9 and 17 on the nature of work. How do you account for the positive view of paragraph 9 and the negative view of paragraph 17?

3. Why, in paragraph 12, does Bly allude to John Keats's famous ode, "To Autumn" (1819)? Can you appreciate what she is doing if you've never read the

poem? How quickly can you find it in your college library? Aside from the collected poems of John Keats, what would be the surest source for the poem?

4. Notice when Bly changes suddenly from past to present tense. Why does she make the shift? Is something gained by the change?

5. Think about Bly's generalizations in her final paragraph. Selecting an appropriate piece of machinery—a car, a computer, a television set—respond to Bly's generalizations.

Daniel Boorstin (b. 1914) attended Oxford University as a Rhodes Scholar after graduating from Harvard University. He was admitted to the bar, and taught history for twenty-five years at the University of Chicago. Later, he served as Librarian of Congress from 1975 to 1987. Author of many books, his The Americans: The Colonial Experience *won the Bancroft Award in 1959;* The Americans: The National Experience *won the Francis Parkman Prize in 1966;* The Americans: The Democratic Experience *won the Pulitzer Prize in 1974.* The Discoverers, *subtitled "A History of Man's Search to Know His World and Himself," appeared in 1983.*

13

DANIEL J. BOORSTIN
The Pseudo-Event*

Admiring Friend: "My, that's a beautiful baby you have there!"
Mother: "Oh, that's nothing—you should see his photograph!"

1   The simplest of our extravagant expectations concerns the amount of novelty in the world. There was a time when the reader of an unexciting newspaper would remark, "How dull is the world today!" Nowadays he says, "What a dull newspaper!" When the first American newspaper, Benjamin Harris' *Publick Occurrences Both Forreign and Domestick,* appeared in Boston on September 25, 1690, it promised to furnish news regularly once a month. But, the editor explained, it might appear oftener "if any Glut of Occurrences happen." The responsibility for making news was entirely God's—or the Devil's. The newsman's task was only to give "an Account of such considerable things as have arrived unto our Notice."

From *The Image* by Daniel J. Boorstin. Copyright © 1961 by Daniel J. Boorstin. Reprinted by permission of Atheneum Publishers, an imprint of Macmillan Publishing Company.
    * Title chosen by the editors.

Although the theology behind this way of looking at events soon   2
dissolved, this view of the news lasted longer. "The skilled and faithful
journalist," James Parton observed in 1866, "recording with exactness
and power the thing that has come to pass, is Providence addressing
men." The story is told of a Southern Baptist clergyman before the Civil
War who used to say, when a newspaper was brought in the room, "Be
kind enough to let me have it a few minutes, till I see how the Supreme
Being is governing the world." Charles A. Dana, one of the great American editors of the nineteenth century, once defended his extensive
reporting of crime in the New York *Sun* by saying, "I have always felt
that whatever the Divine Providence permitted to occur I was not too
proud to report."

Of course, this is now a very old-fashioned way of thinking. Our   3
current point of view is better expressed in the definition by Arthur
MacEwen, whom William Randolph Hearst made his first editor of the
San Francisco *Examiner*: "News is anything that makes a reader say,
'Gee whiz!'" Or, put more soberly, "News is whatever a good editor
chooses to print."

We need not be theologians to see that we have shifted responsibil-   4
ity for making the world interesting from God to the newspaperman.
We used to believe there were only so many "events" in the world. If
there were not many intriguing or startling occurrences, it was no fault
of the reporter. He could not be expected to report what did not exist.

Within the last hundred years, however, and especially in the   5
twentieth century, all this has changed. We expect the papers to be full
of news. If there is no news visible to the naked eye, or to the average
citizen, we still expect it to be there for the enterprising newsman. The
successful reporter is one who can find a story, even if there is no
earthquake or assassination or civil war. If he cannot find a story, then
he must make one—by the questions he asks of public figures, by the
surprising human interest he unfolds from some commonplace event,
or by "the news behind the news." If all this fails, then he must give us a
"think piece"—an embroidering of well-known facts, or a speculation
about startling things to come.

This change in our attitude toward "news" is not merely a basic   6
fact about the history of American newspapers. It is a symptom of a
revolutionary change in our attitude toward what happens in the world,
how much of it is new, and surprising, and important. Toward how life
can be enlivened, toward our power and the power of those who inform
and educate and guide us, to provide synthetic happenings to make up
for the lack of spontaneous events. Demanding more than the world can

give us, we require that something be fabricated to make up for the world's deficiency. This is only one example of our demand for illusions.

7   Many historical forces help explain how we have come to our present immoderate hopes. But there can be no doubt about what we now expect, nor that it is immoderate. Every American knows the anticipation with which he picks up his morning newspaper at breakfast or opens his evening paper before dinner, or listens to the newscasts every hour on the hour as he drives across country, or watches his favorite commentator on television interpret the events of the day. Many enterprising Americans are now at work to help us satisfy these expectations. Many might be put out of work if we should suddenly moderate our expectations. But it is we who keep them in business and demand that they fill our consciousness with novelties, that they play God for us.

8   The new kind of synthetic novelty which has flooded our experience I will call "pseudo-events." The common prefix "pseudo" comes from the Greek word meaning false, or intended to deceive. Before I recall the historical forces which have made these pseudo-events possible, have increased the supply of them and the demand for them, I will give a commonplace example.

9   The owners of a hotel, in an illustration offered by Edward L. Bernays in his pioneer *Crystallizing Public Opinion* (1923), consult a public relations counsel. They ask how to increase their hotel's prestige and so improve their business. In less sophisticated times, the answer might have been to hire a new chef, to improve the plumbing, to paint the rooms, or to install a crystal chandelier in the lobby. The public relations counsel's technique is more indirect. He proposes that the management stage a celebration of the hotel's thirtieth anniversay. A committee is formed, including a prominent banker, a leading society matron, a well-known lawyer, an influential preacher, and an "event" is planned (say a banquet) to call attention to the distinguished service the hotel has been rendering the community. The celebration is held, photographs are taken, the occasion is widely reported, and the object is accomplished. Now this occasion is a pseudo-event, and will illustrate all the essential features of pseudo-events.

10   This celebration, we can see at the outset, is somewhat—but not entirely—misleading. Presumably the public relations counsel would not have been able to form his committee of prominent citizens if the hotel had not actually been rendering service to the community. On the other hand, if the hotel's services had been all that important, instigation by public relations counsel might not have been necessary. Once

the celebration has been held, the celebration itself becomes evidence that the hotel really is a distinguished institution. The occasion actually gives the hotel the prestige to which it is pretending.

It is obvious, too, that the value of such a celebration to the owners 11 depends on its being photographed and reported in newspapers, magazines, newsreels, on radio, and over television. It is the report that gives the event its force in the minds of potential customers. The power to make a reportable event is thus the power to make experience. One is reminded of Napoleon's apocryphal reply to his general, who objected that circumstances were unfavorable to a proposed campaign. "Bah, I make circumstances!" The modern public relations counsel—and he is, of course, only one of many twentieth-century creators of pseudo-events—has come close to fulfilling Napoleon's idle boast. "The counsel on public relations," Mr. Bernays explains, "not only knows what news value is, but knowing it, he is in a position to *make news happen*. He is a creator of events."

The intriguing feature of the modern situation, however, comes 12 precisely from the fact that the modern news makers are not God. The news they make happen, the events they create, are somehow not quite real. There remains a tantalizing difference between man-made and God-made events.

A pseudo-event, then, is a happening that possesses the following 13 characteristics:

1. It is not spontaneous, but comes about because someone has planned, planted, or incited it. Typically, it is not a train wreck or an earthquake, but an interview.
2. It is planted primarily (not always exclusively) for the immediate purpose of being reported or reproduced. Therefore, its occurrence is arranged for the convenience of the reporting or reproducing media. Its success is measured by how widely it is reported. Time relations in it are commonly fictitious or factitious; the announcement is given out in advance "for future release" and written as if the event had occurred in the past. The question, "Is it real?" is less important than, "Is it newsworthy?"
3. Its relation to the underlying reality of the situation is ambiguous. Its interest arises largely from this very ambiguity. Concerning a pseudo-event the question, "What does it mean?" has a new dimension. While the news interest in a train wreck is in *what* happened and in the real consequences, the interest in an interview is always, in a sense, in *whether* it really happened

and in what might have been the motives. Did the statement really mean what it said? Without some of this ambiguity a pseudo-event cannot be very interesting.

4. Usually it is intended to be a self-fulfilling prophecy. The hotel's thirtieth-anniversary celebration, by saying that the hotel is a distinguished institution, actually makes it one.

14　　A perfect example of how pseudo-events can dominate is the recent popularity of the quiz show format. Its original appeal came less from the fact that such shows were tests of intelligence (or of dissimulation) than from the fact that the situations were elaborately contrived—with isolation booths, armed bank guards, and all the rest—and they purported to inform the public.

15　　The application of the quiz show format to the so-called "Great Debates" between Presidential candidates in the election of 1960 is only another example. These four campaign programs, pompously and self-righteously advertised by the broadcasting networks, were remarkably successful in reducing great national issues to trivial dimensions. With appropriate vulgarity, they might have been called the $400,000 Question (Prize: a $100,000-a-year job for four years). They were a clinical example of the pseudo-event, of how it is made, why it appeals, and of its consequences for democracy in America.

16　　In origin the Great Debates were confusedly collaborative between politicians and news makers. Public interest centered around the pseudo-event itself: the lighting, make-up, ground rules, whether notes would be allowed, etc. Far more interest was shown in the performance than in what was said. The pseudo-events spawned in turn by the Great Debates were numberless. People who had seen the shows read about them the more avidly, and listened eagerly for interpretations by news commentators. Representatives of both parties made "statements" on the probable effects of the debates. Numerous interviews and discussion programs were broadcast exploring their meaning. Opinion polls kept us informed on the nuances of our own and other people's reactions. Topics of speculation multiplied. Even the question whether there should be a fifth debate became for a while a lively "issue."

17　　The drama of the situation was mostly specious, or at least had an extremely ambiguous relevance to the main (but forgotten) issue: which participant was better qualified for the Presidency. Of course, a man's ability, while standing under klieg lights, without notes, to answer in two and a half minutes a question kept secret until that moment, had only the most dubious relevance—if any at all—to his real qualifications to make deliberate Presidential decisions on long-standing public questions after being instructed by a corps of advisers. The great Presidents in our history (with the possible exception of F.D.R.) would have done miserably; but our most notorious demagogues would have shone. A number of exciting pseudo-events were created—for example, the Quemoy–Matsu issue.[1] But that, too, was a good example of a pseudo-event: it was created to be reported, it concerned a then-quiescent problem, and it put into the most factitious and trivial terms the great and real issue of our relation to Communist China.

The television medium shapes this new kind of political quiz-show spectacular in many crucial ways. Theodore H. White has proven this with copious detail in his *The Making of the President: 1960* (1961). All the circumstances of this particular competition for votes were far more novel than the old word "debate" and the comparisons with the Lincoln-Douglas Debates suggested. Kennedy's great strength in the critical first debate, according to White, was that he was in fact not "debating" at all, but was seizing the opportunity to address the whole nation; while Nixon stuck close to the issues raised by his opponent, rebutting them one by one. Nixon, moreover, suffered a handicap that was serious only on television: he has a light, naturally transparent skin. On an ordinary camera that takes pictures by optical projection, this skin photographs well. But a television camera projects electronically, by an "image-orthicon tube" which has an x-ray effect. This camera penetrates Nixon's transparent skin and brings out (even just after a shave) the tiniest hair growing in the follicles beneath the surface. For the decisive first program Nixon wore a make-up called "Lazy Shave" which was ineffective under these conditions. He therefore looked haggard and heavy-bearded by contrast to Kennedy, who looked pert and clean-cut.

This greatest opportunity in American history to educate the voters by debating the large issues of the campaign failed. The main reason, as White points out, was the compulsions of the medium. "The nature of both TV and radio is that they abhor silence and 'dead time.' All TV and radio discussion programs are compelled to snap question and answer back and forth as if the contestants were adversaries in an intellectual tennis match. Although every experienced newspaperman

18

19

[1] Hotly debated by Kennedy and Nixon in 1960: should these islands off the Chinese mainland be defended by the United States as part of Nationalist China's territory?

and inquirer knows that the most thoughtful and responsive answers to any difficult question come after long pause, and that the longer the pause the more illuminating the thought that follows it, nonetheless the electronic media cannot bear to suffer a pause of more than five seconds; a pause of thirty seconds of dead time on air seems interminable. Thus, snapping their two-and-a-half-minute answers back and forth, both candidates could only react for the cameras and the people, they could not think." Whenever either candidate found himself touching a thought too large for two-minute exploration, he quickly retreated. Finally the television-watching voter was left to judge, not on issues explored by thoughtful men, but on the relative capacity of the two candidates to perform under television stress.

20   Pseudo-events thus lead to emphasis on pseudo-qualifications. Again the self-fulfilling prophecy. If we test Presidential candidates by their talents on TV quiz performances, we will, of course, choose presidents for precisely these qualifications. In a democracy, reality tends to conform to the pseudo-event. Nature imitates art.

21   We are frustrated by our very efforts publicly to unmask the pseudo-event. Whenever we describe the lighting, the make-up, the studio setting, the rehearsals, etc., we simply arouse more interest. One newsman's interpretation makes us more eager to hear another's. One commentator's speculation that the debates may have little significance makes us curious to hear whether another commentator disagrees.

22   Pseudo-events do, of course, increase our illusion of grasp on the world, what some have called the American illusion of omnipotence. Perhaps, we come to think, the world's problems can really be settled by "statements," by "Summit" meetings, by a competition of "prestige," by overshadowing images, and by political quiz shows.

23   Once we have tasted the charm of pseudo-events, we are tempted to believe they are the only important events. Our progress poisons the sources of our experience. And the poison tastes so sweet that it spoils our appetite for plain fact. Our seeming ability to satisfy our exaggerated expectations makes us forget that they are exaggerated.

---- **CONSIDERATIONS** _____

1. "VIKING PROMOTION HITS TOWN THIS WEEK"—banner headline on page 1 of the *Park Rapids* (Minnesota) *Enterprise*, July 30, 1986. Hard news or pseudo-event? Explain.

2. Daniel J. Boorstin, a professor of history, distinguishes between spontaneous events and events that are staged to advance a position or to promote a person or an institution. He argues that there "remains a tantalizing difference between man-made and God-made events." In what sense is that difference "tantalizing"?

3. Use Boorstin's criteria to find an example of a pseudo-event in a newspaper or a news magazine. Analyze the piece to determine if it possesses the characteristics he lists. Does it, for example, contain ambiguities?

4. Why, according to Boorstin, are these pseudo-events harmful? Do you agree?

5. Through the first two paragraphs of his essay, Boorstin makes extensive use of short quotations carefully chosen to illustrate his point. Is there a limit to the number of quotations a given essay can employ effectively? Explain. Where might you find several quotations on a particular subject?

6. Study Boorstin's essay as an example of argument. Which of his techniques reveal the argumentative nature of his writing? (Don't ignore the epigraph that precedes his first paragraph.)

Gwendolyn Brooks (b. 1917) grew up in Chicago. She lives there still, and has been Poet Laureate of Illinois since 1968. Her books of poems began with A Street in Brownsville (1945); Annie Allen (1949) won the Pulitzer Prize. "The Bean Eaters" was the title poem of a volume published in 1960. She has written autobiography and work for children.

14

GWENDOLYN BROOKS
The Bean Eaters

They eat beans mostly, this old yellow pair.
Dinner is a casual affair.
Plain chipware on a plain and creaking wood,
Tin flatware.

5   Two who are Mostly Good.
Two who have lived their day,
But keep on putting on their clothes
And putting things away.

And remembering . . .
10 Remembering, with twinklings and twinges,
As they lean over the beans in their rented back room
     that is full of beads and receipts and dolls and cloths,
     tobacco crumbs, vases and fringes.

Bruce Catton (1899–1978) became a historian while working as a newspaper reporter and magazine editor. His books, many on the Civil War, include Mr. Lincoln's Army *(1951) and* A Stillness at Appomattox *(1953). Catton received both the Pulitzer Prize and the National Book Award.*

15

BRUCE CATTON

Grant and Lee: A Study in Contrasts

When Ulysses S. Grant and Robert E. Lee met in the parlor of a 1 modest house at Appomattox Court House, Virginia, on April 9, 1865, to work out the terms for the surrender of Lee's Army of Northern Virginia, a great chapter in American life came to a close, and a great new chapter began.

These men were bringing the Civil War to its virtual finish. To be 2 sure, other armies had yet to surrender, and for a few days the fugitive Confederate government would struggle desperately and vainly, trying to find some way to go on living now that its chief support was gone. But in effect it was all over when Grant and Lee signed the papers. And the little room where they wrote out the terms was the scene of one of the poignant, dramatic contrasts in American history.

They were two strong men, these oddly different generals, and 3 they represented the strengths of two conflicting currents that, through them, had come into final collision.

Back of Robert E. Lee was the notion that the old aristocratic 4 concept might somehow survive and be dominant in American life.

Lee was tidewater Virginia, and in his background were family, 5 culture, and tradition . . . the age of chivalry transplanted to a New World which was making its own legends and its own myths. He embodied a way of life that had come down through the age of knight-hood and the English country squire. America was a land that was beginning all over again, dedicated to nothing much more complicated than the rather hazy belief that all men had equal rights and should have an equal chance in the world. In such a land Lee stood for the feeling that it was somehow of advantage to human society to have a pronounced inequality in the social structure. There should be a leisure class, backed by ownership of land; in turn, society itself should be keyed to the land as the chief source of wealth and influence. It would bring forth (according to this ideal) a class of men with a strong sense of obligation to the community; men who lived not to gain advantage for themselves, but to meet the solemn obligations which had been laid on them by the very fact that they were privileged. From them the country would get its leadership; to them it could look for the higher values—of thought, of conduct, of personal deportment—to give it strength and virtue.

6   Lee embodied the noblest elements of this aristocratic ideal. Through him, the landed nobility justified itself. For four years, the Southern states had fought a desperate war to uphold the ideals for which Lee stood. In the end, it almost seemed as if the Confederacy fought for Lee; as if he himself was the Confederacy . . . the best thing that the way of life for which the Confederacy stood could ever have to offer. He had passed into legend before Appomattox. Thousands of tired, underfed, poorly clothed Confederate soldiers, long since past the simple enthusiasm of the early days of the struggle, somehow con-sidered Lee the symbol of everything for which they had been willing to die. But they could not quite put this feeling into words. If the Lost Cause, sanctified by so much heroism and so many deaths, had a living justification, its justification was General Lee.

7   Grant, the son of a tanner on the Western frontier, was everything Lee was not. He had come up the hard way and embodied nothing in particular except the eternal toughness and sinewy fiber of the men who grew up beyond the mountains. He was one of a body of men who owed reverence and obeisance to no one, who were self-reliant to a fault, who cared hardly anything for the past but who had a sharp eye for the future.

8   These frontier men were the precise opposites of the tidewater aristocrats. Back of them, in the great surge that had taken people over the Alleghenies and into the opening Western country, there was a deep, implicit dissatisfaction with a past that had settled into grooves. They stood for democracy, not from any reasoned conclusion about the

proper ordering of human society, but simply because they had grown up in the middle of democracy and knew how it worked. Their society might have privileges, but they would be privileges each man had won for himself. Forms and patterns meant nothing. No man was born to anything except perhaps to a chance to show how far he could rise. Life was competition.

Yet along with this feeling had come a deep sense of belonging to a national community. The Westerner, who developed a farm, opened a shop, or set up in business as a trader, could hope to prosper only as his own community prospered—and his community ran from the Atlantic to the Pacific and from Canada down to Mexico. If the land was settled, with towns and highways and accessible markets, he could better himself. He saw his fate in terms of the nation's own destiny. As its horizons expanded so did his. He had, in other words, an acute dollars-and-cents stake in the continued growth and development of his country.   9

And that, perhaps, is where the contrast between Grant and Lee becomes most striking. The Virginia aristocrat, inevitably, saw himself in relation to his own region. He lived in a static society which could endure almost anything except change. Instinctively, his first loyalty would go to the locality in which that society existed. He would fight to the limit of endurance to defend it, because in defending it he was defending everything that gave his own life its deepest meaning.   10

The Westerner, on the other hand, would fight with an equal tenacity for the broader concept of society. He fought so because everything he lived by was tied to growth, expansion, and a constantly widening horizon. What he lived by would survive or fall with the nation itself. He could not possibly stand by unmoved in the face of an attempt to destroy the Union. He would combat it with everything he had, because he could only see it as an effort to cut the ground out from under his feet.   11

So Grant and Lee were in complete contrast, representing two diametrically opposed elements in American life. Grant was the modern man emerging; beyond him, ready to come on the stage, was the great age of steel and machinery, of crowded cities and a restless burgeoning vitality. Lee might have ridden down from the old age of chivalry, lance in hand, silken banner fluttering over his head. Each man was the perfect champion of his cause, drawing both his strengths and his weaknesses from the people he led.   12

Yet it was not all contrast, after all. Different as they were—in background, in personality, in underlying aspiration—these two great   13 soldiers had much in common. Under everything else, they were marvelous fighters. Furthermore, their fighting qualities were really very much alike.

14   Each man had, to begin with, the great virtue of utter tenacity and fidelity. Grant fought his way down the Mississippi Valley in spite of acute personal discouragement and profound military handicaps. Lee hung on in the trenches at Petersburg after hope itself had died. In each man there was an indomitable quality . . . the born fighter's refusal to give up as long as he can still remain on his feet and lift his two fists.

15   Daring and resourcefulness they had, too; the ability to think faster and move faster than the enemy. These were the qualities which gave Lee the dazzling campaigns of Second Manassas and Chancellorsville and won Vicksburg for Grant.

16   Lastly, and perhaps greatest of all, there was the ability, at the end, to turn quickly from war to peace once the fighting was over. Out of the way these two men behaved at Appomattox came the possibility of a peace of reconciliation. It was a possibility not wholly realized, in the years to come, but which did, in the end, help the two sections to become one nation again . . . after a war whose bitterness might have seemed to make such a reunion wholly impossible. No part of either man's life became him more than the part he played in their brief meeting in the McLean house at Appomattox. Their behavior there put all succeeding generations of Americans in their debt. Two great Americans, Grant and Lee—very different, yet under everything very much alike. Their encounter at Appomattox was one of the great moments of American history.

____ CONSIDERATIONS _____

1. Bruce Catton's "Grant and Lee" is a classic example of the comparison–contrast essay, both in subject matter and organization. Select equally different figures of your own time and write about them, following Catton's organizational method.

2. After studying the contrast Catton offers in paragraphs 10 and 11, consider an essay on similar trends in modern American life—for example, adherents of no-growth against those who argue for expansion.

3. "Two great Americans, Grant and Lee," writes Catton in his last paragraph. Do you find evidence that Catton favored either?

4. In paragraph 6, Catton describes Lee as a "symbol." A symbol of what? How can you recognize a symbol when you see one? Why would anyone fight for a symbol?

5. Nowhere in his essay does Catton describe physical appearances. A half-hour's research in your college library should give you enough description to add at least a paragraph to Catton's essay. Where in the essay would you insert such an addition? Would physical description contribute to or confuse Catton's character study?

6. Judging by the proportions of this essay, decide whether Catton found the differences between the two men more interesting than their similarities.

Lynne V. Cheney (b. 1941) was appointed Chairman of the National Endowment for the Humanities in Washington by President Reagan in 1986. She has published two novels and written a history of the House of Representatives called Kings of the Hill. *She took her Bachelor's Degree with highest honors from Colorado College, followed by a Master's Degree from the University of Colorado and a Ph.D. in nineteenth-century British literature from the University of Wisconsin.*

This brief essay appeared in the Newsweek *column "My Turn" in 1986.*

16

LYNNE V. CHENEY
Students of Success

1   Not long ago, my college-age daughter read about a software genius who became a multimillionaire before he was 30. "That does it," she said, "I'm going into computers."

2   This daughter, who has never met a political-science course she didn't like, was only joking. But a study conducted by the Carnegie Foundation shows that many young people do think seriously along these lines. Instead of choosing college majors—and careers—according to their interests, they are channeling themselves into fields that promise to be profitable: business, engineering, computer science, allied health programs.

3   Given the high cost of a college education, this trend is not surprising. A bachelor's degree now costs $40,000 at an average independent college. Can we expect students to major in the liberal arts when their starting salaries will be significantly lower than they are for business and professional majors? Shouldn't they get the best possible return on their investment?

They should, but I would suggest that there are better ways to   4
calculate profit and loss than by looking at starting salaries. Consider,
first of all, that very few people stay in the same line of work over a
lifetime. They switch jobs, even change professions, and what is crucial for advancement is not specialized training but the ability to
think critically and judge wisely. Given the difficulty of predict-
ing which skills will be in demand even five years from now, let
alone over a lifetime, a student's best career preparation is one
that emphasizes general understanding and intellectual curiosity: a
knowledge of how to learn and the desire to do it. Literature, history, philosophy and the social sciences—majors that students avoid
today—are the ones traditionally believed to develop such habits of
mind.

I recently conducted an informal survey of successful Americans,   5
and while several dozen phone calls aren't proof of the value of a
liberal-arts major, the results are suggestive. The communications
world, for example, is dominated by liberal-arts majors. Thomas H.
Wyman, chairman of CBS, majored in English, as did Cathleen
Black, publisher of USA Today. Washington Post columnist William
Raspberry studied history; NBC News anchorman Tom Brokaw, political science.

In public life, too, leaders more often than not were students of the   6
liberal arts. They form a majority in the president's cabinet. Secretary of
State George Shultz and Secretary of Energy John Herrington majored
in economics. Interior Secretary Donald Hodel majored in government, and Transportation Secretary Elizabeth Dole, political science.
Secretary of the Treasury James Baker read history with a minor
in classics; Secretary of Education William Bennett studied philosophy.

The president himself majored in economics and sociology. His   7
communications director, Pat Buchanan, majored in English and philosophy. White House chief of staff (and former treasury secretary)
Donald Regan was an English major and before he came to government
had a remarkably successful business career as the head of Merrill
Lynch. Secretary of Commerce Malcolm Baldrige headed Scovill Manufacturing, and now the former English major is leading a campaign for
clear writing in government.

Executives like Regan and Baldrige are not unusual. According to a   8
recent report in Fortune magazine, 38 percent of today's CEO's majored
in the liberal arts, and a close reading of The New York Times shows
that 9 of the top 13 executives at IBM are liberal-arts majors. At AT&T,

a study showed social-science and humanities graduates moving into middle management faster than engineers and doing at least as well as their business and engineering counterparts in reaching top management levels.

9   For several years now, corporate executives have extolled the wide range of knowledge and interests that a study of the liberal arts encourages. And now under Tom Wyman's direction, CBS has funded an organization that investigates exactly why it is that liberal-arts training is valuable to the American corporation. "In an increasingly competitive, internationally oriented and technologically innovative society," Wyman recently wrote, "successful executives will be those who can understand—and interpret—complex relationships and who are capable of continually reconsidering assumptions underlying old operating practices."

10   In the past, such top-level views did not always filter down to where entry-level hiring is done. But reports from that front are encouraging. A study by Northwestern University shows that many major companies plan to increase their hiring of liberal-arts graduates by some 20 percent in 1986. Or as one employer recently told "Today" show viewers, "Those that are involved in recruiting people to the company are looking for . . . broader skills . . . Then we will worry about teaching them terminology, specifics of the jobs."

11   I don't mean to argue that liberal arts is the only road to success. The average starting salary for engineers remains impressively high, almost $30,000 compared to $21,000 for a liberal-arts graduate. In fact, my informal survey also shows that engineers are doing well in a variety of fields. Chrysler chairman Lee Iacocca was an engineering major, as was former Delaware Gov. Pete du Pont. My point is that there are many paths to success and students shouldn't force themselves down any single one if their true interests lie elsewhere. College should be a time for intellectual enthusiasm, for trying to read one's way through the library, for heated debate with those who see the world differently. College should be a time for learning to enjoy the life of the mind rather than for learning to tolerate what one doesn't find interesting.

12   Students who follow their hearts in choosing majors will most likely end up laboring at what they love. They're the ones who will put in the long hours and intense effort that achievement requires. And they're the ones who will find the sense of purpose that underlies most human happiness.

_____ **CONSIDERATIONS** _____

1. "College should be a time for learning to enjoy the life of the mind rather than for learning to tolerate what one doesn't find interesting," writes Lynne Cheney, deploring the tendency of many students to think of college as vocational training. Read Caroline Bird's "Where College Fails Us" for a different view, and decide where you stand.

2. Cheney's essay questions trends of thought she sees in today's college students, but she uses as the opening of her piece a joking decision made by her daughter. How could you employ a similar device to begin an essay on a serious topic like crime, the threat of the nuclear arms race, or the destruction of the natural environment?

3. Cheney made a telephone survey to test her own convictions. She points out that such a survey may not provide realistic results. Does it have any value? Consider taking a similar survey among your friends as a way of testing your views on a topic you intend to write about.

4. Think of an older teacher, employer, or relative whom Cheney might have used as an illustration of her closing paragraph. Write a realistic interview with that person.

Andrei Codrescu (b. 1946) emigrated from Romania to the United States when he was twenty years old. Best known for weekly pieces delivered on National Public Radio's "All Things Considered"—we reprint two of them, from the collection A Craving for Swan *(1986)—Codrescu teaches at Louisiana State University and writes poetry, fiction, and autobiography. He is one of the great titlers of our time, author of books called* Ectoplasm Is My Hobby *(1971),* Comrade Past and Mister Present *(1986), and* Raised by Puppets Only to Be Killed by Research *(1989). Also, he edits a magazine called* Exquisite Corpse.

17

ANDREI CODRESCU
The End of the Person

When the perennial question of what to wear came up, I noticed that I didn't much care. I just threw on a leather jacket over a T-shirt and kept my professor pants on. My wife put on some kind of Indian skirt and then an old velvet dress on top of that, with a short padded Army jacket over that, and combat boots for good measure. The art opening we went to was attended mostly by folks who looked so instantly familiar I immediately forgot what they were wearing. The one exception was a woman in a leather miniskirt with fake Barbie hair and spiked hi-heeled shoes. And I only remember her because she reminded me vaguely of sex. At the bar we went to after the opening, there were semi-punks drinking champagne, and guys in suits drinking whiskey. The punks were probably businessmen who'd taken off their suits, and the businessmen were probably punks who'd put them on. Later we went to another place, a nightclub where you had to wait in line. A girl in back of us said to her girlfriend: "I'm wearing everything I got. I came here with a suitcase, and I'm wearing everything in it." She looked perfectly normal to me. A little of this and a little of that. That's just it, I thought to myself. Not so long ago, people really agonized when they went out. It wasn't just a matter of clothes: they had to decide *who* they wanted to be. There was a time there in the seventies when everybody worried about their persona: they wouldn't go out if they couldn't project a certain image, be some *thing*. Before that, in let's say, the sixties, there were only two kinds of folk, straight and hip. You dressed like one or the other. Way back in the fifties, everybody was square. You wore whatever everybody else did. Before that, in prehistory, people dressed like what they *really* were. Peasants dressed like peasants. Soldiers like soldiers. Judges like judges. Bums like bums. But we've come to the end of history: we are all one thing today: bored humans: it doesn't matter what we wear, it doesn't even matter who we are. We're back to the basics.

——— CONSIDERATIONS ———————————————

1. Codrescu's mini-essay is one long paragraph. It might look as if he "didn't much care," or just threw in "a little of this and a little of that," and quit when he was tired. To find this essay's structural logic, try breaking it up into conventional paragraphs. How many paragraph breaks do you come up with? Where do they occur? Why? Why doesn't Codrescu indicate those breaks?

2. Consider and discuss the several possible directions in which Codrescu's closing phrase, "back to the basics," might start our minds moving. Which of these has the most relevance to his conclusion, "we are all one thing today: bored humans: it doesn't matter what we wear, it doesn't even matter who we are"?

3. Codrescu uses the word "persona," then explains it as the image one would like to project of himself or herself. Mark Twain, for example, in writing *The Adventures of Huckleberry Finn*, adopted the persona of the river boy, Huck Finn, writing the novel as he imagined Huck would tell the story. Can you find other examples of persona in this book? Have you ever used a persona in your own writing? If not, why not?

4. What do you think of Codrescu's history of human dress? Does it seem complete and accurate enough to justify his conclusion that "we've come to the end of history"? Explain.

18

ANDREI CODRESCU
Time's Fingers

1   A little noticed change has been taking place in our time-world. The advent of digital time has been changing the way we act and think. I believe that it has graduated us to a higher level of anxiety, with greater expectations of efficiency.

2   The old, round, hand-moved time still retained a certain connection to the natural flow of things, to the roundness of the earth and to the changes of light and seasons. Old, round time was outside ourselves, far enough removed from us so we could ignore it if we so chose.

3   Not so with digital time, which is a pulse. It beats instead of turning. It imitates the sound of the heart and thus insinuates itself into the body. More and more, we mistake its rhythmic pulse for our own, thus mistaking the demands of the world with our own desires.

4   Before wrist watches, time used to reside in towers in the centers of towns. At that distance, it could be seen by everybody, but only if they so wished. It took an effort, an actual visit with "time." But then something happened: time first began to live *with* us, and now it is beginning to live *in* us.

5   I remember what it was like to be a child, immersed in the infinitely stretchable substance of time. For me there was only child time, divided arbitrarily and quite painfully by the edicts of the grownups into Bedtime, Wakeup Time, and Schooltime. But within each of those divisions, Eternity still reigned. Later, of course, they managed to infect me with the anxious demands of clock time. Very soon, all that remained was the anxiety of precision. The swift strokes of the time-piece chopped Eternity to pieces.

6   Occasionally, I stop long enough to recapture the dimensions of childhood. But not often enough. Like everybody else, I am helpless before the new technologies.

7   Time is a virus, and it is growing stronger.

—— **CONSIDERATIONS** ———————————————————————

1. Codrescu concludes his "Time's Fingers" by identifying time as "a virus and it is growing stronger." Considering the negative connotations of viruses, explain your opinion of the author's choice of that word and its emphatic placement at the end of his essay.

2. In paragraph 2, the author implies that "the old, round, hand-moved time" was somehow more natural than digital time. Use this as the jumping-off point for an essay on the notion that technology advances while removing us farther and farther from nature. What other examples might you use? What examples might you use to refute the idea?

3. Many children growing up in these push-button times do not understand the expression "dial a number," referring to the older dial telephones. Older folk may not understand the boy who says, "Hey, Mom, let's make this a fast-forward day." Discuss the ways that new technologies affect our language.

4. Philosophers have often pondered the nature of time, the arbitrary ways we measure it, the difficulty of defining it, the dramatically subjective ways we perceive it (see Codrescu's paragraph 5 for an example of the latter). Some people resent tampering with time, such as switching from standard to daylight savings time. Travelers are often perplexed by the apparent loss or gain of time that occurs when they cross time zones. Given such a background, develop an essay from the following statement in William Faulkner's novel *The Sound and the Fury* (1929): "Time is dead as long as it is being clicked off by little wheels; only when the clock stops does time come to life."

Frank Conroy (b. 1936) grew up in various towns along the eastern seaboard, and attended Haverford College in Pennsylvania. He plays jazz piano, was director of the literature program at the National Endowment for the Arts from 1982 to 1987, and now directs the writing program at the University of Iowa. He writes about his early life in Stop-Time, *from which we take this episode. His prose possesses the qualities that make the best reminiscence: details feel exact and bright, though miniature with distance, like the landscape crafted for background to model trains. In 1985 he published a collection of short stories called* Midair.

19

FRANK CONROY
A Yo-Yo Going Down

1   The common yo-yo is crudely made, with a thick shank between two widely spaced wooden disks. The string is knotted or stapled to the shank. With such an instrument nothing can be done except the simple up-down movement. My yo-yo, on the other hand, was a perfectly balanced construction of hard wood, slightly weighted, flat, with only a sixteenth of an inch between the halves. The string was not attached to the shank, but looped over it in such a way as to allow the wooden part to spin freely on its own axis. The gyroscopic effect thus created kept the yo-yo stable in all attitudes.

2   I started at the beginning of the book and quickly mastered the novice, intermediate, and advanced stages, practicing all day every day in the woods across the street from my house. Hour after hour of practice, never moving to the next trick until the one at hand was mastered.

3   The string was tied to my middle finger, just behind the nail. As I threw—with your palm up, make a fist; throw down your hand, fingers

unfolding, as if you were casting grain—a short bit of string would tighten across the sensitive pad of flesh at the tip of my finger. That was the critical area. After a number of weeks I could interpret the condition of the string, the presence of any imperfections on the shank, but most importantly the exact amount of spin or inertial energy left in the yo-yo at any given moment—all from that bit of string on my fingertip. As the throwing motion became more and more natural I found I could make the yo-yo "sleep" for an astonishing length of time—fourteen or fifteen seconds—and still have enough spin left to bring it back to my hand. Gradually the basic moves became reflexes. Sleeping, twirling, swinging, and precise aim. Without thinking, without even looking, I could run through trick after trick involving various combinations of the elemental skills, switching from one to the other in a smooth continuous flow. On particularly good days I would hum a tune under my breath and do it all in time to the music.

Flicking the yo-yo expressed something. The sudden, potentially 4 comic extension of one's arm to twice its length. The precise neatness of it, intrinsically soothing, as if relieving an inner tension too slight to be noticeable, the way a man might hitch up his pants simply to enact a reassuring gesture. It felt good. The comfortable weight in one's hand, the smooth, rapid-descent down the string, ending with a barely audible snap as the yo-yo hung balanced, spinning, pregnant with force and the slave of one's fingertip. That it was vaguely masturbatory seems inescapable. I doubt that half the pubescent boys in America could have been captured by any other means, as, in the heat of the fad, half of them were. A single Loop-the-Loop might represent, in some mysterious way, the act of masturbation, but to break down the entire repertoire into the three stages of throw, trick, and return representing erection, climax, and detumescence seems immoderate.

The greatest pleasure in yo-yoing was an abstract pleasure — 5 watching the dramatization of simple physical laws, and realizing they would never fail if a trick was done correctly. The geometric purity of it! The string wasn't just a string, it was a tool in the enactment of theorems. It was a line, an idea. And the top was an entirely different sort of idea, a gyroscope, capable of storing energy and of interacting with the line. I remember the first time I did a particularly lovely trick, one in which the sleeping yo-yo is swung from right to left while the string is interrupted by an extended index finger. Momentum carries the yo-yo in a circular path around the finger, but instead of completing the arc the yo-yo falls on the taut string between the performer's hands, where it continues to spin in an upright position. My pleasure at that moment was as much from the beauty of the experiment as from pride. Snapping apart my hands I sent the yo-yo into the air above my head, bouncing it off nothing, back into my palm.

6   I practiced the yo-yo because it pleased me to do so, without the slightest application of will power. It wasn't ambition that drove me, but the nature of yo-yoing. The yo-yo represented my first organized attempt to control the outside world. It fascinated me because I could see my progress in clearly defined stages, and because the intimacy of it, the almost spooky closeness I began to feel with the instrument in my hand, seemed to ensure that nothing irrelevant would interfere. I was, in the language of jazz, "up tight" with my yo-yo, and finally free, in one small area at least, of the paralyzing sloppiness of life in general.

7   The first significant problem arose in the attempt to do fifty consecutive Loop-the-Loops. After ten or fifteen the yo-yo invariably started to lean and the throws became less clean, resulting in loss of control. I almost skipped the whole thing because fifty seemed excessive. Ten made the point. But there it was, written out in the book. To qualify as an expert you had to do fifty, so fifty I would do.

8   It took me two days, and I wouldn't have spent a moment more. All those Loop-the-Loops were hard on the strings. Time after time the shank cut them and the yo-yo went sailing off into the air. It was irritating, not only because of the expense (strings were a nickel each, and fabricating your own was unsatisfactory), but because a random element had been introduced. About the only unforeseeable disaster in yo-yoing was to have your string break, and here was a trick designed to do exactly that. Twenty-five would have been enough. If you could do twenty-five clean Loop-the-Loops you could do fifty or a hundred. I supposed they were simply trying to sell strings and went back to the more interesting tricks.

9   The witty nonsense of Eating Spaghetti, the surprise of The Twirl, the complex neatness of Cannonball, Backwards Round the World, or Halfway Round the World—I could do them all, without false starts or sloppy endings. I could do every trick in the book. Perfectly.

10   The day was marked on the kitchen calendar (God Gave Us Bluebell Natural Bottled Gas). I got on my bike and rode into town. Pedaling along the highway I worked out with the yo-yo to break in a new string. The twins were appearing at the dime store.

11   I could hear the crowd before I turned the corner. Kids were coming on bikes and on foot from every corner of town, rushing down

the streets like madmen. Three or four policemen were busy keeping the street clear directly in front of the store, and in a small open space around the doors some of the more adept kids were running through their tricks, showing off to the general audience or stopping to compare notes with their peers. Standing at the edge with my yo-yo safe in my pocket, it didn't take me long to see I had them all covered. A boy in a sailor hat could do some of the harder tricks, but he missed too often to be a serious threat. I went inside.

As Ramos and Ricardo performed I watched their hands carefully, noticing little differences in style, and technique. Ricardo was a shade classier, I thought, although Ramos held an edge in the showy two-handed stuff. When they were through we went outside for the contest. 12

"Everybody in the alley!" Ramos shouted, his head bobbing an inch or two above the others. "Contest starting now in the alley!" A hundred excited children followed the twins into an alley beside the dime store and lined up against the wall. 13

"Attention all kids!" Ramos yelled, facing us from the middle of the street like a drill sergeant. "To qualify for contest you got to Rock the Cradle. You got to rock yo-yo in cradle four time. Four time! Okay? Three time no good. Okay. Everybody happy?" There were murmurs of disappointment and some of the kids stepped out of line. The rest of us closed ranks. Yo-yos flicked nervously as we waited. "Winner receive grand prize. Special Black Beauty Prize Yo-Yo with Diamonds," said Ramos, gesturing to his brother who smiled and held up the prize, turning it in the air so we could see the four stones set on each side. ("The crowd gasped . . ." I want to write. Of course they didn't. They didn't make a sound, but the impact of the diamond yo-yo was obvious.) We'd never seen anything like it. One imagined how the stones would gleam as it revolved, and how much prettier the tricks would be. The ultimate yo-yo! The only one in town! Who knew what feats were possible with such an instrument? All around me a fierce, nervous resolve was settling into the contestants, suddenly skittish as race-horses. 14

"Ricardo will show trick with Grand Prize Yo-Yo. Rock the Cradle four time!" 15

"One!" cried Ramos. 16

"Two!" the kids joined in. 17

"Three!" It was really beautiful. He did it so slowly you would have thought he had all the time in the world. I counted seconds under my breath to see how long he made it sleep. 18

19   "Four!" said the crowd.

20   "Thirteen" I said to myself as the yo-yo snapped back into his hand. Thirteen seconds. Excellent time for that particular trick.

21   "Attention all kids!" Ramos announced. "Contest start now at head of line."

22   The first boy did a sloppy job of gathering his string but managed to rock the cradle quickly four times.

23   "Okay." Ramos tapped him on the shoulder and moved to the next boy, who fumbled. "Out." Ricardo followed, doing an occasional Loop-the-Loop with the diamond yo-yo. "Out . . . out . . . okay," said Ramos as he worked down the line.

24   There was something about the man's inexorable advance that unnerved me. His decisions were fast, and there was no appeal. To my surprise I felt my palms begin to sweat. Closer and closer he came, his voice growing louder, and then suddenly he was standing in front of me. Amazed, I stared at him. It was as if he'd appeared out of thin air.

25   "What happen boy, you swarrow bubble gum?"

26   The laughter jolted me out of it. Blushing, I threw down my yo-yo and executed a slow Rock the Cradle, counting the four passes and hesitating a moment at the end so as not to appear rushed.

27   "Okay." He tapped my shoulder. "Good."

28   I wiped my hands on my blue jeans and watched him move down the line. "Out . . . out . . . out." He had a large mole on the back of his neck.

29   Seven boys qualified. Coming back, Ramos called out, "Next trick Backward Round the World! Okay? Go!"

30   The first two boys missed, but the third was the kid in the sailor hat. Glancing quickly to see that no one was behind him, he hunched up his shoulder, threw, and just barely made the catch. There was some loose string in his hand, but not enough to disqualify him.

31   Number four missed, as did number five, and it was my turn. I stepped forward, threw the yo-yo almost straight up over my head, and as it began to fall pulled very gentle to add some speed. It zipped neatly behind my legs and there was nothing more to do. My head turned to one side, I stood absolutely still and watched the yo-yo come in over my shoulder and slap into my hand. I added a Loop-the-Loop just to show the tightness of the string.

32   "Did you see that?" I heard someone say.

33   Number seven missed, so it was between myself and the boy in the sailor hat. His hair was bleached by the sun and combed up over his forehead in a pompadour, held from behind by the white hat. He was a

year or two older than me. Blinking his blue eyes nervously, he adjusted the tension of his string.

"Next trick Cannonball! Cannonball! You go first this time," 34 Ramos said to me.

Kids had gathered in a circle around us, those in front quiet and 35 attentive, those in back jumping up and down to get a view. "Move back for room," Ricardo said, pushing them back. "More room, please."

I stepped into the center and paused, looking down at the ground. 36 It was a difficult trick. The yo-yo had to land exactly on the string and there was a chance I'd miss the first time. I knew I wouldn't miss twice. "Can I have one practice?"

Ramos and Ricardo consulted in their mother tongue, and then 37 Ramos held up his hands. "Attention all kids! Each boy have one practice before trick."

The crowd was then silent, watching me. I took a deep breath and 38 threw, following the fall of the yo-yo with my eyes, turning slightly, matador-fashion, as it passed me. My finger caught the string, the yo-yo came up and over, and missed. Without pausing I threw again. "Second time," I yelled, so there would be no misunderstanding. The circle had been too big. This time I made it small, sacrificing beauty for security. The yo-yo fell where it belonged and spun for a moment. (A moment I don't rush, my arms widespread, my eyes locked on the spinning toy. The Trick! There it is, brief and magic right before your eyes! My hands are frozen in the middle of a deaf-and-dumb sentence, holding the whole airy, tenuous statement aloft for everyone to see.) With a quick snap I broke up the trick and made my catch.

Ramos nodded. "Okay. Very good. Now next boy." 39

Sailor-hat stepped forward, wiping his nose with the back of his 40 hand. He threw once to clear the string.

"One practice," said Ramos. 41

He nodded. 42

"C'mon Bobby," someone said. "You can do it." 43

Bobby threw the yo-yo out to the side, made his move, and missed. 44 "Damn," he whispered. (He said "dahyum.") The second time he got halfway through the trick before his yo-yo ran out of gas and fell impotently off the string. He picked it up and walked away, winding slowly.

Ramos came over and held my hand in the air. "The winner!" he 45 yelled. "Grand prize Black Beauty Diamond Yo-Yo will now be awarded."

Ricardo stood in front of me. "Take off old yo-yo." I loosened the 46 knot and slipped it off. "Put out hand." I held out my hand and he looped the new string on my finger, just behind the nail, where the mark was. "You like Black Beauty," he said, smiling as he stepped back. "Diamond make pretty colors in the sun."

47   "Thank you," I said.

48   "Very good with yo-yo. Later we have contest for whole town. Winner go to Miami for State Championship. Maybe you win. Okay?"

49   "Okay." I nodded. "Thank you."

50   A few kids came up to look at Black Beauty. I threw it once or twice to get the feel. It seemed a bit heavier than my old one. Ramos and Ricardo were surrounded as the kids called out their favorite tricks.

51   "Do Pickpocket! Pickpocket!"

52   "Do the Double Cannonball!"

53   "Ramos! Ramos! Do the Turkish Army!"

54   Smiling, waving their hands to ward off the barrage of requests, the twins worked their way through the crowd toward the mouth of the alley. I watched them moving away and was immediately struck by a wave of fierce and irrational panic. "Wait," I yelled, pushing through after them. "Wait!"

55   I caught them on the street.

56   "No more today," Ricardo said, and then paused when he saw it was me. "Okay. The champ. What's wrong? Yo-yo no good?"

57   "No. It's fine."

58   "Good. You take care of it."

59   "I wanted to ask when the contest is. The one where you get to go to Miami."

60   "Later. After school begins." They began to move away. "We have to go home now."

61   "Just one more thing," I said, walking after them. "What is the hardest trick you know?"

62   Ricardo laughed. "Hardest trick is killing flies in air."

63   "No, no. I mean a real trick."

64   They stopped and looked at me. "There is a very hard trick," Ricardo said. "I don't do it, but Ramos does. Because you won the contest he will show you. But only once, so watch carefully."

65   We stepped into the lobby of the Sunset Theater. Ramos cleared his string. "Watch," he said, and threw. The trick started out like a Cannonball, and then unexpectedly folded up, opened again, and as I watched breathlessly the entire complex web spun around in the air, propelled by Ramos' two hands making slow circles like a swimmer. The end was like the end of a Cannonball.

"That's beautiful," I said, genuinely awed. "What's it called?" 66
"The Universe." 67
"The Universe," I repeated. 68
"Because it goes around and around," said Ramos, "like the 69
planets."

_____ **CONSIDERATIONS** _____

1. List the ways in which Conroy says one can get pleasure from the yo-yo.

2. How much of performance is play? Would you use the word performance for the work of a painter, an opera singer, a tennis star, a poet? Are professional athletes paid to play? What is the difference between work and play?

3. One respected writer says that "play is the direct opposite of seriousness," yet writers like Conroy are serious in recalling their childhood play. Can you resolve this apparent contradiction?

4. Conroy's essay might be divided into two major sections. Where would you draw the dividing line? Describe the two sections in terms of the author's intention. In the second section, the author makes constant use of dialogue; in the first, there is none. Why?

5. "I practiced the yo-yo because it pleased me to do so, without the slightest application of will power." Consider the relevance or irrelevance of will power to pleasure. Are they mutually exclusive?

6. In paragraph 14, Conroy interrupts his narrative with a parenthetical remark about himself as the writer: "('The crowd gasped . . .' I want to write. Of course they didn't. They didn't make a sound, but the impact of the diamond yo-yo was obvious.)" Are such glimpses of the writer useful or merely distracting? Discuss.

Emily Dickinson (1830–1886) was little known as a poet in her lifetime, but now is acknowledged as among the greatest American poets. She lived her entire life in Amherst, Massachusetts, and spent her later years as a virtual recluse in the Dickinsons' brick homestead on Main Street. She always remained close to her family, and kept contact with the outside world through a vast correspondence.

She published little poetry in her lifetime. After her death, however, more than a thousand poems were discovered neatly arranged in the bureau of the upstairs bedroom where she wrote. In 1955, a definitive edition of The Poems of Emily Dickinson *was published, containing 1,775 poems and fragments.*

20

EMILY DICKINSON
There's a certain Slant of light

There's a certain Slant of light,
Winter Afternoons—
That oppresses, like the Heft
Of Cathedral Tunes—

5   Heavenly Hurt, it gives us—
We can find no scar,
But internal difference,
Where the Meanings, are—

None may teach it—Any—
10   'Tis the Seal Despair—
An imperial affliction
Sent us of the Air—

When it comes, the Landscape listens—   15
Shadows—hold their breath—
When it goes, 'tis like the Distance
On the look of Death—

*Joan Didion (b. 1934) worked as an editor in New York for
some years, and then returned to her native California where
she supports herself by writing. She has collaborated on
screenplays (often with her husband, John Gregory Dunne),
including* Panic in Needle Park *(1971) and* A Star is Born *(1976).
Best known for her novels—*Play It As It Lays *appeared in 1971,*
A Book of Common Prayer *in 1977, and* Democracy *in 1984—
she is also admired for her essays, collected in* Slouching
Towards Bethlehem *(1969), from which we take this piece, and*
The White Album *(1979). Her long essay,* Salvador, *appeared as
a book in 1983 and* Miami *in 1987. Students who keep journals
or notebooks, or who practice daily writing, may learn a thing or
two from Joan Didion.*

21

JOAN DIDION
On Keeping a Notebook

1   " 'That woman Estelle,' " the note reads, " 'is partly the reason
why George Sharp and I are separated today.' *Dirty crepe-de-Chine
wrapper, hotel bar, Wilmington RR, 9:45* A.M. August Monday
morning."

2   Since the note is in my notebook, it presumably has some meaning to me. I study it for a long while. At first I have only the most general
notion of what I was doing on an August Monday morning in the bar of
the hotel across from the Pennsylvania Railroad station in Wilmington,
Delaware (waiting for a train? missing one? 1960? 1961? why Wilmington?), but I do remember being there. The woman in the dirty
crepe-de-Chine wrapper had come down from her room for a beer, and
the bartender had heard before the reason why George Sharp and she
were separated today. "Sure," he said, and went on mopping the floor.
"You told me." At the other end of the bar is a girl. She is talking,

pointedly, not to the man beside her but to a cat lying in the triangle of sunlight cast through the open door. She is wearing a plaid silk dress from Peck & Peck, and the hem is coming down.

Here is what it is: the girl has been on the Eastern Shore, and now 3 she is going back to the city, leaving the man beside her, and all she can see ahead are the viscous summer sidewalks and the 3 A.M. long-distance calls that will make her lie awake and then sleep drugged through all the steaming mornings left in August (1960? 1961?). Because she must go directly from the train to lunch in New York, she wishes that she had a safety pin for the hem of the plaid silk dress, and she also wishes that she could forget about the hem and the lunch and stay in the cool bar that smells of disinfectant and malt and make friends with the woman in the crepe-de-Chine wrapper. She is afflicted by a little self-pity, and she wants to compare Estelles. That is what that was all about.

Why did I write it down? In order to remember, of course, but 4 exactly what was it I wanted to remember? How much of it actually happened? Did any of it? Why do I keep a notebook at all? It is easy to deceive oneself on all those scores. The impulse to write things down is a peculiarly compulsive one, inexplicable to those who do not share it, useful only accidentally, only secondarily, in the way that any compulsion tries to justify itself. I suppose that it begins or does not begin in the cradle. Although I have felt compelled to write things down since I was five years old, I doubt that my daughter ever will, for she is a singularly blessed and accepting child, delighted with life exactly as life presents itself to her, unafraid to go to sleep and unafraid to wake up. Keepers of private notebooks are a different breed altogether, lonely and resistant rearrangers of things, anxious malcontents, children afflicted apparently at birth with some presentiment of loss.

My first notebook was a Big Five tablet, given to me by my mother 5 with the sensible suggestion that I stop whining and learn to amuse myself by writing down my thoughts. She returned the tablet to me a few years ago; the first entry is an account of a woman who believed herself to be freezing to death in the Arctic night, only to find when day broke, that she had stumbled onto the Sahara Desert, where she would die of the heat before lunch. I have no idea what turn of a five-year-old's mind could have prompted so insistently "ironic" and exotic a story, but it does reveal a certain predilection for the extreme which has dogged me into adult life; perhaps if I were analytically inclined I would find it a truer story than any I might have told about Donald Johnson's birthday party or the day my cousin Brenda put Kitty Litter in the aquarium.

6   So the point of my keeping a notebook has never been, nor is it now, to have an accurate factual record of what I have been doing or thinking. That would be a different impulse entirely, an instinct for reality which I sometimes envy but do not possess. At no point have I ever been able successfully to keep a diary; my approach to daily life ranges from the grossly negligent to the merely absent, and on those few occasions when I have tried dutifully to record a day's events, boredom has so overcome me that the results are mysterious at best. What is this business about "shopping, typing piece, dinner with E, depressed"? Shopping for what? Typing what piece? Who is E? Was this "E" depressed, or was I depressed? Who cares?

7   In fact I have abandoned altogether that kind of pointless entry; instead I tell what some would call lies. "That's simply not true," the members of my family frequently tell me when they come up against my memory of a shared event. "The party was *not* for you, the spider was *not* a black widow, *it wasn't that way at all.*" Very likely they are right, for not only have I always had trouble distinguishing between what happened and what merely might have happened, but I remain unconvinced that the distinction, for my purposes, matters. The cracked crab that I recall having for lunch the day my father came home from Detroit in 1945 must certainly be embroidery, worked into the day's pattern to lend verisimilitude; I was ten years old and would not now remember the cracked crab. The day's events did not turn on cracked crab. And yet it is precisely that fictitious crab that makes me see the afternoon all over again, a home movie run all too often, the father bearing gifts, the child weeping, an exercise in family love and guilt. Or that is what it was to me. Similarly, perhaps it never did snow that August in Vermont; perhaps there never were flurries in the night wind, and maybe no one else felt the ground hardening and summer already dead even as we pretended to bask in it, but that was how it felt to me, and it might as well have snowed, could have snowed, did snow.

8   *How it felt to me:* that is getting closer to the truth about a notebook. I sometimes delude myself about why I keep a notebook, imagine that some thrifty virtue derives from preserving everything observed. See enough and write it down, I tell myself, and then some morning when the world seems drained of wonder, some day when I am only going through the motions of doing what I am supposed to do, which is write—on that bankrupt morning I will simply open my notebook and there it will all be, a forgotten account with accumulated interest, paid passage back to the world out there: dialogue overheard in hotels and elevators and at the hat-check counter in Pavillon (one

middle-aged man shows his hat check to another and says, "That's my old football number"); impressions of Bettina Aptheker and Benjamin Sonnenberg and Teddy ("Mr. Acapulco") Stauffer; careful *aperçus* about tennis bums and failed fashion models and Greek shipping heiresses, one of whom taught me a significant lesson (a lesson I could have learned from F. Scott Fitzgerald, but perhaps we must meet the very rich for ourselves) by asking, when I arrived to interview her in her orchid-filled sitting room on the second day of a paralyzing New York blizzard, whether it was snowing outside.

I imagine, in other words, that the notebook is about other people. But of course it is not. I have no real business with what one stranger said to another at the hat-check counter in Pavillon; in fact I suspect that the line "That's my old football number" touched not my own imagination at all, but merely some memory of something once read, probably "The Eighty-Yard Run." Nor is my concern with a woman in a dirty crepe-de-Chine wrapper in a Wilmington bar. My stake is always, of course, in the unmentioned girl in the plaid silk dress. *Remember what it was to be me:* that is always the point. 9

It is a difficult point to admit. We are brought up in the ethic that others, any others, all others, are by definition more interesting than ourselves; taught to be diffident, just this side of self-effacing. ("You're the least important person in the room and don't forget it," Jessica Mitford's governess would hiss in her ear on the advent of any social occasion; I copied that into my notebook because it is only recently that I have been able to enter a room without hearing some such phrase in my inner ear.) Only the very young and the very old may recount their dreams at breakfast, dwell upon self, interrupt with memories of beach picnics and favorite Liberty lawn dresses and the rainbow trout in a creek near Colorado Springs. The rest of us are expected, rightly, to affect absorption in other people's favorite dresses, other people's trout. 10

And so we do. But our notebooks give us away, for however dutifully we record what we see around us, the common denominator of all we see is always, transparently, shamelessly, the implacable "I." We are not talking here about the kind of notebook that is patently for public consumption, a structural conceit for binding together a series of graceful *pensées:* we are talking about something private, about bits of the mind's string too short to use, an indiscriminate and erratic assemblage with meaning only for its maker. 11

And sometimes even the maker has difficulty with the meaning. There does not seem to be, for example, any point in my knowing for the rest of my life that, during 1964, 720 tons of soot fell on every square 12 mile of New York City, yet there it is in my notebook, labeled "FACT." Nor do I really need to remember that Ambrose Bierce liked to spell Leland Stanford's[1] name "£eland $tanford" or that "smart women almost always wear black in Cuba," a fashion hint without much potential for practical application. And does not the relevance of these notes seem marginal at best?:

> In the basement museum of the Inyo County Courthouse in Independence, California, sign pinned to a mandarin coat: "This MANDARIN COAT was often worn by Mrs. Minnie S. Brooks when giving lectures on her TEAPOT COLLECTION."

> Redhead getting out of car in front of Beverly Wilshire Hotel, chinchilla stole, Vuitton bags with tags reading:
>
>
> MRS LOU FOX
>
> HOTEL SAHARA
>
> VEGAS
>

13   Well perhaps not entirely marginal. As a matter of fact, Mrs. Minnie S. Brooks and her MANDARIN COAT pull me back into my own childhood, for although I never knew Mrs. Brooks and did not visit Inyo County until I was thirty, I grew up in just such a world, in houses cluttered with Indian relics and bits of gold ore and ambergris and the souvenirs my Aunt Mercy Farnsworth brought back from the Orient. It is a long way from that world to Mrs. Lou Fox's world, where we all live now, and is it not just as well to remember that? Might not Mrs. Minnie S. Brooks help me to remember what I am? Might not Mrs. Lou Fox help me to remember what I am not?

14   But sometimes the point is harder to discern. What exactly did I have in mind when I noted down that it cost the father of someone I know $650 a month to light the place on the Hudson in which he lived before the Crash? What use was I planning to make of this line by Jimmy Hoffa: "I may have my faults, but being wrong ain't one of them"? And although I think it interesting to know where the girls who travel with the Syndicate have their hair done when they find themselves on the West Coast, will I ever make suitable use of it? Might I not be better off just passing it on to John O'Hara? What is a recipe for sauerkraut doing in my notebook? What kind of magpie keeps this notebook? *"He was born the night the Titanic went down."* That seems a nice enough line, and I even recall who said it, but is it not really a better line in life than it could ever be in fiction?

---

[1] Railroad magnate (1834–1893) who founded the university.—ED.

But of course that is exactly it: not that I should ever use the line,   15
but that I should remember the woman who said it and the afternoon I
heard it. We were on her terrace by the sea, and we were finishing the
wine left from lunch, trying to get what sun there was, a California
winter sun. The woman whose husband was born the night the *Titanic*
went down wanted to rent her house, wanted to go back to her children
in Paris. I remember wishing that I could afford the house, which cost
$1,000 a month. "Someday you will," she said lazily. "Someday it all
comes." There in the sun on her terrace it seemed easy to believe in
someday, but later I had a low-grade afternoon hangover and ran over a
black snake on the way to the supermarket and was flooded with
inexplicable fear when I heard the checkout clerk explaining to the man
ahead of me why she was finally divorcing her husband. "He left me no
choice," she said over and over as she punched the register. "He has a
little seven-month-old baby by her, he left me no choice." I would like
to believe that my dread then was for the human condition, but of
course it was for me, because I wanted a baby and did not then have one
and because I wanted to own the house that cost $1,000 a month to rent
and because I had a hangover.

It all comes back. Perhaps it is difficult to see the value in having   16
one's self back in that kind of mood, but I do see it; I think we are well
advised to keep on nodding terms with the people we used to be,
whether we find them attractive company or not. Otherwise they turn
up unannounced and surprise us, come hammering on the mind's door
at 4 A.M. of a bad night and demand to know who deserted them, who
betrayed them, who is going to make amends. We forget all too soon the
things we thought we could never forget. We forget the loves and the
betrayals alike, forget what we whispered and what we screamed, forget
who we were. I have already lost touch with a couple of people I used to
be; one of them, a seventeen-year-old, presents little threat, although it
would be of some interest to me to know again what it feels like to sit
on a river levee drinking vodka-and-orange-juice and listening to Les
Paul and Mary Ford and their echoes sing "How High the Moon" on the
car radio. (You see I still have the scenes, but I no longer perceive myself
among those present, no longer could even improvise the dialogue.) The
other one, a twenty-three-year-old, bothers me more. She was always a
good deal of trouble, and I suspect she will reappear when I least want to
see her, skirts too long, shy to the point of aggravation, always the
injured party, full of recriminations and little hurts and stories I do not
want to hear again, at once saddening me and angering me with her
vulnerability and ignorance, an apparition all the more insistent for
being so long banished.

17   It is a good idea, then, to keep in touch, and I suppose that keeping in touch is what notebooks are all about. And we are all on our own when it comes to keeping those lines open to ourselves: your notebook will never help me, nor mine you. *"So what's new in the whiskey business?"* What could that possibly mean to you? To me it means a blonde in a Pucci bathing suit sitting with a couple of fat men by the pool at the Beverly Hills Hotel. Another man approaches, and they all regard one another in silence for a while. "So what's new in the whiskey business?" one of the fat men finally says by way of welcome, and the blonde stands up, arches one foot and dips it in the pool, looking all the while at the cabaña where Baby Pignatari is talking on the telephone. That is all there is to that, except that several years later I saw the blonde coming out of Saks Fifth Avenue in New York with her California complexion and a voluminous mink coat. In the harsh wind that day she looked old and irrevocably tired to me, and even the skins in the mink coat were not worked the way they were doing them that year, not the way she would have wanted them done, and there is the point of the story. For a while after that I did not like to look in the mirror, and my eyes would skim the newspapers and pick out only the deaths, the cancer victims, the premature coronaries, the suicides, and I stopped riding the Lexington Avenue IRT because I noticed for the first time that all the strangers I had seen for years—the man with the seeing-eye dog, the spinster who read the classified pages every day, the fat girl who always got off with me at Grand Central—looked older than they once had.

18   It all comes back. Even that recipe for sauerkraut: even that brings it back. I was on Fire Island when I first made that sauerkraut, and it was raining, and we drank a lot of bourbon and ate the sauerkraut and went to bed at ten, and I listened to the rain and the Atlantic and felt safe. I made the sauerkraut again last night and it did not make me feel any safer, but that is, as they say, another story.

_____ CONSIDERATIONS _____

1. Read the selections from Henry David Thoreau's journal and comment on the differences you find between his idea of a journal and Didion's idea of a writer's notebook.

2. How far must you read in Didion's piece before you know her real reason for keeping a journal? Why does she delay that announcement so long? Might such a delay work well in one of your essays?

3. "You're the least important person in the room and don't forget it" is a line from Didion's journal. Does she believe that statement? If not, why does she include it in her essay?

4. Didion discusses the randomness of a notebook. How does she use this randomness, or lack of order or purpose, to bring order and purpose to her essay? Take paragraphs 14 and 15 and study the method she derives from her seeming madness.

5. In paragraph 16, Didion says she has already "lost touch with a couple of people I used to be." How does this awareness relate to the last line of James Agee's "Knoxville: Summer 1915"? Have you ever had similar feelings about some of the people you used to be? What significant details in your memory come to mind?

6. Using a periodical index in your college library, see how quickly you can locate one of Didion's many journalistic essays.

Annie Dillard (b. 1945) was born in Pittsburgh, went to Hollins College, and lived for a while in Virginia in the Roanoke Valley—the area she describes so beautifully in her writing. She currently lives in Connecticut. In 1974 she published her first book of poems, Tickets for a Prayer Wheel, *and her first book of prose,* Pilgrim at Tinker Creek, *which won a Pulitzer Prize. In 1977 she published* Holy the Firm, *and in 1982* Living by Fiction.*

Teaching a Stone to Talk (1982) gathers Annie Dillard's miscellaneous essays from periodicals. Book reviewers often condescend to such collections; in her introduction to the work Annie Dillard wants to be certain that readers understand and tells us ". . . this is my real work." Indeed, the brief essay is her literary form, and she masters it as Chekhov mastered the short story.

22

ANNIE DILLARD
Sojourner

1   If survival is an art, then mangroves are artists of the beautiful: not only that they exist at all—smooth-barked, glossy-leaved, thickets of lapped mystery—but that they can and do exist as floating islands, as trees upright and loose, alive and homeless on the water.

2   I have seen mangroves, always on tropical ocean shores, in Florida and in the Galápagos. There is the red mangrove, the yellow, the button, and the black. They are all short, messy trees, waxy-leaved, laced all over with aerial roots, woody arching buttresses, and weird leathery berry pods. All this tangles from a black muck soil, a black muck matted like a mud-sopped rag, a muck without any other plants, shaded, cold to the touch, tracked at the water's edge by herons and nosed by sharks.

120

It is these shoreline trees which, by a fairly common accident, can become floating islands. A hurricane flood or a riptide can wrest a tree from the shore, or from the mouth of a tidal river, and hurl it into the ocean. It floats. It is a mangrove island, blown.

There are floating islands on the planet; it amazes me. Credulous Pliny described some islands thought to be mangrove islands floating on a river. The people called these river islands *the dancers*, "because in any consort of musicians singing, they stir and move at the stroke of the feet, keeping time and measure."

Trees floating on rivers are less amazing than trees floating on the poisonous sea. A tree cannot live in salt. Mangrove trees exude salt from their leaves; you can see it, even on shoreline black mangroves, as a thin white crust. Lick a leaf and your tongue curls and coils; your mouth's a heap of salt.

Nor can a tree live without soil. A hurricane-born mangrove island may bring its own soil to the sea. But other mangrove trees make their own soil—and their own islands—from scratch. These are the ones which interest me. The seeds germinate in the fruit on the tree. The germinated embryo can drop anywhere— say, onto a dab of floating muck. The heavy root end sinks; a leafy plumule unfurls. The tiny seedling, afloat, is on its way. Soon aerial roots shooting out in all directions trap debris. The sapling's networks twine, the interstices narrow, and water calms in the lee. Bacteria thrive on organic broth; amphipods swarm. These creatures grow and die at the trees' wet feet. The soil thickens, accumulating rainwater, leaf rot, seashells, and guano; the island spreads.

More seeds and more muck yield more trees on the new island. A society grows, interlocked in a tangle of dependencies. The island rocks less in the swells. Fish throng to the backwaters stilled in snarled roots. Soon, Asian mudskippers—little four-inch fish—clamber up the mangrove roots into the air and peer about from periscope eyes on stalks, like snails. Oysters clamp to submersed roots, as do starfish, dog whelk, and the creatures that live among tangled kelp. Shrimp seek shelter there, limpets a holdfast, pelagic birds a rest.

And the mangrove island wanders on, afloat and adrift. It walks teetering and wanton before the wind. Its fate and direction are random. It may bob across an ocean and catch on another mainland's shores. It may starve or dry while it is still a sapling. It may topple in a storm, or pitchpole. By the rarest of chances, it may stave into another mangrove island in a crash of clacking roots, and mesh. What it is most likely to do is drift anywhere in the alien ocean, feeding on death and growing, netting a makeshift soil as it goes, shrimp in its toes and terns in its hair.

9   We could do worse.

10   I alternate between thinking of the planet as home—dear and familiar stone hearth and garden—and as a hard land of exile in which we are all sojourners. Today I favor the latter view. The word "sojourner" occurs often in the English Old Testament. It invokes a nomadic people's sense of vagrancy, a praying people's knowledge of estrangement, a thinking people's intuition of sharp loss: "For we are strangers before thee, and sojourners, as were all our fathers: our days on the earth are as a shadow, and there is none abiding."

11   We don't know where we belong, but in times of sorrow it doesn't seem to be here, here with these silly pansies and witless mountains, here with sponges and hard-eyed birds. In times of sorrow the innocence of the other creatures—from whom and with whom we evolved— seems a mockery. Their ways are not our ways. We seem set among them as among lifelike props for a tragedy—or a broad lampoon—on a thrust rock stage.

12   It doesn't seem to be here that we belong, here where space is curved, the earth is round, we're all going to die, and it seems as wise to stay in bed as budge. It is strange here, not quite warm enough, or too warm, too leafy, or inedible, or windy, or dead. It is not, frankly, the sort of home for people one would have thought of—although I lack the fancy to imagine another.

13   The planet itself is a sojourner in airless space, a wet ball flung across nowhere. The few objects in the universe scatter. The coherence of matter dwindles and crumbles toward stillness. I have read, and repeated, that our solar system as a whole is careering through space toward a point east of Hercules. Now I wonder: what could that possibly mean, east of Hercules? Isn't space curved? When we get "there," how will our course change, and why? Will we slide down the universe's inside arc like mud slung at a wall? Or what sort of welcoming shore is this east of Hercules? Surely we don't anchor there, and disembark, and sweep into dinner with our host. Does someone cry, "Last stop, last stop"? At any rate, east of Hercules, like east of Eden, isn't a place to call home. It is a course without direction; it is "out." And we are cast.

14   These are enervating thoughts, the thoughts of despair. They

crowd back, unbidden, when human life as it unrolls goes ill, when we lose control of our lives or the illusion of control, and it seems that we are not moving toward any end but merely blown. Our life seems cursed to be a wiggle merely, and a wandering without end. Even nature is hostile and poisonous, as though it were impossible for our vulnerability to survive on these acrid stones.

Whether these thoughts are true or not I find less interesting than   15
the possibilities for beauty they may hold. We are down here in time, where beauty grows. Even if things are as bad as they could possibly be, and as meaningless, then matters of truth are themselves indifferent; we may as well please our sensibilities and, with as much spirit as we can muster, go out with a buck and wing.

The planet is less like an enclosed spaceship—spaceship earth—   16
than it is like an exposed mangrove island beautiful and loose. We the people started small and have since accumulated a great and solacing muck of soil, of human culture. We are rooted in it; we are bearing it with us across nowhere. The word "nowhere" is our cue: the consort of musicians strikes up, and we in the chorus stir and move and start twirling our hats. A mangrove island turns drift to dance. It creates its own soil as it goes, rocking over the salt sea at random, rocking day and night and round the sun, rocking round the sun and out toward east of Hercules.

_____ CONSIDERATIONS _____

1. In many passages, Annie Dillard's prose verges on poetry, particularly in her high degree of compression in alluding to persons ("Pliny," paragraph 4), places ("Galápagos," paragraph 2, "east of Hercules," paragraph 13), and sources (see Psalms 39 for the quotation in paragraph 10) that may not be immediately recognizable to the hurried reader. You will enjoy her essay more and appreciate her skill if you take the time to determine the significance of these allusions.

2. One of the hallmarks of an accomplished writer like Dillard is the ability to integrate the various materials of an essay. As one example, study her closing paragraph to see how tightly she brings together elements she has introduced earlier.

3. Explain why a reader would be foolish to conclude that Dillard's essay is simply a study of the mangrove islands, of interest only to students of natural history. What elements of the essay might account for such a conclusion?

4. Dillard's diction (choice of words) mixes vocabularies. Find a few other contrasts, such as the scientific ("plumule," "amphipods," "pelagic") versus

the imaginative ("matted like a mud-sopped rag," or "shrimp in its toes and terns in its hair") versus the nautical ("pitchpole," "stave," "lee"), and discuss the delights and difficulties for a reader encountering such diversity.

5. Does Dillard offer any consolation for the sense of despairing rootlessness she expresses in paragraph 13? Explain in a short essay based on your own ideas about the destiny or purpose of humankind's presence on the planet.

Frederick Douglass (1817–1895) was born a slave in Maryland, and escaped to Massachusetts in 1838. Later, he lectured against slavery and wrote of his experience. "Plantation Life" comes from A Narrative of the Life of Frederick Douglass, an American Slave, Written by Himself *(1845). During the Civil War he organized two regiments of black troops in Massachusetts; in the Reconstruction period he worked for the government.*

23

FREDERICK DOUGLASS
Plantation Life

My master's family consisted of two sons, Andrew and Richard; 1
one daughter, Lucretia, and her husband, Captain Thomas Auld. They
lived in one house, upon the home plantation of Colonel Edward Lloyd.
My master was Colonel Lloyd's clerk and superintendent. He was what
might be called the overseer of the overseers. I spent two years of
childhood on this plantation in my old master's family. . . . As I received my first impressions of slavery on this plantation, I will give
some description of it, and of slavery as it there existed. The plantation
is about twelve miles north of Easton, in Talbot county, and is situated
on the border of Miles River. The principal products raised upon it were
tobacco, corn, and wheat. These were raised in great abundance; so that,
with the products of this and the other farms belonging to him, he was
able to keep in almost constant employment a large sloop, in carrying
them to market at Baltimore. This sloop was named Sally Lloyd, in
honor of one of the colonel's daughters. My master's son-in-law, Captain Auld, was master of the vessel; she was otherwise manned by the
colonel's own slaves. Their names were Peter, Isaac, Rich, and Jake.
These were esteemed very highly by the other slaves, and looked upon
as the privileged ones of the plantation; for it was no small affair, in the
eyes of the slaves, to be allowed to see Baltimore.

Colonel Lloyd kept from three to four hundred slaves on his home 2 plantation, and owned a large number more on the neighboring farms belonging to him. The names of the farms nearest to the home plantation were Wye Town and New Design. "Wye Town" was under the overseership of a man named Noah Willis. New Design was under the overseership of a Mr. Townsend. The overseers of these, and all the rest of the farms, numbering over twenty, received advice and direction from the managers of the home plantation. This was the great business place. It was the seat of government for the whole twenty farms. All disputes among the overseers were settled here. If a slave was convicted of any high misdemeanor, became unmanageable, or evinced a determination to run away, he was brought immediately here, severely whipped, put on board the sloop, carried to Baltimore, and sold to Austin Woolfolk, or some other slave-trader, as a warning to the slaves remaining.

3   Here, too, the slaves of all the other farms received their monthly allowance of food, and their yearly clothing. The men and women slaves received, as their monthly allowance of food, eight pounds of pork, or its equivalent in fish, and one bushel of corn meal. Their yearly clothing consisted of two coarse linen shirts, one pair of linen trousers, like the shirts, one jacket, one pair of trousers for winter, made of coarse negro cloth, one pair of stockings, and one pair of shoes; the whole of which could not have cost more than seven dollars. The allowance of the slave children was given to their mothers, or the old women having the care of them. The children unable to work in the field had neither shoes, stockings, jackets, nor trousers, given to them; their clothing consisted of two coarse linen shirts per year. When these failed them, they went naked until the next allowance-day. Children from seven to ten years old, of both sexes, almost naked, might be seen at all seasons of the year.

4   There were no beds given the slaves, unless one coarse blanket be considered such, and none but the men and women had these. This, however, is not considered a very great privation. They find less difficulty from the want of beds, than from the want of time to sleep; for when their day's work in the field is done, the most of them having their washing, mending, and cooking to do, and having few or none of the ordinary facilities for doing either of these, very many of their sleeping hours are consumed in preparing for the field the coming day; and when this is done, old and young, male and female, married and single, drop down side by side, on one common bed,—the cold, damp floor,—each covering himself or herself with their miserable blankets; and here they sleep till they are summoned to the field by the driver's horn. At the

sound of this, all must rise, and be off to the field. There must be no halting; every one must be at his or her post; and woe betides them who hear not this morning summons to the field; for if they are not awakened by the sense of hearing, they are by the sense of feeling: no age nor sex finds any favor. Mr. Severe, the overseer, used to stand by the door of the quarter, armed with a large hickory stick and heavy cowskin, ready to whip any one who was so unfortunate as not to hear, or, from any other cause, was prevented from being ready to start for the field at the sound of the horn.

Mr. Severe was rightly named: he was a cruel man. I have seen him   5
whip a woman, causing the blood to run half an hour at the time; and this, too, in the midst of her crying children, pleading for their mother's release. He seemed to take pleasure in manifesting his fiendish barbarity. Added to his cruelty, he was a profane swearer. It was enough to chill the blood and stiffen the hair of an ordinary man to hear him talk. Scarce a sentence escaped him but that was commenced or concluded by some horrid oath. The field was the place to witness his cruelty and profanity. His presence made it both the field of blood and of blasphemy. From the rising till the going down of the sun, he was cursing, raving, cutting, and slashing among the slaves of the field, in the most frightful manner. His career was short. He died very soon after I went to Colonel Lloyd's; and he died as he lived, uttering, with his dying groans, bitter curses and horrid oaths. His death was regarded by the slaves as the result of a merciful providence.

Mr. Severe's place was filled by a Mr. Hopkins. He was a very   6
different man. He was less cruel, less profane, and made less noise, than Mr. Severe. His course was characterized by no extraordinary demonstrations of cruelty. He whipped, but seemed to take no pleasure in it. He was called by the slaves a good overseer.

The home plantation of Colonel Lloyd wore the appearance of a   7
country village. All the mechanical operations for all the farms were performed here. The shoemaking and mending, the blacksmithing, cartwrighting, coopering, weaving, and grain-grinding, were all performed by the slaves on the home plantation. The whole place wore a businesslike aspect very unlike the neighboring farms. The number of houses, too, conspired to give it advantage over the neighboring farms. It was called by the slaves the *Great House Farm.* Few privileges were esteemed higher, by the slaves of the out-farms, than that of being selected to do errands at the Great House Farm. It was associated in their minds with greatness. A representative could not be prouder of his election to a seat in the American Congress, than a slave on one of the

out-farms would be of his election to do errands at the Great House
Farm. They regarded it as evidence of great confidence reposed in them
by their overseers; and it was on this account, as well as a constant
desire to be out of the field from under the driver's lash, that they
esteemed it a high privilege, one worth careful living for. He was called
the smartest and most trusty fellow, who had this honor conferred upon
him the most frequently. The competitors for this office sought as
diligently to please their overseers, as the office-seekers in the political
parties seek to please and deceive the people. The same traits of character might be seen in Colonel Lloyd's slaves, as are seen in the slaves of
the political parties.

8   The slaves selected to go to the Great House Farm, for the monthly
allowance for themselves and their fellow-slaves, were peculiarly enthusiastic. While on their way, they would make the dense old woods,
for miles around, reverberate with their wild songs, revealing at once
the highest joy and the deepest sadness. They would compose and sing
as they went along, consulting neither time nor tune. The thought that
came up, came out—if not in the word, in the sound;—and as frequently in the one as in the other. They would sometimes sing the most
pathetic sentiment in the most rapturous tone, and the most rapturous
sentiment in the most pathetic tone. Into all of their songs they would
manage to weave something of the Great House Farm. Especially would
they do this, when leaving home. They would then sing most exultingly
the following words:—

> I am going away to the Great House Farm!
> A, yea! O, Yea! O!

This they would sing, as a chorus, to words which to many would seem
unmeaning jargon, but which, nevertheless, were full of meaning to
themselves. I have sometimes thought that the mere hearing of those
songs would do more to impress some minds with the horrible character of slavery, than the reading of whole volumes of philosophy on the
subject could do.

9   I did not, when a slave, understand the deep meaning of those rude
and apparently incoherent songs. I was myself within the circle; so that
I neither saw nor heard as those without might see and hear. They told a
tale of woe which was then altogether beyond my feeble comprehension; they were tones loud, long, and deep; they breathed the prayer and
complaint of souls boiling over with the bitterest anguish. Every tone
was a testimony against slavery, and a prayer to God for deliverance
from chains. The hearing of those wild notes always depressed my

spirit, and filled me with ineffable sadness. I have frequently found myself in tears while hearing them. The mere recurrence of those songs, even now, afflicts me; and while I am writing these lines, an expression of feeling has already found its way down my cheek. To those songs I trace my first glimmering conception of the dehumanizing character of slavery. I can never get rid of that conception. Those songs still follow me, to deepen my hatred of slavery, and quicken my sympathies for my brethren in bonds. If any one wishes to be impressed with the soul-killing effects of slavery, let him go to Colonel Lloyd's plantation, and, on allowance-day, place himself in the deep pine woods, and there let him, in silence, analyze the sounds that shall pass through the chambers of his soul,—and if he is not thus impressed, it will only be because "there is no flesh in his obdurate heart."

I have often been utterly astonished, since I came to the north, to   10
find persons who could speak of the singing, among slaves, as evidence of their contentment and happiness. It is impossible to conceive of a greater mistake. Slaves sing most when they are most unhappy. The songs of the slave represent the sorrows of his heart; and he is relieved by them, only as an aching heart is relieved by its tears. At least, such is my experience. I have often sung to drown my sorrow, but seldom to express my happiness. Crying for joy, and singing for joy, were alike uncommon to me while in the jaws of slavery. The singing of a man cast away upon a desolate island might be as appropriately considered as evidence of contentment and happiness, as the singing of a slave; the songs of the one and of the other are prompted by the same emotion.

___ CONSIDERATIONS ___

1. Is there anything to suggest, at the end of paragraph 7, that Douglass had a talent for satire?

2. In paragraphs 2 and 7, Douglass sketches the operations of the home plantation and its relationship to the outlying farms owned by the same man. Does the arrangement sound feudal? How did the plantation system differ from feudalism?

3. "I was myself within the circle; so that I neither saw nor heard as those without might see and hear," writes Douglass in paragraph 9. Is a fish aware that its medium is water? Are you, as a student, always conscious of the knowledge you acquire?

4. What single phenomenon, according to Douglass, taught him the most moving and enduring lesson about the dehumanizing character of slavery? In

what way did that lesson surprise those who had not had Douglass's experience?

5. Paragraph 5 offers a good example of Douglass's typical sentence structure: a linear series of independent clauses, with little or no subordination, all of which produces a blunt, stop-and-go effect. Without losing any of the information provided, rewrite the paragraph, reducing the number of sentences from twelve to six. Do this by converting some of the sentences to phrases, modifying clauses, or, in some cases, single-word modifiers.

6. Read Brent Staples's essay "Just Walk On By" and write an essay on the changes in race relations through the 146 years between Douglass's and Staple's accounts.

Gretel Ehrlich (b. 1946) grew up in California, went East to study, and eventually settled in Wyoming, which she first visited in 1976 to film a documentary for PBS. From making films and writing poems—she has published two poetry collections—she has more recently turned to prose. "About Men" comes from her essay collection, The Solace of Open Spaces, *which appeared in 1985. In 1988 she published a novel called* Heart Mountain, *which she plans to follow with more essays. She married a Wyoming rancher and lives in the Big Horn Basin ten miles from a paved road.*

24

GRETEL EHRLICH
About Men

When I'm in New York but feeling lonely for Wyoming I look for   1
the Marlboro ads in the subway. What I'm aching to see is horseflesh,
the glint of a spur, a line of distant mountains, brimming creeks, and a
reminder of the ranchers and cowboys I've ridden with for the last eight
years. But the men I see in those posters with their stern, humorless
looks remind me of no one I know here. In our hellbent earnestness to
romanticize the cowboy we've ironically disesteemed his true character. If he's "strong and silent" it's because there's probably no one to
talk to. If he "rides away into the sunset" it's because he's been on
horseback since four in the morning moving cattle and he's trying,
fifteen hours later, to get home to his family. If he's "a rugged individu-
alist" he's also part of a team: ranch work is teamwork and even the
glorified open-range cowboys of the 1880s rode up and down the
Chisholm Trail in the company of twenty or thirty other riders. Instead
of the macho, trigger-happy man our culture has perversely wanted him
to be, the cowboy is more apt to be convivial, quirky, and softhearted.
To be "tough" on a ranch has nothing to do with conquests and displays

From *The Solace of Open Spaces* by Gretel Ehrlich. Reprinted by permission of Viking Penguin, Inc., a division of Penguin Books USA Inc.

of power. More often than not, circumstances—like the colt he's riding or an unexpected blizzard—are overpowering him. It's not toughness but "toughing it out" that counts. In other words, this macho, cultural artifact the cowboy has become is simply a man who possesses resilience, patience, and an instinct for survival. "Cowboys are just like a pile of rocks—everything happens to them. They get climbed on, kicked, rained and snowed on, scuffed up by wind. Their job is 'just to take it,' " one old-timer told me.

2   A cowboy is someone who loves his work. Since the hours are long—ten to fifteen hours a day—and the pay is $30 he has to. What's required of him is an odd mixture of physical vigor and maternalism. His part of the beef-raising industry is to birth and nurture calves and take care of their mothers. For the most part his work is done on horseback and in a lifetime he sees and comes to know more animals than people. The iconic myth surrounding him is built on American notions of heroism: the index of a man's value as measured in physical courage. Such ideas have perverted manliness into a self-absorbed race for cheap thrills. In a rancher's world, courage has less to do with facing danger than with acting spontaneously—usually on behalf of an animal or another rider. If a cow is stuck in a boghole he throws a loop around her neck, takes his dally (a half hitch around the saddle horn), and pulls her out with horsepower. If a calf is born sick, he may take her home, warm her in front of the kitchen fire, and massage her legs until dawn. One friend, whose favorite horse was trying to swim a lake with hobbles on, dove under water and cut her legs loose with a knife, than swam her to shore, his arm around her neck lifeguard-style, and saved her from drowning. Because these incidents are usually linked to someone or something outside himself, the westerner's courage is selfless, a form of compassion.

3   The physical punishment that goes with cowboying is greatly underplayed. Once fear is dispensed with, the threshold of pain rises to meet the demands of the job. When Jane Fonda asked Robert Redford (in the film *Electric Horseman*) if he was sick as he struggled to his feet one morning, he replied, "No, just bent." For once the movies had it right. The cowboys I was sitting with laughed in agreement. Cowboys are rarely complainers; they show their stoicism by laughing at themselves.

4   If a rancher or cowboy has been thought of as a "man's man"—laconic, hard-drinking, inscrutable—there's almost no place in which the balancing act between male and female, manliness and femininity, can be more natural. If he's gruff, handsome, and physically fit on the

outside, he's androgynous at the core. Ranchers are midwives, hunters, nurturers, providers, and conservationists all at once. What we've interpreted as toughness—weathered skin, calloused hands, a squint in the eye and a growl in the voice—only masks the tenderness inside. "Now don't go telling me these lambs are cute," one rancher warned me the first day I walked into the football-field-sized lambing sheds. The next thing I knew he was holding a black lamb. "Ain't this little rat good-lookin'?"

So many of the men who came to the West were southerners— men looking for work and a new life after the Civil War—that chivalrousness and strict codes of honor were soon thought of as western traits. There were very few women in Wyoming during territorial days, so when they did arrive (some as mail-order brides from places like Philadelphia) there was a stand-offishness between the sexes and a formality that persists now. Ranchers still tip their hats and say, "Howdy, ma'am" instead of shaking hands with me. 5

Even young cowboys are often evasive with women. It's not that they're Jekyll and Hyde creatures—gentle with animals and rough on women—but rather, that they don't know how to bring their tenderness into the house and lack the vocabulary to express the complexity of what they feel. Dancing wildly all night becomes a metaphor for the explosive emotions pent up inside, and when these are, on occasion, released, they're so battery-charged and potent that one caress of the face or one "I love you" will peal for a long while. 6

The geographical vastness and the social isolation here make emotional evolution seem impossible. Those contradictions of the heart between respectability, logic, and convention on the one hand, and impulse, passion, and intuition on the other, played out wordlessly against the paradisical beauty of the West, give cowboys a wide-eyed but drawn look. Their lips pucker up, not with kisses but with immutability. They may want to break out, staying up all night with a lover just to talk, but they don't know how and can't imagine what the consequences will be. Those rare occasions when they do bare themselves result in confusion. "I feel as if I'd sprained my heart," one friend told me a month after such a meeting. 7

My friend Ted Hoagland wrote, "No one is as fragile as a woman but no one is as fragile as a man." For all the women here who use "fragileness" to avoid work or as a sexual ploy, there are men who try to hide theirs, all the while clinging to an adolescent dependency on women to cook their meals, wash their clothes, and keep the ranch house warm in winter. But there is true vulnerability in evidence here. 8

Because these men work with animals, not machines or numbers, because they live outside in landscapes of torrential beauty, because they are confined to a place and a routine embellished with awesome variables, because calves die in the arms that pulled others into life, because they go to the mountains as if on a pilgrimage to find out what makes a herd of elk tick, their strength is also a softness, their toughness, a rare delicacy.

—— CONSIDERATIONS ————————————————

1. While Ehrlich writes informally, her vocabulary may give some readers a little trouble. Consider unfamiliar words like "disesteemed," "artifact," "iconic," "stoicism," "laconic," "androgynous." Just looking them up in the dictionary may not be enough. Examine the same words in their immediate context: "we've ironically *disesteemed* his true character"; "this macho, cultural *artifact* the cowboy has become"; "the *iconic* myth surrounding him is built on American notions of heroism"; "cowboys are rarely complainers; they show their *stoicism* by laughing at themselves"; "a man's man—*laconic*, hard-drinking, inscrutable"; "he's *androgynous* at the core. Ranchers are midwives, hunters, nurturers, providers, and conservationists all at once." A third step, if you want to make these new words your own, would be to use them in your own writing.

2. The real nature of the cowboy, writes Ehrlich, is hidden beneath a set of myths and stereotypes implanted deeply in our consciousness by Hollywood movies and cheap fiction. Is this more true of the cowboy than of people in other walks of life, say a policeman, a sailor, an artist, a shopkeeper, a student, a teacher? Build an essay on your responses to the question.

3. Ehrlich closes her essay with a set of contradictions. In what way do such contradictions make sense, and why would an author risk confusing the reader with them?

4. Ehrlich's "About Men," Maxine Kumin's "Building Fence," Carol Bly's "Getting Tired," and Joyce Carol Oates's "On Boxing" are all concerned with habits of life conventionally thought of as masculine. Are these subjects distorted by the fact that the writers are women? Do their approaches differ from the way male writers might have written about the same topics?

5. Read the little anecdote that opens Daniel Boorstin's essay "The Pseudo-Event". Then comment on Ehrlich's turning to Marlboro advertisements in her homesickness for the life she had known in Montana. How does she make the reader aware that she herself is conscious of the irony?

Loren Eiseley (1907–1977) was an anthropologist who taught at the University of Pennsylvania, and a writer of unusual ability. He wrote two books of poems and numerous collections of prose, including The Night Country *(1971) and* All the Strange Hours *(1975). Eiseley was a scientist-poet, a human brooder over the natural world, determined never to distort the real world by his brooding dream, an objective anthropologist with a talent for subjective response.*

Imagination and chemistry equally inform "More Thoughts on Wilderness." When Eiseley writes about an experience in the badlands of Nebraska and South Dakota, he combines not only imagination and chemistry, not only archaeology and imagery, but religious feeling and scientific thought.

25

LOREN EISELEY
More Thoughts on Wilderness

On the maps of the old voyageurs it is called *Mauvaises Terres*, the 1
evil lands, and, slurred a little with the passage through many minds, it
has come down to us anglicized as the badlands. The soft shuffle of
moccasins has passed through its canyons on the grim business of war
and flight, but the last of those slight disturbances of immemorial
silences died out almost a century ago. The land, if one can call it a land,
is a waste as lifeless as that valley in which lie the kings of Egypt. Like
the Valley of the Kings, it is a mausoleum, a place of dry bones in what
once was a place of life. Now it has silences as deep as those in the
moon's airless chasms.

Nothing grows among its pinnacles; there is no shade except 2
under great toadstools of sandstone whose bases have been eaten to the
shape of wine glasses by the wind. Everything is flaking, cracking,

disintegrating, wearing away in the long, imperceptible weather of time. The ash of ancient volcanic outbursts still sterilizes its soil, and its colors in that waste are the colors that flame in the lonely sunsets on dead planets. Men come there but rarely, and for one purpose only, the collection of bones.

3   It was a late hour on a cold, wind-bitten autumn day when I climbed a great hill spined like a dinosaur's back and tried to take my bearings. The tumbled waste fell away in waves in all directions. Blue air was darkening into purple along the bases of the hills. I shifted my knapsack, heavy with the petrified bones of long-vanished creatures, and studied my compass. I wanted to be out of there by nightfall, and already the sun was going sullenly down in the west.

4   It was then that I saw the flight coming on. It was moving like a little close-knit body of black specks that danced and darted and closed again. It was pouring from the north and heading toward me with the undeviating relentlessness of a compass needle. It streamed through the shadows rising out of monstrous gorges. It rushed over towering pinnacles in the red light of the sun or momentarily sank from sight within their shade. Across that desert of eroding clay and windworn stone they came with a faint wild twittering that filled the air about me as those tiny living bullets hurtled past into the night.

5   It may not strike you as a marvel. It would not, perhaps, unless you stood in the middle of a dead world at sunset, but that was where I stood. Fifty million years lay under my feet, fifty million years of bellowing monsters moving in a green world now gone so utterly that its very light was traveling on the farther edge of space. The chemicals of all that vanished age lay about me in the ground. Around me still lay the shearing molars of dead titanotheres, the delicate sabers of soft-stepping cats, the hollow sockets that had held the eyes of many a strange, outmoded beast. Those eyes had looked out upon a world as real as ours: dark, savage brains had roamed and roared their challenges into the steaming night.

6   Now they were still here, or, put it as you will, the chemicals that made them were here about me in the ground. The carbon that had driven them ran blackly in the eroding stone. The stain of iron was in the clays. The iron did not remember the blood it had once moved within, the phosphorus had forgot the savage brain. The little individual moment had ebbed from all those strange combinations of chemicals as it would ebb from our living bodies into the sinks and runnels of oncoming time.

7   I had lifted up a fistful of that ground. I held it while that wild

flight of south-bound warblers hurtled over me into the oncoming dark. There went phosphorus, there went iron, there went carbon, there beat the calcium in those hurrying wings. Alone on a dead planet I watched that incredible miracle speeding past. It ran by some true compass over field and waste land. It cried its individual ecstasies into the air until the gullies rang. It swerved like a single body, it knew itself, and, lonely, it bunched close in the racing darkness, its individual entities feeling about them the rising night. And so, crying to each other their identity, they passed away out of my view.

I dropped my fistful of earth. I heard it roll inanimate back into the   8
gully at the base of the hill: iron, carbon, the chemicals of life. Like men from those wild tribes who had haunted these hills before me seeking visions. I made my sign to the great darkness. It was not a mocking sign, and I was not mocked. As I walked into my camp late that night, one man, rousing from his blankets beside the fire, asked sleepily, "What did you see?"

"I think, a miracle," I said softly, but I said it to myself. Behind me   9
that vast waste began to glow under the rising moon.

_____ CONSIDERATIONS _____

1. Eiseley draws in the reader by enlivening his expository prose with figures of speech. Write a brief study of his figurative writing, beginning with the half-dozen examples presented in paragraphs 2 and 3.

2. As a professional anthropologist and archaeologist, Eiseley had many occasions to write the "process essay," a step by step explanation of a particular process. To what extent could "More Thoughts on Wilderness" be called a process essay? Why would that term be unsatisfactory as a complete description of the piece?

3. Eiseley's reflections take him to the chemical elements of life—carbon, iron, phosphorus. How does he escape the sterile kind of analysis and categorization that Henry David Thoreau criticizes in his "Journal entry for October 12, 1857"?

4. What prompts Eiseley to conclude that he has seen a miracle? Explain.

5. Using the passage of long periods of time, as Eiseley does, write a short, descriptive essay reflecting on a landscape you know well.

Ralph Ellison (b. 1914), born in Oklahoma, won the National Book Award in 1953 for his novel The Invisible Man. *His essays are collected in* Shadow and Act *(1964). For thirty years, Ellison has lectured and written on literature and race.*

26

RALPH ELLISON
On Becoming a Writer

1   In the beginning writing was far from a serious matter; it was a reflex of reading, an extension of a source of pleasure, escape, and instruction. In fact, I had become curious about writing by way of seeking to understand the aesthetic nature of literary power, the devices through which literature could command my mind and emotions. It was not, then, the *process* of writing which initially claimed my attention, but the finished creations, the artifacts, poems, plays, novels. The act of learning writing technique was, therefore, an amusing investigation of what seemed at best a secondary talent, an exploration, like dabbling in sculpture, of one's potentialities as a "Renaissance Man." This, surely, would seem a most unlikely and even comic concept to introduce here; and yet, it is precisely because I come from where I do (the Oklahoma of the years between World War I and the Great Depression) that I must introduce it, and with a straight face.

2   Anything and everything was to be found in the chaos of Oklahoma; thus the concept of the Renaissance Man has lurked long within the shadow of my past, and I shared it with at least a half dozen of my Negro friends. How we actually acquired it I have never learned, and since there is no true sociology of the dispersion of ideas within the American democracy, I doubt if I ever shall. Perhaps we breathed it in with the air of the Negro community of Oklahoma City, the capital of that state whose Negroes were often charged by exasperated white Texans with not knowing their "place." Perhaps we took it defiantly

from one of them. Or perhaps I myself picked it up from some transplanted New Englander whose shoes I had shined of a Saturday afternoon. After all, the most meaningful tips do not always come in the form of money, nor are they intentionally extended. Most likely, however, my friends and I acquired the idea from some book or some idealistic Negro teacher, some dreamer seeking to function responsibly in an environment which at its more normal took on some of the mixed character of nightmare and of dream.

One thing is certain, ours was a chaotic community, still characterized by frontier attitudes and by that strange mixture of the naive and sophisticated, the benign and malignant, which makes the American past so puzzling and its present so confusing; that mixture which often affords the minds of the young who grow up in the far provinces such wide and unstructured latitude, and which encourages the individual's imagination—up to the moment "reality" closes in upon him—to range widely and, sometimes, even to soar.   3

We hear the effects of this in the Southwestern jazz of the 30's, that joint creation of artistically free and exuberantly creative adventurers, of artists who had stumbled upon the freedom lying within the restrictions of their musical tradition as within the limitations of their social background, and who in their own unconscious way have set an example for any Americans, Negro or white, who would find themselves in the arts. They accepted themselves and the complexity of life as they knew it, they loved their art and through it they celebrated American experience definitively in sound. Whatever others thought or felt, this was their own powerful statement, and only non-musical assaults upon their artistic integrity—mainly economically inspired changes of fashion—were able to compromise their vision.   4

Much of so-called Kansas City jazz was actually brought to perfection in Oklahoma by Oklahomans. It is an important circumstance for me as a writer to remember, because while these musicians and their fellows were busy creating out of tradition, imagination, and the sounds and emotions around them, a freer, more complex, and driving form of jazz, my friends and I were exploring an idea of human versatility and possibility which went against the barbs or over the palings of almost every fence which those who controlled social and political power had erected to restrict our roles in the life of the country. Looking back, one might say that the jazzmen, some of whom we idolized, were in their own way better examples for youth to follow than were most judges and ministers, legislators and governors (we were stuck with the notorious Alfalfa Bill Murray). For as we viewed these pillars of society from the   5 confines of our segregated community we almost always saw crooks, clowns, or hypocrites. Even the best were revealed by their attitudes toward us as lacking the respectable qualities to which they pretended and for which they were accepted outside by others, while despite the outlaw nature of their art, the jazzmen were less torn and damaged by the moral compromises and insincerities which have so sickened the life of our country.

6   Be that as it may, our youthful sense of life, like that of many Negro children (though no one bothers to note it—especially the specialists and "friends of the Negro" who view our Negro-American life as essentially non-human) was very much like that of Huckleberry Finn, who is universally so praised and enjoyed for the clarity and courage of his moral vision. Like Huck, we observed, we judged, we imitated and evaded as we could the dullness, corruption, and blindness of "civilization." We were undoubtedly comic because, as the saying goes, we weren't supposed to know what it was all about. But to ourselves we were "boys," members of a wild, free, outlaw tribe which transcended the category of race. Rather we were Americans born into the forty-sixth state, and thus, into the context of Negro-American post-Civil War history, "frontiersmen." And isn't one of the implicit functions of the American frontier to encourage the individual to a kind of dreamy wakefulness, a state in which he makes—in all ignorance of the accepted limitations of the possible—rash efforts, quixotic gestures, hopeful testings of the complexity of the known and the given?

7   Spurring us on in our controlled and benign madness was the voracious reading of which most of us were guilty and the vicarious identification and empathetic adventuring which it encouraged. This was due, in part, perhaps to the fact that some of us were fatherless— my own father had died when I was three—but most likely it was because boys are natural romantics. We were seeking examples, patterns to live by, out of a freedom which for all its being ignored by the sociologists and subtle thinkers, was implicit in the Negro situation. Father and mother substitutes also have a role to play in aiding the child to help create himself. Thus we fabricated our own heroes and ideals catch-as-catch-can; and with an outrageous and irreverent sense of freedom. Yes, and in complete disregard of ideas of respectability or the surreal incongruity of some of our projections. Gamblers and scholars, jazz musicians and scientists, Negro cowboys and soldiers from the Spanish-American and First World Wars, movie stars and stunt men, figures from the Italian Renaissance and literature, both classical and popular, were combined with the special virtues of some local bootleg-

ger, the eloquence of some Negro preacher, the strength and grace of some local athlete, the ruthlessness of some businessman-physician, the elegance in dress and manners of some head-waiter or hotel doorman.

Looking back through the shadows upon this absurd activity, I realize now that we were projecting archetypes, recreating folk figures, legendary heroes, monsters even, most of which violated all ideas of social hierarchy and order and all accepted conceptions of the hero handed down by cultural, religious, and racist tradition. But we remember, were under the intense spell of the early movies, the silents as well as the talkies; and in our community, life was not so tightly structured as it would have been in the traditional South—or even in deceptively *"free"* Harlem. And our imaginations processed reality and dream, natural man and traditional hero, literature and folklore, like maniacal editors turned loose in some frantic film-cutting room. Remember, too, that being boys, yet in the play-stage of our development, we were dream-serious in our efforts. But serious nevertheless, for *culturally* play is a preparation, and we felt that somehow the human ideal lay in the vague and constantly shifting figures—sometimes comic but always versatile, picaresque, and self-effacingly heroic— which evolved from our wildly improvisatory projections: figures neither white nor black, Christian nor Jewish, but representative of certain desirable essences, of skills and powers, physical, aesthetic, and moral.

The proper response to these figures was, we felt, to develop ourselves for the performance of many and diverse roles, and the fact that certain definite limitations had been imposed upon our freedom did not lessen our sense of obligation. Not only were we to prepare but we were to perform—not with mere competence but with an almost reckless verve, with, may we say (without evoking the quaint and questionable notion of *négritude*) Negro-American style? Behind each artist there stands a traditional sense of style, a sense of the felt tension indicative of expressive completeness; a mode of humanizing reality and of evoking a feeling of being at home in the world. It is something which the artist shares with the group, and part of our boyish activity expressed a yearning to make any and everything of quality *Negro-American*; to appropriate it, possess it, recreate it in our own group and individual images.

And we recognized and were proud of our group's own style wherever we discerned it, in jazzmen and prize-fighters, ballplayers, and tap dancers; in gesture, inflection, intonation, timbre, and phrasing. Indeed, in all those nuances of expression and attitude which reveal a culture. We did not fully understand the cost of that style, but we recognized within it an affirmation of life beyond all question of our difficulties as Negroes.

11   Contrary to the notion currently projected by certain specialists in the "Negro problem" which characterizes the Negro American as self-hating and defensive, we did not so regard ourselves. We felt, among ourselves at least, that we were supposed to be whoever we would and could be and do anything and everything which other boys did, and do it better. Not defensively, because we were ordered to do so; nor because it was held in the society at large that we were naturally, as Negroes, limited—but because we demanded it of ourselves. Because to measure up to our own standards was the only way of affirming our notion of manhood.

12   Hence it was no more incongruous, as seen from our own particular perspective in this land of incongruities, for young Negro Oklahomans to project themselves as Renaissance men than for white Mississippians to see themselves as ancient Greeks or noblemen out of Sir Walter Scott. Surely our fantasies have caused far less damage to the nation's sense of reality, if for no other reason than that ours were expressive of a more democratic ideal. Remember, too, as William Faulkner made us so vividly aware, that the slaves often took the essence of the aristocratic ideal (as they took Christianity) with far more seriousness than their masters, and that we, thanks to the tight telescoping of American history, were but two generations from that previous condition. Renaissance men, indeed!

13   I managed, by keeping quiet about it, to cling to our boyish ideal during three years in Alabama, and I brought it with me to New York, where it not only gave silent support to my explorations of what was then an unknown territory, but served to mock and caution me when I became interested in the Communist ideal. And when it was suggested that I try my hand at writing it was still with me.

14   The act of writing requires a constant plunging back into the shadow of the past where time hovers ghostlike. When I began writing in earnest I was forced, thus, to relate myself consciously and imaginatively to my mixed background as American, as Negro-American, and as a Negro from what in its own belated way was a pioneer background. More important, and inseparable from this particular effort, was the necessity of determining my true relationship to that body of American literature to which I was most attracted and through which, aided by what I could learn from the literatures of Europe, I would find my own

voice and to which I was challenged, by way of achieving myself, to make some small contribution, and to whose composite picture of reality I was obligated to offer some necessary modifications.

This was no matter of sudden insight but of slow and blundering discovery, of a struggle to stare down the deadly and hypnotic temptation to interpret the world and all its devices in terms of race. To avoid this was very important to me, and in light of my background far from simple. Indeed, it was quite complex, involving as it did, a ceaseless questioning of all those formulas which historians, politicians, sociologists, and an older generation of Negro leaders and writers—those of the so-called "Negro Renaissance"—had evolved to describe my group's identity, its predicament, its fate, and its relation to the larger society and the culture which we share. 15

Here the question of reality and personal identity merge. Yes, and the question of the nature of the reality which underlies American fiction and thus the human truth which gives fiction viability. In this quest, for such it soon became, I learned that nothing could go unchallenged; especially that feverish industry dedicated to telling Negroes who and what they are, and which can usually be counted upon to deprive both humanity and culture of their complexity. I had undergone, not too many months before taking the path which led to writing, the humiliation of being taught in a class in sociology at a Negro college (from Park and Burgess, the leading textbook in the field) that Negroes represented the "lady of the races." This contention the Negro instructor passed blandly along to us without even bothering to wash his hands, much less his teeth. Well, I had no intention of being bound by any such humiliating definition of my relationship to American literature. Not even to those works which depicted Negroes negatively. Negro Americans have a highly developed ability to abstract desirable qualities from those around them, even from their enemies, and my sense of reality could reject bias while appreciating the truth revealed by achieved art. The pleasure which I derived from reading had long been a necessity, and in the *act* of reading, that marvelous collaboration between the writer's artful vision and the reader's sense of life, I had become acquainted with other possible selves; freer, more courageous and ingenuous and, during the course of the narrative at least, even wise. 16

At the time I was under the influence of Ernest Hemingway, and his description, in *Death in the Afternoon*, of his thinking when he first went to Spain became very important as translated in my own naïve fashion. He was trying to write, he tells us, 17 and I found the greatest difficulty aside from knowing truly what you really felt, rather than what you were supposed to feel, and had been taught to feel, was to put down what really happened in action; what the actual things were which produced the emotion that you experienced. . . .

18   His statement of moral and aesthetic purpose which followed focused my own search to relate myself to American life through literature. For I found the greatest difficulty for a Negro writer was the problem of revealing what he truly felt, rather than serving up what Negroes were supposed to feel, and were encouraged to feel. And linked to this was the difficulty, based upon our long habit of deception and evasion, of depicting what really happened within our areas of American life, and putting down with honesty and without bowing to ideological expediencies the attitudes and values which give Negro-American life, its sense of wholeness and which render its bearable and human and, when measured by our own terms, desirable.

19   I was forced to this awareness through my struggles with the craft of fiction; yes, and by my attraction (soon rejected) to Marxist political theory, which was my response to the inferior status which society sought to impose upon me (I did not then, now, or ever *consider* myself inferior).

20   I did not know my true relationship to America—what citizen of the U.S. really does?—but I did know and accept how I felt inside. And I also knew, thanks to the old Renaissance Man, what I expected of myself in the matter of personal discipline and creative quality. Since by the grace of the past and the examples of manhood picked willy-nilly from the continuing-present of my background, I rejected all negative definitions imposed upon me by others, there was nothing to do but search for those relationships which were fundamental.

21   In this sense fiction became the agency of my efforts to answer the questions, Who am I, what am I, how did I come to be? What shall I make of the life around me, what celebrate, what reject, how confront the snarl of good and evil which is inevitable? What does American society *mean* when regarded out of my *own* eyes, when informed by my *own* sense of the past and viewed by my *own* complex sense of the present? How, in other words, should I think of myself and my pluralistic sense of the world, how express my vision of the human predicament, without reducing it to a point which would render it sterile before that necessary and tragic—though enhancing—reduction which must occur before the fictive vision can come alive? It is quite

possible that much potential fiction by Negro Americans fails precisely at this point: through the writers' refusal (often through provincialism or lack of courage or through opportunism) to achieve a vision of life and a resourcefulness of craft commensurate with the complexity of their actual situation. Too often they fear to leave the uneasy sanctuary of race to take their chances in the world of art.

—— CONSIDERATIONS ——

1. Ellison's opening statement that writing was "a reflex of reading" points to the experience of many other students and writers (see Richard Wright's "The Library Card") and implies an important relationship between the two activities. Are reading and writing two sides of the same coin? (See also the editors' "Preface" to this volume.)

2. Look in a good dictionary for a definition of "Renaissance man" and explain why this concept is central to an understanding of Ellison's essay.

3. How, in paragraph 7, does Ellison specify, and thus clarify, what he means by "ours was a chaotic community" in paragraph 3?

4. At several points in his essay, Ellison is critical of "specialists and 'friends of the Negro.'" What is his primary criticism of their efforts?

5. Does Ellison's remark "boys are natural romantics" in paragraph 7 help explain his first sentence in paragraph 8? Do you think that sentence is limited to the boys of one race or class? Use your own experience to write an essay on the subject.

6. Would Eiseley's short essay "More Thoughts on Wilderness" be an example of what Ellison expresses in the first sentence of his paragraph 14?

Nora Ephron (b. 1941), daughter of two screenwriters, grew up in Hollywood wanting to move to New York and become a writer. She did. She began by working for Newsweek, *and soon was contributing articles to the* New Yorker *and a monthly column to* Esquire. *Most of her writing is about women, and manages to be at once funny and serious, profound and irreverent—and on occasion outrageous. In 1983 she published a novel entitled* Heartburn *which, in 1986, was made into a film. Her essays are collected in* Wallflower at the Orgy *(1970) and* Crazy Salad *(1975), from which we take this essay on growing up flat-chested.*

27

NORA EPHRON
A Few Words About Breasts: Shaping Up Absurd

1   I have to begin with a few words about androgyny. In grammar school, in the fifth and sixth grades, we were all tyrannized by a rigid set of rules that supposedly determined whether we were boys or girls. The episode in *Huckleberry Finn* where Huck is disguised as a girl and gives himself away by the way he threads a needle and catches a ball—that kind of thing. We learned that the way you sat, crossed your legs, held a cigarette and looked at your nails, your wristwatch, the way you did these things instinctively was absolute proof of your sex. Now obviously most children did not take this literally, but I did. I thought that just one slip, just one incorrect cross of my legs or flick of an imaginary cigarette ash would turn me from whatever I was into the other thing; that would be all it took, really. Even though I was outwardly a girl and had many of the trappings generally associated with the field of girldom—a girl's name, for example, and dresses, my own telephone, an autograph book—I spent the early years of my adolescence absolutely

certain that I might at any point gum it up. I did not feel at all like a girl. I was boyish. I was athletic, ambitious, outspoken, competitive, noisy, rambunctious. I had scabs on my knees and my socks slid into my loafers and I could throw a football. I wanted desperately not to be that way, not to be a mixture of both things but instead just one, a girl, a definite indisputable girl. As soft and as pink as a nursery. And nothing would do that for me, I felt, but breasts.

I was about six months younger than everyone in my class, and so 2 for about six months after it began, for six months after my friends had begun to develop—that was the word we used, develop—I was not particularly worried. I would sit in the bathtub and look down at my breasts and know that any day now, any second now, they would start growing like everyone else's. They didn't. "I want to buy a bra," I said to my mother one night. "What for?" she said. My mother was really hateful about bras, and by the time my third sister had gotten to the point where she was ready to want one, my mother had worked the whole business into a comedy routine. "Why not use a Band-Aid instead?" she would say. It was a source of great pride to my mother that she had never even had to wear a brassiere until she had her fourth child, and then only because her gynecologist made her. It was incomprehensible to me that anyone would ever be proud of something like that. It was the 1950s, for God's sake. Jane Russell. Cashmere sweaters. Couldn't my mother see that? *"I am too old to wear an undershirt."* Screaming. Weeping. Shouting. "Then don't wear an undershirt," said my mother. "But I want to buy a bra," "What for?"

I suppose that for most girls, breasts, brassieres, that entire thing, 3 has more trauma, more to do with the coming of adolescence, of becoming a woman, than anything else. Certainly more than getting your period, although that too was traumatic, symbolic. But you could *see* breasts; they were there; they were visible. Whereas a girl could claim to have her period for months before she actually got it and nobody would ever know the difference. Which is exactly what I did. All you had to do was make a great fuss over having enough nickels for the Kotex machine and walk around clutching your stomach and moaning for three to five days a month about The Curse and you could convince anybody. There is a school of thought somewhere in the women's lib/women's mag/gynecology establishment that claims that menstrual cramps are purely psychological, and I lean toward it. Not that I didn't have them finally. Agonizing cramps, heating-pad cramps, go-down-to-the-school-nurse-and-lie-on-the-cot cramps. But unlike any pain I have ever suffered, I adored the pain of cramps, welcomed it, wallowed in it, bragged about it. "I can't go. I have cramps." "I can't do that. I have cramps." And most of all, gigglingly, blushingly: "I can't swim. I have cramps." Nobody ever used the hard-core word. Menstruation. God, what an awful word. Never that. "I have cramps."

4   The morning I first got my period, I went into my mother's bedroom to tell her. And my mother, my utterly-hateful-about-bras mother, burst into tears. It was really a lovely moment, and I remember it so clearly not just because it was one of the two times I ever saw my mother cry on my account (the other was when I was caught being a six-year-old kleptomaniac), but also because the incident did not mean to me what it meant to her. Her little girl, her firstborn, had finally become a woman. That was what she was crying about. My reaction to the event, however, was that I might well be a woman in some scientific, textbook sense (and could at least stop faking every month and stop wasting all those nickels). But in another sense—in a visible sense—I was an androgynous and as liable to tip over into boyhood as ever.

5   I started with a 28AA bra. I don't think they made them any smaller in those days, although I gather that now you can buy bras for five year olds that don't have any cups whatsoever in them; trainer bras they are called. My first brassiere came from Robinson's Department Store in Beverly Hills. I went there alone, shaking, positive they would look me over and smile and tell me to come back next year. An actual fitter took me into the dressing room and stood over me while I took off my blouse and tried the first one on. The little puffs stood out on my chest. "Lean over," said the fitter (to this day I am not sure what fitters in bra departments do except to tell you to lean over). I leaned over, with the fleeing hope that my breasts would miraculously fall out of my body and into the puffs. Nothing.

6   "Don't worry about it," said my friend Libby some months later, when things had not improved. "You'll get them after you're married."

7   "What are you talking about?" I said.

8   "When you get married," Libby explained, "your husband will touch your breasts and rub them and kiss them and they'll grow."

9   That was the killer. Necking I could deal with. Intercourse I could deal with. But it had never crossed my mind that a man was going to touch my breasts, that breasts had something to do with all that, petting, my God they never mentioned petting in my little sex manual about fertilization of the ovum. I became dizzy. For I knew instantly— as naïve as I had been only a moment before—that only part of what she

was saying was true: the touching, rubbing, kissing part, not the growing part. And I knew that no one would ever want to marry me. I had no
breasts. I would never have breasts.

My best friend in school was Diana Raskob. She lived a block from   10
me in a house full of wonders. English muffins, for instance. The
Raskobs were the first people in Beverly Hills to have English muffins
for breakfast. They also had an apricot tree in the back, and a badminton
court, and a subscription to *Seventeen* magazine, and hundreds of
games like Sorry and Parcheesi and Treasure Hunt and Anagrams.
Diana and I spent three or four afternoons a week in their den reading
and playing and eating. Diana's mother's kitchen was full of the most
colossal assortment of junk food I have ever been exposed to. My house
was full of apples and peaches and milk and homemade chocolate-
chip cookies—which were nice, and good for you, but-not-right-before-
dinner-or-you'll-spoil-your-appetite. Diana's house had nothing in it
that was good for you, and what's more, you could stuff it in right up
until dinner and nobody cared. Bar-B-Q potato chips (they were the first
in them, too), giant bottles of ginger ale, fresh popcorn with melted
butter, hot fudge sauce on Baskin-Robbins jamoca ice cream, powdered-
sugar doughnuts from Van de Kamps. Diana and I had been best friends
since we were seven; we were about equally popular in school (which is
to say, not particularly), we had about the same success with boys
(extremely intermittent) and we looked much the same. Dark. Tall.
Gangly.

It is September, just before school begins. I am eleven years old,   11
about to enter the seventh grade, and Diana and I have not seen each
other all summer. I have been to camp and she has been somewhere like
Banff with her parents. We are meeting, as we often do, on the street
midway between our two houses and we will walk back to Diana's and
eat junk and talk about what has happened to each of us that summer. I
am walking down Walden Drive in my jeans and my father's shirt
hanging out and my old red loafers with the socks falling into them and
coming toward me is . . . I take a deep breath . . . a young woman.
Diana. Her hair is curled and she has a waist and hips and a bust and she
is wearing a straight skirt, an article of clothing I have been repeatedly
told that I will be unable to wear until I have the hips to hold it up. My
jaw drops, and suddenly I am crying, crying hysterically, can't catch my
breath sobbing. My best friend has betrayed me. She has gone ahead
without me and done it. She has shaped up.

12   Here are some things I did to help:

13   Bought a Mark Eden Bust Developer.

14   Slept on my back for four years.

15   Splashed cold water on them every night because some French actress said in *Life* magazine that that was what *she* did for her perfect bustline.

16   Ultimately, I resigned myself to a bad toss and began to wear padded bras. I think about them now, think about all those years in high school I went around in them, my three padded bras, every single one of them with different sized breasts. Each time I changed bras I changed sizes: one week nice perky but not too obtrusive breasts, the next medium-sized slightly pointed ones, the next week knockers, true knockers; all the time, whatever size I was, carrying around this rubber-ized appendage on my chest that occasionally crashed into a wall and was poked inward and had to be poked outward—I think about all that and wonder how anyone kept a straight face through it. My parents, who normally had no restraints about needling me—why did they say nothing as they watched my chest go up and down? My friends, who would periodically inspect my breasts for signs of growth and reassure me—why didn't they at least counsel consistency?

17   And the bathing suits. I die when I think about the bathing suits. That was the era when you could lay an uninhabited bathing suit on the beach and someone would make a pass at it. I would put one on, an absurd swimsuit with its enormous bust built into it, the bones from the suit stabbing me in the rib cage and leaving little red welts on my body, and there I would be, my chest plunging straight downward absolutely vertically from my collarbone to the top of my suit and then suddenly, wham, out came all that padding and material and wiring absolutely horizontally.

18   Buster Klepper was the first boy who ever touched them. He was my boyfriend my senior year of high school. There is a picture of him in my high-school yearbook that makes him look quite attractive in a Jewish, horn-rimmed glasses sort of way, but the picture does not show the pimples, which were air-brushed out, or the dumbness. Well, that isn't really fair. He wasn't dumb. He just wasn't terribly bright. His mother refused to accept it, refused to accept the relentlessly average report cards, refused to deal with her son's inevitable destiny in some junior college or other. "He was tested," she would say to me, apropos of nothing, "and it came out 145. That's near-genius." Had the word underachiever been coined, she probably would have lobbed that one at

me, too. Anyway, Buster was really very sweet—which is, I know, damning with faint praise, but there it is. I was the editor of the front page of the high-school newspaper and he was editor of the back page; we had to work together, side by side, in the print shop, and that was how it started. On our first date, we went to see *April Love* starring Pat Boone. Then we started going together. Buster had a green coupe, a 1950 Ford with an engine he had handchromed until it shone, dazzled, reflected the image of anyone who looked into it, anyone usually being Buster polishing it or the gas-station attendants he constantly asked to check the oil in order for them to be overwhelmed by the sparkle on the valves. The car also had a boot stretched over the back seat for reasons I never understood; hanging from the rearview mirror, as was the custom, was a pair of angora dice. A previous girl friend named Solange who was famous throughout Beverly Hills High School for having no pigment in her right eyebrow had knitted them for him. Buster and I would ride around town, the two of us seated to the left of the steering wheel. I would shift gears. It was nice.

There was necking. Terrific necking. First in the car, overlooking   19
Los Angeles from what is now the Trousdale Estates. Then on the bed of his parents' cabana at Ocean House. Incredibly wonderful, frustrating necking, I loved it, really, but no further than necking, please don't, please, because there I was absolutely terrified of the general implications of going-a-step-further with a near-dummy and also terrified of his finding out there was next to nothing there (which he knew, of course; he wasn't that dumb).

I broke up with him at one point. I think we were apart for about   20
two weeks. At the end of that time I drove down to see a friend at a boarding school in Palos Verdes Estates and a disc jockey played *April Love* on the radio four times during the trip. I took it as a sign. I drove straight back to Griffith Park to a golf tournament Buster was playing in (he was the sixth-seeded teen-age golf player in Southern California) and presented myself back to him on the green of the 18th hole. It was all very dramatic. That night we went to a drive-in and I let him get his hand under my protuberances and onto my breasts. He really didn't seem to mind at all.

"Do you want to marry my son?" the woman asked me.   21
"Yes," I said.   22
I was nineteen years old, a virgin, going with this woman's son,   23
this big strange woman who was married to a Lutheran minister in New Hampshire and pretended she was Gentile and had this son, by

her first husband, this total fool of a son who ran the hero-sandwich concession at Harvard Business School and whom for one moment one December in New Hampshire I said—as much out of politeness as anything else—that I wanted to marry.

24   *"Fine," she said. "Now, here's what you do. Always make sure you're on top of him so you won't seem so small. My bust is very large, you see, so I always lie on my back to make it look smaller, but you'll have to be on top most of the time."*

25   *I nodded. "Thank you," I said.*

26   *"I have a book for you to read," she went on. "Take it with you when you leave. Keep it." She went to the bookshelf, found it, and gave it to me. It was a book on frigidity.*

27   *"Thank you," I said.*

28   That is a true story. Everything in this article is a true story, but I feel I have to point out that that story in particular is true. It happened on December 30, 1960. I think about it often. When it first happened, I naturally assumed that the woman's son, my boyfriend, was responsible. I invented a scenario where he had had a little heart-to-heart with his mother and had confessed that his only objection to me was that my breasts were small; his mother then took it upon herself to help out. Now I think I was wrong about the incident. The mother was acting on her own, I think: that was her way of being cruel and competitive under the guise of being helpful and maternal. You have small breasts, she was saying; therefore you will never make him as happy as I have. Or you have small breasts; therefore you will doubtless have sexual problems. Or you have small breasts; therefore you are less woman than I am. She was, as it happens, only the first of what seems to me to be a never-ending string of women who have made competitive remarks to me about breast size. "I would love to wear a dress like that," my friend Emily says to me, "but my bust is too big." Like that. Why do women say these things to me? Do I attract these remarks the way other women attract married men or alcoholics or homosexuals? This summer, for example. I am at a party in East Hampton and I am introduced to a woman from Washington. She is a minor celebrity, very pretty and Southern and blonde and outspoken and I am flattered because she has read something I have written. We are talking animatedly, we have been talking no more than five minutes, when a man comes up to join us. "Look at the two of us," the woman says to the man, indicating me and her. "The two of us together couldn't fill an A cup." Why does she say that? It isn't even true, dammit, so why? Is she even more addled

than I am on this subject? Does she honestly believe there is something wrong with her size breasts, which, it seems to me, now that I look hard at them, are just right. Do I unconsciously bring out competitiveness in women? In that form? What did I do to deserve it?

As for men.   29

There were men who minded and let me know they minded.   30 There were men who did not mind. In any case, I always minded.

And even now, now that I have been countlessly reassured that my   31 figure is a good one, now that I am grown up enough to understand that most of my feelings have very little to do with the reality of my shape, I am nonetheless obsessed by breasts. I cannot help it. I grew up in the terrible Fifties—with rigid stereotypical sex roles, the insistence that men be men and dress like men and women be women and dress like women, the intolerance of androgyny—and I cannot shake it, cannot shake my feelings of inadequacy. Well, that time is gone, right? All those exaggerated examples of breast worship are gone, right? Those women were freaks, right? I know all that. And yet, here I am, stuck with the psychological remains of it all, stuck with my own peculiar version of breast worship. You probably think I am crazy to go on like this: here I have set out to write a confession that is meant to hit you with the shock of recognition and instead you are sitting there thinking I am thoroughly warped. Well, what can I tell you? If I had had them, I would have been a completely different person. I honestly believe that.

After I went into therapy, a process that made it possible for me to   32 tell total strangers at cocktail parties that breasts were the hang-up of my life, I was often told that I was insane to have been bothered by my condition. I was also frequently told, by close friends, that I was extremely boring on the subject. And my girl friends, the ones with nice big breasts, would go on endlessly about how their lives had been far more miserable than mine. Their bra straps were snapped in class. They couldn't sleep on their stomachs. They were stared at whenever the word "mountain" cropped up in geography. And *Evangeline*, good God what they went through every time someone had to stand up and recite the Prologue to Longfellow's *Evangeline: ". . . stand like druids of eld . . ./With beards that rest on their bosoms."* It was much worse for them, they tell me. They had a terrible time of it, they assure me. I don't know how lucky I was, they say.

I have thought about their remarks, tried to put myself in their   33 place, considered their point of view. I think they are full of shit.

_____ **CONSIDERATIONS** _____

1. Nora Ephron's account offends some readers and attracts others for the same reason—the frank and casual exploration of a subject that generations have believed unmentionable. This problem is worth investigating: Are there, in fact, subjects that should not be discussed in the popular press? Are there words a writer must not use? Why? And who should make the list of things not to be talked about?

2. Imagine an argument about Ephron's article between a feminist and an antifeminist. What ammunition could each find in the article? Write the dialogue as you hear it.

3. Ephron reports that from a very early age she worried that she might not be "a girl, a definite indisputable girl." Is this anxiety as uncommon as she thought it was? Is worry about one's sex an exclusively female problem?

4. Are our ideas about masculinity and femininity changing? How are such ideas determined? How important are they in shaping personality and in channeling thoughts?

5. Ephron's article is a good example of the very informal essay. What does she do that makes it so informal? Consider both diction and sentence structure.

6. How can one smile at others' problems—or at one's own disappointments, for that matter? How can Ephron see humor now in what she thought of as tragic then? Provide an example from your own experience.

Daniel Mark Epstein (b. 1948) lives in Baltimore and teaches at Towson State University. The most recent of his five books of poetry is Spirits *(1987). This essay comes from a collection of reminiscences and expository essays called* Star of Wonder *(1986), which Epstein followed with a book of essays on varieties of love,* Love's Compass *(1990). He has received both a prix de Rome and a Guggenheim Fellowship.*

28

DANIEL MARK EPSTEIN
The Case of Harry Houdini

When my grandfather was a boy he saw the wild-haired magician 1
escape from a riveted boiler. He would remember that image as long as
he lived, and how Harry Houdini, the rabbi's son, defeated the German
Imperial Police at the beginning of the twentieth century. Hearing
those tales and others even more incredible, sixty years after the magician's death we cannot help but wonder: what did the historical
Houdini *really* do? And how on earth did he do it?

The newspaper accounts are voluminous, and consistent. The 2
mere cataloguing of Houdini's escapes soon grows tedious, which they
were not, to be sure, in the flesh. But quickly: the police stripped him
naked and searched him thoroughly before binding his wrists and ankles with five pairs of irons. Then they would slam him into a cell and
turn the key of a three-bond burglar-proof lock. He escaped, hundreds of
times, from the most secure prisons in the world. He hung upside down
in a straitjacket from the tallest buildings in America, and escaped in
full view of the populace. He was chained hand and foot and nailed into
a packing case weighted with lead; the packing case was dropped from a
tugboat into New York's East River and ninety seconds later Houdini
surfaced. The packing case was hauled up intact, with the manacles

inside, still fastened. He was sealed into a paper bag and got out without disturbing the seal. He was sewn into a huge football, into the belly of a whale, and escaped. In California he was buried six feet underground, and clawed his way out. He did this, he did that. These are facts that cannot be exaggerated, for they were conceived as exaggerations. We know he did these things because his actions were more public than the proceedings of Congress, and most of them he performed over and over, so no one would miss the point.

3   How did he do such things? For all rational people who are curious, sixty years after the magician's death, there is good news and bad news. The good news is that we know how the vast majority of Houdini's tricks were done, and the explanations are as fascinating as the mystery was. Much of our knowledge comes from the magician's writings, for Houdini kept ahead of his imitators by exposing his cast-off tricks. We have additional information from technicians and theater historians. No magician will reveal Houdini's secrets—their code forbids it. But so much controversy has arisen concerning his powers—so much conjecture they may have been supernatural—that extraordinary measures have been taken to assure us Houdini was a *mortal* genius. Many secrets have leaked out, and others have been discovered from examining the props. So at last we know more about Houdini's technique than any other magician's.

4   The disturbing news is that, sixty years after his last performance, some of his more spectacular escapes remain unexplained. And while magicians such as Doug Henning are bound not to expose their colleagues, they are free to admit what mystifies them. They know how Houdini walked through the brick wall at Hammerstein's Roof Garden, in 1914, but they do not know how he made the elephant disappear in 1918. This trick he performed only for a few months in New York. And when people asked him why he did not continue he told them that Teddy Roosevelt, a great hunter, had begged him to stop before he exhausted the world's supply of pachyderms.

5   But before we grapple with the mysteries, let us begin with what we can understand. Let us begin with my grandfather's favorite story, the case of Harry Houdini versus the German police. Houdini's first tour of Europe depended upon the good will and cooperation of the law. When he arrived in London in 1900 the twenty-six-year-old magician did not have a single booking. His news clippings eventually inspired an English agent, who had Houdini manacled to a pillar in Scotland Yard. Seeing that Houdini was securely fastened, Superintendent Melville of the Criminal Investigation Department said he would return in a

couple of hours, when the escapist had worn himself out. By the time Melville got to the door the magician was free to open it for him.

The publicity surrounding his escape from the most prestigious police force in the world opened up many another door for the young magician. Booked at the Alhambra Theater in London, he performed his "Challenge" handcuff act, which had made him famous on the vaude- ville circuit. After some card tricks and standard illusions, Houdini would stand before the proscenium and challenge the world to restrain him with ropes, straitjackets, handcuffs, whatever they could bring on, from lockshops, prisons, and museums. A single failure might have ruined him. There is no evidence that he ever failed, though in several cases he nearly died from the effort required to escape from sadistic shackles. The "Challenge" act filled the Alhambra Theater for two months. Houdini might have stayed there if Germany had not already booked him; the Germans could hardly wait to get a look at Houdini. 6

As he had done in America and England, Houdini began his tour of Germany with a visit to police headquarters. The Dresden officers were not enthusiastic, yet they could hardly refuse the magician's invitation to lock him up. That might suggest a crisis of confidence. And like their colleagues the world over, the Dresden police viewed Houdini's news clippings as so much paper in the balance with their locks and chains. Of course the Dresden police had no more success than those of Kansas City, or San Francisco, or Scotland Yard. Their manacles were paper to him. The police chief reluctantly signed the certificate Houdini demanded, but the newspapers gave him little coverage. 7

So on his opening night at Dresden's Central Theater, Houdini arranged to be fettered in the leg irons and manacles of the Mathil- degasse Prison. Some of the locks weighed forty pounds. The audience, packed to the walls, went wild over his escape, and the fact that he spoke their language further endeared him. If anything could have held him captive it would have been the adoring burghers of Dresden, who mobbed the theater for weeks. The manager wanted to buy out Hou- dini's contract with the Wintergarten of Berlin, so as to hold him over in Dresden, but the people of Berlin could not wait to see the magician. 8

Houdini arrived in Berlin in October of 1900. The first thing he did was march into the police station, strip stark naked, and challenge the jailors. They could not hold him. This time Count von Windheim, the highest ranking policeman in Germany, signed the certificate of Houdini's escape. The Wintergarten was overrun. The management appealed to the theater of Houdini's next engagement, in Vienna, so they might hold him over an extra month in Berlin. The Viennese 9 finally yielded, demanding an indemnity equal to Houdini's salary for one month. When the magician, at long last, opened at the Olympic Theater in Paris, in December of 1901, he was the highest paid foreign entertainer in French history.

10   But meanwhile there was big trouble brewing in Germany. It seems the police there had little sense of humor about Houdini's peculiar gifts, and the Jew had quickly exhausted what little there was. In Dortmund he escaped from the irons that had bound Glowisky, a notorious murderer, beheaded three days before. At Hanover the police chief, Count von Schwerin, plotted to disgrace Houdini, challenging him to escape from a special straitjacket reinforced with thick leather. Houdini agonized for one and a half hours while von Schwerin looked on, his jubilant smile melting in wonder, then rage, as the magician worked himself free.

11   The cumulative anger of the German police went public in July of 1901. Inspector Werner Graff witnessed Houdini's escape from all the manacles at the Cologne police station and vowed to end the humiliation. It was not a simple matter of pride. Graff, along with von Schwerin and other officials, feared Houdini was weakening their authority and inviting jailbreaks, if not other kinds of antisocial behavior. So Graff wrote a letter to Cologne's newspaper, the *Rheinische Zeitung*. The letter stated that Houdini had escaped from simple restraints at the police headquarters, by trickery; but his publicity boasted he could escape from restraints *of any kind.* Such a claim, Graff wrote, was a lie, and Houdini ought to be prosecuted for fraud.

12   Though he knew the letter was nonsense, the magician could not ignore it, for it was dangerous nonsense. If the police began calling him a fraud in every town he visited, Houdini would lose his audience. So he demanded that Graff apologize and the newspaper publish a retraction. Graff refused, and other German dailies reprinted his letter. Should Harry Houdini sue the German policeman for libel? Consider the circumstances. Germany, even in 1901, was one of the most authoritarian states in the world. Houdini was an American, a Jew who embarrassed the police. A libel case against Graff would turn upon the magician's claim that he could escape from *any* restraint, and the courtroom would become an international theater. There a German judge and jury would try his skill, and, should they find it wanting, Houdini would be washed up, exiled to play beer halls and dime museums. Only an artist with colossal pride and total confidence in his methods would act as Houdini did. He hired the most prominent trial lawyer in Cologne, and ordered him to sue Werner Graff and the Imperial Police of Germany for criminal libel.

There was standing room only in the Cologne *Schöffengericht.*   13
The judge allowed Werner Graff to seek out the most stubborn locks
and chains he could find, and tangle Houdini in them, in full view of
everyone. Here was a hitch, for Houdini did not wish to show the crowd
his technique. He asked the judge to clear the courtroom, and in the
ensuing turmoil the magician released himself so quickly no one knew
how he had done it. The *Schöffengericht* fined the astonished policeman and ordered a public apology. So Graff's lawyer appealed the case.

Two months later Graff was better prepared. In the *Strafkammer*,   14
or court of appeals, he presented thirty letters from legal authorities
declaring that the escape artist could not justify his advertisements.
And Graff had a shiny new pair of handcuffs. The premier locksmith of
Germany had engineered the cuffs especially for the occasion. Werner
Graff explained to the judge that the lock, once closed, could never be
opened, even with its own key. Let Houdini try to get out of these.

This time the court permitted Houdini to work in privacy, and a   15
guard led the magician to an adjacent chamber. Everyone else settled
down for a long wait, in a chatter of anticipation. They were interrupted
four minutes later by the entrance of Houdini, who tossed the manacles
on the judge's bench. So the *Strafkammer* upheld the lower court's
decision, as did the *Oberlandesgericht* in a "paper" appeal. The court
fined Werner Graff thirty marks and ordered him to pay for the trials as
well as a published apology. Houdini's next poster showed him in
evening dress, his hands manacled, standing before the judge, jurors,
and a battery of mustachioed policemen. Looking down on the scene
was a bust of the Kaiser against a crimson background, and a scroll that
read: "The Imperial Police of Cologne slandered Harry Houdini . . .
were compelled to advertise 'An Honorary Apology' and pay costs of the
trials. By command of Kaiser Wilhelm II, Emperor of Germany."

Now this is surely a wondrous tale, like something out of the   16
Arabian Nights, and it will seem no less wonderful when we understand the technique that made it come true. In 1901, when Houdini
took on the Imperial Police, he was not whistling in the dark. By
the time he left America at the end of the nineteenth century he
had dissected every kind of lock he could find in the New World,
and whatever he could import from the old one. Arriving in London,
Houdini could write that there were only a few kinds of British handcuffs, "seven or eight at the utmost," and these were some of the
simplest he had ever seen. He searched the markets, antique shops, and
locksmiths, buying up all the European locks he could find so he could
dismantle and study them.

17   Then during his Berlin engagement he worked up to ten hours a day at Mueller's locksmith on the Mittelstrasse, studying restraints. He was the Bobby Fischer of locks. With a chessmaster's foresight Houdini devised a set of picks to release every lock in existence, as well as *any he could imagine*. Such tireless ingenuity produced the incandescent light bulb and the atom bomb. Houdini's creation of a theatrical metaphor made a comparable impact on the human spirit. He had a message that he delivered so forcefully that it goes without mentioning in theater courses: humankind cannot be held in chains. The European middle class had reached an impressionable age, and the meaning of Houdini's theater was not lost upon them. Nor was he mistaken by the aristocracy, who stayed away in droves. The spectacle of this American Jew bursting from chains by dint of ingenuity did not amuse the rich. They wanted desperately to demythologize him.

18   It was not about to happen in the German courtroom. When Werner Graff snapped the "new" handcuffs on Houdini, they were not strange to the magician. He had already invented them, so to speak, as well as the pick to open them, and the pick was in his pocket. Only a locksmith whose knowledge surpassed Houdini's could stop him; diligent study assured him that, as of 1901, there could be no such locksmith on the face of the earth.

19   What else can we understand about the methods of Harry Houdini, born Ehrich Weiss? We know he was a superbly conditioned athlete who did not smoke or take a drop of alcohol. His straitjacket escapes he performed in full view of the world so they could see it was by main force and flexibility that he freed himself. He may or may not have been able to dislocate his shoulders at will—he said he could, and it seems no more marvelous than certain other skills he demonstrated. Friends reported that his toes could untie knots most of us could not manage with our fingers. And routinely the magician would hold his breath for as long as four minutes to work underwater escapes. To cheapen the supernatural claims of the fakir Rahman Bey, Houdini remained underwater in an iron box for ninety minutes, as against the Egyptian's sixty. Examining Houdini, a physician testified that the fifty-year-old wizard had halved his blood pressure while doubling his pulse. Of course, more wonderful than any of these skills was the courage allowing him to employ them, in predicaments where any normal person would panic.

20   These things are known about Houdini. The same tireless ingenuity, when applied to locks and jails, packing cases and riveted boilers; the same athletic prowess, when applied at the bottom of the East River, or while dangling from a rope attached to the cornice of the *Sun*

building in Baltimore—these talents account for the vast majority of Houdini's exploits. As we have mentioned, theater historians, notably Raymund Fitzsimons in his *Death and the Magician*, have carefully exposed Houdini's ingenuity, knowing that nothing can tarnish the miracle of the man's existence. Their accounts are technical and we need not dwell on them, except to say they *mostly* support Houdini's oath that his effects were achieved by natural, or mechanical, means. The Houdini problem arises from certain outrageous effects no one has ever been able to explain, though capable technicians have been trying for more than sixty years.

Let us briefly recall those effects. We have mentioned the disap- 21 pearing elephant. On January 7, 1918, Houdini had a ten-thousand-pound elephant led onto the bright stage of the Hippodrome in New York City. A trainer marched the elephant around a cabinet large enough for an elephant, proving there was space behind. There was no trap door in the floor of the Hippodrome, and the elephant could not fly. Houdini ushered the pachyderm into the cabinet and closed the curtains. Then he opened them, and where the elephant had stood there was nothing but empty space. Houdini went on with his program, which might have been making the Hippodrome disappear, for all the audience knew. A reporter for the *Brooklyn Eagle* noted: "The program says that the elephant vanished into thin air. The trick is performed fifteen feet from the backdrop and the cabinet is slightly elevated. That explanation is as good as any." After Houdini stopped making elephants disappear, nineteen weeks later, the trick would never be precisely duplicated.

That is the single "conventional" illusion of Houdini's repertoire 22 that remains unexplained. He was not the greatest illusionist of his time, though he was among the better ones. His expertise was the escape act, that specialty of magic furthest removed from theater, for its challenges are quite real and sometimes beyond the magician's control. It was the escapes, as his wife later wrote, that were truly dangerous, and Houdini privately admitted some anxieties about them. Give a wizard twenty years to build a cabinet that snuffs an elephant, and you will applaud his cleverness if he succeeds, in the controlled environment of his theater. But surrender the same man, stark naked, to the Russian police, who stake their honor upon detaining him in a convict van, and you may well suspect the intercession of angels should he get out.

And that is exactly what Houdini did, in one of the strangest and 23 most celebrated escapes of his career. Strange, because it was Houdini's habit to escape only from barred jail cells where the locks were within easy reach, and then only after inspection, so he might hide picks in crannies, or excuse himself if he foresaw failure. But the Siberian transport cell made his blood boil. On May 11, 1903, the chief of the Russian secret police searched the naked Houdini inside and out. The revolt of 1905 was in its planning stages and the Imperial Police were understandably touchy. The magician's wrists were padlocked and his ankles fettered before the police locked him into the *carette*. Mounted on a wagon, the zinc-lined steel cell stood in the prison courtyard in view of Chief Lebedoeff, his staff, and a number of civilians. Twenty-eight minutes later Houdini was walking around the courtyard, stretching. Nobody saw him get out, but he was out. The police ran to the door of the *carette*. The door was still locked and the shackles lay on the floor of the undamaged van. The police were so furious they would not sign the certificate of escape, but so many people had witnessed the event that the news was soon being shouted all over Moscow. Doug Henning has written: "It remains one of his escapes about which the real method is pure conjecture."

24   In the Houdini Museum at Niagara Falls, Canada, you may view the famous *Mirror* handcuffs. If you are a scholar you can inspect them. In March of 1904 the London *Daily Mirror* discovered a blacksmith who had been working for five years to build a set of handcuffs no mortal man could pick. Examining the cuffs, the best locksmiths in London agreed they had never seen such an ingenious mechanism. The newspaper challenged Houdini to escape from them. On March 17, before a house of four thousand in the London Hippodrome, a journalist fastened the cuffs on Houdini's wrists and turned the key six times. The magician retired to his cabinet onstage, and the band struck up a march. He did not emerge for twenty minutes. When he did, it was to hold the lock up to the light. Remember that most "Challenge" handcuffs were regulation, and familiar to Houdini. He studied the lock in the light, and then went back into the cabinet as the band played a waltz.

25   Ten minutes later Houdini stuck his head out, asking if he could have a cushion to kneel on. He was denied. After almost an hour Houdini came out of the cabinet again, obviously worn out, and his audience groaned. He wanted the handcuffs to be unlocked for a moment so he could take off his coat, as he was sweating profusely. The journalist denied the request, since Houdini had never before seen the handcuffs unlocked, and that might give him an advantage. Whereupon Houdini, in full view of the four thousand, extracted a penknife from his pocket and opened it with his teeth. Turning the coat inside out over his

head, he shredded it loose with the penknife and returned to the cabinet. Someone called out that Houdini had been handcuffed for more than an hour. As the band played on, the journalists of the *Daily Mirror* could taste the greatest scoop of the twentieth century. But ten minutes later there was a cry from the cabinet and Houdini leaped out of it, free, waving the handcuffs high in the air. While the crowd roared, several men from the audience carried Houdini on their shoulders around the theater. He was crying as if his heart would break.

For all his other talents, Houdini was a notoriously wooden actor, and we may assume the rare tears were altogether real, the product of an uncounterfeitable emotion. It is as if the man himself had been overwhelmed by his escape. Eighty years of technological progress have shed no light upon it. We know how Houdini got out of other handcuffs, but not these. As far as anyone can tell, the *Mirror* handcuffs remain as the blacksmith described them—a set of handcuffs no mortal man could pick. One is tempted to dismiss the whole affair as mass hypnosis. 26

In the same Canadian museum you may view the Chinese water torture cell, in which the magician was hung upside down in water, his ankles padlocked to the riveted roof. His escape from this cell was the crowning achievement of his stage career, and though he performed it on tour during the last ten years of his life, no one has the slightest notion of how he did it. The gifted Doug Henning revived the act in 1975 on television. But he would be the first to tell you his was *not* Houdini's version but his own, and he would not do it onstage before a live audience seven nights a week, with matinees on Wednesday and Saturday, because the trick would be unspeakably dangerous even if he could perform it there. When Houdini died he willed the contraption to his brother Hardeen, a fine magician in his own right. But Hardeen would not get in it either, and the instructions were to be burned upon his death. Again, as with the vanishing elephant, we are reviewing a stage illusion under controlled conditions, and may bow to a master's technical superiority without fretting that he had used supernatural powers. 27

But the *Mirror* handcuffs and the Siberian van escape are troublesome, as are certain of Houdini's escapes from reinforced straitjackets and packing cases under water. So is the fact that he was buried six feet underground and clawed his way out. He only tried it once, and nearly died in the struggle, but the feat was attested, and you do not need a degree in physics to know it is as preposterous as rising from the dead. 28

The weight of the earth is so crushing you could not lift it in the open air. Try doing this with no oxygen. The maestro himself misjudged the weight and, realizing his folly, tried to signal his crew when the grave was not yet full. They could not hear him and kept right on shoveling as fast as they could, so as not to keep him waiting. Then they stood back to watch. A while later they saw his bleeding hands appear above the ground.

29   If we find Houdini's record unsettling, imagine what our grandparents must have thought of him. They knew almost nothing of his technique. Where we remain troubled by a few of his illusions and escapes, our ancestors were horrified by most of them. The European journalists thought he was some kind of hobgoblin, a shapeshifter who could crawl through keyholes or dematerialize and reappear at will. One can hardly blame them. Despite his constant reassurances that his effects were technical, and natural, the practical-minded layman could not believe it, and even fellow magicians were disturbed by his behavior.

30   So we come to the central issue in the case of Harry Houdini. It is an issue he carefully avoided in public while studying it diligently in private. To wit: Can a magician, by the ultimate perfection of a technique, generate a force that, at critical moments, will achieve a supernatural result? Houdini's writings show this was the abiding concern of his intellectual life. It is, of course, the essential mystery of classical magic since before the Babylonians. Yet it remained a private and professional concern until Houdini's career forced it upon the public.

31   With the same determination that opened the world's locks, Houdini searched for an answer. His own technique was so highly evolved that its practice might have satisfied him, but his curiosity was unquenchable. He amassed the world's largest collection of books pertaining to magic and the occult, and no less a scholar than Edmund Wilson honored Houdini's authority. The son of a rabbi, Houdini pursued his studies with rabbinic thoroughness. And, from the beginning of his career, he sought out the living legends of magic and badgered them in retirement, sometimes with tragicomic results.

32   As far back as 1895 it seemed to Houdini something peculiar was going on when he performed the metamorphosis with his wife, Beatrice, who was known as Bess. You have probably seen this classic illusion. Two friends of mine once acted it in my living room as a birthday present. When the Houdinis performed the metamorphosis, Bess would handcuff Harry, tie him in a sack, and lock him in a trunk.

She would draw a curtain hiding the trunk, and then it would open, showing Houdini free upon the stage. Where was Bess? Inside the trunk, inside the sack, handcuffed—there was Bess. The method of the trick is only mysterious if you cannot pay for it. But the Houdinis' *timing* of the metamorphosis got very mysterious indeed. They polished the act until it happened in less than three seconds—three rather blurred seconds in their own minds. Believe me, you cannot get *into* the trunk in less than three seconds. So when the Houdinis had done the trick they were often as stunned as their audience. It seemed a sure case of technique unleashing a supernatural force. Perplexed, Houdini planned to interview Hermann the Great, the pre-eminent conjuror in America in 1895, and ask Hermann what was up. But Hermann died as Houdini was about to ask him the question.

And Houdini shadowed the marvelous Harry Kellar, cross-   33 examining him, and Alexander Heimburger, and the decrepit Ira Davenport, who had been a medium as well as a magician. But the great magicians flatly denied the psychic possibility, and Davenport would not answer to Houdini's satisfaction. In 1903 he discovered that Wiljalba Frikell, a seemingly mythic wizard of the nineteenth century, was still alive, in retirement near Dresden. When the ancient mage would not acknowledge his letters, Houdini grew convinced Wiljalba Frikell was the man to answer his question. He took the train to Dresden and knocked on Frikell's door. His wife sent Houdini away. On the road in Germany and Russia, Houdini continued to send letters and gifts to Frikell. And at last, six months after he had been turned away from Frikell's door, the reclusive magician agreed to see him.

Houdini rang the doorbell at two P.M. on October 8, 1903, the exact   34 hour of his appointment. An hour earlier, Wiljalba Frikell had dressed in his best suit and laid out his scrapbooks, programs, and medals for Houdini to view. Houdini excitedly followed Frikell's wife into the room where the master sat surrounded by the mementos of his glorious career. But he would not be answering any of the questions that buzzed in Houdini's brain. The old man was stone dead.

Throughout his life Houdini categorically denied that any of his   35 effects were achieved by supernatural means. He crusaded against mediums, clairvoyants, and all who claimed psychic power, advertising that he would reproduce any of their manifestations by mechanical means. In the face of spiritualists who accused *him* of being a physical medium, he protested that all his escapes and illusions were tricks. He was probably telling the truth as he understood it. But Rabbi Drachman, who spoke at Houdini's funeral and had been in a position to receive confidences, said: "Houdini possessed a wondrous power that he never understood, and which he never revealed to anyone in life."

36   Houdini was not Solomon; he was a vaudeville specialist. If he ever experienced a psychic power, it surely humbled his understanding. And to admit such a power, in his position, would have been a monumental stupidity. Why? If for no other reason, Talmudic law forbids the performance of miracles, and Houdini was the obedient son of Rabbi Weiss. Also, in case he should forget the Jewish law, it is strictly against the magician's code to claim a supernatural power, for reasons impossible to ignore. Mediums made such claims at their own risk. Two of the more famous mediums of the nineteenth century, Ira and William Davenport, achieved manifestations similar to Houdini's. Audiences in Liverpool, Leeds, and Paris rioted, stormed the stage, and ran the mediums out of town, crying their performances were an outrage against God and a danger to man. Whether or not the acts were supernatural is beside the point—billing them as such was bad business and hazardous to life and limb. Yet the Davenports were no more than a sideshow compared to Houdini. The man was blinding. There had not been such a public display of apparent miracles in nearly two thousand years. Had the Jew so much as hinted his powers were spiritual, he might have expected no better treatment than the renegade Hebrew of Nazareth.

37   Houdini was the self-proclaimed avatar of nothing but good old American know-how, and that is how he wished to be remembered. Bess, his wife of thirty years, was loyal to him in this, as in all other things. Pestered for revelations about Houdini's magic long after his death, the widow swore by her husband's account. But against her best intentions, Bess clouded the issue by saying just a little more than was necessary. It was in a letter to Sir Arthur Conan Doyle, who had been a close friend of hers and Houdini's.

38   The friendship was an odd one. The author of Sherlock Holmes believed in spiritualism, and championed the séance with all the fervor with which Houdini opposed it. There were two great mysteries in Doyle's life: the powers of Sherlock Holmes and Harry Houdini. Doyle knew the Houdinis intimately, and nothing the magician said could shake Sir Arthur's conviction that certain of Houdini's escapes were supernatural. Doyle never stopped trying to get Houdini to confess. In 1922 it was more than a personal issue. The séance had become big business in America, with millions of bereaved relatives paying to communicate with their dear departed. Spiritualism was a homegrown, persuasive religious movement, a bizarre reaction to American

science and pragmatism. The great critic Edmund Wilson, who admired Houdini and understood his gifts, recognized that the magician had appeared at a critical moment in the history of spiritualism. Houdini was the only man living who had the authority, and the competence, to expose the predatory mediums, and his success was decisive.

Yet Houdini's lecture-demonstrations, and exposures of false mediums, only fueled Doyle's suspicions that his friend was the real thing, a physical medium. In all fairness, Sir Arthur Conan Doyle was a credulous old gentleman who knew nothing of Houdini's techniques. But his instinct was sound. Two months after Houdini died, Sir Arthur wrote to Bess in despair of ever learning the truth from the magician's lips, and she wrote Doyle a long letter. What concerns us here are a few sentences that, coming from the woman who shared his life and work and who maintained her loyalty to Houdini alive and dead, we must regard as altogether startling.

> I will never be offended by anything you say for him or about him, but that he possessed psychic powers—he never knew it. As I told Lady Doyle often he would get a difficult lock, I stood by the cabinet and I would hear him say, "This is beyond me," and after many minutes when the audience became restless I nervously would say, "Harry, if there is anything in this belief in Spiritism,—why don't you call on them to assist you," and before many minutes had passed Houdini had mastered the lock.
>
> We never attributed this to psychic help. We just knew that that particular instrument was the one to open that lock, and so did all his tricks.

The tone of this letter penned so soon after her husband's death is somber throughout, painfully sincere. This was not a subject for levity, this being the central issue in the life of Harry Houdini. So what on earth is Bess trying to tell Sir Arthur when she testifies to the invocation of spirits in one sentence and repudiates psychic help in the next? What kind of double-talk is this, when the widow refers to the summoning of spiritual aid as "that particular instrument," as if a spirit were no different from any other skeleton key? It sounds like sheer euphemism; it sounds like the Houdinis' lifetime of work had uncovered a power so terrifying they would not admit it to each other, let alone the world. Would that Albert Einstein had been so discreet in 1905.

So what if Harry Houdini, once in a while, "spirited" himself out of a Siberian van, or a pair of *Mirror* handcuffs, or a packing case at the bottom of the East River? It is perhaps no more remarkable than that an

39

40

41

American Jew won a verdict against the German police for criminal libel in 1901, or reversed a religious movement in America in 1922. Houdini died in Detroit on Halloween in 1926, of acute appendicitis. He was born in Budapest on March 24, 1874, but told the world he was born in Appleton, Wisconsin, on April 6. Not until after World War II did Americans discover that their greatest magician was an alien. Houdini's work was no more miraculous than his life. His life was no more miraculous than the opening and closing of a flower.

—— CONSIDERATIONS ————————————————

1. Why did Houdini stubbornly insist that none of his feats was supernatural?

2. Summing up Houdini's miraculous escapes, Epstein writes, "There are facts that cannot be exaggerated, for they were conceived as exaggerations." In what way does that last clause make sense—if, indeed, it does?

3. In detailing the struggle between Houdini and the German police inspector, Graff, the author implies that the American escape artist was also fighting anti-semitism. Study the account, in paragraphs 10 through 15, to isolate the way Epstein expresses that implication and to determine whether he provides grounds for it.

4. What were some of Houdini's tricks that are still unexplained? (See paragraphs 21, 22, 23, 24, 25, and 28.) What does the author call "the crowning achievement" of Houdini's stage career?

5. In paragraph 17, Epstein describes Houdini's career as "a theatrical metaphor," a vehicle for delivering a message of great importance to the human spirit: "humankind cannot be held in chains." Do you find any evidence in the essay that such chains need not be limited to physical ones?

6. Study the last sentence of the essay. It is a fine example of a writer achieving real emphasis through apparent understatement. Why is it such a satisfying ending to the piece?

7. Study other writers of biographical essays—Peter Gay and Bruce Catton. Compare and contrast their techniques with Epstein's.

*William Faulkner (1897–1962) was a great novelist, born in
Mississippi, who supported himself much of his life by writing
screenplays and short fiction for magazines. He received the
Nobel Prize for literature in 1950. Among his novels are* The
Sound and the Fury *(1929),* As I Lay Dying *(1930),* Light in
August *(1932), and a comic series:* The Hamlet *(1940),* The
Town *(1957), and* The Mansion *(1960). "A Rose for Emily" is an
expert piece of magazine fiction; remarkably, it also makes an
emblem for the disease and decease of a society.*

29

WILLIAM FAULKNER
A Rose for Emily

I

When Miss Emily Grierson died, our whole town went to her   1
funeral: the men through a sort of respectful affection for a fallen
monument, the women mostly out of curiosity to see the inside of her
house, which no one save an old manservant—a combined gardener and
cook—had seen in at least ten years.

It was a big, squarish frame house that had once been white,   2
decorated with cupolas and spires and scrolled balconies in the heavily
lightsome style of the seventies, set on what had once been our most
select street. But garages and cotton gins had encroached and obliter-
ated even the august names of that neighborhood; only Miss Emily's
house was left, lifting its stubborn and coquettish decay above the
cotton wagons and the gasoline pumps—an eyesore among eyesores.
And now Miss Emily had gone to join the representatives of those
august names where they lay in the cedar-bemused cemetery among
the ranked and anonymous graves of Union and Confederate soldiers
who fell at the battle of Jefferson.

Alive, Miss Emily had been a tradition, a duty, and a care; a sort of   3

hereditary obligation upon the town, dating from that day in 1894 when
Colonel Sartoris, the mayor—he who fathered the edict that no Negro
woman should appear on the streets without an apron—remitted her
taxes, the dispensation dating from the death of her father on into
perpetuity. Not that Miss Emily would have accepted charity. Colonel
Sartoris invented an involved tale to the effect that Miss Emily's father
had loaned money to the town, which the town, as a matter of business,
preferred this way of repaying. Only a man of Colonel Sartoris' generation and thought could have invented it, and only a woman could have
believed it.

4   When the next generation, with its more modern ideas, became
mayors and aldermen, this arrangement created some little dissatisfaction. On the first of the year they mailed her a tax notice. February
came, and there was no reply. They wrote her a formal letter, asking her
to call at the sheriff's office at her convenience. A week later the mayor
wrote her himself, offering to call or to send his car for her, and received
in reply a note on paper of an archaic shape, in a thin, flowing calligra-
phy in faded ink, to the effect that she no longer went out at all. The tax
notice was also enclosed, without comment.

5   They called a special meeting of the Board of Aldermen. A depu-
tation waited upon her, knocked at the door through which no visitor
had passed since she ceased giving china-painting lessons eight or ten
years earlier. They were admitted by the old Negro into a dim hall from
which a staircase mounted into still more shadow. It smelled of dust
and disuse—a close, dank smell. The Negro led them into the parlor. It
was furnished in heavy, leather-covered furniture. When the Negro
opened the blinds of one window, a faint dust rose sluggishly about
their thighs, spinning with slow motes in the single sun-ray. On a
tarnished gilt easel before the fireplace stood a crayon portrait of Miss
Emily's father.

6   They rose when she entered—a small, fat woman in black, with a
thin gold chain descending to her waist and vanishing into her belt,
leaning on an ebony cane with a tarnished gold head. Her skeleton was
small and spare; perhaps that was why what would have been merely
plumpness in another was obesity in her. She looked bloated, like a
body long submerged in motionless water, and of that pallid hue. Her
eyes, lost in the fatty ridges of her face, looked like two small pieces of
coal pressed into a lump of dough as they moved from one face to
another while the visitors stated their errand.

7   She did not ask them to sit. She just stood in the door and listened
quietly until the spokesman came to a stumbling halt. Then they could
hear the invisible watch ticking at the end of the gold chain.

Her voice was dry and cold. "I have no taxes in Jefferson. Colonel 8
Sartoris explained it to me. Perhaps one of you can gain access to the
city records and satisfy yourselves."

"But we have. We are the city authorities, Miss Emily. Didn't you 9
get a notice from the sheriff, signed by him?"

"I received a paper, yes," Miss Emily said. "Perhaps he considers 10
himself the sheriff. . . . I have no taxes in Jefferson."

"But there is nothing on the books to show that, you see. We must 11
go by the—"

"See Colonel Sartoris. I have no taxes in Jefferson." 12

"But, Miss Emily—" 13

"See Colonel Sartoris." (Colonel Sartoris had been dead almost ten 14
years.) "I have no taxes in Jefferson. Tobe!" The Negro appeared. "Show
these gentlemen out."

II

So she vanquished them, horse and foot, just as she had van- 15
quished their fathers thirty years before about the smell. That was two
years after her father's death and a short time after her sweetheart—the
one we believed would marry her—had deserted her. After her father's
death she went out very little; after her sweetheart went away, people
hardly saw her at all. A few of the ladies had the temerity to call, but
were not received, and the only sign of life about the place was the
Negro man—a young man then—going in and out with a market
basket.

"Just as if a man—any man—could keep a kitchen properly," the 16
ladies said, so they were not surprised when the smell developed. It was
another link between the gross, teeming world and the high and mighty
Griersons.

A neighbor, a woman, complained to the mayor, Judge Stevens, 17
eighty years old.

"But what will you have me do about it, madam?" he said. 18

"Why, send her word to stop it," the woman said. "Isn't there a 19
law?"

"I'm sure that won't be necessary," Judge Stevens said. "It's proba- 20
bly just a snake or a rat that nigger of hers killed in the yard. I'll speak to
him about it."

The next day he received two more complaints, one from a man 21
who came in diffident deprecation. "We really must do something
about it, Judge. I'd be the last one in the world to bother Miss Emily, but
we've got to do something." That night the Board of Aldermen met—

three graybeards and one younger man, a member of the rising generation.

22   "It's simple enough," he said. "Send her word to have her place cleaned up. Give her a certain time to do it in, and if she don't . . ."

23   "Dammit, sir," Judge Stevens said, "will you accuse a lady to her face of smelling bad?"

24   So the next night, after midnight, four men crossed Miss Emily's lawn and slunk about the house like burglars, sniffing along the base of the brickwork and at the cellar openings while one of them performed a regular sowing motion with his hand out of a sack slung from his shoulder. They broke open the cellar door and sprinkled lime there, and in all the out-buildings. As they recrossed the lawn, a window that had been dark was lighted and Miss Emily sat in it, the light behind her, and her upright torso motionless as that of an idol. They crept quietly across the lawn and into the shadow of the locusts that lined the street. After a week or two the smell went away.

25   That was when people had begun to feel really sorry for her. People in our town remembering how old lady Wyatt, her great-aunt, had gone completely crazy at last, believed that the Griersons held themselves a little too high for what they really were. None of the young men were quite good enough for Miss Emily and such. We had long thought of them as a tableau: Miss Emily a slender figure in white in the background, her father a spraddled silhouette in the foreground, his back to her and clutching a horsewhip, the two of them framed by the back-flung front door. So when she got to be thirty and was still single, we were not pleased exactly, but vindicated; even with insanity in the family she wouldn't have turned down all of her chances if they had really materialized.

26   When her father died, it got about that the house was all that was left to her; and in a way, people were glad. At last they could pity Miss Emily. Being left alone, and a pauper, she had become humanized. Now she too would know the old thrill and the old despair of a penny more or less.

27   The day after his death all the ladies prepared to call at the house and offer condolence and aid, as is our custom. Miss Emily met them at the door, dressed as usual and with no trace of grief on her face. She told them that her father was not dead. She did that for three days, with the ministers calling on her, and the doctors trying to persuade her to let them dispose of the body. Just as they were about to resort to law and force, she broke down, and they buried her father quickly.

28   We did not say she was crazy then. We believed she had to do that.

We remembered all the young men her father had driven away, and we knew that with nothing left, she would have to cling to that which had robbed her, as people will.

III

She was sick for a long time. When we saw her again, her hair was   29
cut short, making her look like a girl, with a vague resemblance to those angels in colored church windows—sort of tragic and serene.

The town had just let the contracts for paving the sidewalks, and   30
in the summer after her father's death they began to work. The construction company came with niggers and mules and machinery, and a foreman named Homer Barron, a Yankee—a big, dark, ready man, with a big voice and eyes lighter than his face. The little boys would follow in groups to hear him cuss the niggers, and the niggers singing in time to the rise and fall of picks. Pretty soon he knew everybody in town. Whenever you heard a lot of laughing anywhere about the square, Homer Barron would be in the center of the group. Presently we began to see him and Miss Emily on Sunday afternoons driving in the yellow-wheeled buggy and the matched team of bays from the livery stable.

At first we were glad that Miss Emily would have an interest,   31
because the ladies all said, "Of course a Grierson would not think seriously of a Northener, a day laborer." But there were still others, older people, who said that even grief could not cause a real lady to forget *noblesse oblige*—without calling it *noblesse oblige*. They just said, "Poor Emily. Her kinsfolk should come to her." She had some kin in Alabama; but years ago her father had fallen out with them over the estate of old lady Wyatt, the crazy woman, and there was no communication between the two families. They had not even been represented at the funeral.

And as soon as the old people said, "Poor Emily," the whispering   32
began. "Do you suppose it's really so?" they said to one another. "Of course it is. What else could . . ." This behind their hands; rustling of craned silk and satin behind jalousies closed upon the sun of Sunday afternoon as the thin, swift clop-clop-clop of the matched team passed: "Poor Emily."

She carried her head high enough—even when we believed that   33
she was fallen. It was as if she demanded more than ever the recognition of her dignity as the last Grierson; as if it had wanted that touch of earthliness to reaffirm her imperviousness. Like when she bought the rat poison, the arsenic. That was over a year after they had begun to say "Poor Emily," and while the two female cousins were visiting her.

34   "I want some poison," she said to the druggist. She was over thirty then, still a slight woman, though thinner than usual, with cold, haughty black eyes in a face the flesh of which was strained across the temples and about the eyesockets as you imagine a lighthouse-keeper's face ought to look. "I want some poison," she said.

35   "Yes, Miss Emily. What kind? For rats and such? I'd recom—"

36   "I want the best you have. I don't care what kind."

37   The druggist named several. "They'll kill anything up to an elephant. But what you want is—"

38   "Arsenic," Miss Emily said. "Is that a good one?"

39   "Is . . . arsenic? Yes ma'am. But what you want—"

40   "I want arsenic."

41   The druggist looked down at her. She looked back at him, erect, her face like a strained flag. "Why, of course," the druggist said. "If that's what you want. But the law requires you to tell what you are going to use it for."

42   Miss Emily just stared at him, her head tilted back in order to look him eye for eye, until he looked away and went and got the arsenic and wrapped it up. The Negro delivery boy brought her the package; the druggist didn't come back. When she opened the package at home there was written on the box, under the skull and bones: "For rats."

IV

43   So the next day we all said, "She will kill herself"; and we said it would be the best thing. When she had first begun to be seen with Homer Barron, we had said, "She will marry him." Then we said, "She will persuade him yet," because Homer himself had remarked—he liked men, and it was known that he drank with the younger men in the Elk's Club—that he was not a marrying man. Later we said, "Poor Emily," behind the jalousies as they passed on Sunday afternoon in the glittering buggy, Miss Emily with her head high and Homer Barron with his hat cocked and a cigar in his teeth, reins and whip in a yellow glove.

44   Then some of the ladies began to say that it was a disgrace to the town and a bad example to the young people. The men did not want to interfere, but at last the ladies forced the Baptist minister—Miss Emily's people were Episcopal—to call upon her. He would never divulge what happened during that interview, but he refused to go back again. The next Sunday they again drove about the streets and the following day the minister's wife wrote to Miss Emily's relations in Alabama.

45   So she had blood-kin under her roof again and we sat back to watch

developments. At first nothing happened. Then we were sure that they had to be married. We learned that Miss Emily had been to the jeweler's and ordered a man's toilet set in silver, with the letters H.B. on each piece. Two days later we learned that she had bought a complete outfit of men's clothing, including a nightshirt, and we said "They are married." We were really glad. We were glad because the two female cousins were even more Grierson than Miss Emily had ever been.

So we were surprised when Homer Barron—the streets had been finished some time since—was gone. We were a little disappointed that there was not a public blowing-off, but we believed that he had gone on to prepare for Miss Emily's coming, or to give a chance to get rid of the cousins. (By that time it was a cabal, and we were all Miss Emily's allies to help circumvent the cousins.) Sure enough, after another week they departed. And, as we had expected all along, within three days Homer Barron was back in town. A neighbor saw the Negro man admit him at the kitchen door at dusk one evening. 46

And that was the last we saw of Homer Barron. And of Miss Emily for some time. The Negro man went in and out with the market basket, but the front door remained closed. Now and then we would see her at a window for a moment, as the men did that night when they sprinkled the lime, but for almost six months she did not appear on the streets. Then we knew that this was to be expected too; as if that quality of her father which had thwarted her woman's life so many times had been too virulent and too furious to die. 47

When we next saw Miss Emily, she had grown fat and her hair was turning gray. During the next few years it grew grayer and grayer until it attained an even pepper-and-salt iron-gray, when it ceased turning. Up to the day of her death at seventy-four it was still that vigorous iron-gray, like the hair of an active man. 48

From that time on her front door remained closed, save for a period of six or seven years, when she was about forty, during which she gave lessons in china-painting. She fitted up a studio in one of the downstairs rooms, where the daughters and granddaughters of Colonel Sartoris' contemporaries were sent to her with the same regularity and in the same spirit that they were sent on Sundays with a twenty-five cent piece for the collection plate. Meanwhile her taxes had been remitted. 49

Then the newer generation became the backbone and the spirit of the town, and the painting pupils grew up and fell away and did not send their children to her with boxes of color and tedious brushes and pictures cut from the ladies' magazines. The front door closed upon the last one and remained closed for good. When the town got free postal deliv- 50 ery Miss Emily alone refused to let them fasten the metal numbers above her door and attach a mailbox to it. She would not listen to them.

51   Daily, monthly, yearly we watched the Negro grow grayer and more stooped, going in and out with the market basket. Each December we sent her a tax notice, which would be returned by the post office a week later, unclaimed. Now and then we would see her in one of the downstairs windows—she had evidently shut up the top floor of the house—like the carven torso of an idol in a niche, looking or not looking at us, we could never tell which. Thus she passed from generation to generation—dear, inescapable, impervious, tranquil, and perverse.

52   And so she died. Fell ill in the house filled with dust and shadows, with only a doddering Negro man to wait on her. We did not even know she was sick; we had long since given up trying to get any information from the Negro. He talked to no one, probably not even to her, for his voice had grown harsh and rusty, as if from disuse.

53   She died in one of the downstairs rooms, in a heavy walnut bed with a curtain, her gray head propped on a pillow yellow and moldy with age and lack of sunlight.

V

54   The Negro met the first of the ladies at the front door and let them in, with their hushed, sibilant voices and their quick, curious glances, and then he disappeared. He walked right through the house and out the back and was not seen again.

55   The two female cousins came at once. They held the funeral on the second day, with the town coming to look at Miss Emily beneath a mass of bought flowers, with the crayon face of her father musing profoundly above the bier and the ladies sibilant and macabre; and the very old men—some in their brushed Confederate uniforms—on the porch and the lawn, talking of Miss Emily as if she had been a contemporary of theirs, believing that they had danced with her and courted her perhaps, confusing time with its mathematical progression, as the old do, to whom all the past is not a diminishing road, but, instead, a huge meadow which no winter ever quite touches, divided from them now by the narrow bottleneck of the most recent decade of years.

56   Already we knew that there was one room in the region above the stairs which no one had seen in forty years, and which would have to be forced. They waited until Miss Emily was decently in the ground before they opened it.

57   The violence of breaking down the door seemed to fill this room

with pervading dust. A thin, acrid pall as of the tomb seemed to lie everywhere upon this room decked and furnished as for a bridal: upon the valance curtains of faded rose color, upon the rose-shaded lights, upon the dressing table, upon the delicate array of crystal and the man's toilet things backed with tarnished silver, silver so tarnished that the monogram was obscured. Among them lay a collar and tie, as if they had just been removed, which, lifted, left upon the surface a pale crescent in the dust. Upon a chair hung the suit, carefully folded; beneath it the two mute shoes and the discarded socks.

The man himself lay in the bed.   58

For a long while we just stood there, looking down at the profound   59
and fleshless grin. The body had apparently once lain in the attitude of an embrace, but now the long sleep that outlasts love, that conquers even the grimace of love, had cuckolded him. What was left of him, rotted beneath what was left of the nightshirt, had become inextricable from the bed in which he lay; and upon him and upon the pillow beside him lay that even coating of the patient and biding dust.

Then we noticed that in the second pillow was the indentation of a   60
head. One of us lifted something from it, and leaning foward, that faint and invisible dust dry and acrid in the nostrils, we saw a long strand of iron-gray hair.

——— CONSIDERATIONS ————————————————

1. The art of narration, some say, is the successful management of a significant sequence of actions through time. But "through time" does not necessarily imply chronological order. Identify the major events of Faulkner's story according to when they actually happened, then arrange them in the order in which they are given by the author. Try the same technique with "A Worn Path" by Eudora Welty.

2. Faulkner uses the terms "Negro" and "nigger" to refer to nonwhite persons in the story. Does he intend distinction between the two words? If he were writing the story today, instead of in 1930, might he substitute the word "black"? Why? Can you think of parallel terms used to designate other minority peoples, say, Jews, Catholics, Italians, or Japanese? Of what significance is the variety of such terms?

3. In what ways, if any, is Emily Grierson presented as a sympathetic character? Why?

4. In part III, Faulkner puts considerable emphasis on the phrase *noblesse oblige*. Look up the meaning of that phrase, then comment on the author's use of it.

5. Who is the "we" in the story? Does "we" play any significant part?

6. Obviously death is a significant element in this story. Could Faulkner also have had in mind the death of a particular society or a way of life? Discuss Faulkner's use of symbolism, using examples from the story.

7. While the events of Faulkner's story span a considerable period of time, they fall roughly halfway between the accounts of Frederick Douglass (1845) and Shelby Steele (1988). Looking through the eyes of these three writers, what changes do you see in attitudes toward African Americans over the 143 years?

Robert Finch (b. 1943) was born in New Jersey beside the Passaic River, which he has called "one of the ten dirtiest rivers in America." He settled on Cape Cod full-time in 1972, where he has been director of publications for the Cape Cod Museum of Natural History. He has written Common Ground: A Naturalist's Cape Cod *(1981) and* The Primal Place *(1983). The essays in* Common Ground, *from which we take "Very Like a Whale," first appeared as weekly columns syndicated in four Cape Cod newspapers.*

30

ROBERT FINCH
Very Like a Whale

One day last week at sunset I went back to Corporation Beach in Dennis to see what traces, if any, might be left of the great, dead finback whale that had washed up there several weeks before. The beach was not as hospitable as it had been that sunny Saturday morning after Thanksgiving when thousands of us streamed over the sand to gaze and look. A few cars were parked in the lot, but these kept their inhabitants. Bundled up against a sharp wind, I set off along the twelve-foot swath of trampled beach grass, a raw highway made in a few hours by ten thousand feet that day.

I came to the spot where the whale had beached and marveled that such a magnitude of flesh could have been there one day and gone the next. But the carcass had been hauled off and the tide had smoothed and licked clean whatever vestiges had remained. The cold, salt wind had lifted from the sands the last trace of that pervasive stench of decay that clung to our clothes for days, and now blew clean and sharp into my nostrils.

The only sign that anything unusual had been there was that the beach was a little too clean, not quite so pebbly and littered as the

1

2

3

surrounding areas, as the grass above a new grave is always fresher and greener. What had so manifestly occupied this space a short while ago was now utterly gone. And yet the whale still lay heavily on my mind; a question lingered, like a persistent odor in the air. And its dark shape, though now sunken somewhere beneath the waves, still loomed before me, beckoning, asking something.

4   What was it? What had we seen? Even the several thousand of us that managed to get down to the beach before it was closed off did not see much. Whales, dead or alive, are protected these days under the Federal Marine Mammals Act, and shortly after we arrived, local police kept anyone from actually touching the whale. I could hardly regret this, since in the past beached whales, still alive, have had cigarettes put out in their eyes and bits of flesh hacked off with pocket knives by souvenir seekers. And so, kept at a distance, we looked on while the specialists worked, white-coated, plastic-gloved autopsists from the New England Aquarium, hacking open the thick hide with carving knives and plumbing its depth for samples to be shipped to Canada for analysis and determination of causes of death. What was it they were pulling out? What fetid mystery would they pluck from that huge coffin of dead flesh? We would have to trust them for the answer.

5   But as the crowds continued to grow around the whale's body like flies around carrion, the question seemed to me, and still seems, not so much why did the whale die, but why had we come to see it? What made this dark bulk such a human magnet, spilling us over onto private lawns and fields? I watched electricians and oil truck drivers pulling their vehicles off the road and clambering down to the beach. Women in high heels and pearls, on their way to Filene's, stumbled through the loose sand to gaze at a corpse. The normal human pattern was broken and a carnival atmosphere was created, appropriate enough in the literal sense of "a farewell to the flesh." But there was also a sense of pilgrimage in those trekking across the beach, an obligation to view such a thing. But for what? Are we really such novices to death? Or so reverent toward it?

6   I could understand my own semiprofessional interest in the whale, but what had drawn these hordes? There are some obvious answers, of course: a break in the dull routine, "something different." An old human desire to associate ourselves with great and extraordinary events. We placed children and sweethearts in front of the corpse and clicked cameras. "Ruthie and the whale." "Having a whale of a time on Cape Cod."

7   Curiosity, the simplest answer, doesn't really answer anything.

What, after all, did we learn by being there? We were more like children at a zoo, pointing and poking, or Indians on a pristine beach, gazing in innocent wonder at strange European ships come ashore. Yet, as the biologists looted it with vials and plastic bags and the press captured it on film, the spectators also tried to *make* something of the whale. Circling around it as though for some hold on its slippery bulk, we grappled it with metaphors, lashed similes around its immense girth. It lay upside down, overturned "like a trailer truck." Its black skin was cracked and peeling, red underneath, "like a used tire." The distended, corrugated lower jaw, "a giant accordion," was afloat with the gas of putrefaction and, when pushed, oscillated slowly "like an enormous waterbed." Like our primitive ancestors, we still tend to make images to try to comprehend the unknown.

But what were we looking at? Or more to the point, from what 8 perspective were we looking at it? What did we see in it that might tell us why we had come? A male finback whale—*Balaenoptera physalus*—a baleen cetacean. The second largest creature ever to live on earth. An intelligent and complex mammal. A cause for conservationists. A remarkably adapted swimming and eating machine. Perfume, pet food, engineering oil. A magnificent scientific specimen. A tourist attraction. A media event, a "day to remember." A health menace, a "possible carrier of a communicable disease." A municipal headache and a navigational hazard. Material for an essay.

On the whale's own hide seemed to be written its life history, 9 which we could remark but not read. The right fluke was almost entirely gone, lost in some distant accident or battle and now healed over with a white scar. The red eye, unexpectedly small and mammalian, gazed out at us with fiery blankness. Like the glacial scratches sometimes found on our boulders, there were strange marks or grooves in the skin around the anal area, perhaps caused by scraping the ocean bottom.

Yet we could not seem to scratch its surface. The whale—dead, 10 immobile, in full view—nonetheless shifted kaleidoscopically before our eyes. The following morning it was gone, efficiently and sanitarily removed, like the week's garbage. What was it we saw? I have a theory, though probably (as they say in New England) it hardly does.

There is a tendency these days to defend whales and other endan- 11 gered animals by pointing out their similarities to human beings. Cetaceans, we are told, are very intelligent. They possess a highly complex language and have developed sophisticated communications systems that transmit over long distances. They form family groups, develop social structures and personal relationships, and express loyalty and affection toward one another. Much of their behavior seems to be recreational: they sing, they play. And so on.

12   These are not sentimental claims. Whales apparently do these things, at least as far as our sketchy information about their habits warrants such interpretations. And for my money, any argument that helps to preserve these magnificent creatures can't be all bad.

13   I take exception to this approach not because it is wrong, but because it is wrongheaded and misleading. It is exclusive, anthropocentric, and does not recognize nature in its own right. It implies that whales and other creatures have value only insofar as they reflect man himself and conform to his ideas of beauty and achievement. This attitude is not really far removed from that of the whalers themselves. To consume whales solely for their nourishment of human values is only a step from consuming them for meat and corset staves. It is not only presumptuous and patronizing, but it is misleading and does both whales and men a grave disservice. Whales have an inalienable right to exist, not because they resemble man *or* because they are useful to him, but simply because they do exist, because they have a proven fitness to the exactitudes of being on a global scale matched by few other species. If they deserve our admiration and respect, it is because, as Henry Beston put it, "They are other nations, caught with ourselves in the net of life and time, fellow prisoners of the splendour and travail of life."

14   But that still doesn't explain the throngs who came pell-mell to stare and conjecture at the dead whale that washed up at Corporation Beach and dominated it for a day like some extravagant *memento mori*. Surely we were not flattering ourselves, consciously or unconsciously, with any human comparisons to that rotting hulk. Nor was there much, in its degenerate state, that it had to teach us. And yet we came—why?

15   The answer may be so obvious that we have ceased to recognize it. Man, I believe, has a crying need to confront otherness in the universe. Call it nature, wilderness, the "great outdoors," or what you will—we crave to look out and behold something other than our own human faces staring back at us, expectantly and increasingly frustrated. What the human spirit wants, as Robert Frost said, "Is not its own love back in copy-speech,/ But counter-love, original response."

16   This sense of otherness is, I feel, as necessary a requirement to our personalities as food and warmth are to our bodies. Just as an individual, cut off from human contact and stimulation, may atrophy and die of loneliness and neglect, so mankind is today in a similar, though more subtle, danger of cutting himself off from the natural world he shares with all creatures. If our physical survival depends upon our devising a

proper use of earth's materials and produce, our growth as a species depends equally upon our establishing a vital and generative relationship with what surrounds us.

We need plants, animals, weather, unfettered shores and un- 17
broken woodland, not merely for a stable and healthy environment, but as an antidote to introversion, a preventive against human inbreeding. Here in particular, in the splendor of natural life, we have an extraordinary reservoir of the Cape's untapped possibilities and modes of being, ways of experiencing life, of knowing wind and wave. After all, how many neighborhoods have whales wash up in their backyards? To confine this world in zoos or in exclusive human terms does injustice not only to nature, but to ourselves as well.

Ever since his beginnings, when primitive man adopted totems 18
and animal spirits to himself and assumed their shapes in ritual dance, *Homo sapiens* has been a superbly imitative animal. He has looked out across the fields and seen and learned. Somewhere along the line, though, he decided that nature was his enemy, not his ally, and needed to be confined and controlled. He abstracted nature and lost sight of it. Only now are we slowly realizing that nature can be confined only by narrowing our own concepts of it, which in turn narrows us. That is why we came to see the whale.

We substitute human myth for natural reality and wonder why we 19
starve for nourishment. "Your Cape" becomes "your Mall," as the local radio jingle has it. Thoreau's "huge and real Cape Cod . . . a wild, rank place with no flattery in it," becomes the Chamber of Commerce's "Rural Seaside Charm"—until forty tons of dead flesh wash ashore and give the lie to such thin, flattering conceptions, flesh whose stench is still the stench of life that stirs us to reaction and response. That is why we came to see the whale. Its mute, immobile bulk represented that ultimate, unknowable otherness that we both seek and recoil from, and shouted at us louder than the policeman's bullhorn that the universe is fraught, not merely with response or indifference, but incarnate assertion.

Later that day the Dennis Board of Health declared the whale 20
carcass to be a "health menace" and warned us off the beach. A health menace? More likely an intoxicating, if strong, medicine that might literally bring us to our senses.

But if those of us in the crowd failed to grasp the whale that day, 21
others did not have much better luck. Even in death the whale escaped us: the tissue samples taken in the autopsy proved insufficient for analysis and the biologists concluded, "We will never know why the

whale died." The carcass, being towed tail-first by a Coast Guard cutter for a final dumping beyond Provincetown, snapped a six-inch hawser. Eluding further attempts to reattach it, it finally sank from sight. Even our powers of disposal, it seemed, were questioned that day.

22 And so, while we are left on shore with the memory of a deflated and stinking carcass and of bullhorns that blared and scattered us like flies, somewhere out beyond the rolled waters and the shining winter sun, the whale sings its own death in matchless, sirenian strains.

—— CONSIDERATIONS —————————————————

1. A feature of Finch's style in "Very Like a Whale" is his skillful use of figurative language. In paragraph 3, for example, he compares the cleaned up beach to "grass above a new grave," and his question to the whale which "still lay heavily on my mind." Other examples are the question which "lingered like a persistent odor," and the dark shape of the whale, long gone beneath the waves, that "still loomed" before him. Locate and underline a dozen more figures of speech in the essay. Decide whether they are merely decorative or significantly functional in the essay.

2. Does Finch's title sound familiar, but you just can't place it? Look up the phrase in *Familiar Quotations* by John Bartlett. Does it take on a new meaning when used as the title of this essay? How much thought do you give to the titles of your own essays?

3. Where does Finch first set forth the thesis of his essay? What responsibility does a thesis expressed as a question place upon the writer? Does Finch meet that responsibility?

4. With the exception of the first three lines, what is the conspicuous grammatical form used in paragraph 8? Try changing each of the items in the series to a more conventional form. Can you now justify Finch's style in this paragraph?

5. "Curiosity, the simplest answer, doesn't really answer anything," writes Finch in paragraph 7. Read Peter Steinhart's essay, "The Old Curiosity," and imagine the kind of response Steinhart might offer to the quoted statement.

6. Why does Finch object to a common approach by people concerned about preserving "nature"? See paragraph 13. Would he, for instance, find George Orwell's response to the death of an elephant (see "Shooting an Elephant") "sentimental," "exclusive," or "anthropocentric"?

7. What is the significance of the next to last word of Finch's essay?

*Robert Frost (1874–1963) was born in California and became
the great poet of New England. He published many books of
poetry and won the Pulitzer Prize three times. A popular figure,
Frost was admired as a gentle, affectionate, avuncular figure
given to country sayings. The private Frost, however, was
another man—guilty, jealous, bitter, sophisticated, occasionally
triumphant, and always complicated.*

*"Design" is a brief but complicated poem. As far back as we
find record, humankind has worried about the place of malice or
bad luck in the scheme of things. We have attributed
misfortunes to the retribution of a just God, to the Fates, to
divine caprice, to broken taboos, to evil spirits, witches, demons.
It is possible that Robert Frost here names the greatest fear
of all.*

31

ROBERT FROST
Design

I found a dimpled spider, fat and white,
On a white heal-all, holding up a moth
Like a white piece of rigid satin cloth—
Assorted characters of death and blight
Mixed ready to begin the morning right,   5
Like the ingredients of a witches' broth—
A snow-drop spider, a flower like a froth,
And dead wings carried like a paper kite.
What had that flower to do with being white,
The wayside blue and innocent heal-all?   10
What brought the kindred spider to that height,
Then steered the white moth thither in the night?
What but design of darkness to appall?—
If design govern in a thing so small.

In 1912 Frost sent "In White" to a friend in a letter. At the time he was teaching psychology at the Plymouth Normal School in Plymouth, New Hampshire. In the decade that followed, Frost revised the poem; he first printed "Design" as we know it in 1922.

32

ROBERT FROST
In White

A dented spider like a snowdrop white
On a white Heal-all, holding up a moth
Like a white piece of lifeless satin cloth—
Saw ever curious eye so strange a sight?

5 Portent in little, assorted death and blight
Like the ingredients of a witches' broth?
The beady spider, the flower like a froth,
And the moth carried like a paper kite.

What had that flower to do with being white,
10 The blue Brunella every child's delight?
What brought the kindred spider to that height?
(Make we no thesis of the miller's plight.)
What but design of darkness and of night?
Design, design! Do I use the word aright?

Martin Gansberg (b. 1920) edited and reported for the New York Times *for forty years. This story, written in 1964, has been widely reprinted. Largely because of Gansberg's account, the murder of Kitty Genovese has become an infamous example of citizen apathy. When Gansberg returned to the neighborhood fifteen years afterward, revisiting the place of the murder with a television crew, the people had not changed: still, no one wanted to get involved.*

33

MARTIN GANSBERG

38 Who Saw Murder Didn't Call the Police

For more than half an hour 38 respectable, law-abiding citizens in 1
Queens watched a killer stalk and stab a woman in three separate
attacks in Kew Gardens.

Twice their chatter and the sudden glow of their bedroom lights 2
interrupted him and frightened him off. Each time he returned, sought
her out, and stabbed her again. Not one person telephoned the police
during the assault; one witness called after the woman was dead.

That was two weeks ago today. 3

Still shocked is Assistant Chief Inspector Frederick M. Lussen, in 4
charge of the borough's detectives and a veteran of 25 years of homicide
investigations. He can give a matter-of-fact recitation on many murders. But the Kew Gardens slaying baffles him—not because it is a
murder, but because the "good people" failed to call the police.

"As we have reconstructed the crime," he said, "the assailant had 5
three chances to kill this woman during a 35-minute period. He returned twice to complete the job. If we had been called when he first
attacked, the woman might not be dead now."

6   This is what the police say happened beginning at 3:20 A.M. in the staid, middle-class, tree-lined Austin Street area:

7   Twenty-eight-year-old Catherine Genovese, who was called Kitty by almost everyone in the neighborhood, was returning home from her job as manager of a bar in Hollis. She parked her red Fiat in a lot adjacent to the Kew Gardens Long Island Rail Road Station, facing Mowbray Place. Like many residents of the neighborhood, she had parked there day after day since her arrival from Connecticut a year ago, although the railroad frowns on the practice.

8   She turned off the lights of her car, locked the door, and started to walk the 100 feet to the entrance of her apartment at 82–70 Austin Street, which is in a Tudor building, with stores in the first floor and apartments on the second.

9   The entrance to the apartment is in the rear of the building because the front is rented to retail stores. At night the quiet neighborhood is shrouded in the slumbering darkness that marks most residential areas.

10   Miss Genovese noticed a man at the far end of the lot, near a seven-story apartment house at 82–40 Austin Street. She halted. Then nervously, she headed up Austin Street toward Lefferts Boulevard, where there is a call box to the 102nd Police Precinct in nearby Richmond Hill.

11   She got as far as a street light in front of a bookstore before the man grabbed her. She screamed. Lights went on in the 10-story apartment house at 82–67 Austin Street, which faces the bookstore. Windows slid open and voices punctuated the early-morning stillness.

12   Miss Genovese screamed: "Oh, my God, he stabbed me! Please help me! Please help me!"

13   From one of the upper windows in the apartment house, a man called down: "Let that girl alone!"

14   The assailant looked up at him, shrugged and walked down Austin Street toward a white sedan parked a short distance away. Miss Genovese struggled to her feet.

15   Lights went out. The killer returned to Miss Genovese, now trying to make her way around the side of the building by her parking lot to get to her apartment. The assailant stabbed her again.

16   "I'm dying!" she shrieked. "I'm dying!"

17   Windows were opened again, and lights went on in many apartments. The assailant got into his car and drove away. Miss Genovese staggered to her feet. A city bus, O–10, the Lefferts Boulevard line to Kennedy International Airport, passed. It was 3:35 A.M.

The assailant returned. By then, Miss Genovese had crawled to the 18
back of the building where the freshly painted brown doors to the
apartment house held out hope for safety. The killer tried the first door;
she wasn't there. At the second door, 82–62 Austin Street, he saw her
slumped on the floor at the foot of the stairs. He stabbed her a third
time—fatally.

It was 3:50 by the time the police received their first call, from a 19
man who was a neighbor of Miss Genovese. In two minutes they were
at the scene. The neighbor, a 70-year-old woman, and another woman
were the only persons on the street. Nobody else came forward.

The man explained that he had called the police after much delib- 20
eration. He had phoned a friend in Nassau County for advice and then
he had crossed the roof of the building to the apartment of the elderly
woman to get her to make the call.

"I didn't want to get involved," he sheepishly told the police. 21

Six days later, the police arrested Winston Moseley, a 29-year-old 22
business-machine operator, and charged him with homicide. Moseley
had no previous record. He is married, has two children and owns a
home at 133–19 Sutter Avenue, South Ozone Park, Queens. On
Wednesday, a court committed him to Kings County Hospital for psy-
chiatric observation.

When questioned by the police, Moseley also said that he had slain 23
Mrs. Annie May Johnson, 24, of 146–12 133rd Avenue, Jamaica, on Feb.
29 and Barbara Kralik, 15, of 174–17 140th Avenue, Springfield Gardens, last July. In the Kralik case, the police are holding Alvin L.
Mitchell, who is said to have confessed that slaying.

The police stressed how simple it would have been to have gotten 24
in touch with them. "A phone call," said one of the detectives, "would
have done it." The police may be reached by dialing "O" for operator or
SPring 7–3100.

Today witnesses from the neighborhood, which is made up of 25
one-family homes in the $35,000 to $60,000 range with the exception of
the two apartment houses near the railroad station, find it difficult to
explain why they didn't call the police.

A housewife, knowingly if quite casually, said, "We thought it 26
was a lover's quarrel." A husband and wife both said, "Frankly, we were
afraid." They seemed aware of the fact that events might have been
different. A distraught woman, wiping her hands on her apron, said, "I
didn't want my husband to get involved."

One couple, now willing to talk about that night, said they heard 27
the first screams. The husband looked thoughtfully at the bookstore
where the killer first grabbed Miss Genovese.

28   "We went to the window to see what was happening," he said, "but the light from our bedroom made it difficult to see the street." The wife, still apprehensive, added: "I put out the light and we were able to see better."

29   Asked why they hadn't called the police, she shrugged and replied: "I don't know."

30   A man peeked out from a light opening in the doorway to his apartment and rattled off an account of the killer's second attack. Why hadn't he called the police at the time? "I was tired," he said without emotion. "I went back to bed."

31   It was 4:25 A.M. when the ambulance arrived to take the body of Miss Genovese. It drove off. "Then," a solemn police detective said, "the people came out."

____ CONSIDERATIONS ____

1. Obviously—though not overtly—Gansberg's newspaper account condemns the failure of ordinary citizens to feel socially responsible. Explain how the writer makes his purpose obvious without openly stating it. Compare his method with Orwell's use of implication in "A Hanging."

2. In paragraph 7, Gansberg tells us that Catherine Genovese was called Kitty and that she drove a red Fiat. Are these essential details? If not, why does this writer use them?

3. Newspapers use short paragraphs for visual relief. If you were making this story into a narrative essay, how might you change the paragraphing?

4. Is Gansberg's opening sentence a distortion of the facts? Read his account carefully before you answer; then explain and support your answer with reference to other parts of the story.

5. Gansberg's newspaper report was published nearly twenty years ago. Are similar incidents more common now? Were they more common in the 1960s than in the 1940s, 1920s, 1900s? In what way does media coverage affect our impressions? What sources could you use to find the facts?

*Peter Gay (b. 1923) was born in Berlin and came to the
United States in 1941. He took his Ph.D. in history at Columbia
University and has taught at Yale University since 1959. As a
historian, he has written a study of* The Enlightenment *(rev. ed.,
1985) but he writes out of another passion as well. While he was
already a professor of history at Yale, he undertook professional
training at the Western New England Institute for
Psychoanalysis—not in order to become a practitioner but in
order to understand the discipline of psychoanalysis. Among the
results of this understanding is his monumental biography,*
Freud: A Life of Our Time *(1988). He has been a Guggenheim
Fellow and in 1989 was elected to the National Institute of Arts
and Letters.*

This essay is Peter Gay's introduction to Karl Marx, *for
American college students, taken from the third volume of*
Historians at Work *(1975), which Gay edited with Victor G.
Wexler.*

34

PETER GAY
Karl Marx

Of all the historians who appear in this series, none has caused   1
more controversy, attracted more followers, or gathered as many detractors as Karl Marx. Considering Marx's influence and the fact that he
was a pioneer, if not a very judicious practitioner, of economic history,
it is difficult to imagine that with the exception of the *Communist
Manifesto* and perhaps a small fraction of *Das Kapital*, his major works
were virtually unread during his lifetime. Marx, however, was not an
obscure figure in the middle of the nineteenth century. As a political
pamphleteer, as a journalist with a truculent pen, as a radical in exile
from his native Germany, as an implacable foe to all those who dis-

agreed with him, and as a leader of the International Workingmen's Association, he was well known in the Western World. Today his name and the interpretation of history which bears his name are anathema to some, a cause for argument among many, and the objects of veneration in parts of the world he never knew himself. Much of the heat generated by Marxist studies follows the example of Marx's particular style, for it was not enough for him to state his case. He had to insult and denigrate even those from whom he had learned a good deal in order to establish that his doctrine constituted a science; other socialists, who were also economic and social theorists, were to his mind dreamers, idlers, unconscious pawns of the reactionary forces of bourgeois society.

2   The year before Marx was born, his father renounced the Jewish religion and adopted the Lutheranism of his neighbors in the German Rhineland. Marx's antipathy to religion is sometimes attributed to a combination of guilt feelings and resentment that he may have felt as a result of his father's conversion. Actually, the elder Marx's inveterate skepticism made this move far less dramatic than it might seem. What probably impressed the young Marx was the repressive atmosphere of the German Restoration after the defeat of Napoleon and the abolition of the French reforms, which included religious toleration. Marx grew up believing that the Europe of his time was hostile as well as reactionary. When he transferred from the University of Bonn to the University of Berlin in 1836, he was a strong and hardened young man, in addition to being a brilliant student.

3   The dominant intellectual presence at the University of Berlin at that time was Hegel, even though he had died in 1833. His philosophy was taught and debated throughout the University, and it remained a powerful force in German intellectual circles throughout the nineteenth century. Hegel opposed the empiricism and the materialism of the Enlightenment with an elaborate philosophy of history. He maintained that the dynamic factor in the development of peoples and civilizations was not a matter of individual choices or decisive acts. Behind the actual movement of history, Hegel insisted, lay an unfolding spirit that was at once an abstract, rational, and unalterable force constituting the real history of mankind. Such a theory could be interpreted and adapted by students of varying political persuasions. Marx came under the influence of a Hegelian leftist, Moses Hess, who helped him understand how Hegelianism might provide the framework, if not the substance, of a radical political theory.

4   After a brief career as editor-in-chief of the *Rheinische Zeitung*, which he transformed into an organ of vehement protest against the

Prussian government, Marx emigrated to Paris, where, during the years 1843 to 1845, he launched his critique of the conservative interpretation of Hegelianism. Having read the French socialists Fourier and Proudhon, as well as Ludwig Feuerbach's *Theses on Hegelian Philosophy*, Marx, together with Friedrich Engels, his lifelong friend and collaborator, wrote *The German Ideology* in the summer of 1846. In this youthful work the authors claim that "life is not determined by consciousness, but consciousness by life." Hegel was correct in his belief that laws govern history, but those laws themselves, not being the product of ideas or an absolute will, are the product of the material conditions of life. The fabric of the Hegelian dialectic might be preserved, according to Marx and Engels, but it had to be reordered. "In direct contrast to German philosophy," the authors wrote, "which descends from heaven to earth, here we ascend from earth to heaven."

To this early period of Marx's life also belong his *Economic and* 5 *Philosophical Manuscripts of 1844*, which were not published until the twentieth century, as well as his virulent attack on Proudhon, *The Poverty of Philosophy*, published in 1847. Each of these works represents different aspects of Marx's critique of bourgeois society and of those who would reform it. In the 1844 *Manuscripts*, Marx offers an analysis of the role and function of workingmen in the capitalist system, and concludes that the "filthy self-interest" of the owners of private property is responsible for the alienation of the worker from the product of his labor. Whenever the worker is not needed by the capitalist, "he is shunned like the plague." Proudhon sent Marx a copy of his book *The Philosophy of Poverty* before it reached the public in order to elicit what he believed would be sympathetic advice from a fellow critic of industrial society. What Proudhon received was harsh, biting invective, which became Marx's hallmark throughout the remainder of his life. Marx dismissed Proudhon as totally ignorant of the true nature of the Hegelian dialectic and of the scientific inevitability of revolution. With his naïve reforms, Proudhon, like the other socialists and Utopians, was merely prolonging the existing agony of the vast majority of the population.

With the publication of the *Communist Manifesto*, published just 6 a few weeks before the revolution in Paris in 1848, Marx's name became inextricably bound to the Communist League for which he and Engels had written this daring and confident summary of the meaning of world history. The phrases which open and close this work have become part of a catechism for those who accept Marx's argument that capitalism lives on borrowed time allotted to it by the exploitation of the proletariat. Marx is far more than a historian in the *Manifesto;* he is a prophet, an inciter, a thoroughgoing revolutionary. As far as he is concerned, capitalism contains the kernel of its own destruction; because, as it exploits the proletariat, it organizes it, and thus helps precipitate the inevitable revolution. For those who would alter this process with piecemeal reform and gradual improvement of the condition of the working class, he expresses nothing but contempt. Fruitlessly and destructively these socialists endeavor "to deaden the class struggle and reconcile class antagonisms."

7   For all his boldness and swagger, Marx proved to be a poor prophet. Within a year after the appearance of the *Manifesto*, the revolution it was supposed to herald had failed, and Marx was living the life of a penurious exile in London. In 1852, he wrote *The Eighteenth Brumaire* of Louis Napoleon*, which purports to describe the failure of the revolution in France in 1848, and the establishment of the Second Empire under the nephew of Napoleon Bonaparte. Marx's self-imposed task in this history, as is evident in our selections from it, is to unmask the means by which the bourgeoisie swindled the proletariat during this revolution, thus accounting for its egregious failure. The revolution he constructs is a logical retrogressive development. From a bourgeois monarchy to a bourgeois republic, to the restoration of a bourgeois empire, the propertied class made sure that the proletariat would serve only as a means to their ends, and wind up cheated in the end. But Marx concluded with what was for him a sanguine prophecy: the government of Louis Napoleon would be no more successful than that of his uncle nor would any other regime which attempted to exist in defiance of the inexorable march of history, a process that would finally bring the victory to the proletariat, and an end to the class struggle.

8   The chief work of Marx's long isolation in London was *Das Kapital*. He provided in this formidable study an elaborate economic theory, and treated it historically. In the first volume, the only one to appear in his lifetime, he applied his economic theories to the rise of the Industrial Revolution. The later volumes, which Engels edited, discuss the methods employed in the capitalist system to sell products and determine wages and profits. He maintained here, as he always had, that the bourgeoisie exploited the proletariat in holding on to the surplus value of labor, the unearned increment which it did not deserve. He predicted that this exploitation as well as the other ills of the capitalist system, including ruthless competition and overproduction, would eventually

---

* Second month of the calendar of the first French Republic, October 22–November 20.

bring that system to destruction, "when the capitalist husk bursts asunder. The knell of private property sounds. The expropriators are expropriated." At this point, the state, which had been an instrument of oppression, would no longer be needed. The pre-history of mankind would have come to an end.

In London, when he was not at the British Museum library work- 9 ing on *Das Kapital*, or pitifully looking for some work so that his family could eat, he pushed the workers' International in the direction of a single centralized revolution, directed from a common source and toward a common end. Disillusioned by the failure of the Paris Commune of 1871, and heartbroken by the death of his wife, Jenny, Marx went in 1881 to Africa in search of sun and consolation. But he found neither. In 1883, seated in his study in the north of London, he died. He was a powerful indicter of the society that surrounded him, and his memory has been an inspiration to countless social critics, even when those critics no longer accept his philosophy of history. It is also safe to say that his influence on twentieth-century historiography is more pervasive than any other historian's of his time.

___ CONSIDERATIONS _____

1. In paragraph 6, Peter Gay describes Karl Marx as a historian, a prophet, an inciter, a thoroughgoing revolutionary. Which of these aspects did Gay select as a means of organizing his essay?

2. A reader following Marx's political development in Gay's essay must contend with a number of terms that are important to such a discussion yet confusing. They, like other words, not only have a variety of meanings, but have changed in their usage through history. Select one or two examples of such words in "Karl Marx," extract their meanings from a variety of dictionaries, and discuss your conclusions.

3. To give his readers a substantial yet succinct introduction to Marx, Gay employs a variety of devices to compress his material. One is his skillful use of sentence structure. Study the fourth sentence in paragraph 1 to see how structure helped him compact several biographical facts into a single sentence. Try your hand at composing such a sentence.

4. How does Gay make use of Marx's little-known book *The Poverty of Philosophy* to make a general point about his lifetime of writing?

5. Why does Gay conclude his essay with a relatively minor point of interest aimed primarily at a small group of specialists?

6. Is the author of "Karl Marx" himself a Marxist? That is, can you find evidence in the essay that Gay is a proponent or opponent of Marx or of a Marxist version of history?

Stephen Jay Gould (b. 1941) is a paleontologist who teaches at Harvard and writes scientific essays for the general reader. He calls himself "an evolutionist," for Darwin and the theory of evolution live at the center of his mind. He has written five books, of which three collect his periodical essays: Ever Since Darwin *(1977),* The Panda's Thumb *(1980), and* Hen's Teeth and Horse's Toes *(1983). Gould's lively mind, eager to use scientific method for public thinking, seeks out diverse subjects and often discovers a political flavor in matters not usually perceived as political.*

35

STEPHEN JAY GOULD
Wide Hats and Narrow Minds

1   In 1861, from February to June, the ghost of Baron Georges Cuvier haunted the Anthropological Society of Paris. The great Cuvier, Aristotle of French biology (an immodest designation from which he did not shrink), died in 1832, but the physical vault of his spirit lived on as Paul Broca and Louis Pierre Gratiolet squared off to debate whether or not the size of a brain has anything to do with the intelligence of its bearer.

2   In the opening round, Gratiolet dared to argue that the best and brightest could not be recognized by their big heads. (Gratiolet, a confirmed monarchist, was no egalitarian. He merely sought other measures to affirm the superiority of white European males.) Broca, founder of the Anthropological Society and the world's greatest craniometrician, or head measurer, replied that "study of the brains of human races would lose most of its interest and utility" if variation in size counted for nothing. Why, he asked, had anthropologists spent so much time measuring heads if the results had no bearing upon what he regarded as

the most important question of all—the relative worth of different peoples:

> Among the questions heretofore discussed within the Anthropo-
> logical Society, none is equal in interest and importance to the
> question before us now. . . . The great importance of craniology
> has struck anthropologists with such force that many among us
> have neglected the other parts of our science in order to devote
> ourselves almost exclusively to the study of skulls. . . . In such
> data, we hope to find some information relevant to the intellec-
> tual value of the various human races.

Broca and Gratiolet battled for five months and through nearly 200   3
pages of the published bulletin. Tempers flared. In the heat of battle,
one of Broca's lieutenants struck the lowest blow of all: "I have noticed
for a long time that, in general, those who deny the intellectual importance of the brain's volume have small heads." In the end, Broca won,
hands down. During the debate, no item of information had been more
valuable to Broca, none more widely discussed or more vigorously
contended, than the brain of Georges Cuvier.

Cuvier, the greatest anatomist of his time, the man who revised   4
our understanding of animals by classifying them according to
function—how they work—rather than by rank in an anthropocentric
scale of lower to higher. Cuvier, the founder of paleontology, the man
who first established the fact of extinction and who stressed the importance of catastrophes in understanding the history both of life and the
earth. Cuvier, the great statesman who, like Talleyrand, managed to
serve all French governments, from revolution to monarchy, and die in
bed. (Actually, Cuvier passed the most tumultuous years of the revolution as a private tutor in Normandy, although he feigned revolutionary
sympathies in his letters. He arrived in Paris in 1795 and never left.)
F. Bourdier, a recent biographer, describes Cuvier's corporeal ontogeny,
but his words also serve as a good metaphor for Cuvier's power and
influence: "Cuvier was short and during the Revolution he was very
thin; he became stouter during the Empire; and he grew enormously fat
after the Restoration."

Cuvier's contemporaries marveled at his "massive head." One   5
admirer affirmed that it "gave to his entire person an undeniable cachet
of majesty and to his face an expression of profound meditation." Thus,
when Cuvier died, his colleagues, in the interests of science and curiosity, decided to open the great skull. On Tuesday, May 15, 1832, at
seven o'clock in the morning, a group of the greatest doctors and biolo-

gists of France gathered to dissect the body of Georges Cuvier. They began with the internal organs and, finding "nothing very remarkable," switched their attention to Cuvier's skull. "Thus," wrote the physician in charge, "we were about to contemplate the instrument of this powerful intelligence." And their expectations were rewarded. The brain of Georges Cuvier weighed 1,830 grams, more than 400 grams above average and 200 grams larger than any nondiseased brain previously weighed. Unconfirmed reports and uncertain inference placed the brains of Oliver Cromwell, Jonathan Swift, and Lord Byron in the same range, but Cuvier had provided the first direct evidence that brilliance and brain size go together.

6   Broca pushed his advantage and rested a good part of his case on Cuvier's brain. But Gratiolet probed and found a weak spot. In their awe and enthusiasm, Cuvier's doctors had neglected to save either his brain or his skull. Moreover, they reported no measures on the skull at all. The figure of 1,830 g for the brain could not be checked; perhaps it was simply wrong. Gratiolet sought an existing surrogate and had a flash of inspiration: "All brains are not weighed by doctors," he stated, "but all heads are measured by hatters and I have managed to acquire, from this new source, information which, I dare to hope, will not appear to you as devoid of interest." In short, Gratiolet presented something almost bathetic in comparison with the great man's brain: he had found Cuvier's hat! And thus, for two meetings, some of France's greatest minds pondered seriously the meaning of a worn bit of felt.

7   Cuvier's hat, Gratiolet reported, measured 21.8 cm in length and 18.0 cm in width. He then consulted a certain M. Puriau, "one of the most intelligent and widely known hatters of Paris." Puriau told him that the largest standard size for hats measured 21.5 by 18.5 cm. Although very few men wore a hat so big, Cuvier was not off scale. Moreover, Gratiolet reported with evident pleasure, the hat was extremely flexible and "softened by very long usage." It had probably not been so large when Cuvier bought it. Moreover, Cuvier had an exceptionally thick head of hair, and he wore it bushy. "This seems to prove quite clearly," Gratiolet proclaimed, "that if Cuvier's head was very large, its size was not absolutely exceptional or unique."

8   Gratiolet's opponents preferred to believe the doctors and refused to grant much weight to a bit of cloth. More than twenty years later, in 1883, G. Hervé again took up the subject of Cuvier's brain and discovered a missing item: Cuvier's head had been measured after all, but the figures had been omitted from the autopsy report. The skull was big indeed. Shaved of that famous mat of hair, as it was for the autopsy, its

greatest circumference could be equaled by only 6 percent of "scientists and men of letters" (measured in life with their hair at that) and zero percent of domestic servants. As for the infamous hat, Hervé pleaded ignorance, but he did cite the following anecdote: "Cuvier had a habit of leaving his hat on a table in his waiting room. It often happened that a professor or a statesman tried it on. The hat descended below their eyes."

Yet, just as the doctrine of more-is-better stood on the verge of triumph, Hervé snatched potential defeat from the jaws of Broca's victory. Too much of a good thing can be as troubling as a deficiency, and Hervé began to worry. Why did Cuvier's brain exceed those of other "men of genius" by so much? He reviewed both details of the autopsy and records of Cuvier's frail early health and constructed a circumstantial case for "transient juvenile hydrocephaly," or water on the brain. If Cuvier's skull had been artificially enlarged by the pressure of fluids early during its growth, then a brain of normal size might simply have expanded—by decreasing in density, not by growing larger—into the space available. Or did an enlarged space permit the brain to grow to an unusual size after all? Hervé could not resolve this cardinal question because Cuvier's brain had been measured and then tossed out. All that remained was the magisterial number, 1,830 grams. "With the brain of Cuvier," wrote Hervé, "science has lost one of the most precious documents it ever possessed."

On the surface, this tale seems ludicrous. The thought of France's finest anthropologists arguing passionately about the meaning of a dead colleague's hat could easily provoke the most misleading and dangerous inference of all about history—a view of the past as a domain of naive half-wits, the path of history as a tale of progress, and the present as sophisticated and enlightened.

But if we laugh with derision, we will never understand. Human intellectual capacity has not altered for thousands of years so far as we can tell. If intelligent people invested intense energy in issues that now seem foolish to us, then the failure lies in our understanding of their world, not in their distorted perceptions. Even the standard example of ancient nonsense—the debate about angels on pinheads—makes sense once you realize that theologians were not discussing whether five or eighteen would fit, but whether a pin could house a finite or an infinite number. In certain theological systems, the corporeality or noncorporeality of angels is an important matter indeed.

In this case, a clue to the vital importance of Cuvier's brain for nineteenth-century anthropology lies in the last line of Broca's

9

10

11

12

statement, quoted above: "In such data, we hope to find some information relevant to the intellectual value of the various human races." Broca and his school wanted to show that brain size, through its link with intelligence, could resolve what they regarded as the primary question for a "science of man"—explaining why some individuals and groups are more successful than others. To do this, they separated people according to a priori convictions about their worth—men versus women, whites versus blacks, "men of genius" versus ordinary folks— and tried to demonstrate differences in brain size. The brains of eminent men (literally males) formed an essential link in their argument— and Cuvier was the *crème de la crème.* Broca concluded:

> In general, the brain is larger in men than in women, in eminent men than in men of mediocre talent, in superior races than in inferior races. Other things equal, there is a remarkable relationship between the development of intelligence and the volume of the brain.

13   Broca died in 1880, but disciples continued his catalog of eminent brains (indeed, they added Broca's own to the list—although it weighed in at an undistinguished 1,484 grams). The dissection of famous colleagues became something of a cottage industry among anatomists and anthropologists. E.A. Spitzka, the most prominent American practitioner of the trade, cajoled his eminent friends: "To me the thought of an autopsy is certainly less repugnant than I imagine the process of cadaveric decomposition in the grave to be." The two premier American ethnologists, John Wesley Powell and W. J. McGee made a wager over who had the larger brain—and Spitzka contracted to resolve the issue for them posthumously. (It was a toss-up. The brains of Powell and McGee differed very little, no more than varying body size might require.)

14   By 1907, Spitzka could present a tabulation of 115 eminent men. As the list grew in length, ambiguity of results increased apace. At the upper end, Cuvier was finally overtaken when Turgenev broke the 2,000-gram barrier in 1883. But embarrassment and insult stalked the other end. Walt Whitman managed to hear the varied carols of America singing with only 1,282 g. Franz Josef Gall, a founder of phrenology— the original "science" of judging mental worth by the size of localized brain areas—could muster only 1,198 g. Later, in 1924, Anatole France almost halved Turgenev's 2,012 and weighed in at a mere 1,017 g.

15   Spitzka, nonetheless, was undaunted. In an outrageous example of data selected to conform with a priori prejudice, he arranged, in order, a

large brain from an eminent white male, a bushwoman from Africa, and a gorilla. (He could easily have reversed the first two by choosing a larger black and a smaller white.) Spitzka concluded, again invoking the shade of Georges Cuvier: "The jump from a Cuvier or a Thackeray to a Zulu or a Bushman is no greater than from the latter to the gorilla or the orang."

Such overt racism is no longer common among scientists, and I 16 trust that no one would now try to rank races or sexes by the average size of their brains. Yet our fascination with the physical basis of intelligence persists (as it should), and the naïve hope remains in some quarters that size of some other unambiguous external feature might capture the subtlety within. Indeed, the crassest form of more-is-better—using an easily measured quantity to assess improperly a far more subtle and elusive quality—is still with us. And the method that some men use to judge the worth of their penises or their automobiles is still being applied to brains. This essay was inspired by recent reports on the whereabouts of Einstein's brain. Yes, Einstein's brain was removed for study, but a quarter century after his death, the results have not been published. The remaining pieces—others were farmed out to various specialists—now rest in a Mason jar packed in a cardboard box marked "Costa Cider" and housed in an office in Wichita, Kansas. Nothing has been published because nothing unusual has been found. "So far it's fallen within normal limits for a man his age," remarked the owner of the Mason jar.

Did I just hear Cuvier and Anatole France laughing in concert from 17 on high? Are they repeating a famous motto of their native land: *plus ça change, plus c'est la même chose* ("the more things change, the more they remain the same"). The physical structure of the brain must record intelligence in some way, but gross size and external shape are not likely to capture anything of value. I am, somehow, less interested in the weight and convolutions of Einstein's brain than in the near certainty that people of equal talent have lived and died in cotton fields and sweatshops.

_____ CONSIDERATIONS _____

1. Stephen Jay Gould's essays typically reveal the writer's lively interest in research. Read a few of his other short pieces—see titles of his collections in the headnote preceding this essay—and comment on some of the other qualities they share.

2. Why, according to Gould, is the-bigger-the-better the "crassest form" of classifying quality? Cite an example from a current advertisement.

3. Gould's essay might well be taken as a satire if it were not for paragraph 11. Explain how that passage runs counter to the usual pursuits of satirists.

4. What very specific detail mentioned in paragraph 16 expresses Gould's opinion of the importance of the research conducted by Gratiolet, Broca, Spitzka, and others. Explain. (The detail has nothing to do with brain size.)

5. What does Gould mean in paragraph 15 when he accuses Spitzka of "an outrageous example of data selected to conform with a priori prejudice"? Concoct your own example in a paragraph satirizing distortion of some recent bit of market or consumer research.

John Haines (b. 1924), who homesteaded in Alaska from 1947 through 1969, still lives there, when he can, at the address "Mile 68, Richardson Highway." He is first of all a poet, with his many books including News from the Glacier: Selected Poems 1960–1980 *(1982); his essays are collected in* Living Off the Country: Essays on Poetry and Place *(1981) and* The Stars, The Snow, The Fire *(1989).*

36

JOHN HAINES
Snow

To one who lives in the snow and watches it day by day, it is a 1 book to be read. The pages turn as the wind blows; the characters shift and the images formed by their combinations change in meaning, but the language remains the same. It is a shadow language, spoken by things that have gone by and will come again. The same text has been written there for thousands of years, though I was not here, and will not be here in winters to come, to read it. These seemingly random ways, these paths, these beds, these footprints, these hard, round pellets in the snow: they all have meaning. Dark things may be written there, news of other lives, their sorties and excursions, their terrors and deaths. The tiny feet of a shrew or a vole make a brief, erratic pattern across the snow, and here is a hole down which the animal goes. And now the track of an ermine comes this way, swift and searching, and he too goes down that white shadow of a hole.

A wolverine, and the loping, toed-in track I followed uphill for two 2 miles one spring morning, until it finally dropped away into another watershed and I gave up following it. I wanted to see where he would go and what he would do. But he just went on, certain of where he was going, and nothing came of it for me to see but that sure and steady track in the snowcrust, and the sunlight strong in my eyes.

203

3   Snow blows across the highway before me as I walk—little, wavering trails of it swept along like a people dispersed. The snow people—where are they going? Some great danger must pursue them. They hurry and fall; the wind gives them a push, they get up and go on again.

4   I was walking home from Redmond Creek one morning late in January. On a divide between two watersheds I came upon the scene of a battle between a moose and three wolves. The story was written plainly in the snow at my feet. The wolves had come in from the west, following an old trail from the Salcha River, and had found the moose feeding in an open stretch of the overgrown road I was walking.

5   The sign was fresh, it must have happened the night before. The snow was torn up, with chunks of frozen moss and broken sticks scattered about; here and there, swatches of moose hair. A confusion of tracks in the trampled snow—the splayed, stabbing feet of the moose, the big, furred pads and spread toenails of the wolves.

6   I walked on, watching the snow. The moose was large and alone, almost certainly a bull. In one place he backed himself into a low, brush-hung bank to protect his rear. The wolves moved away from him—those moose feet are dangerous. The moose turned, ran on for fifty yards, and the fight began again. It became a running, broken fight that went on for nearly half a mile in the changing, rutted terrain, the red morning light coming across the hills from the sun low in the south. A pattern shifting and uncertain; the wolves relenting, running out into the brush in a wide circle, and closing again: another patch of moose hair in the trodden snow.

7   I felt that I knew those wolves. I had seen their tracks several times before during that winter, and once they had taken a marten from one of my traps. I believed them to be a female and two nearly grown pups. If I was right, she may have been teaching them how to hunt, and all that turmoil in the snow may have been the serious play of things that must kill to live. But I saw no blood sign that morning, and the moose seemed to have gotten the better of the fight. At the end of it he plunged away into thick alder brush. I saw his tracks, moving more slowly now, as he climbed through a low saddle, going north in the shallow, unbroken snow. The three wolves trotted east toward Banner Creek.

8   What might have been silence, an unwritten page, an absence, spoke to me as clearly as if I had been there to see it. I have imagined a

man who might live as the coldest scholar on earth, who followed each clue in the snow, writing a book as he went. It would be the history of snow, the book of winter. A thousand-year text to be read by a people hunting these hills in a distant time. Who was here, and who has gone? What were their names? What did they kill and eat? Whom did they leave behind?

____ CONSIDERATIONS ____

1. John Haines's first paragraph is pleasant to read; it also demonstrates a particular literary device we all know but, more commonly than not, forget to use ourselves. Study how Haines chose to introduce his subject in that paragraph until you're sure you have identified that device and understand how it works. Then try using it yourself in a paragraph on a different subject of your own choosing. What special requirement is imposed on you if you are to extend that device through a whole paragraph?

2. Since nothing happened when he followed the wolverine in paragraph 2, why does Haines tell us about it?

3. John Haines "reads" snow. Other than words on a page, what do you "read"?

4. After teaching us something about seeing and interpreting—that is, "reading"—what does Haines do that is sobering?

Jean Hegland (b. 1956) did graduate work and taught
composition at Eastern Washington University. Now she lives
with her family in northern California, writing fiction and
essays, and teaches creative writing at Santa Rosa Junior
College. "Fourth Month"—part of the forthcoming Life Within:
Celebration of a Pregnancy—*appeared in* Spiritual Mothering *in*
1989.

37

JEAN HEGLAND
Fourth Month

Woman is the artist of the imagination and the child in the
womb is the canvas whereon she painteth her pictures.

Paracelsus (1493–1541)

1   For several days I thought they were just the soft rumblings of my
own guts, these dim twistings low in my belly. But then one morning as
we lay in bed, the twister's father put his hand on my stomach and felt a
nudge at the same time I felt a poke. After months of gyrating unob-
served, this creature had finally made itself indisputably known, its
delicate flutters like a message from a distant planet or a deserted
island—there is life here, too! It tapped against its father's palm once
more, and then was still, indifferent to our sudden joy, to the hot blaze
of tears in its parents' eyes.

2   It feels like a kiss, this quickening, like another's tongue slipping
and curling inside my mouth. The Eskimos said that the aurora borealis
was the playing of unborn children. I have seen only the dim, southern
version of those northern lights, but still, this sensation is like that,
ghostly, lovely, a dance performed in the darkness of another world.

Now as I go about my days, I am aware of the baby brewing inside 3
me, and it suprises me that the pattern of my life is not completely
transformed by this quickening. At night, when I lie next to Douglas, I
feel the tumbling of the child we have set in motion, and I think I am
a priestess privy to the mysteries of the gods. But at other times
this tickling in my guts comes as no suprise. Like the passing of
gas, or the beating of a heart, it is a familiar feeling, comfortable,
homey, and often it seems usual, normal, to have this movement inside me.

I feel newly fond of this old body, now that it is more than just the 4
vehicle of my own continuance. I have forgiven its many curves and
softnesses, and I am proud of the neat little bulge of my belly, pleased
with my swollen breasts and their thick brown nipples. No longer
mine, more than myself, I have become a catalyst, a resource, a riddle. I
am a boat which contains an ocean, a basket filling with a single egg. I
am a cradle, a crucible, a garden.

"Quicken" means to come to life, and it does seem as though this 5
baby had just begun, now that I can feel its presence. And now that I can
distinguish between us, I feel more connection to it than I did before.
With these first quiet nudges comes the nascence of love.

In Egypt, they say that the heart sees the baby before the eye. But 6
even a heart must be able to see before it can love. Our organs cannot
love themselves, and even a heart can only love what is outside of and
other than itself, because such a great part of loving is that longing to
bridge that distance. Now that it is tangibly separate from me, I find
myself asking the lover's question of this finger-length child tucked
beneath my heart: dear Trout, what is it like for you? They say that
already your face, with its newly finished lips, is like no one else's face.
Already, the lines that tell your fortune are etched into your pea-sized
palms. Already, the whorls have risen on the pads of your fingertips and
in the flesh of your feet. What is it like to have that face, those feet and
hands?

I wish I could be a twin in your womb, to know what it is you 7
know. I wish I could hear the sounds and silences that your ears have
just begun to hear, could feel the currents of amniotic fluid on your raw
skin, and the elastic give of the walls that contain you. I wish I could
learn exactly what this time is like for you. But as I ask those questions
to which I know I will never find answers, I learn something else. I learn
that imagination is the essence of love.

—— **CONSIDERATIONS** ————————————————————

1. In what way does the author of "Fourth Month" prepare us for the surprising conclusion: "I learn that imagination is the essence of love"?

2. Although "Fourth Month" is a subjective expression of what the pregnant woman experiences, the writer's research is skillfully put to work in this short essay. Find examples of that research.

3. How does her awareness of her developing baby affect the mother's image of herself?

4. Each of the chapters of Hegland's book, *The Life Within*, from which "Fourth Month" was taken, begins with a quotation from a different source. What do you think of an author's use of such material? Can you imagine using one of Ambrose Bierce's "Devil's Definitions" at the head of an essay you might write?

Lillian Hellman (1905–1984) was a playwright, born in New Orleans, who grew up in New Orleans and New York City. After graduating from New York University, she went to work in publishing. The Children's Hour *(1934), her first great success on Broadway, was followed by her most famous play,* The Little Foxes *(1939), and* Watch on the Rhine *(1941). She also wrote the book for Leonard Bernstein's musical* Candide.

Hellman's later works were autobiographical, and include Pentimento *(1973),* Scoundrel Time *(1977), and* An Unfinished Woman, *which won the National Book Award in 1970. These narratives were collected into one volume with new commentary by the author:* Three *(1979). In 1980 she published* Maybe: A Story.

The anecdote below, which is from An Unfinished Woman, *tells of a climactic episode in the transition from childhood to adolescence, and shows the rebelliousness, strong feeling, and independence that become themes of the autobiography.*

38

LILLIAN HELLMAN
Runaway

It was that night that I disappeared, and that night that Fizzy said I   1
was disgusting mean, and Mr. Stillman said I would forever pain my mother and father, and my father turned on both of them and said he would handle his family affairs himself without comments from strangers. But he said it too late. He had come home very angry with me: the jeweler, after my father's complaints about his unreliability, had found the lock of hair in the back of the watch. What started out to be a mild reproof on my father's part soon turned angry when I wouldn't explain about the hair. (My father was often angry when I was most like him.) He was so angry that he forgot that he was attacking me in front of the Stillmans, my old rival Fizzy, and the delighted Mrs. Dreyfus, a

new, rich boarder who only that afternoon had complained about my bad manners. My mother left the room when my father grew angry with me. Hannah, passing through, put up her hand as if to stop my father and then, frightened of the look he gave her, went out to the porch. I sat on the couch, astonished at the pain in my head. I tried to get up from the couch, but one ankle turned and I sat down again, knowing for the first time the rampage that could be caused in me by anger. The room began to have other forms, the people were no longer men and women, my head was not my own. I told myself that my head had gone somewhere and I have little memory of anything after my Aunt Jenny came into the room and said to my father, "Don't you remember?" I have never known what she meant, but I knew that soon after I was moving up the staircase, that I slipped and fell a few steps, that when I woke up hours later in my bed, I found a piece of angel cake—an old love, an old custom—left by my mother on my pillow. The headache was worse and I vomited out of the window. Then I dressed, took my red purse, and walked a long way down St. Charles Avenue. A St. Charles Avenue mansion had on its back lawn a famous doll's-house, an elaborate copy of the mansion itself, built years before for the small daughter of the house. As I passed this showpiece, I saw a policeman and moved swiftly back to the doll palace and crawled inside. If I had known about the fantasies of the frightened, that ridiculous small house would not have been so terrible for me. I was surrounded by ornate, carved reproductions of the mansion furniture, scaled for children, bisque figurines in miniature, a working toilet seat of gold leaf in suitable size, small draperies of damask with a sign that said "From the damask of Marie Antoinette," a miniature samovar with small bronze cups, and a tiny Madame Récamier couch on which I spent the night, my legs on the floor. I must have slept, because I woke from a nightmare and knocked over a bisque figurine. The noise frightened me, and since it was now almost light, in one of those lovely mist mornings of late spring when every flower in New Orleans seems to melt and mix with the air, I crawled out. Most of that day I spent walking, although I had a long session in the ladies' room of the railroad station. I had four dollars and two bits, but that wasn't much when you meant it to last forever and when you knew it would not be easy for a fourteen-year-old girl to find work in a city where too many people knew her. Three times I stood in line at the railroad ticket windows to ask where I could go for four dollars, but each time the question seemed too dangerous and I knew no other way of asking.

2   Toward evening, I moved to the French Quarter, feeling sad and

envious as people went home to dinner. I bought a few Tootsie Rolls
and a half loaf of bread and went to the St. Louis Cathedral in Jackson
Square. (It was that night that I composed the prayer that was to become, in the next five years, an obsession, mumbled over and over
through the days and nights: "God forgive me, Papa forgive me, Mama
forgive me, Sophronia, Jenny, Hannah, and all others, through this time
and that time, in life and in death." When I was nineteen, my father,
who had made several attempts through the years to find out what my
lip movements meant as I repeated the prayer, said, "How much would
you take to stop that? Name it and you've got it." I suppose I was sick of
the nonsense by that time because I said, "A leather coat and a feather
fan," and the next day he bought them for me.) After my loaf of bread, I
went looking for a bottle of soda pop and discovered, for the first time,
the whorehouse section around Bourbon Street. The women were
ranged in the doorways of the cribs, making the first early evening offers
to sailors, who were the only men in the streets. I wanted to stick
around and see how things like that worked, but the second or third
time I circled the block, one of the girls called out to me. I couldn't
understand the words, but the voice was angry enough to make me run
toward the French Market.

The Market was empty except for two old men. One of them called   3
to me as I went past, and I turned to see that he had opened his pants and
was shaking what my circle called "his thing." I flew across the street
into the coffee stand, forgetting that the owner had known me since I
was a small child when my Aunt Jenny would rest from her marketing
tour with a cup of fine, strong coffee.

He said, in the patois, "*Que faites, ma 'fant? Je suis fermé.*"   4

I said, "*Rien. My tante attend*"—Could I have a doughnut?   5

He brought me two doughnuts, saying one was *lagniappe*, but I   6
took my doughnuts outside when he said, "*Mais ou est vo' tante à
c'heure?*"

I fell asleep with my doughnuts behind a shrub in Jackson Square.   7
The night was damp and hot and through the sleep were many voices
and, much later, there was music from somewhere near the river. When
all sounds had ended, I woke, turned my head, and knew I was being
watched. Two rats were sitting a few feet from me. I urinated on my
dress, crawled backwards to stand up, screamed as I ran up the steps of
St. Louis Cathedral and pounded on the doors. I don't know when I
stopped screaming or how I got to the railroad station, but I stood
against the wall trying to tear off my dress and only knew I was doing it
when two women stopped to stare at me. I began to have cramps in my

stomach of a kind I had never known before. I went to the ladies' room and sat bent in a chair, whimpering with pain. After a while the cramps stopped, but I had an intimation, when I looked into the mirror, of something happening to me: my face was blotched, and there seemed to be circles and twirls I had never seen before, the straight blonde hair was damp with sweat, and a paste of green from the shrub had made lines on my jaw. I had gotten older.

8   Sometime during that early morning I half washed my dress, threw away my pants, put cold water on my hair. Later in the morning a cleaning woman appeared, and after a while began to ask questions that frightened me. When she put down her mop and went out of the room, I ran out of the station. I walked, I guess, for many hours, but when I saw a man on Canal Street who worked in Hannah's office, I realized that the sections of New Orleans that were known to me were dangerous for me.

9   Years before, when I was a small child, Sophronia and I would go to pick up, or try on, pretty embroidered dresses that were made for me by a colored dressmaker called Bibettera. A block up from Bibettera's there had been a large ruin of a house with a sign, ROOMS—CLEAN—CHEAP, and cheerful people seemed always to be moving in and out of the house. The door of the house was painted a bright pink. I liked that and would discuss with Sophronia why we didn't live in a house with a pink door.

10   Bibettera was long since dead, so I knew I was safe in this Negro neighborhood. I went up and down the block several times, praying that things would work and I could take my cramps to bed. I knocked on the pink door. It was answered immediately by a small young man.

11   I said, "Hello." He said nothing.

12   I said, "I would like to rent a room, please."

13   He closed the door but I waited, thinking he had gone to get the lady of the house. After a long time, a middle-aged woman put her head out of a second-floor window and said, "What you at?"

14   I said, "I would like to rent a room, please. My mama is a widow and has gone to work across the river. She gave me money and said to come here until she called for me."

15   "Who your mama?"

16   "Er. My mama."

17   "What you at? Speak out."

18   "I told you. I have money . . ." But as I tried to open my purse, the voice grew angry.

19   "This is a nigger house. Get you off. *Vite.*"

20   I said, in a whisper, "I know. I'm part nigger."

The small young man opened the front door. He was laughing.   21
"You part mischief. Get the hell out of here."

I said, "Please"—and then, "I'm related to Sophronia Mason. She   22
told me to come. Ask her."

Sophronia and her family were respected figures in New Orleans   23
Negro circles, and because I had some vague memory of her stately bow
to somebody as she passed this house, I believed they knew her. If they
told her about me I would be in trouble, but phones were not usual then
in poor neighborhoods, and I had no other place to go.

The woman opened the door. Slowly I went into the hall.   24

I said, "I won't stay long. I have four dollars and Sophronia will   25
give more if . . ."

The woman pointed up the stairs. She opened the door of a small   26
room. "Washbasin place down the hall. Toilet place behind the kitchen.
Two-fifty and no fuss, no bother."

I said, "Yes, ma'am, yes ma'am," but as she started to close the   27
door, the young man appeared.

"Where your bag?"   28

"Bag?"   29

"Nobody put up here without no bag."   30

"Oh. You mean the bag with my clothes? It's at the station. I'll go   31
and get it later . . ." I stopped because I knew I was about to say I'm
sick, I'm in pain, I'm frightened.

He said, "I say you lie. I say you trouble. I say you get out."   32

I said, "And I say you shut up."   33

Years later, I was to understand why the command worked, and to   34
be sorry that it did, but that day I was very happy when he turned and
closed the door. I was asleep within minutes.

Toward evening, I went down the stairs, saw nobody, walked a few   35
blocks and bought myself an oyster loaf. But the first bite made me feel
sick, so I took my loaf back to the house. This time, as I climbed the
steps, there were three women in the parlor, and they stopped talking
when they saw me. I went back to sleep immediately, dizzy and nauseated.

I woke to a high, hot sun and my father standing at the foot of the   36
bed staring at the oyster loaf.

He said, "Get up now and get dressed."   37

I was crying as I said, "Thank you, Papa, but I can't."   38

From the hall, Sophronia said, "Get along up now. *Vite.* The   39
morning is late."

My father left the room. I dressed and came into the hall carrying   40 my oyster loaf. Sophronia was standing at the head of the stairs. She pointed out, meaning my father was on the street.

41   I said, "He humiliated me. He did. I won't . . ."

42   She said, "Get you going or I will never see you whenever again."

43   I ran past her to the street. I stood with my father until Sophronia joined us, and then we walked slowly, without speaking, to the street-car line. Sophronia bowed to us, but she refused my father's hand when he attempted to help her into the car. I ran to the car meaning to ask her to take me with her, but the car moved and she raised her hand as if to stop me. My father and I walked again for a long time.

44   He pointed to a trash can sitting in front of a house. "Please put that oyster loaf in the can."

45   At Vanalli's restaurant, he took my arm. "Hungry?"

46   I said, "No, thank you, Papa."

47   But we went through the door. It was, in those days, a New Orleans custom to have an early black coffee, go to the office, and after a few hours have a large breakfast at a restaurant. Vanalli's was crowded, the headwaiter was so sorry, but after my father took him aside, a very small table was put up for us—too small for my large father, who was accommodating himself to it in a manner most unlike him.

48   He said, "Jack, my rumpled daughter would like cold crayfish, a nice piece of pompano, separate bowl of Béarnaise sauce, don't ask me why, French fried potatoes . . ."

49   I said, "Thank you, Papa, but I am not hungry. I don't want to be here."

50   My father waved the waiter away and we sat in silence until the crayfish came. My hand reached out instinctively and then drew back.

51   My father said, "Your mother and I have had an awful time."

52   I said, "I'm sorry about that. But I don't want to go home, Papa."

53   He said, angrily, "Yes, you do. But you want me to apologize first. I do apologize but you should not have made me say it."

54   After a while I mumbled, "God forgive me, Papa forgive me, Mama forgive me, Sophronia, Jenny, Hannah . . ."

55   "Eat your crayfish."

56   I ate everything he had ordered and then a small steak. I suppose I had been mumbling throughout my breakfast.

57   My father said, "You're talking to yourself. I can't hear you. What are you saying.?"

58   "God forgive me, Papa forgive me, Mama forgive me, Sophronia, Jenny . . ."

My father said, "Where do we start your training as the first Jewish   59
nun on Prytania Street?"

When I finished laughing, I liked him again. I said, "Papa, I'll tell   60
you a secret. I've had very bad cramps and I am beginning to bleed. I'm
changing life."

He stared at me for a while. Then he said, "Well, it's not the way   61
it's usually described, but it's accurate, I guess. Let's go home now to
your mother."

We were never, as long as my mother and father lived, to mention   62
that time again. But it was of great importance to them and I've thought
about it all my life. From that day on I knew my power over my parents.
That was not to be too important: I was ashamed of it and did not abuse
it too much. But I found out something more useful and more dangerous: if you are willing to take the punishment, you are halfway through
the battle. That the issue may be trivial, the battle ugly, is another
point.

_____ CONSIDERATIONS _____

1. Hellman's recollection of running away at fourteen is complicated by
her refusal to tell it in strict chronology. Instead, she interrupts the narrative
with flashbacks and episodes of later years. How can one justify such interrup-
tions?

2. On page 213, as she is trying to talk her way into the rooming house in
the black district, Hellman tells a young man to shut up and then adds, "Years
later, I was to understand why the command worked, and to be sorry that it
did." What did she later understand?

3. What was the "power over my parents" that Hellman learned from her
runaway experience? Have you ever wielded such power?

4. Accounts of childhood escapades often suffer as the author idealizes or
glamorizes them. Does Hellman successfully resist the temptation? What is
your evidence?

5. The bases the fourteen-year-old runaway touched in her flight were
actually part of a familiar world; a doll's house, a cathedral, a market, a railroad
station. How does Hellman give her flight more than a touch of horror?

6. In what specific ways did her first menstrual period heighten and
distort some of the things that happened—or seemed to happen—to the
fourteen-year-old runaway? Discuss the ways in which physiological and
psychological conditions seem to feed on each other.

Ernest Hemingway (1899–1961) was an ambulance driver and a soldier in World War I, and made use of these experiences in his novel A Farewell to Arms *(1929). One of the Lost Generation of expatriate American writers who lived in Paris in the twenties—a time described in his memoir,* A Moveable Feast *(1964)—he was a great prose stylist and innovator, who received a Nobel Prize for literature in 1954. Other Hemingway novels include* The Sun Also Rises *(1926),* To Have and Have Not *(1937),* For Whom the Bell Tolls *(1940), and* The Garden of Eden, *which was discovered recently and published posthumously in 1986. His* Selected Letters, *edited by Carlos Baker, appeared in 1981.*

Many critics prefer Hemingway's short stories to his novels, and his early stories—"Hills Like White Elephants" among them—to his later ones. This early prose is plain, simple, and clean. This story is dialogue virtually without narrative or description or interpretation; yet when we have finished it we have met two people whom we will not easily forget.

39

ERNEST HEMINGWAY
Hills Like White Elephants

The hills across the valley of the Ebro were long and white. On this side there was no shade and no trees and the station was between two lines of rails in the sun. Close against the side of the station there was the warm shadow of the building and a curtain, made of strings of bamboo beads, hung across the open door into the bar, to keep out flies. The American and the girl with him sat at a table in the shade, outside the building. It was very hot and the express from Barcelona would come in forty minutes. It stopped at this junction for two minutes and went on to Madrid.

"What should we drink?" the girl asked. She had taken off her hat 10
and put it on the table.

"It's pretty hot," the man said.

"Let's drink beer."

"Dos cervezas," the man said into the curtain.

"Big ones?" a woman asked from the doorway. 15

"Yes. Two big ones."

The woman brought two glasses of beer and two felt pads. She put
the felt pads and the beer glasses on the table and looked at the man and
the girl. The girl was looking off at the line of hills. They were white in
the sun and the country was brown and dry. 20

"They look like white elephants," she said.

"I've never seen one." The man drank his beer.

"No, you wouldn't have."

"I might have," the man said. "Just because you say I wouldn't
have doesn't prove anything." 25

The girl looked at the bead curtain. "They've painted something
on it," she said. "What does it say?"

"Anis del Toro. It's a drink."

"Could we try it?"

The man called "Listen" through the curtain. 30

The woman came out from the bar.

"Four reales."

"We want two Anis del Toros."

"With water?"

"Do you want it with water?" 35

"I don't know," the girl said. "Is it good with water?"

"It's all right."

"You want them with water?" asked the woman.

"Yes, with water."

"It tastes like licorice," the girl said and put the glass down. 40

"That's the way with everything."

"Yes," said the girl. "Everything tastes of licorice. Especially all
the things you've waited so long for, like absinthe."

"Oh, cut it out."

"You started it," the girl said. "I was being amused. I was having a 45
fine time."

"Well, let's try and have a fine time."

"All right. I was trying. I said the mountains looked like white
elephants. Wasn't that bright?"

"That was bright." 50

"I wanted to try this new drink. That's all we do, isn't it—look at things and try new drinks?"

"I guess so."

The girl looked across at the hills.

55 "They're lovely hills," she said. "They don't really look like white elephants. I just meant the colouring of their skin through the trees."

"Should we have another drink?"

"All right."

The warm wind blew the bead curtain against the table.

60 "The beer's nice and cool," the man said.

"It's lovely," the girl said.

"It's really an awfully simple operation, Jig," the man said. "It's not really an operation at all."

The girl looked at the ground the table legs rested on.

65 "I know you wouldn't mind it, Jig. It's really not anything. It's just to let the air in."

The girl did not say anything.

"I'll go with you and I'll stay with you all the time. They just let the air in and then it's all perfectly natural."

70 "Then what will we do afterwards?"

"We'll be fine afterwards. Just like we were before."

"What makes you think so?"

"That's the only thing that bothers us. It's the only thing that's made us unhappy."

75 The girl looked at the bead curtain, put her hand out and took hold of two of the strings of beads.

"And you think then we'll be all right and be happy."

"I know we will. You don't have to be afraid. I've known lots of people that have done it."

80 "So have I," said the girl. "And afterward they were all so happy."

"Well," the man said, "if you don't want to you don't have to. I wouldn't have you do it if you didn't want to. But I know it's perfectly simple."

"And you really want to?"

85 "I think it's the best thing to do. But I don't want you to do it if you don't really want to."

"And if I do it you'll be happy and things will be like they were and you'll love me?"

"I love you now. You know I love you."

90 "I know. But if I do it, then it will be nice again if I say things are like white elephants, and you'll like it?"

"I'll love it. I love it now but I just can't think about it. You know how I get when I worry."

"If I do it you won't ever worry?"

"I won't worry about that because it's perfectly simple." 95

"Then I'll do it. Because I don't care about me."

"What do you mean?"

"I don't care about me."

"Well, I care about you."

"Oh, yes. But I don't care about me. And I'll do it and then every- 100
thing will be fine."

"I don't want you to do it if you feel that way."

The girl stood up and walked to the end of the station. Across, on the other side, were fields of grain and trees along the banks of the Ebro. Far away, beyond the river, were mountains. The shadow of a cloud 105
moved across the field of grain and she saw the river through the trees.

"And we could have all this," she said. "And we could have everything and every day we make it more impossible."

"What did you say?"

"I said we could have everything." 110

"We can have everything."

"No, we can't."

"We can have the whole world."

"No, we can't."

"We can go everywhere." 115

"No we can't. It isn't ours any more."

"It's ours."

"No, it isn't. And once they take it away, you never get it back."

"But they haven't taken it away."

"We'll wait and see." 120

"Come on back in the shade," he said. "You mustn't feel that way."

"I don't feel any way," the girl said. "I just know things."

"I don't want you to do anything that you don't want to do—"

"Nor that isn't good for me," she said. "I know. Could we have another beer?" 125

"All right. But you've got to realize—"

"I realize," the girl said. "Can't we maybe stop talking?"

They sat down at the table and the girl looked across at the hills on the dry side of the valley and the man looked at her and at the table.

"You've got to realize," he said, "that I don't want you to do it if 130
you don't want to. I'm perfectly willing to go through with it if it means anything to you."

"Doesn't it mean anything to you? We could get along."

"Of course it does. But I don't want anybody but you. I don't want
135   anyone else. And I know it's perfectly simple."

"Yes, you know it's perfectly simple."

"It's all right for you to say that, but I do know it."

"Would you do something for me now?"

"I'd do anything for you."

140   "Would you please please please please please please please stop
talking?"

He did not say anything but looked at the bags against the wall of
the station. There were labels on them from all the hotels where they
had spent nights.

145   "But I don't want you to," he said. "I don't care anything about it."

"I'll scream," the girl said.

The woman came out through the curtains with two glasses of
beer and put them down on the damp felt pads. "The train comes in five
minutes," she said.

150   "What did she say?" asked the girl.

"That the train is coming in five minutes."

The girl smiled brightly at the woman, to thank her.

"I'd better take the bags over to the other side of the station," the
man said. She smiled at him.

155   "All right. Then come back and we'll finish the beer."

He picked up the two heavy bags and carried them around the
station to the other tracks. He looked up the tracks but could not see the
train. Coming back, he walked through the bar-room, where people
waiting for the train were drinking. He drank an Anis at the bar and
160   looked at the people. They were all waiting reasonably for the train. He
went out through the bead curtain. She was sitting at the table and
smiled at him.

"Do you feel better?" he asked.

"I feel fine," she said. "There's nothing wrong with me. I feel
165   fine."

___ CONSIDERATIONS _____

1. Nearly all of Hemingway's story is dialogue, often without identifying
phrases such as "he said" or "she said." Does the lack of these phrases make it
difficult to decide which character is speaking? What, if anything, does Hemingway do to make up for missing dialogue tags? Compare his practice with the

way other short story writers in this book handle dialogue. See also how the following nonfiction writers make use of dialogue: Frank Conroy, Lillian Hellman, and Richard Wright.

2. If you have ever questioned the common statement that writers must pay careful attention to *every* word they use, spend a little time examining the way Hemingway uses "it," beginning where the couple start talking about the operation. Try to determine the various possible antecedents for that neutral pronoun in each context where it occurs. Such an effort may help you discover one reason why Hemingway's spare, almost skeletal style is so powerful.

3. Try to put the central conflict of this story in your own words. Imagine yourself the writer suddenly getting the idea for this story and quickly writing a sentence or two to record the idea in your journal. Is that idea anything like the thesis statement of an essay?

4. Why is Hemingway *not* explicit about the kind of operation the two characters are discussing? Is he simply trying to mystify the reader? Does this consideration help you to understand other stories or poems that seem difficult at first?

5. Although Hemingway's description of locale is limited to a few brief passages, he presents a distinct place. How does that place contribute to your understanding the point of the story?

6. Why does Hemingway refuse to describe the two characters? From what the story offers, what do you know about them?

7. Hemingway's story was written in the 1920s. Have the questions he raises about the operation been resolved since then?

Edward Hoagland (b. 1932) was born in New York City and lives there much of the year, alternating between Manhattan and the countryside of northern Vermont. He has written novels but is best known for his essays in volumes like The Courage of Turtles, Walking the Dead Diamond River, *and* The Edward Hoagland Reader. *"The Urge for an End" was published in* Harper's, *March, 1988.*

40

EDWARD HOAGLAND
The Urge for an End

1   A friend of mine, a peaceable soul who has been riding the New York subways for thirty years, finds himself stepping back from the tracks once in a while and closing his eyes as the train rolls in. This, he says, is not only to suppress an urge to throw himself in front of it but because every couple of weeks an impulse rises in him to push a stranger onto the tracks, any stranger, thus ending his own life too. He blames this partly on apartment living—"pigeonholes without being able to fly."

2   It is profoundly startling not to trust oneself after decades of doing so. I don't dare keep ammunition in my country house for a small rifle I bought secondhand two decades ago. The gun sat in a cupboard in the back room with the original box of .22 bullets under the muzzle all that time, seldom fired except at a few apples hanging in a tree every fall to remind me of my army training near the era of the Korean War, when I'd been considered quite a marksman. When I bought the gun I didn't trust either my professional competence as a writer or my competence as a father as much as I came to do, but certainly believed I could keep myself alive. I bought it for protection, and the idea that someday I might be afraid of shooting myself with the gun would have seemed inconceivable—laughable.

3   One's fifties can be giddy years, as anybody fifty knows. Chest

pains, back pains, cancer scares, menopausal or prostate complications are not the least of it, and the fidelities of a lifetime, both personal and professional, may be called into question. Was it a mistake to have stuck so long with one's marriage, and to have stayed with a lackluster well-paying job? (Or *not* to have stayed and stuck?) People not only lose faith in their talents and their dreams or values; some simply tire of them. Grow tired, too, of the smell of fried-chicken grease, once such a delight, and the cold glutinosity of ice cream, the boredom of beer, the stop-go of travel, the hiccups of laughter, and of two rush hours a day, then the languor of weekends, of athletes as well as accountants, and even the frantic birdsong of spring—red-eyed vireos that have been clocked singing 22,000 times in a day. Life is a matter of cultivating the five senses (the sixth too), and an equilibrium with nature and what I think of as its subdivision, human nature, trusting no one completely but almost everyone at least a little; but this is easier said than done.

More than 30,000 Americans took their own lives last year, men 4 mostly, with the highest rate being among those older than sixty-five. When I asked a friend of mine why three times as many men kill themselves as members of her own sex, she replied with sudden anger, "I'm not going to go into the self-indulgence of men." Suicide is an exasperating act as often as it is pitiable. "Committing" suicide is in bad odor in our culture even among those who don't believe that to cash in your chips ahead of time and hand back to God his gifts to you is a blasphemous sin. We the living, in any case, are likely to feel accused by this person who "voted with his feet." It appears to cast a subversive judgment upon the social polity as a whole that what was supposed to work in life—religion, family, friendship, commerce, and industry—did not; and furthermore, it "frightens the horses in the street," as Virginia Woolf once defined wrongful behavior (before she killed herself).

Many suicides inflict outrageous trauma, burning permanent inju- 5 ries into the minds of their children, though they may have joked beforehand only of "taking a dive." And sometimes the gesture has a peevish or cowardly aspect, or seems to have been senselessly short-sighted as far as an outside observer can tell. There are desperate suicides and crafty suicides, people who do it to cause others trouble and people who do it to save others trouble, deranged exhibitionists who yell from a building ledge and closedmouthed, secretive souls who swim out into the ocean's anonymity. Suicide may in fact be an attempt to escape death, shortcut the dreadful deteriorating processes, abort one's natural trajectory, elude "the ruffian on the stairs," in A. E.

Housman's phrase for a cruelly painful and anarchic death—make it neat and not messy. The deed can be grandiose or self-abnegating, vindictive or drably mousy, rationally plotted or plainly insane. People sidle toward death, intent upon outwitting their own bodies' defenses, or they may dramatize the chance to make one last, unambiguous, irrevocable decision, like a captain scuttling his ship—death before dishonor—leaping toward oblivion through a curtain of pain, like a frog going down the throat of a snake. One man I knew hosted a quietly affectionate evening with several unknowing friends on the night before he swallowed too many pills. Another waved an apologetic good-bye to a bystander on a bridge; rarely considerate, he turned apologetic in the last moment of life. Never physically inclined, he made a great vault toward the ice on the Mississippi.

6   In the army, we wore dog tags with a notch at one end by which these numbered pieces of metal could be jammed between our teeth, if we lay dead and nameless on a battlefield, for later sorting. As "servicemen" our job would be to kill people who were pointed out to us as enemies, or make "the supreme sacrifice" for a higher good than enjoying the rest of our lives. Life was very much a possession, in other words—not only God's, but the soldier's own to dispose of. Working in an army hospital, I frequently did handle dead bodies, but this never made me feel I would refuse to kill another man whose uniform was pointed out to me as being inimical, or value my life more tremulously and vigilantly. The notion of dying for my country didn't appeal to me as much as dying free-lance for my ideas (in the unlikely event I *could* do that), but I was ready. People were taught during the 1940s and '50s that one should be ready to die for one's beliefs. Heroes were revered because they had deliberately chosen to give up their lives. Life would not be worth living under the tyranny of an invader, and Nathan Hale apparently hadn't paused to consider whether God might have other uses for him besides being hanged. Nor did the pilot Colin Kelly hesitate before crashing his plane into a Japanese battleship, becoming America's first well-publicized hero in World War II.

7   I've sometimes wondered why people who know that they are terminally ill, or who are headed for suicide, so very seldom have paused to take a bad guy along with them. It is lawless to consider an act of assassination, yet hardly more lawless, really, than suicide is regarded in some quarters. Government bureaucracies, including our own, in their majesty and as the executors of laws, regularly weigh the pros and cons of murdering foreign antagonists. Of course the answer is

that most individuals are fortunately more timid as well as humbler in their judgment than government officialdom; but beyond that, when dying or suicidal, people no longer care enough to devote their final energies to doing good works of any kind—Hitler himself in their gun sights they would have passed up. Some suicides become so crushed and despairing that they can't recognize the consequences of anything they do; and it's not primarily vindictiveness that wreaks such havoc upon their survivors but their derangement from ordinary life.

Courting the idea is different from the real impulse. "When he begged for help, we took him and locked him up," another friend of mine says, speaking of her husband. "Not till then. Wishing to be out of the situation you are in—feeling helpless and unable to cope—is not the same as wishing to be dead. If I actually wished to be dead, even my children's welfare would have no meaning."   8

You might think the ready option of divorce available lately would have cut suicide rates, offering an escape to battered wives, lovelorn husbands, and other people in despair. But it doesn't work that way. When the number of choices people have is increased, an entire range of possibilities opens up. The suicide rate among teenagers has nearly quadrupled since 1950, although the standard of comfort that their families enjoy has gone up. Black Americans, less affluent than white Americans, have a suicide rate about half that of whites.   9

Still, if a fiftyish fellow with fine teeth and a foolproof pension plan, a cottage at the beach and the Fourth of July weekend coming up, kills himself, it seems truculent. We would look at him bafflingly if he told us he no longer likes the Sturm und Drang of banging fireworks.   10

Then stay at your hideaway! we'd argue with him.   11

"Big mouths eat little mouths. Nature isn't 'timeless.' Whole lives are squeezed into three months or three days."   12

What about your marriage?   13

"She's become more mannish than me. I loved women. I don't believe in marriage between men."   14

Remarry, then!   15

"I've gone impotent, and besides, when I see somebody young and pretty I guess I feel like dandling her on my knee."   16

Marriage is friendship. You can find someone your own age.   17

"I'm tired of it."   18

But how about your company?—it's positioned itself on the cutting edge of the silicon frontier. That's interesting.   19

"I know what wins. It's less and less appetizing."   20

21   *You're not scared of death anymore?*
22   "It interests me less than it did."
23   *What are you so sick of? The rest of us keep going.*
24   "I'm tired of weathermen and sportscasters on the screen. Of being patient and also of impatience. I'm tired of the President, whoever the President happens to be, and sleeping badly, with forty-eight half hours in the day—of breaking two eggs every morning and putting sugar on something. I'm tired of the drone of my voice, but also of us jabbering like parrots at each other—of all our stumpy ways of doing everything."
25   *You're bored with yourself?*
26   "I'm maybe the least interesting person I know."
27   *But to kill yourself?*
28   "You know, it's a tradition, too," he remarks quietly, not making so bold as to suggest that the tradition is an honorable one, though his tone of voice might be imagined to imply this. "I guess I've always been a latent maverick."
29   Except in circumstances which are themselves a matter of life and death, I'm reluctant to agree with the idea that suicide is not the result of mental illness. No matter how reasonably the person appears to have examined his options, it goes against the grain of nature for him to destroy himself. And any illness that threatens his life changes a person. Suicidal thinking, if serious, can be a kind of death scare, comparable to suffering a heart attack or undergoing a cancer operation. One survives such a phase both warier and chastened. When—two years ago—I emerged from a bad dip into suicidal speculation, I felt utterly exhausted and yet quite fearless of ordinary dangers, vastly afraid of myself but much less scared of extraneous eventualities. The fact of death may not be tragic; many people die with a bit of a smile that captures their mouths at the last instant, and some who are revived after a deadly accident are reluctant to be brought to life, resisting resuscitation, and carrying back confusing, beamish, or ecstatic memories. But the same impetuosity that made him throw himself out of a window might have enabled that person to love life all the more if he'd been calibrated somewhat differently at the time of the emergency. Death's edge is so abrupt and near that many who expect a short, momentary dive may be astounded to find that it is bottomless and change their minds and start to scream when they are only halfway down.
30   Although my fright at my mind's anarchy superseded my fear of death in the conventional guise of heart seizures, airplane crashes, and

so on, nightmares are more primitive, and in my dreams I continued to be scared of a death not sought after—dying from driving too fast and losing control of the car, breaking through thin ice while skating and drowning in the cold, or falling off a cliff. When I am tense and sleeping raggedly, my worst nightmare isn't drawn from anxious prep-school memories or the bad spells of my marriages or any of adulthood's vicissitudes. Nothing else from the past half-century has the staying power in my mind of the elevated train rides that my father and I used to take down Third Avenue to the Battery in New York City on Sunday afternoons when I was three or four or five, so I could see the fish at the aquarium. We were probably pretty good companions in those years, but the wooden platforms forty feet up shook terribly as trains from both directions pulled in and out. To me they seemed worse than rickety—ready to topple. And the roar was fearful, and the railings left large gaps for a child to fall through, after the steep climb up the slatsided, windy, shaking stairway from street level. It's a rare dream, but several times a year I still find myself on such a perch, without his company or anybody else's, on a boyish or a grown-up's mission, when the elevated platform begins to rattle desperately, seesaw, heel over, and finally come apart, disintegrate, while I cling to struts and trusses.

My father, as he lay dying at home of bowel cancer, used to enjoy watching Tarzan reruns on the children's hour of television. Like a strong green vine, they swung him far away from his deathbed to a world of skinnydipping, friendly animals, and scenic beauty linked to the lost realities of his adolescence in Kansas City. Earlier, when he was still able to walk without much pain, he'd paced the house for several hours at night, contemplating suicide, I expect, along with other anguishing thoughts, regrets, remembrances, and yearnings, while the rest of us slept. But he decided to lie down and die the slower way. I don't know how much of that decision was for his wife and children, how much was because he didn't want to be a "quitter," as he sometimes put it, and how much was due to his believing that life belongs to God (which I'm not even sure he did). He was not a churchgoer after his thirties. He had belonged to J. P. Morgan's church, St. George's, on Stuyvesant Square—Morgan was a hero of his—but when things went a little wrong for him at the Wall Street law firm he worked for, and he changed jobs and moved out to the suburbs, he became a skeptic on religious matters, and gradually, in the absence of faith of that previous kind, he adhered to a determined allegiance to the social order. Dwight D. Eisenhower instead of J. P. Morgan became the sort of hero he

31

admired, and suicide would have seemed an act of insurrection against the laws and conventions of the society, internationalist-Republican, that he believed in.

32   I was never particularly afraid that I might plan a suicide, swallowing a bunch of pills and keeping them down—only of what I think of as Anna Karenina's kind of death. This most plausible self-killing in all of literature is frightening because it was unwilled, regretted at midpoint, and came as a complete surprise to Anna herself. After rushing impulsively, in great misery, to the Moscow railway station to catch a train, she ended up underneath another one, dismayed, astonished, and trying to climb out from under the wheels even as they crushed her. Many people who briefly verge on suicide undergo a mental somersault for a terrifying interval during which they're upside down, their perspective topsy-turvy, skidding, churning; and this is why I got rid of the bullets for my .22.

33   Nobody expects to trust his body overmuch after the age of fifty. Incipient cataracts or arthritis, outlandish snores, tooth-grinding, ankles that threaten to turn are part of the game. But not to trust one's *mind!* That's a surprise. The single attribute that older people were sure to have (we thought as boys) was a stodgy dependability, a steady temperance and caution. Adults might be vain, unimaginative, pompous, and callous, but they did have their affairs tightly in hand. It was not till my thirties that I began to know friends who were in their fifties on equal terms, and I remember being amused, piqued, and bewildered to learn that some of them still felt as marginal or rebellious or in a quandary about what to do with themselves for the next dozen years as my contemporaries were likely to. Even that close to retirement, some of them harbored a deep-seated contempt for the organizations they had been working for, ready to walk away from almost everybody they had known and the efforts of whole decades with very little sentiment. Nor did twenty years of marriage necessarily mean more than two or three—they might be just as ready to walk away from that also, and didn't really register it as twenty years at all. Rather, life could be about to begin all over again. "Bummish" was how one man described himself, with a raffish smile—"Lucky to have a roof over my head"—though he'd just put a child through Yale. He was quitting his job and claimed with exasperation that his wife still cried for her mother in her sleep, as if they'd never been married.

The great English traveler Richard Burton quoted an Arab proverb 34
that speaks for many middle-aged men of the old-fashioned variety:
"Conceal thy Tenets, thy Treasure and thy Travelling." These are
serious matters, in other words. People didn't conceal their tenets in
order to betray them, but to fight for them more opportunely. And
except for kings and princelings, concealing whatever treasure one had
went without saying. As for travel, a man's travels were also a matter of
gravity. Travel was knowledge, ambiguity, dalliances or misalliances,
divided loyalty, forbidden thinking; and besides, someday he might
need to make a run for it and go to ground someplace where he had made
some secret friends. Friends of mine whose husbands or whose wives
have died have been quite startled afterward to discover caches of
money or traveler's checks concealed around the house, or a bundle of
cash in a safe-deposit box.

Burton, like any other desert adage-spinner (and most individuals 35
over fifty), would have agreed to an addition so obvious that it wasn't
included to begin with: "Conceal thy Illnesses." I can remember how
urgently my father worried that word would get out, after a preliminary
operation for his cancer. He didn't want to be written off, counted out of
the running at the corporation he worked for and in other enclaves of
competition. Men often compete with one another until the day they
die; comradeship consists of rubbing shoulders jocularly with a competitor. As breadwinners, they must be considered fit and sound by
friend as well as foe, and so there's lots of truth to the most common
answer I heard when asking why three times as many men as women
kill themselves: "They keep their troubles to themselves"; "They don't
know how to ask for help."

I'm not entirely like that, and I discovered that when I confided 36
something of my perturbation to a woman friend, she was likely to keep
telephoning me or mailing cheery postcards, whereas a man would
usually listen with concern, communicate his sympathy, and maybe
intimate that he had pondered the same drastic course of action himself
a few years back and would end up respecting my decision either way.
Open-mindedness seems an important attribute to a good many men
who pride themselves on being objective, hearing all sides of an issue,
on knowing that truth and honesty do not always coincide with social
dicta, and who may even cherish a subterranean outlaw streak that, like
being ready to violently defend one's family, reputation, and country, is
by tradition male.

Men, having been so much freer than women in society, used to 37 feel they had less of a stake in the maintenance of certain churchly conventions and enjoyed speaking irreverently about various social truisms, including even the principle that people ought to die on schedule, not cutting in ahead of their assigned place in line. Contemporary women, after their triumphant irreverence during the 1960s and 1970s, cannot be generalized about so easily. They turn as skeptical and saturnine as any man. In fact, women attempt suicide more frequently, but favor pills or other methods, whereas two-thirds of the men who kill themselves use a gun: in 1985, 85 percent of suicides by means of firearms were committed by men. An overdose of medication hasn't the same finality. It may be reversible if the person is discovered quickly, or be subject to benign miscalculation to start with. Even if it works, perhaps it can be fudged by a kindly doctor in the recordkeeping. Like an enigmatic drowning or a single-car accident that baffles the suspicions of the insurance company, a suicide by drugs can be a way to avoid making a loud statement, and merely illustrate the final modesty of a person who didn't wish to ask for too much of the world's attention.

38   Unconsummated attempts at suicide can strike the rest of us as self-pitying, self-aggrandizing, or as plaintive plea-bargaining—"childish," we say, though actually the helplessness that echoes through a child's suicide is ghastly beyond any stunt of self-mutilation an adult may indulge in. It would be hard to define chaos better than as a world where children decide that they don't want to live.

39   Love is the solution to all dilemmas, we sometimes hear; and in those moments when the spirit bathes itself in beneficence and manages to transcend the static of personalities rubbing fur off of each other, indeed it is. Without love nothing matters, Paul told the Corinthians, a mystery which, if true, has no ready Darwinian explanation. Love without a significant sexual component and for people who are unrelated to us serves little practical purpose. It doesn't help us feed our families, win struggles, thrive, and prosper. It distracts us from the ordinary business of sizing people up and making a living, and is not even conducive to intellectual observation, because instead of seeing them, we see right through them to the bewildered child and dreaming adolescent who inhabited their bodies earlier, the now tired idealist who fell in and out of love, got hired and quit, bought cars and wore them out, liked black-eyed susans, blueberry muffins, and roosters crowing—liked roosters crowing better than skyscrapers but now likes skyscrapers better than roosters crowing. As swift as thought, we select the details that we need to see in order to be able to love them.

40   Yet at other times we'll dispense with these same poignancies and

choose only their grunginess to look at, their pinched mouths and shifty eyes, their thirst for gin at noon and indifference to their kids, their greed for the best tidbit on the buffet table, and their penchant for poking their penises up the excretory end of other human beings. I tend to gaze quite closely at the faces of priests I meet on the street to see if a lifetime of love has marked them noticeably. Real serenity or asceticism I no longer expect, and I take for granted the beefy calm that often goes with Catholic celibacy, but I am watching for the marks of love and often see mere resignation or tenacity.

Many men are romantics, likely to plunge, go for broke, take action in a spirit of exigency rather than waiting for the problem to resolve itself. Then, still as romantics, they may drift into despairing passivity, stare at the TV all day long, and binge with a bottle. Women too may turn frenetic for a while and then throw up their hands; but though they may not seem as grandiosely fanciful and romantic at the outset, they are more frequently believers—at least they seem to me to believe in God or in humanity, the future, and so on. We have above us the inviting eternity of "the heavens," if we choose to look at it, lying on our backs in the summer grass under starlight, some of which had left its source before mankind became man. But because we live in our heads more than in nature nowadays, even the summer sky is a mine field for people whose memories are mined. With the sky no longer humbling, and sunshine only a sort of convenience, and no godhead located anywhere outside of our own heads, every problem may seem insolubly interlocked. When the telephone has become impossible to answer at home, sometimes it finally becomes impossible to stride down the gangplank of a cruise ship in Mombasa too, although no telephones will ring for you there. 41

But if escapist travel is ruled out in certain emergencies, surely you can *pray?* Pray, yes; but to whom? That requires a bit of preparation. Rarely do people obtain much relief from praying if they haven't stood in line awhile to get a visa. It's an appealing idea that you can just *go*, and in a previous era perhaps you could have. But it's not so simple now. What do you believe in? Whom are you praying to? What are you praying for? There's no crèche on the courthouse lawn; you're not supposed to adhere exactly even to what your parents believed. Like psychotherapy, praying takes time, even if you know which direction to face when you kneel. 42

Love is powerfully helpful when the roof falls in—loving other people with a high and hopeful heart and as a kind of prayer. That feat 43 too, however, requires new and sudden insights or long practice. The beatitude of loving strangers as well as friends—loving them on sight with a leap of empathy and intuition—is a form of inspiration, edging, of course, in some cases toward madness, as other states of beatitude can do. But there's no question that a genuine love for the living will stymie suicidal depressions not chemical in origin. Love is an elixir, changing the life of the lover. And many of us have experienced this—a temporary lightening of our leery, prickly disapproval of much of the rest of the world, when at a wedding or a funeral of shared emotion, or when we have fallen in love.

44   Yet the zest for life of those unusual men and women who make a great zealous success of living is due more often in good part to the crafty pertinacity with which they manage to overlook the misery of others. You can watch them watch life beat the stuffing out of the faces of their friends and acquaintances, yet they themselves seem to outwit the dense delays of social custom, the tedious tick-tock of bureaucratic obfuscation, accepting loss and age and change and disappointment without suffering punctures in their stomach lining. Breathlessness or strange dull pains from their nether organs don't nonplus them. They fret and doubt in moderation, and love a lobster roast, squeeze lemon juice on living clams on the half shell to prove that the clams are alive, laugh as a robin tussles a worm out of the ground or a kitten flees a dog. Like the problem drinkers, pork eaters, and chain smokers who nevertheless finish out their allotted years, succumbing to a stroke at a nice round biblical age when the best vitamin-eating vegetarian has long since died, their faces become veritable walnuts of fine character, with the same smile lines as the rarer individual whose grin has been affectionate all of his life.

45   We spend our lives getting to know ourselves, yet wonders never cease. During my adolescent years my states of mind, though undulant, seemed seamless; even when I was unhappy, no cracks or fissures made me wonder if I was a danger to myself. My confidence was such that I treaded the slippery lips of waterfalls, fought forest fires, drove ancient cars cross-country night and day, and scratched the necks of menagerie leopards in the course of various adventures which enhanced the joy of being alive. The chemistry of the mind, because unfathomable, is more frightening. In the city, I live on the waterfront and occasionally will notice an agitated-looking figure picking his way along the pilings and stringpieces of the timbered piers nearby, staring at the sliding whorls on the surface of the Hudson as if teetering over an abyss. Our building, across the street, seems imposing from the water and over the years has

acted as a magnet for a number of suicides—people who have dreaded the clammy chill, the onerous smothering essential to their first plan. One woman climbed out after jumping in and took the elevator to our roof (my neighbors remember how wringing wet she was), and leapt off, banging window ledges on the way down, and hit with the whap of a sack of potatoes, as others have.

But what is more remarkable than that a tiny minority of souls   46
reach a point where they entrust their bodies to the force of gravity is that so few of the rest of us splurge an hour of a summer day gazing at the trees and sky. How many summers do we *have?*

47

People with sunny natures do seem to live longer than people who are nervous wrecks; yet mankind didn't evolve out of the animal kingdom by being unduly sunny-minded. Life was fearful and phantasmagoric, supernatural and preternatural, as well as encompassing the kind of clockwork regularity of our well-governed day. It had numerous superstitious elements, such as we are likely to catch a whiff of only when we're peering at a dead body. And it was not just our optimism but our pessimistic premonitions, our dark moments as a species, our irrational, frightful speculations, our strange mutations upon the simple theme of love, and our sleepless, obsessive inventiveness—our dread as well as our faith—that made us human beings. Staking one's life on the more general good came to include risking suicide also. Brilliant, fecund people sometimes kill themselves.   48

Joy to the world! . . . Let heaven and nature sing, and heaven and nature sing. The famous Christmas carol invokes not only glee but unity: heaven with nature, not always a Christian combination. It's a rapturous hymn, and no one should refuse to surrender to such a pitch of revelation when it comes. But the flip side of rapture can be a riptide of panic, or hysterical gloom. Our faces are not molded as if joy were a preponderant experience. (Nor is a caribou's or a thrush's.) Our faces in repose look stoic or battered, and people of the sunniest temperament sometimes die utterly unstrung, doubting everything they have ever believed in.   49

Let heaven and nature sing! But *is* there such harmony? Are God and Mother Nature really the same? And will we risk burning our wings if we mount high enough to try to see? I've noticed that woods soil in Italy smells the same as woods soil in New England when you pick up a handful of it and enjoy its aromas—but is God there the same? It can be precarious to wonder. I don't rule out suicide as being unthinkable for people who have tried to live full lives, and don't regard it as negating the work and faith and even ecstasy they may have known before. In killing himself a person acknowledges his failures during a time span when perhaps heaven and earth had caught him like a pair of scissors— but not his life span. Man is different from animals in that he speculates, a high-risk activity.

___ CONSIDERATIONS _____

1. In paragraph 3, Hoagland includes the one reason for suicide with which it is probably most difficult to argue. Identify that reason.

2. What do you see as the unifying idea of paragraph 5, in which no main idea is overtly stated?

3. Why, according to Hoagland, do so few people—terminally ill or headed for suicide—seize the opportunity to rid the world of a public enemy?

4. "The Urge for an End" is an informal, personal essay in that Hoagland writes in the first person, relies heavily upon his personal experience, and adopts a casual, slangy, almost playful tone. With an eye (and an ear) open to Hoagland's tone, study the essay and collect examples of language that creates and maintains the writer's attitude.

5. Our expectations of each other figure frequently in Hoagland's essay. In paragraph 33, what was he surprised to learn about his expectations of older people?

6. In paragraphs 34 and 35, Hoagland refers to the tendency among older people to conceal their illnesses. Use your own experience with older people and/or your reading to build an essay confirming or refuting Hoagland's idea.

7. In the last third of his essay, Hoagland presents what he calls the world's best definition of chaos. What has that to do with suicide? (Hint: In paragraph 9, he reports that "The suicide rate among teenagers has nearly quadrupled since 1950. . . .")

8. In paragraph 41, the author writes ". . . we live in our heads more than in nature nowadays," and in paragraph 46, he wonders that "so few of the rest of us splurge an hour of a summer day gazing at the trees and sky." Read Robert Finch's essay "Very Like a Whale," especially paragraphs 15, 16, 17, and 18, and/or Peter Steinhart's "The Old Curiosity," especially paragraph 14, and/or the entry from Henry David Thoreau's journal of November 30, 1858. Draw from those readings and your own life to develop into an essay Hoagland's implications that nature might have a preventive or curative effect on would-be suicides.

Andrew Holleran (b. 1943) has written essays for New York
magazine *and* Christopher Street, *as well as two novels:* Dancer
from the Dance *(1978) and* Nights in Aruba *(1984).* Ground Zero
(1988) collects his essays, including "Bedside Manners."

41

ANDREW HOLLERAN
Bedside Manners

"There is no difference between men so profound," wrote Scott 1
Fitzgerald, "as that between the sick and the well."

There are many thoughts that fill someone's head as he walks 2
across town on a warm July afternoon to visit a friend confined to a
hospital room—and that is one of them. Another occurs to you as you
wait for the light to change and watch the handsome young basketball
players playing on the public court behind a chicken wire fence: Health
is everywhere. The world has a surreal quality to it when you are on
your way to the hospital to visit someone you care for who is seriously
ill: Everyone in it, walking down the sidewalk, driving by in cars,
rushing about on a basketball court with sweat-stained chests, exhausted faces, and wide eyes, seems to you extremely peculiar. They are
peculiar because they are free: walking under their own power, nicely
dressed, sometimes beautiful. Beauty does not lose its allure under the
spell of grief. The hospital visitor still notices the smooth chests of the
athletes in their cotton shorts as they leap to recover the basketball
after it bounces off the rim. But everything seems strangely quiet—
speechless—as if you were watching a movie on television with the
sound turned off, as if everyone else in the world but you is totally
unaware of something: that the act of walking across York Avenue
under one's own power is essentially miraculous.

Every time he enters a hospital, the visitor enters with two simul- 3
taneous thoughts: He hates hospitals, and only people working in them

lead serious lives. Everything else is selfish. Entering a hospital he always thinks, *I should work for a year as a nurse, an aide, a volunteer helping people, coming to terms with disease and death.* This feeling will pass the moment he leaves the hospital. In reality the visitor hopes his fear and depression are not evident on his face as he walks down the gleaming, silent hall from the elevator to his friend's room. He is trying hard to stay calm.

4   The door of the room the receptionist downstairs has told the visitor his friend is in is closed—and on it are taped four signs that are not on any of the other doors and are headlined, WARNING. The visitor stops as much to read them as to allow his heartbeat to subside before going in. He knows—from the accounts of friends who have already visited—he must don a robe, gloves, mask, and even a plastic cap. He is not sure if the door is closed because his friend is asleep inside or because the door to this room is always kept closed. So he pushes it open a crack and peers in. His friend is turned on his side, a white mound of bed linen, apparently sleeping.

5   The visitor is immensely relieved. He goes down the hall and asks a nurse if he may leave the *Life* magazine he brought for his friend and writes a note to him saying he was here. Then he leaves the hospital and walks west through the summer twilight as if swimming through an enchanted lagoon. The next day—once more crossing town—he is in that surreal mood, under a blue sky decorated with a few photogenic, puffy white clouds, certain that no one else knows . . . knows he or she is absurdly, preposterously, incalculably fortunate to be walking on the street. He feels once again that either the sound has been turned off or some other element (his ego, perhaps with all its anger, ambition, jealousy) has been removed from the world. The basketball players are different youths today but just as much worth pausing to look at. He enters the hospital one block east more calmly this time and requests to see his friend—who is allowed only two visitors at a time, and visits lasting no more than ten minutes. He goes upstairs, peeks around the door, and sees his friend utterly awake. The visitor's heart races as he steps back and puts on the gloves, mask, cap, and robe he has been told his friends all look so comical in. He smiles because he hopes the photograph that made him bring the copy of *Life* to the hospital— Russian women leaning against a wall in Leningrad in bikinis and winter coats, taking the sun on a February day—has amused his friend as much as it tickled him.

6   "Richard?" the visitor says as he opens the door and peeks in. His friend blinks at him. Two plastic tubes are fixed in his nostrils bringing

him oxygen. His face is emaciated and gaunt, his hair longer, softer in appearance, wisps rising above his head. But the one feature the visitor cannot get over are his friend's eyes. His eyes are black, huge, and furious. Perhaps because his face is gaunt or perhaps because they really are larger than usual, they seem the only thing alive in his face; as if his whole being were distilled and concentrated, poured, drained, into his eyes. They are shining, alarmed, and—there is no other word—furious. He looks altogether like an angry baby—or an angry old man—or an angry bald eagle.

And just as the hospital visitor is absorbing the shock of these livid eyes, the sick man says in a furious whisper, "Why did you bring me that dreadful magazine? I hate *Life* magazine! With that stupid picture! I wasn't amused! I wasn't amused at all! You should never have brought that dreck into this room!" 7

The visitor is momentarily speechless: It is the first time in their friendship of ten years that anything abusive or insulting has ever been said; it is as astonishing as the gaunt face in which two huge black eyes burn and shine. But he sits down and recovers his breath and apologizes. The visitor thinks, *He's angry because I haven't visited him till now. He's angry that he's here at all, that he's sick.* And they begin to talk. They talk of the hospital food (which he hates too), of the impending visit of his mother (whose arrival he dreads), of the drug he is taking (which is experimental), and of the other visitors he has had. The patient asks the visitor to pick up a towel at the base of the bed and give it to him. The visitor complies. The patient places it across his forehead—and the visitor, who, like most people, is unsure what to say in this situation, stifles the question he wants to ask, *Why do you have a towel on your forehead?* The patient finally says, "Don't you think I look like Mother Theresa?" And the visitor realizes his friend has made a joke—as he did years ago in their house on Fire Island: doing drag with bedspreads, pillow cases, towels, whatever was at hand. The visitor does not smile—he is so unprepared for a joke in these circumstances— but he realizes, with relief, he is forgiven. He realizes what people who visit the sick often learn: It is the patient who puts the visitor at ease. In a few moments his ten minutes are up. He rises and says, "I don't want to tire you." He goes to the door and once beyond it he turns and looks back. His friend says to him, "I'm proud of you for coming." 8

"Oh—!" the visitor says and shakes his head. "Proud of *me* for coming!" he tells a friend later that evening, after he has stripped off his gown and mask and gone home, through the unreal city of people in perfect health. "Proud of me! Can you imagine! To say that to me, to 9 make *me* feel good! When he's the one in bed!" The truth is he is proud of himself the next time he visits his friend, for he is one of those people who looks away when a nurse takes a blood test and finds respirators frightening. He is like almost everyone—everyone except these extraordinary people who work in hospitals, he thinks, as he walks into the building. The second visit is easier, partly because it is the second, and partly because the patient is better—the drug has worked.

10   But he cannot forget the sight of those dark, angry eyes and the plastic tubes and emaciated visage—and as he goes home that evening, he knows there is a place whose existence he was not aware of before: the foyer of death. It is a place many of us will see at least once in our lives. Because modern medicine fights for patients who a century ago would have died without its intervention, it has created an odd place between life and death. One no longer steps into Charon's boat to be ferried across the River Styx—ill people are now detained, with one foot in the boat and the other still on shore. It is a place where mercy looks exactly like cruelty to the average visitor. It is a place that one leaves, if one is only a visitor, with the conviction that ordinary life is utterly miraculous, so that, going home from the hospital on the subway, one is filled with things one cannot express to the crowd that walks up out of the station or throngs the street of the block where he lives. But if the people caught in the revolving door between health and death could speak, would they not say—as Patrick Cowley reportedly did as he watched the men dancing to his music while he was fatally ill, "Look at those stupid queens. Don't they *know?*" Guard your health. It is all you have. It is the thin line that stands between you and hell. It is your miraculous possession. Do nothing to threaten it. Treat each other with kindness. Comfort your suffering friends. Help one another. Revere life. Do not throw it away for the momentous pleasures of lust, or even the obliteration of loneliness.

11   Many homosexuals wonder how they will die: where, with whom. Auden went back to Oxford, Santayana to the Blue Nuns in Rome. We are not all so lucky. Some men afflicted with AIDS returned to die in their family's home. Others have died with friends. Some have died bitterly and repudiated the homosexual friends who came to see them; others have counted on these people. Volunteers from the Gay Men's Health Crisis have cooked, cleaned, shopped, visited, taken care of people they did not even know until they decided to help. One thing is sure—we are learning how to help one another. We are discovering the strength and goodness of people we knew only in discotheques or as faces on Fire Island. We are following a great moral precept by visiting

the sick. We are once again learning the awful truth Robert Penn Warren wrote years ago: "Only through the suffering of the innocent is the brotherhood of man confirmed." The most profound difference between men may well be that between the sick and the well, but compassionate people try to reach across the chasm and bridge it. The hospital visitor who conquers his own fear of something facing us all takes the first step on a journey that others less fearful than he have already traveled much further on: They are combining eros and agape as they rally round their stricken friends. As for the courage and dignity and sense of humor of those who are sick, these are beyond praise, and one hesitates where words are so flimsy. As for a disease whose latency period is measured in years, not months, there is no telling which side of the line dividing the sick and the well each of us will be on before this affliction is conquered. We may disdain the hysteria of policemen and firemen who call for masks, and people who ask if it is safe to ride the subway, and television crews who will not interview AIDS patients. For they are not at risk—those who are, are fearlessly helping their own. This is the greatest story of the plague.

CONSIDERATIONS

1. In his long closing paragraph, Holleran uses the words "eros" and "agape" in the same clause. Both Greek words could be translated "love." What difference is the author after? Or is he careless and guilty of redundancy?

2. Locate in that same closing paragraph the theme Holleran borrows from the Scott Fitzgerald quotation that opens the essay. Note that the sentence following that restatement begins with a "but," as though to imply that what follows the "but" is more important than what precedes it. How does that "but" alter Holleran's thesis?

3. In paragraph 2, Holleran uses on four occasions a device of punctuation few writers employ. Review what you know of that device, study Holleran's use of it to determine what function(s) it performs in this passage, then try using it yourself in one of your own essays.

4. Holleran does not mention the word "AIDS" until his closing paragraph. How soon do you suspect that this is the disease his friend suffers from? What clues does Holleran give you?

5. In explaining what he means by "the foyer of death" (paragraph 10), Holleran reminds his readers of Charon, a figure in Greek mythology. What is the most immediately available source that you could expect to tell you enough about that figure to understand the author's use of it in "Bedside Manners"? What are some alternative sources?

6. How does Holleran avoid thrusting himself unduly into the reader's attention in discussing a situation as obviously intimate and personal as Holleran's concern for his friend hospitalized with AIDS?

7. Would Holleran's essay be as effective if the friend were dying of cancer rather than AIDS? What elements of important interest to contemporary Americans would be missing? What elements would remain the same?

Langston Hughes (1902–1967) was a poet, novelist, playwright, and essayist who wrote with wit and energy; he was a leader in the emergence of black American literature in the twentieth century. More than twenty of his books remain in print, including Selected Poems; *his autobiography,* I Wonder as I Wander; *and* The Langston Hughes Reader. *He argues as well as he sings the blues—and he knows how to tell a story.*

42

LANGSTON HUGHES
Salvation

I was saved from sin when I was going on thirteen. But not really 1
saved. It happened like this. There was a big revival at my Auntie Reed's church. Every night for weeks there had been much preaching, singing, praying, and shouting, and some very hardened sinners had been brought to Christ, and the membership of the church had grown by leaps and bounds. Then just before the revival ended, they held a special meeting for children, "to bring the young lambs to the fold." My aunt spoke of it for days ahead. That night I was escorted to the front row and placed on the mourners' bench with all the other young sinners, who had not yet been brought to Jesus.

My aunt told me that when you were saved you saw a light, and 2
something happened to you inside! And Jesus came into your life! And God was with you from then on! She said you could see and hear and feel Jesus in your soul. I believed her. I had heard a great many old people say the same thing and it seemed to me they ought to know. So I sat there calmly in the hot, crowded church, waiting for Jesus to come to me.

The preacher preached a wonderful rhythmical sermon, all moans 3
and shouts and lonely cries and dire pictures of hell, and then he sang a

song about the ninety and nine safe in the fold, but one little lamb was left out in the cold. Then he said: "Won't you come? Won't you come to Jesus? Young lambs, won't you come?" And he held out his arms to all us young sinners there on the mourners' bench. All the little girls cried. And some of them jumped up and went to Jesus right away. But most of us just sat there.

4   A great many old people came and knelt around us and prayed, old women with jet-black faces and braided hair, old men with work-gnarled hands. And the church sang a song about the lower lights are burning, some poor sinners to be saved. And the whole building rocked with prayer and song.

5   Still I kept waiting to *see* Jesus.

6   Finally all the young people had gone to the altar and were saved, but one boy and me. He was a rounder's son named Westley. Westley and I were surrounded by sisters and deacons praying. It was very hot in the church, and getting late now. Finally Westley said to me in a whisper: "God damn! I'm tired o' sitting here. Let's get up and be saved." So he got up and was saved.

7   Then I was left all alone on the mourners' bench. My aunt came and knelt at my knees and cried, while prayers and songs swirled all around me in the little church. The whole congregation prayed for me alone, in a mighty wail of moans and voices. And I kept waiting se-renely for Jesus, waiting, waiting—but he didn't come. I wanted to see him, but nothing happened to me. Nothing! I wanted something to happen to me, but nothing happened.

8   I heard the songs and the minister saying: "Why don't you come? My dear child, why don't you come to Jesus? Jesus is waiting for you. He wants you. Why don't you come? Sister Reed, what is this child's name?"

9   "Langston," my aunt sobbed.

10   "Langston, why don't you come? Why don't you come and be saved? Oh, Lamb of God! Why don't you come?"

11   Now it was really getting late. I began to be ashamed of myself, holding everything up so long. I began to wonder what God thought about Westley, who certainly hadn't seen Jesus either, but who was now sitting proudly on the platform, swinging his knickerbockered legs and grinning down at me, surrounded by deacons and old women on their knees praying. God had not struck Westley dead for taking his name in vain or for lying in the temple. So I decided that maybe to save further trouble, I'd better lie, too, and say that Jesus had come, and get up and be saved.

So I got up.   12

Suddenly the whole room broke into a sea of shouting, as they saw   13
me rise. Waves of rejoicing swept the place. Women leaped in the air.
My aunt threw her arms around me. The minister took me by the hand
and led me to the platform.

When things quieted down, in a hushed silence, punctuated by a   14
few ecstatic "Amens," all the new young lambs were blessed in the
name of God. Then joyous singing filled the room.

That night, for the last time in my life but one—for I was a big boy   15
twelve years old—I cried. I cried, in my bed alone, and couldn't stop. I
buried my head under the quilts, but my aunt heard me. She woke up
and told my uncle I was crying because the Holy Ghost had come into
my life, and because I had seen Jesus. But I was really crying because I
couldn't bear to tell her that I had lied, that I had deceived everybody in
the church, and I hadn't seen Jesus, and that now I didn't believe there
was a Jesus any more, since he didn't come to help me.

—— CONSIDERATIONS ——————————————————

1. Hughes tells this critical episode of his childhood in a simple, straightforward, unelaborated fashion, almost as though he were still a child telling the
story as it happened. Why is it necessary to say "*almost* as though he were still a
child"? How would you go about recounting a critical moment in your
childhood? Where does simple childhood memory stop and adult judgment take
over?

2. Hughes's disillusionment is an example of what people call "an initia-
tion story." Compare it with the Ernest Hemingway short story, or John Updike's story, or the autobiographical essay by Lillian Hellman. Discuss the
degrees of awareness noticeable among these varied characters.

3. Why is it so important to the congregation of Auntie Reed's church
that everyone, children included, acknowledge their salvation?

4. Why does Westley finally proclaim that he is saved?

5. In his final paragraph, Hughes writes, "That night, for the last time in
my life but one . . . I cried." He does not tell us, in this account, what that other
time was. Read a little more about his life, or simply use your imagination, and
write a brief account of the other time.

Thomas Jefferson (1743–1826) was the third president of the United States, and perhaps more truly the Father of his Country than George Washington was; or maybe we would only like to think so, for such paternity flatters the offspring. Jefferson was a politician, philosopher, architect, inventor, and writer. With an energy equal to his curiosity, he acted to improve the world: he wrote the Declaration of Independence; he wrote a life of Jesus; and he founded the University of Virginia, whose original buildings he designed. An arch-republican, fearful of Alexander Hamilton's monarchical reverence for authority, Jefferson withheld support from the Constitution until he saw the Bill of Rights added to it.

We take this text from Garry Wills's Inventing America *(1978); by juxtaposition, Wills demonstrates the revision of a classic.*

43

THOMAS JEFFERSON

The Declarations of Jefferson and of the Congress

I will state the form of the declaration as originally reported. The parts struck out by Congress shall be distinguished by a black line drawn under them; & those inserted by them shall be placed in the margin or in a concurrent column:

1   A Declaration by the representatives of the United states of America, in [General] Congress assembled.

2   When in the course of human events it becomes necessary for one people to dissolve the political bands which have connected them with another, and to assume among the powers of the earth the separate & equal station to which the laws of nature and of nature's god entitle them, a decent respect to the opinions of

Taken from Jefferson's Notes and Proceedings—*Papers*, 1:315–319.

mankind requires that they should declare the causes which impel them to the separation.

3   We hold these truths to be self evident: that all men are created equal; that they are endowed by their creator with ∧ [inherent and] inalienable rights; that among these are life, liberty & the pursuit of happiness: that to secure these rights, governments are instituted among men, deriving their just powers from the consent of the governed; that whenever any form of government becomes destructive of these ends, it is the right of the people to alter or to abolish it, & to institute new government, laying it's foundation on such principles, & organising it's powers in such form, as to them shall seem most likely to effect their safety & happiness. Prudence indeed will dictate that governments long established should not be changed for light & transient causes; and accordingly all experience hath shewn that mankind are more disposed to suffer while evils are sufferable than to right themselves by abolishing the forms to which they are accustomed. But when a long train of abuses & usurpations [begun at a distinguished period and] pursuing invariably the same object, evinces a design to reduce them under absolute despotism it is their right, it is their duty to throw off such government, & to provide new guards for their future security. Such has been the patient sufferance of these colonies; & such is now the necessity which constrains them to ∧ [expunge] their former systems of government. The history of the present king of Great Britain is a history of ∧ [unremitting] injuries & usurpations, [among which appears no solitary fact to contradict the uniform tenor of the rest but all have] ∧ in direct object the establishment of an absolute tyranny over these states. To prove this let facts be submitted to a candid world [for the truth of which we pledge a faith yet unsullied by falsehood.]

[margin: certain]

[margin: alter]

[margin: repeated]

[margin: all having]

4   He has refused his assent to laws the most wholesome & necessary for the public good.

5   He has forbidden his governors to pass laws of immediate & pressing importance, unless suspended in their operation till his assent should be obtained; & when so suspended, he has utterly neglected to attend to them.

6   He has refused to pass other laws for the accommodation of large districts of people, unless those people would relinquish the right of representation in the legislature, a right inestimable to them, & formidable to tyrants only.

7   He has called together legislative bodies at places unusual, uncomfortable, and distant from the depository of their public records, for the sole purpose of fatiguing them into compliance with his measures.

8   He has dissolved representative houses repeatedly [& continu-
ally] for opposing with manly firmness his invasions on the
rights of the people.

9   He has refused for a long time after such dissolutions to cause
others to be elected, whereby the legislative powers, incapable of
annihilation, have returned to the people at large for their exercise, the state remaining in the mean time exposed to all the
dangers of invasion from without & convulsions within.

10   He has endeavored to prevent the population of these states;
for that purpose obstructing the laws for naturalization of for-
eigners, refusing to pass others to encourage their migrations
hither, & raising the conditions of new appropriations of lands.

11   He has ∧ [suffered] the administration of justice [totally to   obstructed
cease in some of these states]∧ refusing his assent to laws for   by
establishing judiciary powers.

12   He has made [our] judges dependant on his will alone, for the
tenure of their offices, & the amount & paiment of their salaries.

13   He has erected a multitude of new offices [by a self assumed
power] and sent hither swarms of new officers to harrass our
people and eat out their substance.

14   He has kept among us in times of peace standing armies [and
ships of war] without the consent of our legislatures.

15   He has affected to render the military independent of, &
superior to the civil power.

16   He has combined with others to subject us to jurisdiction
foreign to our constitutions & unacknowledged by our laws,
giving his assent to their acts of pretended legislation for quarter-
ing large bodies of armed troops among us; for protecting them
by a mock-trial from punishment for any murders which they
should commit on the inhabitants of these states; for cutting off
our trade with all parts of the world; for imposing taxes on us
without our consent; for depriving us ∧ of the benefits of trial by   in many
jury; for transporting us beyond seas to be tried for pretended   cases
offences; for abolishing the free system of English laws in a
neighboring province, establishing therein an arbitrary government, and enlarging it's boundaries, so as to render it at once an
example and fit instrument for introducing the same absolute
rule into these ∧ [states]; for taking away our charters, abolishing   colonies
our most valuable laws, and altering fundamentally the forms of
our governments; for suspending our own legislatures, & declar-   by declaring
ing themselves invested with power to legislate for us in all cases   us out of his
whatsoever.   protection &
                                                                    waging war
17   He has abdicated government here ∧ [withdrawing his gover-   against us
nors, and declaring us out of his allegiance & protection.]

18   He has plundered our seas, ravaged our coasts, burnt our towns, & destroyed the lives of our people.

19   He is at this time transporting large armies of foreign merce-naries to compleat the works of death, desolation & tyranny already begun with circumstances of cruelty and perfidy ∧ un-worthy the head of a civilized nation.   *[margin: scarcely paralleled in the most barbarous ages, & totally]*

20   He has constrained our fellow citizens taken captive on the high seas to bear arms against their country, to become the executioners of their friends & brethren, or to fall themselves by their hands.

21   He has ∧ endeavored to bring on the inhabitants of our fron-tiers the merciless Indian savages, whose known rule of warfare is an undistinguished destruction of all ages, sexes, & conditions [of existence.]   *[margin: excited domestic insurrections amongst us, & has]*

22   [He has incited treasonable insurrections of our fellow-citizens, with the allurements of forfeiture & confiscation of our property.

23   He has waged cruel war against human nature itself, violat-ing it's most sacred rights of life and liberty in the persons of a distant people who never offended him, captivating & carrying them into slavery in another hemisphere or to incur miserable death in their transportation thither. This piratical warfare, the opprobrium of *infidel* powers, is the warfare of the *Christian* king of Great Britain. Determined to keep open a market where *Men* should be bought & sold, he has prostituted his negative for suppressing every legislative attempt to prohibit or to restrain this execrable commerce. And that this assemblage of horrors might want no fact of distinguished die, he is now exciting those very people to rise in arms among us, and to purchase that liberty of which he has deprived them, by murdering the people on whom he also obtruded them: thus paying off former crimes committed against the *Liberties* of one people, with crimes which he urges them to commit against the *lives* of another.]

24   In every stage of these oppressions we have petitioned for redress in the most humble terms: our repeated petitions have been answered only by repeated injuries. A prince whose charac-ter is thus marked by every act which may define a tyrant is unfit to be the ruler of a ∧ people [who mean to be free. Future ages will scarcely believe that the hardiness of one man adventured, within the short compass of twelve years only, to lay a founda-tion so broad & so undisguised for tyranny over a people fostered & fixed in principles of freedom.]   *[margin: free]*

25   Nor have we been wanting in attentions to our British breth-ren. We have warned them from time to time of attempts by their

legislature to extend ∧ [a] jurisdiction over ∧ [these our states.]   an unwarranta
We have reminded them of the circumstances of our emigration   us
& settlement here, [no one of which could warrant so strange a
pretension: that these were effected at the expence of our own
blood & treasure, unassisted by the wealth or the strength of
Great Britain: that in constituting indeed our several forms of
government, we had adopted one common king, thereby laying a
foundation for perpetual league & amity with them: but that
submission to their parliament was no part of our constitution,
nor ever in idea, if history may be credited: and,] we ∧ appealed to   have
their native justice and magnanimity ∧ [as well as to] the ties of
our common kindred to disavow these usurpations which ∧   and we have
[were likely to] interrupt our connection and correspondence.   conjured them
They too have been deaf to the voice of justice & of consan-   would
guinity, [and when occasions have been given them, by the regu-   inevitably
lar course of their laws, of removing from their councils the
disturbers of our harmony, they have, by their free election,
reestablished them in power. At this very time too they are
permitting their chief magistrate to send over not only souldiers
of our common blood, but Scotch & foreign mercenaries to in-
vade & destroy us. These facts have given the last stab to agonizing affection, and manly spirit bids us to renounce for ever these
unfeeling brethren. We must endeavor to forget our former love
for them, and to hold them as we hold the rest of mankind
enemies in war, in peace friends. We might have been a free and a
great people together; but a communication of grandeur & of
freedom it seems is below their dignity. Be it so, since they will
have it. The road to happiness & to glory is open to us too. We
will tread it apart from them, and] ∧ acquiesce in the necessity   we must the
which denounces our [eternal] separation ∧!   and hold
                                                  them as we
26   We therefore the representa-   liament of Great Britain: & fi-   hold the rest
tives of the United states of   nally we do assert & declare   of mankind
America in General Congress   these colonies to be free & inde-   enemies in
assembled do in the name, & by   pendant states,] & that as free &   war in peace
the authority of the good people   independant states, they have   friends.
of these [states reject & re-   full power to levy war, conclude
nounce all allegiance & sub-   peace, contract alliances, estab-
jection to the kings of Great   lish commerce, & to do all other
Britain & all others who may   acts & things which independ-
hereafter claim by, through or   ant states may of right do. And
under them: we utterly dissolve   for the support of this declara-
all political connection which   tion we mutually pledge to each
may heretofore have subsisted   other our lives, our fortunes &
between us & the people or par-   our sacred honour.

We therefore the representatives of the United states of America in General Congress assembled, appealing to the supreme judge of the world for the rectitude of our intentions, do in the name, & by the authority of the good people of these colonies, solemnly publish & declare that these United colonies are & of right ought to be free & independant states; that they are absolved from all allegiance to the British crown, and that all political connection between them & the state of Great Britain is, & ought to be, totally dissolved; & that as free & independant states they have full power to levy war, conclude peace, contract alliances, establish commerce & to do all other acts & things which independant states may of right do.

And for the support of this declaration, with a firm reliance on the protection of divine providence we mutually pledge to each other our lives, our fortunes & our sacred honour.

—— CONSIDERATIONS

1. What part of the original declaration deleted by Congress most surprises you? Why?

2. Make a careful study of the first eight or ten changes imposed by Congress on Jefferson's original declaration. Why do you think each was made? Would any of them have made good examples for George Orwell to use in his "Politics and the English Language"?

3. Garry Wills says in his book *Inventing America* that the declaration is easy to misunderstand because it "is written in the lost language of the Enlightenment." What was the Enlightenment? How does the language of that period differ from that of today? Perhaps the declaration should be rewritten in modern English?

4. If you conclude that the declaration should be rewritten, try your hand at it. Try, for instance, rewriting the famous third paragraph: "We hold these truths. . . ." Can you be sure you're not writing a parody?

5. How is the declaration organized? Does it break down into distinct parts? If so, what is the function of those parts?

*Verlyn Klinkenborg (b. 1952) grew up in Iowa, son of a teacher
and a nurse who were themselves children of farmers. Through
visits to relatives, he returned to the hayfields his parents had
left. While he wrote about haying in the midwest, he lived in
the East: It is a commonplace that writers write best about
winter during summer, and about home when they are far away.
Klinkenborg took a Ph.D. at Princeton University and is now a
Briggs Copeland Lecturer at Harvard University.*

44

VERLYN KLINKENBORG
While We Waited

1   While we waited, here are the things we did.

2   Chores twice every day. Standing with a feed wagon at the silo,
waiting for it to fill with corn and sorghum silage for the cattle in the
lower feedlot. Two bales of hay for the yearling calves. A half-bale for
the young Simmenthal bull that Reggie named Nelson because it was
purchased from the Rockefeller herd. Check the twenty-six calves and
their mothers in the pasture that straddles the river. Milk for the wild
kittens in the calf barn. Pork liver for their parents. Feed Sam the dog.
Feed ourselves, and give ourselves coffee. (The pigs take care of themselves, day and night. Self-feeders.)

3   Preparing for chores, stand by the corn dryer as an auger ships corn
into the IH feed grinder, which turns it into a rough powder. A sign on
the corn dryer says: "Work with safety line. Avoid center. Avoid flowing grain. Danger of suffocation." In Louie's boyhood, when flax was
still grown in this region, men drowned in flax seed. When one of the
belts on the feed grinder breaks, replace it.

4   Drive to Kanaranzi Elevator on Monday morning, when the temperature is forty degrees, to buy sorghum seed and the herbicide 2,4-D,
which kills broadleaf plants by causing them to grow to death, and

Banvel (three quarts of each to 200 gallons of water, about a half pint per acre). The elevator man has sold half of Louie's sorghum seed to someone else. Louie talks of a two-hour wait in line to dump beans at the elevator during harvest. Kanaranzi may be the only town, hardly a town, just a small herd of buildings, in the country whose bank was held up by men driving snowmobiles. They fled across open fields, ditched the machines, and escaped in a car. They were never caught.

On the IH 656 I spray the young beans, which requires a windless, rainless day. So does the rest of the county. I listen to KEW and KQAD on the radio. I shiver in the cold, except when I drive into the wind. I get the point of closed-cab tractors. I keep my eyes peeled for killdeer and yellow-headed blackbirds. Janelle and Louie begin cultivating corn. The cultivating goes on for three days. Louie drills sorghum in a small field north of the house where beans washed out. 5

We pay some visits. To my dad's next-older brother, Kenneth, and his wife, Frieda. Ken and Frieda are the only town dwellers among my dad's siblings. Ken runs the NAPA parts store in Rock Rapids. Behind it he garages an immense white Cadillac (1959). When my dad is in town he sits at Frieda's organ and plays "Danke Schön." Ken is a cheerful man who collects Jim Beam decanters. All the bourbon remains intact, sealed, except what gradually evaporates through the porcelain. Ken specializes in Jim Beam autos and trains. He showed me two shelves full of original Jim Beam boxes and receipts. 6

We visit my dad's oldest brother, Everon, who has just returned from China where he and the rest of his World War II Flying Tiger squadron revisited their old bases. The living room is filled with Chinese gifts. Everon was a Norden bombsight specialist and lives on the home place, where my father was raised, the farm I know best. With Esther, his wife, he has raised a flock of boys (seven) and a single girl, Donna. 7

Bruce and another neighbor, name of Gary, stop by and ask for our help moving calves. Louie hitches his trailer to the pickup and we head a couple of miles north. Bruce's Holstein calves have escaped and high-tailed it down the road to a deserted farmstead where Bruce and Gary have penned them in an old dairy yard. The house stands vacant, drapes sagging, but the farm buildings are filled with pigs. In coveralls and workboots, Gary and Bruce wade deep into the thick green muck of the yard and work the cattle toward a gate—I work them away from the barn. It takes two trips to trailer them back where they belong. While we are at Bruce's we pick up Louie's other bull, a Limousin called (unofficially) Red Nuts. Red Nuts and Nelson will be put out to pasture 8 with the heifers in July and next spring there will be a new crop of calves. For the moment, Red Nuts and Nelson engage in some chivalrous combat.

9   Stopped to see W. Ray, who is always called W. (pronounced *dub-ya*) Ray. Louie has run out of square-baled alfalfa for his calves and W. Ray has some extra. W. Ray has a high wheezing laugh that explodes out of nowhere. His dog Ginger has just killed a skunk. "Git, Ginger, git outta here. And I gotta spend the rest of the day with her"—then that big surprising laugh from a man with wire-rim glasses. W. Ray built a fine new ranch house within three feet of a two-story stucco house that is gradually falling in. It took seven years to finish the new house. When W. Ray decided to build it, he immediately lost interest in the old one. Louie says, "He used to make you walk right in with your shit boots on." W. Ray and I toss down bales of second-cut hay from the hayloft of the most cavernous, heavily timbered barn I have ever seen. W. Ray recommends leather gloves for slinging bales. W. Ray is the kind of man (say Louie and Janelle, who both get a bang out of him) who will borrow your feed wagon, haul it all the way to Ellsworth and back, and then, to repay you, take you out to the Magnolia Lounge Bar and Steak Restaurant in Magnolia and get angry if you don't order the most expensive item on the menu. The Magnolia Lounge Bar and Steak Restaurant, with its $6.95 filets, may be the best place to eat in all of Minnesota.

10   We fix fence. Down where the Rock River curves around the beanfield, some wires are down and we find, flashlights in hand, news on the TV, a couple of cows standing dumbly among the beans. They hup back over the fence. The next night Louie and I decide to do a little catfish angling down where the cattle leaped the fence. We take a lunch (it is 8:00 p.m.), a thermos, and some beef liver. We thread the liver onto hooks and sling them into the river with rods and reels I found behind the bar in the basement. We fish for ten minutes, then agree it is too damn cold for June and head back to the house. Louie wonders if I am the angler he has heard I am.

11   Neighbors stop by in the evening to order seed from Louie, who represents Jacques Seed. My parents' house in California is filled with Jacques Seed paraphernalia—pitchers, calendars, hats, vests—as well as pig paraphernalia. Janelle and Louie are pork boosters and a portion of profits on their hogs goes to the Pork Producers' Association for advertising.

12   We go to Harlan's to pick up Louie's IH 1066. We go to Harlan's to pick up a short battery cable. We go to J & M in Luverne to pick up a battery for the township's Allis and some sisal baling twine from Du-

buque. We also stop in at Mark Jacobson's Luverne International dealership so Louie can pick up the electronic monitor for his corn planter after a forty-four dollar repair. The monitor tells the tractor driver whether the planter is seeding the ground uniformly. Last spring it blew a transistor no bigger than a corn kernel and omitted every eighth row in one of the upper fields, which Louie had to fill in as best he could.

And every day we walk out to the alfalfa and kick the swath we cut 13 on Saturday. It has not dried. Nothing has dried. For three days it is cloudy and cold. I mow the lawn and the grove and around the implements beside the granary. I pretend I am windrowing alfalfa. I take walks through the alfalfa with Sam the dog. I come to know alfalfa.

_____ **CONSIDERATIONS** _____

1. How does Klinkenborg's style change as one moves from the first two or three paragraphs into the remainder of the piece?

2. Compared with almost any other essay in this text, "While We Waited" seems to lack all of the qualities that essayists strive for. Why, then, is it included in the text?

3. Why does the author not explain such terms as "IH 656," "NAPA," "Danke Schön," "Jim Beam decanters," and "J & M"?

4. What is another characteristic of Klinkenborg's style that suggests oral (as opposed to written) language or the language of a private journal?

5. In what sense is Klinkenborg's last sentence an understatement?

Maxine Kumin (b. 1925) came north from Philadelphia to attend Radcliffe College and has remained in New England, since 1976 in her beloved New Hampshire countryside, where she farms and raises horses. She is a poet, with a Pulitzer Prize won in 1973 for her collection Up Country. *Her other books include* Our Ground Time Here Will Be Brief *(1982) and most recently* Nurture *(1989). In 1989 she became Poet Laureate of New Hampshire. She has also published novels, a collection of short stories, many children's books, and two essay collections. We take this essay from* In Deep *(1987).*

45

MAXINE KUMIN
Building Fence

1   Making fences presupposes not only pastures but a storehouse of diligence. When you start from a tangle of sumac and blackberry, every reclaimed square yard seems more precious than an acre of riverbottom land. For a dozen years we've been pushing back the forest, clearing, seeding, and sustaining what now adds up to fourteen up-and-down acres of the once two hundred-odd that nurtured a dairy herd between the two world wars.

2   Building the fence itself is an imperfect science. Despite actual measurements, you have to yield to the contours of the land. Post holes are soul destroyers. Technology hasn't done much for the fence line on a hill farm. Even if you hire a neighbor's tractor with auger attachment, at least half the holes will have to be hand crafted as you ease them this side or that of expectation. Stones annoy, rocks impede, boulders break your heart as you tunnel down at a slant, hunting in vain for the earth bottom. If obdurate ledge or obstinate pudding stone does not require acts of faith and leaps of imagination, here and there you can count on a slope too steep for machinery to navigate. The gasoline-powered two-

From *In Deep* by Maxine Kumin. Reprinted by permission of Viking Penguin, Inc., a division of Penguin Books USA Inc.

man auger is more adaptable, but even that ingenious tool will not maneuver between stump and bedrock with the same agility as the old manual clamshell tool.

Setting the posts exacts more faith from the dogged fence-pilgrim. 3 Somehow there is never enough dirt in the pile you took out, even after you've placed a ring of stones in the bottom of the hole to brace the post. Even with a ring of stones stomped in nearly at the top for further support, your supply of loose dirt has vanished. You end up digging part of a second hole to make enough friable earth to hold the first pole solid. Clearly, you do not come out even.

You've set 225 posts, roughly ten feet apart. From an appropriate 4 distance, if you squint, it's merely a toothpick stockade, inconclusive and raw-looking. You long to get on with it, to establish the feeling of fence, the ethos of enclosure.

The best part of building the fence is tacking up the string that 5 denotes where the line of top boards means to be. You go around importantly to do this light work, trailing your ball of twine, wearing your apron of nails. You measure with your fold-up rule fifty-two inches from the ground—but where exactly *is* the ground? This mound, this declivity, this solitary flat patch? You tap in a nail, pull the string taut from the previous post, catch it with a few easy twists around, and so on. String stands in for wood, a notion, a suggestion of what's to come. Foreshadowing, you could call it.

Because this is New England, the fence travels uphill and down; 6 only little bits of it are on the level. Although string lightheartedly imitates the contours of the land, boards have to be held in place, the angle of cut defined by pencil. Invariably, both ends of the boards want cutting. The eye wants readjustments despite the ruler. Sometimes bottom boards catch on hummocks, outcroppings, or earth bulges which must be shoveled out or the board rearranged. But let's say you've tacked up your whole top line for the day, you've stepped back, eye-balled and readjusted it. Oh, the hammering home! The joy and vigor of sending nails through hemlock into the treated four-by-four uprights. Such satisfying whacks, such permanence, such vengeance against the mass bustications of horses and heifers through the puny electric wire of yore. Visions of acres and acres of fences, field after field tamed, groomed, boarded in; that is the meaning of gluttony.

Finishing the fence—painting, staining, or applying preserva- 7 tive—requires the same constancy as the slow crafting of it. You put in your two hours a day, rejoice when rain interrupts the schedule and your Calvinist soul is permitted to tackle some other chore. Cleaning tack, for example, provides a pleasurable monotony compared to the servitude of the four-inch roller and the can of Noxious Mixture. In our case, it's composed of one-third diesel oil, one-third used crankcase oil, and one-third creosote. You are properly garbed to apply this Grade C syrup, wearing cast-off overalls, a battered felt hat, decayed boots, and thick neoprene gloves. You stand almost an arm's length away from the fence in order to get enough leverage so the mixture will penetrate wood grain—here tough, there smooth, here cracked and warty, there slick as a duck's feather. You invent methods for relieving the dreary sameness of the job. On one course you begin left to right, top to bottom, back to front. On the next you reverse the order. Sometimes you do all the undersides first, or all the backs. Sometimes you spring ahead, lavishly staining all the front-facing boards just to admire the dark wood lines dancing against the hummocky terrain of these young—yea, virginal— fields. The process gets you in the shoulder blades, later in the knees. You spatter freckles of the stuff on your protected body. Your protective eyeglasses are now freckled with iridescent dots. The stench of the mix permeates your hair, your gloved hands, becomes a way of life. You can no longer gain a new day without putting in your two hours staining board fences. More compelling than tobacco or alcohol, that addictive odor of char, of disinfectant, of grease pits. The horses follow you along the fence line, curious, but even the fresh-faced filly keeps a respectful distance from you and your repellent mixture.

8   A year later you sit atop the remnants of a six-foot-wide stone wall unearthed along the perimeter of number two field and look across to the remarkable pear tree that stands alone in the third and newest field. Behind you, the first field; behind it, the barn. Between fields, hedgerow and hickory trees, red pine and hemlock. An intermittent brook further defines the boundary between number one and number two. A tributary meanders at the foot of number three. Beyond, a life-time of second-growth woodland awaits. In your mind's eye, an infinity of fenced fields recedes but never vanishes. And all the livestock of a lifetime safely graze.

——— **CONSIDERATIONS** ————————————————————————

1. Make a little list of products you have seen advertised as "hand crafted." Then look at Kumin's use of the term to describe a hole in the ground. Is there something odd about that usage?

2. Can you remember jobs in which you had to invent "methods for relieving the dreary sameness" of a job, as Kumin puts it in paragraph 7? See also "Getting Tired," especially paragraph 13, for Carol Bly's method of keeping herself awake while driving a tractor back and forth across a field in Minnesota. Write an essay about the tricks and diversions we invent to get ourselves through a tedious job.

3. Do you find the word "bustications," as used in paragraph 6, in your dictionary? Neither do we. What does that suggest to you, first, about that particular word, and, second, about any newly invented word?

4. What phrase in paragraph 4 do the last two sentences of paragraph 8 elucidate?

Thomas Lynch (b. 1948) was born in Detroit and now lives in the town of Milford, Michigan, where he has been a funeral director since 1974. His first book of poems, Skating with Heather Grace, *was published by Knopf in 1988. "Burying" appeared in the* Quarterly.

46

THOMAS LYNCH

Burying

1   Every year I bury one hundred and fifty of my townspeople. Another dozen or two I take to the crematory to be burned. I sell caskets, burial vaults, and urns for the ashes. I have a sideline in headstones and monuments. I do flowers on commission.

2   Apart from the tangibles, I sell the use of my building eleven thousand square feet, furnished and fixtured with an abundance of pastel and chair rail and crown moldings. The whole lash-up is mortgaged and remortgaged well into the next century. My rolling stock includes a hearse, a limo, two Fleetwoods, and a mini-van with darkened windows our price list calls a service vehicle and everyone in town calls the Dead Wagon.

3   I used to use the "unit pricing method"—the old package deal. It meant you had only one number to look at. It was a large number. Now everything is itemized. It's the law. So now there is a long list of items and numbers and italicized disclaimers, something like a menu or the Sears, Roebuck wish book, and sometimes the federally mandated options begin to look like cruise control or rear-window defrost. I wear black most of the time, to keep folks in mind of the fact we're not talking Buicks here. At the bottom of the list there is still a large number.

4   In a good year the gross is close to half a million, 5 percent of which we hope to call profit. I am the only undertaker in this town. I have a corner on the market.

From the *Quarterly*. Reprinted by permission of the author.

The market, such as it is, is figured on what is called the "crude 5
death rate"—the number of deaths every year out of every thousand of
persons.

Here is how it works. 6

Imagine a large room into which you coax one thousand people. 7
You slam the doors in January, leaving them plenty of food and drink,
color TVs, magazines, condoms. Your sample should have an age distribution heavy on Baby Boomers and their children—1.2 children per
boomer. For every four normal people, there is one Old-Timer, who, if
he or she wasn't in this big room, would probably be in Florida or
Arizona or a nursing home. You get the idea. The group will include
fifteen lawyers, one faith healer, three dozen real-estate agents, a video
technician, several licensed counselors, and an Amway distributor. The
rest will be between jobs, middle managers, ne'er-do-wells, or retired.

Now the magic part—come late December, when you throw open 8
the doors, only 991.3, give or take, will shuffle out upright. Two hundred and sixty will now be selling Amway. The other 8.7 have become
the crude death rate.

Here's another stat. 9

Of the 8.7 corpses, two-thirds will have been Old-Timers, 5 per- 10
cent will be children, and the rest (2.75) will be Boomers—realtors and
attorneys—one of whom was, no doubt, elected to public office during
the year. What's more, three will have died of cerebral vascular or
coronary difficulties, two of cancer, one each of vehicular mayhem,
diabetes, and domestic violence. The spare change will be by act of God
or suicide—most likely the faith healer.

The figure most often and most conspicuously missing from the 11
insurance charts and demographics is the one I call THE BIG ONE, which
refers to the number of people out of every one hundred born who will
die. Over the long haul, THE BIG ONE hovers right around . . . well—
dead nuts on 100. If this were on the charts, they would call it "Death
expectancy" and no one would buy futures of any kind. But it is a useful
number and has its lessons. Maybe you will want to figure out what to
do with your life. Maybe it will make you feel a certain kinship to the
rest of us. Maybe it will make you hysterical. Whatever the implications of a one hundred death expectancy, calculate how big a town this
is and why mine produces for me steady, if sometimes unpredictable,
labor.

They die around the clock here, without apparent preference for a 12
day of the week, month of the year; there is no clear favorite in the way
of season. Nor does the alignment of the stars, fullness of moon, or

liturgical calendar have very much to do with it. The whereabouts are neither here nor there. They go off upright or horizontally, in Chevrolets and nursing homes, in bathtubs, on the interstates, in ERs, ORs, BMWs. And while it may be so that we assign more equipment or more importance to deaths that create themselves in places marked by initials—ICU being somehow better than Greenbrier Convalescent Home—it is also true that the dead don't care. In this way, the dead I bury and burn are like the dead before them, for whom time and space have become mortally unimportant. This loss of interest is, in fact, one of the first sure signs that something serious is about to happen. The next thing is they quit breathing. At this point, to be sure, a "gunshot wound to the chest" or "shock and trauma" will get more ink than a CVA or ASHD, but no condition of death is any less permanent than any other. All will do. The dead don't care.

13   Nor does *who* much matter, either. To say "I'm okay, you're okay, and by the way, he's dead!" is, for the living, a kind of comfort.

14   It is why we drag rivers and comb plane wrecks.

15   It is why MIA is more painful than DOA.

16   It is why we have open caskets and classified obits.

17   Knowing is better than not knowing, and knowing it is you is terrifically better than knowing it is me. Once I'm the dead guy, whether you're okay or he's okay won't much interest me. You can both go bag your asses, because the dead don't care.

18   Of course, the living, bound by their adverbs and their actuarials, still do. Now there's the difference and why I'm in business. The living are careful and oftentimes caring. The dead are careless, or maybe it's care-less. Either way, they don't care. These are unremarkable and verifiable truths.

19   My former mother-in-law, herself an unremarkable and verifiable truth, was always fond of holding forth with Cagneyesque bravado—to wit, "When I'm dead, just put me in a box and throw me in a hole." But whenever I would remind her that we did substantially that with *everyone,* the woman would grow sullen and a little cranky.

20   Later, over meat loaf and green beans, she would invariably give out with "When I'm dead, just cremate me and scatter the ashes."

21   My former mother-in-law was trying to make carelessness sound like fearlessness. The kids would stop eating and look at each other. The kids' mother would whine, "Oh, Mom, don't talk like that." I'd take out my lighter and begin to play with it.

22   In the same way, the priest that married me to this woman's

daughter—a man who loved golf and gold ciboria and vestments made of Irish linen; a man who drove a great black sedan with a wine-red interior and who always had his eye on the cardinal's job—this same fellow, leaving the cemetery one day, felt called upon to instruct me thus: "No bronze coffin for me. No sir! No orchids or roses or limousines. The plain pine box is the one I want, a quiet Low Mass, and the pauper's grave. No pomp or circumstance."

He wanted, he explained, to be an example of simplicity, of 23 prudence, of piety and austerity—all priestly and, apparently, Christian virtues. When I told him that he needn't wait, that he could begin his ministry of good example yet today, that he could quit the country club and do his hacking at the public links and trade his brougham for a used Chevette, that free of his Florsheims and cashmeres and prime ribs, free of his bingo nights and building funds, he could become, for Christ's sake, the very incarnation of Francis himself, or Anthony of Padua; when I said, in fact, that I would be willing to assist him in this, that I would gladly distribute his CDs and credit cards among the needy of the parish, and that I would, when the sad duty called, bury him for nothing in the manner he would have by then become accustomed to; when I told the priest who had married me these things, he said nothing at all, but turned his wild eye on me in the manner in which the cleric must have looked on Sweeney years ago, before he cursed him, irreversibly, into a bird.*

What I was trying to tell the fellow was, of course, that being a 24 dead saint is no more worthwhile than being a dead philodendron or a dead angelfish. Living is the rub, and always has been. Living saints still feel the flames and stigmata, the ache of chastity and the pangs of conscience. Once dead, they let their relics do the legwork, because, as I was trying to tell this priest, the dead don't care.

Only the living care. 25

And I am sorry to be repeating myself, but this is the central fact of 26 my business—that there is nothing, once you are dead, that can be done *to you* or *for you* or *with you* or *about you* that will do you any good or any harm; that any damage or decency we do accrues to the living, to whom your death happens if it really happens to anyone. The living have to live with it; you don't. Theirs is the grief or gladness your death brings. And there is the truth, abundantly self-evident, that seems, now

---

* Lynch alludes to a medieval Irish poem in which Sweeney attacks a priest, who puts a curse on Sweeney and changes him into a bird. The poem was recently translated from the Celtic by the Irish poet Seamus Heaney who called it, "Sweeney Astray."

that I think of it, the one most elusive to my old in-laws, to the parish priest, and to perfect strangers who are forever accosting me in barbershops and in cocktail bars and at parent-teacher conferences, hellbent or duty-bound on telling me what it is they want done with them when they are dead.

27   Give it a rest is the thing I say.

28   Once you are dead, put your feet up, call it a day, and let the old man or the missus or the thankless kids decide whether you are to be buried or burned or blown out of a cannon or left to dry out in a ditch. It's not your day to watch it, because the dead don't care.

29   Another reason people are always rehearsing their obsequies with me has to do with the fear of death, which is something anyone in his right mind has. It is healthy. It keeps us from playing in the traffic. I say pass it on to the kids.

30   There is a belief—widespread among the women I have dated, local Rotarians, and friends of my children—that I, being the undertaker here, have some irregular fascination with, special interest in, inside information about, even attachment to, *the dead.* They assume, these people, some perhaps with good reason, that I want their bodies.

31   It is an interesting concept.

32   But here's the truth.

33   Being dead is one—the worst, the last—but only one in a series of calamities that afflicts our own and several other species. The list may include, but is not limited to, gingivitis, bowel obstruction, contested divorce, tax audit, spiritual vexation, money trouble, political mischief, and on and on and on. There is no shortage of *misery.* And I am no more attracted to the dead than the dentist is to your bad gums, the doctor to your rotten innards, or the accountant to your sloppy expense records. I have no more stomach for misery than the banker or the lawyer, the pastor or the politico—because misery is careless and is everywhere. Misery is the bad check, the exwife, the mob in the street, and the IRS—who, like the dead, feel nothing, and, like the dead, *don't care.*

34   Which is not to say that the dead do not matter.

35   They do.

36   Last Monday morning, Milo Hornsby died. Mrs. Hornsby called at 2:00 A.M. to say that Milo had "expired" and would I take care of it, as if his condition were like any other that could be renewed or somehow improved upon. At 2:00 A.M., yanked from sleep, I am thinking, Put a quarter in Milo and call me in the morning. But Milo is dead. In a moment, in a twinkling, Milo has slipped irretrievably out of our reach, beyond Mrs. Hornsby and the children, beyond the women at the laun-

dromat he owned, beyond his comrades at the Legion Hall, the Grand
Master of the Masonic Lodge, his pastor at First Baptist, beyond the
mailman, zoning board, town council, and Chamber of Commerce;
beyond us all, and any treachery or any kindness we had in mind
for him.

Milo is dead.   37

X's on his eyes, lights out, curtains.   38

Helpless, harmless.   39

Milo's dead.   40

Which is why I do not haul to my senses, coffee and a quick shave,   41
Homburg and great coat, warm up the Dead Wagon, and make for the
freeway in the early o'clock for Milo's sake but for his missus's sake, for
she who has become, in the same moment and same twinkling, like
water to ice, the widow Hornsby. I go for her—because she still can cry
and care and pray and pay my bill.

The hospital that Milo died in is state of the art. There are signs on   42
every door declaring a part or process or bodily function. I like to think
that, taken together, the words would add up to something like the
Human Condition, but they never do. What's left of Milo, the remains,
are in the basement, between SHIPPING & RECEIVING and LAUNDRY
ROOM. Milo would like that if he were still liking anything. Milo's room
is called PATHOLOGY.

The medical-technical parlance of death emphasizes disorder. We   43
are forever dying of failures, of anomalies, of insufficiencies, of dysfunctions, arrests, accidents. These are either chronic or acute. The language of death certificates—Milo's says "Cardiopulmonary Failure"—
is like the language of weakness. Likewise, Mrs. Hornsby, in her grief,
will be said to be breaking down or falling apart or going to pieces, as if
there were something structurally awry with her. It is as if death and
grief were not part of the Order of Things, as if Milo's failure and his
widow's weeping were, or ought to be, sources of embarrassment. "Doing well" for Mrs. Hornsby would mean that she is bearing up, braving
the storm, or being strong for the children. We have willing pharmacists
to help her with this. Of course, for Milo, doing well would mean he was
back upstairs, holding his own, keeping the meters and monitors
bleeping.

But Milo is downstairs, between SHIPPING & RECEIVING and LAUN-   44
DRY ROOM, in a stainless-steel drawer, wrapped in white plastic top to
toe, and—because of his small head, wide shoulders, ponderous belly,
and skinny legs, and the trailing white binding cord from his ankles and
toe tags—he looks, for all the world, like a larger than life-size sperm.

45   I sign for him and get him out of there. At some level, I am still thinking Milo gives a shit, which by now we all know he doesn't—because the dead don't care.

46   Back at my place of business, upstairs in the embalming room, behind a door marked PRIVATE, Milo Hornsby is floating on a porcelain table under fluorescent lights. Unwrapped, outstretched, Milo is beginning to look a little more like himself—eyes wide open, mouth agape, returning to our gravity. I shave him, close his eyes, his mouth. We call this "setting the features." These are the features—eyes and mouth—that, in death, will never look the way they would look in life, when they are always opening, closing, focusing, signaling, telling us something. In death, what they tell us is they will not be doing anything anymore. The last detail to be managed is Milo's hands—one folded over the other, over the umbilicus, in an attitude of ease, of repose, of retirement.

47   They will not be doing anything anymore, either.

48   I wash his hands before positioning them.

49   When my wife moved out some years ago, I kept the children and the dirty laundry. It was big news in a small town. There was the gossip and the goodwill that places like this are famous for. And while there was plenty of talk, no one knew exactly what to say to me. They felt hopeless, I suppose. So they brought casseroles and beef stews, took the kids out to the movies or canoeing, brought their younger sisters around to visit me. What Milo did was send his laundry van by twice a week for two months, until I had found a housekeeper. Milo would pick up five loads in the morning and return them by lunchtime, fresh and folded. I never asked him to do this. I hardly knew him. I had never been in his home or in his laundromat. His wife had never known my wife. His children were too old to play with my children.

50   After my housekeeper was installed, I went to thank Milo and to pay my bill. The invoices detailed the number of loads, the washers and the dryers, detergent, bleaches, fabric softeners. I think the total came to sixty dollars. When I asked Milo what the charges were for pickup and delivery, for stacking and folding, for saving my life and the lives of my children, for keeping us in clean clothes and towels and bed linens, "Never mind that," Milo said, "one hand washes the other."

51   I place Milo's right hand over his heft hand, then try the other way. Then back again. Then I decide that it does not matter, that one hand washes the other either way.

52   The embalming takes me about two hours.

53   It is daylight by the time I am done.

Every Monday morning Paddy Fulton comes to my office. He was   54
damaged in some profound way in Korea. The details of his damage are
unknown to the locals. Paddy Fulton has no limp or anything missing—
so everyone thinks it was something he saw in Korea that left him a
little simple, occasionally perplexed, the type to draw rein abruptly in
his daylong walks, to consider the meaning of litter, pausing over bottle
caps and gum wrappers. Paddy Fulton has a nervous smile and a dead-
fish handshake. He wears a baseball cap and thick eyeglasses. Every
Sunday night Paddy goes to the I.G.A. and buys up the tabloids at the
checkout stands with headlines that usually involve Siamese twins or
movie stars or UFOs. Paddy is a speed reader and a math whiz—but
because of his damage, he has never held a job and never applied for one.
Every Monday morning, Paddy brings me clippings of stories under
headlines like: 601 LB. MAN FALLS THRU COFFIN— A GRAVE SITUATION or
EMBALMER FOR THE STARS SAYS ELVIS IS FOREVER. The Monday morning
Milo died, Paddy's clipping had to do with an urn full of ashes that made
grunting and groaning noises, that whistled sometimes, and that was
expected to begin talking. Certain scientists in England could make no
sense of it. They had run several tests. The ashes' widow, however—left
with nine children and no estate—is convinced that her dearly beloved
and greatly reduced husband is trying to give her winning numbers for
the lottery. "Jacky would never leave us without good prospects," she
says. "He loved his family more than anything." There is a picture of
the two of them—the widow and the urn, the living and the dead, flesh
and bronze, the Victrola and the Victrola's dog. She has her ear cocked,
waiting.

We are always waiting. Waiting for some good word or for the   55
winning numbers. Waiting for a sign or wonder, some signal from our
dear dead that the dead still care. We are gladdened when they do
outstanding things, when they arise from their graves or appear to us in
dreams or fall from their caskets. It pleases us no end, as if there were no
end; as if the dead still cared, had agendas, were yet alive.

But the sad and well-known fact of the matter is that most of us   56
will stay in our caskets and be dead a long time, and that our urns and
graves will never make a sound. Our reason and requiems, our headstones and High Masses, will neither get us in nor keep us out of
heaven. The meaning of our lives, and the memories of them, will
belong only to the living, just as our funerals do.

We heat graves here for winter burials, as a kind of foreplay before   57
digging in, to loosen the frost's hold on the ground before the sexton and
his backhoe do the opening. We buried Milo in the ground last Wednesday. It was, by then, the only thing to do. The mercy is that what we

buried there, in an oak casket, just under the frost line, had ceased to be Milo. It was something else. Milo had become the idea of himself, a permanent fixture of the third person and past tense, his widow's loss of appetite and trouble sleeping, the absence in places where we look for him, our habits of him breaking, our phantom limb, our one hand washing the other.

—— CONSIDERATIONS ————————————————

1. Why is Thomas Lynch less than reverential toward the dead? Is he disrespectful toward them?

2. Are the following words synonymous: ironic, satiric, sardonic, cynical, humorous, witty, sarcastic? After comparing their definitions in a good dictionary, which one would you select as the most descriptive of Lynch's tone (attitude) in his essay? Be prepared to back up your choice by referring to illustrative words, phrases, or passages in "Burying." If you think none of these words is appropriate, make a case for any other word you think would be better.

3. In paragraph 43, Lynch tells us of something he discovers by looking at the "parlance of death." What is his criticism of that jargon?

4. In paragraph 46, find an example of Lynch making fun of his own parlance. What other evidence do you find that Lynch enjoys playing with language?

5. Some readers feel that Lynch is coldly commercial about his work. What passages might give them that impression? What evidence do you find that Lynch is not without feelings about the dead and their survivors?

6. What do you make of Lynch's method of explaining the "crude death rate"?

7. Look at some of Lynch's one-sentence paragraphs. How do you suppose he might defend them as paragraphs?

8. What did Milo's remark "One hand washes the other" mean to Lynch?

*John McPhee (b. 1931) was born in Princeton, New Jersey,
where he graduated from college, and where he still lives. His
writing, largely for the* **New Yorker**, *has taken him far afield, to
Florida for a book about oranges, to Maine for a book about
birchbark canoes, and all over the country for encounters with
the American wilderness. In 1977 he published a report on
Alaska called* Coming into the Country.

47

JOHN McPHEE
Ice Pond

Summer, 1981

At Princeton University, off and on since winter, I have observed   1
the physicist Theodore B. Taylor standing like a mountaineer on the
summit of what appears to be a five-hundred-ton Sno-Kone. Taylor now
calls himself a "nuclear dropout." His has been, at any rate, a semicir-
cular career, beginning at Los Alamos Scientific Laboratory, where, as
an imaginative youth in his twenties, he not only miniaturized the
atomic bomb but also designed the largest-yield fission bomb that had
ever been exploded anywhere. In his thirties, he moved on to General
Atomic, in La Jolla, to lead a project called Orion, his purpose being to
construct a spaceship sixteen stories high and as voluminous as a
college dormitory, in which he personally meant to take off from a
Nevada basin and set a course for Pluto, with intermediate stops on
Ganymede, Rhea, and Dione—ice-covered satellites of Jupiter and Sat-
urn. The spaceship Orion, with its wide flat base, would resemble the
nose of a bullet, the head of a rocket, the ogival hat of a bishop. It would
travel at a hundred thousand miles an hour and be driven by two
thousand fission bombs. Taylor's colleague Freeman Dyson meant to go
along, too, extending spectacularly a leave of absence from the Institute

for Advanced Study, in Princeton. The project was developing splendidly when the nuclear treaty of 1963 banned explosions in space and the atmosphere. Taylor quelled his dreams, and turned to a sombre subject. Long worried about the possibility of clandestine manufacture of nuclear bombs by individuals or small groups of terrorists, he spent his forties enhancing the protection of weapons-grade uranium and plutonium where it exists in private industries throughout the world. And now, in his fifties—and with the exception of his service as a member of the President's Commission on the Accident at Three Mile Island—he has gone flat-out full-time in pursuit of sources of energy that avoid the use of fission and of fossil fuel, one example of which is the globe of ice he has caused to be made in Princeton. "This isn't Ganymede," he informs me, scuffing big crystals under his feet. "But it's almost as exciting."

2   Taylor's hair is salt-and-peppery now but still stands in a thick youthful wave above his dark eyebrows and luminous brown eyes. He is tall, and he remains slim. What he has set out to do is to air-condition large buildings or whole suburban neighborhoods using less than ten per cent of the electricity required to cool them by conventional means, thereby saving more than ninety per cent of the oil that might be used to make the electricity. This way and that, he wants to take the "E" out of OPEC. The ice concept is simple. He grins and calls it "simple-minded—putting old and new ideas together in a technology appropriate to our time." You scoop out a depression in the ground, he explains—say, fifteen feet deep and sixty feet across—and line it with plastic. In winter, you fill it with a ball of ice. In summer, you suck ice water from the bottom and pump it indoors to an exchanger that looks something like an automobile radiator and cools air that is flowing through ducts. The water, having picked up some heat from the building, is about forty-five degrees as it goes back outside, where it emerges through shower heads and rains on the porous ice. Percolating to the bottom, the water is cooled as it descends, back to thirty-two degrees. Taylor calls this an ice pond. A modest number of ice ponds could cool, for example, the District of Columbia, saving the energy equivalent of one and a half million barrels of oil each summer.

3   The initial problem was how to make the ice. Taylor first brooded about this some years ago when he was researching the theoretical possibilities of constructing greenhouses that would aggregately cover tens of millions of acres and solve the pollution problems of modern agriculture. The greenhouses had to be cooled. He thought of making ice in winter and using it in summer. For various regions, he calculated

how much ice you would have to make in order to have something left on Labor Day. How much with insulation? How much without insulation? The volumes were small enough to be appealing. How to make the ice? If you were to create a pond of water and merely let it freeze, all you would get, of course, would be a veneer that would break up with the arrival of spring. Ice could be compiled by freezing layer upon layer, but in most places in the United States six or eight feet would be the maximum thickness attainable in an average winter, and that would not be enough. Eventually, he thought of artificial snow. Ski trails were covered with it not only in Vermont and New Hampshire but also in New Jersey and Pennsylvania, and even in North Carolina, Georgia, and Alabama. To make ice, Taylor imagined, one might increase the amount of water moving through a ski-resort snow machine. The product would be slush. In a pondlike receptacle, water would drain away from the slush. It could be pumped out and put back through the machine. What remained in the end would be a ball of ice.

Taylor had meanwhile become a part-time professor at Princeton, and on one of his frequent visits to the university from his home in Maryland he showed his paper ice ponds to colleagues at the university's Center for Energy and Environmental Studies. The Center spent a couple of years seeking funds from the federal government for an ice-pond experiment, but the government was not interested. In 1979, the Prudential Insurance Company of America asked the university to help design a pair of office buildings—to be built just outside Princeton—that would be energy-efficient and innovative in as many ways as possible. Robert Socolow, a physicist who is the Center's director, brought Taylor into the Prudential project, and Taylor soon had funds for his snow machine, his submersible pumps, his hole in the ground.   4

At Los Alamos, when Taylor got together on paper the components of a novel bomb he turned over his numbers and his ideas to other people, who actually made the device. Had such a job been his to do, there would have been no bombs at all. His mind is replete with technology but innocent of technique. He cannot competently change a tire. He has difficulty opening doors. The university hired Don Kirkpatrick, a consulting solar engineer, to assemble and operate appropriate hardware, while unskilled laborers such as Taylor and Freeman Dyson would spread insulating materials over the ice or just stand by to comment.   5

"The first rule of technology is that no one can tell in advance whether a piece of technology is any good," Dyson said one day. "It will   6 hang on things that are unforeseeable. In groping around, one wants to try things out that are quick and cheap and find out what doesn't work. The Department of Energy has many programs and projects—solar-energy towers and other grandiose schemes—with a common characteristic: no one can tell whether they're any good or not, and they're so big it will take at least five years and probably ten to find out. This ice pond is something you can do cheaply and quickly, and see whether it works."

7   A prototype pond was tried in the summer of 1980. It was dug beside a decrepit university storage building, leaky with respect to air and water, that had cinder-block walls and a flat roof. Size of an average house, there were twenty-four hundred square feet of space inside. Summer temperatures in the nineties are commonplace in New Jersey, and in musty rooms under that flat roof temperatures before the ice pond were sometimes close to a hundred and thirty. The 1980 pond was square—seventy-five feet across and fifteen feet deep. It contained a thousand tons of ice for a while, but more than half of that melted before insulation was applied: six inches of dry straw between sheets of polyethylene, weighed down with bald tires. Even so, the old building was filled most of the time from June to September with crisp October air. Something under seven tons of ice would melt away on a hot day. Nonetheless, at the end of summer a hundred tons remained. "It's a nice alternative to fossil fuels," Robert Socolow commented. "It has worked too well to be forgotten."

8   The concept having been successfully tested, the next imperative was to refine the art—technically, economically, and aesthetically. "The point is to make it elegant this time," said Freeman Dyson, and, from its hexagonal concrete skirt to its pure-white reflective cover, "elegant" is the word for the 1981 pond. Concealing the ice is a tentlike Dacron-covered free-span steel structure with six ogival sides—a cryodesic dome—which seems to emerge from the earth like the nose of a bullet, the head of a rocket, the hat of a bishop. Lift a flap and step inside. Look up at the summit of a white tower under insulation. Five hundred tons of ice—fifty-eight feet across the middle—rise to a conical peak, under layers of polyethylene foam, sewn into fabric like enormous quilts. It is as if the tip of the Finsteraarhorn had been wrapped by Christo.

9   Taylor, up on the foam, completes his inspection of the ice within, whose crystals are jagged when they first fall from the snow machine, and later, like glacier ice, recrystallize more than once into spheres of increasing diameter until the ultimate substance is very hard and re-

sembles a conglomerate of stream gravel. The U.S. Army's Cold Regions Research and Engineering Laboratory has cored it with instruments of the type used on glaciers in Alaska. Suspended from a girder high above Taylor's head and pointing at the summit of the ice is something that appears to be a small naval cannon with a big daisy stuck in its muzzle. This is SMI SnowStream 320, the machine that made the ice. In its days of winter operation, particles plumed away from it like clouds of falling smoke. Unlike many such machines, it does not require compressed air but depends solely on its daisy-petalled propeller blades of varying length for maximum effectiveness in disassembling water. "We are harvesting the cold of winter for use in the summer," Taylor says. "This is natural solar refrigeration, powered by the wind. Wind brings cold air to us, freezes the falling water, and takes the heat away. We are rolling with nature—trying to make use of nature instead of fighting it. That machine cost seven thousand dollars. It can make about eight thousand tons of ice in an average winter here in Princeton—for thirty-five dollars a hundred tons. A hundred tons is enough to air-condition almost any house, spring to fall. In the course of a winter, that machine could make ten thousand tons of ice in Boston, seven thousand in Washington, D.C., fifteen thousand in Chicago, thirty thousand in Casper, Wyoming, fifty thousand in Minneapolis, and, if anybody cares, a hundred thousand tons of ice in Fairbanks. The lower the temperature, the more water you can move through the machine. We don't want dry snow, of course. Snow is too fluffy. We want slop. We want wet sherbet. At twenty degrees Fahrenheit, we can move fifty gallons a minute through the machine. The electricity that drives the snow machine amounts to a very small fraction of the electricity that is saved by the cooling capacity of the ice. In summer, electrical pumps circulate the ice water from the bottom of the pond for a few tenths of a cent a ton. The cost of moving air in ducts through the building is the same as in a conventional system and is negligible in comparison with the electrical cost of cooling air. We're substituting ice water made with winter winds for the cold fluid in a refrigerated-air-conditioner, using less than a tenth as much electrical energy as a conventional air-conditioning system. Our goal is to make the over-all cost lower than the cost of a conventional system and use less than one-tenth of the energy. We're just about there."

The Prudential's new buildings—a hundred and thirty thousand   10
square feet each, by Princeton's School of Architecture and Skidmore, Owings & Merrill—will be started this summer on a site a mile away. They are low, discretionary structures, provident in use of resources,

durable, sensible, actuarial—with windows shaded just enough for summer but not too much for winter, with heat developing in a passive solar manner and brought in as well by heat pumps using water from the ground—and incorporating so many other features thrifty with energy that God will probably owe something to the insurance company after the account is totted up. An ice pond occupying less than half an acre can be expected to compound His debt.

11   A man who could devise atomic bombs and then plan to use them to drive himself to Pluto might be expected to expand his thinking if he were to create a little hill of ice. Taylor has lately been mulling the potentialities of abandoned rock quarries. You could fill an old rock quarry a quarter of a mile wide with several million tons of ice and then pile up more ice above ground as high as the Washington Monument. One of those could air-condition a hundred thousand homes. With all that volume, there would be no need for insulation. You would build pipelines at least ten feet in diameter and aim them at sweltering cities, where heat waves and crime waves would flatten in the water-cooled air. You could make ice reservoirs comparable in size to New York's water reservoirs and pipe ice water to the city from a hundred miles away. After the water had served as a coolant, it would be fed into the city's water supply.

12   "You could store grain at fifty degrees in India," Taylor goes on. "We're exploring that. The idea is to build an aqueduct to carry an ice slurry from the foothills of the Himalayas down to the Gangetic plain. With an insulated cover over the aqueduct, the amount of ice lost in, say, two hundred miles would be trivial—if the aqueduct is more than ten feet across. In place of electric refrigeration, dairies could use ice ponds to cool milk. Most cheese factories could use at least fifty thousand tons of ice a year. If all the cheese factories in the United States were to do that, they alone would save, annually, about six million barrels of oil. When natural gas comes out of the earth, it often contains too much water vapor to be suitable for distribution. One way to get rid of most of the water is to cool the gas to forty degrees. If ice ponds were used to cool, say, half the natural gas that is produced in this country, they would save the equivalent of ten million barrels of oil each year. Massive construction projects, such as dams, use amazing amounts of electricity to cool concrete while it hardens, sometimes for as much as three years. Ice ponds could replace the electricity. Ice ponds could cool power plants more effectively than environmental water does, and therefore make the power plants more efficient. Ice would also get rid of

the waste heat in a manner more acceptable than heating up a river. In places like North Dakota, you can make ice with one of these machines for a few cents a ton—and the coolant would be economically advantageous in all sorts of industrial processing."

Taylor shivers a little, standing on the ice, and, to warm himself, he lights a cigarette. "You could also use snow machines to freeze seawater," he continues. "As seawater freezes, impurities migrate away from it, and you are left with a concentrated brine rich in minerals, and with frozen water that is almost pure—containing so little salt you can't taste it. As seawater comes out of the snow machine and the spray is freezing in the air, the brine separates from the pure frozen water as it falls. To use conventional refrigeration—to use an electric motor to run a compressor to circulate Freon to freeze seawater—is basically too costly. The cost of freezing seawater with a ski-slope machine is less than a hundredth the cost of freezing seawater by the conventional system. There are sixty-six pounds of table salt in a ton of seawater, almost three pounds of magnesium, a couple of pounds of sulphur, nearly a pound of calcium, lesser amounts of potassium, bromine, boron, and so forth. Suppose you had a ship making ice from seawater with snow machines that had been enlarged and adapted for the purpose. You would produce a brine about ten times as concentrated with useful compounds as the original seawater. It would be a multifarious ore. Subsequent extraction of table salt, magnesium, fertilizers, and other useful material from the brine would make all these products cheaper than they would be if they were extracted from unconcentrated seawater by other methods. The table salt alone would pay for the ship. You could separate it out for a dollar a ton. A ship as large as a supertanker could operate most of the year, shuttling back and forth from the Arctic to the Antarctic. At latitudes like that, you can make twenty times as much ice as you can in Princeton."

"What do you do with the ice?"

"Your options are to return it to the sea or to put it in a skirt and haul it as an iceberg to a place where they need fresh water. The Saudis and the French have been looking into harvesting icebergs in Antarctica and towing them to the Red Sea. Someone has described this as bringing the mountain to Muhammad. I would add that if you happen to live in a place like New York the mountain is right at your doorstep—all you have to do is make it. The cost of making fresh water for New York City with snow machines and seawater would be less than the cost of delivered water there now. Boston looks awfully good—twice as good as Princeton. Boston could make fresh water, become a major producer of table salt and magnesium and sulphur, and air-condition itself—in one operation. All they have to do is make ice. It would renew Boston. More than a hundred years ago, people cut ice out of ponds there and shipped it around Cape Horn to San Francisco. When this country was getting going, one of Boston's main exports was ice."

—— **CONSIDERATIONS** ————————————————————————

1. Standing on top of his 500-ton Sno-Kone, Theodore Taylor told McPhee, "This isn't Ganymede, but it's almost as exciting." Why was his reference to Ganymede appropriate?

2. In paragraph 2, McPhee says that Taylor "wants to take the 'E' out of OPEC." What does the "E" stand for and why would getting rid of it fit in with Taylor's aims?

3. Why does McPhee lump Taylor with "unskilled laborers" in paragraph 5?

4. At the end of paragraph 8, McPhee, trying to describe Taylor's cone of ice wrapped in layers of polyethylene foam, writes, "It is as if the tip of the Finsteraarhorn had been wrapped by Christo." Assuming that neither of the capitalized words means anything to you, how do you assimilate them? Why do writers use such allusions?

Nancy Mairs (b. 1943) began life in California, went East to attend college in Massachusetts, and has worked as a technical writer and editor as well as a teacher at the high school and college levels. She has published a book of poems, In All the Rooms of the Yellow House *(1984), and a collection of essays,* Plain Text: Deciphering a Woman's Life *(1986), as well as* Remembering the Bone House: An Erotics of Place and Space *(1989).*

48

NANCY MAIRS
The Unmaking of a Scientist

My daughter is dissecting a chicken. Her first. Her father, whose job this usually is, has been derelict in his duties, and my hands are now too weak to dissect much more than a zucchini. If she wants dinner (and she does), she will make this pale, flabby carcass into eight pieces I can fit into the skillet. I act as coach. To encourage her, I tell her that her great-great-grandfather was a butcher. This is true, not something I have made up to con her into doing a nasty job. 1

Now that she's gotten going, she is having a wonderful time. She has made the chicken crow and flap and dance all over the cutting board, and now it lies quiet under her short, strong fingers as she slices the length of its breastbone. She pries back the ribs and peers into the cavity. "Oh, look at its mesenteries!" she cries. I tell her I thought mesentery was something you got from drinking the water in Mexico. She pokes at some filmy white webs. Mesenteries, she informs me, are the membranes that hold the chicken's organs in place. My organs too. She flips the chicken over and begins to cut along its spine. As her fingers search out joints and the knife severs wing from breast, leg from thigh, she gives me a lesson in the comparative anatomy of this chicken and the frog she and her friend Emily have recently dissected at school. 2

I am charmed by her enthusiasm and self-assurance. Since she was 3

From *Plain Text: Deciphering a Woman's Life*. Reprinted by permission of the University of Arizona Press.

quite small, she has talked of becoming a veterinarian, and now that she is approaching adulthood, her purpose is growing firmer. During this, her junior year in a special high school, she is taking a college-level introductory course in biology. I took much the same course when I was a freshman in college. But if I entered that course with Anne's self-confidence, and I may very well have done so, I certainly had none of it by the time I wrote the last word of my final examination in my blue book and turned it in the following spring. As the result of Miss White and the quadrat report, I am daunted to the point of dysfunction by the notion of thinking or writing "scientifically."

4   That woman—damn that woman!—turned me into a scientific cripple, and did so in the name of science at a prestigious women's college that promised to school me in the liberal arts that I might "have life and have it abundantly." And really, I have had it abundantly, so I suppose I oughtn't to complain if it's been a little short in *Paramecia* and *Amanita phalloides* and *Drosophila melanogaster*, whose eyes I have never seen.

5   Still, Miss White should not have been allowed to teach freshman biology because she had a fatal idiosyncrasy (fatal, that is, to the courage of students, not to herself, though I believe she is dead now of some unrelated cause): She could not bear a well-written report. One could be either a writer or a scientist but not both, she told me one November afternoon, the grey light from a tall window sinking into the grain of the dark woodwork in her cramped office in the old Science Building, her fingers flicking the sheets of my latest lab write-up. She was washing her hands of me, I could tell by the weariness of her tone. She didn't even try to make me a scientist. For that matter, she didn't even point to a spot where I'd gone wrong and show me what she wanted instead. She simply wrinkled her nose at the odor of my writing, handed me the sheets, and sent me away. We never had another conference. At the end of the semester, I wrote my quadrat report, and Miss White failed it. She allowed me to rewrite it. I wrote it again, and she failed it again. Neither of us went for a third try.

6   All the same, I liked my quadrat, which was a twenty-by-twenty plot in the College Woods behind the Library. Mine was drab compared to some others: Pam Weprin's, I remember, had a brook running through it, in which she discovered goldfish. It turned out that her magical discovery had a drab explanation: In a heavy rain the water from Peacock Pond backed up and spilled its resident carp into the brook. Even so, her quadrat briefly held an excitement mine never did. Mine was, in fact, as familiar as a living room, since I had spent large

portions of my youth tramping another such woods sixty miles north. The lichen grew on the north side of the trees. In the rain the humus turned black and rank. Afterwards, a fallen log across one corner would sprout ears of tough, pale fungus.

Each freshman biology student received a quadrat. There were 7 enough of us that we had to double up, but I never met my quadrat-mate or even knew her name. It occurs to me now that I ought to have found out, ought to have asked her what she got on her quadrat report, but I was new to failure and knew no ways to profit from it. I simply did as I was told—visited my quadrat to observe its progress through the seasons and wrote up my observations—and then discovered that I had somehow seen and spoken wrong. I wish now that I had kept the report. I wonder exactly what I said in it. Probably something about ears of fungus. Good God.

With a D+ for the first semester I continued, perversely, to like 8 biology, but I also feared it more and more. Not the discipline itself. I pinned and opened a long earthworm, marvelling at the delicately tinted organs. I dissected a beef heart, carefully, so as not to spoil it for stuffing and roasting at the biology department's annual beef-heart feast. For weeks I explored the interior of my rat, which I had opened neatly, like the shutters over a window. He was a homely thing, stiff, his fur yellow and matted from formaldehyde, and because he was male, not very interesting. Several students got pregnant females, and I envied them the intricate organs, the chains of bluish-pink fetuses. At the end of each lab, I would reluctantly close the shutters, swaddle my rat in his plastic bag, and slip him back into the crock.

No, biology itself held more fascination and delight than fear. But 9 with each report I grew more terrified of my own insidious poetic nature, which Miss White sniffed out in the simplest statement about planaria or left ventricles. Years later, when I became a technical editor and made my living translating the garbled outbursts of scientists, I learned that I had done nothing much wrong. My understanding was limited, to be sure, but Miss White would have forgiven me ignorance, even stupidity I think, if I had sufficiently muddled the language. As it was, I finished biology with a C−, and lucky I was to get it, since the next year the college raised the passing grade from C− to C. I have always thought, indeed, that the biology department awarded me a passing grade simply so that they wouldn't have to deal with me another year.

And they didn't. Nor did anyone else. I never took another science 10 course, although I surprised myself long afterward by becoming, perforce and precipitously, a competent amateur herpetologist. My husband arrived home one afternoon with a shoebox containing a young bull snake, or gopher snake as this desert variety is called, which he had bought for a quarter from some of his students at a school for emotionally disturbed boys so that they wouldn't try to find out how long a snake keeps wriggling without its head. This was Ferdinand, who was followed by two more bull snakes, Squeeze and Beowulf, and by a checkered garter snake named Winslow J. Tweed, a black racer named Jesse Owens, a Yuma king snake named Hrothgar, and numerous nameless and short-lived blind snakes, tiny and translucent, brought to us by our cats Freya, Burton Rustle, and Vanessa Bell. I grew so knowledgeable that when my baby boa constrictor, Crictor, contracted a respiratory ailment, I found that I was more capable of caring for him than were any of the veterinarians in the city. In fact, I learned, veterinarians do not do snakes; I could find only one to give Crictor the shot of a broad-spectrum antibiotic he needed.

11   So I do do snakes. I have read scientific treatises on them. I know that the Latin name for the timber rattlesnake is *Crotalus horridus horridus*. I know that Australia has more varieties of venomous snakes than any other continent, among them the lethal sea snakes and the willfully aggressive tiger snake. I know how long one is likely to live after being bitten by a mamba (not long). I read the treatises; but I don't, of course, write them. Although as a technical editor I grew proficient at unraveling snarls in the writing of scientists. I have never, since Miss White, attempted scientific experimentation or utterance.

12   Aside from my venture into herpetology, I remain a scientific booby. I mind my stupidity. I feel diminished by it. And I know now that it is unnecessary, the consequence of whatever quirk of fate brought me into Miss White's laboratory instead of Miss Chidsey's or Dr. McCoy's. Miss White, who once represented the whole of scientific endeavor to me, was merely a woman with a hobbyhorse. I see through her. Twenty years later, I am now cynical enough to write a quadrat report badly enough to pass her scrutiny, whereas when I had just turned seventeen I didn't even know that cynicism was an option—knowledge that comes, I suppose, from having life abundantly. I've learned, too, that Miss White's bias, though unusually strong, was not peculiar to herself but arose from a cultural rift between the humanities and the sciences resulting in the assumption that scientists will naturally write badly, that they are, in fact, rhetorical boobies. Today I teach technical writing. My students come to me terrified of the word-world from which they feel debarred, and I teach them to breach the bound-

aries in a few places, to step with bravado at least a little way inside. Linguistic courage is the gift I can give them.

In return, they give me gifts that I delight in—explanations of   13
vortex centrifuges, evaluations of copper-smelting processes, plans for extracting gums from paloverde beans. These help me compensate for my deficiencies, as do the works of the popularizers of science. Carl Sagan. Loren Eiseley. Lewis Thomas and his reverential reflections subtitled *Notes of a Biology Watcher*. Stephen Jay Gould. James Burke and Jacob Bronowski. Pierre Teilhard de Chardin. John McPhee, who has made me love rocks. Isaac Asimov. Elaine Morgan. I watch television too. *Nova. Odyssey. The Undersea World of Jacques Cousteau. The Body in Question*. But always I am aware that I am having translated for me the concepts of worlds I will never now explore for myself. I stand with my toes on the boundaries, peering, listening.

Anne has done a valiant job with the chicken. She's had a little   14
trouble keeping its pajamas on, and one of the thighs has a peculiar trapezoidal shape, but she's reduced it to a workable condition. I brown it in butter and olive oil. I press in several cloves of garlic and then splash in some white wine. As I work, I think of the worlds Anne is going to explore. Some of them are listed in the college catalogues she's begun to collect: "Genetics, Energetics, and Evolution"; "Histology of Animals"; "Vertebrate Endocrinology"; "Electron Microscopy"; "Organic Synthesis"; "Animal Morphogenesis."

Anne can write. No one has yet told her that she can be a scientist   15
or a writer but not both, and I trust that no one ever will. The complicated world can ill afford such lies to its children. As she plunges from my view into the thickets of calculus, embryology, and chemical thermodynamics, I will wait here for her to send me back messages. I love messages

—— **CONSIDERATIONS** —————————————————————————

1. What, precisely, is a quadrat? (*Hint:* It is not a member of the family *Muridae* nor of the genus *Rattus*, one specimen of which Mairs dissected as a girl in biology class. It does, however, figure importantly in Mairs's disillusionment with science education.)

2. Mairs does some interesting things with tenses in her essay. Study the changes carefully. How might you try them in your own writing?

3. "The complicated world can ill afford such lies to its children," Mairs writes in her closing paragraph. What lies does she mean? And why is she particularly well qualified to point them out?

4. Another aspect to the preceding question opens up if one thinks about the "cultural rift" Mairs writes about in paragraph 12 "between the humanities and the sciences." And what does she know about that?

5. Are any of the science writers so admired by Mairs in paragraph 13 immediately available to you?

6. What is the meaning of "mesentery," and how do the writer and her daughter have a bit of fun with the word?

Peter Marin (b. 1936) teaches at the University of California at Santa Barbara in the departments of sociology and of English —a double profession which probably makes him unique among American academics. He has taught at colleges all over the country, has directed a free school, has worked for the government, and has written in many genres: poems, a novel, and many essays of social criticism. He likes especially to investigate people and ideas that appear excluded from the center of American society. For several years he has spent much of his time in shelters and on the streets of American cities. He is currently writing a book about the homeless.

49

PETER MARIN
Helping and Hating the Homeless

When I was a child, I had a recurring vision of how I would end as 1 an old man: alone, in a sparsely furnished second-story room I could picture quite precisely, in a walk-up on Fourth Avenue in New York, where the secondhand bookstores then were. It was not a picture which frightened me. I liked it. The idea of anonymity and solitude and marginality must have seemed to me, back then, for reasons I do not care to remember, both inviting and inevitable. Later, out of college, I took to the road, hitchhiking and traveling on freights, doing odd jobs here and there, crisscrossing the country. I liked that too: the anonymity and the absence of constraint and the rough community I sometimes found. I felt at home on the road, perhaps because I felt at home nowhere else, and periodically, for years, I would return to that world, always with a sense of relief and release.

I have been thinking a lot about that these days, now that tran- 2 sience and homelessness have made their way into the national con-

Reprinted by permission of the author.

sciousness, and especially since the town I live in, Santa Barbara, has become well known because of the recent successful campaign to do away with the meanest aspects of its "sleeping ordinances"—a set of foolish laws making it illegal for the homeless to sleep at night in public places. During that campaign I got to know many of the homeless men and women in Santa Barbara, who tend to gather, night and day, in a small park at the lower end of town, not far from the tracks and the harbor, under the rooflike, overarching branches of a gigantic fig tree, said to be the oldest on the continent. There one enters much the same world I thought, as a child, I would die in, and the one in which I traveled as a young man: a "marginal" world inhabited by all those unable to find a place in "our" world. Sometimes, standing on the tracks close to the park, you can sense in the wind, or in the smell of tar and ties, the presence and age of that marginal world: the way it stretches backward and inevitably forward in time, parallel to our own world, always present, always close, and yet separated from us—at least in the mind—by a gulf few of us are interested in crossing.

3   Late last summer, at a city council meeting here in Santa Barbara, I saw, close up, the consequences of that strange combination of proximity and distance. The council was meeting to vote on the repeal of the sleeping ordinances, though not out of any sudden sense of compassion or justice. Council members had been pressured into it by the threat of massive demonstrations—"The Selma of the Eighties" was the slogan one heard among the homeless. But this threat that frightened the council enraged the town's citizens. Hundreds of them turned out for the meeting. One by one they filed to the microphone to curse the council and castigate the homeless. Drinking, doping, loitering, panhandling, defecating, urinating, molesting, stealing—the litany went on and on, was repeated over and over, accompanied by fantasies of disaster: the barbarian hordes at the gates, civilization ended.

4   What astonished me about the meeting was not what was said; one could have predicted that. It was the power and depth of the emotion revealed: the mindlessness of the fear, the vengefulness of the fury. Also, almost none of what was said had anything to do with the homeless people I know—not the ones I once traveled with, not the ones in town. They, the actual homeless men and women, might not have existed at all.

5   If I write about Santa Barbara, it is not because I think the attitudes at work here are unique. They are not. You find them everywhere in America. In the last few months I have visited several cities around the country, and in each of them I have found the same thing: more and

more people in the streets, more and more suffering. (There are at least 350,000 homeless people in the country, perhaps as many as 3 million.) And, in talking to the good citizens of these cities, I found, almost always, the same thing: confusion and ignorance, or simple indifference, but anger too, and fear.

What follows here is an attempt to explain at least some of that 6 anger and fear, to clear up some of the confusion, to chip away at the indifference. It is not meant to be definitive; how could it be? The point is to try to illuminate some of the darker corners of homelessness, those we ordinarily ignore, and those in which the keys to much that is now going on may be hidden.

The trouble begins with the word "homeless." It has become such 7 an abstraction, and is applied to so many different kinds of people, with so many different histories and problems, that it is almost meaningless.

Homelessness, in itself, is nothing more than a condition visited 8 upon men and women (and, increasingly, children) as the final stage of a variety of problems about which the word "homelessness" tells us almost nothing. Or, to put it another way, it is a catch basin into which pour all of the people disenfranchised or marginalized or scared off by processes beyond their control, those which lie close to the heart of American life. Here are the groups packed into the single category of "the homeless":

- Veterans, mainly from the war in Vietnam. In many American cities, vets make up close to 50 percent of all homeless males.
- The mentally ill. In some parts of the country, roughly a quarter of the homeless would, a couple of decades ago, have been institutionalized.
- The physically disabled or chronically ill, who do not receive any benefits or whose benefits do not enable them to afford permanent shelter.
- The elderly on fixed incomes whose funds are no longer sufficient for their needs.
- Men, women, and whole families pauperized by the loss of a job.
- Single parents, usually women, without the resources or skills to establish new lives.
- Runaway children, many of whom have been abused.
- Alcoholics and those in trouble with drugs (whose troubles often begin with one of the other conditions listed here).
- Immigrants, both legal and illegal, who often are not counted

among the homeless because they constitute a "problem" in their own right.

- Traditional tramps, hobos, and transients, who have taken to the road or the streets for a variety of reasons and who prefer to be there.

9   You can quickly learn two things about the homeless from this list. First, you can learn that many of the homeless, before they were homeless, were people more or less like ourselves: members of the working or middle class. And you can learn that the world of the homeless has its roots in various policies, events, and ways of life for which some of us are responsible and from which some of us actually prosper.

10   We decide, as a people, to go to war, we ask our children to kill and to die, and the result, years later, is grown men homeless on the street.

11   We change, with the best intentions, the laws pertaining to the mentally ill, and then, without intention, neglect to provide them with services; and the result, in our streets, drives some of us crazy with rage.

12   We cut taxes and prune budgets, we modernize industry and shift the balance of trade, and the result of all these actions and errors can be read, sleeping form by sleeping form, on our city streets.

13   The liberals cannot blame the conservatives. The conservatives cannot blame the liberals. Homelessness is the *sum total* of our dreams, policies, intentions, errors, omissions, cruelties, kindnesses, all of it recorded, in flesh, in the life of the streets.

14   You can also learn from this list one of the most important things there is to know about the homeless—that they can be roughly divided into two groups: those who have had homelessness forced upon them and want nothing more than to escape it; and those who have at least in part *chosen* it for themselves, and now accept, or in some cases, embrace it.

15   I understand how dangerous it is to introduce the idea of choice into a discussion of homelessness. It can all too easily be used to justify indifference or brutality toward the homeless, or to argue that they are only getting what they "deserve." And yet it seems to me that it is only by taking choice into account, in all of the intricacies of its various forms and expressions, that one can really understand certain kinds of homelessness.

16   The fact is, many of the homeless are not only hapless victims but voluntary exiles, "domestic refugees," people who have turned not against life itself but against *us*, our life, American life. Look for a

moment at the vets. The price of returning to America was to forget what they had seen or learned in Vietnam, to "put it behind them." But some could not do that, and the stress of trying showed up as alcoholism, broken marriages, drug addiction, crime. And it showed up too as life on the street, which was for some vets a desperate choice made in the name of life—the best they could manage. It was a way of avoiding what might have occurred had they stayed where they were: suicide, or violence done to others.

We must learn to accept that there may indeed be people, and not only vets, who have seen so much of our world, or seen it so clearly, that to live in it becomes impossible. Here, for example, is the story of Alice, a homeless middle-aged woman in Los Angeles, where there are, perhaps, 50,000 homeless people. It was set down a few months ago by one of my students at the University of California, Santa Barbara, where I taught for a semester. I had encouraged them to go find the homeless and listen to their stories. And so, one day, when this student saw Alice foraging in a dumpster outside a McDonald's, he stopped and talked to her: 17

> She told me she had led a pretty normal life as she grew up and eventually went to college. From there she went on to Chicago to teach school. She was single and lived in a small apartment.
>
> One night, after she got off the train after school, a man began to follow her to her apartment building. When she got to her door she saw a knife and the man hovering behind her. She had no choice but to let him in. The man raped her.
>
> After that, things got steadily worse. She had a nervous breakdown. She went to a mental institution for three months, and when she went back to her apartment she found her belongings gone. The landlord had sold them to cover the rent she hadn't paid.
>
> She had no place to go and no job because the school had terminated her employment. She slipped into depression. She lived with friends until she could muster enough money for a ticket to Los Angeles. She said she no longer wanted to burden her friends, and that if she had to live outside, at least Los Angeles was warmer than Chicago.
>
> It is as if she began back then to take on the mentality of a street person. She resolved herself to homelessness. She's been out West since 1980, without a home or job. She seems happy, with her best friend being her cat. But the scars of memories still haunt her, and she is running from them, or should I say *him*.

18   This is, in essence, the same story one hears over and over again on the street. You begin with an ordinary life; then an event occurs—traumatic, catastrophic; smaller events follow, each one deepening the original wound; finally, homelessness becomes inevitable, or begins to *seem* inevitable to the person involved—the only way out of an intolerable situation. You are struck continually, hearing these stories, by something seemingly unique in American life, the absolute isolation involved. In what other culture would there be such an absence or failure of support from familial, social, or institutional sources? Even more disturbing is the fact that it is often our supposed sources of support—family, friends, government organizations—that have caused the problem in the first place.

19   Everything that happened to Alice—the rape, the loss of job and apartment, the breakdown—was part and parcel of a world gone radically wrong, a world, for Alice, no longer to be counted on, no longer worth living in. Her homelessness can be seen as flight, as failure of will or nerve, even, perhaps, as *disease*. But it can also be seen as a mute, furious refusal, a self-imposed exile far less appealing to the rest of us than ordinary life, but *better*, in Alice's terms.

20   We like to think, in America, that everything is redeemable, that everything broken can be magically made whole again, and that what has been "dirtied" can be cleansed. Recently I saw on television that one of the soaps had introduced the character of a homeless old woman. A woman in her thirties discovers that her long-lost mother has appeared in town, on the streets. After much searching the mother is located and identified and embraced; and then she is scrubbed and dressed in style, restored in a matter of days to her former upper-class habits and role.

21   A triumph—but one more likely to occur on television than in real life. Yes, many of those on the streets could be transformed, rehabilitated. But there are others whose lives have been irrevocably changed, damaged beyond repair, and who no longer want help, who no longer recognize the need for help, and whose experience in our world has made them want only to be left alone. How, for instance, would one restore Alice's life, or reshape it in a way that would satisfy *our* notion of what a life should be? What would it take to return her to the fold? How to erase the four years of homelessness, which have become as familiar to her, and as much a home, as her "normal" life once was? Whatever we think of the way in which she has resolved her difficulties, it constitutes a sad peace made with the world. Intruding ourselves upon it in the name of redemption is by no means as simple a task—or as justifiable a task—as one might think.

It is important to understand too that however disorderly and dirty   22
and unmanageable the world of homeless men and women like Alice
appears to us, it is not without its significance, and its rules and rituals.
The homeless in our cities mark out for themselves particular neighborhoods, blocks, buildings, doorways. They impose on themselves
often obsessively strict routines. They reduce their world to a small
area, and thereby protect themselves from a world that might otherwise
be too much to bear.

Pavlov, the Russian psychologist, once theorized that the two   23
most fundamental reflexes in all animals, including humans, are those
involving freedom and orientation. Grab any animal, he said, and it will
immediately struggle to accomplish two things: to break free and to
orient itself. And this is what one sees in so many of the homeless.
Having been stripped of all other forms of connection, and of most kinds
of social identity, they are left only with this: the raw stuff of nature,
something encoded in the cells—the desire to be free, the need for
familiar space. Perhaps this is why so many of them struggle so vehe-
mently against us when we offer them aid. They are clinging to their
freedom and their space, and they do not believe that this is what we,
with our programs and our shelters, mean to allow them.

Years ago, when I first came to California, bumming my way west,   24
the marginal world, and the lives of those in it, were very different from
what they are now. In those days I spent much of my time in hobo
jungles or on the skid rows of various cities, and just as it was easier
back then to "get by" in the easygoing beach towns on the California
coast, or in the bohemian and artistic worlds in San Francisco or Los
Angeles or New York, it was also far easier than it is now to survive in
the marginal world.

It is important to remember this—important to recognize the   25
immensity of the changes that have occurred in the marginal world in
the past twenty years. Whole sections of many cities—the Bowery in
New York, the Tenderloin in San Francisco—were once ceded to the
transient. In every skidrow area in America you could find what you
needed to survive: hash houses, saloons offering free lunches,
pawnshops, surplus-clothing stores, and, most important of all, cheap
hotels and flophouses and two-bit employment agencies specializing in
the kinds of labor (seasonal, shape-up) transients have always done.

It was by no means a wonderful world. But it *was* a world. Its   26
rituals were spelled out in ways most of the participants understood. In
hobo jungles up and down the tracks, whatever there was to eat went
into a common pot and was divided equally. Late at night, in empties

crisscrossing the country, men would speak with a certain anonymous openness, as if the shared condition of transience created among them a kind of civility.

27   What most people in that world wanted was simply to be left alone. Some of them had been on the road for years, itinerant workers. Others were recuperating from wounds they could never quite explain. There were young men and a few women with nothing better to do, and older men who had no families or had lost their jobs or wives, or for whom the rigor and pressure of life had proved too demanding. The marginal world offered them a respite from the other world, a world grown too much for them.

28   But things have changed. There began to pour into the marginal world—slowly in the sixties, a bit faster in the seventies, and then faster still in the eighties—more and more people who neither belonged nor knew how to survive there. The sixties brought the counterculture and drugs; the streets filled with young dropouts. Changes in the law loosed upon the streets mentally ill men and women. Inflation took its toll, then recession. Working-class and even middle-class men and women—entire families—began to fall into a world they did not understand.

29   At the same time the transient world was being inundated by new inhabitants, its landscape, its economy, was shrinking radically. Jobs became harder to find. Modernization had something to do with it; machines took the place of men and women. And the influx of workers from Mexico and points farther south created a class of semipermanent workers who took the place of casual transient labor. More important, perhaps, was the fact that the forgotten parts of many cities began to attract attention. Downtown areas were redeveloped, reclaimed. The skid-row sections of smaller cities were turned into "old townes." The old hotels that once catered to transients were upgraded or torn down or became warehouses for welfare families—an arrangement far more profitable to the owners. The price of housing increased; evictions increased. The mentally ill, who once could afford to house themselves in cheap rooms, the alcoholics, who once would drink themselves to sleep at night in their cheap hotels, were out on the street—exposed to the weather and to danger, and also in plain and public view: "problems" to be dealt with.

30   Nor was it only cheap shelter that disappeared. It was also those "open" spaces that had once been available to those without other shelter. As property rose in value, the nooks and crannies in which the homeless had been able to hide became more visible. Doorways, alleys,

abandoned buildings, vacant lots—these "holes" in the cityscape, these gaps in public consciousness, became *real estate.* The homeless, who had been there all the time, were overtaken by economic progress, and they became intruders.

You cannot help thinking, as you watch this process, of what 31 happened in parts of Europe in the eighteenth and nineteenth centuries: the effects of the enclosure laws, which eliminated the "commons" in the countryside and drove the rural poor, now homeless, into the cities. The centuries-old tradition of common access and usage was swept away by the beginnings of industrialism; land became *privatized,* a commodity. At the same time something occurred in the cultural psyche. The world itself, space itself, was subtly altered. It was no longer merely to be lived in; it was now to be owned. What was enclosed was not only the land. It was also *the flesh itself;* it was cut off from, denied access to, the physical world.

And one thinks too, when thinking of the homeless, of the Ameri- 32 can past, the settlement of the "new" world which occurred at precisely the same time that the commons disappeared. The dream of freedom and equality that brought men and women here had something to do with *space,* as if the wilderness itself conferred upon those arriving here a new beginning: the Eden that had been lost. Once God had sent Christ to redeem men; now he provided a new world. Men discovered, or believed, that this world, and perhaps time itself, had no edge, no limit. Space was a sign of God's magnanimity. It was a kind of grace.

Somehow, it is all this that is folded into the sad shapes of the 33 homeless. In their mute presence one can sense, however faintly, the dreams of a world gone aglimmering, and the presence of our failed hopes. A kind of claim is made, silently, an ethic is proffered, or, if you will, a whole cosmology, one older than our own ideas of privilege and property. It is as if flesh itself were seeking, this one last time, the home in the world it has been denied.

Daily the city eddies around the homeless. The crowds flowing 34 past leave a few feet, a gap. We do not touch the homeless world. Perhaps we cannot touch it. It remains separate even as the city surrounds it.

The homeless, simply because they are homeless, are strangers, 35 alien—and therefore a threat. Their presence, in itself, comes to constitute a kind of violence; it deprives us of our sense of safety. Let me use myself as an example. I know, and respect, many of those now homeless on the streets of Santa Barbara. Twenty years ago, some of them would have been my companions and friends. And yet, these days, if I walk through the park near my home and see strangers bedding down for the night, my first reaction, if not fear, is a sense of annoyance and intrusion, of worry and alarm. I think of my teenage daughter, who often walks through the park, and then of my house, a hundred yards away, and I am tempted—only tempted, but tempted, still—to call the "proper" authorities to have the strangers moved on. Out of sight, out of mind.

36   Notice: I do not bring them food. I do not offer them shelter or a shower in the morning. I do not even stop to talk. Instead, I think: my daughter, my house, my privacy. What moves me is not the threat of *danger*—nothing as animal as that. Instead there pops up inside of me, neatly in a row, a set of anxieties, ones you might arrange in a dollhouse living room and label: Family of bourgeois fears. The point is this: our response to the homeless is fed by a complex set of cultural attitudes, habits of thought, and fantasies and fears so familiar to us, so common, that they have become a *second* nature and might as well be instinctive, for all the control we have over them. And it is by no means easy to untangle this snarl of responses. What does seem clear is that the homeless embody all that bourgeois culture has for centuries tried to eradicate and destroy.

37   If you look to the history of Europe you find that homelessness first appears (or is first acknowledged) at the very same moment that bourgeois culture begins to appear. The same processes produced them both: the breakup of feudalism, the rise of commerce and cities, the combined triumphs of capitalism, industrialism, and individualism. The historian Fernand Braudel, in *The Wheels of Commerce*, describes, for instance, the armies of impoverished men and women who began to haunt Europe as far back as the eleventh century. And the makeup of these masses? Essentially the same then as it is now: the unfortunates, the throwaways, the misfits, the deviants.

> In the eighteenth century, all sorts and conditions were to be found in this human dross . . . widows, orphans, cripples . . . journeymen who had broken their contracts, out-of-work labourers, homeless priests with no living, old men, fire victims . . . war victims, deserters, discharged soldiers, would-be vendors of useless articles, vagrant preachers with or without licenses, "pregnant servant-girls and unmarried mothers driven from home," children sent out "to find bread or to maraud."

Then, as now, distinctions were made between the "homeless" 38
and the supposedly "deserving" poor, those who knew their place and
willingly sustained, with their labors, the emergent bourgeois world.

> The good paupers were accepted, lined up and registered on the
> official list; they had a right to public charity and were some-
> times allowed to solicit it outside churches in the prosperous
> districts, when the congregation came out, or in market
> places. . . .
> When it comes to beggars and vagrants, it is a very different
> story, and different pictures meet the eye: crowds, mobs,
> processions, sometimes mass emigrations, "along the country
> highways or the streets of the Towns and Villages," by beggars
> "whom hunger and nakedness has driven from home.". . . The
> towns dreaded these alarming visitors and drove them out as
> soon as they appeared on the horizon.

And just as the distinctions made about these masses were the 39
same then as they are now, so too was the way society saw them. They
seemed to bourgeois eyes (as they still do) the one segment of society
that remained resistant to progress, unassimilable and incorrigible,
inimical to all order.

It is in the nineteenth century, in the Victorian era, that you can 40
find the beginnings of our modern strategies for dealing with the homeless: the notion that they should be controlled and perhaps eliminated
through "help." With the Victorians we begin to see the entangling of
self-protection with social obligation, the strategy of masking self-
interest and the urge to control as *moral duty* Michel Foucault has
spelled this out in his books on madness and punishment: the zeal with
which the overseers of early bourgeois culture tried to purge, improve,
and purify all of urban civilization whether through schools and
prisons, or, quite literally, with public baths and massive new water and
sewage systems. Order, ordure—this is, in essence, the tension at the
heart of bourgeois culture, and it was the singular genius of the Victorians to make it the main component of their medical, aesthetic, *and*
moral systems. It was not a sense of justice or even empathy which
called for charity or new attitudes toward the poor; it was *hygiene.* The
very same attitudes appear in nineteenth-century America. Charles
Loring Brace, in an essay on homeless and vagrant children written in
1876, described the treatment of delinquents in this way: "Many of
their vices drop from them like the old and verminous clothing they left
behind. . . . The entire change of circumstances seems to cleanse

them of bad habits." Here you have it all: *vices, verminous clothing, cleansing them of bad habits*—the triple association of poverty with vice with dirt, an equation in which each term comes to stand for all of them.

41   These attitudes are with us still; that is the point. In our own century the person who has written most revealingly about such things is George Orwell, who tried to analyze his own middle-class attitudes toward the poor. In 1933, in *Down and Out in Paris and London,* he wrote about tramps:

> In childhood we are taught that tramps are blackguards . . . a repulsive, rather dangerous creature, who would rather die than work or wash, and wants nothing but to beg, drink or rob hen-houses. The tramp monster is no truer to life than the sinister Chinaman of the magazines, but he is very hard to get rid of. The very word "tramp" evokes his image.

42   All of this is still true in America, though now it is not the word "tramp" but the word "homeless" that evokes the images we fear. It is the homeless who smell. Here, for instance, is part of a paper a student of mine wrote about her first visit to a Rescue Mission on skid row.

> The sermon began. The room was stuffy and smelly. The mixture of body odors and cooking was nauseating. I remember thinking: how can these people share this facility? They must be repulsed by each other. They had strange habits and dispositions. They were a group of dirty, dishonored, weird people to me.
>
> When it was over I ran to my car, went home, and took a shower. I felt extremely dirty. Through the day I would get flashes of that disgusting smell.

43   To put it as bluntly as I can, for many of us the homeless are *shit.* And our policies toward them, our spontaneous sense of disgust and horror, our wish to be rid of them—all of this has hidden in it, close to its heart, our feelings about excrement. Even Marx, that most bourgeois of revolutionaries, described the deviant *lumpen* in *The Eighteenth Brumaire of Louis Bonaparte* as "scum, offal, refuse of all classes." These days, in puritanical Marxist nations, they are called "parasites" —a word, perhaps not incidentally, one also associates with human waste.

44   What I am getting at here is the *nature* of the desire to help the homeless—what is hidden behind it and why it so often does harm. Every government program, almost every private project, is geared as

much to the needs of those giving help as it is to the needs of the homeless. Go to any government agency, or, for that matter, to most private charities, and you will find yourself enmeshed, at once, in a bureaucracy so tangled and oppressive, or confronted with so much moral arrogance and contempt, that you will be driven back out into the streets for relief.

Santa Barbara, where I live, is as good an example as any. There are 45 three main shelters in the city—all of them private. Between them they provide fewer than a hundred beds a night for the homeless. Two of the three shelters are religious in nature: the Rescue Mission and the Salvation Army. In the mission, as in most places in the country, there are elaborate and stringent rules. Beds go first to those who have not been there for two months, and you can stay for only two nights in any two-month period. No shelter is given to those who are not sober. Even if you go to the mission only for a meal, you are required to listen to sermons and participate in prayer, and you are regularly proselytized— sometimes overtly, sometimes subtly. There are obligatory, regimented showers. You go to bed precisely at ten: lights out, no reading, no talking. After the lights go out you will find fifteen men in a room with double-decker bunks. As the night progresses the room grows stuffier and hotter. Men toss, turn, cough, and moan. In the morning you are awakened precisely at five forty-five. Then breakfast. At seventhirty you are back on the street.

The town's newest shelter was opened almost a year ago by a 46 consortium of local churches. Families and those who are employed have first call on the beds—a policy which excludes the congenitally homeless. Alcohol is not simply forbidden *in* the shelter; those with a history of alcoholism must sign a "contract" pledging to remain sober and chemical-free. Finally, in a paroxysm of therapeutic bullying, the shelter has added a new wrinkle: if you stay more than two days you are required to fill out and then discuss with a social worker a complex form listing what you perceive as your personal failings, goals, and strategies—all of this for men and women who simply want a place to lie down out of the rain!

It is these attitudes, in various forms and permutations, that you 47 find repeated endlessly in America. We are moved either to "redeem" the homeless or to punish them. Perhaps there is nothing consciously hostile about it. Perhaps it is simply that as the machinery of bureaucracy cranks itself up to deal with these problems, attitudes assert themselves automatically. But whatever the case, the fact remains that almost every one of our strategies for helping the homeless is simply an attempt to rearrange the world *cosmetically*, in terms of how it looks and smells to *us*. Compassion is little more than the passion for control.

48   The central question emerging from all this is, What does a society owe to its members in trouble, and *how* is that debt to be paid? It is a question which must be answered in two parts: first, in relation to the men and women who have been marginalized against their will, and then, in a slightly different way, in relation to those who have chosen (or accept or even prize) their marginality.

49   As for those who have been marginalized against their wills, I think the general answer is obvious: A society owes its members whatever it takes for them to regain their places in the social order. And when it comes to specific remedies, one need only read backward the various processes which have created homelessness and then figure out where help is likely to do the most good. But the real point here is not the specific remedies required—affordable housing, say—but the basis upon which they must be offered, the necessary underlying ethical notion we seem in this nation unable to grasp: that those who are the inevitable casualties of modern industrial capitalism and the free-market system are entitled, *by right*, and by the simple virtue of their participation in that system, to whatever help they need. They are entitled to help to find and hold their places in the society whose social contract they have, in effect, signed and observed.

50   Look at that for just a moment: the notion of a contract. The majority of homeless Americans have kept, insofar as they could, to the terms of that contract. In any shelter these days you can find men and women who have worked ten, twenty, forty years, and whose lives have nonetheless come to nothing. These are people who cannot afford a place in the world they helped create. And in return? Is it life on the street they have earned? Or the cruel charity we so grudgingly grant them?

51   But those marginalized against their will are only half the problem. There remains, still, the question of whether we owe anything to those who are voluntarily marginal. What about them: the street people, the rebels, and the recalcitrants, those who have torn up their social contracts or returned them unsigned?

52   I was in Las Vegas last fall, and I went out to the Rescue Mission at the lower end of town, on the edge of the black ghetto, where I first stayed years ago on my way west. It was twilight, still hot; in the vacant lot next door to the mission 200 men were lining up for supper. A warm

wind blew along the street lined with small houses and salvage yards, and in the distance I could see the desert's edge and the smudge of low hills in the fading light. There were elderly alcoholics in line, and derelicts, but mainly the men were the same sort I had seen here years ago: youngish, out of work restless and talkative, the drifters and wanderers for whom the word "wanderlust" was invented.

At supper—long communal tables, thin gruel, stale sweet rolls, 53 ice water—a huge black man in his twenties, fierce and muscular, sat across from me. "I'm from the Coast, man," he said. "Never been away from home before. Ain't sure I like it. Sure don't like *this* place. But I lost my job back home a couple of weeks ago and figured, why wait around for another. I thought I'd come out here, see me something of the world."

After supper, a squat Portuguese man in his mid-thirties, hun- 54 kered down against the mission wall, offered me a smoke and told me: "Been sleeping in my car, up the street, for a week. Had my own business back in Omaha. But I got bored, man. Sold everything, got a little dough, came out here. Thought I'd work construction. Let me tell you, this is one tough town."

In a world better than ours, I suppose, men (or women) like this 55 might not exist. Conservatives seem to have no trouble imagining a society so well disciplined and moral that deviance of this kind would disappear. And leftists envision a world so just, so generous, that deviance would vanish along with inequity. But I suspect that there will always be something at work in some men and women to make them restless with the systems others devise for them, and to move them outward toward the edges of the world, where life is always riskier, less organized, and easier going.

Do we owe anything to these men and women, who reject our 56 company and what we offer and yet nonetheless seem to demand *some-thing* from us?

We owe them, I think, at least a place to exist, a way to exist. That 57 may not be a *moral* obligation, in the sense that our obligation to the involuntarily marginal is clearly a moral one, but it is an obligation nevertheless, one you might call an existential obligation.

Of course, it may be that I think we owe these men something 58 because I have liked men like them, and because I want their world to be there always, as a place to hide or rest. But there is more to it than that. I think we as a society need men like these. A society needs its margins as much as it needs art and literature. It needs holes and gaps, *breathing spaces*, let us say, into which men and women can escape and live, when necessary, in ways otherwise denied them. Margins guarantee to society a flexibility, an elasticity, and allow it to accommodate itself to the natures and needs of its members. When margins vanish, society becomes too rigid, too oppressive by far, and therefore inimical to life.

59   It is for such reasons that, in cultures like our own, marginal men and women take on a special significance. They are all we have left to remind us of the narrowness of the received truths we take for granted. "Beyond the pale," they somehow redefine the pale, or remind us, at least, that *something* is still out there, beyond the pale. They preserve, perhaps unconsciously, a dream that would otherwise cease to exist, the dream of having a place in the world, and of being *left alone.*

60   Quixotic? Infantile? Perhaps. But remember Pavlov and his reflexes coded in the flesh: animal, and therefore as if given by God. What we are talking about here is *freedom,* and with it, perhaps, an echo of the dream men brought, long ago, to wilderness America. I use the word "freedom" gingerly, in relation to lives like these: skewed, crippled, emptied of everything we associate with a full, or realized, freedom. But perhaps this is the condition into which freedom has fallen among us. Art has been "appreciated" out of existence; literature has become an extension of the university, replete with tenure and pensions; and as for politics, the ideologies which ring us round seem too silly or shrill by far to speak for life. What is left, then, is this mute and intransigent independence, this "waste" of life which refuses even interpretation, and which cannot be assimilated to any ideology, and which therefore can be put to no one's use. In its crippled innocence and the perfection of its superfluity it amounts, almost, to a rebellion against history, and that is no small thing.

61   Let me put it as simply as I can: what we see on the streets of our cities are two dramas, both of which cut to the troubled heart of the culture and demand from us a response we may not be able to make. There is the drama of those struggling to survive by regaining their place in the social order. And there is the drama of those struggling to survive outside of it.

62   The resolution of both struggles depends on a third drama occurring at the heart of the culture: the tension and contention between the magnanimity we owe to life and the darker tendings of the human psyche: our fear of strangeness, our hatred of deviance, our love of order and control. How we mediate by default or design between those contrary forces will determine not only the destinies of the homeless but also something crucial about the nation, and perhaps—let me say it—about our own souls.

——— CONSIDERATIONS ——————————————

1. What advantage does Marin gain by starting his essay with his own youthful experience on the road?

2. What causes a word like "homeless" to lose much of its meaning?

3. Paragraphs 10, 11, and 12 form a sequence of short, one-sentence units of very similar construction: "We decide . . . ," "We change . . . ," "We cut . . . ." What, if anything, does the writer gain that is worth the risk of sounding monotonous?

4. In more than one place in his essay, Marin divides the homeless into the involuntary and the voluntary. Why, then, in paragraph 15, does he say that it is "dangerous to introduce the idea of choice into a discussion of homelessness"?

5. Why, according to Marin, do some of the homeless react violently to any offer of aid?

6. Marin's paragraph 29, in which he talks about what has happened to old neighborhoods, brings to mind a word that Marin does not use— "gentrification." Why might it have been an idea to work into that paragraph?

7. In paragraph 43, Marin puts it as "bluntly" as he can. Do you find his bluntness offensive or justifiable in this context?

Joyce Carol Oates (b. 1938) grew up in New York State and attended Syracuse University. She has published many novels, collections of short stories, essay collections, and books of poetry. A Guggenheim Fellow and winner of the National Book Award, she currently teaches at Princeton University. Recent fiction includes Bellefleur *(1987),* The Assignation *(1988), and* Because It Is Bitter and Because It Is My Heart *(1990). Her book* On Boxing, *from which the following is excerpted, appeared in 1987.*

50

JOYCE CAROL OATES
On Boxing

1   No sport is more physical, more direct, than boxing. No sport appears more powerfully homoerotic: the confrontation in the ring— the disrobing—the sweaty, heated combat that is part dance, courtship, coupling—the frequent urgent pursuit by one boxer of the other in the fight's natural and violent movement toward the "knockout." Surely boxing derives much of its appeal from this mimicry of a species of erotic love in which one man overcomes the other in an exhibition of superior strength.

2   Most fights, however fought, lead to an embrace between the boxers after the final bell—a gesture of mutual respect and apparent affection that appears to the onlooker to be more than perfunctory. Rocky Graziano, often derided for being a slugger rather than a "classic" boxer, sometimes kissed his opponents out of gratitude for the fight. Does the boxing match, one almost wonders, lead irresistibly to this moment: the public embrace of two men who otherwise, in public or in private, could not approach each other with such passion. Are men privileged to embrace with love only after having fought? A woman is

struck by the tenderness men will express for boxers who have been hurt, even if it is only by way of commentary on photographs: the startling picture of Ray (Boom Boom) Mancini after his second losing fight with Livingstone Bramble, for instance, when Mancini's face was hideously battered (photographs in *Sports Illustrated* and elsewhere were gory, near-pornographic); the much-reprinted photograph of the defeated Thomas Hearns being carried to his corner in the arms of an enormous black man in formal attire—the "Hit Man" from Detroit now helpless, only semiconscious, looking precisely like a black Christ taken from the cross. These are powerful, haunting, unsettling images, cruelly beautiful, very much bound up with the primitive appeal of the sport.

Yet to suggest that men might love one another directly without 3 the violent ritual of combat is to misread man's greatest passion—for war, not peace. Love, if there is to be love, comes second.

Boxing is, after all, about lying. It is about cultivating a double 4 personality. As José Torres, the ex-light-heavyweight champion who is now the New York State Boxing Commissioner, says: "We fighters understand lies. What's a feint? What's a left hook off the jab? What's an opening? What's thinking one thing and doing another . . . ?"

There is nothing fundamentally playful about boxing, nothing 5 that seems to belong to daylight, to pleasure. At its moments of greatest intensity it seems to contain so complete and so powerful an image of life—life's beauty, vulnerability, despair, incalculable and often reckless courage—that boxing *is* life, and hardly a mere game. During a superior boxing match we are deeply moved by the body's communion with itself by way of another's flesh. The body's dialogue with its shadow-self—or Death. Baseball, football, basketball—these quintessentially American pastimes are recognizably sports because they involve play: They are games. One *plays* football; one doesn't *play* boxing.

Observing team sports, teams of adult men, one sees how men are 6 children in the most felicitous sense of the word. But boxing in its elemental ferocity cannot be assimilated into childhood—though very young men box, even professionally, and numerous world champions began boxing when they were hardly more than children. Spectators at public games derive much of their pleasure from reliving the communal emotions of childhood, but spectators at boxing matches relive the murderous infancy of the race. Hence the notorious cruelty of boxing crowds and the excitement when a man begins to bleed. ("When I see blood," says Marvin Hagler, "I become a bull." He means his own.)

7   The boxing ring comes to seem an altar of sorts, one of those legendary magical spaces where the laws of a nation are suspended: Inside the ropes, during an officially regulated three-minute round, a man may be killed at his opponent's hands but he cannot be legally murdered. Boxing inhabits a sacred space predating civilization; or, to use D. H. Lawrence's phrase, before God was love. If it suggests a savage ceremony or a rite of atonement, it also suggests the futility of such rites. For what atonement is the fight waged, if it must shortly be waged again . . . ?

8   All this is to speak of the paradox of boxing—its obsessive appeal for many who find in it not only a spectacle involving sensational feats of physical skill but an emotional experience impossible to convey in words; an art form, as I have suggested, with no natural analogue in the arts. And of course this accounts, too, for the extreme revulsion it arouses in many people. ("Brutal," "disgusting," "barbaric," "inhuman," "a terrible, terrible sport"—typical comments on the subject.)

9   In December 1984, the American Medical Association passed a resolution calling for the abolition of boxing on the principle that it is the only sport in which the *objective* is to cause injury. This is not surprising. Humanitarians have always wanted to reform boxing—or abolish it altogether. The 1896 heavyweight title match between Ruby Robert Fitzsimmons and Peter Maher was outlawed in many parts of the United States, so canny promoters staged it across the Mexican border four hundred miles from El Paso. (Some three hundred people made the arduous journey to see what must have been one of the most disappointing bouts in boxing history—Fitzsimmons knocked out his opponent in a mere ninety-five seconds.)

10   During the prime of Jack Dempsey's career in the 1920s, boxing was illegal in many states, like alcohol, and like alcohol, seems to have aroused a hysterical public enthusiasm. Photographs of jammed outdoor arenas taken in the 1920s with boxing rings like postage-sized altars at their centers, the boxers themselves scarcely visible, testify to the extraordinary emotional appeal boxing had at that time, even as reform movements were lobbying against it. When Jack Johnson won the heavyweight title in 1908 (he had to pursue the white champion Tommy Burns all the way to Australia to confront him), the special "danger" of boxing was also that it might expose and humiliate white men in the ring. After Johnson's victory over the "White Hope" contender Jim Jeffries, there were race riots and lynchings throughout the United States; even films of some of Johnson's fights were outlawed in many states. And because boxing has become a sport in which black and Hispanic men have lately excelled, it is particularly vulnerable to at-

tack by white middle-class reformers, who seem uninterested in lobbying against equally dangerous but "establishment" sports like football, auto racing, and thoroughbred horse racing.

There is something peculiarly American in the fact that, while   11
boxing is our most controversial sport, it is also the sport that pays its top athletes the most money. In spite of the controversy, boxing has never been healthier financially. The three highest paid athletes in the world in both 1983 and 1984 were boxers; a boxer with a long career like heavyweight champion Larry Holmes—forty-eight fights in thirteen years as a professional—can expect to earn somewhere beyond $50 million. (Holmes said that after retirement what he would miss about boxing is his million-dollar checks.) Dempsey, who said that a man fights for one thing only—money—made somewhere beyond $3,500,000 in the ring in his long and varied career. Now $1.5 million is a fairly common figure for a single fight. Thomas Hearns made at least $7 million in his fight with Hagler while Hagler made at least $7.5 million. For the first of his highly publicized matches with Roberto Duran in 1980—which he lost on a decision—the popular black welterweight champion Sugar Ray Leonard received a staggering $10 million to Duran's $1.3 million. And none of these figures takes into account various subsidiary earnings (from television commercials, for instance) which in Leonard's case are probably as high as his income was from boxing.

Money has drawn any number of retired boxers back into the ring,   12
very often with tragic results. The most notorious example is perhaps Joe Louis, who, owing huge sums in back taxes, continued boxing well beyond the point at which he could perform capably. After a career of seventeen years he was stopped by Rocky Marciano—who was said to have felt as upset by his victory as Louis by the defeat. (Louis then went on to a degrading second career as a professional wrestler. This, too, ended abruptly when 300-pound Rocky Lee stepped on the forty-two-year-old Louis's chest and damaged his heart.) Ezzard Charles, Jersey Joe Walcott, Joe Frazier, Muhammad Ali—each continued fighting when he was no longer in condition to defend himself against young heavyweight boxers on the way up. Of all heavyweight champions, only Rocky Marciano, to whom fame and money were not of paramount significance, was prudent enough to retire before he was defeated. In any case, the prodigious sums of money a few boxers earn do not account for the sums the public is willing to pay them.

Though boxing has long been popular in many countries and   13
under many forms of government, its popularity in the United States since the days of John L. Sullivan has a good deal to do with what is felt

as the spirit of the individual—his "physical" spirit—in conflict with the constrictions of the state. The rise of boxing in the 1920s in particular might well be seen as a consequence of the diminution of the individual vis-à-vis society; the gradual attrition of personal freedom, will, and strength—whether "masculine" or otherwise. In the Eastern bloc of nations, totalitarianism is a function of the state; in the Western bloc it has come to seem a function of technology, or history—"fate." The individual exists in his physical supremacy, but does the individual matter?

14   In the magical space of the boxing ring so disquieting a question has no claim. There, as in no other public arena, the individual as a unique physical being asserts himself; there, for a dramatic if fleeting period of time, the great world with its moral and political complexities, its terrifying impersonality, simply ceases to exist. Men fighting one another with only their fists and their cunning are all contemporaries, all brothers, belonging to no historical time. "He can run, but he can't hide"—so said Joe Louis before his famous fight with young Billy Conn in 1941. In the brightly lighted ring, man is *in extremis*, performing an atavistic rite or agon for the mysterious solace of those who can participate only vicariously in such drama: the drama of life in the flesh. Boxing has become America's tragic theater.

_____ CONSIDERATIONS _____

1. In her opening paragraph, Oates uses the term "homoerotic." How does this differ from "homosexual"? Or does it?

2. What, according to Oates, is "man's greatest passion"? How does she try to support this assertion?

3. In paragraphs 11 and 12, Oates cites remarks by great fighters like Larry Holmes and Jack Dempsey, who claim that the most important thing about boxing is the money. How do their statements affect the writer's assertion (in paragraph 5) that boxing is hardly a game, it is life itself?

4. A research question: What happened to the resolution passed in 1984 by the American Medical Association calling for the abolition of boxing? Does Oates's essay provide any answers? How would you go about finding an answer in your college library?

5. In what way does it make sense for Oates to describe gory photographs of battered boxers as "near-pornographic"?

6. Oates compares boxing to love (paragraph 2), sacrifice (paragraph 6), religious rites (paragraph 7), and the theater (paragraph 14). Are such notions merely fanciful or do they point up significant aspects of the sport?

Flannery O'Connor (1925–1964) was born in Savannah and moved with her family to her mother's birthplace, Milledgeville, Georgia, at the age of twelve. When she was fifteen her father died of the inherited degenerative disease lupus. She took her B.A. at Milledgeville's Georgia State College for Women (now Georgia College) and then studied fiction writing at the University of Iowa. From 1947 until 1951 she spent time in New York, Connecticut, and Georgia. When she discovered that she was ill, she returned to live with her mother on the Milledgeville farm called Andalusia, surrounded by pet peacocks and peahens, writing her remarkable fiction and staying in touch with friends by letter. She died of lupus when she was thirty-eight.

In 1979 a selection of Flannery O'Connor's letters, edited by Sally Fitzgerald, appeared as The Habit of Being. The letters are affectionate, often funny, rich with literary and religious thought.

The following excerpts begin with two letters about "A Good Man Is Hard to Find." The first is a passage from a letter addressed to the novelist John Hawkes, a leading writer of O'Connor's generation, author of The Lime Twig, The Blood Oranges, and The Passion Artist among other novels. In the passage found here, O'Connor speaks of the theology of her story. The second letter, "To a Professor of English," is prefaced by Sally Fitzgerald's explanatory note. The letter that follows is another to John Hawkes. In it O'Connor's Catholicism is clear and certain; Hawkes is of another mind. The last letter is addressed to Alfred Corn, who is now a well-known poet. In 1962 he was an undergraduate at Emory University in Atlanta, Georgia; when he heard Flannery O'Connor speak to an English class, he wrote her about a subject that troubled him.

51

FLANNERY O'CONNOR
From Flannery O'Connor's Letters

TO JOHN HAWKES

14 April 60

1 Thanks for your letter of some time back. I have been busy keeping my blood pressure down while reading various reviews of my book. Some of the favorable ones are as bad as the unfavorable; most reviewers seem to have read the book in fifteen minutes and written the review in ten. . . . I hope that when yours comes out you'll fare better.

2 It's interesting to me that your students naturally work their way to the idea that the Grandmother in "A Good Man" is not pure evil and may be a medium for Grace. If they were Southern students I would say this was because they all had grandmothers like her at home. These old ladies exactly reflect the banalities of the society and the effect of the comical rather than the seriously evil. But Andrew [Lytle] insists that she is a witch, even down to the cat. These children, yr. students, know their grandmothers aren't witches.

3 Perhaps it is a difference in theology, or rather the difference that ingrained theology makes in the sensibility. Grace, to the Catholic way of thinking, can and does use as its medium the imperfect, purely human, and even hypocritical. Cutting yourself off from Grace is a very decided matter, requiring a real choice, act of will, and affecting the very ground of the soul. The Misfit is touched by the Grace that comes through the old lady when she recognizes him as her child, as she has been touched by the Grace that comes through him in his particular suffering. His shooting her is a recoil, a horror at her humanness, but after he has done it and cleaned his glasses, the Grace has worked in him and he pronounces his judgment: she would have been a good woman if *he* had been there every moment of her life. True enough. In the

Protestant view, I think Grace and nature don't have much to do with each other. The old lady, because of her hypocrisy and humanness and banality couldn't be a medium for Grace. In the sense that I see things the other way, I'm a Catholic writer.

TO A PROFESSOR OF ENGLISH

A professor of English had sent Flannery the following letter: "I am writing as spokesman for three members of our department and some ninety university students in three classes who for a week now have been discussing your story 'A Good Man Is Hard to Find.' We have debated at length several possible interpretations, none of which fully satisfies us. In general we believe that the appearance of the Misfit is not "real" in the same sense that the incidents of the first half of the story are real. Bailey, we believe, imagines the appearance of the Misfit, whose activities have been called to his attention on the night before the trip and again during the stopover at the roadside restaurant. Bailey, we further believe, identifies himself with the Misfit and so plays two roles in the imaginary last half of the story. But we cannot, after great effort, determine the point at which reality fades into illusion or reverie. Does the accident literally occur, or is it a part of Bailey's dream? Please believe me when I say we are not seeking an easy way out of our difficulty. We admire your story and have examined it with great care, but we are convinced that we are missing something important which you intended for us to grasp. We will all be very grateful if you comment on the interpretation which I have outlined above and if you will give us further comments about your intention in writing 'A Good Man Is Hard to Find.'"

She replied:

28 March 61

1   The interpretation of your ninety students and three teachers is fantastic and about as far from my intentions as it could get to be. If it were a legitimate interpretation, the story would be little more than a trick and its interest would be simply for abnormal psychology. I am not interested in abnormal psychology.

2   There is a change of tension from the first part of the story to the second where the Misfit enters, but this is no lessening of reality. This story is, of course, not meant to be realistic in the sense that it portrays

the everyday doings of people in Georgia. It is stylized and its conventions are comic even though its meaning is serious.

3   Bailey's only importance is as the Grandmother's boy and the driver of the car. It is the Grandmother who first recognizes the Misfit and who is most concerned with him throughout. The story is a duel of sorts between the Grandmother and her superficial beliefs and the Misfit's more profoundly felt involvement with Christ's action which set the world off balance for him.

4   The meaning of a story should go on expanding for the reader the more he thinks about it, but meaning cannot be captured in an interpretation. If teachers are in the habit of approaching a story as if it were a research problem for which any answer is believable so long as it is not obvious, then I think students will never learn to enjoy fiction. Too much interpretation is certainly worse than too little, and where feeling for a story is absent, theory will not supply it.

5   My tone is not meant to be obnoxious. I am in a state of shock.

TO JOHN HAWKES

28 November 61

1   I have been fixing to write you ever since last summer when we saw the goat man.[1] We went up to north Georgia to buy a bull and when we were somewhere above Conyers we saw up ahead a pile of rubble some eight feet high on the side of the road. When we got about fifty feet from it, we could begin to make out that some of the rubble was distributed around something like a cart and that some of it was alive. Then we began to make out the goats. We stopped in front of it and looked back. About half the goats were asleep, venerable and exhausted, in a kind of heap. I didn't see Chess. Then my mother located an arm around the neck of one of the goats. We also saw a knee. The old man was lying on the road, asleep amongst them, but we never located his face.

2   That is wonderful about the new baby. I can't equal that but I do have some new additions to my ménage. For the last few years I have been hunting a pair of swans that I could afford. Swans cost $250 a pair and that was beyond me. My friend in Florida, the one I wrote you about once, took upon herself to comb Florida for cheap swans. What she sets

---

[1] The founder of the Free Thinking Christian Mission, a wandering witness who traveled with a cart and a clutch of goats.

out to do, she does. . . . So now I am the owner of a one-eyed swan and her consort. They are Polish, or immutable swans and very tractable and I radiate satisfaction every time I look at them.

I had brief notes from Andrew [Lytle][2] a couple of times lately. In   3 fact he has a story of mine but I haven't heard from him whether he's going to use it or not. He said he had asked you to write an article about my fiction and that if he used my story I might want to send it to you. If he does take it and you write an article and want to see the story ["The Lame Shall Enter First"], I'll send it. It's about one of Tarwater's terrible cousins, a lad named Rufus Johnson, and it will add fuel to your theory though not legitimately I think.

You haven't convinced me that I write with the Devil's will or   4 belong in the romantic tradition and I'm prepared to argue some more with you on this if I can remember where we left off at. I think the reason we can't agree on this is because there is a difference in our two devils. My Devil has a name, a history and a definite plan. His name is Lucifer, he's a fallen angel, his sin is pride, and his aim is the destruction of the Divine plan. Now I judge that your Devil is co-equal to God, not his creature; that pride is his virtue, not his sin; and that his aim is not to destroy the Divine plan because there isn't any Divine plan to destroy. My Devil is objective and yours is subjective. You say one becomes "evil" when one leaves the herd. I say that depends entirely on what the herd is doing.

The herd has been known to be right, in which case the one who   5 leaves it is doing evil. When the herd is wrong, the one who leaves it is not doing evil but the right thing. If I remember rightly, you put that word, evil, in quotation marks which means the standards you judge it by there are relative; in fact you would be looking at it there with the eyes of the herd.

I think I would admit to writing what Hawthorne called "ro-   6 mances," but I don't think that has anything to do with the romantic mentality. Hawthorne interests me considerably. I feel more of a kinship with him than with any other American, though some of what he wrote I can't make myself read through to the end.

I didn't write the note to *Wise Blood.* I just let it go as is. I thought   7 here I am wasting my time saying what I've written when I've already written it and I could be writing something else. I couldn't hope to convince anybody anyway. A friend of mine wrote me that he had read a review in one of the university magazines of *The Violent Bear etc.* that

[2] Novelist, editor at this time of the *Sewanee Review.*

said that since the seeds that had opened one at a time in Tarwater's blood were put there in the first place by the great uncle that the book was about homosexual incest. When you have a generation of students who are being taught to think like that, there's nothing to do but wait for another generation to come along and hope it won't be worse. . . .

8   I've introduced *The Lime Twig* to several people and they're all enthusiastic. Somebody has gone off with my copy now. I hope you are at another one.

TO ALFRED CORN

30 May 62

1   I think that this experience you are having of losing your faith, or as you think, of having lost it, is an experience that in the long run belongs to faith; or at least it can belong to faith if faith is still valuable to you, and it must be or you would not have written me about this.

2   I don't know how the kind of faith required of a Christian living in the 20th century can be at all if it is not grounded on this experience that you are having right now of unbelief. This may be the case always and not just in the 20th century. Peter said, "Lord, I believe. Help my unbelief." It is the most natural and most human and most agonizing prayer in the gospels, and I think it is the foundation prayer of faith.

3   As a freshman in college you are bombarded with new ideas, or rather pieces of ideas, new frames of reference, an activation of the intellectual life which is only beginning, but which is already running ahead of your lived experience. After a year of this, you think you cannot believe. You are just beginning to realize how difficult it is to have faith and the measure of a commitment to it, but you are too young to decide you don't have faith just because you feel you can't believe. About the only way we know whether we believe or not is by what we do, and I think from your letter that you will not take the path of least resistance in this matter and simply decide that you have lost your faith and that there is nothing you can do about it.

4   One result of the stimulation of your intellectual life that takes place in college is usually a shrinking of the imaginative life. This sounds like a paradox, but I have often found it to be true. Students get so bound up with difficulties such as reconciling the clashing of so many different faiths such as Buddhism, Mohammedanism, etc., that they cease to look for God in other ways. Bridges once wrote Gerard Manley Hopkins and asked him to tell him how he, Bridges, could

believe. He must have expected from Hopkins a long philosophical answer. Hopkins wrote back, "Give alms." He was trying to say to Bridges that God is to be experienced in Charity (in the sense of love for the divine image in human beings). Don't get so entangled with intellectual difficulties that you fail to look for God in this way.

The intellectual difficulties have to be met, however, and you will 5
be meeting them for the rest of your life. When you get a reasonable hold on one, another will come to take its place. At one time, the clash of the different world religions was a difficulty for me. Where you have absolute solutions, however, you have no need of faith. Faith is what you have in the absence of knowledge. The reason this clash doesn't bother me any longer is because I have got, over the years, a sense of the immense sweep of creation, of the evolutionary process in everything, of how incomprehensible God must necessarily be to be the God of heaven and earth. You can't fit the Almighty into your intellectual categories. I might suggest that you look into some of the works of Pierre Teilhard de Chardin (*The Phenomenon of Man* et al.). He was a paleontologist—helped to discover Peking man—and also a man of God. I don't suggest you go to him for answers but for different questions, for that stretching of the imagination that you need to make you a sceptic in the face of much that you are learning, much of which is new and shocking but which when boiled down becomes less so and takes its place in the general scheme of things. What kept me a sceptic in college was precisely my Christian faith. It always said: wait, don't bite on this, get a wider picture, continue to read.

If you want your faith, you have to work for it. It is a gift, but for 6
very few is it a gift given without any demand for equal time devoted to its cultivation. For every book you read that is anti-Christian, make it your business to read one that presents the other side of the picture; if one isn't satisfactory read others. Don't think that you have to abandon reason to be a Christian. A book that might help you is *The Unity of Philosophical Experience* by Etienne Gilson. Another is Newman's *The Grammar of Assent*. To find out about faith, you have to go to the people who have it and you have to go to the most intelligent ones if you are going to stand up intellectually to agnostics and the general run of pagans that you are going to find in the majority of people around you. Much of the criticism of belief that you find today comes from people who are judging it from the standpoint of another and narrower discipline. The Biblical criticism of the 19th century, for instance, was the product of historical disciplines. It has been entirely revamped in the 20th century by applying broader criteria to it, and those people who

lost their faith in the 19th century because of it, could better have hung on in blind trust.

7   Even in the life of a Christian, faith rises and falls like the tides of an invisible sea. It's there, even where he can't see it or feel it, if he wants it to be there. You realize, I think, that it is more valuable, more mysterious, altogether more immense than anything you can learn or decide upon in college. Learn what you can, but cultivate Christian scepticism. It will keep you free—not free to do anything you please, but free to be formed by something larger than your own intellect or the intellects of those around you.

8   I don't know if this is the kind of answer that can help you, but any time you care to write me, I can try to do better.

—— CONSIDERATIONS ———————————————————————

Letter to John Hawkes, April 14, 1960

1. What does O'Connor mean when she says that some of the favorable reviews of her book "are as bad as the unfavorable"? How do you go about judging the quality of a book review? As a writer, how do you judge your instructors' comments on your own papers?

2. In paragraph 2, O'Connor suggests that the grandmother in her story is like a lot of grandmothers in the South, but in her letter to the Professor of English she says her story is not realistic in the "everyday" sense. Can you reconcile this apparent contradiction?

3. O'Connor's comments on the term "grace" in paragraph 3 might be more understandable if you pursued the word itself in a good dictionary where you will find at least a dozen different definitions of the word. Keep in mind that she is using the word according to her own view of Catholic theology.

4. O'Connor says at the end of paragraph 3 that she is a Catholic writer. Does she mean that Protestant readers are not welcome or that Protestants could not understand her work? Is it possible to disagree with—or even disapprove of—a writer's ideas and still appreciate that writer's work? Explain.

5. While she does not always agree with John Hawkes's interpretations of her stories, O'Connor's letters to him (see also that of 11/28/61) express a good deal more respect for his ideas than can be found in her letter to a professor of English. Read a little of the work of John Hawkes to see if you can discover qualities he shares with O'Connor.

Letter to a Professor of English, March 28, 1961

1. O'Connor says her story is realistic, not in an "everyday" but "stylized" sense. Compare a paragraph or two of her story with a passage in Eudora

Welty's "A Worn Path" to see if you can determine what O'Connor means by "stylized." You might also get some help on that word by consulting a history of art.

2. Find passages in "A Good Man Is Hard to Find" that will illustrate what O'Connor means by the grandmother's "superficial beliefs" and the Misfit's "more profoundly felt involvement." Does such a close examination of the story push you closer to or further away from O'Connor's belief that the heart of the story is a "duel of sorts" between the grandmother and the Misfit?

3. In paragraph 4, O'Connor makes an interesting distinction between "meaning" and "interpretation" as she deplores the "habit of approaching a story as if it were a research problem for which any answer is believable so long as it is not obvious." Discuss some experience of your own in which insistence upon a particular interpretation (yours or anyone else's) interfered with the expanded meaning O'Connor mentions.

4. O'Connor says in her last paragraph that her tone in the letter "is not meant to be obnoxious." If you were the professor to whom she had written, what particular lines or words in the letter might you think gave it an obnoxious tone? Can you find any other writers in this book whose tone is obnoxious? Explain.

5. In what sense, if any, do you think a short story (or poem or novel or play or essay for that matter) can be taught? What assistance do you expect or want from your own instructor and/or text in reading a story like O'Connor's?

Letter to John Hawkes, November 28, 1961

1. O'Connor's remarkable versatility in the use of the English language is demonstrated in her letters as well as in her stories. This letter to John Hawkes, for example, shows her ability to shift from one voice to another at will. Find examples.

2. At the end of paragraph 4, O'Connor tells Hawkes, "You say one becomes 'evil' when one leaves the herd. I say that depends entirely on what the herd is doing." Write an essay on relative versus absolute morality.

3. O'Connor, speaking of her interest in Hawthorne, makes a distinction between writing "romances" and having a "romantic mentality." What did Hawthorne mean by "romances," and why does O'Connor "feel more of a kinship with him than with any other American"?

4. O'Connor's letters are filled with brief reports on local events and people, like the one on the goat man in the letter to John Hawkes. Eudora Welty, in discussing one of her own short stories—see her essay "The Point of the Story"—says that her story began when she observed an old woman in Mississippi. How might O'Connor's observations of her surroundings have contributed to "A Good Man Is Hard to Find"?

Letter to Alfred Corn, May 30, 1962

1. "You can't fit the Almighty into your intellectual categories," says O'Connor. Does she advise her correspondent to ignore the intellectual challenges of college? Study her discussion of the clash between intellectual inquiry and faith, especially in paragraphs 5 and 6, and write an essay on her conclusions.

2. How, according to O'Connor, can we know whether we believe or not?

3. Look over consideration 1 regarding O'Connor's 1961 letter to John Hawkes and think about voice. How would you describe the voice in this letter to Alfred Corn? Does O'Connor play with changes of voice in this letter? Why?

4. Read Langston Hughes's essay "Salvation"; how might O'Connor have consoled the disillusioned boy?

Flannery O'Connor's first novel, Wise Blood, *appeared in 1952;
her second and last,* The Violent Bear It Away, *in 1960. Most
critics prefer her stories to her novels. All of her fiction—stories
and novels together—is gathered together in one volume of The
Library of America. During her lifetime she published one
collection of stories, bearing the title of the story that follows.
This was the story she usually read aloud when asked to read.*

52

FLANNERY O'CONNOR
A Good Man Is Hard to Find

The grandmother didn't want to go to Florida. She wanted to visit   1
some of her connections in east Tennessee and she was seizing every
chance to change Bailey's mind. Bailey was the son she lived with, her
only boy. He was sitting on the edge of his chair at the table, bent over
the orange sports section of the *Journal.* "Now look here, Bailey," she
said, "see here, read this," and she stood with one hand on her thin hip
and the other rattling the newspaper at his bald head. "Here this fellow
that calls himself The Misfit is aloose from the Federal Pen and headed
toward Florida and you read here what it says he did to these people. Just
you read it. I wouldn't take my children in any direction with a criminal
like that aloose in it. I couldn't answer to my conscience if I did."

Bailey didn't look up from his reading so she wheeled around then   2
and faced the children's mother, a young woman in slacks, whose face
was as broad and innocent as a cabbage and was tied around with a green
headkerchief that had two points on the top like rabbit's ears. She was
sitting on the sofa, feeding the baby his apricots out of a jar. "The
children have been to Florida before," the old lady said. "You all ought
to take them somewhere else for a change so they would see different

parts of the world and be broad. They never have been to east Tennessee.''

3   The children's mother didn't seem to hear her, but the eight-year-old boy, John Wesley, a stocky child with glasses, said, "If you don't want to go to Florida, why dontcha stay at home?" He and the little girl, June Star, were reading the funny papers on the floor.

4   "She wouldn't stay at home to be queen for a day," June Star said without raising her yellow head.

5   "Yes, and what would you do if this fellow, The Misfit, caught you?" the grandmother asked.

6   "I'd smack his face," John Wesley said.

7   "She wouldn't stay at home for a million bucks," June Star said. "Afraid she'd miss something. She has to go everywhere we go."

8   "All right, Miss," the grandmother said. "Just remember that the next time you want me to curl your hair."

9   June Star said her hair was naturally curly.

10   The next morning the grandmother was the first one in the car, ready to go. She had her big black valise that looked like the head of a hippopotamus in one corner, and underneath it she was hiding a basket with Pitty Sing, the cat, in it. She didn't intend for the cat to be left alone in the house for three days because he would miss her too much and she was afraid he might brush against one of the gas burners and accidentally asphyxiate himself. Her son, Bailey, didn't like to arrive at a motel with a cat.

11   She sat in the middle of the back seat with John Wesley and June Star on either side of her. Bailey and the children's mother and the baby sat in the front and they left Atlanta at eight forty-five with the mileage on the car at 55890. The grandmother wrote this down because she thought it would be interesting to say how many miles they had been when they got back. It took them twenty minutes to reach the outskirts of the city.

12   The old lady settled herself comfortably, removing her white cotton gloves and putting them up with her purse on the shelf in front of the back window. The children's mother still had on slacks and still had her head tied up in a green kerchief, but the grandmother had on a navy blue straw sailor hat with a bunch of white violets on the brim and a navy blue dress with a small white dot in the print. Her collar and cuffs were white organdy trimmed with lace and at her neckline she had pinned a purple spray of cloth violets containing a sachet. In case of an accident, anyone seeing her dead on the highway would know at once that she was a lady.

She said she thought it was going to be a good day for driving, 13
neither too hot nor too cold, and she cautioned Bailey that the speed
limit was fifty-five miles an hour and that the patrolmen hid themselves behind bill-boards and small clumps of trees and sped out after
you before you had a chance to slow down. She pointed out interesting
details of the scenery: Stone Mountain; the blue granite that in some
places came up to both sides of the highway; the brilliant red clay banks
slightly streaked with purple; and the various crops that made rows of
green lace-work on the ground. The trees were full of silver-white
sunlights and the meanest of them sparkled. The children were reading
comic magazines and their mother had gone back to sleep.

"Let's go through Georgia fast so we don't have to look at it 14
much," John Wesley said.

"If I were a little boy," said the grandmother, "I wouldn't talk 15
about my native state that way. Tennessee has the mountains and
Georgia has the hills."

"Tennessee is just a hillbilly dumping ground," John Wesley said, 16
"and Georgia is a lousy state too."

"You said it," June Star said. 17

"In my time," said the grandmother, folding her thin veined fin- 18
gers, "children were more respectful of their native states and their
parents and everything else. People did right then. Oh look at the cute
little pickaninny!" she said and pointed to a Negro child standing in the
door of a shack. "Wouldn't that make a picture, now?" she asked and
they all turned and looked at the little Negro out of the back window.
He waved.

"He didn't have any britches on," June Star said. 19

"He probably didn't have any," the grandmother explained. "Lit 20
tle niggers in the country don't have things like we do. If I could paint,
I'd paint that picture," she said.

The children exchanged comic books. 21

The grandmother offered to hold the baby and the children's 22
mother passed him over the front seat to her. She set him on her knee
and bounced him and told him about the things they were passing. She
rolled her eyes and screwed up her mouth and stuck her leathery thin
face into his smooth bland one. Occasionally he gave her a faraway
smile. They passed a large cotton field with five or six graves fenced in
the middle of it, like a small island. "Look at the graveyard!" the
grandmother said, pointing it out. "That was the old family burying
ground. That belonged to the plantation."

"Where's the plantation?" John Wesley asked. 23

24   "Gone With the Wind," said the grandmother. "Ha. Ha."

25   When the children finished all the comic books they had brought, they opened the lunch and ate it. The grandmother ate a peanut butter sandwich and an olive and would not let the children throw the box and the paper napkins out the window. When there was nothing else to do they played a game by choosing a cloud and making the other two guess what shape it suggested. John Wesley took one the shape of a cow and June Star guessed a cow and John Wesley said, no, an automobile, and June Star said he didn't play fair, and they began to slap each other over the grandmother.

26   The grandmother said she would tell them a story if they would keep quiet. When she told a story, she rolled her eyes and waved her head and was very dramatic. She said once when she was a maiden lady she had been courted by a Mr. Edgar Atkins Teagarden from Jasper, Georgia. She said he was a very good-looking man and a gentleman and that he brought her a watermelon every Saturday afternoon with his initials cut in it, E.A.T. Well, one Saturday, she said, Mr. Teagarden brought the watermelon and there was nobody at home and he left it on the front porch and returned in his buggy to Jasper, but she never got the watermelon, she said, because a nigger boy ate it when he saw the initials, E.A.T.! This story tickled John Wesley's funny bone and he giggled and giggled but June Star didn't think it was any good. She said she wouldn't marry a man that just brought her a watermelon on Saturday. The grandmother said she would have done well to marry Mr. Teagarden because he was a gentleman and had bought Coca-Cola stock when it first came out and that he had died only a few years ago, a very wealthy man.

27   They stopped at The Tower for barbecued sandwiches. The Tower was a part-stucco and part-wood filling station and dance hall set in a clearing outside of Timothy. A fat man named Red Sammy Butts ran it and there were signs stuck here and there on the building and for miles up and down the highway saying, TRY RED SAMMY'S FAMOUS BARBECUE. NONE LIKE FAMOUS RED SAMMY'S! RED SAM! THE FAT BOY WITH THE HAPPY LAUGH. A VETERAN! RED SAMMY'S YOUR MAN!

28   Red Sammy was lying on the bare ground outside The Tower with his head under a truck while a gray monkey about a foot high, chained to a small chinaberry tree, chattered nearby. The monkey sprang back into the tree and got on the highest limb as soon as he saw the children jump out of the car and run toward him.

29   Inside, The Tower was a long dark room with a counter at one end

and tables at the other and dancing space in the middle. They all sat down at a broad table next to the nickelodeon and Red Sam's wife, a tall burnt-brown woman with hair and eyes lighter than her skin, came and took their order. The children's mother put a dime in the machine and played "The Tennessee Waltz," and the grandmother said that tune always made her want to dance. She asked Bailey if he would like to dance but he only glared at her. He didn't have a naturally sunny disposition like she did and trips made him nervous. The grandmother's brown eyes were very bright. She swayed her head from side to side and pretended she was dancing in her chair. June Star said play something she could tap to so the children's mother put in another dime and played a fast number and June Star stepped out onto the dance floor and did her tap routine.

"Ain't she cute?" Red Sam's wife said, leaning over the counter. 30
"Would you like to come be my little girl?"

"No, I certainly wouldn't," June Star said. "I wouldn't live in a 31
broken-down place like this for a million bucks!" and she ran back to the table.

"Ain't she cute?" the woman repeated, stretching her mouth 32
politely.

"Aren't you ashamed?" hissed the grandmother. 33

Red Sam came in and told his wife to quit lounging on the counter 34
and hurry up with these people's order. His khaki trousers reached just to his hip bones and his stomach hung over them like a sack of meal swaying under his shirt. He came over and sat down at a table nearby and let out a combination sigh and yodel. "You can't win," he said. "You can't win," and he wiped his sweating red face off with a gray handkerchief. "These days you don't know who to trust," he said. "Ain't that the truth?"

"People are certainly not nice like they used to be," said the 35
grandmother.

"Two fellers come in here last week," Red Sammy said, "driving a 36
Chrysler. It was an old beat-up car but it was a good one and these boys looked all right to me. Said they worked at the mill and you know I let them fellers charge the gas they bought? Now why did I do that?"

"Because you're a good man!" the grandmother said at once. 37

"Yes'm, I suppose so," Red Sam said as if he were struck with this 38
answer.

His wife brought the orders, carrying the five plates all at once 39
without a tray, two in each hand and one balanced on her arm. "It isn't a

soul in this green world of God's that you can trust," she said. "And I don't count nobody out of that, not nobody," she repeated, looking at Red Sammy.

40   "Did you read about that criminal, The Misfit, that's escaped?" asked the grandmother.

41   "I wouldn't be a bit surprised if he didn't attack this place right here," said the woman. "If he hears about it being here, I wouldn't be none surprised to see him. If he hears it's two cent in the cash register, I wouldn't be a tall surprised if he . . ."

42   "That'll do," Red Sam said. "Go bring these people their Co'-Colas," and the woman went off to get the rest of the order.

43   "A good man is hard to find," Red Sammy said. "Everything is getting terrible. I remember the day you could go off and leave your screen door unlatched. Not no more."

44   He and the grandmother discussed better times. The old lady said that in her opinion Europe was entirely to blame for the way things were now. She said the way Europe acted you would think we were made of money and Red Sam said it was no use talking about it, she was exactly right. The children ran outside into the white sunlight and looked at the monkey in the lacy chinaberry tree. He was busy catching fleas on himself and biting each one carefully between his teeth as if it were a delicacy.

45   They drove off again into the hot afternoon. The grandmother took cat naps and woke up every few minutes with her own snoring. Outside of Toombsboro she woke up and recalled an old plantation that she had visited in this neighborhood once when she was a young lady. She said the house had six white columns across the front and that there was an avenue of oaks leading up to it and two little wooden trellis arbors on either side in front where you sat down with your suitor after a stroll in the garden. She recalled exactly which road to turn off to get to it. She knew that Bailey would not be willing to lose any time looking at an old house, but the more she talked about it, the more she wanted to see it once again and find out if the little twin arbors were still standing. "There was a secret panel in this house," she said craftily, not telling the truth but wishing that she were, "and the story went that all the family silver was hidden in it when Sherman came through but it was never found. . . ."

46   "Hey!" John Wesley said. "Let's go see it! We'll find it! We'll poke all the wood work and find it! Who lives there? Where do you turn off at? Hey Pop, can't we turn off there?"

"We never have seen a house with a secret panel!" June Star 47
shrieked. "Let's go to the house with the secret panel! Hey, Pop, can't
we go see the house with the secret panel!"

"It's not far from here, I know," the grandmother said. "It 48
wouldn't take over twenty minutes."

Bailey was looking straight ahead. His jaw was as rigid as a 49
horseshoe. "No," he said.

The children began to yell and scream that they wanted to see the 50
house with the secret panel. John Wesley kicked the back of the front
seat and June Star hung over her mother's shoulder and whined desperately into her ear that they never had any fun even on their vacation,
that they could never do what THEY wanted to do. The baby began to
scream and John Wesley kicked the back of the seat so hard that his
father could feel the blows in his kidney.

"All right!" he shouted and drew the car to a stop at the side of the 51
road. "Will you all shut up? Will you all just shut up for one second? If
you don't shut up, we won't go anywhere."

"It would be very educational for them," the grandmother mur- 52
mured.

"All right," Bailey said, "but get this. This is the only time 53
we're going to stop for anything like this. This is the one and only
time."

"The dirt road that you have to turn down is about a mile back," 54
the grandmother directed. "I marked it when we passed."

"A dirt road," Bailey groaned. 55

After they had turned around and were headed toward the dirt 56
road, the grandmother recalled other points about the house, the beautiful glass over the front doorway and the candle lamp in the hall. John
Wesley said that the secret panel was probably in the fireplace.

"You can't go inside the house," Bailey said. "You don't know 57
who lives there."

"While you all talk to the people in front, I'll run around behind 58
and get in a window," John Wesley suggested.

"We'll all stay in the car," his mother said. 59

They turned onto the dirt road and the car raced roughly along in a 60
swirl of pink dust. The grandmother recalled the times when there were
no paved roads and thirty miles was a day's journey. The dirt road was
hilly and there were sudden washes in it and sharp curves on dangerous
embankments. All at once they would be on a hill, looking down over
the blue tops of trees for miles around, then the next minute, they

would be in a red depression with the dust-coated trees looking down on them.

61   "This place had better turn up in a minute," Bailey said, "or I'm going to turn around."

62   The road looked as if no one had traveled on it in months.

63   "It's not much further," the grandmother said and just as she said it, a horrible thought came to her. The thought was so embarrassing that she turned red in the face and her eyes dilated and her feet jumped up, upsetting her valise in the corner. The instant the valise moved, the newspaper top she had over the basket under it rose with a snarl and Pitty Sing, the cat, sprang onto Bailey's shoulder.

64   The children were thrown to the floor and their mother, clutching the baby, was thrown out the door onto the ground; the old lady was thrown into the front seat. The car turned over once and landed right-side-up in a gulch on the side of the road. Bailey remained in the driver's seat with the cat—gray-striped with a broad white face and an orange nose—clinging to his neck like a caterpillar.

65   As soon as the children saw they could move their arms and legs, they scrambled out of the car shouting, "We've had an ACCIDENT!" The grandmother was curled up under the dashboard, hoping she was injured so that Bailey's wrath would not come down on her all at once. The horrible thought she had had before the accident was that the house she had remembered so vividly was not in Georgia but in Tennessee.

66   Bailey removed the cat from his neck with both hands and flung it out the window against the side of a pine tree. Then he got out of the car and started looking for the children's mother. She was sitting against the side of the red gutted ditch, holding the screaming baby, but she only had a cut down her face and a broken shoulder. "We've had an ACCIDENT!" the children screamed in a frenzy of delight.

67   "But nobody's killed," June Star said with disappointment as the grandmother limped out of the car, her hat still pinned to her head but the broken front brim standing up at a jaunty angle and the violet spray hanging off the side. They all sat down in the ditch, except the children, to recover from the shock. They were all shaking.

68   "Maybe a car will come along," said the children's mother hoarsely.

69   "I believe I have injured an organ," said the grandmother, pressing her side, but no one answered her. Bailey's teeth were clattering. He had on a yellow sport shirt with bright blue parrots designed in it and his face was as yellow as the shirt. The grandmother decided that she would not mention that the house was in Tennessee.

The road was about ten feet above and they could see only the tops 70
of the trees on the other side of it. Behind the ditch they were sitting in
there were more woods, tall and dark and deep. In a few minutes they
saw a car some distance away on top of a hill, coming slowly as if the
occupants were watching them. The grandmother stood up and waved
both arms dramatically to attract their attention. The car continued to
come on slowly, disappeared around a bend and appeared again, moving
even slower, on top of the hill they had gone over. It was a big black
battered hearselike automobile. There were three men in it.

It came to a stop just over them and for some minutes, the driver 71
looked down with a steady expressionless gaze to where they were
sitting, and didn't speak. Then he turned his head and muttered something to the other two and they got out. One was a fat boy in black
trousers and a red sweat shirt with a silver stallion embossed on the
front of it. He moved around on the right side of them and stood staring,
his mouth partly open in a kind of loose grin. The other had on khaki
pants and a blue striped coat and a gray hat pulled down very low, hiding
most of his face. He came around slowly on the left side. Neither spoke.

The driver got out of the car and stood by the side of it, looking 72
down at them. He was an older man than the other two. His hair was
just beginning to gray and he wore silver-rimmed spectacles that gave
him a scholarly look. He had a long creased face and didn't have on any
shirt or undershirt. He had on blue jeans that were too tight for him and
he was holding a black hat and a gun. The two boys also had guns.

"We've had an ACCIDENT!" the children screamed. 73

The grandmother had the peculiar feeling that the bespectacled 74
man was someone she knew. His face was as familiar to her as if she had
known him all her life but she could not recall who he was. He moved
away from the car and began to come down the embankment, placing
his feet carefully so that he wouldn't slip. He had on tan and white
shoes and no socks, and his ankles were red and thin. "Good afternoon,"
he said, "I see you all had you a little spill."

"We turned over twice!" said the grandmother. 75

"Oncet," he corrected. "We see it happen. Try their car and see 76
will it run, Hiram," he said quietly to the boy with the gray hat.

"What you got that gun for?" John Wesley asked. "Whatcha gonna 77
do with that gun?"

"Lady," the man said to the children's mother, "would you mind 78
calling them children to sit down by you? Children make me nervous. I
want all you all to sit down right together there where you're at."

"What are you telling us what to do for?" June Star asked. 79

80   Behind them the line of woods gaped like a dark open mouth. "Come here," said their mother.

81   "Look here now," Bailey began suddenly, "we're in a predicament! We're in . . ."

82   The grandmother shrieked. She scrambled to her feet and stood staring.

83   "You're the Misfit!" she said. "I recognized you at once!"

84   "Yes'm," the man said, smiling slightly as if he were pleased in spite of himself to be known. "But it would have been better for all of you, lady, if you hadn't of reckernized me."

85   Bailey turned his head sharply and said something to his mother that shocked even the children. The old lady began to cry and The Misfit reddened.

86   "Lady," he said, "don't you get upset. Sometimes a man says things he don't mean. I don't reckon he meant to talk to you thataway."

87   "You wouldn't shoot a lady, would you?" the grandmother said and removed a clean handkerchief from her cuff and began to slap at her eyes with it.

88   The Misfit pointed the toe of his shoe into the ground and made a little hole and then covered it up again. "I would hate to have to," he said.

89   "Listen," the grandmother almost screamed, "I know you're a good man. You don't look a bit like you have common blood. I know you must come from nice people!"

90   "Yes mam," he said, "finest people in the world." When he smiled he showed a row of strong white teeth. "God never made a finer woman than my mother and my daddy's heart was pure gold," he said. The boy with the red sweat shirt had come around behind them and was standing with his gun at his hip. The Misfit squatted down on the ground. "Watch them children, Bobby Lee," he said. "You know they make me nervous." He looked at the six of them huddled together in front of him and he seemed to be embarrassed as if he couldn't think of anything to say. "Ain't a cloud in the sky," he remarked, looking up at it. "Don't see no sun but don't see no cloud neither."

91   "Yes, it's a beautiful day," said the grandmother. "Listen," she said, "you shouldn't call yourself The Misfit because I know you're a good man at heart. I can just look at you and tell."

92   "Hush!" Bailey yelled. "Hush! Everybody shut up and let me handle this!" He was squatting in the position of a runner about to spring forward but he didn't move.

"I pre-chate that, lady," The Misfit said and drew a little circle in 93
the ground with the butt of his gun.

"It'll take a half a hour to fix this here car," Hiram called, looking 94
over the raised hood of it.

"Well, first you and Bobby Lee get him and that little boy to step 95
over yonder with you," The Misfit said, pointing to Bailey and John
Wesley. "The boys want to ask you something," he said to Bailey.
"Would you mind stepping back in them woods there with them?"

"Listen," Bailey began, "we're in a terrible predicament! Nobody 96
realizes what this is," and his voice cracked. His eyes were as blue and
intense as the parrots in his shirt and he remained perfectly still.

The grandmother reached up to adjust her hat brim as if she were 97
going to the woods with him but it came off in her hand. She stood
staring at it and after a second she let it fall on the ground. Hiram pulled
Bailey up by the arm as if he were assisting an old man. John Wesley
caught hold of his father's hand and Bobby Lee followed. They went off
toward the woods and just as they reached the dark edge, Bailey turned
and supporting himself against a gray naked pine trunk, he shouted,
"I'll be back in a minute, Mamma, wait on me!"

"Come back this instant!" his mother shrilled but they all disap- 98
peared into the woods.

"Bailey Boy!" the grandmother called in tragic voice but she found 99
she was looking at The Misfit squatting on the ground in front of her. "I
just know you're a good man," she said desperately. "You're not a bit
common!"

"Nome, I ain't a good man," The Misfit said after a second as if he 100
had considered her statement carefully, "but I ain't the worst in the
world neither. My daddy said I was a different breed of dog from my
brothers and sisters. 'You know,' Daddy said, 'it's some that can live
their whole life out without asking about it and it's others has to know
why it is, and this boy is one of the latters. He's going to be into
everything!'" He put on his black hat and looked up suddenly and then
away deep into the woods as if he were embarrassed again. "I'm sorry, I
don't have on a shirt before you ladies," he said, hunching his shoulders
slightly. "We buried our clothes that we had on when we escaped and
we're just making do until we can get better. We borrowed these from
some folks we met," he explained.

"That's perfectly all right," the grandmother said. "Maybe Bailey 101
has an extra shirt in his suitcase."

"I'll look and see terrectly," The Misfit said. 102

103   "Where are they taking him?" the children's mother screamed.

104   "Daddy was a card himself," The Misfit said. "You couldn't put anything over on him. He never got in trouble with the Authorities though. Just had the knack of handling them."

105   "You could be honest too if you'd only try," said the grandmother. "Think how wonderful it would be to settle down and live a comfortable life and not have to think about somebody chasing you all the time."

106   The Misfit kept scratching in the ground with the butt of his gun as if he were thinking about it. "Yes'm, somebody is always after you," he murmured.

107   The grandmother noticed how thin his shoulder blades were just behind his hat because she was standing up looking down on him. "Do you ever pray?" she asked.

108   He shook his head. All she saw was the black hat wiggle between his shoulder blades. "Nome," he said.

109   There was a pistol shot from the woods, followed closely by another. Then silence. The old lady's head jerked around. She could hear the wind move through the tree tops like a long satisfied insuck of breath. "Bailey Boy!" she called.

110   "I was a gospel singer for a while," The Misfit said. "I been most everything. Been in the arm service, both land and sea, at home and abroad, been twict married, been an undertaker, been with the railroads, plowed Mother Earth, been in a tornado, seen a man burnt alive oncet," and he looked up at the children's mother and the little girl who were sitting close together, their faces white and their eyes glassy; "I even seen a woman flogged," he said.

111   "Pray, pray," the grandmother began, "pray, pray . . ."

112   "I never was a bad boy that I remember of," The Misfit said in an almost dreamy voice, "but somewheres along the line I done something wrong and got sent to the penitentiary. I was buried alive," and he looked up and held her attention to him by a steady stare.

113   "That's when you should have started to pray,"she said. "What did you do to get sent to the penitentiary that first time?"

114   "Turn to the right, it was a wall," The Misfit said, looking up again at the cloudless sky. "Turn to the left, it was a wall. Look up it was a ceiling, look down it was a floor. I forgot what I done, lady. I set there and set there, trying to remember what it was I done and I ain't recalled it to this day. Oncet in a while, I would think it was coming to me, but it never come."

"Maybe they put you in by mistake," the old lady said vaguely. 115

"Nome," he said. "It wasn't no mistake. They had the papers 116
on me."

"You must have stolen something," she said. 117

The Misfit sneered slightly. "Nobody had nothing I wanted," he 118
said. "It was a head-doctor at the penitentiary said what I had done was
kill my daddy but I known that for a lie. My daddy died in nineteen
ought nineteen of the epidemic flu and I never had a thing to do with it.
He was buried in the Mount Hopewell Baptist churchyard and you can
go there and see for yourself."

"If you would pray," the old lady said, "Jesus would help you." 119

"That's right," The Misfit said. 120

"Well then, why don't you pray?" she asked trembling with de- 121
light suddenly.

"I don't want no hep," he said, "I'm doing all right by myself." 122

Bobby Lee and Hiram came ambling back from the woods. Bobby 123
Lee was dragging a yellow shirt with bright blue parrots in it.

"Throw me that shirt, Bobby Lee," The Misfit said. The shirt came 124
flying at him and landed on his shoulder and he put it on. The grandmother couldn't name what the shirt reminded her of. "No, lady," The
Misfit said while he was buttoning it up, "I found out the crime don't
matter. You can do one thing or you can do another, kill a man or take a
tire off his car, because sooner or later you're going to forget what it was
you done and just be punished for it."

The children's mother had begun to make heaving noises as if she 125
couldn't get her breath. "Lady," he asked, "would you and that little girl
like to step off yonder with Bobby Lee and Hiram and join your
husband?"

"Yes, thank you," the mother said faintly. Her left arm dangled 126
helplessly and she was holding the baby, who had gone to sleep, in the
other. "Hep that lady up, Hiram," The Misfit said as she struggled to
climb out of the ditch, "and Bobby Lee, you hold onto that little girl's
hand."

"I don't want to hold hands with him," June Star said. "He 127
reminds me of a pig."

The fat boy blushed and laughed and caught her by the arm and 128
pulled her off into the woods after Hiram and her mother.

Alone with The Misfit, the grandmother found that she had lost 129
her voice. There was not a cloud in the sky nor any sun. There was
nothing around her but woods. She wanted to tell him that he must

pray. She opened and closed her mouth several times before anything came out. Finally she found herself saying, "Jesus. Jesus," meaning, Jesus will help you, but the way she was saying it, it sounded as if she might be cursing.

130   "Yes'm," The Misfit said as if he agreed. "Jesus thrown everything off balance. It was the same case with Him as with me except He hadn't committed any crime and they could prove I had committed one because they had the papers on me. Of course," he said, "they never shown me any papers. That's why I sign myself now, I said long ago, you get you a signature and sign everything you do and keep a copy of it. Then you'll know what you done and you can hold up the crime to the punishment and see do they match and in the end you'll have something to prove you ain't been treated right. I call myself The Misfit," he said, "because I can't make what all I done wrong fit what all I gone through in punishment."

131   There was a piercing scream from the woods, followed closely by a pistol report. "Does it seem right to you, lady, that one is punished a heap and another ain't punished at all?"

132   "Jesus!" the old lady cried. "You've got blood! I know you wouldn't shoot a lady! I know you come from nice people! Pray! Jesus, you ought not to shoot a lady. I'll give you all the money I've got!"

133   "Lady," The Misfit said, looking beyond her far into the woods, "there was never a body that give the undertaker a tip."

134   There were two more pistol reports and the grandmother raised her head like a parched old turkey hen crying for water and called, "Bailey Boy, Bailey Boy!" as if her heart would break.

135   "Jesus was the only One that ever raised the dead," The Misfit continued, "and He shouldn't have done it. He thrown everything off balance. If He did what He said, then it's nothing for you to do but throw away everything and follow Him, and if He didn't then it's nothing for you to do but enjoy the few minutes you got left the best way you can—by killing somebody or burning down his house or doing some other meanness to him. No pleasure but meanness," he said and his voice had become almost a snarl.

136   "Maybe He didn't raise the dead," the old lady mumbled, not knowing what she was saying and feeling so dizzy that she sank down in the ditch with her legs twisted under her.

137   "I wasn't there so I can't say He didn't," The Misfit said. "I wisht I had of been there," he said, hitting the ground with his fist. "It ain't right I wasn't there because if I had of been there I would of known.

Listen lady," he said in a high voice, "if I had of been there I would of known and I wouldn't be like I am now." His voice seemed about to crack and the grandmother's head cleared for an instant. She saw the man's face twisted close to her own as if he were going to cry and she murmured, "Why, you're one of my babies. You're one of my own children!" She reached out and touched him on the shoulder. The Misfit sprang back as if a snake had bitten him and shot her three times through the chest. Then he put his gun down on the ground and took off his glasses and began to clean them.

Hiram and Bobby Lee returned from the woods and stood over the 138 ditch, looking down at the grandmother who half sat and half lay in a puddle of blood with her legs crossed under her like a child's and her face smiling up at the cloudless sky.

Without his glasses, The Misfit's eyes were red-rimmed and pale 139 and defenseless-looking. "Take her off and throw her where you thrown the others," he said, picking up the cat that was rubbing itself against his leg.

"She was a talker, wasn't she?" Bobby Lee said, sliding down the 140 ditch with a yodel.

"She would of been a good woman," The Misfit said, "if it had 141 been somebody there to shoot her every minute of her life."

"Some fun!" Bobby Lee said. 142

"Shut up, Bobby Lee," The Misfit said. "It's no real pleasure in 143 life."

_____ **CONSIDERATIONS** _____

1. To keep the children quiet, the grandmother tells the ridiculous story of Mr. Edgar Atkins Teagarden, who cut his initials E.A.T. in a watermelon. How do you account for O'Connor's including such an anecdote in a story about a psychopathic murderer?

2. One respected scholar and critic describes O'Connor's story as a "satire on the half-and-half Christian faced with nihilism and death." In what sense would the grandmother qualify as a "half-and-half Christian"? Is there anything in O'Connor's letters to John Hawkes and Alfred Corn that might help you understand what O'Connor thought a real Christian was?

3. Does this story contain characteristics of satire as seen in Jonathan Swift's "A Modest Proposal," Don Sharp's "Under the Hood," or Woody Allen's "Death Knocks"?

4. O'Connor borrows a line from her own story to serve as a title. Find the line, study the context and comment on it as a title.

5. When the Misfit tells the grandmother, "it would have been better for all of you, lady, if you hadn't of reckernized me," what purpose does his warning serve, in furthering the story?

6. Study three elderly women: the grandmother in this story, Faulkner's Emily, and Welty's Phoenix Jackson. Do you think it fair to say that all three are used to convey the point of their respective authors' stories? Explain.

Flannery O'Connor also wrote essays, collected after her death in a volume called Mystery and Manners *(1969). This essay, which originally appeared in the* Georgia Bulletin *in 1963, addressed local and immediate problems. In the American nineties its insights remain urgent, as our culture, in O'Connor's word, becomes increasingly "fractured."*

53

FLANNERY O'CONNOR
The Total Effect and the Eighth Grade

In two recent instances in Georgia, parents have objected to their   1
eighth- and ninth-grade children's reading assignments in modern fiction. This seems to happen with some regularity in cases throughout the country. The unwitting parent picks up his child's book, glances through it, comes upon passages of erotic detail or profanity, and takes off at once to complain to the school board. Sometimes, as in one of the Georgia cases, the teacher is dismissed and hackles rise in liberal circles everywhere.

The two cases in Georgia, which involved Steinbeck's *East of*   2
Eden and John Hersey's *A Bell for Adano*, provoked considerable newspaper comment. One columnist, in commending the enterprise of the teachers, announced that students do not like to read the fusty works of the nineteenth century, that their attention can best be held by novels dealing with the realities of our own time, and that the Bible, too, is full of racy stories.

Mr. Hersey himself addressed a letter to the State School Superin-   3
tendent in behalf of the teacher who had been dismissed. He pointed out

that his book is not scandalous, that it attempts to convey an earnest message about the nature of democracy, and that it falls well within the limits of the principle of "total effect," that principle followed in legal cases by which a book is judged not for isolated parts but by the final effect of the whole book upon the general reader.

4   I do not want to comment on the merits of these particular cases. What concerns me is what novels ought to be assigned in the eighth and ninth grades as a matter of course, for if these cases indicate anything, they indicate the haphazard way in which fiction is approached in our high schools. Presumably there is a state reading list which contains "safe" books for teachers to assign; after that it is up to the teacher.

5   English teachers come in Good, Bad, and Indifferent, but too frequently in high schools anyone who can speak English is allowed to teach it. Since several novels can't easily be gathered into one textbook, the fiction that students are assigned depends upon their teacher's knowledge, ability, and taste: variable factors at best. More often than not, the teacher assigns what he thinks will hold the attention and interest of the students. Modern fiction will certainly hold it.

6   Ours is the first age in history which has asked the child what he would tolerate learning, but that is a part of the problem with which I am not equipped to deal. The devil of Educationism that possesses us is the kind that can be "cast out only by prayer and fasting." No one has yet come along strong enough to do it. In other ages the attention of children was held by Homer and Virgil, among others, but, by the reverse evolutionary process, that is no longer possible; our children are too stupid now to enter the past imaginatively. No one asks the student if algebra pleases him or if he finds it satisfactory that some French verbs are irregular, but if he prefers Hersey to Hawthorne, his taste must prevail.

7   I would like to put forward the proposition, repugnant to most English teachers, that fiction, if it is going to be taught in the high schools, should be taught as a subject and as a subject with a history. The total effect of a novel depends not only on its innate impact, but upon the experience, literary and otherwise, with which it is approached. No child needs to be assigned Hersey or Steinbeck until he is familiar with a certain amount of the best work of Cooper, Hawthorne, Melville, the early James, and Crane, and he does not need to be assigned these until he has been introduced to some of the better English novelists of the eighteenth and nineteenth centuries.

8   The fact that these works do not present him with the realities of his own time is all to the good. He is surrounded by the realities of his

own time, and he has no perspective whatever from which to view them. Like the college student who wrote in her paper on Lincoln that he went to the movies and got shot, many students go to college unaware that the world was not made yesterday; their studies began with the present and dipped backward occasionally when it seemed necessary or unavoidable.

There is much to be enjoyed in the great British novels of the   9 nineteenth century, much that a good teacher can open up in them for the young student. There is no reason why these novels should be either too simple or too difficult for the eighth grade. For the simple, they offer simple pleasures; for the more precocious, they can be made to yield subtler ones if the teacher is up to it. Let the student discover, after reading the nineteenth-century British novel, that the nineteenth-century American novel is quite different as to its literary characteristics, and he will thereby learn something not only about these individual works but about the sea-change which a new historical situation can effect in a literary form. Let him come to modern fiction with this experience behind him, and he will be better able to see and to deal with the more complicated demands of the best twentieth-century fiction.

Modern fiction often looks simpler than the fiction that preceded   10 it, but in reality is more complex. A natural evolution has taken place. The author has for the most part absented himself from direct participation in the work and has left the reader to make his own way amid experiences dramatically rendered and symbolically ordered. The modern novelist merges the reader in experience; he tends to raise the passions he touches upon. If he is a good novelist, he raises them to effect by their order and clarity a new experience—the total effect— which is not in itself sensuous or simply of the moment. Unless the child has had some literary experience before, he is not going to be able to resolve the immediate passions the book arouses into any true, total picture.

It is here the moral problem will arise. It is one thing for a child to   11 read about adultery in the Bible or in *Anna Karenina*, and quite another for him to read about it in most modern fiction. This is not only because in both the former instances adultery is considered a sin, and in the latter, at most, an inconvenience, but because modern writing involves the reader in the action with a new degree of intensity, and literary mores now permit him to be involved in any action a human being can perform.

In our fractured culture, we cannot agree on morals; we cannot   12 even agree that moral matters should come before literary ones when there is a conflict between them. All this is another reason why the high schools would do well to return to their proper business of preparing foundations. Whether in the senior year students should be assigned modern novelists should depend both on their parents' consent and on what they have already read and understood.

13   The high-school English teacher will be fulfilling his responsibility if he furnishes the student a guided opportunity, through the best writing of the past, to come, in time, to an understanding of the best writing of the present. He will teach literature, not social studies or little lessons in democracy or the customs of many lands.

14   And if the student finds that this is not to his taste? Well, that is regrettable. Most regrettable. His taste should not be consulted; it is being formed.

_____ CONSIDERATIONS _____

1. How far must you read in O'Connor's essay before you know her chief concern? Does it occupy her attention in her first three paragraphs? If not, how can you defend the organization of this essay?

2. O'Connor argues in paragraph 8 that "it is all to the good" that the so-called classics do not present the child with realities of his own time. How does her reference to the college student writing about Lincoln apply to her argument? How would she offset a reader's insistence that the child's reading be relevant to his or her own time?

3. To what extent does O'Connor's paragraph 10 help explain the principle of "total effect" mentioned in paragraph 3? Do you consider that principle a reasonable means of sorting out acceptable from unacceptable reading matter?

4. How would Margaret Atwood (see "Pornography") respond to O'Connor's solution to the moral problem mentioned in paragraph 12?

5. Write a response to O'Connor's answer to her question at the beginning of paragraph 14. Take into account the rest of her essay as well as your own feelings.

6. What nineteenth-century British and American novels do you remember well enough to compare with modern novels? If your answer is "none," are you in any position to argue with O'Connor?

Frank O'Connor (1903–1966), the pseudonym of Michael Francis O'Donovan, was a great Irish storywriter born in Cork. He wrote novels, criticism (most notably The Lonely Voice: A Study of the Short Story, *in 1962), and biography, but his short stories are his most celebrated work. We take "Christmas" from his volume of autobiography called* An Only Child *(1961).*

54

FRANK O'CONNOR
Christmas

Christmas was always the worst time of the year for me, though it 1 began well, weeks before Christmas itself, with the Christmas numbers. Normally I read only boys' weeklies, but at this time of year all papers, juvenile and adult, seemed equally desirable, as though the general magic of the season transcended the particular magic of any one paper. School stories, detective stories, and adventure stories all emerged into one great Christmas story.

Christmas numbers were, of course, double numbers; their pale- 2 green and red covers suddenly bloomed into glossy colours, with borders of red-berried holly. Even their titles dripped with snow. As for the pictures within, they showed roads under snow, and old houses under snow, with diamond-paned windows that were brilliant in the darkness. I never knew what magic there was in snow for me because in Ireland we rarely saw it for more than two or three days in the year, and that was usually in the late spring. In real life it meant little to me except that Father—who was always trying to make a manly boy of me as he believed himself to have been at my age—made me wash my face and hands in it to avert chilblains. I think its magic in the Christmas numbers depended on the contrast between it and the Christmas candles, the holly branches with the red berries, the log fires, and the gleaming windows. It was the contrast between light and dark, life and

From *An Only Child* by Frank O'Connor. Reprinted by permission of Joan Daves.

death; the cold and darkness that reigned when life came into the world. Going about her work, Mother would suddenly break into song:

> *Natum videte*
> *Regem angelorum . . .**

and I would join in. It was the season of imagination. My trouble was that I already had more than my share of imagination.

3   Then there were no more Christmas numbers, but I managed to preserve the spirit of them, sitting at my table with pencil and paper, trying to draw Christmas scenes of my own—dark skies and walls, bright snow and windows. When I was older and could trace figures, these turned into the figures of the manger scene, cut out and mounted on cardboard to make a proper crib.

4   Christmas Eve was the culmination of this season, the day when the promise of the Christmas numbers should be fulfilled. The shops already had their green and red streamers, and in the morning Mother decorated the house with holly and ivy. Much as I longed for it, we never had red-berried holly, which cost more. The Christmas candle, two feet high and a couple of inches thick, was set in a jam crock, wrapped in coloured paper, and twined about with holly. Everything was ready for the feast. For a lot of the day I leaned against the front door or wandered slowly down the road to the corner, trying to appear careless and indifferent so that no one should know I was really waiting for the postman. Most of the Christmas mail we got came on Christmas Eve, and though I don't think I ever got a present through the post, that did not in the least diminish my expectations of one. Whatever experience might have taught me, the Christmas numbers taught differently.

5   Father had a half-day on Christmas Eve, and came home at noon with his week's pay in his pocket—that is, when he got home at all. Mother and I knew well how easily he was led astray by out-of-works who waited at the street corners for men in regular jobs, knowing that on Christmas Eve no one could refuse them a pint. But I never gave that aspect of it much thought. It wasn't for anything so commonplace as Father's weekly pay that I was waiting. I even ignored the fact that when he did come in, there was usually an argument and sometimes a quarrel. At ordinary times when he did not give Mother enough to pay the bills, she took it with resignation, and if there was a row it was he who provoked it by asking: 'Well, isn't that enough for you?' But at

---

* From the 17th-century Latin hymn, "Adeste Fideles" ("O Come, All Ye Faithful"). ("Behold the birth of the King of angels.") St. Stephen's Day is observed in Catholic communities. O'Connor explains the custom in paragraphs 12 and 13.

Christmas she would fight and fight desperately. One Christmas Eve he came home and handed her the housekeeping money with a complacent air, and she looked at the coins in her hand and went white. 'Lord God, what am I to do with that?' I heard her whisper despairingly, and I listened in terror because she never invoked the name of God. Father suddenly blew up into the fury he had been cooking up all the way home—a poor, hard-working man deprived of his little bit of pleasure at Christmas time because of an extravagant wife and child. 'Well, what do you want it for?' he snarled. 'What do I want it for?' she asked distractedly, and went through her shopping list, which, God knows, must have been modest enough. And then he said something that I did not understand, and I heard her whispering in reply and there was a frenzy in her voice that I would not have believed possible; 'Do you think I'll leave him without it on the one day of the year?'

Years later I suddenly remembered the phrase because of its   6
beauty, and realized that it was I who was to be left without a toy, and on this one day of the year that seemed to her intolerable. And yet I did not allow it to disturb me; I had other expectations, and I was very happy when the pair of us went shopping together, down Blarney Lane, past the shop in the big old house islanded in Goulnaspurra, where they sold the coloured cardboard cribs I coveted, with shepherds and snow, manger and star, and across the bridge to Myles's Toy Shop on the North Main Street. There in the rainy dusk, jostled by prams and drunken women in shawls, and thrust on one side by barefooted children from the lanes, I stood in wonder, thinking which treasure Santa Claus would bring me from the ends of the earth to show his appreciation of the way I had behaved in the past twelve months. As he was a most superior man, and I a most superior child, I saw no limit to the possibilities of the period, and no reason why Mother should not join in my speculations.

It was usually dark when we tramped home together, up Wyse's   7
Hill, from which we saw the whole city lit up beneath us and the trams reflected in the water under Patrick's Bridge; or later—when we lived in Barrackton, up Summerhill, Mother carrying the few scraps of meat and the plum pudding from Thompson's and me something from the Penny Bazaar. We had been out a long time, and I was full of expectations of what the postman might have brought in the meantime. Even when he hadn't brought anything, I didn't allow myself to be upset, for I knew that the poor postmen were dreadfully overworked at this time of year. And even if he didn't come later, there was always the final Christmas-morning delivery. I was an optimistic child, and the holly over the

mirror in the kitchen and the red paper in the lighted window of the huxter shop across the street assured me that the Christmas numbers were right and anything might happen.

8   There were lesser pleasures to look forward to, like the lighting of the Christmas candle and the cutting of the Christmas cake. As the youngest of the household I had the job of lighting the candle and saying solemnly: 'The light of Heaven to our souls on the last day', and Mother's principal worry was that before the time came Father might slip out to the pub and spoil the ritual, for it was supposed to be carried out by the oldest and the youngest, and Father, by convention, was the oldest, though, in fact, as I later discovered, he was younger than Mother.

9   In those days the cake and candle were supposed to be presented by the small shopkeeper from whom we bought the tea, sugar, paraffin oil, and so on. We could not afford to shop in the big stores where everything was cheaper, because they did not give credit to poor people, and most of the time we lived on credit. But each year our 'presents' seemed to grow smaller, and Mother would comment impatiently on the meanness of Miss O' or Miss Mac in giving us a tiny candle or a stale cake. (When the 1914 War began they stopped giving us the cake.) Mother could never believe that people could be so mean, but, where we were concerned, they seemed to be capable of anything. The lighted candle still left me with two expectations. However late it grew I never ceased to expect the postman's knock, and even when that failed, there was the certainty that Christmas Morning would set everything right.

10   But when I woke on Christmas Morning, I felt the season of imagination slipping away from me and the world of reality breaking in. If all Santa Claus could bring me from the North Pole was something I could have bought in Myles's Toy Shop for a couple of pence, he seemed to me to be wasting his time. Then the postman came, on his final round before a holiday that already had begun to seem eternal, and either he brought nothing for us, or else he brought the dregs of the Christmas mail, like a Christmas card from somebody who had just got Mother's card and remembered her existence at the last moment. Often, even this would be in an unsealed envelope and it would upset her for hours. It was strange in a woman to whom a penny was money that an unsealed envelope seemed to her the worst of ill-breeding, equivalent to the small candle or the stale cake—not a simple measure of economy, but plain, unadulterated bad taste.

11   Comparing Christmas gifts with other kids didn't take long or give much satisfaction, and even then the day was overshadowed by the

harsh rule that I was not supposed to call at other children's houses or they at mine. This, Mother said, was the family season, which was all very well for those who had families but death to an only child. It was the end of the season of imagination, and there was no reason to think it would ever come again. Nothing had happened as it happened in the Christmas numbers. There was no snow; no relative had returned from the States with presents for everyone; there was nothing but Christmas Mass and the choir thundering out *Natum videte regem angelorum* as though they believed it, when any fool could see that things were just going on in the same old way. Mother would sigh and say: 'I never believe it's really Christmas until I hear the *Adeste*,' but if that was all that Christmas meant to her she was welcome to it. Most Christmas days I could have screamed with misery. I argued with Mother that other kids were just as depressed as I was, and dying to see me, but I never remember that she allowed me to stray far from the front door.

But, bad as Christmas Day was, St. Stephen's Day was terrible. It 12
needed no imagination, only as much as was required to believe that you really had a dead wren on the holly bush you carried from door to door, singing:

> I up with me stick and I gave him a fall,
> And I brought him here to visit ye all.

Father was very contemptuous, watching this, and took it as an- 13
other sign of the disappearance of youthful manliness, for in his young days not only did they wash their faces in snow, but on Christmas Day they raised the countryside with big sticks, killing wrens—or droleens, as we called them. Everyone knew that it was the droleen's chirping that had alerted the Roman soldiers in the Garden of Gethsemane and pointed out to them where Christ was concealed, and in Father's young days they had carried it around with great pomp, all the mummers disguised. It seemed to him positively indecent to ask for money on the strength of a dead wren that you didn't have. It wasn't the absence of the wren that worried Mother, even if he was an informer, for she adored birds and supported a whole regiment of them through the winter, but the fear that I would be a nuisance to other women as poor as herself who didn't have a penny to give the wren boys.

In the afternoon she and I went to see the cribs in the chapels. 14
(There were none in the parish churches.) She was never strong enough to visit the seven cribs you had to visit to get the special blessing, but we always went to the chapel of the Good Shepherd Convent in Sunday's

Well where she had gone to school. She was very loyal to those she called 'the old nuns', the nuns who had been kind to her when she was a child.

15   One Christmas Santa Claus brought me a toy engine. As it was the only present I had received, I took it with me to the convent, and played with it on the floor while Mother and 'the old nuns' discussed old times and how much nicer girls used to be then. But it was a young man who brought us in to see the crib. When I saw the Holy Child in the manger I was very distressed, because little as I had, he had nothing at all. For me it was fresh proof of the incompetence of Santa Claus—an elderly man who hadn't even remembered to give the Infant Jesus a toy and who should have been retired long ago. I asked the young nun politely if the Holy Child didn't like toys, and she replied composedly enough: 'Oh, he does, but his mother is too poor to afford them.' That settled it. My mother was poor too, but at Christmas she at least managed to buy me something, even if it was only a box of crayons. I distinctly remember getting into the crib and putting the engine between his outstretched arms. I probably showed him how to wind it as well, because a small baby like that would not be clever enough to know. I remember too the tearful feeling of reckless generosity with which I left him there in the nightly darkness of the chapel, clutching my toy engine to his chest.

16   Because somehow I knew even then exactly how that child felt— the utter despondency of realizing that he had been forgotten and that nobody had brought him anything; the longing for the dreary, dreadful holidays to pass till his father got to hell out of the house, and the postman returned again with the promise of better things.

⎯⎯ CONSIDERATIONS ⎯⎯⎯⎯⎯⎯⎯⎯⎯⎯⎯⎯⎯⎯⎯⎯⎯⎯⎯⎯⎯⎯⎯⎯⎯

1. The pleasures of anticipation, we are told, rarely match the reality that follows. Does O'Connor's account of his boyhood Christmas support this commonplace? Referring to "Christmas," write an argumentative essay on the subject.

2. O'Connor's preoccupation with the "magic" of snow, in paragraph 2, prompts a question: Why did snow and holly berries and the red and green covers of the Christmas magazines strike the adult writer as he tells of his boyhood?

3. O'Connor describes himself on Christmas Eve, loitering about, "trying to appear careless and indifferent," as he waited for the postman to bring the

Christmas mail. What current slang word would perfectly fit the boy's behavior, and why didn't O'Connor use it?

4. What happened to the toy engine O'Connor remembers receiving one Christmas, and what had it to do with the boy's feeling that Santa Claus was an incompetent old man "who should have been retired long ago"?

5. If the O'Connors were so poor, how did they manage a Christmas cake and a Christmas candle?

*George Orwell (1903–1950) was the pen name of Eric Blair,
who was born in India of English parents, attended Eton on a
scholarship, and returned to the East as a member of the
Imperial Police. He quit his position after five years because he
wanted to write, and because he came to feel that imperialism
was "very largely a racket." For eight years he wrote with small
success and lived in considerable poverty. His first book,* Down
and Out in Paris and London *(1933), described those years.
Further memoirs and novels followed, including* Burmese Days
(1935) and Keep the Aspidistra Flying *(1938). His last books
were the political fable* Animal Farm *(1945) and his great anti-
utopia* 1984, *which appeared in 1949, shortly before his death.
He died of tuberculosis, his health first afflicted when he was a
policeman in Burma, undermined by years of poverty, and
further worsened by a wound he received during the civil war in
Spain.*

*Best known for his fiction, Orwell was essentially an essayist;
even his novels are essays. He made his living most of his adult
life by writing reviews and articles for English weeklies. His
collected essays, reviews, and letters form an impressive four
volumes. Politics is at the center of his work—a personal
politics. After his disaffection from imperialism, he became a
leftist and fought on the Loyalist side against Franco in Spain.
(*Homage to Catalonia *comes out of this time.) But his experience
of Communist duplicity there, and his early understanding of
the paranoid totalitarianism of Stalin, turned him anti-
Communist. He could swear allegiance to no party. His anti-
Communism made him in no way conservative; he considered
himself a socialist until his death, but other socialists would
have nothing to do with him. He found politics shabby and
politicians dishonest. With an empirical, English turn of mind,
he looked skeptically at all saviors and panaceas.*

55

GEORGE ORWELL
A Hanging

It was in Burma, a sodden morning of the rains. A sickly light, like   1
yellow tinfoil, was slanting over the high walls into the jail yard. We
were waiting outside the condemned cells, a row of sheds fronted with
double bars, like small animal cages. Each cell measured about ten feet
by ten and was quite bare within except for a plank bed and a pot for
drinking water. In some of them brown, silent men were squatting at
the inner bars, with their blankets draped round them. These were the
condemned men, due to be hanged within the next week or two.

One prisoner had been brought out of his cell. He was a Hindu, a   2
puny wisp of a man, with a shaven head and vague liquid eyes. He had a
thick, sprouting moustache, absurdly too big for his body, rather like
the moustache of a comic man on the films. Six tall Indian warders were
guarding him and getting him ready for the gallows. Two of them stood
by with rifles and fixed bayonets, while the others handcuffed him,
passed a chain through his handcuffs and fixed it to their belts, and
lashed his arms tight to his sides. They crowded very close about him,
with their hands always on him in a careful, caressing grip, as though all
the while feeling him to make sure he was there. It was like men
handling a fish which is still alive and may jump back into the water.
But he stood quite unresisting, yielding his arms limply to the ropes, as
though he hardly noticed what was happening.

Eight o'clock struck and a bugle call, desolately thin in the wet air,   3
floated from the distant barracks. The superintendent of the jail, who
was standing apart from the rest of us, moodily prodding the gravel with
his stick, raised his head at the sound. He was an army doctor, with a
grey toothbrush moustache and a gruff voice. "For God's sake hurry up,
Francis," he said irritably. "The man ought to have been dead by this
time. Aren't you ready yet?"

Francis, the head jailer, a fat Dravidian in a white drill suit and   4 gold spectacles, waved his black hand. "Yes sir, yes sir," he bubbled. "All iss satisfactorily prepared. The hangman iss waiting. We shall proceed."

5   "Well, quick march, then. The prisoners can't get their breakfast till this job's over."

6   We set out for the gallows. Two warders marched on either side of the prisoner, with their rifles at the slope; two others marched close against him, gripping him by arm and shoulder, as though at once pushing and supporting him. The rest of us, magistrates and the like, followed behind. Suddenly, when we had gone ten yards, the procession stopped short without any order or warning. A dreadful thing had happened—a dog, come goodness knows whence, had appeared in the yard. It came bounding among us with a loud volley of barks and leapt round us wagging its whole body, wild with glee at finding so many human beings together. It was a large woolly dog, half Airedale, half pariah. For a moment it pranced around us, and then, before anyone could stop it, it had made a dash for the prisoner, and jumping up tried to lick his face. Everybody stood aghast, too taken aback even to grab the dog.

7   "Who let that bloody brute in here?" said the superintendent angrily. "Catch it, someone!"

8   A warder detached from the escort, charged clumsily after the dog, but it danced and gambolled just out of his reach, taking everything as part of the game. A young Eurasian jailer picked up a handful of gravel and tried to stone the dog away, but it dodged the stones and came after us again. Its yaps echoed from the jail walls. The prisoner, in the grasp of the two warders, looked on incuriously, as though this was another formality of the hanging. It was several minutes before someone managed to catch the dog. Then we put my handkerchief through its collar and moved off once more, with the dog still straining and whimpering.

9   It was about forty yards to the gallows. I watched the bare brown back of the prisoner marching in front of me. He walked clumsily with his bound arms, but quite steadily, with that bobbing gait of the Indian who never straightens his knees. At each step his muscles slid neatly into place, the lock of hair on his scalp danced up and down, his feet printed themselves on the wet gravel. And once, in spite of the men who gripped him by each shoulder, he stepped lightly aside to avoid a puddle on the path.

10   It is curious; but till that moment I had never realized what it means to destroy a healthy, conscious man. When I saw the prisoner step aside to avoid the puddle I saw the mystery, the unspeakable

wrongness, of cutting a life short when it is in full tide. This man was not dying, he was alive just as we are alive. All the organs of his body were working—bowels digesting food, skin renewing itself, nails growing, tissues forming—all toiling away in solemn foolery. His nails would still be growing when he stood on the drop, when he was falling through the air with a tenth-of-a-second to live. His eyes saw the yellow gravel and the grey walls, and his brain still remembered, foresaw, reasoned—even about puddles. He and we were a party of men walking together, seeing, hearing, feeling, understanding the same world; and in two minutes, with a sudden snap, one of us would be gone—one mind less, one world less.

The gallows stood in a small yard, separate from the main grounds 11 of the prison, and overgrown with tall prickly weeds. It was a brick erection like three sides of a shed, with planking on top, and above that two beams and a crossbar with the rope dangling. The hangman, a greyhaired convict in the white uniform of the prison, was waiting beside his machine. He greeted us with a servile crouch as we entered. At a word from Francis the two wards, gripping the prisoner more closely than ever, half led, half pushed him to the gallows and helped him clumsily up the ladder. Then the hangman climbed up and fixed the rope round the prisoner's neck.

We stood waiting, five yards away. The warders had formed in a 12 rough circle round the gallows. And then, when the noose was fixed, the prisoner began crying out to his god. It was a high, reiterated cry of "Ram! Ram! Ram! Ram!" not urgent and fearful like a prayer or cry for help, but steady, rhythmical, almost like the tolling of a bell. The dog answered the sound with a whine. The hangman, still standing on the gallows, produced a small cotton bag like a flour bag and drew it down over the prisoner's face. But the sound, muffled by the cloth, still pcrointed, over and over again: "Ram! Ram! Ram! Ram! Ram!"

The hangman climbed down and stood ready, holding the lever. 13 Minutes seemed to pass. The steady, muffled crying from the prisoner went on and on, "Ram! Ram! Ram!" never faltering for an instant. The superintendent, his head on his chest, was slowly poking the ground with his stick; perhaps he was counting the cries, allowing the prisoner a fixed number—fifty, perhaps, or a hundred. Everyone had changed colour. The Indians had gone grey like bad coffee, and one or two of the bayonets were wavering. We looked at the lashed, hooded man on the drop, and listened to his cries—each cry another second of life; the same thought was in all our minds; oh, kill him quickly, get it over, stop that abominable noise!

14   Suddenly the superintendent made up his mind. Throwing up his head he made a swift motion with his stick. "Chalo!" he shouted almost fiercely.

15   There was a clanking noise, and then dead silence. The prisoner had vanished, and the rope was twisting on itself. I let go of the dog, and it galloped immediately to the back of the gallows; but when it got there it stopped short, barked, and then retreated into a corner of the yard, where it stood among the weeds, looking timorously out at us. We went round the gallows to inspect the prisoner's body. He was dangling with his toes pointed straight downwards, very slowly revolving, as dead as a stone.

16   The superintendent reached out with his stick and poked the bare brown body; it oscillated slightly. "*He's* all right," said the superintendent. He backed out from under the gallows, and blew out a deep breath. The moody look had gone out of his face quite suddenly. He glanced at his wrist-watch. "Eight minutes past eight. Well, that's all for this morning, thank God."

17   The warders unfixed bayonets and marched away. The dog, sobered and conscious of having misbehaved itself, slipped after them. We walked out of the gallows yard, past the condemned cells with their waiting prisoners, into the big central yard of the prison. The convicts, under the command of warders armed with lathis, were already receiving their breakfast. They squatted in long rows, each man holding a tin pannikin, while two warders with buckets marched round ladling out rice; it seemed quite a homely, jolly scene, after the hanging. An enormous relief had come upon us now that the job was done. One felt an impulse to sing, to break into a run, to snigger. All at once everyone began chatting gaily.

18   The Eurasian boy walking beside me nodded towards the way we had come, with a knowing smile: "Do you know, sir, our friend (he meant the dead man) when he heard his appeal had been dismissed, he pissed on the floor of his cell. From fright. Kindly take one of my cigarettes, sir. Do you not admire my new silver case, sir? From the boxwallah, two rupees eight annas. Classy European style."

19   Several people laughted—at what, nobody seemed certain.

20   Francis was walking by the superintendent, talking garrulously: "Well, sir, all has passed off with the utmost satisfactoriness. It was all finished—flick! Like that. It iss not always so—oah, no! I have known cases where the doctor wass obliged to go beneath the gallows and pull the prissoner's legs to ensure decease. Most disagreeable!"

21   "Wriggling about, eh? That's bad," said the superintendent.

"Ach, sir, it iss worse when they become refractory! One man, I   22
recall, clung to the bars of hiss cage when we went to take him out. You
will scarcely credit, sir, that it took six wards to dislodge him, three
pulling at each leg. We reasoned with him, 'My dear fellow,'" we said,
'think of all the pain and trouble you are causing to us!' But no, he
would not listen! Ach, he wass very troublesome!"

I found that I was laughing quite loudly. Everyone was laughing.   23
Even the superintendent grinned in a tolerant way. "You'd better all
come out and have a drink," he said quite genially. "I've got a bottle of
whiskey in the car. We could do with it."

We went through the big double gates of the prison into the road.   24
"Pulling at his legs!" exclaimed a Burmese magistrate suddenly, and
burst into a loud chuckling. We all began laughing again. At that moment Francis' anecdote seemed extraordinarily funny. We all had a
drink together, native and European alike, quite amicably. The dead
man was a hundred yards away.

—— CONSIDERATIONS ——

1. Many readers have described Orwell's "A Hanging" as a powerful
condemnation of capital punishment. Study Orwell's technique in drawing
from his readers the desired inference. It might be helpful to read another
master of implication—Ernest Hemingway in his short story "Hills Like White
Elephants."

2. Point out examples of Orwell's skillful use of detail to establish the
place and mood of "A Hanging." Adapt his technique to your purpose in your
next essay.

3. What minor incident caused Orwell suddenly to see "the unspeakable
wrongness . . . of cutting a life short"? Why?

4. What effect, in paragraph 6, does the boisterous dog have on the players
of this scene? On you, the reader? Explain in terms of the whole essay.

5. "One mind, one world less" is the way Orwell sums up the demise of
the Hindu prisoner. Obviously, Orwell's statement is highly compressed, jam-
ming into its short length many ideas, hopes, and fears. Write a short essay,
opening up his aphorism so that your readers get some idea of what can be
packed into five short words. For additional examples of compressed expression, see Ambrose Bierce's "Devil's Dictionary," and any of the poems in this
book.

6. The warden and others present were increasingly disconcerted by the
prisoner's continued cry, "Ram! Ram! Ram! Ram!" But note Orwell's description of that cry in paragraphs 12 and 13. Does that description give you a clue as
to the nature of the man's cry? Why doesn't Orwell explain it?

In this famous essay, Orwell attacks the rhetoric of politics.
He largely attacks the left—because his audience was an
English intellectual class that was largely leftist.

56

GEORGE ORWELL
Politics and the English Language

1   Most people who bother with the matter at all would admit that
the English language is in a bad way, but it is generally assumed that we
cannot by conscious action do anything about it. Our civilization is
decadent and our language—so the argument runs—must inevitably
share in the general collapse. It follows that any struggle against the
abuse of language is a sentimental archaism, like preferring candles to
electric light or hansom cabs to aeroplanes. Underneath this lies the
half-conscious belief that language is a natural growth and not an
instrument which we shape for our own purposes.

2   Now, it is clear that the decline of a language must ultimately
have political and economic causes: it is not due simply to the bad
influence of this or that individual writer. But an effect can become a
cause, reinforcing the original cause and producing the same effect in an
intensified form, and so indefinitely. A man may take to drink because
he feels himself to be a failure, and then fail all the more completely
because he drinks. It is rather the same thing that is happening to the
English language. It becomes ugly and inaccurate because our thoughts

are foolish, but the slovenliness of our language makes it easier for us to have foolish thoughts. The point is that the process is reversible. Modern English, especially written English, is full of bad habits which spread by imitation and which can be avoided if one is willing to take the necessary trouble. If one gets rid of these habits one can think more clearly, and to think clearly is a necessary first step towards political regeneration: so that the fight against bad English is not frivolous and is not the exclusive concern of professional writers. I will come back to this presently, and I hope that by that time the meaning of what I have said here will have become clearer. Meanwhile, here are five specimens of the English language as it is now habitually written.

These five passages have not been picked out because they are 　3 especially bad—I could have quoted far worse if I had chosen—but because they illustrate various of the mental vices from which we now suffer. They are a little below the average, but are fairly representative samples. I number them so that I can refer back to them when necessary:

> (1) I am not, indeed, sure whether it is not true to say that the Milton who once seemed not unlike a seventeenth-century Shelley had not become, out of an experience ever more bitter in each year, more alien [*sic*] to the founder of that Jesuit sect which nothing could induce him to tolerate.
>
> <div align="right">Professor Harold Laski
[Essay in <i>Freedom of Expression</i>]</div>

> (2) Above all, we cannot play ducks and drakes with a native battery of idioms which prescribes such egregious collocations of vocables as the Basic *put up with* for *tolerate* or *put at a loss* for *bewilder*.
>
> <div align="right">Professor Lancelot Hogben [<i>Interglossa</i>]</div>

> (3) On the one side we have the free personality: by definition it is not neurotic, for it has neither conflict nor dream. Its desires, such as they are, are transparent, for they are just what institutional approval keeps in the forefront of consciousness; another institutional pattern would alter their number and intensity; there is little in them that is natural, irreducible, or culturally dangerous. But *on the other side*, the social bond itself is nothing but the mutual reflection of these self-secure integrities. Recall the definition of love. Is not this the very picture of a small academic? Where is there a place in this hall of mirrors for either personality or fraternity?
>
> <div align="right">Essay on psychology in <i>Politics</i> [New York]</div>

(4) All the "best people" from the gentlemen's clubs, and all the frantic fascist captains, united in common hatred of Socialism and bestial horror of the rising tide of the mass revolutionary movement, have turned to acts of provocation, to foul incendiarism, to medieval legends of poisoned wells, to legalize their own destruction of proletarian organizations, and rouse the agitated petty-bourgeoisie to chauvinistic fervor on behalf of the fight against the revolutionary way out of the crisis.

Communist pamphlet

(5) If a new spirit is to be infused into this old country, there is one thorny and contentious reform which must be tackled, and that is the humanization and galvanization of the B.C.C. Timidity here will bespeak canker and atrophy of the soul. The heart of Britain may be sound and of strong beat, for instance, but the British lion's roar at present is like that of Bottom in Shakespeare's *Midsummer Night's Dream*—as gentle as any sucking dove. A virile new Britain cannot continue indefinitely to be traduced in the eyes, or rather ears, of the world by the effete languors of Langham Place brazenly masquerading as "standard English." When the Voice of Britain is heard at nine o'clock, better far and infinitely less ludicrous to hear aitches honestly dropped than the present priggish, inflated, inhibited, schoolma'amish arch braying of blameless bashful mewing maidens!

Letter in *Tribune*

4   Each of these passages has faults of its own, but, quite apart from avoidable ugliness, two qualities are common to all of them. The first is staleness of imagery; the other is lack of precision. The writer either has a meaning and cannot express it, or he inadvertently says something else, or he is almost indifferent as to whether his words mean anything or not. This mixture of vagueness and sheer incompetence is the most marked characteristic of modern English prose, and especially of any kind of political writing. As soon as certain topics are raised, the concrete melts into the abstract and no one seems able to think of turns of speech that are not hackneyed: prose consists less and less of *words* chosen for the sake of their meaning, and more and more of *phrases* tacked together like the sections of a prefabricated hen-house. I list below, with notes and examples, various of the tricks by means of which the work of prose-construction is habitually dodged:

DYING METAPHORS

A newly invented metaphor assists thought by evoking a visual   5
image, while on the other hand a metaphor which is technically "dead"
(e.g. *iron resolution*) has in effect reverted to being an ordinary word and
can generally be used without loss of vividness. But in between these
two classes there is a huge dump of worn-out metaphors which have
lost all evocative power and are merely used because they save people
the trouble of inventing phrases for themselves. Examples are: *Ring the
changes on, take up the cudgels for, toe the line, ride roughshod over,
stand shoulder to shoulder with, play into the hands of, no axe to grind,
grist to the mill, fishing in troubled waters, on the order of the day,
Achilles' heel, swan song, hotbed.* Many of these are used without
knowledge of their meaning (what is a "rift," for instance?), and incompatible metaphors are frequently mixed, a sure sign that the writer is
not interested in what he is saying. Some metaphors now current have
been twisted out of their original meaning without those who use them
even being aware of the fact. For example, *toe the line* is sometimes
written *tow the line.* Another example is *the hammer and the anvil,*
now always used with the implication that the anvil gets the worst of it.
In real life it is always the anvil that breaks the hammer, never the other
way about: a writer who stopped to think what he was saying would be
aware of this, and would avoid perverting the original phrase.

OPERATORS OR VERBAL FALSE LIMBS

These save the trouble of picking out appropriate verbs and nouns,   6
and at the same time pad each sentence with extra syllables which give
it an appearance of symmetry. Characteristic phrases are *render inoperative, militate against, make contact with, be subjected to, give rise to,
give grounds for, have the effect of, play a leading part (role) in, make
itself felt, take effect, exhibit a tendency to, serve the purpose of,* etc.,
etc. The keynote is the elimination of simple verbs. Instead of being a
single word, such as *break, stop, spoil, men, kill* a verb becomes a
phrase, made up of a noun or adjective tacked on to some general-
purpose verb such as *prove, serve, form, play, render.* In addition, the
passive voice is wherever possible used in preference to the active, and
noun constructions are used instead of gerunds (*by examination of*
instead of *by examining*). The range of verbs is further cut down by

means of the *-ize* and *de-* formations, and the banal statements are given an appearance of profundity by means of the *not un-* formation. Simple conjunctions and prepositions are replaced by such phrases as *with respect to, having regard to, the fact that, by dint of, in view of, in the interests of, on the hypothesis that;* and the ends of sentences are saved from anticlimax by such resounding commonplaces as *greatly to be desired, cannot be left out of account, a development to be expected in the near future, deserving of serious consideration, brought to a satisfactory conclusion* and so on and so forth.

PRETENTIOUS DICTION

7   Words like *phenomenon, element, individual* (as noun), *objective, categorical, effective, virtual, basic, primary, promote, constitute, exhibit, exploit, utilize, eliminate, liquidate,* are used to dress up simple statements and give an air of scientific impartiality to biased judgments. Adjectives like *epoch-making, epic, historic, unforgettable, triumphant, age-old, inevitable, inexorable, veritable,* are used to dignify the sordid processes of international politics, while writing that aims at glorifying war usually takes on an archaic color, its characteristic words being: *realm, throne, chariot, mailed fist, trident, sword, shield, buckler, banner, jackboot, clarion.* Foreign words and expressions such as *cul de sac, ancien régime, deux ex machina, mutatis mutandis, status quo, gleichschaltung, weltanschauung,* are used to give an air of culture and elegance. Except for the useful abbrecations *i.e., e.g.,* and *etc.,* there is no real need for any of the hundreds of foreign phrases now current in English. Bad writers, and especially scientific, political and sociological writers, are nearly always haunted by the notion that Latin or Greek words are grander than Saxon ones, and unnecessary words like *expedite, ameliorate, predict, extraneous, deracinated, clandestine, subaqueous* and hundreds of others constantly gain ground from their Anglo-Saxon opposite numbers.[1] The jargon peculiar to Marxist writing (*hyena, hangman, cannibal, petty bourgeois, these gentry, lacquey, flunkey, mad dog, White Guard,* etc.) consists largely of words and phrases translated from Russian, German or French; but the normal way of coining a new word is to use a Latin or Greek root with the

---

[1] An interesting illustration of this is the way in which the English flower names which were in use till very recently are being ousted by Greek ones, *snapdragon* becoming *antirrhinum, forget-me-not* becoming *myosotis,* etc. It is hard to see any practical reason for this change of fashion: it is probably due to an instinctive turning-away from the more homely word and a vague feeling that the Greek is scientific.

appropriate affix and, where necessary, the *-ize* formation. It is often easier to make up words of this kind (*deregionalize, impermissible, extramarital, nonfragmentary* and so forth) than to think up the English words that will cover one's meaning. The result, in general, is an increase in slovenliness and vagueness.

MEANINGLESS WORDS

In certain kinds of writing, particularly in art criticism and literary criticism, it is normal to come across long passages which are almost completely lacking in meaning.[2] Words like *romantic, plastic, values, human, dead, sentimental, natural, vitality,* as used in art criticism, are strictly meaningless, in the sense that they not only do not point to any discoverable object, but are hardly ever expected to do so by the reader. When one critic writes, "The outstanding features of Mr. X's work is its living quality," while another writes, "The immediately striking thing about Mr. X's work is its peculiar deadness," the reader accepts this as a simple difference of opinion. If words like *black* and *white* were involved, instead of the jargon words *dead* and *living,* he would see at once that language was being used in an improper way. Many political words are similarly abused. The word *Fascism* has now no meaning in so far as it signifies "something not desirable." The words *democracy, socialism, freedom, patriotic, realistic, justice,* have each of them several different meanings which cannot be reconciled with one another. In the case of a word like *democracy,* not only is there no agreed definition, but the attempt to make one is resisted from all sides. It is almost universally felt that when we call a country democratic we are praising it: consequently the defenders of every kind of régime claim that it is a democracy, and fear that they might have to stop using the word if it were tied down to any one meaning. Words of this kind are often used in a consciously dishonest way. That is, the person who uses them has his own private definition, but allows his hearer to think he means something quite different. Statements like *Marshal Pétain was a true patriot, The Soviet Press is the freest in the world, The Catholic Church is opposed to persecution,* are almost always made with intent to deceive. Other words used in variable

8

---

[2] Example: "Comfort's catholicity of perception and image, strangely Whitman-esque in range, almost the exact opposite in aesthetic compulsion, continues to evoke that trembling atmospheric accumulative hinting at a cruel, an inexorably serene time-lessness. . . . Wrey Gardiner scores by aiming at simple bull's-eyes with precision. Only they are not so simple, and through his contented sadness runs more than the surface bitter-sweet of resignation." (*Poetry Quarterly.*)

meanings, in most cases more or less dishonestly, are: *class, totalitarian, science, progressive, reactionary, bourgeois, equality.*

9   Now that I have made this catalogue of swindles and perversions, let me give another example of the kind of writing that they lead to. This time it must of its nature be an imaginary one. I am going to translate a passage of good English into modern English of the worst sort. Here is a well-known verse from *Ecclesiastes:*

> *I returned and saw under the sun, that the race is not to the swift, nor the battle to the strong, neither yet bread to the wise, nor yet riches to men of understanding, nor yet favour to men of skill, but time and chance happeneth to them all.*

10   Here it is in modern English:

> Objective consideration of contemporary phenomena compels the conclusion that success or failure in competitive activities exhibits no tendency to be commensurate with innate capacity, but that a considerable element of the unpredictable must invariably be taken into account.

11   This is a parody, but not a very gross one. Exhibit (3), above, for instance, contains several patches of the same kind of English. It will be seen that I have not made a full translation. The beginning and ending of the sentence follow the original meaning fairly closely, but in the middle the concrete illustrations—race, battle, bread—dissolve into the vague phrase "success or failure in competitive activities." This had to be so, because no modern writer of the kind I am discussing—no one capable of using phrases like "objective consideration of contemporary phenomena"—would ever tabulate his thoughts in that precise and detailed way. The whole tendency of modern prose is away from concreteness. Now analyse these two sentences a little more closely. The first contains forty-nine words but only sixty syllables, and all its words are those of everyday life. The second contains thirty-eight words of ninety syllables: eighteen of its words are from Latin roots, and one from Greek. The first sentence contains six vivid images, and only one phrase ("time and chance") that could be called vague. The second contains not a single fresh, arresting phrase, and in spite of its ninety syllables it gives only a shortened version of the meaning contained in the first. Yet without a doubt it is the second kind of sentence that is gaining ground in modern English. I do not want to exaggerate. This kind of writing is not yet universal, and outcrops of simplicity will occur here and there in the worst-written page. Still, if you or I were told to write a few lines on the uncertainty of human fortunes, we should

probably come much nearer to my imaginary sentence than to the one from *Ecclesiastes.*

As I have tried to show, modern writing at its worst does not 12 consist in picking out words for the sake of their meaning and inventing images in order to make the meaning clearer. It consists in gumming together long strips of words which have already been set in order by someone else, and making the results presentable by sheer humbug. The attraction of this way of writing is that it is easy. It is easier—even quicker, once you have the habit—to say *In my opinion it is not an unjustifiable assumption that* than to say *I think.* If you use ready made phrases, you not only don't have to hunt about for words; you also don't have to bother with the rhythms of your sentences, since these phrases are generally so arranged as to be more or less euphonious. When you are composing in a hurry—when you are dictating to a stenographer, for instance, or making a public speech—it is natural to fall into a pretentious, Latinized style. Tags like *a consideration which we should do well to bear in mind* or *a conclusion to which all of us would readily assent* will save many a sentence from coming down with a bump. By using stale metaphors, similes and idioms, you save much mental effort, at the cost of leaving your meaning vague, not only for your reader but for yourself. This is the significance of mixed metaphors. The sole aim of a metaphor is to call up visual image. When these images clash—as in *The Fascist octopus has sung its swan song, the jackboot is thrown into the melting pot*—it can be taken as certain that the writer is not seeing a mental image of the objects he is naming; in other words he is not really thinking. Look again at the examples I gave at the beginning of this essay. Professor Laski (1) uses five negatives in fifty-three words. One of these is superfluous, making nonsense of the whole passage, and in addition there is the slip *alien* for *akin,* making further nonsense, and several avoidable pieces of clumsiness which increase the general vagueness. Professor Hogben (2) plays ducks and drakes with a battery which is able to write prescriptions, and, while disapproving of the everyday phrase *put up with,* is unwilling to look *egregious* up in the dictionary and see what it means; (3), if one takes an uncharitable attitude towards it, is simply meaningless: probably one could work out its intended meaning by reading the whole of the article in which it occurs. In (4), the writer knows more or less what he wants to say, but an accumulation of stale phrases chokes him, like tea leaves blocking a sink. In (5), words and meaning have almost parted company. People who write in this manner usually have a general emotional meaning—they dislike one thing and want to express solidarity with another—but they are not interested in the detail of what they are saying. A scrupulous writer, in every sentence that he writes, will ask himself at least four questions, thus: What am I trying to say? What words will express it? What image or idiom will make it clearer? Is this image fresh enough to have an effect? And he will probably ask himself two more: Could I put it more shortly? Have I said anything that is avoidably ugly? But you are not obliged to go to all this trouble. You can shirk it by simply throwing your mind open and letting the ready-made phrases come crowding in. They will construct your sentences for you—even think your thoughts for you, to a certain extent—and at need they will perform the important service of partially concealing your meaning even from yourself. It is at this point that the special connection between politics and the debasement of language becomes clear.

13   In our time it is broadly true that political writing is bad writing. Where it is not true, it will generally be found that the writer is some kind of rebel, expressing his private opinions and not a "party line." Orthodoxy, of whatever color, seems to demand a lifeless, imitative style. The political dialects to be found in pamphlets, leading articles, manifestos, White Papers and the speeches of undersecretaries do, of course, vary from party to party, but they are all alike in that one almost never finds in them a fresh, vivid, home-made turn of speech. When one watches some tired hack on the platform mechanically repeating the familiar phrases—*bestial atrocities, iron heel, blood-stained tyranny, free people of the world, stand shoulder to shoulder*—one often has a curious feeling that one is not watching a live human being but some kind of dummy: a feeling which suddenly becomes stronger at moments when the light catches the speaker's spectacles and turns them into blank discs which seem to have no eyes behind them. And this is not altogether fanciful. A speaker who uses that kind of phraseology has gone some distance towards turning himself into a machine. The appropriate noises are coming out of his larynx, but his brain is not involved as it would be if he were choosing his words for himself. If the speech he is making is one that he is accustomed to make over and over again, he may be almost unconscious of what he is saying, as one is when one utters the responses in church. And this reduced state of consciousness, if not indispensable, is at any rate favorable to political conformity.

14   In our time, political speech and writing are largely the defence of the indefensible. Things like the continuance of British rule in India, the Russian purges and deportations, the dropping of the atom bombs on Japan, can indeed be defended, but only by arguments which are too brutal for most people to face, and which do not square with the

professed aims of political parties. Thus political language has to consist largely of euphemism, question-begging and sheer cloudy vagueness. Defenceless villages are bombarded from the air, the inhabitants driven out into the countryside, the cattle machine-gunned, the huts set on fire with incendiary bullets: this is called *pacification*. Millions of peasants are robbed of their farms and sent trudging along the roads with no more than they can carry: this is called *transfer of population* or *rectification of frontiers*. People are imprisoned for years without trial, or shot in the back of the neck or sent to die of scurvy in Arctic lumber camps: this is called *elimination of unreliable elements*. Such phraseology is needed if one wants to name things without calling up mental pictures of them. Consider for instance some comfortable English professor defending Russian totalitarianism. He cannot say outright: "I believe in killing off your opponents when you can get good results by doing so." Probably, therefore, he will say something like this:

"While freely conceding that the Soviet régime exhibits certain   15
features which the humanitarian may be inclined to deplore, we must, I think, agree that a certain curtailment of the right to political opposition is an unavoidable concomitant of transitional periods, and that the rigors which the Russian people have been called upon to undergo have been amply justified in the sphere of concrete achievement."

The inflated style is itself a kind of euphemism. A mass of Latin   16
words falls upon the facts like soft snow, blurring the outlines and covering up all the details. The great enemy of clear language is insincerity. When there is a gap between one's real and one's declared aims, one turns as it were instinctively to long words and exhausted idioms, like a cuttlefish squirting out ink. In our age there is no such thing as "keeping out of politics." All issues are political issues, and politics itself is a mass of lies, evasions, folly, hatred and schizophrenia. When the general atmosphere is bad, language must suffer. I should expect to find—this is a guess which I have not sufficient knowledge to verify—that the German, Russian and Italian languages have all deteriorated in the last ten or fifteen years, as a result of dictatorship.

But if thought corrupts language, language can also corrupt   17
thought. A bad usage can spread by tradition and imitation, even among people who should and do know better. The debased language that I have been discussing is in some ways very convenient. Phrases like *a not unjustifiable assumption, leaves much to be desired, would serve no good purpose, a consideration which we should do well to bear in mind,* are a continuous temptation, a packet of aspirins always at one's elbow. Look back through this essay, and for certain you will find that I have again and again committed the very faults I am protesting against.

By this morning's post I have received a pamphlet dealing with condi-tions in Germany. The author tells me that he "felt impelled" to write it. I open it at random, and here is almost the first sentence that I see: "[The Allies] have an opportunity not only of achieving a radical trans-formation of Germany's social and political structure in such a way as to avoid a nationalistic reaction in Germany itself, but at the same time of laying the foundations of a co-operative and unified Europe." You see, he "feels impelled" to write—feels, presumably, that he has some-thing new to say—and yet his words, like cavalry horses answering the bugle, group themselves automatically into the familiar dreary pattern. This invasion of one's mind by ready-made phrases (*lay the founda-tions, achieve a radical transformation*) can only be prevented if one is constantly on guard against them, and every such phrase anaesthetizes a portion of one's brain.

18   I said earlier that the decadence of our language is probably cur-able. Those who deny this would argue, if they produced an argument at all, that language merely reflects existing social conditions, and that we cannot influence its development by any direct tinkering with words and constructions. So far as the general tone or spirit of a language goes, this may be true, but it is not true in detail. Silly words and expressions have often disappeared, not through any evolutionary process but ow-ing to the conscious action of a minority. Two recent examples were *explore every avenue* and *leave no stone unturned*, which were killed by the jeers of a few journalists. There is a long list of flyblown meta-phors which could similarly be got rid of if enough people would inter-est themselves in the job; and it should also be possible to laugh the *not un-* formation out of existence,[3] to reduce the amount of Latin and Greek in the average sentence, to drive out foreign phrases and strayed scientific words, and, in general, to make pretentiousness unfashion-able. But all these are minor points. The defence of the English language implies more than this, and perhaps it is best to start by saying what it does *not* imply.

19   To begin with it has nothing to do with archaism, with the salvag-ing of obsolete words and turns of speech, or with the setting up of a "standard English" which must never be departed from. On the con-trary, it is especially concerned with the scrapping of every word or idiom which has outworn its usefulness. It has nothing to do with correct grammar and syntax, which are of no importance so long as one makes one's meaning clear, or with the avoidance of Americanisms, or

[3] One can cure oneself of the *not un-* formation by memorizing this sentence: *A not unblack dog was chasing a not unsmall rabbit across a not ungreen field.*

with having what is called a "good prose style." On the other hand it is not concerned with fake simplicity and the attempt to make written English colloquial. Nor does it even imply in every case preferring the Saxon word to the Latin one, though it does imply using the fewest and shortest words that will cover one's meaning. What is above all needed is to let the meaning choose the word, and not the other way about. In prose, the worst thing one can do with words is to surrender to them. When you think of a concrete object, you think wordlessly, and then, if you want to describe the thing you have been visualizing you probably hunt about till you find the exact words that seem to fit it. When you think of something abstract you are more inclined to use words from the start, and unless you make a conscious effort to prevent it, the existing dialect will come rushing in and do the job for you, at the expense of blurring or even changing your meaning. Probably it is better to put off using words as long as possible and get one's meaning as clear as one can through pictures or sensations. Afterwards one can choose— not simply *accept*—the phrases that will best cover the meaning, and then switch round and decide what impression one's words are likely to make on another person. This last effort of the mind cuts out all stale or mixed images, all prefabricated phrases, needless repetitions, and humbug and vagueness generally. But one can often be in doubt about the effect of a word or a phrase, and one needs rules that one can rely on when instinct fails. I think the following rules will cover most cases:

(i) Never use a metaphor, simile or other figure of speech which you are used to seeing in print.
(ii) Never use a long word where a short one will do.
(iii) If it is possible to cut a word out, always cut it out.
(iv) Never use the passive where you can use the active.
(v) Never use a foreign phrase, a scientific word or a jargon word if you can think of an everyday English equivalent.
(vi) Break any of these rules sooner than say anything outright barbarous.

These rules sound elementary, and so they are, but they demand a deep change of attitude in anyone who has grown used to writing in the style now fashionable. One could keep all of them and still write bad English, but one could not write the kind of stuff that I quoted in those five specimens at the beginning of this article.

I have not here been considering the literary use of language, but merely language as an instrument for expressing and not for concealing or preventing thought. Stuart Chase and others have come near to claiming that all abstract words are meaningless, and have used this as a

20

pretext for advocating a kind of political quietism. Since you don't know what Fascism is, how can you struggle against Fascism? One need not swallow such absurdities as this, but one ought to recognize that the present political chaos is connected with the decay of language, and that one can probably bring about some improvement by starting at the verbal end. If you simplify your English, you are freed from the worst follies of orthodoxy. You cannot speak any of the necessary dialects, and when you make a stupid remark its stupidity will be obvious, even to yourself. Political language—and with variations this is true of all political parties, from Conservatives to Anarchists—is designed to make lies sound truthful and murder respectable, and to give an appearance of solidity to pure wind. One cannot change this all in a moment, but one can at least change one's own habits, and from time to time one can even, if one jeers loudly enough, send some worn-out and useless phrase—some *jackboot, Achilles' heel, hotbed, melting pot, acid test, veritable inferno* or other lump of verbal refuse—into the dustbin where it belongs.

—— **CONSIDERATIONS** ————————————————

1. "Style is the man himself." How well, and in what ways, does Orwell's essay illustrate Buffon's aphorism? Select another author in the text, someone with a distinct style, and test it against Buffon's statement.

2. Assuming that Orwell's statement in paragraph 2, "the fight against bad English is not frivolous and is not the exclusive concern of professional writers," is the conclusion of a syllogism, reconstruct the major and minor premises of that syllogism by studying the steps Orwell takes to reach his conclusion.

3. Orwell documents his argument by quoting five passages by writers who wrote in the forties. From comparable sources, assemble a gallery of current specimens to help confirm or refute his contention that "the English language is in a bad way."

4. Orwell concludes with six rules. From the rest of his essay, how do you think he would define "anything outright barbarous" (in rule vi)?

5. Has Orwell broken some of his own rules? Point out and explain any examples you find. Look over his "Shooting an Elephant" and "A Hanging" as well as "Politics and the English Language."

6. In paragraph 16, Orwell asserts that "The inflated style is itself a kind of euphemism." Look up the meaning of "euphemism" and compile examples from your local newspaper. Do you agree with Orwell that they are "swindles and perversions"? Note how Ambrose Bierce counts on our understanding of euphemisms in his Devil's Dictionary.

Some of George Orwell's best essays, like "A Hanging" and this one, derive from his experience as a colonial policeman, upholder of law and order for the British empire. Many political thinkers develop an ideology from thought and theory; Orwell's politics grew empirically from the life he lived. He provides us models for learning by living—and for learning by writing out of one's life.

57

GEORGE ORWELL
Shooting an Elephant

In Moulmein, in Lower Burma, I was hated by large numbers of people—the only time in my life that I have been important enough for this to happen to me. I was sub-divisional police officer of the town, and in an aimless, petty kind of way anti-European feeling was very bitter. No one had the guts to raise a riot, but if a European woman went through the bazaars alone somebody would probably spit betel juice over her dress. As a police officer I was an obvious target and was baited whenever it seemed safe to do so. When a nimble Burman tripped me up on the football field and the referee (another Burman) looked the other way, the crowd yelled with hideous laughter. This happened more than once. In the end the sneering yellow faces of young men that met me everywhere, the insults hooted after me when I was at a safe distance, got badly on my nerves. The young Buddhist priests were the worst of all. There were several thousands of them in the town and none of them seemed to have anything to do except stand on street corners and jeer at Europeans.

All this was perplexing and upsetting. For at that time I had already made up my mind that imperialism was an evil thing and the sooner I chucked up my job and got out of it the better. Theoretically—

and secretly, of course—I was all for the Burmese and all against their oppressors, the British. As for the job I was doing, I hated it more bitterly than I can perhaps make clear. In a job like that you see the dirty work of Empire at close quarters. The wretched prisoners huddling in the stinking cages of the lock-ups, the grey, cowed faces of the long-term convicts, the scarred buttocks of the men who had been flogged with bamboos—all these oppressed me with an intolerable sense of guilt. But I could get nothing into perspective. I was young and ill-educated and I had had to think out my problems in the utter silence that is imposed on every Englishman in the East. I did not even know that the British Empire is dying, still less did I know that it is a great deal better than the younger empires that are going to supplant it. All I knew was that I was stuck between my hatred of the empire I served and my rage against the evil-spirited little beasts who tried to make my job impossible. With one part of my mind I thought of the British Raj as an unbreakable tyranny, as something clamped down, in *saecula saeculorum*, upon the will of prostrate peoples; with another part I thought that the greatest joy in the world would be to drive a bayonet into a Buddhist priest's guts. Feelings like these are the normal by-products of imperialism; ask any Anglo-Indian official, if you can catch him off duty.

3   One day something happened which in a roundabout way was enlightening. It was a tiny incident in itself, but it gave me a better glimpse than I had had before of the real nature of imperialism—the real motives for which despotic governments act. Early one morning the sub-inspector at a police station the other end of town rang me up on the phone and said that an elephant was ravaging the bazaar. Would I please come and do something about it? I did not know what I could do, but I wanted to see what was happening and I got on to a pony and started out. I took my rifle, an old .44 Winchester and much too small to kill an elephant, but I thought the noise might be useful *in terrorem*. Various Burmans stopped me on the way and told me about the elephant's doings. It was not, of course, a wild elephant, but a tame one which had gone "must." It had been chained up, as tame elephants always are when their attack of "must" is due, but on the previous night it had broken its chain and escaped. Its mahout, the only person who could manage it when it was in that state, had set out in pursuit, but had taken the wrong direction and was now twelve hours' journey away, and in the morning the elephant had suddenly reappeared in the town. The Burmese population had no weapons and were quite helpless against it. It had already destroyed somebody's bamboo hut, killed a cow and raided some fruit-stalls and devoured the stock; also it had met the

municipal rubbish van and, when the driver jumped out and took to his heels, had turned the van over and inflicted violences upon it.

The Burmese sub-inspector and some Indian constables were   4 waiting for me in the quarter where the elephant had been seen. It was a very poor quarter, a labyrinth of squalid bamboo huts, thatched with palmleaf, winding all over a steep hillside. I remember that it was a cloudy, stuffy morning at the beginning of the rains. We began questioning the people as to where the elephant had gone and, as usual, failed to get any definite information. That is invariably the case in the East; a story always sounds clear enough at a distance, but the nearer you get to the scene of events the vaguer it becomes. Some of the people said that the elephant had gone in one direction, some said that he had gone in another, some professed not even to have heard of any elephant. I had almost made up my mind that the whole story was a pack of lies, when we heard yells a little distance away. There was a loud, scandalized cry of "Go away, child! Go away this instant!" and an old woman with a switch in her hand came round the corner of hut, violently shooing away a crowd of naked children. Some more women followed, clicking their tongues and exclaiming; evidently there was something that the children ought not to have seen. I rounded the hut and saw a man's dead body sprawling in the mud. He was an Indian, a black Dravidian coolie, almost naked, and he could not have been dead many minutes. The people said that the elephant had come suddenly upon him round the corner of the hut, caught him with its trunk, put its foot on his back and ground him into the earth. This was the rainy season and the ground was soft, and his face had scored a trench a foot deep and a couple of yards long. He was lying on his belly with arms crucified and head sharply twisted to one side. His face was coated with mud, the eyes wide open, the teeth bared and grinning with an expression of unendurable agony. (Never tell me, by the way, that the dead look peaceful. Most of the corpses I have seen looked devilish.) The friction of the great beast's foot had stripped the skin from his back as neatly as one skins a rabbit. As soon as I saw the dead man I sent an orderly to a friend's house nearby to borrow an elephant rifle. I had already sent back the pony, not wanting it to go mad with fright and throw me if it smelt the elephant.

The orderly came back in a few minutes with a rifle and five   5 cartridges, and meanwhile some Burmans had arrived and told us that the elephant was in the paddy fields below, only a few hundred yards away. As I started forward practically the whole population of the quarter flocked out of the houses and followed me. They had seen the rifle and were all shouting excitedly that I was going to shoot the elephant. They had not shown much interest in the elephant when he was merely ravaging their homes, but it was different now that he was going to be shot. It was a bit of fun to them, as it would be to an English crowd; besides they wanted the meat. It made me vaguely uneasy. I had no intention of shooting the elephant—I had merely sent for the rifle to defend myself if necessary—and it is always unnerving to have a crowd following you. I marched down the hill, looking and feeling a fool, with the rifle over my shoulder and an ever-growing army of people jostling at my heels. At the bottom, when you got away from the huts, there was a metalled road and beyond that a miry waste of paddy fields a thousand yards across, not yet ploughed but soggy from the first rains and dotted with coarse grass. The elephant was standing eight yards from the road, his left side towards us. He took not the slightest notice of the crowd's approach. He was tearing up bunches of grass, beating them against his knees to clean them and stuffing them into his mouth.

6   I had halted on the road. As soon as I saw the elephant I knew with perfect certainty that I ought not to shoot him. It is a serious matter to shoot a working elephant—it is comparable to destroying a huge and costly piece of machinery—and obviously one ought not to do it if it can possibly be avoided. And at that distance, peacefully eating, the elephant looked no more dangerous than a cow. I thought then and I think now that his attack of "must" was already passing off; in which case he would merely wander harmlessly about until the mahout came back and caught him. Moreover, I did not in the least want to shoot him. I decided that I would watch him for a little while to make sure that he did not turn savage again, and then go home.

7   But at that moment, I glanced round at the crowd that had followed me. It was an immense crowd, two thousand at the least and growing every minute. It blocked the road for a long distance on either side. I looked at the sea of yellow faces above the garish clothes—faces all happy and excited over this bit of fun, all certain that the elephant was going to be shot. They were watching me as they would watch a conjuror about to perform a trick. They did not like me, but with the magical rifle in my hands I was momentarily worth watching. And suddenly I realized that I should have to shoot the elephant after all. The people expected it of me and I had got to do it; I could feel their two thousand wills pressing me forward, irresistibly. And it was at this moment, as I stood there with the rifle in my hands, that I first grasped the hollowness, the futility of the white man's dominion in the East.

Here was I, the white man with his gun, standing in front of the unarmed native crowd—seemingly the leading actor of the piece; but in reality I was only an absurd puppet pushed to and fro by the will of those yellow faces behind. I perceived in this moment that when the white man turns tyrant it is his own freedom that he destroys. He becomes a sort of hollow, posing dummy, the conventionalized figure of a sahib. For it is the condition of his rule that he shall spend his life in trying to impress the "natives," and so in every crisis he has got to do what the "natives" expect of him. He wears a mask, and his face grows to fit it. I had got to shoot the elephant. I had committed myself to doing it when I sent for the rifle. A sahib has got to act like a sahib; he has got to appear resolute, to know his own mind and do definite things. To come all that way, rifle in hand, with two thousand people marching at my heels, and then to trail feebly away, having done nothing—no, that was impossible. The crowd would laugh at me. And my whole life, every white man's life in the East, was one long struggle not to be laughed at.

But I did not want to shoot the elephant. I watched him beating his   8
bunch of grass against his knees, with that preoccupied grandmotherly air that elephants have. It seemed to me that it would be murder to shoot him. At that age I was not squeamish about killing animals, but I had never shot an elephant and never wanted to. (Somehow it always seems worse to kill a *large* animal.) Besides, there was the beast's owner to be considered. Alive, the elephant was worth at least a hundred pounds; dead, he would only be worth the value of his tusks, five pounds, possibly. But I had got to act quickly. I turned to some experienced-looking Burmans who had been there when we arrived, and asked them how the elephant had been behaving. They all said the same things: he took no notice of you if you left him alone, but he might charge if you went too close to him.

It was perfectly clear to me what I ought to do. I ought to walk up   9
to within, say, twenty-five yards of the elephant and test his behavior. If he charged, I could shoot; if he took no notice of me, it would be safe to leave him until the mahout came back. But also I knew that I was going to do no such thing. I was a poor shot with a rifle and the ground was soft mud into which one would sink at every step. If the elephant charged and I missed him, I should have about as much chance as a toad under a steam-roller. But even then I was not thinking particularly of my own skin, only of the watchful yellow faces behind. For at that moment, with the crowd watching me, I was not afraid in the ordinary sense, as I would have been if I had been alone. A white man mustn't be frightened in front of "natives"; and so, in general, he isn't frightened. The sole

thought in my mind was that if anything went wrong those two thousand Burmans would see me pursued, caught, trampled on and reduced to a grinning corpse like that Indian up the hill. And if that happened it was quite probable that some of them would laugh. That would never do. There was only one alternative. I shoved the cartridges into the magazine and lay down on the road to get a better aim.

10   The crowd grew very still, and a deep, low, happy sigh, as of people who see the theatre curtain go up at last, breathed from innumerable throats. They were going to have their bit of fun after all. The rifle was a beautiful German thing with cross-hair sights. I did not then know that in shooting an elephant one would shoot to cut an imaginary bar running from ear-hole to ear-hole. I ought, therefore, as the elephant was sideways on, to have aimed straight at his ear-hole; actually I aimed several inches in front of this, thinking the brain would be further forward.

11   When I pulled the trigger I did not hear the bang or feel the kick—one never does when a shot goes home—but I heard the devilish roar of glee that went up from the crowd. In that instant, in too short a time, one would have thought, even for the bullet to get there, a mysterious, terrible change had come over the elephant. He neither stirred nor fell, but every line of his body had altered. He looked suddenly stricken, shrunken, immensely old, as though the frightful impact of the bullet had paralysed him without knocking him down. At last, after what seemed a long time—it might have been five seconds, I dare say—he sagged flabbily to his knees. His mouth slobbered. An enormous senility seemed to have settled upon him. One could have imagined him thousands of years old. I fired again into the same spot. At the second shot he did not collapse but climbed with desperate slowness to his feet and stood weakly upright, with legs sagging and head drooping. I fired a third time. That was the shot that did for him. You could see the agony of it jolt his whole body and knock the last remnant of strength from his legs. But in falling he seemed for a moment to rise, for as his hind legs collapsed beneath him he seemed to tower upward like a huge rock toppling, his trunk reaching skywards like a tree. He trumpeted, for the first and only time. And then down he came, his belly towards me, with a crash that seemed to shake the ground even where I lay.

12   I got up. The Burmans were already racing past me across the mud. It was obvious that the elephant would never rise again, but he was not dead. He was breathing very rhythmically with long rattling gasps, his great mound of a side painfully rising and falling. His mouth was wide open. I could see far down into caverns of pale pink throat. I waited a

long time for him to die, but his breathing did not weaken. Finally I fired my two remaining shots into the spot where I thought his heart must be. The thick blood welled out of him like red velvet, but still he did not die. His body did not even jerk when the shots hit him, the tortured breathing continued without pause. He was dying, very slowly and in great agony, but in some world remote from me where not even a bullet could damage him further. I felt I had got to put an end to that dreadful noise. It seemed dreadful to see the great beast lying there, powerless to move and yet powerless to die, and not even to be able to finish him. I sent back for my small rifle and poured shot after shot into his head and down his throat. They seemed to make no impression. The tortured gasps continued as steadily as the ticking of a clock.

In the end I could not stand it any longer and went away. I heard 13 later that it took him half an hour to die. Burmans were bringing dahs and baskets even before I left, and I was told they had stripped his body almost to the bones by the afternoon.

Afterwards, of course, there were endless discussions about the 14 shooting of the elephant. The owner was furious, but he was only an Indian and could do nothing. Besides, legally I had done the right thing, for a mad elephant has to be killed, like a mad dog, if its owner fails to control it. Among the Europeans opinion was divided. The older men said I was right, the younger men said it was a damn shame to shoot an elephant for killing a coolie, because the elephant was worth more than any damn Coringhee coolie. And afterwards I was very glad that the coolie had been killed; it put me legally in the right and it gave me sufficient pretext for shooting the elephant. I often wondered whether any of the others grasped that I had done it solely to avoid looking a fool.

_____ CONSIDERATIONS _____   ▬   ▬

1. Some of Orwell's remarks about the Burmese make him sound like a racist; collect a half-dozen of them on a separate sheet of paper, then look for lines or phrases that counter the first samples. Discuss your findings, bearing in mind the purpose of Orwell's essay.

2. "In a job like that you see the dirty work of Empire at close quarters." If you ponder Orwell's capitalizing "Empire" (paragraph 2) and then substitute other abstract terms for "Empire"—say, Government, Poverty, War, Hatred— you may discover one of the most important principles of effective writing, a principle beautifully demonstrated by Orwell's whole account.

3. In paragraph 4, Orwell says, "the nearer you get to the scene of events

the vaguer it becomes." Have you had an experience that would help you understand his remark? Would it hold true for the soldier caught in battle, a couple suffering a divorce, a football player caught in a pile-up on the scrimmage line?

4. Some years after his experience in Burma, Orwell became a well-known opponent of fascism. How might shooting the elephant have taught him to detest totalitarianism?

5. "Somehow it always seems worse to kill a *large* animal," Orwell writes in paragraph 8. Why? Are some lives more equal than others?

6. In paragraph 10, Orwell describes his rifle as a "beautiful German thing." Does he use the word "beautiful" in the same way Don Sharp uses it in the last paragraph of his essay "Under the Hood"? Neither of the writers means "pulchritude" when he uses "beautiful." What synonyms might fit their sense of the word?

7. After two substantial paragraphs of agonizing detail, Orwell's elephant is still dying. Why does the writer inflict this punishment on the reader?

Joyce Peseroff (b. 1948) lives in Massachusetts, where she coedits a poetry magazine called Green House. *She grew up in the Bronx, studied in California, and spent three years as a Junior Fellow in the Michigan Society of Fellows. In 1977, her first book of poems used this as its title poem. Note how a course in geology can turn into a poem. She has also edited a collection of essays about the poet Robert Bly,* When Sleepers Awake *(1984), and an anthology,* The Ploughshares Poetry Reader *(1987).*

58

JOYCE PESEROFF
The Hardness Scale

Diamonds are forever so I gave you quartz
which is #7 on the hardness scale
and it's hard enough to get to know anybody these days
if only to scratch the surface
and quartz will scratch six other mineral surfaces: 5
it will scratch glass
it will scratch gold
it will even
scratch your eyes out one morning—you can't be
too careful.   10
Diamonds are industrial so I bought
a ring of topaz
which is #8 on the hardness scale.
I wear it on my right hand, the way it was
supposed to be, right? No tears and fewer regrets   15
for reasons smooth and clear as glass. Topaz will scratch glass,
it will scratch your quartz,

and all your radio crystals. You'll have to be silent
the rest of your days
20   not to mention your nights. Not to mention
the night you ran away very drunk very
very drunk and you tried to cross the border
but couldn't make it across the lake.
Stirring up geysers with the oars you drove the red canoe
25   in circles, tried to pole it but
your left hand didn't know
what the right hand was doing.
You fell asleep
and let everyone know it when you woke up.
30   In a gin-soaked morning (hair of the dog) you went
hunting for geese,
shot three lake trout in violation of the game laws,
told me to clean them and that
my eyes were bright as sapphires
35   which is #9 on the hardness scale.
A sapphire will cut a pearl
it will cut stainless steel
it will cut vinyl and mylar and will probably
cut a record this fall
40   to be released on an obscure label known only to aficionados.
I will buy a copy.
I may buy you a copy
depending on how your tastes have changed.
I will buy copies for my friends
45   we'll get a new needle,
a diamond needle,
which is #10 on the hardness scale
and will cut anything.
It will cut wood and mortar,
50   plaster and iron,
it will cut the sapphires in my eyes and I will bleed
blind as 4 A.M. in the subways when even degenerates
are dreaming, blind as the time
you shot up the room with a new hunting rifle
55   blind drunk
as you were.
You were #11 on the hardness scale

later that night
apologetic as
you worked your way up
slowly from the knees
and you worked your way down
from the open-throated blouse.
Diamonds are forever so I give you softer things.

60

*Chet Raymo (b. 1936) teaches physics and astronomy at
Stonehill College in Massachusetts. He writes a weekly column
about science for the* Boston Globe, *from which we take this
essay. His six books on science include* The Soul of the Night,
*which became a Book of the Month Club selection. In 1987 he
published* Honey from Stone, *and in 1990 branched out into
fiction, with* In the Falcon's Claw, A Novel of the Year 1000.

_59

CHET RAYMO
Dinosaurs and Creationists

1   Down on the Paluxy River in Texas there are fossil footprints of
human beings in the stratum of sedimentary rock that bears the tracks
of dinosaurs. Or so claim the adherents of some fundamentalist religious groups. The Paluxy tracks, and similar markings at other sites in
the American West, have become one of the centerpieces of the fundamentalist anti-evolution crusade. For a decade, the purported "man
tracks" in Texas have been touted by creationists as proof, once and for
all, of the falsity of evolution.

2   The Paluxy River sedimentary strata date from the Cretaceous
Period of geologic history, 120 million years ago. Creationists claim the
rocks are only thousands of years old, and, they say, the Paluxy River
tracks show that humans and dinosaurs coexisted, most likely in the
time preceding the flood of Noah.

3   Of course, there are no human footprints in the Cretaceous rocks
of Texas, or in any other rocks that date from the time of the dinosaurs.
The purported man tracks have been examined by geologists. Some are
not tracks at all, but only erosion features that are typical of river beds.
Other, poorly defined "human" footprints are similar to dinosaur tracks
in size, pace and step angles. So devastating has been the scientific

From the *Boston Globe*, November 17, 1986. Reprinted by permission of the
author.

critique that in recent months some creationists have begun to hedge their bets regarding a human origin for the Paluxy River tracks.

None of this would be worth talking about if it were not for the 4 fact that science is under a growing attack by people who take things like the Paluxy River "man tracks" seriously. In Louisiana the state legislature has mandated that "creation science" be taught in schools along with evolution. The law has been judged unconstitutional by lower federal courts and is now before the U.S. Supreme Court.

In spite of setbacks in the courts, fundamentalists maintain pres- 5 sure on school boards, state legislatures and textbook publishers to include creation science in school curricula or, failing that, to end the teaching of evolution.

At issue is not freedom of religion. People have the right to believe 6 what they want about how and when the world was made. At issue is whether there is such a thing as creation science that should be taught in our public schools.

Science is not a collection of truths about the world. If I say that 7 "the Earth is 4.5 billion years old," or that "humans evolved from lower orders of life," I have made a scientific statement, but such a statement is not itself science. Science is not what we know; science is a way of knowing.

Observation is an important criterion for the validity of scientific 8 truth, but it is not the only criterion. Different people can interpret the same observations differently. The Paluxy River tracks are a case in point. An equally important criterion for truth in science is consistency. What we hold to be true in one area of science must not contradict what is held to be true in another area.

Science is not a smorgasbord of truths from which we can pick and 9 choose. A better image for science is a spider's web. Confidence in any one strand of the web is maintained by the tension and resiliency of the entire web. If one strand of the web is broken, a certain relaxation of tension is felt throughout the web.

Our belief in the evolution of life through geologic time is based on 10 what we have learned in many other areas of science. Our confidence is assured by the success of the entire ensemble of scientific truths. Scientific truths are tentative and partial, and subject to continual revision and refinement, but as we tinker with truth in science we always keep our ear attuned to the timbre of the web.

Fundamentalists use film, video, electronics, computer and com- 11 munication satellites to spread the anti-evolution message. Ironically, these technologies are based on the same ensemble of physical principles that lead us to believe that life evolved over eons of geologic time. You can't tear down one part of the web of science unless you are willing and able to rebuild a structure of understanding that works as well or better than the one you have disassembled. This is what the creationists are unable to do. And this is why there is no such thing as creation science.

12   There is more risk in the anti-evolution crusade than a particular view of the origin of the world. At risk is the ability of the next generation of Americans to distinguish science from nonscience. Science is confidence in the human mind to discover some measure of truth about the world. Science is humility in the face of nature's complexity. And above all, science is a respect for consistency as a hallmark of truth.

13   In at least one thing the creationists are right. If humans walked with dinosaurs, then evolution is false. And by the same test, much of what we know about geology, astronomy, physics, chemistry, biology, and medicine can be thrown out too.

_____ CONSIDERATIONS _____

1. How does Raymo distinguish a "scientific statement" from "science" itself? Why does he pause in his argument against "creation science" to make that distinction?

2. Raymo uses the metaphor of "the web" in his argument. Is he being fanciful or is the metaphor integral to his explanation? Explain.

3. What is Raymo's strategy in delaying his thesis statement until paragraph 4?

4. Is Raymo chiefly concerned about freedom of religion, the integrity of science, or the nature of tracks found along the Paluxy River in Texas? Does the organization of his essay help you decide?

Rainer Maria Rilke (1875–1926) wrote his Letters to a Young Poet *while he was himself still a young poet. The student poet, Franz Kappus (1883–1966), addressed him in 1903 at the age of twenty, when Rilke was only twenty-eight years old. Rilke, famously solitary, relieved his solitude with much correspondence. We excerpt this passage from Rilke's seventh letter to Kappus, dated May 14, 1904, and written while he visited Rome.*

Rilke is acknowledged to be the greatest modern German poet and one of the greatest in any language. There are many translations of his poetry into English, notably the Selected Poems *translated by Stephen Mitchell, who also translated the* Letters to a Young Poet. *Mitchell lives in Berkeley, California, and has won prizes for his translations of Rilke's poems and his novel* The Notebooks of Malte Laurids Brigge.

60

RAINER MARIA RILKE
On Love

It is also good to love: because love is difficult. For one human 1
being to love another human being: that is perhaps the most difficult
task that has been entrusted to us, the ultimate task, the final test and
proof, the work for which all other work is merely preparation. That is
why young people, who are beginners in everything, are not yet *capable*
of love: it is something they must learn. With their whole being, with
all their forces, gathered around their solitary, anxious, upward-beating
heart, they must learn to love. But learning-time is always a long,
secluded time, and therefore loving, for a long time ahead and far on
into life, is—: solitude, a heightened and deepened kind of aloneness for
the person who loves. Loving does not at first mean merging, surrender-

ing, and uniting with another person (for what would a union be of two people who are unclarified, unfinished, and still incoherent—?), it is a high inducement for the individual to ripen, to become something in himself, to become world, to become world in himself for the sake of another person; it is a great, demanding claim on him, something that chooses him and calls him to vast distances. Only in this sense, as the task of working on themselves ("to hearken and to hammer day and night"), may young people use the love that is given to them. Merging and surrendering and every kind of communion is not for them (who must still, for a long, long time, save and gather themselves); it is the ultimate, is perhaps that for which human lives are as yet barely large enough.

2 But this is what young people are so often and so disastrously wrong in doing: they (who by their very nature are impatient) fling themselves at each other when love takes hold of them, they scatter themselves, just as they are, in all their messiness, disorder, bewilderment . . . : And what can happen then? What can life do with this heap of half-broken things that they call their communion and that they would like to call their happiness, if that were possible, and their future? And so each of them loses himself for the sake of the other person, and loses the other, and many others who still wanted to come. And loses the vast distances and possibilities, gives up the approaching and fleeing of gentle, prescient Things in exchange for an unfruitful confusion, out of which nothing more can come; nothing but a bit of disgust, disappointment, and poverty, and the escape into one of the many conventions that have been put up in great numbers like public shelters on this most dangerous road. No area of human experience is so extensively provided with conventions as this one is: there are life-preservers of the most varied invention, boats and water wings; society has been able to create refuges of every sort, for since it preferred to take love-life as an amusement, it also had to give it an easy form, cheap, safe, and sure, as public amusements are.

3 It is true that many young people who love falsely, i.e., simply surrendering themselves and giving up their solitude (the average person will of course always go on doing that—), feel oppressed by their failure and want to make the situation they have landed in livable and fruitful in their own, personal way—. For their nature tells them that the questions of love, even more than everything else that is important, cannot be resolved publicly and according to this or that agreement; that they are questions, intimate questions from one human being to another, which in any case require a new, special, *wholly* personal

answer—. But how can they, who have already flung themselves together and can no longer tell whose outlines are whose, who thus no
longer possess anything of their own, how can they find a way out of
themselves, out of the depths of their already buried solitude?

They act out of mutual helplessness, and then if, with the best of   4
intentions, they try to escape the convention that is approaching them
(marriage, for example), they fall into the clutches of some less obvious
but just as deadly conventional solution. For then everything around
them is—convention. Wherever people act out of a prematurely fused,
muddy communion, *every* action is conventional: every relation that
such confusion leads to has its own convention, however unusual (i.e.,
in the ordinary sense immoral) it may be; even separating would be a
conventional step, an impersonal, accidental decision without strength
and without fruit.

Whoever looks seriously will find that neither for death, which is   5
difficult, nor for difficult love has any clarification, any solution, any
hint of a path been perceived; and for both these tasks, which we carry
wrapped up and hand on without opening, there is no general, agreed-
upon rule that can be discovered. But in the same measure in which we
begin to test life as individuals, these great Things will come to meet us,
the individuals, with greater intimacy. The claims that the difficult
work of love makes upon our development are greater than life, and we,
as beginners, are not equal to them. But if we nevertheless endure and
take this love upon us as burden and apprenticeship, instead of losing
ourselves in the whole easy and frivolous game behind which people
have hidden from the most solemn solemnity of their being,—then a
small advance and a lightening will perhaps be perceptible to those who
come long after us. That would be much.

We are only just now beginning to consider the relation of one   6
individual to a second individual objectively and without prejudice, and
our attempts to live such relationships have no model before them. And
yet in the changes that time has brought about there are already many
things that can help our timid novitiate.

The girl and the woman, in their new, individual unfolding, will   7
only in passing be imitators of male behavior and misbehavior and
repeaters of male professions. After the uncertainty of such transitions,
it will become obvious that women were going through the abundance
and variation of those (often ridiculous) disguises just so that they could
purify their own essential nature and wash out the deforming influ-
ences of the other sex. Women, in whom life lingers and dwells more
immediately, more fruitfully, and more confidently, must surely have

become riper and more human in their depths than light, easygoing man, who is not pulled down beneath the surface of life by the weight of any bodily fruit and who, arrogant and hasty, undervalues what he thinks he loves. This humanity of woman, carried in her womb through all her suffering and humiliation, will come to light when she has stripped off the conventions of mere femaleness in the transformations of her outward status, and those men who do not yet feel it approaching will be astonished by it. Someday (and even now, especially in the countries of northern Europe, trustworthy signs are already speaking and shining), someday there will be girls and women whose name will no longer mean the mere opposite of the male, but something in itself, something that makes one think not of any complement and limit, but only of life and reality: the female human being.

8   This advance (at first very much against the will of the outdistanced men) will transform the love experience, which is now filled with error, will change it from the ground up, and reshape it into a relationship that is meant to be between one human being and another, no longer one that flows from man to woman. And this more human love (which will fulfill itself with infinite consideration and gentleness, and kindness and clarity in binding and releasing) will resemble what we are now preparing painfully and with great struggle: the love that consists in this: that two solitudes protect and border and greet each other.

———— CONSIDERATIONS ————

1. Rilke's disquisition—one is tempted to call it a sermon, for he certainly urges and proclaims as a preacher might—differs from almost every other essay in this text, and thus may prove difficult to read. What contributes to this difficulty?

2. What is his principal reason for saying that the young are incapable of love? How does this belief relate to his comments later in the essay on the evolution of women?

3. Rilke mentions marriage as one of the conventional escapes that so many take instead of persisting along the "dangerous" road to love. He does not specify others. Can you derive some of them from his discussion?

4. Read Flannery O'Connor's short story, "A Good Man Is Hard to Find" and her letter to John Hawkes. In the last paragraph of that letter, she tries to help Hawkes and his students understand the difficult concept of "grace." As she describes grace, does it have any connection with Rilke's concept of love? Explain.

5. Rilke's letter was written in May 1904. Does paragraph 7 prophesy stages of women's liberation? What examples or illustrations can you cite to support your answer?

6. Put into your own words Rilke's definition of love, which closes his final sentence in this selection. What difficulties do you find in accomplishing this task? Why?

Ann Farrer Scott (b. 1947) was born in Iowa, practiced law in Pennsylvania, and now lives in Minnesota with her family, writing essays for a variety of publications. "Feeling 'Kind of Temporary'" appeared in the New York Times *in 1984.*

61

ANN FARRER SCOTT
Feeling "Kind of Temporary"

1   I grew up air-conditioned. By that I mean that as a child I lived in tract houses on what had once been prairie, where buffalo had grazed and where, as it always had, the summer sun shone relentlessly on the land. The houses I lived in were like all the other houses around them: air-conditioned, one story, with bedroom windows placed too high, so we could not look out. The arms of the sofa looked like upswept tailfins. There was a hi-fi and a television set. That sofa has long been junked. The hi-fi gave way to a stereo system and the television simply gave out.

2   I was a baby boomer, a child of the affluent society, the throwaway culture. Mine was the new! improved! postwar generation, brought up on Wonder Bread to build our bodies 12 different ways. We were taught, if nothing else, to consume—and to discard, so that we could consume all the more. A successful lesson it was: today each person in this country throws away three to five pounds of garbage a day, according to Arthur Purcell, author of "The Waste Watchers." I wonder, though, if we haven't been throwing away more than we know.

3   In my mind I did not inhabit those low-slung, climate-controlled houses but an old gabled one with high ceilings and tall windows, a house filled with light, where I climbed creaky stairs to an attic. Musty and shadowed, the attic held treasures—a horsehair trunk in which I found a china doll, her pelisse dusty, her kid boots cracked, and a barrel of old books, stored wisdom, the pages yellowed.

As a child I preferred to read books about the past. I did not read   4
much fantasy. Neither did I believe in fairies. It was hard enough to
believe in buffalo. I was seeking not escape but history. I wanted to
know about this odd place where I had landed.

In third grade, after lunch, Mrs. Schroeder read to us in that   5
dimmed room, the shades half pulled, the cement-block walls a dark
yellow, the electric clock clicking, quietly marking the passing of our
time. For several weeks she read to us "The Boxcar Children," an
execrable book in many ways—too much virtue, too many rewards—
but for a year after that I kept a suitcase packed and hidden under my
bed. I knew that at some point I would pull up stakes, and one starry
night I would want to run off to the woods (there were no woods, only
highways and subdivisions) and find there a rusty boxcar, its door half
open. The tracks would be overgrown with weeds. Nearby a clear brook
would ripple. There would be large rocks for building a fireplace. I
would make a bed of pine needles. Not far would be a dump where I
would find a cracked pink cup.

Excavating our dump today, I would be as likely to find polychlori-   6
nated biphenyls as I would a cracked pink cup. Michael Brown describes
our lives in "Laying Waste: The Poisoning of America by Toxic
Chemicals": "We brush our teeth with fluoride compounds, rub on
propylene glycol deodorants, clothe ourselves in rayon and nylon or
treated cotton and wool, drive cars filled with the products of a liver
carcinogen called vinyl chloride, talk on plastic phones, walk on synthetic tiles, live within walls coated with chemical-laden paint. Our
food, kept fresh in refrigerators by heat-absorbent refrigerants, contains
preservatives and chemical additives. And, of course, it has been grown
with the aid of chemical fertilizers and insecticides." All these products
of American abundance and more, Mr. Brown writes, have an underside
of waste. It is strange to find ourselves mortal, finite in a world where
the garbage may last forever.

The dump of Wallace Stegner's childhood, the town dump of   7
Whitemud, Saskatchewan, circa 1913–19, contained relics of everyone
who had ever lived there. It was, Stegner wrote, "our poetry and our
history." Stegner found evidence in the dump even of his own young
life—the carcass of his crippled colt, some fire-damaged volumes of
Shakespeare that had belonged to his father. The children of the town
mined that dump, they dug, they sought. They loaded stuff from the
dump into their wagons and carried back home what the town had
thrown away. Their parents, of course, dispatched the booty back to the
dump.

8   There is not much poetry or history, it seems to me, in what we throw away these days.

9   "Fine quality is a distinct disadvantage in articles made for great numbers of people who do not want a thing that 'wears,' but who want change—a succession of new things that are quickly threadbare and can be lightly thrown away," Willa Cather wrote. She knew that there are stories in things, she saw certain loved objects as tangible memories, and so do her characters. In "Shadows on the Rock" a young girl makes for her father a meal with the kettle and pots that had been her mother's. With these tools, the young girl thinks, "one made a climate within a climate; one made the days—the complexion, the special flavor, the special happiness of each day as it passed; one made life." I am not sure that this is what we do with Tupperware and paper plates.

10   This past year the house where my mother grew up was torn down and replaced by a parking lot. This is the house where my grandmother made potato soup for my mother when she came home from school. It was in the alley behind this house where my mother learned to drive a Model A, denting all the garbage cans along the way. This is the house where my mother went to cry when my father left for the war.

11   It's all right, though, my mother says about her childhood home that was bulldozed into rubble. The last owner, who operated a photography studio there, had ruined it. What had once been mellow woodwork was plywood paneling. Mirrors had been torn out. "So it's all right," she tells me now. "I'd rather just remember it the way it was."

12   But I do not remember that house, and the past is something I need to touch and to hold—to care for and polish and dust. I wear my grandmother's wedding ring. In my daughter's bedroom are two oak chests from my grandmother's summer cottage. When I make chocolate pudding I use my grandmother's recipe. These things are important to me, but, altogether, it's not exactly what you'd call a history, a heritage.

13   You work with what you have, but not much has been made to last. A lot has been thrown away. Here, in my middle years, I find myself doubting the future, struggling with the present, still looking for the past and feeling, as did Willy Loman in 1949, "kind of temporary about myself."

_____ **CONSIDERATIONS** _____

1. In paragraph 7, Scott alludes to a well-known and often reprinted essay, "The Town Dump," taken from Wallace Stegner's book, *Wolf Willow*

(New York: Viking Press, 1959). To what extent, if any, does the effect of Scott's essay depend on a reader's acquaintance with Stegner's? Explain.

2. In paragraph 6, Scott mentions several toxic substances that might be found in her local dump. Is there any connection between her concern about that and her obvious dissatisfaction with being "a child . . . of the throwaway culture"? Or has she momentarily forgotten her thesis?

3. In what way is the material of paragraphs 4 and 5 relevant to Scott's concern that "I wonder, though, if we haven't been throwing away more than we know"?

4. Why, according to Scott, is it important to her that when she makes chocolate pudding, "I use my grandmother's recipe"? What has that to do with her fears about a consumer-oriented way of life?

5. How does Scott shape the end of paragraph 5 so that it ties in with the rest of her essay?

6. Aside from her own observations, does Scott provide any additional substantiation for her statements about our "throwaway culture"?

7. Read paragraph 10 again, paying particular attention to Scott's sentence structure. What is distinctive about it?

8. If you examine the last sentence of paragraph 6, you may find something like a paradox. Consider the nature of a paradox and draw some conclusions about what a writer might hope to gain from such a device.

William Shakespeare (1564–1616) wrote three long poems and a sequence of sonnets, as well as the plays for which we know him best. He was born in Stratford-on-Avon to a middle-class family, moved to London in his twenties, and began his theatrical career as an actor. His writing for the theater started with plays based on English history: the three parts of Henry VI *and* Richard III. The Tempest *was his last play, and by 1611 he had retired to Stratford with the money he had made on the stage.*

This sonnet develops a common poetic theme with metaphors at once profuse and precise.

62

WILLIAM SHAKESPEARE

That Time of Year Thou Mayst in Me Behold

That time of year thou mayst in me behold
When yellow leaves, or none, or few, do hang
Upon those boughs which shake against the cold,
Bare ruined choirs, where late the sweet birds sang.
5   In me thou see'st the twilight of such day
As after sunset fadeth in the west;
Which by and by black night doth take away,
Death's second self, that seals up all in rest.
In me thou see'st the glowing of such fire,
10 That on the ashes of his youth doth lie,
As the deathbed whereon it must expire,
Consumed with that which it was nourished by.
This thou perceiv'st, which makes thy love more strong,
To love that well which thou must leave ere long.

Don Sharp (b. 1938) has taught in Alaska, Hawaii, and Australia, and once owned and operated a garage in Pennsylvania called Discriminating Services. He now lives in Massachusetts, where he writes for magazines and works on old cars. This essay won the Ken Purdy Award for Excellence in Automobile Journalism in 1981.

63

DON SHARP
Under the Hood

The owner of this 1966 Plymouth Valiant has made the rounds of 1 car dealers. They will gladly sell him a new car—the latest model of government regulation and industrial enterprise—for $8,000, but they don't want his clattering, emphysemic old vehicle in trade. It isn't worth enough to justify the paperwork, a classified ad, and space on the used-car lot. "Sell it for junk," they tell him. "Scrap iron is high now, and they'll give you $25 for it."

The owner is hurt. He likes his car. It has served him well for 2 90,000-odd miles. It has a functional shape and he can get in and out of it easily. He can roll down his window in a light rain and not get his shoulder wet. The rear windows roll down, and he doesn't need an air conditioner. He can see out of it fore, aft, and abeam. He can hazard it on urban parking lots without fear of drastic, insurance-deductible casualty loss. His teenage children reject it as passé, so it is always available to him. It has no buzzers, and the only flashing lights are those he controls himself when signaling a turn. The owner, clearly one of a vanishing tribe, brings the car to a kindred spirit and asks me to rebuild it.

We do not discuss the cost. I do not advertise my services and my 3 sign is discreet. My shop is known by word of mouth, and those who spread the word emphasize my house rule: "A blank check and a free hand." That is, I do to your car what I think it needs and you pay for it; you trust me not to take advantage, I guarantee you good brakes, sound steering, and prompt starting, and you pay without quarrel. This kind of arrangement saves a lot of time spent in making estimates and a lot of time haggling over the bill. It also imposes a tremendous burden of responsibility on me and on those who spread the word, and it puts a burden of trust on those who deliver their cars into my custody.

4   A relationship of that sort is about as profound as any that two people can enjoy, even if it lasts no longer than the time required to reline a set of brakes. I think of hometown farmers who made share-cropping deals for the season on a handshake; then I go into a large garage and see the white-coated service writer noting the customer's every specification, calling attention to the fine print at the bottom of the work order, and requiring a contractual signature before even a brake-light bulb is replaced. I perceive in their transaction that ignorance of cause and effect breeds suspicion, and I wonder who is the smaller, the customer or the service writer, and how they came to be so small of spirit.

5   Under the hood of this ailing Valiant, I note a glistening line of seeping oil where the oil pan meets the engine block. For thousands of miles, a piece of cork—a strip of bark from a Spanish tree—has stood firm between the pan and block against churning oil heated to nearly 200 degrees, oil that sought vainly to escape its duty and was forced back to work by a stalwart gasket. But now, after years of perseverance, the gasket has lost its resilience and the craven oil escapes. Ecclesiastes allows a time for all things, and the time for this gasket has passed.

6   Higher up, between the block casting that forms the foundation of the engine and the cylinder-head casting that admits fresh air and exhausts oxidized air and fuel, is the head gasket, a piece of sheet metal as thin as a matchbook cover that has confined the multiple fires built within the engine to their proper domains. Now, a whitish-gray deposit betrays an eroded area from which blue flame spits every time the cylinder fires. The gasket is "blown."

7   Let us stop and think of large numbers. In the four-cycle engines that power all modern cars, a spark jumps a spark-plug gap and sets off a fire in a cylinder every time the crankshaft goes around twice. The crankshaft turns the transmission shaft, which turns the driveshaft, which turns the differential gears, which turn the rear axles, which turn the wheels (what could Aquinas have done with something like that, had he addressed himself to the source of the spark or the final destina-

tion of the wheels?). In 100,000 miles—a common life for modern engines—the engine will make some 260 million turns, and in half of those turns, 130 million of them, a gasoline-fueled fire with a maximum temperature of 2,000 degrees (quickly falling to about 1,200 degrees) is built in each cylinder. The heat generated by the fire raises the pressure in the cylinder to about 700 pounds per square inch, if only for a brief instant before the piston moves and the pressure falls. A head gasket has to contend with heat and pressure like this all the time the engine is running, and, barring mishap, it will put up with it indefinitely.

This Plymouth has suffered mishap. I know it as soon as I raise the   8
hood and see the telltale line of rust running across the underside of the hood: the mark of overheating. A water pump bearing or seal gave way, water leaked out, and was flung off the fan blades with enough force to embed particles of rust in the undercoating. Without cooling water, the engine grew too hot, and that's why the head gasket blew. In an engine, no cause exists without an effect. Unlike a court of law, wherein criminals are frequently absolved of wrongdoing, no engine component is without duty and responsibility, and failure cannot be mitigated by dubious explanations such as parental neglect or a crummy neighborhood.

Just as Sherlock Holmes would not be satisfied with one clue if he   9
could find others, I study the oil filter. The block and oil pan are caked with seepings and drippings, but below the filter the caking is visibly less thick and somewhat soft. So: once upon a time, a careless service-station attendant must have ruined the gasket while installing a new oil filter. Oil en route to the bearings escaped and washed away the grime that had accumulated. Odds are that the oil level fell too low and the crankshaft bearings were starved for oil.

Bearings are flat strips of metal, formed into half-circles about as   10
thick as a matchbook match and about an inch wide. The bearing surface itself—the surface that *bears* the crankshaft and that *bears* the load imposed by the fire-induced pressure above the piston—is half as thick. Bearing metal is a drab, gray alloy, the principal component of which is *babbitt*, a low-friction metal porous enough to absorb oil but so soft that it must be allowed to withstand high pressures. (I like to think that Sinclair Lewis had metallurgy in mind when he named his protagonist George Babbitt.) When the fire goes off above the piston and the pressure is transmitted to the crankshaft via the connecting rod, the babbitt-alloyed bearing pushes downward with a force of about 3,500

pounds per square inch. And it must not give way, must not be peened into foil and driven from its place in fragments.

11   Regard the fleshy end joint of your thumb and invite a 100-pound woman (or a pre-teen child, if no such woman be near to hand) to stand on it. Multiply the sensation by thirty-five and you get an idea of what the bearing is up against. Of course, the bearing enjoys a favorable handicap in the comparison because it works in a metal-to-metal environment heated to 180 degrees or so. The bearing is equal to its task so long as it is protected from direct metal-to-metal contact by a layer of lubricating oil, oil that must be forced into the space between the bearing and the crankshaft against that 3,500 pounds of force. True, the oil gets a lot of help from hydrodynamic action as the spinning crankshaft drags oil along with it, but lubrication depends primarily on a pump that forces oil through the engine at around 40 pounds of pressure.

12   If the oil level falls too low, the oil pump sucks in air. The oil gets as frothy as whipped cream and doesn't flow. In time, oil pressure will fall so low that the "idiot" light on the dashboard will flash, but long before then the bearing may have run "dry" and suffered considerable amounts of its metal to be peened away by those 3,500-pound hammer blows. "Considerable" may mean only 0.005 inches, or about the thickness of one sheet of 75-percent-cotton, 25-pound-per-ream dissertation bond—not much metal, but enough to allow oil to escape from the bearing even after the defective filter gasket is replaced and the oil supply replenished. From the time of oil starvation onward, the beaten bearing is a little disaster waiting to spoil a vacation or a commute to an important meeting.

13   Curious, that an unseen 0.005 inches of drab, gray metal worthy only to inspire the name of a poltroonish bourgeois should enjoy more consequence for human life than almost any equal thickness of a randomly chosen doctoral dissertation. Life is full of ironies.

14   The car I confront does not have an "idiot" light. It has an old-fashioned oil-pressure gauge. As the driver made his rounds from condominium to committee room, he could—if he cared or was ever so alert—monitor the health of his engine bearings by noting the oil pressure. Virtually all cars had these gauges in the old days, but they began to disappear in the mid-'50s, and nowadays hardly any cars have them. In eliminating oil-pressure gauges, the car makers pleaded that, in their dismal experience, people didn't pay much attention to gauges. Accordingly, Detroit switched to the warning light, which was cheaper to manufacture anyway (and having saved a few bucks on the mechani-

cals, the manufacturer could afford to etch a design in the opera windows; this is called "progress"). Curious, in the midst of all this, that Chrysler Corporation, the maker of Plymouths and the victim of so much bad management over the past fifteen years, should have been the one car manufacturer to constantly assert, via a standard-equipment oil-pressure gauge, a faith in the awareness, judgment, and responsibility of drivers. That Chrysler did so may have something to do with its current problems.

The other car makers were probably right. Time was when most   15
men knew how to replace their own distributor points, repair a flat tire, and install a battery. Women weren't assumed to know as much, but they were expected to know how to put a gear lever in neutral, set a choke and throttle, and crank a car by hand if the battery was dead. Now, odds are that 75 percent of men and a higher percentage of women don't even know how to work the jacks that come with their cars. To be sure, a bumper jack is an abominable contraption—the triumph of production economies over good sense—but it will do what it is supposed to do, and the fact that most drivers cannot make one work says much about the way motorists have changed over the past forty years.

About all that people will watch on the downslide of this century   16
is the fuel gauge, for they don't like to be balked in their purpose. A lack of fuel will stop a car dead in its tracks and categorically prevent the driver from arriving at the meeting to consider tenure for a male associate professor with a black grandfather and a Chinese mother. Lack of fuel will stall a car in mid-intersection and leave dignity and image prey to the honks and curses of riffraff driving taxicabs and beer trucks, so people watch the fuel gauge as closely as they watch a pubescent daughter or a bearish stock.

But for the most part, once the key goes into the ignition, people   17
assign responsibility for the car's smooth running to someone else—to anybody but themselves. If the engine doesn't start, that's not because the driver has abused it, but because the manufacturer was remiss or the mechanic incompetent. (Both suspicions are reasonable, but they do not justify the driver's spineless passivity.) The driver considers himself merely a client of the vehicle. He proudly disclaims, at club and luncheon, any understanding of the dysfunctions of the machine. He must so disclaim, for to admit knowledge or to seek it actively would require an admission of responsibility and fault. To be wrong about inflation or the political aspirations of the Albanians doesn't cost anybody anything, but to claim to know why the car won't start and then to be proved wrong is both embarrassing and costly.

18   Few people would remove $500 from someone's pocket without a qualm and put it in their own. Yet, the job-lot run of mechanics do it all the time. Mechanics and drivers are alike: they gave up worrying long ago about the intricacies and demands of cause and effect. The mechanics do not attend closely to the behavior of the vehicle. Rather, they consult a book with flow-charts that says, "Try this, and if it doesn't work, try that." Or they hook the engine up to another machine and read gauges or cathode-ray-tube squiggles, but without realizing that gauges and squiggles are not reality but only tools used to aid perception of reality. A microscope is also a wonderful tool, but you still have to comprehend what you're looking for; else, like James Thurber, you get back the reflection of your own eye.

19   Mechanics, like academics and bureaucrats, have retreated too far from the realities of their tasks. An engine runs badly. They consult the book. The book says to replace part A. They replace A. The engine still runs badly, but the mechanic can deny the fact as handily as a socialist can deny that minimum-wage laws eventually lead to unemployment. Just as the driver doesn't care to know why his oil pressure drops from 40 to 30 to 20 pounds and then to zero, so the mechanic cares little for the casuistic distinctions that suggest that part A is in good order but that some subtle conjunction of wholesome part B with defective part C may be causing the trouble. (I don't know about atheists in foxholes, but I doubt that many Jesuits are found among incompetent mechanics.)

20   And why should the mechanic care? He gets paid in any event. From the mechanic's point of view, he should get paid, for he sees a federal judge hire academic consultants to advise about busing, and after the whites have fled before the imperious column of yellow buses and left the schools blacker than ever, the judge hires the consultants again to find out why the whites moved out. The consultant gets paid in public money, whatever effects his action have, even when he causes things he said would never happen.

21   Consider the garden-variety Herr Doktor who has spent a pleasant series of warm fall weekends driving to a retreat in the Catskills; his car has started with alacrity and run well despite a stuck choke. Then, when the first blue norther of the season sends temperatures toward zero, the faithful machine must be haggled into action and proceeds haltingly down the road, gasping and backfiring. "Needs a new carburetor," the mechanic says, and, to be sure, once a new carburetor is installed, the car runs well again. Our Herr Doktor is happy. His car did not run well; it got a new carburetor and ran well again; ergo, the carburetor was at fault. Q.E.D.

Curious that in personal matters the classic *post hoc* fallacy   22
should be so readily accepted when it would be mocked in academic
debate. Our Herr Doktor should know, or at least suspect, that the
carburetor that functioned so well for the past several months could
hardly have changed its nature overnight, and we might expect of him a
more diligent inquiry into its problems. But "I'm no mechanic," he
chuckles to his colleagues, and they nod agreeably. Such skinned-
knuckle expertise would be unfitting in a man whose self-esteem is
equivalent to his uselessness with a wrench. Lilies of the postindustrial
field must concern themselves with weighty matters beyond the ken of
greasy laborers who drink beer at the end of a workday.

Another example will illustrate the point. A battery cable has an   23
end that is designed to connect to a terminal on the battery. Both
cable-end and battery terminal surfaces look smooth, but aren't. Those
smooth surfaces are pitted and peaked, and only the peaks touch each
other. The pits collect water from the air, and the chemistry of elec-
tricity-carrying metals causes lead oxides to form in the pits. The oxides
progressively insulate the cable end and battery terminal from each
other until the day that turning the key produces only a single, resounding *clunk* and no more. The road service mechanics installs a new $75
battery and collects $25 for his trouble. Removing the cables from the
old battery cleans their ends somewhat, so things work for a few days,
and then the car again fails to start. The mechanic installs a $110
alternator, applies a $5 charge to the battery, and collects another
$25; several days later he gives the battery another $5 charge, installs
a $75 starter, and collects $25 more. In these instances, to charge the
battery—to send current backwards from cable end to battery
terminal—disturbs the oxides and temporarily improves their conduc-
tivity. Wriggling the charger clamps on the cable ends probably helps
too. On the driver's last $25 visit, the mechanic sells another $5 battery
charge and a pair of $25 battery cables. Total bill $400, and all the car
needed was to have its cable ends and battery terminals cleaned. The
mechanic wasn't necessarily a thief. Perhaps, like academic education
consultants, he just wasn't very smart—and his ilk abound; they are as
plentiful as the drivers who will pay generously for the privilege of an
aristocratic disdain of elementary cause and effect in a vehicular electrical system.

After a tolerably long practice as a mechanic, I firmly believe that   24
at least two-thirds of the batteries, starters, alternators, ignition coils,
carburetors, and water pumps that are sold are not needed. Batteries,
alternators, and starters are sold because battery-cable ends are dirty. A

maladjusted or stuck automatic choke is cured by a new carburetor. Water pumps and alternators are sold to correct problems from loose fan belts. In the course of the replacement, the fan belt gets properly tightened, so the original problem disappears in the misguided cure, with mechanic and owner never the wiser.

25   I understand the venality (and laziness and ignorance) of mechanics, and understand the shop owner's need to pay a salary to someone to keep up with the IRS and OSHA forms. The shop marks up parts by 50 to 100 percent. When the car with the faulty choke comes in the door, the mechanic must make a choice: he can spend fifteen minutes fixing it and charge a half-hour's labor, or he can spend a half-hour replacing the carburetor (and charge for one hour) with one he buys for $80 and sells for $135. If the shop is a profit-making enterprise, the mechanic can hardly be blamed for selling the unneeded new carburetor, especially if the customer will stand still to be fleeced. Whether the mechanic acts from ignorance or larceny (the odds are about equal), the result is still a waste, one that arises from the driver's refusal to study the cause and effect of events that occur under the hood of his car.

26   The willingness of a people to accept responsibility for the machines they depend on is a fair barometer of their sense of individual worth and of the moral strength of a culture. According to popular reports, the Russian working folk are a sorrowfully vodka-besotted lot; likewise, reports are that Russian drivers abuse their vehicles atrociously. In our unhappy country, as gauges for battery-charging (ammeters), cooling-water temperature, and oil pressure disappeared from the dashboards, they were replaced by a big-brotherly series of cacophonous buzzers and flashing lights, buzzers and lights mandated by regulatory edict for the sole purpose of reminding the driver that the government considers him a hopeless fool. Concurrent with these developments has come social agitation and law known as "consumer protection," which is, in fact, an extension of that philosophy that people are morons for whom the government must provide outpatient care. People pay handsome taxes to be taught that they are not responsible and do not need to be. This is a long way from what the Puritans paid their tithes for, and, Salem witch trials aside, the Puritans got a better product for their money.

27   What is astounding and dismaying is how quickly people came to believe in their own incompetence. In 1951, Eric Hoffer noted in *The True Believer* that a leader so disposed could make free people into

slaves easier than he could turn slaves into free people (cf. Moses). Hoffer must be pained by the accuracy of his perception.

I do not claim that Everyman can be his own expert mechanic, for I know that precious few can. I do claim that disdain for the beautiful series of cause-and-effect relationships ("beautiful" in the way that provoked Archimedes to proclaim "Eureka!") that move machines, and particularly the automobile, measures not only a man's wit but also a society's morals.　　28

____ CONSIDERATIONS _____

1. At the end of paragraph 4, Sharp poses a question. What sentence toward the end of his essay answers this question? Is that sentence the thesis of his essay? What do you think of his choice of a moral barometer?

2. What would James Thurber think of Sharp's use of "which" in paragraph 7? (See Thurber's short essay "Which.")

3. In paragraphs 10, 11, and 12, Sharp offers an exposition of a process. Study his success in explaining technical matters without lapsing into terminology too specialized for the general reader.

4. Sharp calls a particular device on the dashboard an "idiot light." Why? Connect this epithet with other ideas in his essay.

5. Sharp refers (in paragraph 9) to Sherlock Holmes's renowned skill in deduction, and (in paragraph 22) to a common logical fallacy called *post hoc ergo propter hoc.* Consult a good dictionary for the meaning of this Latin phrase.

6. Note Sharp's distinctive word choice throughout the essay. How do his words affect the tone?

Page Smith (b. 1917) has written a long narrative history in eight volumes called The People's History of the United States. *He taught at the University of California at Santa Cruz, where he was also Provost, but he has also worked outside the academy. He has written editorials for the* Los Angeles Times *and collaborated on a famous compendium from the barnyard called* The Chicken Book. *This essay first appeared in the* Newsletter *of the Research Center for Nonviolence.*

64

PAGE SMITH
The New Abolitionism

1   The notion of human slavery, of owning human beings as property, of beating or mutilating them as punishment, of selling children away from their mothers and wives from their husbands, is an idea so repugnant to the modern consciousness that it is hard to comprehend the fact that such practices were commonplace in the United States a little more than a hundred years ago. When we think of such matters they seem infinitely remote, as though they had happened ages past. Such an institution could never have survived into the present age, we assure ourselves. If the Civil War had not plucked up slavery, an enlightened nation would, by the opening decades of the twentieth century, have renounced it as incompatible with everything that America stands for. "Progress," in its inevitable march, would have made slavery an anachronism. Industrialization would have made it uneconomic.

2   The facts are otherwise. From the beginning of the Republic, the institution of slavery put down deeper and deeper roots, becoming increasingly brutal and repressive with each passing decade. Far from deploring the institution, Southerners began to glorify it, comparing the culture it had produced in the South to that of ancient Greece, another slave-holding society. It was the settled determination of the South to

extend the protection of the federal government to slaves as property westward to the Pacific Ocean and northward as far as Canada. Indeed, they wished to add Cuba to the slave empire.

"Progress," however we define that often ambiguous word, has 3 demonstrated no built-in capacity for regenerating the moral fibre of a people. It has, if anything, displayed a disconcerting capacity to come to terms with exploitation and repression in the name of progress.

How then were the slaves freed? Quite simply, by the heroic 4 efforts of individuals who dedicated their lives to the antislavery cause. They took the name abolitionists. Moral gadflies, tireless agitators, proclaimers of a moral order in the universe, champions of Christian brotherhood, they pricked the conscience of their fellow citizens. They allowed them no rest on the issue of slavery. Day in and day out, year in and year out, relentless and indefatigable, they pressed the issue. Mobbed, beaten, denounced, shut out from the company of respectable people, they persisted. They grew from a handful into an army. When Richard Henry Dana undertook to defend runaway slaves in Boston, friends of a lifetime cut him dead on the streets.

The great mass of Americans north of Mason's and Dixon's Line 5 were quite ready to concede the iniquity of slavery, but they simply wished to forget about the whole subject. They didn't want trouble; they didn't like agitators. Agitators were bad for business. Northerners had other things on their minds like making a living or "dropping out" West, or quarreling over "hard" money versus "soft" money. Their relative indifference to the moral dimensions of the slavery issue demonstrated the ability of a people to ignore or suppress crucial moral issues. In this respect Americans were no different from the vast majority of species. We are all disposed to accept things-as-they-are as having a kind of inevitability about them. They seem part of the landscape, part of the complex set of ideas that define the society as a whole. Dangerous things to tamper with.

We find ourselves today in much the same situation that our 6 forefathers did in the era before the Civil War (which of course was not fought primarily to free the slaves). We have allowed an evil, a horror of almost incomprehensible proportions, to grow up in our midst and come indeed to seem like part of the natural order of things, as inevitable as the sunrise in the morning or the passage of the seasons. We have knowingly and deliberately armed ourselves with the most terrible weapons of destruction conceivable. As people originally dedicated to "emancipating" the world, we have devised and built weapons capable of destroying it many times over. Most astonishing of all (and, one might add, most obscene), we have done this in the name of peace. We have solemnly declared a moral enormity of staggering proportions to be our regretted but necessary duty.

7   To inform the world that we may have to destroy the greater part of it in order to save it from communism (or anything else) is an arrogant presumption which, so far as I know, is without precedent in history. (Perhaps the will has been there before but never the capacity.) Indeed, having stated it, one stares at it unbelievingly on the page. Clearly what is involved in part is a dangerously diminished moral sensibility, but perhaps even more important, a badly flawed notion of the meaning of human existence. The world, believe me, was not created (or has not evolved) to be the creature of the United States, to be shaped or destroyed, in accordance with our Will, reinforced by stockpiles of atomic weapons.

8   Peoples throughout history have lived and suffered under governments far more egregiously tyrannical than any communist regime presently existing in the world. At least they or their children survived to see better times. Now the United States declares that it is prepared, if it deems it necessary to do so, to foreclose a future for the human race by employing nuclear weapons against its communist adversary. Assuming the worst scenario—an impending coummunist global takeover—I suspect that the peoples of the world might prefer, for a time at least, to live under communist regimes rather than not to live at all, to have no successors that could be called human. Or at the very least to have a say in the matter.

9   Perhaps the crowning irony is that at the same time that we are preparing to destroy millions upon millions of Russians because they live under a system called communism, we announce that the system itself is collapsing, to quote Karl Marx, from its internal inconsistencies (as every "system" must in time). Moreover, there seems to be some evidence to support the assertion.

10   I do not covet the mantle of prophecy (I have my hands full with the past) but I see no conceivable reasons to believe that the human race will follow undeviatingly either the path of Russian Communism or American Capitalism (indeed the best thing that can be said of the latter is that it has avoided the worst excesses of the former). Surely the future, if we allow it to happen, must hold something better than either.

11   Which brings us back to the abolitionists. There is only one overriding issue facing the United States and the world, a single issue beside which *all* other issues fade to relative insignificance, and that is the complete outlawing and destruction of all nuclear weapons and weap-

ons systems, beginning in the United States. We must begin in the
United States, because the United States is still a democracy, if a highly
imperfect one, and the citizens of this nation can still make their
convictions felt through their elected representatives.

If the day comes when 75 percent of all Americans (or even,   12
perhaps, 55 percent) announce with clarity and conviction, "We will
not tolerate the existence of a nuclear arsenal in a nation that once
called itself Christian and professed to be dedicated to improving the
condition of all peoples, everywhere," that nuclear arsenal will be
dismantled and mankind will breathe more freely. To bring the people
of this Republic to such a conviction will not be quickly or easily
accomplished. It may take as long as it took the abolitionists to free the
slaves and as much heroism and devotion, as much willingness to
endure hostility and abuse, charges of being unpatriotic or of being a
"commie lover" (as the abolitionists were accused of being "nigger
lovers" and proudly confessed to being).

I, for one, am willing to confess myself as a "commie lover,"   13
because my faith so instructs me. Indeed, I love the commies more than
the capitalists—though I deplore the system under which they live—
because I suspect they are substantially more in need of love. Certainly,
the thought of destroying millions or dozens or *one of them* because
they give their allegiance to a different political system than I do fills
me with repugnance and dismay (not to mention, of course, the millions upon millions of those who will, it seems clear, be quite coinci-
dentally annihilated).

IN THE NAME OF GOD, LET US ABOLISH NUCLEAR WEAPONS.   14

Our leaders tell us that such talk is defeatist, un-American. It is   15
true I have no nerve or will for these murderous games, these scenarios
of destruction with their insane calculations of kills and overkills.
Nations as well as individuals can go insane. It seems clear to me that
the United States is at this moment collectively insane in its policies
and attitudes toward the Soviet Union. I know of no other way to
explain our continuing accumulation of the deadliest weapons.

Slavery was such a madness; the cure was slow and ultimately   16
terrible, but we must never for a moment lose sight of the fact that it
was accomplished finally by the conscious, intelligent, sacrificial efforts of a host of individuals not strikingly different from ourselves. A
group of pacifist organizations have joined forces recently to distribute
"The New Abolitionist Covenant." It is most appropriately named.
Only a modern abolitionist covenant to do away with nuclear arms,
utterly and completely, can save mankind from something very like

destruction and the United States from bearing the primary guilt for the holocaust (though most of us presumably will be dead in any event).

_____ CONSIDERATIONS _____

1. What is the curious feature of Page Smith's opening paragraph, a paragraph commonly used to set forth a writer's thesis?

2. How might Smith have used passages from the journals of Henry David Thoreau to amplify the idea developed in paragraph 2?

3. Is "Better Red than Dead" an acceptable summary of Smith's paragraph 8? In what sense is that expression unacceptable—rhetorically, politically, philosophically, religiously? Explain.

4. With the exception of paragraph 14, Smith's paragraphs are about the same length. Does its unusual length add to the effect of paragraph 14? Make a brief study of the functions and sizes of paragraphs, comparing Smith with other writers in the text.

5. What precepts of (presumably) religious faith does Smith have in mind when he says, in paragraph 13, that his faith instructs him to be a "commie lover"?

*William Stafford (b. 1914) is a poet who grew up in Kansas
and taught for many years at Lewis and Clark College in
Oregon. His* Traveling Through the Dark *won the National Book
Award in 1963, and in 1977, Stafford collected his poems into
one volume called* Stories That Could Be True. A Glass Face in
the Rain *followed in 1982 and* An Oregon Message *in 1987. His
essays appear in* Writing the Australian Crawl *(1978) and* You
Must Revise Your Life *(1986). Stafford's poetry and his personal
account of writing poetry look simple at first glance, but their
simplicity deepens as we return and reread. His poetry is simple
and deep, rather than complex and superficial. Reading about
his way of writing, we feel the style of the man as intensely in
his prose as in his poems.*

65

WILLIAM STAFFORD
A Way of Writing

A writer is not so much someone who has something to say as he 1
is someone who has found a process that will bring about new things he
would not have thought of if he had not started to say them. That is, he
does not draw on a reservoir; instead, he engages in an activity that
brings to him a whole succession of unforeseen stories, poems, essays,
plays, laws, philosophies, religions, or—but wait!

Back in school, from the first when I began to try to write things, I 2
felt this richness. One thing would lead to another; the world would
give and give. Now, after twenty years or so of trying, I live by that
certain richness, an idea hard to pin, difficult to say, and perhaps offensive to some. For there are strange implications in it.

One implication is the importance of just plain receptivity. When 3
I write, I like to have an interval before me when I am not likely to be
interrupted. For me, this means usually the early morning, before oth-

From *Field: Contemporary Poetry and Poetics,* #2. Spring 1970. Reprinted by
permission of *Field,* Oberlin College, Oberlin, Ohio.

ers are awake. I get pen and paper, take a glance out the window (often it is dark out there), and wait. It is like fishing. But I do not wait very long, for there is always a nibble—and this is where receptivity comes in. To get started I will accept anything that occurs to me. Something always occurs, of course, to any of us. We can't keep from thinking. Maybe I have to settle for an immediate impression: it's cold, or hot, or dark, or bright, or in between! Or—well, the possibilities are endless. If I put down something, that thing will help the next thing come, and I'm off. If I let the process go on, things will occur to me that were not at all in my mind when I started. These things, odd or trivial as they may be, are somehow connected. And if I let them string out, surprising things will happen.

4   If I let them string out. . . . Along with initial receptivity, then, there is another readiness: I must be willing to fail. If I am to keep on writing, I cannot bother to insist on high standards. I must get into action and not let anything stop me, or even slow me much. By "standards" I do not mean "correctness"—spelling, punctuation, and so on. These details become mechanical for anyone who writes for awhile. I am thinking about what many people would consider "important" standards, such matters as social significance, positive values, consistency, etc. I resolutely disregard these. Something better, greater, is happening! I am following a process that leads so wildly and originally into new territory that no judgment can at the moment be made about values, significance, and so on. I am making something new, something that has not been judged before. Later others—and maybe I myself—will make judgments. Now, I am headlong to discover. Any distraction may harm the creating.

5   So, receptive, careless of failure, I spin out things on the page. And a wonderful freedom comes. If something occurs to me, it is all right to accept it. It has one justification: it occurs to me. No one else can guide me. I must follow my own weak, wandering, diffident impulses.

6   A strange bonus happens. At times, without my insisting on it, my writings become coherent; the successive elements that occur to me are clearly related. They lead by themselves to new connections. Sometimes the language, even the syllables that happen along, may start a trend. Sometimes the materials alert me to something waiting in my mind, ready for sustained attention. At such times, I allow myself to be eloquent, or intentional, or for great swoops (treacherous! not to be trusted!) reasonable. But I do not insist on any of that; for I know that back of my activity there will be the coherence of my self, and that

indulgence of my impulses will bring recurrent patterns and meanings again.

This attitude toward the process of writing creatively suggests a 7 problem for me, in terms of what others say. They talk about "skills" in writing. Without denying that I do have experience, wide reading, automatic orthodoxies and maneuvers of various kinds, I still must insist that I am often baffled about what "skill" has to do with the precious little area of confusion when I do not know what I am going to say and then I find out what I am going to say. That precious interval I am unable to bridge by skill. What can I witness about it? It remains mysterious, just as all of us must feel puzzled about how we are so inventive as to be able to talk along through complexities with our friends, not needing to plan what we are going to say, but never stalled for long in our confident forward progress. Skill? If so, it is the skill we all have, something we must have learned before the age of three or four.

A writer is one who has become accustomed to trusting that grace, 8 or luck, or—skill.

Yet another attitude I find necessary: most of what I write, like 9 most of what I say in casual conversation, will not amount to much. Even I will realize, and even at the time, that it is not negotiable. It will be like practice. In conversation I allow myself random remarks—in fact, as I recall, that is the way I learned to talk—, so in writing I launch many expendable efforts. A result of this free way of writing is that I am not writing for others, mostly; they will not see the product at all unless the activity eventuates in something that later appears to be worthy. My guide is the self, and its adventuring in the language brings about communication.

This process-rather-than-substance view of writing invites a final, 10 dual reflection:

1. Writers may not be special—sensitive or talented in any usual sense. They are simply engaged in sustained use of a language skill we all have. Their "creations" come about through confident reliance on stray impulses that will, with trust, find occasional patterns that are satisfying.

2. But writing itself is one of the great, free human activities. There is scope for individuality, and elation, and discovery, in writing. For the person who follows with trust and forgiveness what occurs to him, the world remains always ready and deep, an inexhaustible environment, with the combined vividness of an actuality and flexibility of

a dream. Working back and forth between experience and thought, writers have more than space and time can offer. They have the whole unexplored realm of human vision.

A sample daily-writing sheet and the poem as revised.

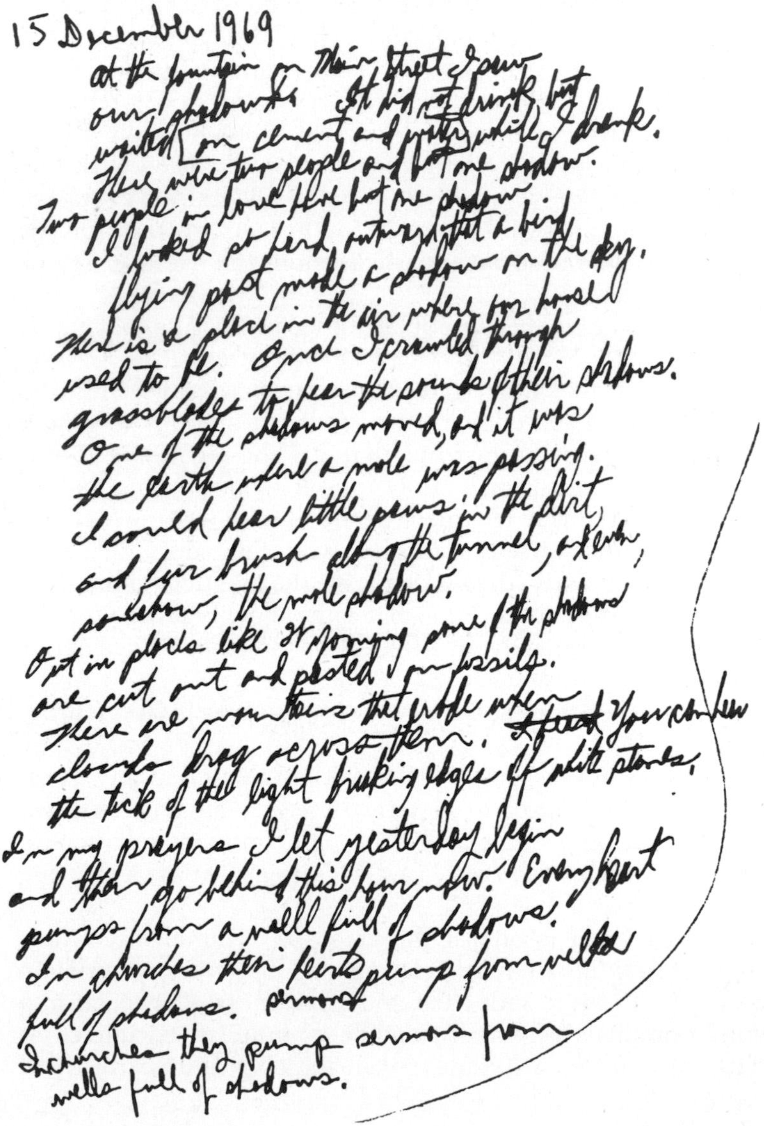

15 December 1969

At the fountain on Main Street I saw
our shadows. They did not drink, but
waited on cement and pretended while I drank.
There were two people and but one shadow.
Two people in love have but one shadow.
I looked at feet, outraged that a bird
flying past made a shadow on the sky.
There is a place in the air where our house
used to be. Once I crawled through
grassblades to hear the sounds of their shadows.
One of the shadows moved, and it was
the earth where a mole was passing.
I could hear little paws in the dirt,
and fur brush along the tunnel, and even,
somehow, the mole shadow.
Out in places like Wyoming some of the shadows
are cut out and pasted down as fossils.
There are mountains that wobble when
clouds drag across them. ~~Speak~~ You can hear
the tick of the light breaking edges off white stones.
In my prayers I let yesterday begin
and then go behind this hour now. Every heart
pumps from a well full of shadows.
In churches their hearts pump from wells
full of shadows. sermons
In churches they pump sermons from
wells full of shadows.

Shadows

I

Out in places like Wyoming some of the shadows
are cut out and pasted on fossils.

There are mountains that erode when
clouds drag across them. You can hear ~~the tick~~ the tick

~~the tick~~ of the light breaking edges off white stones.

At a fountain on Main Street I saw
our shadow. It did not drink but
waited on cement and water while I drank.
There were two people and but one shadow.
I looked up so hard outward that a bird
flying past made a shadow on the sky. X

There is a place in the air where our house
used to be.

Once I crawled through grassblades to hear
the sounds of their shadows. One of the shadows
moved, and it was the earth where a mole
was passing. I could hear little
paws in the dirt, and fur brush along
the tunnel, and even, somehow, the mole shadow.

In churches when hearts pump sermons
from wells full of shadows.
In my prayers I let yesterday begin
and then go behind this hour now.

SHADOWS

Out in places like Wyoming some of the shadows
are cut out and pasted on fossils.
There are mountains that erode when
clouds drag across them. You hear the tick
of sunlight breaking edges off white stones.

At a fountain on Main Street I saw
our shadow. It did not drink but
waited on cement and water while I drank.
There were two people and but one shadow.
I looked up so hard outward that a bird
flying past made a shadow on the sky.
There is a place in the air where
our old house used to be.

Once I crawled through grassblades to hear
the sounds of their shadows. One shadow
moved, and it was the earth where a mole
was passing. I could hear little
paws in the dirt, and fur brush along
the tunnel, and even, somehow, the mole shadow.

In my prayers I let yesterday begin
and then go behind this hour now,
in churches where hearts pump sermons
from wells full of shadows.

—— **CONSIDERATIONS** ——————————————————

1. Stafford is clearly and openly talking about himself—how *he* writes, what writing means to *him*—and yet most readers agree that he successfully avoids the egotism or self-consciousness that sours many first-person essays. Compare his style with three or four other first-person pieces in this book to see how he does it.

2. In his first paragraph, Stafford tells of an idea that might be called writing as discovery. Thinking back through your own writing, can you recall this experience—when, after struggling to write an essay or letter that you *had* to write, you discovered something you *wanted* to write? What did you do about it? More important, what might you do next time it happens?

3. What, according to Stafford, is more important to a writer than "social significance, or positive values, or consistency"?

4. Stafford is talking about writing a poem. How do his discoveries and conclusions bear on *your* problems in writing an essay? Be specific.

5. Do the opening and closing paragraphs differ in style? If so, what is the difference, and why does Stafford allow it?

6. Study the three versions of Stafford's poem "Shadows." Do you find anything that belies the easygoing impression his essay gives of Stafford at work? Explain.

7. Compare Stafford's advice with the suggestions of other authors in the text who talk about writing: Joan Didion, Alice Walker, George Orwell, or Ralph Ellison. What advice is most relevant to your current writing tasks?

Brent Staples (b. 1951) is Assistant Metropolitan Editor at the New York Times. *He grew up in Chester, Pennsylvania, and did his Ph.D. in psychology at the University of Chicago. He taught briefly, then worked for several magazines and newspapers, including the* Chicago Sun-Times, *before moving to New York. Farrar, Straus & Giroux will soon publish his memoir, tentatively titled* Parallel Time. *"Just Walk On By" appeared in* Ms. *magazine in 1986.*

66

BRENT STAPLES
Just Walk On By

1 My first victim was a woman—white, well-dressed, probably in her early twenties. I came upon her late one evening on a deserted street in Hyde Park, a relatively affluent neighborhood in an otherwise mean, impoverished section of Chicago. As I swung onto the avenue behind her, there seemed to be a discreet, uninflammatory distance between us. Not so. She cast back a worried glance. To her, the youngish black man—a broad six feet two inches with a beard and billowing hair, both hands shoved into the pockets of a bulky military jacket—seemed menacingly close. After a few more quick glimpses, she picked up her pace and was soon running in earnest. Within seconds she disappeared into a cross street.

2 That was more than a decade ago. I was 22 years old, a graduate student newly arrived at the University of Chicago. It was in the echo of that terrified woman's footfalls that I first began to know the unwieldy inheritance I'd come into—the ability to alter public space in ugly ways. It was clear that she thought herself the quarry of a mugger, a rapist, or worse. Suffering a bout of insomnia, however, I was stalking sleep, not defenseless wayfarers. As a softy who is scarcely able to take a knife to a raw chicken—let alone hold it to a person's throat—I was surprised, embarrassed, and dismayed all at once. Her flight made me

feel like an accomplice in tyranny. It also made it clear that I was indistinguishable from the muggers who occasionally seeped into the area from the surrounding ghetto. That first encounter, and those that followed, signified that a vast, unnerving gulf lay between nighttime pedestrians—particularly women—and me. And I soon gathered that being perceived as dangerous is a hazard in itself. I only needed to turn a corner into a dicey situation, or crowd some frightened, armed person in a foyer somewhere, or make an errant move after being pulled over by a policeman. Where fear and weapons meet—and they often do in urban America—there is always the possibility of death.

In that first year, my first away from my hometown, I was to   3
become thoroughly familiar with the language of fear. At dark, shadowy intersections in Chicago, I could cross in front of a car stopped at a traffic light and elicit the *thunk, thunk, thunk, thunk* of the driver— black, white, male, or female—hammering down the door locks. On less traveled streets after dark, I grew accustomed to but never comfortable with people who crossed to the other side of the street rather than pass me. Then there were the standard unpleasantries with police, doormen, bouncers, cab drivers, and others whose business it is to screen out troublesome individuals *before* there is any nastiness.

I moved to New York nearly two years ago and I have remained an   4
avid night walker. In central Manhattan, the near-constant crowd cover minimizes tense one-on-one street encounters. Elsewhere—visiting friends in SoHo, where sidewalks are narrow and tightly spaced buildings shut out the sky—things can get very taut indeed.

Black men have a firm place in New York mugging literature.   5
Norman Podhoretz in his famed (or infamous) 1963 essay, "My Negro Problem—And Ours," recalls growing up in terror of black males; they "were tougher than we were, more ruthless," he writes—and as an adult on the Upper West Side of Manhattan, he continues, he cannot constrain his nervousness when he meets black men on certain streets. Similarly, a decade later, the essayist and novelist Edward Hoagland extols a New York where once "Negro bitterness bore down mainly on other Negroes." Where some see mere panhandlers, Hoagland sees "a mugger who is clearly screwing up his nerve to do more than just *ask* for money." But Hoagland has "the New Yorker's quick-hunch posture for broken-field maneuvering," and the bad guy swerves away.

I often witness that "hunch posture," from women after dark on   6
the warrenlike streets of Brooklyn where I live. They seem to set their faces on neutral and, with their purse straps strung across their chests bandolier style, they forge ahead as though bracing themselves against

being tackled. I understand, of course, that the danger they perceive is not a hallucination. Women are particularly vulnerable to street violence, and young black males are drastically overrepresented among the perpetrators of that violence. Yet these truths are no solace against the kind of alienation that comes of being ever the suspect, against being set apart, a fearsome entity with whom pedestrians avoid making eye contact.

7   It is not altogether clear to me how I reached the ripe old age of 22 without being conscious of the lethality nighttime pedestrians attributed to me. Perhaps it was because in Chester, Pennsylvania, the small, angry industrial town where I came of age in the 1960s, I was scarcely noticeable against a backdrop of gang warfare, street knifings, and murders. I grew up one of the good boys, had perhaps a half-dozen fist fights. In retrospect, my shyness of combat has clear sources.

8   Many things go into the making of a young thug. One of those things is the consummation of the male romance with the power to intimidate. An infant discovers that random flailings send the baby bottle flying out of the crib and crashing to the floor. Delighted, the joyful babe repeats those motions again and again, seeking to duplicate the feat. Just so, I recall the points at which some of my boyhood friends were finally seduced by the perception of themselves as tough guys. When a mark cowered and surrendered his money without resistance, myth and reality merged—and paid off. It is, after all, only manly to embrace the power to frighten and intimidate. We, as men, are not supposed to give an inch of our lane on the highway; we are to seize the fighter's edge in work and in play and even in love; we are to be valiant in the face of hostile forces.

9   Unfortunately, poor and powerless young men seem to take all this nonsense literally. As a boy, I saw countless tough guys locked away; I have since buried several, too. They were babies, really—a teenage cousin, a brother of 22, a childhood friend in his mid-twenties—all gone down in episodes of bravado played out in the streets. I came to doubt the virtues of intimidation early on. I chose, perhaps even unconsciously, to remain a shadow—timid, but a survivor.

10   The fearsomeness mistakenly attributed to me in public places often has a perilous flavor. The most frightening of these confusions occurred in the late 1970s and early 1980s when I worked as a journalist in Chicago. One day, rushing into the office of a magazine I was writing for with a deadline story in hand, I was mistaken for a burglar. The office manager called security and, with an ad hoc posse, pursued me through the labyrinthine halls, nearly to my editor's door. I had no way

of proving who I was. I could only move briskly toward the company of someone who knew me.

Another time I was on assignment for a local paper and killing 11 time before an interview. I entered a jewelry store on the city's affluent Near North Side. The proprietor excused herself and returned with an enormous red Doberman pinscher straining at the end of a leash. She stood, the dog extended toward me, silent to my questions, her eyes bulging nearly out of her head. I took a cursory look around, nodded, and bade her good night. Relatively speaking, however, I never fared as badly as another black male journalist. He went to nearby Waukegan, Illinois, a couple of summers ago to work on a story about a murderer who was born there. Mistaking the reporter for the killer, police hauled him from his car at gunpoint and but for his press credentials would probably have tried to book him. Such episodes are not uncommon. Black men trade tales like this all the time.

In "My Negro Problem—And Ours," Podhoretz writes that the 12 hatred he feels for blacks makes itself known to him through a variety of avenues—one being his discomfort with that "special brand of paranoid touchiness" to which he says blacks are prone. No doubt he is speaking here of black men. In time, I learned to smother the rage I felt at so often being taken for a criminal. Not to do so would surely have led to madness—via that special "paranoid touchiness" that so annoyed Podhoretz at the time he wrote the essay.

I began to take precautions to make myself less threatening. I 13 move about with care, particularly late in the evening. I give a wide berth to nervous people on subway platforms during the wee hours, particularly when I have exchanged business clothes for jeans. If I happen to be entering a building behind some people who appear skittish, I may walk by, letting them clear the lobby before I return, so as not to seem to be following them. I have been calm and extremely congenial on those rare occasions when I've been pulled over by the police.

And on late-evening constitutionals along streets less traveled by, 14 I employ what has proved to be an excellent tension-reducing measure: I whistle melodies from Beethoven and Vivaldi and the more popular classical composers. Even steely New Yorkers hunching toward nighttime destinations seem to relax, and occasionally they even join in the tune. Virtually everybody seems to sense that a mugger wouldn't be warbling bright, sunny selections from Vivaldi's *Four Seasons*. It is my equivalent of the cowbell that hikers wear when they know they are in bear country.

—— CONSIDERATIONS ——————————————————

1. "Her flight made me feel like an accomplice in tyranny," writes Staples, in paragraph 2, of the young white woman who was frightened by his mere appearance. What "tyranny" is Staples talking about?

2. Why does Staples say that "being perceived as dangerous is a hazard in itself"?

3. What do hikers wearing cowbells in bear country have to do with Staples's techniques for easing tension on his evening walks?

4. Is there any connection between the fear Staples encounters when he meets lone white men or women on the street at night and the fear of the homeless that many middle class people feel? See Peter Marin's essay "Helping and Hating the Homeless."

5. Why was the word "hunching" a good choice in the second sentence of paragraph 14?

*Shelby Steele (b. 1946) teaches English at San Jose State
University in California. He has published essays in*
Commentary, *the* New York Times Magazine, *and the* American
Scholar, *as well as* Harper's, *which printed "I'm Black, You're
White, Who's Innocent?" in 1988. His "On Being Black and
Middle Class" appeared in* The Best Essays of 1989. *In 1990 St.
Martin's Press published* The Recoloring of America, *his first
collection of essays.*

67

SHELBY STEELE

I'm Black, You're White, Who's Innocent?

It is a warm, windless California evening, and the dying light that 1
covers the redbrick patio is tinted pale orange by the day's smog. Eight
of us, not close friends, sit in lawn chairs sipping chardonnay. A black
engineer and I (we had never met before) integrate the group. A psychologist is also among us, and her presence encourages a surprising openness. But not until well after the lovely twilight dinner has been served,
when the sky has turned to deep black and the drinks have long since
changed to scotch, does the subject of race spring awkwardly upon us.
Out of nowhere the engineer announces, with a coloring of accusation
in his voice, that it bothers him to send his daughter to a school where
she is one of only three black children. "I didn't realize my ambition to
get ahead would pull me into a world where my daughter would lose
touch with her blackness," he says.

Over the course of the evening we have talked about money, 2
infidelity, past and present addictions, child abuse, even politics. Inti-
macies have been revealed, fears named. But this subject, race, sinks us
into one of those shaming silences where eye contact terrorizes. Our
host looks for something in the bottom of his glass. Two women stare

Reprinted by permission of the author.

409

into the black sky as if to locate the Big Dipper and point it out to us. Finally, the psychologist seems to gather herself for a challenge, but it is too late. "Oh, I'm sure she'll be just fine," says our hostess, rising from her chair. When she excuses herself to get the coffee, the two sky gazers offer to help.

3   With three of us now gone, I am surprised to see the engineer still silently holding his ground. There is a willfulness in his eyes, an inner pride. He knows he has said something awkward, but he is determined not to give a damn. His unwavering eyes intimidate me. At last the host's head snaps erect. He has an idea. "The hell with coffee," he says. "How about some of the smoothest brandy you ever tasted?" An idea made exciting by the escape it offers. Gratefully we follow him back into the house, quickly drink his brandy, and say our good-byes.

4   An autopsy of this party might read: death induced by an abrupt and lethal injection of the American race issue. An accurate if super-ficial assessment. Since it has been my fate to live a rather integrated life, I have often witnessed sudden deaths like this. The threat of them, if not the reality, is a part of the texture of integration. In the late 1960s, when I was just out of college, I took a delinquent's delight in playing the engineer's role, and actually developed a small reputation for play-ing it well. Those were the days of flagellatory white guilt; it was such great fun to pinion some professor or housewife or, best of all, a large group of remorseful whites, with the knowledge of both their racism and their denial of it. The adolescent impulse to sneer at convention, to startle the middle-aged with doubt, could be indulged under the guise of racial indignation. And how could I lose? My victims—earnest liberals for the most part—could no more crawl out from under my accusations than Joseph K. in Kafka's *Trial* could escape the amorphous charges brought against him. At this odd moment in history the world was aligned to facilitate my immaturity.

5   About a year of this was enough: the guilt that follows most cheap thrills caught up to me, and I put myself in check. But the impulse to do it faded more slowly. It was one of those petty talents that is tied to vanity, and when there were ebbs in my self-esteem the impulse to use it would come alive again. In integrated situations I can still feel the faint itch. But then there are many youthful impulses that still itch, and now, just inside the door of mid-life, this one is least precious to me.

6   In the literature classes I teach, I often see how the presence of whites all but seduces some black students into provocation. When we come to a novel by a black writer, say Toni Morrison, the white students can easily discuss the human motivations of the black charac-

ters. But, inevitably, a black student, as if by reflex, will begin to set in relief the various racial problems that are the background of these characters' lives. The student's tone will carry a reprimand: the class is afraid to confront the reality of racism. Classes cannot be allowed to die like dinner parties, however. My latest strategy is to thank that student for his or her moral vigilance, and then appoint the young man or woman as the class's official racism monitor. But even if I get a laugh—I usually do, but sometimes the student is particularly indignant, and it gets uncomfortable—the strategy never quite works. Our racial division is suddenly drawn in neon. Overcaution spreads like spilled paint. And, in fact, the black student who started it all does become a kind of monitor. The very presence of this student imposes a new accountability on the class.

I think those who provoke this sort of awkwardness are operating out of a black identity that obliges them to badger white people about race almost on principle. Content hardly matters. (For example, it made no sense for the engineer to expect white people to sympathize with his anguish over sending his daughter to school with *white* children.) Race indeed remains a source of white shame; the goal of these provocations is to put whites, no matter how indirectly, in touch with this collective guilt. In other words, these provocations I speak of are *power* moves, little shows of power that try to freeze the "enemy" in self-consciousness. They gratify and inflate the provocateur. They are the underdog's bite. And whites, far more secure in their power, respond with a self-contained and tolerant silence that is, itself, a show of power. What greater power than that of non-response, the power to let a small enemy sizzle in his own juices, to even feel a little sad at his frustration just as one is also complimented by it. Black anger always, in a way, flatters white power. In America, to know that one is not black is to feel an extra grace, a little boost of impunity. 7

I think the real trouble between the races in America is that the races are not just races but competing power groups—a fact that is easily minimized perhaps because it is so obvious. What is not so obvious is that this is true quite apart from the issue of class. Even the well-situated middle-class (or wealthy) black is never completely immune to that peculiar contest of power that his skin color subjects him to. Race is a separate reality in American society, an entity that carries its own potential for power, a mark of fate that class can soften considerably but not eradicate. 8

The distinction of race has always been used in American life to sanction each race's pursuit of power in relation to the other. The allure 9

of race as a human delineation is the very shallowness of the delineation it makes. Onto this shallowness—mere skin and hair—men
can project a false depth, a system of dismal attributions, a series of
malevolent or ignoble stereotypes that skin and hair lack the substance
to contradict. These dark projections then rationalize the pursuit of
power. Your difference from me makes you bad, and your badness
justifies, even demands, my pursuit of power over you—the oldest
formula for aggression known to man. Whenever much importance is
given to race, power is the primary motive.

10   But the human animal almost never pursues power without first
convincing himself that he is *entitled* to it. And this feeling of entitlement has its own precondition: to be entitled one must first believe in
one's innocence, at least in the area where one wishes to be entitled. By
innocence I mean a feeling of essential goodness in relation to others
and, therefore, superiority to others. Our innocence always inflates us
and deflates those we seek power over. Once inflated we are entitled;
we are in fact licensed to go after the power our innocence tells us we
deserve. In this sense, *innocence is power.* Of course, innocence need
not be genuine or real in any objective sense, as the Nazis demonstrated
not long ago. Its only test is whether or not we can convince ourselves
of it.

11   I think the racial struggle in America has always been primarily a
struggle for innocence. White racism from the beginning has been a
claim of white innocence and, therefore, of white entitlement to sub-
jugate blacks. And in the '60s, as went innocence so went power. Blacks
used the innocence that grew out of their long subjugation to seize more
power, while whites lost some of their innocence and so lost a degree of
power over blacks. Both races instinctively understand that to lose
innocence is to lose power (in relation to each other). Now to be innocent someone else must be guilty, a natural law that leads the races to
forge their innocence on each other's backs. The inferiority of the black
always makes the white man superior; the evil might of whites makes
blacks good. This pattern means that both races have a hidden investment in racism and racial disharmony, despite their good intentions to
the contrary. Power defines their relations, and power requires innocence, which, in turn, requires racism and racial division.

12   I believe it was this hidden investment that the engineer was
protecting when he made his remark—the white "evil" he saw in a
white school "depriving" his daughter of her black heritage confirmed
his innocence. Only the logic of power explained this—he bent reality
to show that he was once again a victim of the white world and, as a
victim, innocent. His determined eyes insisted on this. And the whites,

in their silence, no doubt protected their innocence by seeing him as an ungracious troublemaker—his bad behavior underscoring their goodness. I can only guess how he was talked about after the party. But it isn't hard to imagine that his blunder gave everyone a lift. What none of us saw was the underlying game of power and innocence we were trapped in, or how much we needed a racial impasse to play that game.

When I was a boy of about twelve, a white friend of mine told me one day that his uncle, who would be arriving the next day for a visit, was a racist. Excited by the prospect of seeing such a man, I spent the following afternoon hanging around the alley behind my friend's house, watching from a distance as this uncle worked on the engine of his Buick. Yes, here was evil and I was compelled to look upon it. And I saw evil in the sharp angle of his elbow as he pumped his wrench to tighten nuts, I saw it in the blade-sharp crease of his chinos, in the pack of Lucky Strikes that threatened to slip from his shirt pocket as he bent, and in the way his concentration seemed to shut out the human world. He worked neatly and efficiently, wiping his hands constantly, and I decided that evil worked like this.   13

I felt a compulsion to have this man look upon me so that I could see evil—so that I could see the face of it. But when he noticed me standing beside his toolbox, he said only, "If you're looking for Bobby, I think he went up to the school to play baseball." He smiled nicely and went back to work. I was stunned for a moment, but then I realized that evil could be sly as well, could smile when it wanted to trick you.   14

Need, especially hidden need, puts a strong pressure on perception, and my need to have this man embody white evil was stronger than any contravening evidence. As a black person you always hear about racists but never meet any. And I needed to incarnate this odious category of humanity, those people who hated Martin Luther King Jr. and thought blacks should "go slow" or not at all. So, in my mental dictionary, behind the term "white racist," I inserted this man's likeness. I would think of him and say to myself, "There is no reason for him to hate black people. Only evil explains unmotivated hatred." And this thought soothed me; I felt innocent. If I hated white people, which I did not, at least I had a reason. His evil commanded me to assert in the world the goodness he made me confident of in myself.   15

In looking at this man I was *seeing for innocence*—a form of seeing that has more to do with one's hidden need for innocence (and power) than with the person or group one is looking at. It is quite possible, for example, that the man I saw that day was not a racist. He did absolutely   16 nothing in my presence to indicate that he was. I invested an entire afternoon in seeing not the man but in seeing my innocence through the man. *Seeing for innocence* is, in this way, the essence of racism—the use of others as a means to our own goodness and superiority.

17   The loss of innocence has always to do with guilt, Kierkegaard tells us, and it has never been easy for whites to avoid guilt where blacks are concerned. For whites, *seeing for innocence* means seeing themselves and blacks in ways that minimize white guilt. Often this amounts to a kind of white revisionism, as when President Reagan declares himself "colorblind" in matters of race. The President, like many of us, may aspire to racial color blindness, but few would grant that he has yet reached this sublimely guiltless state. The statement clearly revises reality, moves it forward into some heretofore unknown America where all racial determinism will have vanished. I do not think that Ronald Reagan is a racist, as that term is commonly used, but neither do I think that he is capable of seeing color without making attributions, some of which may be negative—nor am I, or anyone else I've ever met.

18   So why make such a statement? I think Reagan's claim of color blindness with regard to race is really a claim of racial innocence and guiltlessness—the preconditions for entitlement and power. This was the claim that grounded Reagan's campaign against special entitlement programs—affirmative action, racial quotas, and so on—that black power had won in the '60s. Color blindness was a strategic assumption of innocence that licensed Reagan's use of government power against black power.

19   I do not object to Reagan's goals in this so much as the presumption of innocence by which he rationalized them. I, too, am strained to defend racial quotas and any affirmative action that supersedes merit. And I believe there is much that Reagan has to offer blacks. His emphasis on traditional American values—individual initiative, self-sufficiency, strong families—offers what I think is the most enduring solution to the demoralization and poverty that continue to widen the gap between blacks and whites in America. Even his de-emphasis of race is reasonable in a society where race only divides. But Reagan's posture of innocence undermines any beneficial interaction he might have with blacks. For blacks instinctively sense that a claim of racial innocence always precedes a power move against them. Reagan's pretense of innocence makes him an adversary, and makes his quite reasonable message seem vindictive. You cannot be innocent of a man's problem and expect him to listen.

I'm convinced that the secret of Reagan's "teflon" coating, his   20
personal popularity apart from his policies and actions, has been his
ability to offer mainstream America a vision of itself as innocent and
entitled (unlike Jimmy Carter, who seemed to offer only guilt and
obligation). Probably his most far-reaching accomplishment has been to
reverse somewhat the pattern by which innocence came to be distributed in the '60s, when outsiders were innocent and insiders were guilty.
Corporations, the middle class, entrepreneurs, the military—all vil-
lains in the '60s—either took on a new innocence in Reagan's vision or
were designated as protectors of innocence. But again, for one man to be
innocent another man must be bad or guilty. Innocence imposes, *de-*
mands, division and conflict, a right/wrong view of the world. And this,
I feel, has led to the underside of Reagan's achievement. His posture of
innocence draws him into a partisanship that undermines the univer-
sality of his values. He can't sell these values to blacks and others
because he has made blacks into the bad guys and outsiders who justify
his power. It is humiliating for a black person to like Reagan because
Reagan's power is so clearly derived from a distribution of innocence
that leaves a black with less of it, and the white man with more.

Black Americans have always had to find a way to handle white   21
society's presumption of racial innocence whenever they have sought
to enter the American mainstream. Louis Armstrong's exaggerated
smile honored the presumed innocence of white society—I will not
bring you your racial guilt if you will let me play my music. Ralph
Ellison calls this "masking"; I call it bargaining. But whatever it's
called, it points to the power of white society to enforce its innocence. I
believe this power is greatly diminished today. Society has reformed
and transformed—Miles Davis never smiles. Nevertheless, this power
has not faded altogether; blacks must still contend with it.

Historically, blacks have handled white society's presumption of   22
innocence in two ways: they have bargained with it, granting white
society its innocence in exchange for entry into the mainstream; or
they have challenged it, holding that innocence hostage until their
demand for entry (or other concessions) was met. A bargainer says, *I*
already believe you are innocent (good, fair-minded) and have faith
that you will prove it. A challenger says, *If you are innocent, then prove*
it. Bargainers *give* in hope of receiving; challengers *withhold* until they
receive. Of course, there is risk in both approaches, but in each case the
black is negotiating his own self-interest against the presumed racial
innocence of the larger society.

Clearly the most visible black bargainer on the American scene   23 today is Bill Cosby. His television show is a perfect formula for black bargaining in the '80s. The remarkable Huxtable family—with its doctor/lawyer parent combination, its drug-free, college-bound children, and its wise yet youthful grandparents—is a blackface version of the American dream. Cosby is a subscriber to the American identity, and his subscription confirms his belief in its fair-mindedness. His vast audience knows this, knows that Cosby will never assault their innocence with racial guilt. Racial controversy is all but banished from the show. The Huxtable family never discusses affirmative action.

24   The bargain Cosby offers his white viewers—I will confirm your racial innocence if you accept me—is a good deal for all concerned. Not only does it allow whites to enjoy Cosby's humor with no loss of innocence, but it actually enhances their innocence by implying that race is not the serious problem for blacks that it once was. If anything, the success of this handsome, affluent black family points to the fair-mindedness of whites who, out of their essential goodness, changed society so that black families like the Huxtables could succeed. Whites can watch *The Cosby Show* and feel complimented on a job well done.

25   The power that black bargainers wield is the power of absolution. On Thursday nights, Cosby, like a priest, absolves his white viewers, forgives and forgets the sins of the past. (Interestingly, Cosby was one of the first blacks last winter to publicly absolve Jimmy the Greek for his well-publicized faux pas about black athletes.) And for this he is rewarded with an almost sacrosanct status. Cosby benefits from what might be called a gratitude factor. His continued number-one rating may have something to do with the (white) public's gratitude at being offered a commodity so rare in our time; he tells his white viewers each week that they are okay, and that this black man is not going to challenge them.

26   When a black bargains, he may invoke the gratitude factor and find himself cherished beyond the measure of his achievement; when he challenges, he may draw the dark projections of whites and become a source of irritation to them. If he moves back and forth between these two options, as I think many blacks do today, he will likely baffle whites. It is difficult for whites to either accept or reject such blacks. It seems to me that Jesse Jackson is such a figure—many whites see Jackson as a challenger by instinct and a bargainer by political ambition. They are uneasy with him, more than a little suspicious. His powerful speech at the 1984 Democratic convention was a masterpiece of bargaining. In it he offered a Kinglike vision of what America could be, a vision that presupposed Americans had the fair-mindedness to

achieve full equality—an offer in hope of a return. A few days after this speech, looking for rest and privacy at a lodge in Big Sur, he and his wife were greeted with standing ovations three times a day when they entered the dining room for meals. So much about Jackson is deeply American—his underdog striving, his irrepressible faith in himself, the daring of his ambition, and even his stubbornness. These qualities point to his underlying faith that Americans can respond to him despite his race, and this faith is a compliment to Americans, an offer of innocence.

But Jackson does not always stick to the terms of his bargain—he is not like Cosby on TV. When he hugs Arafat, smokes cigars with Castro, refuses to repudiate Farrakhan, threatens a boycott of major league baseball, or, more recently, talks of "corporate barracudas," "pension-fund socialism," and "economic violence," he looks like a challenger in bargainer's clothing, and his positions on the issues look like familiar protests dressed in white-paper formality. At these times he appears to be revoking the innocence so much else about him seems to offer. The old activist seems to come out of hiding once again to take white innocence hostage until whites prove they deserve to have it. In his candidacy there is a suggestion of protest, a fierce insistence on his *right* to run, that sends whites a message that he may secretly see them as a good bit less than innocent. His dilemma is to appear the bargainer while his campaign itself seems to be a challenge.   27

There are, of course, other problems that hamper Jackson's bid for the Democratic presidential nomination. He has held no elective office, he is thought too flamboyant and opportunistic by many, there are rather loud whispers of "character" problems. As an individual he may not be the best test of a black man's chances for winning so high an office. Still, I believe it is the aura of challenge surrounding him that hurts him most. Whether it is right or wrong, fair or unfair, I think no black candidate will have a serious chance at his party's nomination, much less the presidency, until he can convince white Americans that he can be trusted to preserve *their* sense of racial innocence. Such a candidate will have to use his power of absolution; he will have to flatly forgive and forget. He will have to bargain with white innocence out of a genuine belief that it really exists. There can be no faking it. He will have to offer a vision that is passionately raceless, a vision that strongly condemns any form of racial politics. This will require the most courageous kind of leadership, leadership that asks all the people to meet a new standard.   28

Now the other side of American's racial impasse: How do blacks lay claim to their racial innocence?   29

30   The most obvious and unarguable source of black innocence is the victimization that blacks endured for centuries at the hands of a race that insisted on black inferiority as a means to its own innocence and power. Like all victims, what blacks lost in power they gained in innocence—innocence that, in turn, entitled them to pursue power. This was the innocence that fueled the civil rights movement of the '60s, and that gave blacks their first real power in American life— victimization metamorphosed into power via innocence. But this formula carries a drawback that I believe is virtually as devastating to blacks today as victimization once was. It is a formula that binds the victim to his victimization by linking his power to his status as a victim. And this, I'm convinced, is the tragedy of black power in America today. It is primarily a victim's power, grounded too deeply in the entitlement derived from past injustice and in the innocence that Western/Christian tradition has always associated with poverty.

31   Whatever gains this power brings in the short run through political action, it undermines in the long run. Social victims may be collectively entitled, but they are all too often individually demoralized. Since the social victim has been oppressed by society, he comes to feel that his individual life will be improved more by changes *in* society than by his own initiative. Without realizing it, he makes society rather than himself the agent of change. The power he finds in his victimization may lead him to collective action against society, but it also encourages passivity within the sphere of his personal life.

32   This past summer I saw a television documentary that examined life in Detroit's inner city on the twentieth anniversary of the riots there in which forty-three people were killed. A comparison of the inner city then and now showed a decline in the quality of life. Residents feel less safe than they did twenty years ago, drug trafficking is far worse, crimes by blacks against blacks are more frequent, housing remains substandard, and the teenage pregnancy rate has skyrocketed. Twenty years of decline and demoralization, even as opportunities for blacks to better themselves have increased. This paradox is not peculiar to Detroit. By many measures, the majority of blacks—those not yet in the middle class—are further behind whites today than before the victories of the civil rights movement. But there is a reluctance among blacks to examine this paradox, I think, because it suggests that racial victimization is not our real problem. If conditions have worsened for most of us as racism has receded, then much of the problem must be of our own making. But to fully admit this would cause us to lose the innocence we derive from our victimization. And we would jeopardize the entitlement we've always had to challenge society. We are in the odd and

self-defeating position where taking responsibility for bettering ourselves feels like a surrender to white power.

So we have a hidden investment in victimization and poverty. These distressing conditions have been the source of our only real power, and there is an unconscious sort of gravitation toward them, a complaining celebration of them. One sees evidence of this in the near happiness with which certain black leaders recount the horror of Howard Beach and other recent (and I think over-celebrated) instances of racial tension. As one is saddened by these tragic events, one is also repelled at the way some black leaders—agitated to near hysteria by the scent of victim-power inherent in them—leap forward to exploit them as evidence of black innocence and white guilt. It is as though they sense the decline of black victimization as a loss of standing and dive into the middle of these incidents as if they were reservoirs of pure black innocence swollen with potential power.

Seeing for innocence pressures blacks to focus on racism and to neglect the individual initiative that would deliver them from poverty—the only thing that finally delivers anyone from poverty. With our eyes on innocence we see racism everywhere and miss opportunity even as we stumble over it. About 70 percent of black students at my university drop out before graduating—a flight from opportunity that racism cannot explain. It is an injustice that whites can *see for innocence* with more impunity than blacks can. The price whites pay is a certain blindness to themselves. Moreover, for whites *seeing for innocence* continues to engender the bad faith of a long-disgruntled minority. But the price blacks pay is an ever-escalating poverty that threatens to make the worst off of them a permanent underclass. Not fair, but real.

Challenging works best for the collective, while bargaining is more the individual's suit. From this point on, the race's advancement will come from the efforts of its individuals. True, some challenging will be necessary for a long time to come. But bargaining is now—today—a way for the black individual to *join* the larger society, to make a place for himself or herself.

"Innocence is ignorance," Kierkegaard says, and if this is so, the claim of innocence amounts to an insistence on ignorance, a refusal to know. In their assertions of innocence both races carve out very functional areas of ignorance for themselves—territories of blindness that license a misguided pursuit of power. Whites gain superiority by *not* knowing blacks; blacks gain entitlement by *not* seeing their own responsibility for bettering themselves. The power each race seeks in relation to the other is grounded in a double-edged ignorance, ignorance of the self as well as the other.

37   The original sin that brought us to an impasse at the dinner party I mentioned at the outset occurred centuries ago, when it was first decided to exploit racial difference as a means to power. It was the determinism that flowed karmically from this sin that dropped over us like a net that night. What bothered me most was our helplessness. Even the engineer did not know how to go forward. His challenge hadn't worked, and he'd lost the option to bargain. The marriage of race and power depersonalized us, changed us from eight people to six whites and two blacks. The easiest thing was to let silence blanket our situation, our impasse.

38   I think the civil rights movement in its early and middle years offered the best way out of America's racial impasse: in this society, race must not be a source of advantage or disadvantage for anyone. This is fundamentally a *moral* position, one that seeks to breach the corrupt union of race and power with principles of fairness and human equality: if all men are created equal, then racial difference cannot sanction power. The civil rights movement was conceived for no other reason than to redress that corrupt union, and its guiding insight was that only a moral power based on enduring principles of justice, equality, and freedom could offset the lower impulse in man to exploit race as a means to power. Three hundred years of suffering had driven the point home, and in Montgomery, Little Rock, and Selma, racial power was the enemy and moral power the weapon.

39   An important difference between genuine and presumed innocence, I believe, is that the former must be earned through sacrifice, while the latter is unearned and only veils the quest for privilege. And there was much sacrifice in the early civil rights movement. The Gandhian principle of non-violent resistance that gave the movement a spiritual center as well as a method of protest demanded sacrifice, a passive offering of the self in the name of justice. A price was paid in terror and lost life, and from this sacrifice came a hard-earned innocence and a credible moral power.

40   Non-violent passive resistance is a bargainer's strategy. It assumes the power that is the object of the protest has the genuine innocence to morally respond, and puts the protesters at the mercy of that innocence. I think this movement won so many concessions precisely because of its belief in the capacity of whites to be moral. It did not so much demand that whites change as offer them relentlessly the opportunity to live by their own morality—to attain a true innocence based on the sacrifice of their racial privilege, rather than a false innocence based on

presumed racial superiority. Blacks always bargain with or challenge the larger society; but I believe that in the early civil rights years, these forms of negotiation achieved a degree of integrity and genuineness never seen before or since.

In the mid-'60s all this changed. Suddenly a sharp *racial* con-   41
sciousness emerged to compete with the moral consciousness that had defined the movement to that point. Whites were no longer welcome in the movement, and a vocal "black power" minority gained dramatic visibility. Increasingly, the movement began to seek racial as well as moral power, and thus it fell into a fundamental contradiction that plagues it to this day. Moral power precludes racial power by denounc-ing race as a means to power. Now suddenly the movement itself was using race as a means to power, and thereby affirming the very union of race and power it was born to redress. In the end, black power can claim no higher moral standing than white power.

It makes no sense to say this shouldn't have happened. The sacri-   42
fices that moral power demands are difficult to sustain, and it was inevitable that blacks would tire of these sacrifices and seek a more earthly power. Nevertheless, a loss of genuine innocence and moral power followed. The movement, splintered by a burst of racial mili-tancy in the late '60s, lost its hold on the American conscience and descended more and more to the level of secular, interest-group politics. Bargaining and challenging once again became racial rather than moral negotiations.

You hear it asked, why are there no Martin Luther Kings around   43
today? I think one reason is that there are no black leaders willing to resist the seductions of racial power, or to make the sacrifices moral power requires. King understood that racial power subverts moral power, and he pushed the principles of fairness and equality rather than black power because he believed those principles would bring blacks their most complete liberation. He sacrificed race for morality, and his innocence was made genuine by that sacrifice. What made King the most powerful and extraordinary black leader of this century was not his race but his morality.

Black power is a challenge. It grants whites no innocence; it denies   44
their moral capacity and then demands that they be moral. No power can long insist on itself without evoking an opposing power. Doesn't an insistence on black power call up white power? (And could this have something to do with what many are now calling a resurgence of white racism?) I believe that what divided the races at the dinner party I attended, and what divides them in the nation, can only be bridged by an adherence to those moral principles that disallow race as a source of

power, privilege, status, or entitlement of any kind. In our age, principles like fairness and equality are ill-defined and all but drowned in relativity. But this is the fault of people, not principles. We keep them muddied because they are the greatest threat to our presumed innocence and our selective ignorance. Moral principles, even when somewhat ambiguous, have the power to assign responsibility and therefore to provide us with knowledge. At the dinner party we were afraid of so severe an accountability.

45   What both black and white Americans fear are the sacrifices and risks that true racial harmony demands. This fear is the measure of our racial chasm. And though fear always seeks a thousand justifications, none is ever good enough, and the problems we run from only remain to haunt us. It would be right to suggest courage as an antidote to fear, but the glory of the word might only intimidate us into more fear. I prefer the word effort—relentless effort, moral effort. What I like most about this word are its connotations of everydayness, earnestness, and practical sacrifice. No matter how badly it might have gone for us that warm summer night, we should have talked. We should have made the effort.

———— CONSIDERATIONS ————————————————

1. "It was one of those petty talents that is tied to vanity, and when there were ebbs in my self-esteem the impulse to use it would come alive again," writes Steele in paragraph 5. What petty talent is he talking about, and what other similar "talents" can you think of?

2. In paragraph 17, Steele writes, "I do not think that Ronald Reagan is a racist, as that term is commonly used, but neither do I think that he is capable of seeing color without making attributions, some of which may be negative— nor am I, or anyone else I've ever met." Read Brent Staples's short report of his experiences in "Just Walk On By" and decide whether or not he would agree with Steele.

3. In his lengthy discussion of the racial struggle for innocence, beginning with the first sentence of paragraph 11, how does Steele make use of two well-known but different black figures?

4. How does Steele's essay become more than a superficial glance at the racial problems of the United States?

5. How does Steele explain his belief that black power is "the enemy," but moral power is "the weapon" in the blacks' fight for equality?

6. To what extent does Steele employ comparison and contrast in organizing his materials?

7. How could Steele justify devoting his first three paragraphs to a dinner party?

Peter Steinhart (b. 1943) has always lived in California, where he makes his living as a freelance writer. For ten years he has written a column for Audubon Magazine, *and he has published a book—*Tracks in the Sky *(1987)—about wildlife on wetlands inland from the Pacific.*

68

PETER STEINHART
The Old Curiosity

Every now and then, you look up from your wool-braiding and find that you are in a different world. It doesn't happen very often, but it happens. Twice, I have been jogging down country roads and looked up to see a coyote jogging alongside me. It made me feel uncertain of my place in life. I thought perhaps here was some cosmic process server, come with sly grin and pale predatory eyes to laugh at me as I blundered through a seam in the web of time. The alarm lasted an instant, long enough to make me feel the rules had changed. Then, heat kindled across our gazes and the old enmity fell over the encounter. We peeped at each other through pines and manzanitas and then the coyote trotted off, leaving me alone and out of tune. 1

Coyotes seem designed just for such vexing encounters. Coyotes seem to reflect a deep sadness. They move through life like a dispossessed race—hurried, heads low, eyes darting nervously over the landscape, as if expecting a terrible vengeance to strike from ambush. At night they howl in pained and eerie voices, filling the air with lament and hysteria. Our own human disconsolation is there—and more. Beset as they are, coyotes seem knowing—as if, given a wrinkle in time, they could tell us the cause of their sorrows. It might be one of the great secrets. There is a mystery to coyotes as beguiling as the blinking of strange lights in a clear blue sky. It draws me into the night. 2

Several times, I have sat in a mountain meadow late at night while 3 all around me coyotes yipped and shrilled. The noise ran up my spine like mice. Now and then a tawny shadow flitted by. I knew the conclave was the kind of riddle eyes cannot unravel. The thoughts of coyotes would speak, if at all, to the heart and not to the mind. So, I thought, it made more sense to sit among them at night, when the light of reason has faded. If I sat long enough, perhaps I would be asked to tea or offered a trial membership in the group. Perhaps comprehension would drift to me on the vapors of the night air.

4   I confess I have learned nothing of coyotes by sitting up nights with them. I have never understood a word of their gossip or seen them without masks. But my vigils with them have always been exhilarating and memorable. There is something about being out alone with the vast energy and activity of night that fills one's senses and alters one's stature.

5   At such moments, a different part of the mind takes over. We are equipped with two curiosities. One browses through books and calibrates the intervals of time. It is a curiosity about the precise and tangible nature of our world, and it seeks to find the height and texture of the walls immediately around us. It makes us shrewd bankers, politicians, and engineers. But the other is a rarer and older form. It is not a matter of books and calculations, of bending twigs and weighing stones. It is rather a testing of one's own fitness by immersion. Every now and then, something impels us to shut our eyes and leap into the unknown —just to see if we're dressed right for it. The verdict we seek is a blend of thought and feeling. It is something like what an athlete indulges in when he performs beyond his own accepted limits. You jump into the water to see if you float, step outside your refuge, take the lion by the ear, embark upon the adventure.

6   I believe the second curiosity is that of our ancient forebears, of men with lower brows and higher imaginations. I believe this curiosity was born at a time when we felt less confident of the rules, when death and uncertainty came easier into our lives. When, as hunters, we searched the heart and bone and blood of prey, hoping to see how liveliness sneaked in and out of it. When we ventured into new forests and onto unpeopled plains. Such a life made men fearful, reverent, perhaps as harried and nervous and speculative as the coyote, which loses half its yearly population to starvation, inexperience, and bad motives. And I suspect that the old curiosity resides in some other part of our minds than the newer and more cogitative curiosity.

7   Reason has in modern times raised walls of order around us and clothed us in sturdier garments of fact and formula. We are no longer

hunters. Our minds crank out axioms and equations where they once struggled to form questions and tell stories. Our curiosity is different, too. The ancient Apocrypha cautioned, "Be not curious in unnecessary matters, for more things are showed unto thee than men understand." Today, we fear not discovery, but the loss of curiosity. "Life was meant to be lived, and curiosity must be kept alive," we are often told. What we fear to lose today is the feeling that goes with knowing.

That kind of curiosity is alive in children, who cannot separate   8 delight from comprehension. "In youth, before I lost any of my senses, I can remember that I was all alive, and inhabited my body with inexpressible satisfaction," wrote Thoreau. It is the curse of growing up that we lose that satisfaction. Aging is not just a matter of impaired hearing and dimmed vision. It is an impairment of that old curiosity. And as city dwellers we age faster. We invest our senses in order and wear ruts in the concrete because the city is full of novelty and, if we are to accomplish anything at all, we must shut out the distractions. We establish a routine in which our children can find trust and we can find calm. We shut the door to mystery so that we may not have to think.

Even where we boast that life is full of sound and color, we learn to   9 quiet it. California has so much novelty that it overwhelms a newcomer. It has Tahitian houses and Romanesque prisons, bankpaled cowboys and rhinestone Communists, orientals from the dim past and monks from centuries yet unborn. Not long ago, on Spring Street in Los Angeles, I saw a man walking a shoe box on a string, talking to it as if it were a miniature poodle. Nearby, a seven-foot-tall stalk of corn grew out of the sidewalk, defying aridity and the rush of pedestrians. I knew that if I lived there, I would not have looked twice at such things. California has so much novelty that you must grow numb to it. Your senses, already blunted by smoke and noise, the blur of fads, and the glare of artificial lights, yield to your longing for security and quiet. You go blind. It helps you to find your way.

But we can still exercise that old faculty. If we enter an unfamiliar   10 realm, our senses return. Edward Abbey's blossomed in Arches National Park. "A weird, lovely, fantastic object out of nature," he wrote, "has the curious ability to remind us that *out there* is a different world, older and greater and deeper by far than ours . . . For a little while, we are again able to see, as the child sees, a world of marvels."

It we can't travel, we can, nevertheless, change the scene. If we   11 deprive ourselves of the familiar light, open our ears and noses and activate an older part of the brain, the older curiosity comes to life. We do this naturally at night. Perhaps at such times we are more like the way we were in the infancy of our race. We are more emotional then, more given to love, dreams, and terror. Our heart rates, blood chemistry, and brain waves all change at night. We act like other beings.

12   As a youth, I would sneak out of the house after midnight and roam the streets alone, hiding from dog walkers and insomniacs, feeling terror, flight, and triumph. It was as if I were playing an ancient hunting game, the rules of which were locked away in the dusty vaults of the inherited mind. There were new scents riding the night air and in the dark they fired sparks from mind to heart and muscle and blood. The night air carried memories of skunk in passage, the wake of anguish trailing an overworked man, the rumor of a woman's perfume. It was new and delicious. I had entered uncharted latitudes. As I grew older and the challenges of life moved to the city, I walked into Harlem on Saturday nights, chiding myself for taking fruitless risks.

13   But they weren't fruitless. They were expressions of that old curiosity. They were essays of that keen liveliness of which men are, in the age of materials and convenience, less and less capable. They told me that men are most alive when they are engaged and when they are, like the coyote, a little lean, a little harried, pressed enough by circumstance to keep their ears and eyes open.

14   In our urban age, we spend a lot of time trying to restore our senses and re-establish that old link between heart and mind. There are yet people in this world who can hear the songs of moths or see the planet Venus at noon, and they astonish us. They make us want to open our senses to the wider world. And I suspect that the flickering awareness of our outside lives we call the environmental movement has as much to do with our longing to restore the senses as it does with the emergence of ecology as a science. A decade ago, the long-enforced concentration upon common purpose imposed by the Great Depression, World War II, and the Cold War burst like the tired sod of an old earthen dam. What flowed out was an age of curiosity. We pried into the riddles of the moon, the roots of injustice, and the mysteries of drugs and ecstasy. And we looked deeply into nature, unraveling the flow of thought and energy and purpose in the lives of elephants and ants.

15   Not since our hunting days have we looked so hard at nature. And the viewing has stirred strong feelings, for that old curiosity is tuned to nature, just as our eyes are tuned to sunlight, our blood to the chemistry of salt, and our skin to the solvency of water. Our eyes and ears were shaped in the precultural world. Culture has given the world a quantitative, rather than a qualitative, finish. Few men feel individualized by it,

and few can find in it tests of their own stature. Culture is a blind tailor, oblivious of the sags and bulges of an imperfect fit. Biology is more experienced in its craft and has a better eye for the shape of the individual. We still look to nature for tests of our own fitness.

But in the urban age, it becomes harder to find natural objects and   16
harder still to focus our attention upon them. That sends us outdoors and away from cities. One day you look up and see the sky full of swallows or the sea churning with dolphins, and something overturns inside you. You want, suddenly, to be a part of what you see.

For that reason, a largely unmet fraternity of us walk at night. We   17
throw away the light of day and seek instead the rewards that travel over older nerve fibers. The habit turns up in odd places. Dickens walked the streets of London all night. Proust wrote only at night, and then dressed in a special white robe. Thoreau walked at night because by dark "there is less of man in the world." There are many others. For example, ecologist Walter Howard.

Howard is also interested in coyotes. He keeps several dozen of   18
them at a research facility at the University of California at Davis. But his interest in coyotes is more technical than mine. He specializes in vertebrate pest control and has traveled all over the world devising elegant ways to eliminate rats, squirrels, vampire bats, depredating mice, uninvited elephants, and coyotes. His detractors among environmental groups have accused him of being a kind of ecological Dr. Strangelove. And, indeed, Howard has a bristling distrust of nature's motives. "There is no such thing as leaving it to nature," he says. "Nature will destroy our food crops and landscapes. If we lost thousands of vertebrate species tomorrow, man would probably be far better off economically."

But then, he begins to talk of a recent trip to India to consult with   19
officials in Kanha National Park. And he mentions that at night, while the others slept, he went out alone afoot into the forest, listening to the shrieking of langurs, the barking of deer, the moaning of bats, and the coughing of tigers. There is a new warmth and ease to Howard as he describes these walks, and he is almost embarrassed about it. "Every rock and bush you'd think was a tiger or a leopard," he confesses. "But walking out there in the forest at night was exciting."

I knew exactly what he meant. He was not out there intellectu-   20
alizing or rationalizing anything. He was living through his senses. His heart and mind were joined. He was supremely alert and alive. He had shed the skin of calculation and opened the vents of the old curiosity.

CONSIDERATIONS

1. Why does Steinhart devote his first four paragraphs to an experience that taught him nothing?

2. How does Steinhart's interest in coyotes differ from that of his friend, Walter Howard, the ecologist?

3. What does Steinhart suggest, in lieu of traveling, as a means of restoring a childlike wonder and curiosity?

4. How does living in a modern city impair the old curiosity?

5. Do you find it odd that this writer, a scientist himself, urges us to reclaim mystery?

Jonathan Swift (1667–1745), the author of Gulliver's Travels, *was a priest, a poet, and a master of English prose. Some of his strongest satire took the form of reasonable defense of the unthinkable, like his argument in favor of abolishing Christianity in the British Isles. Born in Dublin, he was angry all his life at England's misuse and mistreatment of the subject Irish people. In 1729, he made this modest proposal for solving the Irish problem.*

69

JONATHAN SWIFT
A Modest Proposal

FOR PREVENTING THE CHILDREN OF POOR PEOPLE IN IRELAND
FROM BEING A BURDEN TO THEIR PARENTS OR COUNTRY,
AND FOR MAKING THEM BENEFICIAL TO THE PUBLIC

It is a melancholy object to those who walk through this great 1
town or travel in the country, when they see the streets, the roads, and
cabin doors, crowded with beggars of the female sex, followed by three,
four, or six children, all in rags and importuning every passenger for an
alms. These mothers, instead of being able to work for their honest
livelihood, are forced to employ all their time in strolling to beg sustenance for their helpless infants, who, as they grow up, either turn
thieves for want of work, or leave their dear native country to fight for
the Pretender in Spain, or sell themselves to the Barbadoes.

I think it is agreed by all parties that this prodigious number of 2
children in the arms, or on the backs, or at the heels of their mothers
and frequently of their fathers, is in the present deplorable state of the
kingdom a very great additional grievance; and therefore whoever could
find out a fair, cheap, and easy method of making these children sound
useful members of the commonwealth would deserve so well of the
public as to have his statue set up for a preserver of the nation.

But my intention is very far from being confined to provide only 3
for the children of professed beggars; it is of a much greater extent, and

429

shall take in the whole number of infants at a certain age who are born of parents in effect as little able to support them as those who demand our charity in the streets.

4   As to my own part, having turned my thoughts for many years upon this important subject, and maturely weighed the several schemes of other projectors, I have always found them grossly mistaken in their computation. It is true, a child just dropped from its dam may be supported by her milk for a solar year, with little other nourishment; at most not above the value of two shillings, which the mother may certainly get, or the value in scraps, by her lawful occupation of begging; and it is exactly at one year old that I propose to provide for them in such a manner as instead of being a charge upon their parents or the parish, or wanting food and raiment for the rest of their lives, they shall on the contrary contribute to the feeding, and partly to the clothing, of many thousands.

5   There is likewise another great advantage in my scheme, that it will prevent those voluntary abortions, and that horrid practice of women murdering their bastard children, alas, too frequent among us, sacrificing the poor innocent babes, I doubt, more to avoid the expense than the shame, which would move tears and pity in the most savage and inhuman breast.

6   The number of souls in this kingdom being usually reckoned one million and a half, of these I calculate there may be about two hundred thousand couples whose wives are breeders; from which number I subtract thirty thousand couples who are able to maintain their own children, although I apprehend there cannot be so many under the present distress of the kingdom; but this being granted, there will remain an hundred and seventy thousand breeders. I again subtract fifty thousand for those women who miscarry, or whose children die by accident or disease within the year. There only remain an hundred and twenty thousand children of poor parents actually born. The question therefore is, how this number shall be reared and provided for, which, as I have already said, under the present situation of affairs, is utterly impossible by all the methods hitherto proposed. For we can neither employ them in handicraft or agriculture; we neither build houses (I mean in the country) nor cultivate land. They can very seldom pick up a livelihood by stealing till they arrive at six years old, except where they are of towardly parts; although I confess they learn the rudiments much earlier, during which time they can however be looked upon only as probationers, as I have been informed by a principal gentleman in the country of Cavan, who protested to me that he never knew above one or

two instances under the age of six, even in a part of the kingdom so renowned for the quickest proficiency in that art.

I am assured by our merchants that a boy or a girl before twelve 7 years old is no salable commodity; and even when they come to this age they will not yield above three pounds, or three pounds and half a crown at most on the Exchange; which cannot turn to account either to the parents or the kingdom, the charge of nutriment and rags having been at least four times that value.

I shall now therefore humbly propose my own thoughts, which I 8 hope will not be liable to the least objection.

I have been assured by a very knowing American of my ac- 9 quaintance in London, that a young healthy child well nursed is at a year old a most delicious, nourishing, and wholesome food, whether stewed, roasted, baked, or boiled; and I make no doubt that it will equally serve in a fricassee or a ragout.

I do therefore humbly offer it to public consideration that of the 10 hundred and twenty thousand children, already computed, twenty thousand may be reserved for breed, whereof only one fourth part to be males, which is more than we allow to sheep, black cattle, or swine; and my reason is that these children are seldom the fruits of marriage, a circumstance not much regarded by our savages, therefore one male will be sufficient to serve four females. That the remaining hundred thousand may at a year old be offered in sale to the persons of quality and fortune through the kingdom, always advising the mother to let them suck plentifully in the last month, so as to render them plump and fat for a good table. A child will make two dishes at an entertainment for friends; and when the family dines alone, the fore or hind quarter will make a reasonable dish, and seasoned with a little pepper or salt will be very good boiled on the fourth day, especially in the winter.

I have reckoned upon a medium that a child just born will weigh 11 twelve pounds, and in a solar year if tolerably nursed increaseth to twenty-eight pounds.

I grant this food will be somewhat dear, and therefore very proper 12 for landlords, who, as they have already devoured most of the parents, seem to have the best title to the children.

Infant's flesh will be in season throughout the year, but more 13 plentiful in March, and a little before and after. For we are told by a grave author, an eminent French physician, that fish being a prolific diet, there are more children born in Roman Catholic countries about nine months after Lent than at any other season; therefore, reckoning a year after Lent, the markets will be more glutted than usual, because the number of popish infants is at least three to one in this kingdom; and therefore it will have one other collateral advantage, by lessening the number of Papists among us.

14   I have already computed the charge of nursing a beggar's child (in which list I reckon all cottagers, laborers, and four fifths of the farmers) to be about two shillings per annum, rags included; and I believe no gentleman would repine to give ten shillings for the carcass of a good fat child, which, as I have said, will make four dishes of excellent nutritive meat, when he hath only some particular friend or his own family to dine with him. Thus the squire will learn to be a good landlord, and grow popular among the tenants; the mother will have eight shillings net profit, and be fit for work till she produces another child.

15   Those who are more thrifty (as I must confess the times require) may flay the carcass; the skin of which artificially dressed will make admirable gloves for ladies, and summer boots for fine gentlemen.

16   As to our city of Dublin, shambles may be appointed for this purpose in the most convenient parts of it, and butchers we may be assured will not be wanting; although I rather recommend buying the children alive, and dressing them hot from the knife as we do roasting pigs.

17   A very worthy person, a true lover of his country, and whose virtues I highly esteem, was lately pleased in discoursing on this matter to offer a refinement upon my scheme. He said that many gentlemen of his kingdom, having of late destroyed their deer, he conceived that the want of venison might be well supplied by the bodies of young lads and maidens, not exceeding fourteen years of age nor under twelve, so great a number of both sexes in every county being now ready to starve for want of work and service; and these to be disposed of by their parents, if alive, or otherwise by their nearest relations. But with due deference to so excellent a friend and so deserving a patriot, I cannot be altogether in his sentiments; for as to the males, my American acquaintance assured me from frequent experience that their flesh was generally tough and lean, like that of our schoolboys, by continual exercise, and their taste disagreeable; and to fatten them would not answer the charge. Then as to the females, it would, I think with humble submission, be a loss to the public, because they soon would become breeders themselves: and besides, it is not improbable that some scrupulous people might be apt to censure such a practice (although indeed very unjustly) as a little bordering upon cruelty; which, I confess, hath always been with me the strongest objection against any project, how well soever intended.

18   But in order to justify my friend, he confessed that this expedient

was put into his head by the famous Psalmanazar, a native of the island Formosa, who came from thence to London above twenty years ago, and in conversation told my friend that in his country when any young person happened to be put to death, the executioner sold the carcass to persons of quality as a prime dainty; and that in his time the body of a plump girl of fifteen, who was crucified for an attempt to poison the emperor, was sold to his Imperial Majesty's prime minister of state, and other great mandarins of the court, in joints from the gibbet, at four hundred crowns. Neither indeed can I deny that if the same use were made of several plump young girls in this town, who without one single groat to their fortunes cannot stir abroad without a chair, and appear at the playhouse and assemblies in foreign fineries which they never will pay for, the kingdom would not be the worse.

Some persons of a desponding spirit are in great concern about that 19 vast number of poor people who are aged, diseased, or maimed, and I have been desired to employ my thoughts what course may be taken to ease the nation of so grievous an encumbrance. But I am not in the least pain upon that matter, because it is very well known that they are every day dying and rotting by cold and famine, and filth and vermin, as fast as can be reasonably expected. And as to the younger laborers, they are now in almost as hopeful a condition. They cannot get work, and consequently pine away for want of nourishment to a degree that if at any time they are accidentally hired to common labor, they have not strength to perform it; and thus the country and themselves are happily delivered from the evils to come.

I have too long digressed, and therefore shall return to my subject. I 20 think the advantages by the proposal which I have made are obvious and many, as well as of the highest importance.

For first, as I have already observed, it would greatly lessen the 21 number of Papists, with whom we are yearly overrun, being the principal breeders of the nation as well as our most dangerous enemies; and who stay at home on purpose to deliver the kingdom to the Pretender, hoping to take their advantage by the absence of so many good Protestants, who have chosen rather to leave their country than to stay at home and pay tithes against their conscience to an Episcopal curate.

Secondly, the poorer tenants will have something valuable of their 22 own, which by law may be made liable to distress, and help to pay their landlord's rent, their corn and cattle being already seized and money a thing unknown.

Thirdly, whereas the maintenance of an hundred thousand chil- 23 dren, from two years old and upwards, cannot be computed at less than ten shillings a piece per annum, the nation's stock will be thereby increased fifty thousand pounds per annum, besides the profit of a new dish introduced to the tables of all gentlemen of fortune in the kingdom who have any refinement in taste. And the money will circulate among ourselves, the goods being entirely of our own growth and manufacture.

24   Fourthly, the constant breeders, besides the gain of eight shillings sterling per annum by the sale of their children, will be rid of the charge of maintaining them after the first year.

25   Fifthly, this food would likewise bring great custom to taverns, where the vintners will certainly be so prudent as to procure the best receipts for dressing it to perfection, and consequently have their houses frequented by all the fine gentlemen, who justly value themselves upon their knowledge in good eating; and a skillful cook, who understands how to oblige his guests, will contrive to make it as expensive as they please.

26   Sixthly, this would be a great inducement to marriage, which all wise nations have either encouraged by rewards or enforced by laws and penalties. It would increase the care and tenderness of mothers toward their children, when they were sure of a settlement for life to the poor babes, provided in some sort by the public, to their annual profit instead of expense. We should see an honest emulation among the married women, which of them could bring the fattest child to the market. Men would become as fond of their wives during the time of their pregnancy as they are now of their mares in foal, their cows in calf, or sows when they are ready to farrow; nor offer to beat or kick them (as is too frequent a practice) for fear of a miscarriage.

27   Many other advantages might be enumerated. For instance, the addition of some thousand carcasses in our exportation of barreled beef, the propagation of swine's flesh, and improvements in the art of making good bacon, so much wanted among us by the great destruction of pigs, too frequent at our tables, which are no way comparable in taste or magnificence to a well-grown, fat, yearling child, which roasted whole will make a considerable figure at a lord mayor's feast or any other public entertainment. But this and many others I omit, being studious of brevity.

28   Supposing that one thousand families in this city would be constant customers for infants' flesh, besides others who might have it at merry meetings, particularly weddings and christenings, I compute that Dublin would take off annually about twenty thousand carcasses, and the rest of the kingdom (where probably they will be sold somewhat cheaper) the remaining eighty thousand.

I can think of no one objection that will possibly be raised against   29
this proposal, unless it should be urged that the number of people will
be thereby much lessened in the kingdom. This I freely own, and it was
indeed one principal design in offering it to the world. I desire the reader
will observe, that I calculate my remedy for this one individual kingdom of Ireland and for no other that ever was, is, or I think ever can be
upon earth. Therefore let no man talk to me of other expedients: of
taxing our absentees at five shillings a pound: of using neither clothes
nor household furniture except what is of our own growth and manufacture; of utterly rejecting the materials and instruments that promote
foreign luxury: of curing the expensiveness of pride, vanity, idleness,
and gaming in our women: of introducing a vein of parsimony,
prudence, and temperance: of learning to love our country, in the want
of which we differ even from Laplanders and the inhabitants of To-
pinamboo: of quitting our animosities and factions, nor acting any
longer like the Jews, who were murdering one another at the very
moment their city was taken: of being a little cautious not to sell our
country and conscience for nothing: of teaching landlords to have at
least one degree of mercy toward their tenants: lastly, of putting a spirit
of honesty, industry, and skill into our shopkeepers; who, if a resolution
could now be taken to buy only our native goods, would immediately
unite to cheat and exact upon us in the price, the measure, and the
goodness, nor could ever yet be brought to make one fair proposal of just
dealing, though often and earnestly invited to it.

Therefore, I repeat, let no man talk to me of these and the like   30
expedients, till he hath at least some glimpse of hope that there will
ever be some hearty and sincere attempt to put them in practice.

But as to myself, having been wearied out for many years with   31
offering vain, idle, visionary thoughts, and at length utterly despairing
of success, I fortunately fell upon this proposal, which, as it is wholly
new, so it hath something solid and real, of no expense and little
trouble, full in our own power, and whereby we can incur no danger in
disobliging England. For this kind of commodity will not bear exportation, the flesh being of too tender a consistence to admit a long
continuance in salt, although perhaps I could name a country which
would be glad to eat up our whole nation without it.

After all, I am not so violently bent upon my own opinions as to   32
reject any offer proposed by wise men, which shall be found equally
innocent, cheap, easy, and effectual. But before something of that kind
shall be advanced in contradiction to my scheme, and offering a better, I
desire the author or authors will be pleased maturely to consider two

points. First, as things now stand, how they will be able to find food and raiment for an hundred thousand useless mouths and backs. And secondly, there being a round million of creatures in human figure throughout this kingdom, whose sole subsistence put into a common stock would leave them in debt two millions of pounds sterling, adding those who are beggars by profession to the bulk of farmers, cottagers, and laborers, with their wives and children who are beggars in effect; I desire those politicians who dislike my overture, and may perhaps be so bold to attempt an answer, that they will first ask the parents of these mortals whether they would not at this day think it a great happiness to have been sold for food at a year old in this manner I prescribe, and thereby have avoided such a perpetual scene of misfortunes as they have since gone through by the oppression of landlords, the impossibility of paying rent without money or trade, the want of common sustenance, with neither house nor clothes to cover them from the inclemencies of the weather, and the most inevitable prospect of entailing the like or greater miseries upon their breed forever.

33   I profess, in the sincerity of my heart, that I have not the least personal interest in endeavoring to promote this necessary work, having no other motive than the public good of my country, by advancing our trade, providing for infants, relieving the poor, and giving some pleasure to the rich. I have no children by which I can propose to get a single penny; the youngest being nine years old, and my wife past childbearing.

____ **CONSIDERATIONS** _____

1. The biggest risk a satirist runs is that his reader will be too literal-minded to understand that he or she is reading satire. Can you imagine a reader missing the satiric nature of Swift's "A Modest Proposal"? It has happened many times. What might such a reader think of the author? Consider the same problem with regard to Ambrose Bierce, Nora Ephron, Woody Allen, or Margaret Atwood.

2. One clue to the satire is Swift's diction in certain passages. In paragraph 4, for example, note the phrase, "just dropped from its dam," in reference to a newborn child. How do these words make a sign to the reader? Look for other such words.

3. What words and phrases does Swift use to give the impression of straightforward seriousness?

4. How does Swift turn his satirical talent against religious intolerance?

5. What is the chief target of his satire toward the end of the essay?

Studs Terkel (b. 1912) has been an actor on stage and television, and has conducted a successful radio interview show in Chicago. His best-known books, collections of interviews, are Division Street America *(1966),* Hard Times *(1970),* Working *(1974)—from which we take this example of American speech— and* The Good War *(1984). In 1977 he published* Talking to Myself, *his autobiography, and in 1980* American Dreams Lost and Found. The Great Divide: America in the Eighties *appeared in 1988.*

70

STUDS TERKEL
Phil Stallings, Spot Welder

He is a spot-welder at the Ford assembly plant on the far South 1
Side of Chicago. He is twenty-seven years old; recently married. He
works the third shift: 3:30 P.M. to midnight.

"I start the automobile, the first welds. From there it goes to 2
another line, where the floor's put on, the roof, the trunk hood, the
doors. Then it's put on a frame. There is hundreds of lines.

"The welding gun's got a square handle, with a button on the top 3
for high voltage and a button on the bottom for low. The first is to
clamp the metal together. The second is to fuse it.

"The gun hangs from a ceiling, over tables that ride on a track. It 4
travels in a circle, oblong, like an egg. You stand on a cement platform,
maybe six inches from the ground."

I stand in one spot, about two- or three-feet area, all night. The 5
only time a person stops is when the line stops. We do about thirty-two
jobs per car, per unit. Forty-eight units an hour, eight hours a day.

From *Working: People Talk About What They Do All Day and How They Feel About What They Do* by Studs Terkel. Copyright © 1972, 1974 by Studs Terkel. Reprinted by permission of Pantheon Books, a division of Random House, Inc.

Thirty-two times forty-eight times eight. Figure it out. That's how many times I push that button.

6   The noise, oh it's tremendous. You open your mouth and you're liable to get a mouthful of sparks. (Shows his arms.) That's a burn, these are burns. You don't compete against the noise. You got to yell and at the same time you're straining to maneuver the gun to where you have to weld.

7   You got some guys that are uptight, and they're not sociable. It's too rough. You pretty much stay to yourself. You get involved with yourself. You dream, you think of things you've done. I drift back continuously to when I was a kid and what me and my brothers did. The things you love most are the things you drift back into.

8   Lots of times I worked from the time I started to the time of the break and I never realized I had even worked. When you dream, you reduce the chances of friction with the foreman or with the next guy.

9   It don't stop. It just goes and goes and goes. I bet there's men who have lived and died out there, never seen the end of that line. And they never will—because it's endless. It's like a serpent. It's just all body, no tail. It can do things to you . . . (Laughs.)

10   Repetition is such that if you were to think about the job itself, you'd slowly go out of your mind. You'd let your problems build up, you'd get to a point where you'd be at the fellow next to you—his throat. Every time the foreman came by and looked at you, you'd have something to say. You just strike out at anything you can. So if you involve yourself by yourself, you overcome this.

11   I don't like the pressure, the intimidation. How would you like to go up to someone and say, "I would like to go to the bathroom?" If the foreman doesn't like you, he'll make you hold it, just ignore you. Should I leave this job to go to the bathroom I risk being fired. The line moves all the time.

12   I work next to Jim Grayson and he's preoccupied. The guy on my left, he's a Mexican, speaking Spanish, so it's pretty hard to understand him. You just avoid him. Brophy, he's a young fella, he's going to college. He works catty-corner from me. Him and I talk from time to time. If he ain't in the mood, I don't talk. If I ain't in the mood, he knows it.

13   Oh sure, there's tension here. It's not always obvious, but the whites stay with the whites and the coloreds stay with the coloreds. When you go into Ford, Ford says, "Can you work with other men?" This stops a lot of trouble, 'cause when you're working side by side with a guy, they can't afford to have guys fighting. When two men don't

socialize, that means two guys are gonna do more work, know what I mean?

I don't understand how come more guys don't flip. Because you're 14 nothing more than a machine when you hit this type of thing. They give better care to that machine than they will to you. They'll have more respect, give more attention to that machine. And you *know* this. Somehow you get the feeling that the machine is better than you are. (Laughs.)

You really begin to wonder. What price do they put on me? Look at 15 the price they put on the machine. If that machine breaks down, there's somebody out there to fix it right away. If I break down, I'm just pushed over to the other side till another man takes my place. The only thing they have on their mind is to keep that line running.

I'll do the best I can. I believe in an eight-hour pay for an eight-hour 16 day. But I will not try to outreach my limits. If I can't cut it, I just don't do it. I've been there three years and I keep my nose pretty clean. I never cussed anybody or anything like that. But I've had some real brushes with foremen.

What happened was my job was overloaded. I got cut and it got 17 infected. I got blood poisoning. The drill broke. I took it to the foreman's desk. I says, "Change this as soon as you can." We were running specials for XL hoods. I told him I wasn't a repair man. That's how the conflict began. I says, "If you want, take me to the Green House." Which is a superintendent's office—disciplinary station. This is when he says, "Guys like you I'd like to see in the parking lot."

One foreman I know, he's about the youngest out here, he has this 18 idea: I'm it and if you don't like it, you know what you can do. Anything this other foreman says, he usually overrides. Even in some cases, the foremen don't get along. They're pretty hard to live with, even with each other.

Oh yeah, the foreman's got somebody knuckling down on him, 19 putting the screws to him. But a foreman is still free to go to the bathroom, go get a cup of coffee. He doesn't face the penalties. When I first went in there, I kind of envied foremen. Now, I wouldn't have a foreman's job. I wouldn't give 'em the time of the day.

When a man becomes a foreman, he has to forget about even being 20 human, as far as feelings are concerned. You see a guy there bleeding to death. So what, buddy? That line's gotta keep goin'. I can't live like that. To me, if a man gets hurt, first thing you do is get him some attention.

About the blood poisoning. It came from the inside of a hood 21 rubbin' against me. It caused quite a bit of pain. I went down to the medics. They said it was a boil. Got to my doctor that night. He said blood poisoning. Running fever and all this. Now I've smartened up.

22   They have a department of medics. It's basically first aid. There's no doctor on our shift, just two or three nurses, that's it. They've got a door with a sign on it that says Lab. Another door with a sign on it: Major Surgery. But my own personal opinion, I'm afraid of 'em. I'm afraid if I were to get hurt, I'd get nothin' but back talk. I got hit square in the chest one day with a bar from a rack and it cut me down this side. They didn't take x-rays or nothing. Sent me back on the job. I missed three and a half days two weeks ago. I had bronchitis. They told me I was all right. I didn't have a fever. I went home and my doctor told me I couldn't go back to work for two weeks. I really needed the money, so I had to go back the next day. I woke up still sick, so I took off the rest of the week.

23   I pulled a muscle on my neck, straining. This gun, when you grab this thing from the ceiling, cable, weight, I mean you're pulling everything. Your neck, your shoulders, and your back. I'm very surprised more accidents don't happen. You have to lean over, at the same time holding down the gun. This whole edge here is sharp. I go through a shirt every two weeks, it just goes right through. My coveralls catch on fire. I've had gloves catch on fire. (Indicates arm.) See them little holes? That's what sparks do. I've got burns across here from last night.

24   I know I could find better places to work. But where could I get the money I'm making? Let's face it, $4.32 an hour. That's real good money now. Funny thing is, I don't mind working at body construction. To a great degree, I enjoy it. I love using my hands—more than I do my mind. I love to be able to put things together and see something in the long run. I'll be the first to admit I've got the easiest job on the line. But I'm against this thing where I'm being held back. I'll work like a dog until I get what I want. The job I really want is utility.

25   It's where I can stand and say I can do any job in this department, and nobody has to worry about me. As it is now, out of say, sixty jobs, I can do almost half of 'em. I want to get away from standing in one spot. Utility can do a different job every day. Instead of working right there for eight hours I could work over there for eight, I could work the other place for eight. Every day it would change. I would be around more people. I go out on my lunch break and work on the fork truck for a half-hour—to get the experience. As soon as I got it down pretty good, the foreman in charge says he'll take me. I don't want the other guys to see me. When I hit that fork lift, you just stop your thinking and you concentrate. Something right there in front of you, not in the past, not in the future. This is real healthy.

I don't eat lunch at work. I may grab a candy bar, that's enough. I   26
wouldn't be able to hold it down. The tension your body is put under by
the speed of the line. . . . When you hit them brakes, you just can't
stop. There's a certain momentum that carries you forward. I could hold
the food, but it wouldn't set right.

Proud of my work? How can I feel pride in a job where I call a   27
foreman's attention to a mistake, a bad piece of equipment, and he'll
ignore it. Pretty soon you get the idea they don't care. You keep doing
this and finally you're titled a troublemaker. So you just go about your
work. You *have* to have pride. So you throw it off to something else.
And that's my stamp collection.

I'd break both my legs to get into social work. I see all over so many   28
kids really gettin' a raw deal. I think I'd go into juvenile. I tell kids on
the line, "Man, go out there and get that college." Because it's too late
for me now.

When you go into Ford, first thing they try to do is break your   29
spirit. I seen them bring a tall guy where they needed a short guy. I seen
them bring a short guy where you have to stand on two guys' backs to do
something. Last night, they brought a fifty-eight-year-old man to do the
job I was on. That man's my father's age. I know damn well my father
couldn't do it. To me, this is humanely wrong. A job should be a job, not
a death sentence.

The younger worker, when he gets uptight, he talks back. But you   30
take an old fellow, he's got a year, two years, maybe three years to go. If
it was me, I wouldn't say a word, I wouldn't care what they did. 'Cause,
baby, for another two years I can stick it out. I can't blame this man. I
respect him because he had enough will power to stick it out for thirty
years.

It's gonna change. There's a trend. We're getting younger and   31
younger men. We got this new Thirty and Out. Thirty years seniority
and out. The whole idea is to give a man more time, more time to slow
down and live. While he's still in his fifties, he can settle down in a
camper and go out and fish. I've sat down and thought about it. I've got
twenty-seven years to go. (Laughs.) That's why I don't go around causin'
trouble or lookin' for a cause.

The only time I get involved is when it affects me or it affects a   32
man on the line in a condition that could be me. I don't believe in lost
causes, but when it all happened. . . . (He pauses, appears bewildered.)

The foreman was riding the guy. The guy either told him to go   33
away or pushed him, grabbed him. . . . You can't blame the guy—Jim
Grayson. I don't want nobody stickin' their finger in my face. I'd've
probably hit him beside the head. The whole thing was: Damn it, it's

about time we took a stand. Let's stick up for the guy. We stopped the line. (He pauses, grins.) Ford lost about twenty units. I'd figure about five grand a unit—whattaya got? (Laughs.)

34   I said, "Let's all go home." When the line's down like that, you can go up to one man and say, " You gonna work?" If he says no, they can fire him. See what I mean? But if nobody was there, who the hell were they gonna walk up to and say, "Are you gonna work?" Man, there woulda been nobody there! If it were up to me, we'd gone home.

35   Jim Grayson, the guy I work next to, he's colored. Absolutely. That's the first time I've seen unity on that line. Now it's happened once, it'll happen again. Because everybody just sat down. Believe you me. (Laughs.) It stopped at eight and it didn't start till twenty after eight. Everybody and his brother were down there. It was really nice to see, it really was.

—— **CONSIDERATIONS** ————————————————————————

1. Terkel is famous for his ability to catch the voice of the people he interviews. Study the language of Phil Stallings and list some of the features of his voice.

2. In addition to diction, what removes this selection from the category of "essay"?

3. How does Stallings indicate his opinion that the company puts a higher value on its machines than on its men?

4. Does Stallings agree with what Caroline Bird says in her essay on the value of college?

5. What occurrence on the line, described toward the end of the interview, reveals Stallings's social consciousness?

6. Interview someone you find interesting. Try to shape the material from the interview into something with a point.

*Paul Theroux (b. 1941) is a traveler. He was born in
Massachusetts, and returns to Cape Cod every summer; the rest
of the year he lives in England when he is not taking trains
across China for* Riding the Iron Rooster *(1988) or any place else:*
The Old Patagonian Express: By Train Through the Americas
(1979); The Great Railway Bazaar: By Train Through Asia
(1985). Most of the time he writes novels, including The Family
Arsenal *(1976),* The Mosquito Coast *(1982), and, most recently,*
My Secret History *(1989). Because he has supported himself for
decades as a freelance writer, he has written many articles for
many magazines. He collected his best essays in* Sunrise with
Sea Monsters *(1985), from which we take "Burning Grass."*

71

PAUL THEROUX
Burning Grass

In July, it was very cold in Malawi. On the day that Malawi gained   1
her independence the wind swept down from Soche Hill into the Central stadium bringing with it cold mists. The Africans call this wind
chiperoni and dread it because they don't have enough clothes to withstand its penetration. They also know that it lasts only a few weeks and
that once this difficult period is gotten through they can go out again
into the fields and dig furrows for planting.

Independence was very dark, yet despite the cold winds the people   2
came to see their newly designed flag raised. The Prime Minister told
everyone that Malawi is a black man's country. The cold seemed to turn
everything, everyone, to wood; even the slogans were frozen, the gladness caged in trembling bodies.

Through August it became warmer. The violet flames of the jaca-   3
randa, the deep red of the bougainvillaea, the hibiscus, each bloom a
delicate shell—all suddenly appeared out of the cold of the African
winter.

443

4   In September, two months had passed since that winter, two months since that freezing Independence Day. And now, in this dry season, the people have begun to burn the grass.

5   September 8 was the first day of school. On this same day three members of the cabinet were asked to resign. Shortly afterward all the ministers but two resigned in protest. The Prime Minister, "the Lion of Malawi," was left with only two of his former ministers. Two months after independence the government smoldered in the heat of argument.

6   The custom of burning grass dates back to prehistoric times when there was a great deal of land and only few farmers; much of the land could lie fallow while the rest was burned. It was thought that the burning was necessary for a good crop the following year. The scientists say this is not true, but there are only a handful of scientists in this country of four million farmers. So each year, in the dry season, the grass is burned. A few weeks ago I saw thin trails of blue smoke winding out of valleys and off the hills to disappear in the clouds. And at night I saw the flicker of fires out at a great distance. A short time ago the fires were not great; I could still see the huge Mlanje plateau, a crouching animal, streaked with green, disappearing into Mozambique.

7   Last night I walked outside and saw the fires again. It can be terrifying to see things burning at night, wild bush fires creeping up a mountain like flaming snakes edging sideways to the summit. Even behind the mountains I could see fires, and off into the darkness that is the edge of Malawi I saw the glowing dots of fires just begun. They could burn all night, light the whole sky and make the shadows of trees leap in the flames. During the day the flames would drive the pigs and hyenas out of their thickets; the heat and smoke would turn the fleeing ravens into frightened asterisks of feathers.

8   Today the portent was real. Early this morning the radio said there would be heavy smoke haze. I looked off and Mlanje, Mozambique, even the small hills that had always lain so patiently in the sun, were obscured by the smoke of the bush fires. The horizon has crept close to my house. The horizon is still blue, not the cold blue of the air at a distance, but the heavy pigment of smoke and fresh ashes lingering low over the landscape, close to me.

9   In this season the ministers who have broken from the government are making speeches against the Prime Minister. They are angry. They say that this government is worse than the one it replaced. They say that in two months the Prime Minister has kept none of his prom-

ises; the ministers have spread to all the provinces where, before great numbers of people, they repeat their accusations. The air is heavy with threats and indignation; the people are gathering in groups to talk of this split in the government. They take time off from burning the grass to speak of the government now, after two green months, in flames.

Fire in Africa can go out of control, out of reach of any human   10
being, without disturbing much. It can sweep across the long plains and up the mountains and then, after the fire has burned its length, will flicker and go out. Later the burned ground will be replaced by the woven green of new grass. For a while very little will clear; the smoke will hang in the air and people will either dash about in its arms blindly or will be restless before it, anxiously waiting for it to disperse.

We all know that the horizon will soon move back and back, and   11
another season will come in Malawi. The prolonged fires will delay planting but planting will certainly begin; perhaps the harvest will be later than usual.

Yet now we have the flames and we must somehow live with the   12
heat, the smoke, the urgency of fires on mountains, the terror of fires at night, the burning grass, the dry fields waiting to be lighted, and all the creatures that live in the forest scattering this way and that, away from the charred and smoky ground.

_____ CONSIDERATIONS _____ _____

1. Where and what is Malawi?
2. How does Theroux use two very different subjects: the annual burning of the grasslands and the fate of the new government of Malawi?
3. How does Theroux's short report illustrate the universal conflict between tradition and science?
4. Why are the following vivid images useful: "the violent flames of the jacaranda," "the gladness caged in trembling bodies," "the huge Mlanje plateau, a crouching animal, streaked with green," "turn the fleeing ravens into frightened asterisks of feathers"?

*Lewis Thomas (b. 1913) is a medical doctor, teacher, and
writer. He lives in New York, where he was born, and where he
is now president of the Memorial Sloan-Kettering Cancer Center.
Earlier, he taught medicine at the University of Minnesota, was
department chairman and dean at New York University-
Bellevue, and was a dean at Yale Medical School. We take this
essay from* The Lives of a Cell, *which won a National Book
Award in 1975.* The New England Journal of Medicine *originally
printed the articles collected in that volume, articles that at the
same time make contributions to medicine and to literature. His
scientific mind, like the best minds in whatever field, extends
itself by language to investigate everything human, and to
speculate beyond the human.*

72

LEWIS THOMAS
Ceti

1   Tau Ceti is a relatively nearby star that sufficiently resembles our
sun to make its solar system a plausible candidate for the existence of
life. We are, it appears, ready to begin getting in touch with Ceti, and
with any other interested celestial body in more remote places, out to
the edge. CETI is also, by intention, the acronym of the First International Conference on Communication with Extraterrestrial Intelligence, held in 1972 in Soviet Armenia under the joint sponsorship of the
National Academy of Sciences of the United States and the Soviet
Academy, which involved eminent physicists and astronomers from
various countries, most of whom are convinced that the odds for the
existence of life elsewhere are very high, with a reasonable probability
that there are civilizations, one place or another, with technologic
mastery matching or exceeding ours.

2   On this assumption, the conferees thought it likely that radio-

astronomy would be the generally accepted mode of interstellar communication, on grounds of speed and economy. They made a formal recommendation that we organize an international cooperative program, with new and immense radio telescopes, to probe the reaches of deep space for electromagnetic signals making sense. Eventually, we would plan to send out messages on our own and receive answers, but at the outset it seems more practical to begin by catching snatches of conversation between others.

So, the highest of all our complex technologies in the hardest of 3 our sciences will soon be engaged, full scale, in what is essentially biologic research—and with some aspects of social science, at that.

The earth has become, just in the last decade, too small a place. We 4 have the feeling of being confined—shut in; it is something like outgrowing a small town in a small county. The views of the dark, pocked surface of Mars, still lifeless to judge from the latest photographs, do not seem to have extended our reach; instead, they bring closer, too close, another unsatisfactory feature of our local environment. The blue noonday sky, cloudless, has lost its old look of immensity. The word is out that the sky is not limitless; it is finite. It is, in truth, only a kind of local roof, a membrane under which we live, luminous but confusingly refractile when suffused with sunlight; we can sense its concave surface a few miles over our heads. We know that it is tough and thick enough so that when hard objects strike it from the outside they burst into flames. The color photographs of the earth are more amazing than anything outside: we live inside a blue chamber, a bubble of air blown by ourselves. The other sky beyond, absolutely black and appalling, is wide-open country, irresistible for exploration.

Here we go, then. An extraterrestrial embryologist, having a close 5 look at us from time to time, would probably conclude that the morphogenesis of the earth is coming along well, with the beginnings of a nervous system and fair-sized ganglions in the form of cities, and now with specialized, dish-shaped sensory organs, miles across, ready to receive stimuli. He may well wonder, however, how we will go about responding. We are evolving into the situation of a Skinner pigeon in a Skinner box, peering about in all directions, trying to make connections, probing.

When the first word comes in from outer space, finally, we will 6 probably be used to the idea. We can already provide a quite good explanation for the origin of life, here or elsewhere. Given a moist planet with methane, formaldehyde, ammonia, and some usable minerals, all of which abound, exposed to lightning or ultraviolet irradiation at the right temperature, life might start off almost anywhere. The tricky, unsolved thing is how to get the polymers to arrange in membranes and invent replication. The rest is clear going. If they follow our protocol, it will be anaerobic life at first, then photosynthesis and the first exhalation of oxygen, then respiring life and the great burst of variation, then speciation, and, finally, some kind of consciousness. It is easy, in the telling.

7   I suspect that when we have recovered from the first easy acceptance of signs of life from elsewhere, and finished nodding at each other, and finished smiling, we will be in shock. We have had it our way, relatively speaking, being unique all these years, and it will be hard to deal with the thought that the whole, infinitely huge, spinning, clocklike apparatus around us is itself animate, and can sprout life whenever the conditions are right. We will respond, beyond doubt, by making connections after the fashion of established life, floating out our filaments, extending pili, but we will end up feeling smaller than ever, as small as a single cell, with a quite new sense of continuity. It will take some getting used to.

8   The immediate problem, however, is a much more practical, down-to-earth matter, and must be giving insomnia to the CETI participants. Let us assume that there is, indeed, sentient life in one or another part of remote space, and that we will be successful in getting in touch with it. What on earth are we going to talk about? If, as seems likely, it is a hundred or more light years away, there are going to be some very long pauses. The barest amenities, on which we rely for opening conversations—Hello, are you there?, from us, followed by Yes, hello, from them—will take two hundred years at least. By the time we have our party we may have forgotten what we had in mind.

9   We could begin by gambling on the rightness of our technology and just send out news of ourselves, like a mimeographed Christmas letter, but we would have to choose our items carefully, with durability of meaning in mind. Whatever information we provide must still make sense to us two centuries later, and must still seem important, or the conversation will be an embarrassment to all concerned. In two hundred years it is, as we have found, easy to lose the thread.

10   Perhaps the safest thing to do at the outset, if technology permits, is to send music. This language may be the best we have for explaining what we are like to others in space, with least ambiguity. I would vote for Bach, all of Bach, streamed out into space, over and over again. We would be bragging, of course, but it is surely excusable for us to put the best possible face on at the beginning of such an acquaintance. We can

tell the harder truths later. And, to do ourselves justice, music would give a fairer picture of what we are really like than some of the other things we might be sending, like *Time*, say, or a history of the U.N. or Presidential speeches. We could send out our science, of course, but just think of the wincing at this end when the polite comments arrive two hundred years from now. Whatever we offer as today's items of liveliest interest are bound to be out of date and irrelevant, maybe even ridiculous. I think we should stick to music.

Perhaps, if the technology can be adapted to it, we should send   11
some paintings. Nothing would better describe what this place is like, to an outsider, than the Cézanne demonstrations that an apple is really part fruit, part earth.

What kinds of questions should we ask? The choices will be hard,   12
and everyone will want his special question first. What are your smallest particles? Did you think yourselves unique? Do you have colds? Have you anything quicker than light? Do you always tell the truth? Do you cry? There is no end to the list.

Perhaps we should wait a while, until we are sure we know what   13
we want to know, before we get down to detailed questions. After all, the main question will be the opener: Hello, are you there? If the reply should turn out to be Yes, hello, we might want to stop there and think about that, for quite a long time.

———— CONSIDERATIONS ————————————————

1. If you were to decide on our first communication with life in outer space, what message would you send? Why?

2. Why must people working on interplanetary communication keep time in mind?

3. Like Loren Eiseley (see "More Thoughts on Wilderness"), Thomas skillfully uses figurative language to help us see what he is talking about. Consider, for example, his description of our sky in paragraph 4.

4. Point out some stylistic features in Thomas's essay that account for the highly informal, even jaunty tone.

5. Thomas touches on the shock we will feel when we have proof that mankind is not, after all, unique. What does he mean by saying "we will end up feeling smaller than ever, as small as a single cell, with quite a new sense of continuity"?

6. Why Bach rather than The Beatles or Bob Dylan?

7. How seriously do science fiction stories like *Star Wars* confront the questions raised by Thomas?

Henry David Thoreau (1817–1862) is one of the greatest American writers, and Walden one of the great American books. Thoreau attended Concord Academy, in the Massachusetts town where he was born and lived. Then he went to Harvard and completed his formal education, which was extensive in mathematics, literature, Greek, Latin, and French—and included smatterings of Spanish and Italian and some of the literature of India and China. He and his brother founded a school that lasted four years, and then he was a private tutor to a family. He also worked for his father, manufacturing pencils. But mostly Thoreau walked, meditated, observed nature, and wrote.

A friend of Ralph Waldo Emerson's, Thoreau was influenced by the older man, and by Transcendentalism—a doctrine that recognized the unity of man and nature. For Thoreau, an idea required testing by life itself; it never remained merely mental. In his daily work on his journals, and in the books he carved from them—A Week on the Concord and Merrimack Rivers (1849) as well as Walden (1854)—he observed the detail of daily life, human and natural, and he speculated on the universal laws he could derive from this observation.

"To know it by experience, and be able to give a true account of it"—these words could be carved on Thoreau's gravestone. "To give a true account" he became a great writer, a master of observation.

Thoreau was our greatest observer of nature, but his observations were not limited to fish and elm trees. He was ardently opposed to slavery and disgusted with fellow Northerners who accepted enforcement of the Fugitive Slave Act. Two entries from his journal, on two successive days, respond to one dreadful occasion involving the case of Anthony Burns. When a mob tried to free the fugitive slave, the government called out the militia to ensure that the trial was held. Burns was returned to the South although his identity, as an escaped slave, was doubtful. Never again was the Fugitive Slave Act enforced in Massachusetts.

73

HENRY DAVID THOREAU
June 16, 1854

The effect of a good government is to make life more valuable,—of a bad government, to make it less valuable. We can afford that railroad and all merely material stock should depreciate, for that only compels us to live more simply and economically; but suppose the value of life itself should be depreciated. Every man in New England capable of the sentiment of patriotism must have lived the last three weeks with the sense of having suffered a vast, indefinite loss. I had never respected this government, but I had foolishly thought that I might manage to live here, attending to my private affairs, and forget it. For my part, my old and worthiest pursuits have lost I cannot say how much of their attraction, and I feel that my investment in life here is worth many per cent. less since Massachusetts last deliberately and forcibly restored an innocent man, Anthony Burns, to slavery. I dwelt before in the illusion that my life passed somewhere only *between* heaven and hell, but now I cannot persuade myself that I do not dwell wholly within hell. The sight of that political organization called Massachusetts is to me morally covered with scoriæ and volcanic cinders, such as Milton imagined. If there is any hell more unprincipled than our rulers and our people, I feel curious to visit it. Life itself being worthless, all things with it, that feed it, are worthless. Suppose you have a small library, with pictures to adorn the walls,—a garden laid out around,—and contemplate scientific and literary pursuits, etc., etc., and discover suddenly that your villa, with all its contents, is located in hell, and that the justice of the peace is one of the devil's angels, has a cloven foot and forked tail,—do not these things suddenly lose their value in your eyes? Are you not disposed to sell at a great sacrifice? 1

I feel that, to some extent, the State has fatally interfered with my just and proper business. It has not merely interrupted me in my passage through Court Street on errands of trade, but it has, to some extent, interrupted me and every man on his onward and upward path, on which he had trusted soon to leave Court Street far behind. I have found that hollow which I had relied on for solid. 2

I am surprised to see men going about their business as if nothing 3 had happened, and say to myself, "Unfortunates! they have not heard the news;" that the man whom I just met on horseback should be so earnest to overtake his newly bought cows running away,—since all property is insecure, and if they do not run away again, they may be taken away from him when he gets them. Fool! does he not know that his seed-corn is worth less this year,—that all beneficent harvests fail as he approaches the empire of hell? No prudent man will build a stone house under these circumstances, or engage in any peaceful enterprise which it requires a long time to accomplish. Art is as long as ever, but life is more interrupted and less available for a man's proper pursuits. It is time we had done referring to our ancestors. We have used up all our inherited freedom, like the young bird the albumen in the egg. It is not an era of repose. If we would save our lives, we must fight for them.

4   The discovery is what manner of men your countrymen are. They steadily worship mammon—and on the seventh day curse God with a tintamarre from one end of the *Union* to the other. I heard the other day of a meek and sleek devil of a Bishop Somebody, who commended the law and order with which Burns was given up. I would like before I sit down to a table to inquire if there is one in the company who styles himself or is styled Bishop, and he or I should go out of it. I would have such a man wear his bishop's hat and his clerical bib and tucker, that we may know him.

5   Why will men be such fools as [to] trust to lawyers for a *moral* reform? I do not believe that there is a judge in this country prepared to decide by the principle that a law is immoral and therefore of no force. They put themselves, or rather are by character, exactly on a level with the marine who discharges his musket in any direction in which he is ordered. They are just as much tools, and as little men.

—— **CONSIDERATIONS** ————————————————————

1. In expressing disgust over the Fugitive Slave Act at work in his own state of Massachusetts, Thoreau distinguishes between a high material standard of living and a high valuing of life itself. Thus, he would be willing to dispense with railroads and other creature comforts if the value of life could be preserved. Do you hold similar feelings? Are you willing to trade civil liberties for comforts and conveniences? Is such a trade necessary?

2. To show how the court decisions about Anthony Burns have changed his life, Thoreau makes use of allusion—a literary device—when he refers to

Milton's description of hell. If that allusion does not elicit the dramatic effect Thoreau intends, turn to "Book 1" of Milton's *Paradise Lost*. In your next essay, try to employ an allusion—not necessarily to Milton—to strengthen a point.

3. How does Thoreau use his knowledge of natural history to make credible his statement that "We have used up all our inherited freedom"?

74

HENRY DAVID THOREAU
June 17, 1854

The judges and lawyers, and all men of expediency, consider not whether the Fugitive Slave Law is right, but whether it is what they call constitutional. They try the merits of the case by a very low and incompetent standard. Pray, is virtue constitutional, or vice? Is equity constitutional, or iniquity? It is as impertinent, in important moral and vital questions like this, to ask whether a law is constitutional or not, as to ask whether it is profitable or not. They persist in being the servants of man, and the worst of men, rather than the servants of God. Sir, the question is not whether you or your grandfather, seventy years ago, entered into an agreement to serve the devil, and that service is not accordingly now due; but whether you will not now, for once and at last, serve God,—in spite of your own past recreancy or that of your ancestors,—and obey that eternal and only just Constitution which he, and not any Jefferson or Adams, has written in your being. Is the Constitution a thing to live by? or die by? No, as long as we are alive we forget it, and when we die we have done with it. At most it is only to swear by. While they are hurrying off Christ to the cross, the ruler decides that he cannot *constitutionally* interfere to save him. The Christians, now and always, are they who obey the higher law, who discover it to be according to their constitution to interfere. They at least cut off the ears of the police; the others pocket the thirty pieces of silver. This was meaner than to crucify Christ, for he could better take care of himself.

———— CONSIDERATIONS ————

1. Thoreau groups judges and lawyers into a class he calls "men of expediency." Look up that last word and explain why a man of principle detests those who make their decisions on the basis of expediency.

2. Thoreau questions the wisdom and morality of arguing about a law's constitutionality. Would he have raised the same question had he observed the number of times in recent years that constitutional arguments have been the means of preserving civil liberties?

3. What higher law does Thoreau prefer over Massachusetts law? Why might appeals to that higher law be likely to produce more arguments than it could resolve?

4. In his widely reprinted essay "On the Duty of Civil Disobedience," Thoreau announces that he is a party of one and that "any man more right than his neighbors constitutes a majority of one." Does this position have anything in common with that expressed by Page Smith in the last three or four paragraphs of his essay "The New Abolitionism"? Explain.

The elm tree is fast disappearing. Here Thoreau writes about elms, about vision, about observation—about love of the natural world.

<hr>

75

HENRY DAVID THOREAU
October 12, 1857

<hr>

1   I see a very distant mountain house in a direction a little to the west of Carlisle, and two elms in the horizon on the right of it. Measuring carefully on the map of the county, I think it must be the Baptist Church in North Tewksbury, within a small fraction of fourteen miles from me. I think that this is the greatest distance at which I have seen an elm without a glass. There is another elm in the horizon nearly north, but not so far. It looks very much larger than it is. Perhaps it looms a little. The elm, I think, can be distinguished further than any other tree, and, however faintly seen in the distant horizon, its little dark dome, which the thickness of my nail will conceal, just rising above the line of the horizon, apparently not so big as a prominence on an orange, it suggests ever the same quiet rural and domestic life passing beneath it. It is the vignette to an unseen idyllic poem. Though that little prominence appears so dark there, I know that it is now a rich brownish-yellow canopy of rustling leaves, whose harvest-time is already come, sending down its showers from time to time. Homestead telegraphs to homestead through these distant elms seen from the hilltops. I fancy I hear the house-dog's bark and lowing of the cows asking admittance to their yard beneath it. The tea-table is spread; the master and mistress and the hired men now have just sat down in their shirt-sleeves. Some are so lifted up in the horizon that they seem like portions of the earth detached and floating off by themselves into space. Their dark masses against the sky can be seen as far, at least, as a white spire, though it may be taller. Some of these trees, seen through a glass, are not so large. . . .

2   This was what those scamps did in California. The trees were so

grand and venerable that they could not afford to let them grow a hair's breadth bigger, or live a moment longer to reproach themselves. They were so big that they resolved they should never be bigger. They were so venerable that they cut them right down. It was not for sake of the wood; it was only because they were very grand and venerable.

___ CONSIDERATIONS ___

1. Many readers think of Thoreau as a naturalist, belly-down on the shores of Walden Pond, staring intently at a tiny frog. This excerpt shows a different side. Working from your study of the October 12 journal item, how would you describe what he is doing? How does it affect the conventional view of him?

2. Why, according to Thoreau, did the Californians cut down their giant trees? Who might be more inclined to agree with him: loggers or environmentalists?

3. What have the elms—and Thoreau's way of seeing them—to do with his sense of place?

4. Thoreau's fierce insistence on personal freedom and responsibility is well known. For example, he chose to go to jail rather than to pay an unjust tax. Is his principle of freedom irreconcilable with the daydreaming he does in this excerpt? Explain.

These passages come from his journal, the disciplined daily writing from which Thoreau shaped his finished books. Here he writes about the bream—a small, silvery, flattish freshwater fish—not so much by describing it as by recounting his reaction to it and by ruminating on the relationship between people and the natural world.

76

HENRY DAVID THOREAU
November 30, 1858

1   I cannot but see still in my mind's eye those little striped breams poised in Walden's glaucous water. They balance all the rest of the world in my estimation at present, for this is the bream that I have just found, and for the time I neglect all its brethren and am ready to kill the fatted calf on its account. For more than two centuries have men fished here and have not distinguished this permanent settler of the township. It is not like a new bird, a transient visitor that may not be seen again for years, but there it dwells and has dwelt permanently, who can tell how long? When my eyes first rested on Walden the striped bream was poised in it, though I did not see it, and when Tahatawan paddled his canoe there. How wild it makes the pond and the township to find a new fish in it! America renews her youth here. But in my account of this bream I cannot go a hair's breadth beyond the mere statement that it exists,—the miracle of its existence, my contemporary and neighbor, yet so different from me! I can only poise my thought there by its side and try to think like a bream for a moment. I can only think of precious jewels, of music, poetry, beauty, and the mystery of life. I only see the bream in its orbit, as I see a star, but I care not to measure its distance or weight. The bream, appreciated, floats in the pond as the centre of the system, another image of God. Its life no man can explain more than he can his own. I want you to perceive the mystery of the bream. I have a contemporary in Walden. It has fins where I have legs and arms. I have a friend among the fishes, at least a new acquaintance. Its character will

interest me, I trust, not its clothes and anatomy. I do not want it to eat. Acquaintance with it is to make my life more rich and eventful. It is as if a poet or an anchorite had moved into the town, whom I can see from time to time and think of yet oftener. Perhaps there are a thousand of these striped bream which no one had thought of in that pond,—not their mere impressions in stone, but in the full tide of the bream life.

Though science may sometimes compare herself to a child picking 2 up pebbles on the seashore, that is a rare mood with her; ordinarily her practical belief is that it is only a few pebbles which are *not* known, weighed and measured. A new species of fish signifies hardly more than a new name. See what is contributed in the scientific reports. One counts the fin-rays, another measures the intestines, a third daguerreotypes a scale, etc., etc.; otherwise there's nothing to be said. As if all but this were done, and these were very rich and generous contributions to science. Her votaries may be seen wandering along the shore of the ocean of truth, with their backs to that ocean, ready to seize on the shells which are cast up. You would say that the scientific bodies were terribly put to it for objects and subjects. A dead specimen of an animal, if it is only preserved in alcohol, is just as good for science as a living one preserved in its native element.

What is the amount of my discovery to me? It is not that I have got 3 one in a bottle, that it has got a name in a book, but that I have a little fishy friend in the pond. How was it when the youth first discovered fishes? Was it the number of their fin-rays or their arrangement, or the place of the fish in some system that made the boy dream of them? Is it these things that interest mankind in the fish, the inhabitant of the water? No, but a faint recognition of a living contemporary, a provoking mystery. One boy thinks of fishes and goes a-fishing from the same motive that his brother searches the poets for rare lines. It is the poetry of fishes which is their chief use; their flesh is their lowest use. The beauty of the fish, that is what it is best worth the while to measure. Its place in our systems is of comparatively little importance. Generally the boy loses some of his perception and his interest in the fish; he degenerates into a fisherman or an ichthyologist.

___ **CONSIDERATIONS** _____

1. Thoreau's excitement in describing the bream was generated by his discovery of a species living unnoticed in Walden Pond. But why, according to him, can he do no more than say that it exists? Why is that statement sufficient?

2. What kind of truth—scientific, philosophic, economic, aesthetic— can you find in Thoreau's statement that the bream "is the center of the system, another image of God"? Look carefully at his sentence in paragraph 1. Why pay particular attention to the word "appreciated," which is set off by commas?

3. What does Thoreau's excitement over discovering the bream have in common with Wendell Berry's "A Native Hill"?

4. Why, in his closing statement, does Thoreau consider both the fisherman and the ichthyologist deplorable?

5. "Mystery" is an important word in Thoreau's essay. What is there about the way scientists work that limits their appreciation of the mystery of creation? Loren Eiseley's "More Thoughts on Wilderness" and Peter Steinhart's "The Old Curiosity" may help you with your answer.

James Thurber (1894–1961) was born in Columbus, Ohio, the scene of many of his funniest stories. He graduated from Ohio State University, and after a period as a newspaperman in Paris, began to work for the New Yorker. *For years his comic writing and his cartoons—drawings of sausage-shaped dogs and of men and women forever at battle—were fixtures of that magazine. His collections of essays, short stories, and cartoons include* The Owl in the Attic and Other Perplexities *(1931),* The Seal in the Bedroom and Other Predicaments *(1932),* My Life and Hard Times *(1933),* Men, Women, and Dogs *(1943), and* Alarms and Diversions *(1957). He also wrote an account of life on the* New Yorker *staff,* The Years with Ross *(1959).* Selected Letters of James Thurber *appeared in 1981.*

An elegant stylist, Thurber was always fussy about language. "Which" is an example not only of his fascination with language—which became obsessive at times—but also of his humor.

77

JAMES THURBER
Which

The relative pronoun "which" can cause more trouble than any other word, if recklessly used. Foolhardy persons sometimes get lost in which-clauses and are never heard of again. My distinguished contemporary, Fowler, cites several tragic cases, of which the following is one: "It was rumoured that Beaconsfield intended opening the Conference with a speech in French, his pronounciation of which language leaving everything to be desired . . ." That's as much as Mr. Fowler quotes because, at his age, he was afraid to go any farther. The young man who originally got into that sentence was never found. His fate, however, was not as terrible as that of another adventurer who became involved in a remarkable which-mire. Fowler has followed his devious course as

1

far as he safely could on foot: "Surely what applies to games should also apply to racing, the leaders of which being the very people from whom an example might well be looked for . . ." Not even Henry James could have successfully emerged from a sentence with "which," "whom," and "being" in it. The safest way to avoid such things is to follow in the path of the American author, Ernest Hemingway. In his youth he was trapped in a which-clause one time and barely escaped with his mind. He was going along on solid ground until he got into this: "It was the one thing of which, being very much afraid—for whom has not been warned to fear such things—he . . ." Being a young and powerfully built man, Hemingway was able to fight his way back to where he had started, and begin again. This time he skirted the treacherous morass in this way: "He was afraid of one thing. This was the one thing. He had been warned to fear such things. Everybody has been warned to fear such things." Today Hemingway is alive and well, and many happy writers are following along the trail he blazed.

2   What most people don't realize is that one "which" leads to another. Trying to cross a paragraph by leaping from "which" to "which" is like Eliza crossing the ice. The danger is in missing a "which" and falling in. A case in point is this: "He went up to a pew which was in the gallery, which brought him under a colored window which he loved and always quieted his spirit." The writer, worn out, missed the last "which"—the one that should come just before "always" in that sentence. But supposing he had got it in! We would have: "He went up to a pew which was in the gallery, which brought him under a colored window which he loved and which always quieted his spirit." Your inveterate whicher in this way gives the effect of tweeting like a bird or walking with a crutch, and is not welcome in the best company.

3   It is well to remember that one "which" leads to two and that two "whiches" multiply like rabbits. You should never start out with the idea that you can get by with one "which." Suddenly they are all around you. Take a sentence like this: "It imposes a problem which we either solve, or perish." On a hot night, or after a hard day's work, a man often lets himself get by with a monstrosity like that, but suppose he dictates that sentence bright and early in the morning. It comes to him typed out by his stenographer and he instantly senses that something is the matter with it. He tries to reconstruct the sentence, still clinging to the "which," and gets something like this: "It imposes a problem which we either solve, or which, failing to solve, we must perish on account of." He goes to the water-cooler, gets a drink, sharpens his pencil, and grimly tries again. "It imposes a problem which we either solve or

which we don't solve . . ." He begins once more: "It imposes a problem which we either solve, or which we do not solve, and from which . . ." The more times he does it the more "whiches" he gets. The way out is simple: "We must either solve this problem, or perish." Never monkey with "which." Nothing except getting tangled up in a typewriter ribbon is worse.

—— **CONSIDERATIONS** ————————————————

1. James Thurber concentrates on one word from an important class of function words. These relative pronouns often complicate life for the writer wishing to write clear sentences more complex than "I see Spot. Spot is a dog. Spot sees me." What other words belong to this class? Do you find any of them tripping you up in your sentences?

2. A grammar lesson may seem a peculiar place to find humor, but humor is Thurber's habit, whatever his subject. How does he make his treatment of the relative pronoun "which" entertaining?

3. Compare Fowler's book with an American version such as Wilson Follett's *Modern American Usage.* This could lead you into a study of the concept of usage as the ultimate authority in establishing conventions of grammar, spelling, definition, and punctuation.

4. "One 'which' leads to another" is a play on the old saying "One drink leads to another." Consider how changing one word can revive a thought that George Orwell could call a hackneyed phrase. See how it is done by substituting a key word in several familiar sayings.

5. The two writers Thurber mentions, Henry James and Ernest Hemingway, are not idly chosen. Why not?

*Barbara Tuchman (1912–1989) was born in New York,
graduated from Radcliffe, and began her career as an editor and
writer for the* Nation. *But her interests led her away from the
politics of the moment to the politics of the past, which is to say
history.* The Guns of August, *which won the Pulitzer Prize in
1963, recounted the first weeks of the great war of 1914–1918.*
Stilwell and the American Experience in China *won the Pulitzer
Prize in 1972. Her major work,* A Distant Mirror: The
Calamitous 14th Century *(1973), from which the following essay
was adapted, brought her into the forefront of American
historians. Although she appeared to have deserted modern
history for medieval, she did no such thing. This "six-hundred-
year-old mirror" reflects ourselves. Her last book was* The First
Salute *(1988), an unusual approach to the story of the American
Revolution. Barbara Tuchman wrote clean exposition, laying out
for us clearly what she meant us to understand, supplying detail
adequate to her argument and fascinating in itself. She loved the
feel and shape of an odd and illuminating detail; she collected it
with gusto, and she used it with skill.*

__78__

BARBARA TUCHMAN
History as Mirror

1   At a time when everyone's mind is on the explosions of the moment, it might seem obtuse of me to discuss the fourteenth century. But
I think a backward look at that disordered, violent, bewildered, disintegrating, and calamity-prone age can be consoling and possibly instruc-
tive in a time of similar disarray. Reflected in a six-hundred-year-old
mirror, a more revealing image of ourselves and our species might be
seen than is visible in the clutter of circumstances under our noses. The
value of historical comparison was made keenly apparent to the French
medievalist, Edouard Perroy, when he was writing his book on the

Hundred Years' War while dodging the Gestapo in World War II. "Certain ways of behaving," he wrote, "certain reactions against fate, throw mutual light upon each other."

Besides, if one suspects that the twentieth century's record of inhumanity and folly represents a phase of mankind at its worst, and that our last decade of collapsing assumptions has been one of unprecedented discomfort, it is reassuring to discover that the human race has been in this box before—and emerged. The historian has the comfort of knowing that man (meaning, here and hereafter, the species, not the sex) is always capable of his worst; has indulged in it, painfully struggled up from it, slid back, and gone on again. 2

In what follows, the parallels are not always in physical events but rather in the effect on society, and sometimes in both. 3

The afflictions of the fourteenth century were the classic riders of the Apocalypse—famine, plague, war, and death, this time on a black horse. These combined to produce an epidemic of violence, depopulation, bad government, oppressive taxes, an accelerated breakdown of feudal bonds, working class insurrection, monetary crisis, decline of morals and rise in crime, decay of chivalry, the governing idea of the governing class, and above all, corruption of society's central institution, the Church, whose loss of authority and prestige deprived man of his accustomed guide in a darkening world. 4

Yet amidst the disintegration were sprouting, invisible to contemporaries, the green shoots of the Renaissance to come. In human affairs as in nature, decay is compost for new growth. 5

Some medievalists reject the title of decline for the fourteenth century, asserting instead that it was the dawn of a new age. Since the processes obviously overlap, I am not sure that the question is worth arguing, but it becomes poignantly interesting when applied to ourselves. Do *we* walk amidst trends of a new world without knowing it? How far ahead is the dividing line? Or are we on it? What designation will our age earn from historians six hundred years hence? One wishes one could make a pact with the devil like Enoch Soames, the neglected poet in Max Beerbohm's story, allowing us to return and look ourselves up in the library catalogue. In that future history book, shall we find the chapter title for the twentieth century reading Decline and Fall, or Eve of Revival? 6

The fourteenth century opened with a series of famines brought on when population growth outstripped the techniques of food production. The precarious balance was tipped by a series of heavy rains and 7

floods and by a chilling of the climate in what has been called the Little
Ice Age. Upon a people thus weakened fell the century's central disaster, the Black Death, an eruption of bubonic plague which swept the
known world in the years 1347–1349 and carried off an estimated
one-third of the population in two and a half years. This makes it the
most lethal episode known to history, which is of some interest to an
age equipped with the tools of overkill.

8   The plague raged at terrifying speed, increasing the impression of
horror. In a given locality it accomplished its kill within four to six
months, except in the larger cities, where it struck again in spring after
lying dormant in winter. The death rate in Avignon was said to have
claimed half the population, of whom ten thousand were buried in the
first six weeks in a single mass grave. The mortality was in fact erratic.
Some communities whose last survivors fled in despair were simply
wiped out and disappeared from the map forever, leaving only a grassed-
over hump as their mortal trace.

9   Whole families died, leaving empty houses and property a prey to
looters. Wolves came down from the mountains to attack plague-
stricken villages, crops went unharvested, dikes crumbled, salt water
reinvaded and soured the lowlands, the forest crept back, and second
growth, with the awful energy of nature unchecked, reconverted
cleared land to waste. For lack of hands to cultivate, it was thought
impossible that the world could ever regain its former prosperity.

10   Once the dark bubonic swellings appeared in armpit and groin,
death followed rapidly within one to three days, often overnight. For
lack of gravediggers, corpses piled up in the streets or were buried so
hastily that dogs dug them up and ate them. Doctors were helpless, and
priests lacking to administer that final sacrament so that people died
believing they must go to hell. No bells tolled, the dead were buried
without prayers or funeral rites or tears; families did not weep for the
loss of loved ones, for everyone expected death. Matteo Villani, taking
up the chronicle of Florence from the hands of his dead brother, believed
he was recording the "extermination of mankind."

11   People reacted variously, as they always do: some prayed, some
robbed, some tried to help, most fled if they could, others abandoned
themselves to debauchery on the theory that there would be no tomorrow. On balance, the dominant reaction was fear and a desire to save
one's own skin regardless of the closest ties. "A father did not visit his
son, nor the son his father; charity was dead," wrote one physician, and
that was not an isolated observation. Boccaccio in his famous account
reports that "kinsfolk held aloof, brother was forsaken by brother . . .

often times husband by wife; nay what is more, and scarcely to be believed, fathers and mothers were found to abandon their own children to their fate, untended, unvisited as if they had been strangers."

"Men grew bold," wrote another chronicler, "in their indulgence 12 in pleasure. . . . No fear of God or law of man deterred a criminal. Seeing that all perished alike, they reflected that offenses against human or Divine law would bring no punishment for no one would live long enough to be held to account." This is an accurate summary, but it was written by Thucydides about the Plague of Athens in the fifth century B.C.—which indicates a certain permanence of human behavior.

The nightmare of the plague was compounded for the fourteenth 13 century by the awful mystery of its cause. The idea of disease carried by insect bite was undreamed of. Fleas and rats, which were in fact the carriers, are not mentioned in the plague writings. Contagion could be observed but not explained and thus seemed doubly sinister. The medical faculty of the University of Paris favored a theory of poisonous air spread by a conjunction of the planets, but the general and fundamental belief, made official by a papal bull, was that the pestilence was divine punishment for man's sins. Such horror could only be caused by the wrath of God. "In the year of our Lord, 1348," sadly wrote a professor of law at the University of Pisa, "the hostility of God was greater than the hostility of men."

That belief enhanced the sense of guilt, or rather the conscious- 14 ness of sin (guilt, I suspect, is modern; sin is medieval), which was always so close to the surface throughout the Middle Ages. Out of the effort to appease divine wrath came the flagellants, a morbid frenzy of self-punishment that almost at once found a better object in the Jews.

A storm of pogroms followed in the track of the Black Death, 15 widely stimulated by the flagellants, who often rushed straight for the Jewish quarter, even in towns which had not yet suffered the plague. As outsiders within the unity of Christendom the Jews were natural persons to suspect of evil design on the Christian world. They were accused of poisoning the wells. Although the Pope condemned the attacks as inspired by "that liar the devil," pointing out that Jews died of plague like everyone else, the populace wanted victims, and fell upon them in three hundred communities throughout Europe. Slaughtered and burned alive, the entire colonies of Frankfurt, Cologne, Mainz, and other towns of Germany and the Lowlands were exterminated, despite the restraining efforts of town authorities. Elsewhere the Jews were expelled by judicial process after confession of well-poisoning was extracted by torture. In every case their goods and property, whether looted or confiscated, ended in the hands of the persecutors. The process was lucrative, as it was to be again in our time under the Nazis, although the fourteenth century had no gold teeth to rob from the corpses. Where survivors slowly returned and the communities revived, it was on worse terms than before and in walled isolation. This was the beginning of the ghetto.

16   Men of the fourteenth century were particularly vulnerable because of the loss of credibility by the Church, which alone could absolve sin and offer salvation from hell. When the papal schism dating from 1378 divided the Church under two popes, it brought the highest authority in society into disrepute, a situation with which we are familiar. The schism was the second great calamity of the time, displaying before all the world the unedifying spectacle of twin vicars of God, each trying to bump the other off the chair of St. Peter, each appointing his own college of cardinals, each collecting tithes and revenues and excommunicating the partisans of his rival. No conflict of ideology was involved; the split arose from a simple squabble for the office of the papacy and remained no more than that for the fifty years the schism lasted. Plunged in this scandal, the Church lost moral authority, the more so as its two halves scrambled in the political arena for support. Kingdoms, principalities, even towns, took sides, finding new cause for the endless wars that scourged the times.

17   The Church's corruption by worldliness long antedated the schism. By the fourteenth century the papal court at Avignon was called Babylon and rivaled temporal courts in luxury and magnificence. Its bureaucracy was enormous and its upkeep mired in a commercial traffic in spiritual things. Pardons, indulgences, prayers, every benefice and bishopric, everything the Church had or was, from cardinal's hat to pilgrim's relic, everything that represented man's relation to God, was for sale. Today it is the processes of government that are for sale, especially the electoral process, which is as vital to our political security as salvation was to the emotional security of the fourteenth century.

18   Men still craved God and spun off from the Church in sects and heresies, seeking to purify the realm of the spirit. They too yearned for a greening of the system. The yearning, and disgust with the Establishment, produced freak orders of mystics who lived in coeducational communes, rejected marriage, and glorified sexual indulgence. Passionate reformers ranged from St. Catherine of Siena, who scolded everyone in the hierarchy from the popes down, to John Wycliffe, who plowed the soil of Protestant revolt. Both strove to renew the Church,

which for so long had been the only institution to give order and meaning to the untidy business of living on earth. When in the last quarter of the century the schism brought the Church into scorn and ridicule and fratricidal war, serious men took alarm. The University of Paris made strenuous and ceaseless efforts to find a remedy, finally demanding submission of the conflict to a supreme Council of the Church whose object should be not only reunification but reform.

Without reform, said the University's theologians in their letter to   19
the popes, the damaging effect of the current scandal could be irreversible. In words that could have been addressed to our own secular potentate although he is—happily—not double, they wrote, "The Church will suffer for your overconfidence if you repent too late of having neglected reform. If you postpone it longer the harm will be incurable. Do you think people will suffer forever from your bad government? Who do you think can endure, amid so many other abuses . . . your elevation of men without literacy or virtue to the most eminent positions?" The echo sounds over the gulf of six hundred years with a timeliness almost supernatural.

When the twin popes failed to respond, pressure at last brought   20
about a series of Church councils which endeavored to limit and constitutionalize the powers of the papacy. After a thirty-year struggle, the councils succeeded in ending the schism but the papacy resisted reform. The decades of debate only served to prove that the institution could not be reformed from within. Eighty years of mounting protest were to pass before pressure produced Luther and the great crack.

Despite the parallel with the present struggle between Congress   21
and the presidency, there is no historical law that says the outcome must necessarily be the same. The American presidency at age two hundred is not a massive rock of ages embedded in a thousand years of acceptance as was the medieval Church, and should be easier to reform. One can wish for Congress a better result than the councils had in the effort to curb the executive—or at least one can hope.

The more important parallel lies in the decay of public confidence   22
in our governing institutions, as the fourteenth-century public lost confidence in the Church. Who believes today in the integrity of government?—or of business, or of law or justice or labor unions or the military or the police? Even physicians, the last of the admired, are now in disfavor. I have a theory that the credibility vacuum owes something to our nurture in that conspiracy of fables called advertising, which we daily absorb without believing. Since public affairs and ideas and candidates are now presented to us as a form of advertising, we automatically

suspend belief or suspect fraud as soon as we recognize the familiar slickness. I realize, of course, that the roots of disbelief go down to deeper ground. Meanwhile the effect is a loss of trust in all authority which leaves us guideless and dismayed and cynical—even as in the fourteenth century.

23   Over that whole century hung the smoke of war—dominated by the Anglo-French conflict known to us, though fortunately not to them, as the Hundred Years' War. (With the clock still ticking in Indochina, one wonders how many years there are still to go in that conflict.) Fought on French soil and extending into Flanders and Spain, the Hundred Years' War actually lasted for more than a century, from 1337 to 1453. In addition, the English fought the Scots; the French fought incessant civil wars against Gascons, Bretons, Normans, and Navarrese; the Italian republics fought each other—Florence against Pisa, Venice against Genoa, Milan against everybody; the kingdom of Naples and Sicily was fought over by claimants from Hungary to Aragon; the papacy fought a war that included unbridled massacre to reconquer the Papal States; the Savoyards fought the Lombards; the Swiss fought the Austrians; the tangled wars of Bohemia, Poland, and the German Empire defy listing; crusades were launched against the Saracens, and to fill up any pauses the Teutonic Knights conducted annual campaigns against pagan Lithuania which other knights could join for extra practice. Fighting was the function of the Second Estate, that is, of the landed nobles and knights. A knight without a war or tournament to go to felt as restless as a man who cannot go to the office.

24   Every one of these conflicts threw off Free Companies of mercenaries, organized for brigandage under a professional captain, which became an evil of the period as malignant as the plague. In the money economy of the fourteenth century, armed forces were no longer feudal levies serving under a vassal's obligation who went home after forty days, but were recruited bodies who served for pay. Since this was at great cost to the sovereign, he cut off the payroll as soon as he safely could during halts of truce or negotiation. Thrown on their own resources and having acquired a taste for plunder, the men-at-arms banded together in the Free Companies, whose savage success swelled their ranks with landless knights and squires and roving adventurers.

25   The companies contracted their services to whatever ruler was in need of troops, and between contracts held up towns for huge ransom, ravaged the countryside, and burned, pillaged, raped, and slaughtered their way back and forth across Europe. No one was safe, no town or

village knew when it might be attacked. The leaders, prototypes of the *condottieri* in Italy, became powers and made fortunes and even became respectable like Sir John Hawkwood, commander of the famous White Company. Smaller bands, called in France the *tards-venus* (latecomers), scavenged like jackals, living off the land, plundering, killing, carrying off women, torturing peasants for their small horde of grain or townsmen for their hidden goods, and burning, always burning. They set fire to whatever they left behind, farmhouses, vineyards, abbeys, in a kind of madness to destroy the very sources off which they lived, or would live tomorrow. Destruction and cruelty became self-engendering, not merely for loot but almost one might say for sport. The phenomenon is not peculiar to any one time or people, as we know from the experience of our own century, but in the fourteenth century it seems to have reached a degree and extent beyond explanation.

It must be added that in practice and often personnel the Free   26 Companies were hardly distinguishable from the troops of organized official wars. About 80 percent of the activity of a declared war consisted of raids of plunder and burning through enemy territory. That paragon of chivalry, the Black Prince, could well have earned his name from the blackened ruins he left across France. His baggage train and men-at-arms were often so heavily laden with loot that they moved as slowly as a woman's litter.

The saddest aspect of the Hundred Years' War was the persistent   27 but vain efforts of the belligerents themselves to stop it. As in our case, it spread political damage at home, and the cost was appalling. Moreover it harmed the relations of all the powers at a time when they were anxious to unite to repel the infidel at the gates. For Christendom was now on the defensive against the encroaching Turks. For that reason the Church, too, tried to end the war that was keeping Europe at odds. On the very morning of the fatal battle of Poitiers, two cardinals hurried with offers and counter-offers between the two armed camps, trying in vain to prevent the clash. During periods of truce the parties held long parleys lasting months and sometimes years in the effort to negotiate a definitive peace. It always eluded them, failing over questions of prestige, or put off by the feeling of whichever side held a slight advantage that one more push would bring the desired gains.

All this took place under a code of chivalry whose creed was   28 honor, loyalty, and courtesy and whose purpose, like that of every social code evolved by man in his long search for order, was to civilize and supply a pattern of rules. A knight's task under the code was to uphold the Church, defend his land and vassals, maintain the peace of his province, protect the weak and guard the poor from injustice, shed his blood for his comrade, and lay down his life if needs must. For the land-owning warrior class, chivalry was their ideology, their politics, their system—what democracy is to us or Marxism to the Communists.

29   Originating out of feudal needs, it was already slipping into anachronism by the fourteenth century because the development of monarchy and a royal bureaucracy was taking away the knight's functions, economic facts were forcing him to commute labor dues for money, and a rival element was appearing in the urban magnates. Even his military prowess was being nullified by trained bodies of English longbowmen and Swiss pikemen, nonmembers of the warrior class who in feudal theory had no business in battle at all.

30   Yet in decadence chivalry threw its brightest light; never were its ceremonies more brilliant, its jousts and tournaments so brave, its apparel so splendid, its manners so gay and amorous, its entertainments so festive, its self-glorification more eloquent. The gentry elaborated the forms of chivalry just *because* institutions around them were crumbling. They clung to what gave their status meaning in a desperate embrace of the past. This is the time when the Order of the Garter was founded by the King of England, the Order of the Star by the King of France, the Golden Fleece by the Duke of Burgundy—in deliberate imitation of King Arthur's Knights of the Round Table.

31   The rules still worked well enough among themselves, with occasional notorious exceptions such as Charles of Navarre, a bad man appropriately known as Charles the Bad. Whenever necessity required him to swear loyal reconciliation and fealty to the King of France, his mortal enemy, he promptly engaged in treacherous intrigues with the King of England, leaving his knightly oaths to become, in the White House word, inoperative. On the whole, however, the nobility laid great stress on high standards of honor. It was vis-à-vis the Third Estate that chivalry fell so far short of the theory. Yet it remained an ideal of human relations, as Christianity remained an ideal of faith, that kept men reaching for the unattainable. The effort of society is always toward order, away from anarchy. Sometimes it moves forward, sometimes it slips back. Which is the direction of one's own time may be obscure.

32   The fourteenth century was further afflicted by a series of convulsions and upheavals in the working class, both urban and rural. Causes were various: the cost of constant war was thrown upon the people in hearth taxes, salt taxes, sales taxes, and debasement of coinage. In

France the failure of the knights to protect the populace from incessant ravaging was a factor. It exacerbated the peasants' misery, giving it the energy of anger which erupted in the ferocious mid-century rising called the *Jacquerie*. Shortage of labor caused by the plague had temporarily brought higher wages and rising expectations. When these were met, especially in England, by statutes clamping wages at pre-plague levels, the result was the historic Peasants' Revolt of 1381. In the towns, capitalism was widening the gap between masters and artisans, producing the sustained weavers' revolts in the cloth towns of Flanders and major outbreaks in Florence and Paris. In Paris, too, the merchant class rose against the royal councillors, whom they despised as both corrupt and incompetent. To frighten the regent into submission, they murdered his two chief councillors in his presence.

All these struggles had one thing in common: they were doomed. United against a common threat, the ruling class could summon greater strength than its antagonists and acted to suppress insurrection with savagery equal to the fury from below. Yet discontent had found its voice; dissent and rejection of authority for the first time in the Middle Ages became a social force. Demagogues and determined leaders, reformers and agitators came to the surface. Though all were killed, several by mobs of their own followers, the uprisings they led were the beginning of modern, conscious, class war. 33

Meanwhile, over the second half-century, the plague returned with lesser virulence at intervals of every twelve to fifteen years. It is hardly to be wondered that people of the time saw man's fate as an endless succession of evils. He must indeed be wicked and his enemy Satan finally triumphant. According to a popular belief at the end of the century, no one since the beginning of the schism had entered Paradise. 34

Pessimism was a mark of the age and the *Danse Macabre* or Dance of Death its most vivid expression. Performed at occasions of popular drama and public sermons, it was an actual dance or pantomime in which a figure from every walk of life—king, clerk, lawyer, friar, goldsmith, bailiff, and so on—confronts the loathsome corpse he must become. In the accompanying verses and illustrations which have survived, the theme repeats itself over and over: the end of all life is putrefaction and the grave; no one escapes; no matter what beauty or kingly power or poor man's misery has been the lot in life, all end alike as food for worms. Death is not treated poetically as the soul's flight to reunion with God; it is a skeleton grinning at the vanity of life. 35

Life as well as death was viewed with disgust. The vices and corruptions of the age, a low opinion of one's fellowmen, and nostalgia 36 for the well-ordered past were the favorite themes of literary men. Even Boccaccio in his later works became ill-tempered. "All good customs fail," laments Christine de Pisan of France, "and virtues are held at little worth." Eustache Deschamps complains that "the child of today has become a ruffian. . . . People are gluttons and drunkards, haughty of heart, caring for nought, not honor nor goodness nor kindness . . ." and he ends each verse with the refrain, "Time past had virtue and righteousness but today reigns only vice." In England John Gower denounces Rome for simony, Lollards for heresy, clergy and monks for idleness and lust, kings, nobles, and knights for self-indulgence and rapine, the law for bribery, merchants for usury and fraud, the commons for ignorance, and in general the sins of perjury, lechery, avarice, and pride as displayed in extravagant fashions.

37   These last did indeed, as in all distracted times, reflect a reaching for the absurd, especially in the long pointed shoes which kept getting longer until the points had to be tied up around the knee, and the young men's doublets which kept getting shorter until they revealed the buttocks, to the censure of moralists and snickers of the crowd. Leaving miniskirts to the males, the ladies inexplicably adopted a fashion of gowns and posture designed to make them look pregnant.

38   Self-disgust, it seems to me, has reappeared in our time, not without cause. The succession of events since 1914 has disqualified belief in moral progress, and pollution of the physical world is our bubonic plague. Like the fourteenth century, we have lost confidence in man's capacity to control his fate and even in his capacity to be good. So we have a literature of the anti-hero aimlessly wandering among the perverse, absurd, and depraved; we have porn and pop and blank canvases and anti-music designed to deafen. I am not sure whether in all this the artists are expressing contempt for their fellowman or the loud laugh that bespeaks emptiness of feeling, but whatever the message, it has a faint ring of the *Danse Macabre.*

39   Historians until recently have hurried over the fourteenth century because like most people they prefer not to deal with failure. But it would be a mistake to imply that it was solid gloom. Seen from inside, especially from a position of privilege, it had beauties and wonders, and the ferment itself was exciting. "In these fifty years," said the renowned Comte de Foix to the chronicler Froissart in the year 1389, "there have been more feats of arms and more marvels in the world than in the three hundred years before." The Count himself, a famous huntsman, was known as Phoebus for his personal beauty and splendid court.

40   The streets of cities were bright with colored clothes; crimson

fur-lined gowns of merchants, parti-colored velvets and silks of a noble-
man's retinue, in sky blue and fawn or two shades of scarlet or it might
be the all-emerald liveries of the Green Count of Savoy. Street sounds
were those of human voices: criers of news and official announcements,
shopkeepers in their doorways and itinerant vendors crying fresh eggs,
charcoal at a penny a sack, candlewicks "brighter than the stars," cakes
and waffles, mushrooms, hot baths. Mountebanks entertained the public in the town square or village green with tricks and magic and trained
animals. Jongleurs sang ballads of adventure in Saracen lands. After
church on Sundays, laborers gathered in cookshops and taverns; burghers promenaded in their gardens or visited their vineyards outside the
city walls. Church bells marked the eight times of day from Matins
through Vespers, when shops closed, work ceased, silence succeeded
bustle, and the darkness of unlit night descended.

The gaudy extravagance of noble life was awesome. Now and then   41
its patronage brought forth works of eternal beauty like the exquisite
illuminated Books of Hours commissioned by the Duc de Berry. More
often it was pure ostentation and conspicuous consumption. Charles V
of France owned forty-seven jeweled and golden crowns and sixty-three
complete sets of chapel furnishings, including vestments, gold cruci-
fixes, altarpieces, reliquaries, and prayer books. Jewels and cloth of gold
marked every occasion and every occasion was pretext for a spectacle—
a grand procession, or ceremonial welcome to a visiting prince, a tournament or entertainment with music, and dancing by the light of great
torches. When Gian Galeazzo Visconti, ruler of Milan, gave a wedding
banquet for his daughter, eighteen double courses were served, each of
fish and meat, including trout, quail, herons, eels, sturgeon, and suck-
ling pig spouting fire. The gifts presented after *each* course to several
hundred guests included greyhounds in gem-studded velvet collars,
hawks in tinkling silver bells, suits of armor, rolls of silk and brocade,
garments trimmed with pearls and ermine, fully caparisoned war-
horses, and twelve fat oxen. For the entry into Paris of the new Queen,
Isabel of Bavaria, the entire length of the Rue St. Denis was hung with a
canopy representing the firmament twinkling with stars from which
sweetly singing angels descended bearing a crown, and fountains ran
with wine, distributed to the people in golden cups by lovely maidens
wearing caps of solid gold.

One wonders where all the money came from for such luxury and   42
festivity in a time of devastation. What taxes could burned-out and
destitute people pay? This is a puzzle until one remembers that the Aga
Khan got to be the richest man in the world on the backs of the poorest

people, and that disaster is never as pervasive as it seems from recorded accounts. It is one of the pitfalls for historians that the very fact of being on the record makes a happening appear to have been continuous and all-inclusive, whereas in reality it is more likely to have been sporadic both in time and place. Besides, persistence of the normal is usually greater than the effect of disturbance, as we know from our own times. After absorbing the daily paper and weekly magazine, one expects to face a world consisting entirely of strikes, crimes, power shortages, broken water mains, stalled trains, school shutdowns, Black Panthers, addicts, transvestites, rapists, and militant lesbians. The fact is that one can come home in the evening—on a lucky day—without having encountered more than two or three of these phenomena. This has led me to formulate Tuchman's Law, as follows: "The fact of being reported increases the *apparent* extent of a deplorable development by a factor of ten." (I snatch the figure from the air and will leave it to the quantifiers to justify.)

43   The astonishing fact is that except for Boccaccio, to whom we owe the most vivid account, the Black Death was virtually ignored by the great writers of the time. Petrarch, who was forty-four when it happened, mentions it only as the occasion for the death of Laura; Chaucer, from what I have read, passes it over in silence; Jean Froissart, the Herodotus of his time, gives it no more than one casual paragraph, and even that second Isaiah, the author of *Piers Plowman*, who might have been expected to make it central to his theme of woe, uses it only incidentally. One could argue that in 1348 Chaucer was only eight or nine years old and Froissart ten or eleven and the unknown Langland probably of the same vintage, but that is old enough to absorb and remember a great catastrophe, especially when they lived through several returns of the plague as grown men.

44   Perhaps this tells us that disaster, once survived, leaves less track than one supposed, or that man's instinct for living pushes it down below the surface, or simply that his recuperative powers are remarkable. Or was it just an accident of personality? Is it significant or just chance that Chaucer, the greatest writer of his age, was so uncharacteristic of it in sanguine temperament and good-humored view of his fellow creatures?

45   As for Froissart, never was a man more in love with his age. To him it appeared as a marvelous pageant of glittering armor and the beauty of emblazoned banners fluttering in the breeze and the clear shrill call of the trumpet. Still believing, still enraptured by the chivalric ideal, he reports savagery, treachery, limitless greed, and the pitiless slaughter of the poor when driven to revolt as minor stumbles in

the grand adventure of valor and honor. Yet near the end, even Froissart could not hide from himself the decay made plain by a dissolute court, venality in high places, and a knighthood that kept losing battles. In 1397, the year he turned sixty, the defeat and massacre of the flower of chivalry at the hands of the Turks in the battle of Nicopolis set the seal on the incompetence of his heroes. Lastly, the murder of a King in England shocked him deeply, not for any love of Richard II but because the act was subversive of the whole order that sustained his world. As in Watergate, the underside had rolled to the surface all too visibly. Froissart had not the heart to continue and brought his chronicle to an end.

The sad century closed with a meeting between King Charles VI of France and the Emperor Wenceslaus, the one intermittently mad and the other regularly drunk. They met at Reims in 1397 to consult on means of ending the papal schism, but whenever Charles had a lucid interval, Wenceslaus was in a stupor and so the conference, proving fruitless, was called off.   46

It makes an artistic ending. Yet in that same year Johann Gutenberg, who was to change the world, was born. In the next century appeared Joan of Arc, embodying the new spirit of nationalism, still pure like mountain water before it runs downhill; and Columbus, who opened a new hemisphere; and Copernicus, who revolutionized the concept of the earth's relation to the universe; and Michelangelo, whose sculptured visions gave man a new status; in those proud, superb, unconquered figures, the human being, not God, was captain.   47

As our century enters its final quarter, I am not persuaded, despite the signs, that the end is necessarily doom. The doomsayers work by extrapolation; they take a trend and extend it, forgetting that the doom factor sooner or later generates a coping mechanism. I have a rule for this situation too, which is absolute: you cannot extrapolate any series in which the human element intrudes; history, that is, the human narrative, never follows, and will always fool, the scientific curve. I cannot tell you what twists it will take, but I expect, that like our ancestors, we, too, will muddle through.   48

_____ CONSIDERATIONS _____

1. Barbara Tuchman's essay is built on a useful and classic plan—comparisons and contrasts support and illustrate a main idea or thesis. Find three or four uses of comparison in this essay. Then see whether they do, in fact, undergird the author's major idea.

2. As a professional historian, Tuchman verifies her facts in many kinds

of research materials, although in this relatively informal essay she does not footnote her sources. Notice how she manages to acknowledge those sources and smoothly work the material into her discussion.

3. "Guilt, I suspect," writes Tuchman in paragraph 14, "is modern; sin is medieval." This highly compressed, neatly balanced statement is a good example of aphorism, and, more important, shows us, if we stop to think, a truly economical use of language. What is the point of the distinction?

4. What do you make of "Tuchman's Law," as the author mischievously puts it in paragraph 42? Is she just having fun, or can Tuchman's Law be demonstrated today as the mass media manage our awareness of trends?

5. Tuchman claims that much of the decaying public confidence in governing institutions comes from "our nurture in that conspiracy of fables called advertising." In what specific ways would Daniel Boorstin (see "The Pseudo-Event") agree or disagree with her?

6. History makes sense, students say, when it is clearly related to present life. Is Tuchman successful in bringing the two together? Explain.

*John Updike (b. 1932) grew up in Pennsylvania and went to
Harvard, where he edited the humor magazine, the* Lampoon.
On a fellowship year at Oxford, Updike sold a poem to the New
Yorker *and began his long relationship with that magazine. First
he worked on the staff of the* New Yorker, *contributing to "The
Talk of the Town." When he quit to freelance, he continued to
write stories, poems, reviews, and articles for the magazine.* The
Poorhouse Fair *(1959), his first novel, appeared in the same year
as his first collection of stories,* The Same Door, *from which we
take "Ace in the Hole." This story appears to be the seed of his
second novel,* Rabbit, Run *(1960)—also about an ex-basketball
star with a deteriorating marriage.*

*Updike has published stories, novels, poems, and
miscellaneous collections,* Assorted Prose *(1965),* Picked-up
Pieces *(1975), and* Hugging the Shore *(1983). Among his best-
known novels are* The Centaur *(1963) and* The Witches of
Eastwick *(1984), which was made into a film in 1987. More
recently, he has published new stories collected as* Trust Me
(1987), and a memoir titled Self-Consciousness *(1989).*

79

JOHN UPDIKE
Ace in the Hole

No sooner did his car touch the boulevard heading home than Ace   1
flicked on the radio. He needed the radio, especially today. In the
seconds before the tubes warmed up, he said aloud, doing it just to hear
a human voice, "Jesus. She'll pop her lid." His voice, though familiar,
irked him; it sounded thin and scratchy, as if the bones in his head were
picking up static. In a deeper register Ace added, "She'll murder me."
Then the radio came on, warm and strong, so he stopped worrying. The
Five Kings were doing "Blueberry Hill"; to hear them made Ace feel so
sure inside that from the pack pinched between the car roof and sun

shield he plucked a cigarette, hung it on his lower lip, snapped a match across the rusty place on the dash, held the flame in the instinctive spot near the tip of his nose, dragged, and blew out the match, all in time to the music. He rolled down the window and snapped the match so it spun end-over-end into the gutter. "Two points," he said, and cocked the cigarette toward the roof of the car, sucked powerfully, and exhaled two plumes through his nostrils. He was beginning to feel like himself, Ace Anderson, for the first time that whole day, a bad day. He beat time on the accelerator. The car jerked crazily. "On Blueberry Hill," he sang, "my heart stood still. The wind in the wil-low tree"—he braked for a red light—"played love's suh-*weet* melodee—"

2   "Go, Dad, bust your lungs!" a kid's voice blared. The kid was riding in a '52 Pontiac that had pulled up beside Ace at the light. The profile of the driver, another kid, was dark over his shoulder.

3   Ace looked over at him and smiled slowly, just letting one side of his mouth lift a little. "Shove it," he said, good-naturedly, across the little gap of years that separated them. He knew how they felt, young and mean and shy.

4   But the kid, who looked Greek, lifted his thick upper lip and spat out the window. The spit gleamed on the asphalt like a half-dollar.

5   "Now isn't that pretty?" Ace said, keeping one eye on the light. "You miserable wop. You are *mis*erable." While the kid was trying to think of some smart comeback, the light changed. Ace dug out so hard he smelled burned rubber. In his rear-view mirror he saw the Pontiac lurch forward a few yards, then stop dead, right in the middle of the intersection.

6   The idea of them stalling their fat tin Pontiac kept him in a good humor all the way home. He decided to stop at his mother's place and pick up the baby, instead of waiting for Evey to do it. His mother must have seen him drive up. She came out on the porch holding a plastic spoon and smelling of cake.

7   "You're out early," she told him.

8   "Friedman fired me," Ace told her.

9   "Good for you," his mother said. "I always said he never treated you right." She brought a cigarette out of her apron pocket and tucked it deep into one corner of her mouth, the way she did when something pleased her.

10   Ace lighted it for her. "Friedman was O.K. personally," he said. "He just wanted too much for his money. I didn't mind working Saturdays, but until eleven, twelve Friday nights was too much. Everybody has a right to some leisure."

11   "Well, I don't dare think what Evey will say, but I, for one, thank

dear God you had the brains to get out of it. I always said that job had no future to it—no future of any kind, Freddy."

"I guess," Ace admitted. "But I wanted to keep at it, for the family's sake." 12

"Now, I know I shouldn't be saying this, but any time Evey—this is just between us—any time Evey thinks she can do better, there's room for you *and* Bonnie right in your father's house." She pinched her lips together. He could almost hear the old lady think, *There, I've said it.* 13

"Look, Mom, Evey tries awfully hard, and anyway you know she can't work that way. Not that *that*—I mean, she's a realist, too . . ." He let the rest of the thought fade as he watched a kid across the street dribbling a basketball around a telephone pole that had a backboard and net nailed on it. 14

"Evey's a wonderful girl of her own kind. But I've always said, and your father agrees, Roman Catholics ought to marry among themselves. Now I know I've said it before, but when they get out in the greater world—" 15

"*No*, Mom." 16

She frowned, smoothed herself, and said, "Your name was in the paper today." 17

Ace chose to let that go by. He kept watching the kid with the basketball. It was funny how, though the whole point was to get the ball up into the air, kids grabbed it by the sides and squeezed. Kids just didn't think. 18

"Did you hear?" his mother asked. 19

"Sure, but so what?" Ace said. His mother's lower lip was coming at him, so he changed the subject. "I guess I'll take Bonnie." 20

His mother went into the house and brought back his daughter, wrapped in a blue blanket. The baby looked dopey. "She fussed all day," his mother complained. "I said to your father, 'Bonnie is a dear little girl, but without a doubt she's her mother's daughter.' You were the best-natured boy." 21

"Well I *had* everything," Ace said with an impatience that made his mother blink. He nicely dropped his cigarette into a brown flowerpot on the edge of the porch and took his daughter into his arms. She was getting heavier, solid. When he reached the end of the cement walk, his mother was still on the porch, waving to him. He was so close he could see the fat around her elbow jiggle, and he only lived a half block up the street, yet here she was, waving to him as if he was going to Japan. 22

At the door of his car, it seemed stupid to him to drive the measly 23 half block home. His old coach, Bob Behn, used to say never to ride where you could walk. Cars were the death of legs. Ace left the ignition keys in his pocket and ran along the pavement with Bonnie laughing and bouncing at his chest. He slammed the door of his landlady's house open and shut, pounded up the two flights of stairs, and was panting so hard when he reached the door of his apartment that it took him a couple of seconds to fit the key into the lock.

24   The run must have tuned Bonnie up. As soon as he lowered her into the crib, she began to shout and wave her arms. He didn't want to play with her. He tossed some blocks and a rattle into the crib and walked into the bathroom, where he turned on the hot water and began to comb his hair. Holding the comb under the faucet before every stroke, he combed his hair forward. It was so long, one strand curled under his nose and touched his lips. He whipped the whole mass back with a single pull. He tucked in the tufts around his ears, and ran the comb straight back on both sides of his head. With his fingers he felt for the little ridge at the back where the two sides met. It was there, as it should have been. Finally, he mussed the hair in front enough for one little lock to droop over his forehead, like Alan Ladd. It made the temple seem lower than it was. Every day, his hairline looked higher. He had observed all around him how blond men went bald first. He remembered reading somewhere, though, that baldness shows virility.

25   On his way to the kitchen he flipped the left-hand knob of the television. Bonnie was always quieter with the set on. Ace didn't see how she could understand much of it, but it seemed to mean something to her. He found a can of beer in the refrigerator behind some brownish lettuce and those hot dogs Evey never got around to cooking. She'd be home any time. The clock said 5:12. She'd pop her lid.

26   Ace didn't see what he could do but try and reason with her. "Evey," he'd say, "you ought to thank God I got out of it. It had no future to it at all." He hoped she wouldn't get too mad, because when she was mad he wondered if he should have married her, and doubting that made him feel crowded. It was bad enough, his mother always crowding him. He punched the two triangles in the top of the beer can, the little triangle first, and then the big one, the one he drank from. He hoped Evey wouldn't say anything that couldn't be forgotten. What women didn't seem to realize was that there were things you knew but shouldn't say.

27   He felt sorry he had called the kid in the car a wop.

28   Ace balanced the beer on a corner where two rails of the crib met and looked under the chairs for the morning paper. He had trouble

finding his name, because it was at the bottom of a column on an inside sports page, in a small article about the county basketball statistics:

> "Dusty" Tremwick, Grosvenor Park's sure-fingered center, copped the individual scoring honors with a season's grand (and we do mean grand) total of 376 points. This is within eighteen points of the all-time record of 394 racked up in the 1949–1950 season by Olinger High's Fred Anderson.

Ace angrily sailed the paper into an armchair. Now it was Fred 29
Anderson; it used to be Ace. He hated being called Fred, especially in print, but then the sportswriters were all office boys anyway, Bonn used to say.

"Do not just ask for shoe polish," a man on television said, "but 30
ask for *Emu Shoe Gloss*, the *only* polish that absolutely *guarantees* to make your shoes look shinier than new." Ace turned the sound off, so that the man moved his mouth like a fish blowing bubbles. Right away, Bonnie howled, so Ace turned it up loud enough to drown her out and went into the kitchen, without knowing what he wanted there. He wasn't hungry; his stomach was tight. It used to be like that when he walked to the gymnasium alone in the dark before a game and could see the people from town, kids and parents, crowding in at the lighted doors. But once he was inside, the locker room would be bright and hot, and the other guys would be there, laughing it up and towel-slapping, and the tight feeling would leave. Now there were whole days when it didn't leave.

A key scratched at the door lock. Ace decided to stay in the 31
kitchen. Let *her* find *him*. Her heels clicked on the floor for a step or two; then the television set went off. Bonnie began to cry. "Shut up, honey," Evey said. There was a silence.

"I'm home," Ace called. 32

"No kidding. I thought Bonnie got the beer by herself." 33

Ace laughed. She was in a sarcastic mood, thinking she was 34
Lauren Bacall. That was all right, just so she kept funny. Still smiling, Ace eased into the living room and got hit with, "What are *you* smirking about? Another question: What's the idea running up the street with Bonnie like she was a football?"

"You saw that?" 35

"Your mother told me." 36

"You saw her?" 37

"Of course I saw her. I dropped by to pick up Bonnie. What the hell 38
do you think?—I read her tiny mind?"

39   "Take it easy," Ace said, wondering if Mom had told her about Friedman.

40   "Take it easy? Don't coach *me.* Another question: Why's the car out in front of her place? You give the car to her?"

41   "Look, I parked it there to pick up Bonnie, and I thought I'd leave it there."

42   "Why?"

43   "Whaddeya mean, why? I just did. I just thought I'd walk. It's not that far, you know."

44   "No, I don't know. If you'd been on your feet all day long a block would look like one hell of a long way."

45   "Okay. I'm sorry."

46   She hung up her coat and stepped out of her shoes and walked around the room picking up things. She stuck the newspaper in the wastebasket.

47   Ace said, "My name was in the paper today."

48   "They spell it right?" She shoved the paper deep into the basket with her foot. There was no doubt; she knew about Friedman.

49   "They called me Fred."

50   "Isn't that your name? What *is* your name anyway? Hero J. Great?"

51   There wasn't any answer, so Ace didn't try any. He sat down on the sofa, lighted a cigarette, and waited.

52   Evey picked up Bonnie. "Poor thing stinks. What does your mother do, scrub out the toilet with her?"

53   "Can't you take it easy? I know you're tired."

54   "You should. I'm always tired."

55   Evey and Bonnie went into the bathroom; when they came out, Bonnie was clean and Evey was calm. Evey sat down in an easy chair beside Ace and rested her stocking feet on his knees. "Hit me," she said, twiddling her fingers for the cigarette.

56   The baby crawled up to her chair and tried to stand, to see what he gave her. Leaning over close to Bonnie's nose, Evey grinned, smoke leaking through her teeth, and said, "Only for grownups, honey."

57   "Eve," Ace began, "there was no future in that job. Working all Saturday, and then Friday nights on top of it."

58   "I know. Your mother told *me* all that, too. All I want from you is what happened."

59   She was going to take it like a sport, then. He tried to remember how it *did* happen. "It wasn't my fault," he said. "Friedman told me to back this '51 Chevy into the line that faces Church Street. He just

bought it from an old guy this morning who said it only had thirteen thousand on it. So in I jump and start her up. There was a knock in the engine like a machine gun. I almost told Friedman he'd bought a squirrel, but you know I cut that smart stuff out ever since Palotta laid me off."

"You told me that story. What happens in this one?"   60

"Look, Eve. I *am* telling ya. Do you want me to go out to a movie or   61
something?"

"Suit yourself."   62

"So I jump in the Chevy and snap it back in line, and there was a   63
kind of scrape and thump. I get out and look and Friedman's running
over, his arms going like *this*"—Ace whirled his own arms and
laughed—"and here was the whole back fender of a '49 Merc mashed in.
Just looked like somebody took a planer and shaved off the bulge, you
know, there at the back." He tried to show her with his hands. "The
Chevy, though, didn't have a dent. It even gained some paint. But
Friedman, to *hear* him—Boy, they can rave when their pocketbook's
hit. He said"—Ace laughed again—"never mind."

Evey said, "You're proud of yourself."   64

"No, listen. I'm not happy about it. But there wasn't a thing I could   65
do. It wasn't my driving at all. I looked over on the other side, and there
was just two or three inches between the Chevy and a Buick. *Nobody*
could have gotten into that hole. Even if it had hair on it." He thought
this was pretty good.

She didn't. "You could have looked."   66

"There just wasn't the *space*. Friedman said stick it in; I stuck   67
it in."

"But you could have looked and moved the other cars to make   68
more room."

"I guess that would have been the smart thing."   69

"I guess, too. Now what?"   70

"What do you mean?"   71

"I mean now what? Are you going to give up? Go back to the   72
Army? Your mother? Be a basketball pro? What?"

"You know I'm not tall enough. Anybody under six-six they don't   73
want."

"Is that so? Six-six? Well, please listen to this, Mr. Six-Foot-Five-   74
and-a-Half: I'm fed up. I'm ready as Christ to let you run." She stabbed
her cigarette into an ashtray on the arm of the chair so hard the ashtray
jumped to the floor. Evey flushed and shut up.

What Ace hated most in their arguments was these silences after   75

Evey had said something so ugly she wanted to take it back. "Better ask the priest first," he murmured.

76   She sat right up. "If there's one thing I don't want to hear about from you it's priests. You let the priests to me. You don't know a damn thing about it. Not a damn thing."

77   "Hey, look at Bonnie," he said, trying to make a fresh start with his tone.

78   Evey didn't hear him. "If you think," she went on, "if for one rotten moment you think, Mr. Fred, that the be-all and end-all of my life is you and your hot-shot stunts—"

79   "Look, Mother," Ace pleaded, pointing at Bonnie. The baby had picked up the ashtray and put in on her head for a hat and was waiting for praise.

80   Evey glanced down sharply at the child. "Cute," she said. "Cute as her daddy."

81   The ashtray slid from Bonnie's head and she patted where it had been and looked around puzzled.

82   "Yeah, but watch," Ace said. "Watch her hands. They're really terrific hands."

83   "You're nuts," Evey said.

84   "No, honest. Bonnie's great. She's a natural. Get the rattle for her. Never mind, I'll get it." In two steps, Ace was at Bonnie's crib, picking the rattle out of the mess of blocks and plastic rings and beanbags. He extended the rattle toward his daughter, shaking it delicately. Made wary by this burst of attention, Bonnie reached with both hands; like two separate animals they approached from opposite sides and touched the smooth rattle simultaneously. A smile bubbled up on her face. Ace tugged weakly. She held on, and then tugged back. "She's a natural," Ace said, "and it won't do her any good because she's a girl. Baby, we got to have a boy."

85   "I'm not your baby," Evey said, closing her eyes.

86   Saying "Baby" over and over again, Ace backed up to the radio and, without turning around, switched on the volume knob. In the moment before the tubes warmed up, Evey had time to say, "Wise up, Freddy. What shall we do?"

87   The radio came in on something slow: dinner music. Ace picked Bonnie up and set her in the crib. "Shall we dance?" he asked his wife, bowing.

88   "I want to talk."

89   "Baby. It's the cocktail hour."

"This is getting us no place," she said, rising from her chair, though. 90

"Fred Junior. I can see him now," he said, seeing nothing. 91

"We will have no Juniors." 92

In her crib, Bonnie whimpered at the sight of her mother being 93
seized. Ace fitted his hand into the natural place on Evey's back and she
shuffled stiffly into his lead. When, with a sudden injection of saxo-
phones, the tempo quickened, he spun her out carefully, keeping the
beat with his shoulders. Her hair brushed his lips as she minced in, then
swung away, to the end of his arm; he could feel her toes dig into the
carpet. He flipped his own hair back from his eyes. The music ate
through his skin and mixed with the nerves and small veins; he seemed
to be great again, and all the other kids were around them, in a ring,
clapping time.

___ **CONSIDERATIONS** _____

1. Updike often uses minute physical observations. Do you find any of
these in "Ace in the Hole"? How do they contribute to the story's effect?

2. How old is Ace? What information in the story prompts you to make a
guess? What kind of age do you mean—chronological, mental, emotional? How
important is his age to the story?

3. What are Ace's *real* interests: wife, child, job, future career? How does
Updike help you discriminate between Ace's casual and lasting interests?

4. Which is most important to Ace—the past, the present, or the future?
Cite evidence. Of what thematic significance is this question?

5. If you were a marriage counselor, would you have any advice for this
young couple? Would you say that their marriage is in trouble? What are the
chances that they would even consider consulting a marriage counselor? For
your answers use the story itself.

6. What importance has play had in Ace's life? What particulars in the
story reveal his attitude toward play, sport, games, fun, diversions, recreation?

7. Compare the reactions of Ace's mother and his wife to losing the job.
How do their different attitudes toward this event reveal important things
about Ace's life at this time?

Gore Vidal (b. 1925) entered the army after graduating from
Phillips Exeter Academy and never attended college. He
published his first novel the year he turned twenty-one. Since
then, he has run for Congress and lived in Europe. Vidal's
writing includes plays, essays, and, chiefly, novels, including
Julian (1964), Myra Breckinridge (1968), Burr (1973), Kalki
(1979), Lincoln (1984), and Empire (1987).

80

GORE VIDAL

Drugs

1   It is possible to stop most drug addiction in the United States
within a very short time. Simply make all drugs available and sell them
at cost. Label each drug with a precise description of what effect—good
and bad—the drug will have on the taker. This will require heroic
honesty. Don't say that marijuana is addictive or dangerous when it is
neither, as millions of people know—unlike "speed," which kills most
unpleasantly, or heroin, which is addictive and difficult to kick.

2   For the record, I have tried—once—almost every drug and liked
none, disproving the popular Fu Manchu theory that a single whiff of
opium will enslave the mind. Nevertheless many drugs are bad for
certain people to take and they should be told why in a sensible way.

3   Along with exhortation and warning, it might be good for our
citizens to recall (or learn for the first time) that the United States was
the creation of men who believed that each man has the right to do what
he wants with his own life as long as he does not interfere with his
neighbor's pursuit of happiness (that his neighbor's idea of happiness is
persecuting others does confuse matters a bit).

4   This is a startling notion to the current generation of Americans.
They reflect a system of public education which has made the Bill of
Rights, literally, unacceptable to a majority of high school graduates

(see the annual Purdue reports) who now form the "silent majority"—a phrase which that underestimated wit Richard Nixon took from Homer who used it to describe the dead.

Now one can hear the warning rumble begin: if everyone is al- 5
lowed to take drugs everyone will and the GNP will decrease, the Commies will stop us from making everyone free, and we shall end up a race of Zombies, passively murmuring "groovie" to one another. Alarming thought. Yet it seems most unlikely that any reasonably sane person will become a drug addict if he knows in advance what addiction is going to be like.

Is everyone reasonably sane? No. Some people will always become 6
drug addicts just as some people will always become alcoholics, and it is just too bad. Every man, however, has the power (and should have the legal right) to kill himself if he chooses. But since most men don't, they won't be mainliners either. Nevertheless, forbidding people things they like or think they might enjoy only makes them want those things all the more. This psychological insight is, for some mysterious reason, perennially denied our governors.

It is a lucky thing for the American moralist that our country has 7
always existed in a kind of time-vacuum: we have no public memory of anything that happened before last Tuesday. No one in Washington today recalls what happened during the years alcohol was forbidden to the people by a Congress that thought it had a divine mission to stamp out Demon Rum—launching, in the process, the greatest crime wave in the country's history, causing thousands of deaths from bad alcohol, and creating a general (and persisting) contempt among the citizenry for the laws of the United States.

The same thing is happening today. But the government has 8
learned nothing from past attempts at prohibition, not to mention repression.

Last year when the supply of Mexican marijuana was slightly 9
curtailed by the Feds, the pushers got the kids hooked on heroin and deaths increased dramatically, particularly in New York. Whose fault? Evil men like the Mafiosi? Permissive Dr. Spock? Wild-eyed Dr. Leary? No.

The Government of the United States was responsible for those 10
deaths. The bureaucratic machine has a vested interest in playing cops and robbers. Both the Bureau of Narcotics and the Mafia want strong laws against the sale and use of drugs because if drugs are sold at cost there would be no money in it for anyone.

If there was no money in it for the Mafia, there would be no 11 friendly playground pushers, and addicts would not commit crimes to pay for the next fix. Finally, if there was no money in it, the Bureau of Narcotics would wither away, something they are not about to do without a struggle.

12   Will anything sensible be done? Of course not. The American people are as devoted to the idea of sin and its punishment as they are to making money—and fighting drugs is nearly as big a business as pushing them. Since the combination of sin and money is irresistible (particularly to the professional politician), the situation will only grow worse.

_____ CONSIDERATIONS _____

1. One mark of the experienced arguer is the ability to anticipate and thus neutralize his opponent's rebuttal. Where does Vidal do this? How effective is his attempt?

2. Vidal's argument (paragraphs 10, 11, and 12) that "the bureaucratic machine has a vested interest in playing cops and robbers" rests on his implication that lawmen are at least as interested in preserving their jobs as they are in preserving law and order. Does he present any evidence to support this argument? What kind of evidence could he offer? How could you support a counterargument?

3. Vidal contends that every man "should have the legal right to kill himself." How far would he (or you) extend that "right"? To all varieties of suicide, for instance?

4. Refresh your memory of the Bill of Rights—where do you find it?— and explain why Vidal says it has become "unacceptable to a majority of high school graduates."

5. Is the slang term "groovie"—usually spelled "groovy"—still current? Linguists often study slang because it changes faster than standard language. For the same reason, geneticists study fruit flies because the quick turnover of generations allows them to investigate principles of genetics within a brief period of time. In what way(s) do changes in slang parallel changes in English in general?

6. Given Vidal's belief in freedom of the individual, how do you think he would approach the question of gun control?

7. Write a rebuttal to Vidal's argument, using current statistics and trends in drug abuse.

Alice Walker (b. 1944) grew up in Georgia and went to Sarah Lawrence College in New York City. She first published as a poet, with Once *and* Revolutionary Petunias, *and has added collections of short stories, a biography of Langston Hughes, and novels—notably* The Color Purple *(1982), and more recently* The Temple of My Familiar *(1989).*

She collected her essays as In Search of Our Mothers' Gardens, *from which we take this article originally published in 1970. Elsewhere in* A Writer's Reader *you will find the white Southern writers William Faulkner and Flannery O'Connor, whom Alice Walker mentions in this essay.*

81

ALICE WALKER
The Black Writer and the Southern Experience

My mother tells of an incident that happened to her in the thirties 1
during the Depression. She and my father lived in a small Georgia town and had half a dozen children. They were sharecroppers, and food, especially flour, was almost impossible to obtain. To get flour, which was distributed by the Red Cross, one had to submit vouchers signed by a local official. On the day my mother was to go into town for flour she received a large box of clothes from one of my aunts who was living in the North. The clothes were in good condition, though well worn, and my mother needed a dress, so she immediately put on one of those from the box and wore it into town. When she reached the distribution center and presented her voucher she was confronted by a white woman who looked her up and down with marked anger and envy.

"What'd you come up here for?" the woman asked. 2

"For some flour," said my mother, presenting her voucher. 3

"Humph," said the woman, looking at her more closely and with 4 unconcealed fury. "Anybody dressed up as good as you don't need to come here *begging* for food."

5   "I ain't begging," said my mother; "the government is giving away flour to those that need it, and I need it. I wouldn't be here if I didn't. And these clothes I'm wearing was given to me." But the woman had already turned to the next person in line, saying over her shoulder to the white man who was behind the counter with her, "The *gall* of niggers coming in here dressed better than me!" This thought seemed to make her angrier still, and my mother, pulling three of her small children behind her and crying from humiliation, walked sadly back into the street.

6   "What did you and Daddy do for flour that winter?" I asked my mother.

7   "Well," she said, "Aunt Mandy Aikens lived down the road from us and she got plenty of flour. We had a good stand of corn so we had plenty of meal. Aunt Mandy would swap me a bucket of flour for a bucket of meal. We got by all right."

8   Then she added thoughtfully, "And that old woman that turned me off so short got down so bad in the end that she was walking on *two* sticks." And I knew she was thinking, though she never said it: Here I am today, my eight children healthy and grown and three of them in college and me with hardly a sick day for years. Ain't Jesus wonderful?

9   In this small story is revealed the condition and strength of a people. Outcasts to be used and humiliated by the larger society, the Southern black sharecropper and poor farmer clung to his own kind and to a religion that had been given to pacify him as a slave but which he soon transformed into an antidote against bitterness. Depending on one another, because they had nothing and no one else, the sharecroppers often managed to come through "all right." And when I listen to my mother tell and retell this story I find that the white woman's vindictiveness is less important than Aunt Mandy's resourceful generosity or my mother's ready stand of corn. For their lives were not about that pitiful example of Southern womanhood, but about themselves.

10   What the black Southern writer inherits as a natural right is a sense of *community*. Something simple but surprisingly hard, especially these days, to come by. My mother, who is a walking history of our community, tells me that when each of her children was born the midwife accepted as payment such home-grown or homemade items as a pig, a quilt, jars of canned fruits and vegetables. But there was never any question that the midwife would come when she was needed, whatever the eventual payment for her services. I consider this each

time I hear of a hospital that refuses to admit a woman in labor unless she can hand over a substantial sum of money, cash.

Nor am I nostalgic, as a French philosopher once wrote, for lost 11 poverty. I am nostalgic for the solidarity and sharing a modest existence can sometimes bring. We knew, I suppose, that we were poor. Somebody knew; perhaps the landowner who grudgingly paid my father three hundred dollars a year for twelve months' labor. But we never considered ourselves to be poor, unless, of course, we were deliberately humiliated. And because we never believed we were poor, and therefore worthless, we could depend on one another without shame. And always there were the Burial Societies, the Sick-and-Shut-in Societies, that sprang up out of spontaneous need. And no one seemed terribly upset that black sharecroppers were ignored by white insurance companies. It went without saying, in my mother's day, that birth and death required assistance from the community, and that the magnitude of these events was lost on outsiders.

As a college student I came to reject the Christianity of my par- 12 ents, and it took me years to realize that though they had been force-fed a white man's palliative, in the form of religion, they had made it into something at once simple and noble. True, even today, they can never successfully picture a God who is not white, and that is a major cruelty, but their lives testify to a greater comprehension of the teachings of Jesus than the lives of people who sincerely believe a God *must* have a color and that there can be such a phenomenon as a "white" church.

The richness of the black writer's experience in the South can be 13 remarkable, though some people might not think so. Once, while in college, I told a white middle-aged Northerner that I hoped to be a poet. In the nicest possible language, which still made me as mad as I've ever been, he suggested that a "farmer's daughter" might not be the stuff of which poets are made. On one level, of course, he had a point. A shack with only a dozen or so books is an unlikely place to discover a young Keats. But it is narrow thinking, indeed, to believe that a Keats is the only kind of poet one would want to grow up to be. One wants to write poetry that is understood by one's people, not by the Queen of England. Of course, should she be able to profit by it too, so much the better, but since that is not likely, catering to her tastes would be a waste of time.

For the black Southern writer, coming straight out of the country, 14 as Wright did—Natchez and Jackson are still not as citified as they like to think they are—there is the world of comparisons; between town and country, between the ugly crowding and griminess of the cities and the spacious cleanliness (which actually seems impossible to dirty) of the country. A country person finds the city confining, like a too tight dress. And always, in one's memory, there remain all the rituals of one's growing up: the warmth and vividness of Sunday worship (never mind that you never quite believed) in a little church hidden from the road, and houses set so far back into the woods that at night it is impossible for strangers to find them. The daily dramas that evolve in such a private world are pure gold. But this view of a strictly private and hidden existence, with its triumphs, failures, grotesqueries, is not nearly as valuable to the socially conscious black Southern writer as his double vision is. For not only is he in a position to see his own world, and its close community ("Homecomings" on First Sundays, barbecues to raise money to send to Africa—one of the smaller ironies—the simplicity and eerie calm of a black funeral, where the beloved one is buried way in the middle of a wood with nothing to mark the spot but perhaps a wooden cross already coming apart), but also he is capable of knowing, with remarkably silent accuracy, the people who make up the larger world that surrounds and suppresses his own.

15   It is a credit to a writer like Ernest J. Gaines, a black writer who writes mainly about the people he grew up with in rural Louisiana, that he can write about whites and blacks exactly as he sees them and *knows* them, instead of writing of one group as a vast malignant lump and of the others as a conglomerate of perfect virtues.

16   In large measure, black Southern writers owe their clarity of vision to parents who refused to diminish themselves as human beings by succumbing to racism. Our parents seemed to know that an extreme negative emotion held against other human beings for reasons they do not control can be blinding. Blindness about other human beings, especially for a writer, is equivalent to death. Because of this blindness, which is, above all, racial, the works of many Southern writers have died. Much that we read today is fast expiring.

17   My own slight attachment to William Faulkner was rudely broken by realizing, after reading statements he made in *Faulkner in the University*, that he believed whites superior morally to blacks; that whites had a duty (which at their convenience they would assume) to "bring blacks along" politically, since blacks, in Faulkner's opinion, were "not ready" yet to function properly in a democratic society. He also thought that a black man's intelligence is directly related to the amount of white blood he has.

18   For the black person coming of age in the sixties, where Martin Luther King stands against the murderers of Goodman, Chaney, and Schwerner, there appears no basis for such assumptions. Nor was there

any in Garvey's day, or in Du Bois's or in Douglass's or in Nat Turner's. Nor at any other period in our history, from the very founding of the country; for it was hardly incumbent upon slaves to be slaves and saints too. Unlike Tolstoy, Faulkner was not prepared to struggle to change the structure of the society he was born in. One might concede that in his fiction he did seek to examine the reasons for its decay, but unfortunately, as I have learned while trying to teach Faulkner to black students, it is not possible, from so short a range, to separate the man from his works.

One reads Faulkner knowing that his "colored" people had to 19 come through "Mr. William's" back door, and one feels uneasy, and finally enraged that Faulkner did not burn the whole house down. When the provincial mind starts out *and continues* on a narrow and unprotesting course, "genius" itself must run on a track.

Flannery O'Connor at least had the conviction that "reality" is at 20 best superficial and that the puzzle of humanity is less easy to solve than that of race. But Miss O'Connor was not so much of Georgia, as in it. The majority of Southern writers have been too confined by prevailing social customs to probe deeply into mysteries that the Citizens Councils insist must never be revealed.

Perhaps my Northern brothers will not believe me when I say 21 there is a great deal of positive material I can draw from my "underprivileged" background. But they have never lived, as I have, at the end of a long road in a house that was faced by the edge of the world on one side and nobody for miles on the other. They have never experienced the magnificent quiet of a summer day when the heat is intense and one is so very thirsty, as one moves across the dusty cotton fields, that one learns forever that water is the essence of all life. In the cities it cannot be so clear to one that he is a creature of the earth, feeling the soil between the toes, smelling the dust thrown up by the rain, loving the earth so much that one longs to taste it and sometimes does.

Nor do I intend to romanticize the Southern black country life. I 22 can recall that I hated it, generally. The hard work in the fields, the shabby houses, the evil greedy men who worked my father to death and almost broke the courage of that strong woman, my mother. No, I am simply saying that Southern black writers, like most writers, have a heritage of love and hate, but that they also have enormous richness and beauty to draw from. And, having been placed, as Camus says, "halfway between misery and the sun," they, too, know that "though all is not well under the sun, history is not everything."

No one could wish for a more advantageous heritage than that 23 bequeathed to the black writer in the South: a compassion for the earth, a trust in humanity beyond our knowledge of evil, and an abiding love of justice. We inherit a great responsibility as well, for we must give voice to centuries not only of silent bitterness and hate but also of neighborly kindness and sustaining love.

——— CONSIDERATIONS ———————————————————

1. In paragraph 15, Alice Walker pays tribute to another black novelist, Ernest J. Gaines, for refusing to make his characters into stereotypes of the white villain and the black martyr. She has trouble acknowledging the achievements of another, more famous Southern novelist, William Faulkner. Why? Carefully read paragraph 18 for the answer.

2. Read Eudora Welty's short story, "A Worn Path," and speculate on what Walker might say about Welty's understanding of the black Southern experience.

3. Is Walker sentimental in expressing the values of her poverty-stricken childhood? Find specific statements or phrases to support your answer. Compare her tone with E. B. White's in "Once More to the Lake" or James Agee's in "Knoxville: Summer 1915."

4. "But Miss O'Connor was not so much of Georgia, as in it," writes Walker, in expressing her reservation about Flannery O'Connor's contribution. Why does she distinguish between "of Georgia" and "in it"?

5. Walker mentions several ironies in connection with the black experience in the American South. Isolate a few of these and try explaining the nature and appeal of irony in a writer's work.

6. How does the story in paragraphs 1 through 8 help make Walker's conclusions in paragraph 23 credible?

7. Compare Walker's comments with those of two other black writers: Ralph Ellison (see "On Becoming a Writer") and Shelby Steele (see "I'm Black, You're White, Who's Innocent?").

Eudora Welty (b. 1909) lives in her native Jackson, Mississippi,
where she continues to write, deliberately and slowly, her
perfect stories and novels. A Curtain of Green *(1941) was her*
first volume of collected stories. Her novels include Losing
Battles *(1970) and* The Optimist's Daughter *(1972), which won*
her a Pulitzer Prize. In 1980 The Collected Stories of Eudora
Welty *was published, and in 1984, a reminiscence,* One Writer's
Beginnings. *She has also published volumes of her photographs.*

Here is a passage of reminiscence from One Writer's
Beginnings.

82

EUDORA WELTY
The Baby Question

It was when my mother came out onto the sleeping porch to tell   1
me goodnight that her trial came. The sudden silence in the double bed
meant my younger brothers had both keeled over in sleep, and I in the
single bed at my end of the porch would be lying electrified, waiting for
this to be the night when she'd tell me what she'd promised for so long.
Just as she bent to kiss me I grabbed her and asked: "Where do babies
come from?"

My poor mother! But something saved her every time. Almost any   2
night I put the baby question to her, suddenly, as if the whole outdoors
exploded, Professor Holt would start to sing. The Holts lived next door;
he taught penmanship (the Palmer Method), typing, bookkeeping and
shorthand at the high school. His excitable voice traveled out of their
diningroom windows across the two driveways between our houses,
and up to our upstairs sleeping porch. His wife, usually so quiet and
gentle, was his uncannily spirited accompanist at the piano. "High-ho!

Come to the Fair!" he'd sing, unless he sang "Oho ye oho ye, who's bound for the ferry, the briar's in bud and the sun's going down!"

3   "Dear, this isn't a very good time for you to hear Mother, is it?"

4   She couldn't get started. As soon as she'd whisper something, Professor Holt galloped into the chorus, "And 'tis but a penny to Twickenham town!" "Isn't that enough?" she'd ask me. She'd told me that the mother and the father had to both *want* the baby. This couldn't be enough. I knew she was not trying to fib to me, for she never did fib, but also I could not help but know she was not really *telling* me. And more than that, I was afraid of what I was going to hear next. This was partly because she wanted to tell me in the dark. I thought *she* might be afraid. In something like childish hopelessness I thought she probably *couldn't* tell, just as she *couldn't* lie.

5   On the night we came the closest to having it over with, she started to tell me without being asked, and I ruined it by yelling, "Mother, look at the lightning bugs!"

6   In those days, the dark was dark. And all the dark out there was filled with the soft, near lights of lightning bugs. They were everywhere, flashing on the slow, horizontal move, on the upswings, rising and subsiding in the soundless dark. Lightning bugs signaled and answered back without a stop, from down below all the way to the top of our sycamore tree. My mother just gave me a businesslike kiss and went on back to Daddy in their room at the front of the house. Distracted by lightning bugs, I had missed my chance. The fact is she never did tell me.

7   I doubt that any child I knew ever was told by her mother any more than I was about babies. In fact, I doubt that her own mother ever told her any more than she told me, though there were five brothers who were born after Mother, one after the other, and she was taking care of babies all her childhood.

_____ CONSIDERATIONS _____

1. Welty's account could open up a serious discussion of the controversial matter of sex education. Have you had or heard of an experience in sex education that might be useful for an essay on the subject? Why is the subject so controversial?

2. How does Eudora Welty, the writer, avoid making her mother's failure appear more serious than it was?

3. In Welty's case, how does the child herself complicate her mother's task?

4. What in Welty's account reminds us that she is primarily a storyteller, not a psychologist?

83

EUDORA WELTY
A Worn Path

1   It was December—a bright frozen day in the early morning. Far out in the country there was an old Negro woman with her head tied in a red rag, coming along a path through the pinewoods. Her name was Phoenix Jackson. She was very old and small and she walked slowly in the dark pine shadows, moving a little from side to side in her steps, with the balanced heaviness and lightness of a pendulum in a grandfather clock. She carried a thin, small cane made from an umbrella, and with this she kept tapping the frozen earth in front of her. This made a grave and persistent noise in the still air, that seemed meditative, like the chirping of a solitary little bird.

2   She wore a dark striped dress reaching down to her shoetops, and an equally long apron of bleached sugar sacks, with a full pocket; all neat and tidy, but every time she took a step she might have fallen over her shoelaces, which dragged from her unlaced shoes. She looked straight ahead. Her eyes were blue with age. Her skin had a pattern all its own of numberless branching wrinkles and as though a whole little tree stood in the middle of her forehead, but a golden color ran underneath, and the two knobs of her cheeks were illuminated by a yellow burning under the dark. Under the red rag her hair came down on her neck in the frailest of ringlets, still black, and with an odor like copper.

3   Now and then there was a quivering in the thicket. Old Phoenix said, "Out of my way, all you foxes, owls, beetles, jack rabbits, coons, and wild animals! . . . Keep out from under these feet, little bob-whites. . . . Keep the big wild hogs out of my path. Don't let none of those come running in my direction. I got a long way." Under her small black-freckled hand her cane, limber as a buggy whip, would switch at the brush as if to rouse up any hiding things.

4   On she went. The woods were deep and still. The sun made the pine needles almost too bright to look at, up where the wind rocked. The cones dropped as light as feathers. Down in the hollow was the mourning dove—it was not too late for him.

The path ran up a hill. "Seem like there is chains about my feet, 5
time I get this far," she said, in the voice of argument old people keep to
use with themselves. "Something always take a hold on this hill—
pleads I should stay."

After she got to the top she turned and gave a full, severe look 6
behind her where she had come. "Up through pines," she said at length.
"Now down through oaks."

Her eyes opened their widest and she started down gently. But 7
before she got to the bottom of the hill a bush caught her dress.

Her fingers were busy and intent, but her skirts were full and long, 8
so that before she could pull them free in one place they were caught in
another. It was not possible to allow the dress to tear. "I in the thorny
bush," she said. "Thorns, you doing your appointed work. Never want
to let folks past—no sir. Old eyes thought you was a pretty little *green*
bush."

Finally, trembling all over, she stood free, and after a moment 9
dared to stoop for her cane.

"Sun so high!" she cried, leaning back and looking, while the thick 10
tears went over her eyes. "The time getting all gone here."

At the foot of this hill was a place where a log was laid across the 11
creek.

"Now comes the trial," said Phoenix. 12

Putting her right foot out, she mounted the log and shut her eyes. 13
Lifting her skirt, leveling her cane fiercely before her, like a festival
figure in some parade, she began to march across. Then she opened her
eyes and she was safe on the other side.

"I wasn't as old as I thought," she said. 14

But she sat down to rest. She spread her skirts on the bank around 15
her and folded her hands over her knees. Up above her was a tree in a
pearly cloud of mistletoe. She did not dare to close her eyes, and when a
little boy brought her a little plate with a slice of marble-cake on it she
spoke to him. "That would be acceptable," she said. But when she went
to take it there was just her own hand in the air.

So she left that tree, and had to go through a barbed-wire fence. 16
There she had to creep and crawl, spreading her knees and stretching
her fingers like a baby trying to climb the steps. But she talked loudly to
herself: she could not let her dress be torn now, so late in the day, and
she could not pay for having her arm or leg sawed off if she got caught
fast where she was.

At last she was safe through the fence and risen up out in 17
the clearing. Big dead trees, like black men with one arm, were stand-

ing in the purple stalks of the withered cotton field. There sat a buz-
zard.

18   "Who you watching?"

19   In the furrow she made her way along.

20   "Glad this not the season for bulls," she said, looking sideways,
"and the good Lord made his snakes to curl up and sleep in the winter. A
pleasure I don't see no two-headed snake coming around that tree,
where it come once. It took a while to get by him, back in the summer."

21   She passed through the old cotton and went into a field of dead
corn. It whispered and shook, and was taller than her head. "Through
the maze now," she said, for there was no path.

22   Then there was something tall, black, and skinny there, moving
before her.

23   At first she took it for a man. It could have been a man dancing in
the field. But she stood still and listened, and it did not make a sound. It
was as silent as a ghost.

24   "Ghost," she said sharply, "who be you the ghost of? For I have
heard of nary death close by."

25   But there was no answer, only the ragged dancing in the wind.

26   She shut her eyes, reached out her hand, and touched a sleeve. She
found a coat and inside that an emptiness, cold as ice.

27   "You scarecrow," she said. Her face lighted. "I ought to be shut up
for good," she said with laughter. "My senses is gone. I too old. I the
oldest people I ever know. Dance, old scarecrow," she said, "while I
dancing with you."

28   She kicked her foot over the furrow, and with mouth drawn down
shook her head once or twice in a little strutting way. Some husks blew
down and whirled in streamers about her skirts.

29   Then she went on, parting her way from side to side with the cane,
through the whispering field. At last she came to the end, to a wagon
track, where the silver grass blew between the red ruts. The quail were
walking around like pullets, seeming all dainty and unseen.

30   "Walk pretty," she said. "This the easy place. This the easy
going."

31   She followed the track, swaying through the quiet bare fields,
through the little strings of trees silver in their dead leaves, past cabins
silver from weather, with the doors and windows boarded shut, all like
old women under a spell sitting there. "I walking in their sleep," she
said, nodding her head vigorously.

32   In a ravine she went where a spring was silently flowing through a
hollow log. Old Phoenix bent and drank. "Sweetgum makes the water

sweet," she said, and drank more. "Nobody knows who made this well, for it was here when I was born."

The track crossed a swampy part where the moss hung as white as 33 lace from every limb. "Sleep on, alligators, and blow your bubbles." Then the track went into the road.

Deep, deep the road went down between the high green-colored 34 banks. Overhead the live-oaks met, and it was as dark as a cave.

A black dog with a lolling tongue came up out of the weeds by the 35 ditch. She was meditating, and not ready, and when he came at her she only hit him a little with her cane. Over she went in the ditch, like a little puff of milk-weed.

Down there, her senses drifted away. A dream visited her, and she 36 reached her hand up, but nothing reached down and gave her a pull. So she lay there and presently went to talking. "Old woman," she said to herself, "that black dog come up out of the weeds to stall you off, and now there he sitting on his fine tail, smiling at you."

A white man finally came along and found her—a hunter, a young 37 man, with his dog on a chain.

"Well, Granny!" he laughed. "What are you doing there?" 38

"Lying on my back like a June-bug waiting to be turned over, 39 mister," she said, reaching up her hand.

He lifted her up, gave her a swing in the air, and set her down, 40 "Anything broken, Granny?"

"No sir, them old dead weeds is springy enough," said Phoenix, 41 when she had got her breath. "I thank you for your trouble."

"Where do you live, Granny?" he asked, while the two dogs were 42 growling at each other.

"Away back yonder, sir, behind that ridge. You can't even see it 43 from here."

"On your way home?" 44

"No, sir, I going to town." 45

Why that's too far! That's as far as I walk when I come out myself, 46 and I get something for my trouble." He patted the stuffed bag he carried, and there hung down a little closed claw. It was one of the bobwhites, with its beak hooked bitterly to show it was dead. "Now you go on home, Granny!"

"I bound to go to town, mister," said Phoenix. "The time come 47 around."

He have another laugh, filling the whole landscape. "I know you 48 colored people! Wouldn't miss going to town to see Santa Claus!"

But something held Old Phoenix very still. The deep lines in her 49 face went into a fierce and different radiation. Without warning she had seen with her own eyes a flashing nickel fall out of the man's pocket on to the ground.

50   "How old are you, Granny?" he was saying.

51   "There is no telling, mister," she said, "no telling."

52   Then she gave a little cry and clapped her hands, and said, "Git on away from here, dog! Look! Look at that dog!" She laughed as if in admiration. "He ain't scared of nobody. He a big black dog." She whispered, "Sick him!"

53   "Watch me get rid of that cur," said the man. "Sick him, Pete! Sick him!"

54   Phoenix heard the dogs fighting and heard the man running and throwing sticks. She even heard a gunshot. But she was slowly bending forward by that time, further and further forward, the lids stretched down over her eyes, as if she were doing this in her sleep. Her chin was lowered almost to her knees. The yellow palm of her hand came out from the fold of her apron. Her fingers slid down and along the ground under the piece of money with the grace and care they would have in lifting an egg from under a sitting hen. Then she slowly straightened up, she stood erect, and the nickel was in her apron pocket. A bird flew by. Her lips moved. "God watching me the whole time. I come to stealing."

55   The man came back, and his own dog panted about them. "Well, I scared him off that time," he said, and then he laughed and lifted his gun and pointed it at Phoenix.

56   She stood straight and faced him.

57   "Doesn't the gun scare you?" he said, still pointing it.

58   "No, sir, I seen plenty go off closer by, in my day, and for less what I done," she said, holding utterly still.

59   He smiled, and shouldered the gun. "Well, Granny," he said, "you must be a hundred years old, and scared of nothing. I'd give you a dime if I had any money with me. But you take my advice and stay home, and nothing will happen to you."

60   "I bound to go on my way, mister," said Phoenix. She inclined her head in the red rag. Then they went in different directions, but she could hear the gun shooting again and again over the hill.

61   She walked on. The shadows hung from the oak trees to the road like curtains. Then she smelled wood-smoke, and smelled the river, and she saw a steeple and the cabins on their steep steps. Dozens of little black children whirled around her. There ahead was Natchez shining. Bells were ringing. She walked on.

62   In the paved city it was Christmas time. There were red and green

electric lights strung and crisscrossed everywhere, and all turned on in the daytime. Old Phoenix would have been lost if she had not distrusted her eyesight and depended on her feet to know where to take her.

She paused quietly on the sidewalk, where people were passing by. 63 A lady came along in the crowd, carrying an armful of red-, green-, and silver-wrapped presents; she gave off perfume like the red roses in hot summer, and Phoenix stopped her.

"Please, missy, will you lace up my shoe?" She held up her foot. 64

"What do you want, Grandma?" 65

"See my shoe," said Phoenix. "Do all right for out in the country, 66 but wouldn't look right to go in a big building."

"Stand still then, Grandma," said the lady. She put her packages 67 down carefully on the sidewalk beside her and laced and tied both shoes tightly.

"Can't lace 'em with a cane," said Phoenix. "Thank you, missy. I 68 doesn't mind asking a nice lady to tie up my shoe when I gets out on the street."

Moving slowly and from side to side, she went into the stone 69 building and into a tower of steps, where she walked up and around and around until her feet knew to stop.

She entered a door, and there she saw nailed up on the wall the 70 document that had been stamped with the gold seal and framed in the gold frame which matched the dream that was hung up in her head.

"Here I be," she said. There was a fixed and ceremonial stiffness 71 over her body.

"A charity case, I suppose," said an attendant who sat at the desk 72 before her.

But Phoenix only looked above her head. There was sweat on her 73 face, the wrinkles shone like a bright net.

"Speak up, Grandma," the woman said. "What's your name? We 74 must have your history, you know. Have you been here before? What seems to be the trouble with you?"

Old Phoenix only gave a twitch to her face as if a fly were 75 bothering her.

"Are you deaf?" cried the attendant. 76

But then the nurse came in. 77

"Oh, that's just old Aunt Phoenix," she said. "She doesn't come 78 for herself—she has a little grandson. She makes these trips just as regular as clockwork. She lives away back off the Old Natchez Trace." She bent down. "Well, Aunt Phoenix, why don't you just take a seat? We won't keep you standing after your long trip." She pointed.

79   The old woman sat down, bolt upright in the chair.

80   "Now, how is the boy?" asked the nurse.

81   Old Phoenix did not speak.

82   "I said, how is the boy?"

83   But Phoenix only waited and stared straight ahead, her face very solemn and withdrawn into rigidity.

84   "Is his throat any better?" asked the nurse. "Aunt Phoenix, don't you hear me? Is your grandson's throat any better since the last time you came for the medicine?"

85   With her hand on her knees, the old woman waited, silent, erect, and motionless, just as if she were in armor.

86   "You mustn't take up our time this way, Aunt Phoenix," the nurse said. "Tell us quickly about your grandson, and get it over. He isn't dead, is he?"

87   At last there came a flicker and then a flame of comprehension across her face, and she spoke.

88   "My grandson. It was my memory had left me. There I sat and forgot why I made my long trip."

89   "Forgot?" The nurse frowned. "After you came so far?"

90   Then Phoenix was like an old woman begging a dignified forgiveness for waking up frightened in the night. "I never did go to school—I was too old at the Surrender," she said in a soft voice. "I'm an old woman without an education. It was my memory fail me. My little grandson, he is just the same, and I forgot it in the coming."

91   "Throat never heals, does it?" said the nurse, speaking in a loud, sure voice to Old Phoenix. By now she had a card with something written on it, a little list. "Yes. Swallowed lye. When was it—January— two—three years ago—"

92   Phoenix spoke unasked now. "No, missy, he not dead, he just the same. Every little while his throat begin to close up again, and he not able to swallow. He not get his breath. He not able to help himself. So the time come around, and I go on another trip for soothing medicine."

93   "All right. The doctor said as long as you came to get it you could have it," said the nurse. "But it's an obstinate case."

94   "My little grandson, he sit up there in the house all wrapped up, waiting by himself," Phoenix went on. "We is the only two left in the world. He suffer and it don't seem to put him back at all. He got a sweet look. He going to last. He wear a little patch quilt and peep out, holding his mouth open like a little bird. I remembers so plain now. I not going to forget him again, no, the whole enduring time. I could tell him from all the others in creation."

"All right." The nurse was trying to hush her now. She brought her 95
a bottle of medicine. "Charity," she said, making a check mark in a
book.

Old Phoenix held the bottle close to her eyes and then carefully 96
put it into her pocket.

"I thank you," she said. 97

"It's Christmas time, Grandma," said the attendant. "Could I give 98
you a few pennies out of my purse?"

"Five pennies is a nickel," said Phoenix stiffly. 99

"Here's a nickel," said the attendant. 100

Phoenix rose carefully and held out her hand. She received the 101
nickel and then fished the other nickel out of her pocket and laid it
beside the new one. She stared at her palm closely, with her head on one
side.

Then she gave a tap with her cane on the floor. 102

"This is what come to me to do," she said. "I going to the store and 103
buy my child a little windmill they sells, make out of paper. He going to
find it hard to believe there such a thing in the world. I'll march myself
back where he waiting, holding it straight up in this hand."

She lifted her free hand, gave a little nod, turned round, and walked 104
out of the doctor's office. Then her slow step began on the stairs, going
down.

——— CONSIDERATIONS ———————————————————

1. Some features of Old Phoenix's long journey might bring to mind
Everyman's difficult travel through life. Do specific passages suggest that Old
Phoenix's journey is symbolic or archetypal?

2. Would you say that Old Phoenix is senile, or is she in excellent control
of her thoughts? What evidence can you find for your answer?

3. Is the grandson alive or dead? After you answer this question, read
Welty's own comments on the story in the next selection.

4. Who was the little boy with the slice of marble-cake? Why does he
appear and disappear so abruptly?

5. Eudora Welty makes no comment in the story on Old Phoenix's encounter with the white man. Do the details of that encounter reveal anything
about relations between whites and blacks?

6. What do you learn of Old Phoenix's sense of morality, sense of humor,
and feeling of personal worth?

7. Read William Faulkner's short story, "A Rose for Emily," and write an
essay comparing Emily Grierson and Old Phoenix.

Here is a useful essay Welty wrote about her story "A Worn Path."

84

EUDORA WELTY
The Point of the Story

1   A story writer is more than happy to be read by students; the fact that these serious readers think and feel something in response to his work he finds life-giving. At the same time he may not always be able to reply to their specific questions in kind. I wondered if it might clarify something, for both the questioners and myself, if I set down a general reply to the question that comes to me most often in the mail, from both students and their teachers, after some classroom discussion. The unrivaled favorite is this: "Is Phoenix Jackson's grandson really *dead?*" It refers to a short story I wrote years ago called "A Worn Path," which tells of a day's journey an old woman makes on foot from deep in the country into town and into a doctor's office on behalf of her little grandson; he is at home, periodically ill, and periodically she comes for his medicine; they give it to her as usual, she receives it and starts the journey back.

2   I had not meant to mystify readers by withholding any fact; it is not a writer's business to tease. The story is told through Phoenix's mind as she undertakes her errand. As the author at one with the character as I tell it, I must assume that the boy is alive. As the reader, you are free to think as you like, of course: the story invites you to believe that no matter what happens, Phoenix for as long as she is able to walk and can hold to her purpose will make her journey. The *possibility* that she would keep on even if he were dead is there in her devotion and its single-minded, single-track errand. Certainly the *artistic* truth, which should be good enough for the fact, lies in Phoenix's

own answer to that question. When the nurse asks, "He isn't dead, is he?" she speaks for herself: "He still the same. He going to last."

The grandchild is the incentive. But it is the journey, the going of 3 the errand, that is the story, and the question is not whether the grandchild is in reality alive or dead. It doesn't affect the outcome of the story or its meaning from start to finish. But it is not the question itself that has struck me as much as the idea, almost without exception implied in the asking, that for Phoenix's grandson to be dead would somehow make the story "better."

It's *all right*, I want to say to the students who write to me, for 4 things to be what they appear to be, and for words to mean what they say. It's all right, too, for words and appearances to mean more than one thing—ambiguity is a fact of life. A fiction writer's responsibility covers not only what he presents as the facts of a given story but what he chooses to stir up as their implications; in the end, these implications, too, become facts, in the larger, fictional sense. But it is not all right, not in good faith, for things not to mean what they say.

The grandson's plight was real and it made the truth of the story, 5 which is the story of an errand of love carried out. If the child no longer lived, the truth would persist in the "wornness" of the path. But his being dead can't increase the truth of the story, can't affect it one way or the other. I think I signal this, because the end of the story has been reached before old Phoenix gets home again: she simply starts back. To the question "Is the grandson really dead?" I could reply that it doesn't make any difference. I could also say that I did not make him up in order to let him play a trick on Phoenix. But my best answer would be: "Phoenix is alive."

The origin of a story is sometimes a trustworthy clue to the 6 author—or can provide him with the clue—to its key image; maybe in this case it will do the same for the reader. One day I saw a solitary old woman like Phoenix. She was walking; I saw her, at middle distance, in a winter country landscape, and watched her slowly make her way across my line of vision. That sight of her made me write the story. I invented an errand for her, but that only seemed a living part of the figure she was herself; what errand other than for someone else could be making her go? And her going was the first thing, her persisting in her landscape was the real thing, and the first and the real were what I wanted and worked to keep. I brought her up close enough, by imagination, to describe her face, make her present to the eyes, but the full-length figure moving across the winter fields was the indelible one and the image to keep, and the perspective extending into the vanishing distance the true one to hold in mind.

7   I invented for my character as I wrote, some passing adventures— some dreams and harassments and a small triumph or two, some jolts to her pride, some flights of fancy to console her, one or two encounters to scare her, a moment that gave her cause to feel ashamed, a moment to dance and preen—for it had to be a journey, and all these things belonged to that, parts of life's uncertainty.

8   A narrative line is in its deeper sense, of course, the tracing out of a meaning, and the real continuity of a story lies in this probing forward. The real dramatic force of a story depends on the strength of the emotion that has set it going. The emotional value is the measure of the reach of the story. What gives any such content to "A Worn Path" is not its circumstances but its subject: the deep-grained habit of love.

9   What I hoped would come clear was that in the whole surround of this story, the world it threads through, the only certain thing at all is the worn path. The habit of love cuts through confusion and stumbles or contrives its way out of difficulty, it remembers the way even when it forgets, for a dumbfounded moment, its reason for being. The path is the thing that matters.

10   Her victory—old Phoenix's—is when she sees the diploma in the doctor's office, when she finds "nailed up on the wall the document that had been stamped with the gold seal and framed in the gold frame, which matched the dream that was hung up in her head." The return with the medicine is just a matter of retracing her own footsteps. It is the part of the journey, and of the story, that can now go without saying.

11   In the matter of function, old Phoenix's way might even do as a sort of parallel to your way of work if you are a writer of stories. The way to get there is the all-important, all-absorbing problem, and this problem is your reason for undertaking this story. Your only guide, too, is your sureness about your subject, about what this subject is. Like Phoenix, you work all your life to find your way, through all the obstructions and the false appearances and the upsets you may have brought on yourself, to reach a meaning—using inventions of your imagination, perhaps helped out by your dreams and bits of good luck. And finally too, like Phoenix, you have to assume that what you are working in aid of is life, not death.

12   But you would make the trip anyway—wouldn't you?—just on hope.

CONSIDERATIONS

1. Welty says that Old Phoenix's return trip is "the part of the journey, and of the story, that can now go without saying." If you were writing this story would you choose a different place to end it? Would you follow Old Phoenix all the way back into the hills? Would you show the grandson? Why?

2. How does Welty feel about writers who intentionally mystify their readers?

3. Does "A Worn Path" illustrate what Welty means when she says, "A narrative line is in its deeper sense . . . the tracing out of a meaning"?

4. In paragraph 4, Welty touches on the "factuality" of a work of fiction. This introduces a fascinating (if maddening) question: what is the difference between fiction and nonfiction?

5. Another Southern writer, William Faulkner, wrote a short novel, *As I Lay Dying*, that can be read as a fuller version of "A Worn Path." It too is based on "an errand of love," as Welty puts it. Read the novel and discuss its parallels with Welty's story.

6. What do you think of Welty's response to the question about her story? Does it help you understand and appreciate the story? Does it avoid the initial question?

E. B. White (1899–1985) was born in Mount Vernon, New York, graduated from Cornell in 1921, and joined the staff of the New Yorker *in 1926. For many years, he wrote the brief essay that led off that magazine's "Talk of the Town" and edited other "Talk" segments. In 1929, White collaborated with James Thurber on a book called* Is Sex Necessary? *and from time to time he published collections of essays and poems, most of them taken from the* New Yorker *and* Harper's. *Some of his best-known collections are* One Man's Meat *(1942),* The Second Tree from the Corner *(1953), and* The Points of My Compass *(1962). He is also the author of children's books, most notably* Stuart Little *(1945) and* Charlotte's Web *(1952), and the celebrated book on prose,* The Elements of Style *(with William Strunk, Jr., 1959).*

In 1937, White retired from the New Yorker *and moved to a farm in Maine, where he continued to write those minimal, devastating comments attached to the proofhacks and other errors printed at the ends of the* New Yorker's *columns. There he continued his slow, consistent writing of superb prose. In recent years, the collected* Letters of E. B. White *(1976),* Essays of E. B. White *(1977), and* Poems and Sketches of E. B. White *(1981) have reconfirmed this country's infatuation with the versatile author. A special citation from the Pulitzer Prize Committee in 1978 celebrated the publication of White's letters.*

85

E. B. WHITE
Once More to the Lake

One summer, along about 1904, my father rented a camp on a lake   1
in Maine and took us all there for the month of August. We all got
ringworm from some kittens and had to rub Pond's Extract on our arms
and legs night and morning, and my father rolled over in a canoe with all
his clothes on; but outside of that the vacation was a success and from
then on none of us ever thought there was any place in the world like
that lake in Maine. We returned summer after summer—always on
August 1st for one month. I have since become a salt-water man, but
sometimes in summer there are days when the restlessness of the tides
and the fearful cold of the sea water and the incessant wind that blows
across the afternoon and into the evening make me wish for the placid-
ity of a lake in the woods. A few weeks ago this feeling got so strong I
bought myself a couple of bass hooks and a spinner and returned to the
lake where we used to go, for a week's fishing and to revisit old haunts.

I took along my son, who had never had any fresh water up his   2
nose and who had seen lily pads only from train windows. On the
journey over to the lake I began to wonder what it would be like. I
wondered how time would have marred this unique, this holy spot—
the coves and streams, the hills that the sun set behind, the camps and
the paths behind the camps. I was sure that the tarred road would have
found it out and I wondered in what other ways it would be desolated. It
is strange how much you can remember about places like that once you
allow your mind to return into the grooves that lead back. You remember one thing, and that suddenly reminds you of another thing. I guess I
remembered clearest of all the early mornings, when the lake was cool
and motionless, remembered how the bedroom smelled of the lumber it
was made of and of the wet woods whose scent entered through the
screen. The partitions in the camp were thin and did not extend clear to
the top of the rooms, and as I was always the first up I would dress softly
so as not to wake the others, and sneak out into the sweet outdoors and

start out in the canoe, keeping close along the shore in the long shadows of the pines. I remembered being very careful never to rub my paddle against the gunwale for fear of disturbing the stillness of the cathedral.

3   The lake had never been what you would call a wild lake. There were cottages sprinkled around the shores, and it was in farming country although the shores of the lake were quite heavily wooded. Some of the cottages were owned by nearby farmers, and you would live at the shore and eat your meals at the farmhouse. That's what our family did. But although it wasn't wild, it was a fairly large and undisturbed lake and there were places in it which, to a child at least, seemed infinitely remote and primeval.

4   I was right about the tar: it led to within half a mile of the shore. But when I got back there, with my boy, and we settled into a camp near a farmhouse and into the kind of summertime I had known, I could tell that it was going to be pretty much the same as it had been before—I knew it, lying in bed the first morning, smelling the bedroom, and hearing the boy sneak quietly out and go off along the shore in a boat. I began to sustain the illusion that he was I, and therefore, by simple transposition, that I was my father. This sensation persisted, kept cropping up all the time we were there. It was not an entirely new feeling, but in this setting it grew much stronger. I seemed to be living a dual existence. I would be in the middle of some simple act, I would be picking up a bait box or laying down a table fork, or I would be saying something, and suddenly it would be not I but my father who was saying the words or making the gesture. It gave me a creepy sensation.

5   We went fishing the first morning. I felt the same damp moss covering the worms in the bait can, and saw the dragonfly alight on the tip of my rod as it hovered a few inches from the surface of the water. It was the arrival of this fly that convinced me beyond any doubt that everything was as it always had been, that the years were a mirage and there had been no years. The small waves were the same, chucking the rowboat under the chin as we fished at anchor, and the boat was the same boat, the same color green and the ribs broken in the same places, and under the floor-boards the same fresh-water leavings and débris— the dead hellgrammite, the wisps of moss, the rusty discarded fishhook, the dried blood from yesterday's catch. We stared silently at the tips of our rods, at the dragonflies that came and went. I lowered the tip of mine into the water, tentatively, pensively dislodging the fly, which darted two feet away, poised, darted two feet back, and came to rest again a little farther up the rod. There had been no years between the ducking of this dragonfly and the other one—the one that was part of

memory. I looked at the boy, who was silently watching his fly, and it was my hands that held his rod, my eyes watching. I felt dizzy and didn't know which rod I was at the end of.

We caught two bass, hauling them in briskly as though they were 6 mackerel, pulling them over the side of the boat in a businesslike manner without any landing net, and stunning them with a blow on the back of the head. When we got back for a swim before lunch, the lake was exactly where we had left it, the same number of inches from the dock, and there was only the merest suggestion of a breeze. This seemed an utterly enchanted sea, this lake you could leave to its own devices for a few hours and come back to, and find that it had not stirred, this constant and trustworthy body of water. In the shallows, the dark, water-soaked sticks and twigs, smooth and old, were undulating in clusters on the bottom against the clean ribbed sand, and the track of the mussel was plain. A school of minnows swam by, each minnow with its small individual shadow, doubling the attendance, so clear and sharp in the sunlight. Some of the other campers were in swimming, along the shore, one of them with a cake of soap, and the water felt thin and clear and unsubstantial. Over the years there had been this person with the cake of soap, this cultist, and here he was. There had been no years.

Up to the farmhouse to dinner through the teeming, dusty field, 7 the road under our sneakers was only a two-track road. The middle track was missing, the one with the marks of the hooves and splotches of dried, flaky manure. There had always been three tracks to choose from in choosing which track to walk in; now the choice was narrowed down to two. For a moment I missed terribly the middle alternative. But the way led past the tennis court, and something about the way it lay there in the sun reassured me; the tape had loosened along the backline, the alleys were green with plantains and other weeds, and the net (installed in June and removed in September) sagged in the dry noon, and the whole place steamed with midday heat and hunger and emptiness. There was a choice of pie for dessert, and one was blueberry and one was apple, and the waitresses were the same country girls, there having been no passage of time, only the illusion of it as in a dropped curtain—the waitresses were still fifteen; their hair had been washed, that was the only difference—they had been to the movies and seen the pretty girls with the clean hair.

Summertime, oh summertime, pattern of life indelible, the fade- 8 proof lake, the woods unshatterable, the pasture with the sweetfern and the juniper forever and ever, summer without end; this was the background, and the life along the shore was the design, the cottages with their innocent and tranquil design, their tiny docks with the flagpole and the American flag floating against the white clouds in the blue sky, the little paths over the roots of the trees leading from camp to camp and the paths leading back to the outhouses and the can of lime for sprinkling, and at the souvenir counters at the store the miniature birch-bark canoes and the post cards that showed things looking a little better than they looked. This was the American family at play, escaping the city heat, wondering whether the newcomers in the camp at the head of the cove were "common" or "nice," wondering whether it was true that the people who drove up for Sunday dinner at the farmhouse were turned away because there wasn't enough chicken.

9   It seemed to me, as I kept remembering all this, that those times and those summers had been infinitely precious and worth saving. There had been jollity and peace and goodness. The arriving (at the beginning of August) had been so big a business in itself, at the railway station the farm wagon drawn up, the first smell of the pine-laden air, the first glimpse of the smiling farmer, and the great importance of the trunks and your father's enormous authority in such matters, and the feel of the wagon under you for the long ten-mile haul, and at the top of the last long hill catching the first view of the lake after eleven months of not seeing this cherished body of water. The shouts and cries of the other campers when they saw you, and the trunks to be unpacked, to give up their rich burden. (Arriving was less exciting nowadays, when you sneaked up in your car and parked it under a tree near the camp and took out the bags and in five minutes it was all over, no fuss, no loud wonderful fuss about trunks.)

10   Peace and goodness and jollity. The only thing that was wrong now, really, was the sound of the place, an unfamiliar nervous sound of the outboard motors. This was the note that jarred, the one thing that would sometimes break the illusion and set the years moving. In those other summertimes all motors were inboard; and when they were at a little distance, the noise they made was a sedative, an ingredient of summer sleep. They were one-cylinder and two-cylinder engines, and some were make-and-break and some were jump-spark, but they all made a sleepy sound across the lake. The one-lungers throbbed and fluttered, and the twin-cylinder ones purred and purred and that was a quiet sound too. But now the campers all had outboards. In the daytime, in the hot mornings, these motors made a petulant, irritable sound; at night, in the still evening when the afterglow lit the water, they whined about one's ears like mosquitoes. My boy loved our rented outboard,

and his great desire was to achieve singlehanded mastery over it, and authority, and he soon learned the trick of choking it a little (but not too much), and the adjustment of the needle valve. Watching him I would remember the things you could do with the old one-cylinder engine with the heavy flywheel, how you could have it eating out of your hand if you got really close to it spiritually. Motor boats in those days didn't have clutches, and you would make a landing by shutting off the motor at the proper time and coasting in with a dead rudder. But there was a way of reversing them, if you learned the trick, by cutting the switch and putting it on again exactly on the final dying revolution of the flywheel, so that it would kick back against compression and begin reversing. Approaching a dock in a strong following breeze, it was difficult to slow up sufficiently by the ordinary coasting method, and if a boy felt he had complete mastery over his motor, he was tempted to keep it running beyond its time and then reverse it a few feet from the dock. It took a cool nerve, because if you threw the switch a twentieth of a second too soon you could catch the flywheel when it still had speed enough to go up past center, and the boat would leap ahead, charging bull-fashion at the dock.

We had a good week at the camp. The bass were biting well and the sun shone endlessly, day after day. We would be tired at night and lie down in the accumulated heat of the little bedrooms after the long hot day and the breeze would stir almost imperceptibly outside and the smell of the swamp drift in through the rusty screens. Sleep would come easily and in the morning the red squirrel would be on the roof, tapping out his gay routine. I kept remembering everything, lying in bed in the mornings—the small steamboat that had a long rounded stern like the lip of a Ubangi, and how quietly she ran on the moonlight sails, when the older boys played their mandolins and the girls sang and we ate doughnuts dipped in sugar, and how sweet the music was on the water in the shining light, and what it had felt like to think about girls then. After breakfast we would go up to the store and the things were in the same place—the minnows in a bottle, the plugs and spinners disarranged and pawed over by the youngsters from the boys' camp, the fig newtons and the Beeman's gum. Outside, the road was tarred and cars stood in front of the store. Inside, all was just as it had always been, except there was more Coca-Cola and not so much Moxie and root beer and birch beer and sarsaparilla. We would walk out with a bottle of pop apiece and sometimes the pop would backfire up our noses and hurt. We explored the streams, quietly, where the turtles slid off the sunny logs and dug their way into the soft bottom; and we lay on the town wharf

11

and fed worms to the tame bass. Everywhere we went I had trouble making out which was I, the one walking at my side, the one walking in my pants.

12   One afternoon while we were there at that lake a thunderstorm came up. It was like the revival of an old melodrama that I had seen long ago with childish awe. The second-act climax of the drama of the electrical disturbance over a lake in America had not changed in any important respect. This was the big scene, still the big scene. The whole thing was so familiar, the first feeling of oppression and heat and a general air around camp of not wanting to go very far away. In midafternoon (it was all the same) a curious darkening of the sky, and a lull in everything that had made life tick; and then the way the boats suddenly swung the other way at their moorings with the coming of a breeze out of the new quarter, and the premonitory rumble. Then the kettle drum, then the snare, then the bass drum and cymbals, then crackling light against the dark, and the gods grinning and licking their chops in the hills. Afterward the calm, the rain steadily rustling in the calm lake, the return of light and hope and spirits, and the campers running out in joy and relief to go swimming in the rain, their bright cries perpetuating the deathless joke about how they were getting simply drenched, and the children screaming with delight at the new sensation of bathing in the rain, and the joke about getting drenched linking the generations in a strong indestructible chain. And the comedian who waded in carrying an umbrella.

13   When the others went swimming my son said he was going in too. He pulled his dripping trunks from the line where thay had hung all through the shower, and wrung them out. Languidly, and with no thought of going in, I watched him, his hard little body, skinny and bare, saw him wince slightly as he pulled up around his vitals the small, soggy, icy garment. As he buckled the swollen belt suddenly my groin felt the chill of death.

—— CONSIDERATIONS ——————————————

1. A master of the personal essay, E. B. White transforms an exercise in memory into something universal, timeless, and profound. Study paragraph 4 to see how.

2. White rejuvenates bits and pieces of language that have become worn and lackluster through repetition. Can you find an example of this technique in paragraph 2?

3. White notes many changes at the old summer place, but he is more moved by the sameness. Locate examples of his feeling of sameness and consider how these examples contribute to his themes.

4. The author expresses a predictable dislike of outboard motors on the otherwise quiet lake. Does he avoid stereotype when he writes about motors elsewhere in this essay?

5. What device does White use in his description of the thunderstorm in paragraph 12?

6. How is the last sentence of the essay a surprise? How has White prepared us for it?

*George F. Will (b. 1941) was born in Illinois and graduated
from Princeton University. He has taught politics—at Michigan
State University, the University of Illinois, and the University of
Toronto—and worked as an aid to a Senator. His newspaper
columns on politics, originally printed in the* Washington Post,
*are syndicated nationwide, and have been collected into three
books:* The Pursuit of Happiness and Other Sobering Thoughts
(1979), The Pursuit of Virtue and Other Tory Notions *(1982),
and* The Morning After *(1986), from which we take this column.
A witty conservative, artful and allusive in his prose style, Will
has received the ultimate accolade—Garry Trudeau's
"Doonesbury" strip has satirized him.*

*Well known for his eloquent tributes to baseball, this political
columnist does indeed write about lighter things than politics—
as well as the darker sides of lighter things.*

86

GEORGE F. WILL
Exploring the Racer's Edge

1   It has been said that someone who cheats in an amateur contest is
a cheat, whereas a professional who cheats to feed his family is a
competitor. Piffle. All sports should conform to the International
Olympic Committee's ban on "the use by a competing athlete of any
substance foreign to the body or of any physiological substance taken in
abnormal quantity or taken by an abnormal route of entry into the body,
with the sole intention of increasing in an artifical and an unfair manner his performance in competition." But even this careful language
contains crucial ambiguities—"foreign to the body," "abnormal quantity," "an artificial and unfair manner." Define "fair" and you are home
free. Let's start at the fringe of the subject and nibble in.

2   Seven U.S. Olympic cyclists, including four medal winners, prac-

From *The Morning After: American Successes and Excesses 1981–1986* by George
F. Will. Copyright © 1986 by The Washington Post Company. Reprinted with permission
of The Free Press, a Division of Macmillan, Inc.

ticed "blood doping." They received infusions of blood from relatives or others with the same blood type, in an attempt—it is not clear this works—to increase their red-cell count and accelerate the transfer of oxygen to muscles during endurance events. An eighth cyclist had a reinfusion of his own blood that had been drawn several weeks earlier. Was his blood (or any blood) "foreign to the body?" Clearly blood doping involves an abnormal quantity of blood entering the body through an abnormal route to increase performance in an artificial (and therefore unfair?) manner.

Steroids can enhance muscle mass. They also can kill you, if they 3 do not just decrease sexual capacity, injure your liver and heart, and do sundry other damages. Some people say: It's the athlete's body, he can mess it up as he pleases—besides, sports often involve injuries. But it is one thing to injure yourself in exertion, another to injure yourself with chemicals in pursuit of the ultimate competitive "edge." And it is surely unfair to force your opponent to choose between similarly risking harm and competing at a disadvantage.

It is said that the improper pursuit of edge derives from valuing 4 winning too much. Actually, it derives from misunderstanding why winning is properly valued.

There is a broad gray area of difficult judgments. For example, 5 what, precisely, is the moral difference between eating energy-giving glucose pills and taking a steroid that increases muscle mass? What is the difference between taking vitamins—or, for that matter, eating spinach—in "abnormal quantities" and taking a drug that deadens the pain of an injured foot or (watch it—we are crossing some kind of line here) a drug that increases aggressiveness?

The science of sports medicine is no longer just about the 6 prevention or treatment of injuries. It uses kinesiology and biomechanics and computer analysis of movement—high tech stuff that would make even Gary Hart's head swim—to improve performance. Just as the launching of Sputnik I aroused American interest in science education, minds were concentrated on sports medicine by another embarrassment—the 1976 Montreal Olympics, where East Germany won more gold medals than the United States. (Of course the phrase "East German amateur athlete" is as much an oxymoron as "married bachelor," and some of those East German, er, ladies probably had interesting concoctions of hormones.)

As sports medicine and related technologies become more sophis- 7 ticated, there is anxiety about the integrity of sport. This anxiety is an intuition in search of clarifying criteria. When sprinters began using starting blocks (remember in *Chariots of Fire* each runner carried a trowel to dig toeholds in the track at the starting line) the new equipment was available to all competitors and improved performances without altering the performers. When pole vaulters abandoned stiff bamboo and metal poles in favor of flexible fiberglass poles that fling vaulters skyward, the competition remained essentially the same, although at a previously undreamed-of plateau of achievement. Perhaps we are getting close to the key that unlocks the puzzle: Techniques and technologies are unobjectionable when they improve performance without devaluing it. Proper athletics are activities all of us can attempt. The use of certain exotic drugs or techniques alters the character of an activity and devalues it by making it exotic—no longer a shared activity.

8   We should listen to the promptings of our intuitions about appropriate language. It is one thing to be intense, even obsessive about training, including nutrition. It is different to pursue edge by means of chemical technologies—drugs—that we instinctively speak of as "unnatural" manipulations of the body. Intense training should involve enhancing powers by means of measures or materials that are part of the body's normal functioning, rather than by radical interventions in the body. Interventions are radical when they are designed not just to enhance normal functioning but to cause the body to behave abnormally—not unusually well but unnaturally well.

9   Illegitimate technologies are subverting the integrity of a sport when we feel inclined to speak of "the body," not "the athlete," performing well. Technologies can blur the sense of the self-involved. We admire people who run fast, not bodies that are made fast by chemical boosters. Some athletes probably are nagged by thoughts like: "My weight-lifting achievement is not mine, it belongs to my medicine cabinet."

10   The ancient Greeks, who invented the Olympics and political philosophy, believed that sport was a religious and civic—in a word, moral—undertaking. Sport, they said, is morally serious because a noble aim of life is appreciation of worthy things, such as beauty and bravery. By using their bodies beautifully, athletes teach our souls to appreciate beauty. By competing bravely, athletes make bravery vivid and exemplary.

11   Sport is competition to demonstrate excellence in admired activities. The excellence is most praiseworthy when the activity demands virtues of the spirit—of character—as well as physical prowess. Admirable athletic attainments involve mental mastery of pain and ex-

haustion—the triumph of character, not chemistry, over adversity. We want sport to reward true grit, not sophisticated science. We do not want a child to ask an athlete, "Can I get the autograph of your pharmacist?"

—— CONSIDERATIONS ——————————————————————

1. To understand Will's parenthetical statement at the end of paragraph 6, look up "oxymoron." Find examples of that literary device and explain how it works.

2. Will mentions and deplores methods some athletes have used to gain the "competitive edge." Could these methods be labeled "hi-tech"? Might it follow that Will also would deplore advanced technology in other competitive fields: automobile manufacture, the work of popular musicians, photography, food preparation, the media? If Will were with Frank Conroy (see "A Yo-Yo Going Down") in the yo-yo contest, would he find it unfair if a boy showed up with a synthetic string that would not become snared or tangled?

3. In paragraph 4, Will overturns a common remark about winning in order to point the reader to his major concerns. How does this help him reveal his anxieties about the "integrity of sport"?

4. Will quotes the International Olympic Committee's ban in paragraph 1 and then points out certain ambiguities. Do you agree that these phrases are ambiguous? Why are we to understand ambiguity as a fault? Why is it so difficult to avoid ambiguous language? Is ambiguity ever useful? Reread Eudora Welty's comments on ambiguity in "The Point of the Story."

5. Some of Will's argument presupposes our accepting that sports are "a shared activity." To what extent are America's most popular sports football, baseball, basketball—"shared activities"? Shared with whom?

6. Admitting the difficulty of pinning down our "anxieties" and doubts about some athletic achievements, Will falls back on "intuition" and on the ideals that motivated athletes in ancient Greece. Are these ideas effective in his argument?

7. If you read the title of Will's essay aloud, you may be amused and surprised. Is the word play merely clever or does it add to the essay? Look again at Consideration 4.

Virginia Woolf (1882–1941) is best known as a novelist. The
Voyage Out *appeared in 1915, followed by* Night and Day *(1919),*
Jacob's Room *(1922),* Mrs. Dalloway *(1925),* To The Lighthouse
(1927), Orlando *(1928),* The Waves *(1931),* The Years *(1937), and*
Between the Acts, *published shortly after her death. Daughter of
Sir Leslie Stephen, Victorian critic and essayist who edited the*
Dictionary of National Biography, *she was educated at home
and began her literary career as a critic for the* Times Literary
Supplement. *She wrote essays regularly until her death; four
volumes of her* Collected Essays *appeared in the United States
in 1967. More recently, her publishers have issued six volumes
of her collected letters, and her diary is being published.*

*With her sister Vanessa, a painter, her husband Leonard
Woolf, an editor and writer, and Vanessa's husband Clive Bell,
an art critic, Woolf lived at the center of the Bloomsbury
group—artists and intellectuals who gathered informally to talk
and to amuse each other, and whose unconventional ideas and
habits, when they were known, shocked the stolid British
public. John Maynard Keynes, the economist, was a member of
the varied group, which also included the biographer Lytton
Strachey, the novelist E. M. Forster, and eventually the
expatriate American poet, T. S. Eliot. With her husband, Virginia
Woolf founded The Hogarth Press, a small firm dedicated to
publishing superior works. Among its authors were Eliot and
Woolf herself.*

Virginia Woolf, *a recent biography by her nephew Quentin
Bell, gives an intimate picture of the whole group. Of all the
Bloomsbury people, Woolf was perhaps the most talented.
Through most of her life, she struggled against recurring mental
illness, which brought intense depression and suicidal impulses.
When she was fifty-nine she drowned herself in the River Ouse.
The following famous passage from* A Room of One's Own
*(1929) presents a feminist argument by means of a memorable
supposition.*

87

VIRGINIA WOOLF

If Shakespeare Had Had a Sister

It is a perennial puzzle why no woman wrote a word of that 1
extraordinary [Elizabethan] literature when every other man, it seemed,
was capable of song or sonnet. What were the conditions in which
women lived, I asked myself; for fiction, imaginative work that is, is
not dropped like a pebble upon the ground, as science may be; fiction is
like a spider's web, attached ever so lightly perhaps, but still attached
to life at all four corners. Often the attachment is scarcely perceptible;
Shakespeare's plays, for instance, seem to hang there complete by
themselves. But when the web is pulled askew, hooked up at the edge,
torn in the middle, one remembers that these webs are not spun in
midair by incorporeal creatures, but are the work of suffering human
beings, and are attached to grossly material things, like health and
money and the house we live in. . . .

But what I find . . . is that nothing is known about women before 2
the eighteenth century. I have no model in my mind to turn about this
way and that. Here am I asking why women did not write poetry in the
Elizabethan age, and I am not sure how they were educated; whether
they were taught to write; whether they had sitting-rooms to themselves; how many women had children before they were twenty-one;
what, in short, they did from eight in the morning till eight at night.
They had no money, evidently; according to Professor Trevelyan they
were married whether they liked it or not before they were out of the
nursery, at fifteen or sixteen very likely. It would have been extremely
odd, even upon this showing, had one of them suddenly written the
plays of Shakespeare, I concluded, and I thought of that old gentleman,
who is dead now, but was a bishop, I think, who declared that it was
impossible for any woman, past, present, or to come, to have the genius
of Shakespeare. He wrote to the papers about it. He also told a lady who
applied to him for information that cats do not as a matter of fact go to

heaven, though they have, he added, souls of a sort. How much thinking those old gentlemen used to save one! How the borders of ignorance shrank back at their approach! Cats do not go to heaven. Women cannot write the plays of Shakespeare.

3   Be that as it may, I could not help thinking, as I looked at the works of Shakespeare on the shelf, that the bishop was right at least in this; it would have been impossible, completely and entirely, for any woman to have written the plays of Shakespeare in the age of Shakespeare. Let me imagine, since facts are so hard to come by, what would have happened had Shakespeare had a wonderfully gifted sister, called Judith, let us say. Shakespeare himself went, very probably—his mother was an heiress—to the grammar school, where he may have learnt Latin—Ovid, Virgil and Horace—and the elements of grammar and logic. He was, it is well known, a wild boy who poached rabbits, perhaps shot a deer, and had, rather sooner than he should have done, to marry a woman in the neighbourhood, who bore him a child rather quicker than was right. That escapade sent him to seek his fortune in London. He had, it seemed, a taste for the theatre; he began by holding horses at the stage door. Very soon he got work in the theatre, became a successful actor, and lived at the hub of the universe, meeting everybody, knowing everybody, practising his art on the boards, exercising his wits in the streets, and even getting access to the palace of the queen. Meanwhile his extraordinarily gifted sister, let us suppose, remained at home. She was as adventurous, as imaginative, as agog to see the world as he was. But she was not sent to school. She had no chance of learning grammar and logic, let alone of reading Horace and Virgil. She picked up a book now and then, one of her brother's perhaps, and read a few pages. But then her parents came in and told her to mend the stockings or mind the stew and not moon about with books and papers. They would have spoken sharply but kindly, for they were substantial people who knew the conditions of life for a woman and loved their daughter—indeed, more likely than not she was the apple of her father's eye. Perhaps she scribbled some pages up in an apple loft on the sly, but was careful to hide them or set fire to them. Soon, however, before she was out of her teens, she was to be betrothed to the son of a neighbouring wool-stapler. She cried out that marriage was hateful to her, and for that she was severely beaten by her father. Then he ceased to scold her. He begged her instead not to hurt him, not to shame him in this matter of her marriage. He would give her a chain of beads or a fine petticoat, he said; and there were tears in his eyes. How could she disobey him? How could she break his heart? The force of her own gift alone drove her to it.

She made up a small parcel of her belongings, let herself down by a rope one summer's night and took the road to London. She was not seventeen. The birds that sang in the hedge were not more musical than she was. She had the quickest fancy, a gift like her brother's, for the tune of words. Like him, she had a taste for the theatre. She stood at the stage door; she wanted to act, she said. Men laughed in her face. The manager—a fat, loose-lipped man—guffawed. He bellowed something about poodles dancing and women acting—no woman, he said, could possibly be an actress. He hinted—you can imagine what. She could get no training in her craft. Could she even seek her dinner in a tavern or roam the streets at midnight? Yet her genius was for fiction and lusted to feed abundantly upon the lives of men and women and the study of their ways. At last—for she was very young, oddly like Shakespeare the poet in her face, with the same grey eyes and rounded brows—at last Nick Greene the actor-manager took pity on her; she found herself with child by that gentleman and so—who shall measure the heat and violence of the poet's heart when caught and tangled in a woman's body?— killed herself one winter's night and lies buried at some cross-roads where the omnibuses now stop outside the Elephant and Castle.

That, more or less, is how the story would run, I think, if a woman 4 in Shakespeare's day had had Shakespeare's genius. But for my part, I agree with the deceased bishop, if such he was—it is unthinkable that any woman in Shakespeare's day should have had Shakespeare's genius. For genius like Shakespeare's is not born among labouring, uneducated, servile people. It was not born in England among the Saxons and the Britons. It is not born today among the working classes. How, then, could it have been born among women whose work began, according to Professor Trevelyan, almost before they were out of the nursery, who were forced to it by their parents and held to it by all the power of law and custom?

_____ **CONSIDERATIONS** _____

1. In paragraph 3, Woolf develops at length an imaginary sister of Shakespeare. Why does the writer call that sister Judith rather than Priscilla or Elizabeth or Megan? A quick look at Shakespeare's biography will give you the answer and alert you to a mischievous side of Woolf.

2. At the end of paragraph 2, Woolf says, "How the borders of ignorance shrank back at their approach!" Is this a straight statement, or does she mean something other than what the words say? Study the differences among the

following terms, which often are used mistakenly as synonyms: sarcasm, satire, irony, wit, humor, cynicism, invective, the sardonic.

3. Woolf's essay consists of four paragraphs, one of which accounts for more than half of the composition. Can you find a justification for this disproportionately long paragraph?

4. Concoct an imaginary biography, with a purpose, like Woolf's account of Judith: for example, Mozart's daughter, Napoleon's father, the brother of Jesus Christ, the Queen of Luxembourg, Tolstoy's nephew or niece.

5. "... for fiction ... is not dropped like a pebble upon the ground, as science may be ..." (paragraph 1). In what sense is science dropped like a pebble upon the ground? What is the point of this odd comparison?

6. If you were to invite three authors from this book to an informal discussion of Woolf's essay, whom would you select? Why? Make your selections on the basis of some relationship between their ideas and hers. What sort of outcome would you expect from such a conversation? Write a page of this dialogue.

7. Woolf wrote in the informal idiom of an educated Englishwoman of the 1920s; there are a number of differences between her language and ours. Circle a half dozen such differences and contrast British English with American English.

*Richard Wright (1908–1960) was born on a plantation in
Natchez, Mississippi. A restless and unruly child, he left home
at fifteen and supported himself doing unskilled work, gradually
improving his employment until he became a clerk in a post
office. In this essay from his autobiography* Black Boy *(1944) he
writes about an occasion that transformed his life. By chance he
became obsessed with the notion of reading H. L. Mencken, the
iconoclastic editor and essayist. He schemed and plotted to
borrow Mencken's books from the library, and when he
succeeded, his career as a writer began.*

*Determined to be a successful writer, Richard Wright worked
on the Federal Writers' Project, wrote for the* New Masses, *and
finally won a prize from* Story *magazine for a short novel called*
Uncle Tom's Children. *The following year, he was awarded a
Guggenheim Fellowship, and in 1940 he published his novel*
Native Son, *which has become an American classic. In 1946 he
emigrated to Paris, where he lived until his death. His later
novels include* The Outsider *(1953) and* The Long Dream *(1958).
In 1977, his publisher issued the second half of* Black Boy,
entitled American Hunger.

88

RICHARD WRIGHT
The Library Card

One morning I arrived early at work and went into the bank lobby   1
where the Negro porter was mopping. I stood at a counter and picked up
the Memphis *Commercial Appeal* and began my free reading of the
press. I came finally to the editorial page and saw an article dealing with
one H. L. Mencken. I knew by hearsay that he was the editor of the
American Mercury, but aside from that I knew nothing about him. The

article was a furious denunciation of Mencken, concluding with one, hot, short sentence: Mencken is a fool.

2 I wondered what on earth this Mencken had done to call down upon him the scorn of the South. The only people I had ever heard denounced in the South were Negroes, and this man was not a Negro. Then what ideas did Mencken hold that made a newspaper like the *Commercial Appeal* castigate him publicly? Undoubtedly he must be advocating ideas that the South did not like. Were there, then, people other than Negroes who criticized the South? I knew that during the Civil War the South had hated northern whites, but I had not encountered such hate during my life. Knowing no more of Mencken than I did at that moment, I felt a vague sympathy for him. Had not the South, which had assigned me the role of a non-man, cast at him its hardest words?

3 Now, how could I find out about this Mencken? There was a huge library near the riverfront, but I knew that Negroes were not allowed to patronize its shelves any more than they were the parks and playgrounds of the city. I had gone into the library several times to get books for the white men on the job. Which of them would now help me to get books? And how could I read them without causing concern to the white men with whom I worked? I had so far been successful in hiding my thoughts and feelings from them, but I knew that I would create hostility if I went about the business of reading in a clumsy way.

4 I weighed the personalities of the men on the job. There was Don, a Jew; but I distrusted him. His position was not much better than mine and I knew that he was uneasy and insecure; he had always treated me in an offhand, bantering way that barely concealed his contempt. I was afraid to ask him to help me get books; his frantic desire to demonstrate a racial solidarity with the whites against Negroes might make him betray me.

5 Then how about the boss? No, he was a Baptist and I had the suspicion that he would not be quite able to comprehend why a black boy would want to read Mencken. There were other white men on the job whose attitudes showed clearly that they were Kluxers or sympathizers, and they were out of the question.

6 There remained only one man whose attitude did not fit into an anti-Negro category, for I had heard the white men refer to him as a "Pope lover." He was an Irish Catholic and was hated by the white Southerners. I knew that he read books, because I had got him volumes from the library several times. Since he, too, was an object of hatred, I felt that he might refuse me but would hardly betray me. I hesitated, weighing and balancing the imponderable realities.

One morning I paused before the Catholic fellow's desk.   7

"I want to ask you a favor," I whispered to him.   8

"What is it?"   9

"I want to read. I can't get books from the library. I wonder if you'd   10
let me use your card?"

He looked at me suspiciously.   11

"My card is full most of the time," he said.   12

"I see," I said and waited, posing my question silently.   13

"You're not trying to get me into trouble, are you, boy?" he asked,   14
staring at me.

"Oh, no, sir."   15

"What book do you want?"   16

"A book by H. L. Mencken."   17

"Which one?"   18

"I don't know. Has he written more than one?"   19

"He has written several."   20

"I didn't know that."   21

"What makes you want to read Mencken?"   22

"Oh, I just saw his name in the newspaper," I said.   23

"It's good of you to want to read," he said. "But you ought to read   24
the right things."

I said nothing. Would he want to supervise my reading?   25

"Let me think," he said. "I'll figure out something."   26

I turned from him and he called me back. He stared at me quizzi-   27
cally.

"Richard, don't mention this to the other white men," he said.   28

"I understand," I said. "I won't say a word."   29

A few days later he called me to him.   30

"I've got a card in my wife's name," he said. "Here's mine."   31

"Thank you, sir."   32

"Do you think you can manage it?"   33

"I'll manage fine," I said.   34

"If they suspect you, you'll get in trouble," he said.   35

"I'll write the same kind of notes to the library that you wrote   36
when you sent me for books," I told him. "I'll sign your name."

He laughed.   37

"Go ahead. Let me see what you get," he said.   38

That afternoon I addressed myself to forging a note. Now, what   39
were the names of books written by H. L. Mencken? I did not know any
of them. I finally wrote what I thought would be a foolproof note: *Dear
Madam: Will you please let this nigger boy*—I used the word "nigger"
to make the librarian feel that I could not possibly be the author of the

note—*have some books by H. L. Mencken?* I forged the white man's name.

40   I entered the library as I had always done when on errands for whites, but I felt that I would somehow slip up and betray myself. I doffed my hat, stood a respectful distance from the desk, looked as unbookish as possible, and waited for the white patrons to be taken care of. When the desk was clear of people, I still waited. The white librarian looked at me.

41   "What do you want, boy?"

42   As though I did not possess the power of speech, I stepped forward and simply handed her the forged note, not parting my lips.

43   "What books by Mencken does he want?" she asked.

44   "I don't know, ma'am," I said, avoiding her eyes.

45   "Who gave you this card?"

46   "Mr. Falk," I said.

47   "Where is he?"

48   "He's at work, at the M——— Optical Company," I said. "I've been in here for him before."

49   "I remember," the woman said. "But he never wrote notes like this."

50   Oh, God, she's suspicious. Perhaps she would not let me have the books? If she had turned her back at that moment, I would have ducked out the door and never gone back. Then I thought of a bold idea.

51   "You can call him up, ma'am," I said, my heart pounding.

52   "You're not using these books, are you?" she asked pointedly.

53   "Oh, no, ma'am. I can't read."

54   "I don't know what he wants by Mencken," she said under her breath.

55   I knew now that I had won; she was thinking of other things and the race question had gone out of her mind. She went to the shelves. Once or twice she looked over her shoulder at me, as though she was still doubtful. Finally she came forward with two books in her hand.

56   "I'm sending him two books," she said. "But tell Mr. Falk to come in next time, or send me the names of the books he wants. I don't know what he wants to read."

57   I said nothing. She stamped the card and handed me the books. Not daring to glance at them, I went out of the library, fearing that the woman would call me back for further questioning. A block away from the library I opened one of the books and read a title: *A Book of Prefaces.* I was nearing my nineteenth birthday and I did not know how to pronounce the word "preface." I thumbed the pages and saw strange

words and strange names. I shook my head, disappointed. I looked at the other book; it was called *Prejudices.* I knew what that word meant; I had heard it all my life. And right off I was on guard against Mencken's books. Why would a man want to call a book *Prejudices?* The word was so stained with all my memories of racial hate that I could not conceive of anybody using it for a title. Perhaps I had made a mistake about Mencken? A man who had prejudices must be wrong.

When I showed the books to Mr. Falk, he looked at me and frowned. 58

"That librarian might telephone you," I warned him. 59

"That's all right," he said. "But when you're through reading those books, I want you to tell me what you get out of them." 60

That night in my rented room, while letting the hot water run over my can of pork and beans in the sink, I opened *A Book of Prefaces* and began to read. I was jarred and shocked by the style, the clear, clean sweeping sentences. Why did he write like that? And how did one write like that? I pictured the man as a raging demon, slashing with his pen, consumed with hate, denouncing everything American, extolling everything European or German, laughing at the weaknesses of people, mocking God, authority. What was this? I stood up, trying to realize what reality lay behind the meaning of the words. . . . Yes, this man was fighting, fighting with words. He was using words as a weapon, using them as one would use a club. Could words be weapons? Well, yes, for here they were. Then, maybe, perhaps, I could use them as a weapon? No. It frightened me. I read on and what amazed me was not what he said, but how on earth anybody had the courage to say it. 61

Occasionally I glanced up to reassure myself that I was alone in the room. Who were these men about whom Mencken was talking so passionately? Who was Anatole France? Joseph Conrad? Sinclair Lewis, Sherwood Anderson, Dostoevski, George Moore, Gustave Flaubert, Maupassant, Tolstoy, Frank Harris, Mark Twain, Thomas Hardy, Arnold Bennett, Stephen Crane, Zola, Norris, Gorky, Bergson, Ibsen, Balzac, Bernard Shaw, Dumas, Poe, Thomas Mann, O. Henry, Dreiser, H. G. Wells, Gogol, T. S. Eliot, Gide, Baudelaire, Edgar Lee Masters, Stendhal, Turgenev, Huneker, Nietzsche, and scores of others? Were these men real? Did they exist or had they existed? And how did one pronounce their names? 62

I ran across many words whose meanings I did not know, and I either looked them up in a dictionary or, before I had a chance to do that, encountered the word in a context that made its meaning clear. But what strange world was this? I concluded the book with the conviction 63 that I had somehow overlooked something terribly important in life. I had once tried to write, had once reveled in feeling, had let my crude imagination roam, but the impulse to dream had been slowly beaten out of me by experience. Now it surged up again and I hungered for books, new ways of looking and seeing. It was not a matter of believing or disbelieving what I read, but of feeling something new, of being affected by something that made the look of the world different.

64   As dawn broke I ate my pork and beans, feeling dopey, sleepy. I went to work, but the mood of the book would not die; it lingered, coloring everything I saw, heard, did. I now felt that I knew what the white men were feeling. Merely because I had read a book that had spoken of how they lived and thought, I identified myself with that book. I felt vaguely guilty. Would I, filled with bookish notions, act in a manner that would make the whites dislike me?

65   I forged more notes and my trips to the library became frequent. Reading grew into a passion. My first serious novel was Sinclair Lewis's *Main Street*. It made me see my boss, Mr. Gerald, and identify him as an American type. I would smile when I saw him lugging his golf bags into the office. I had always felt a vast distance separating me from the boss, and now I felt closer to him, though still distant. I felt now that I knew him, that I could feel the very limits of his narrow life. And this had happened because I had read a novel about a mythical man called George F. Babbitt.

66   The plots and stories in the novels did not interest me so much as the point of view revealed. I gave myself over to each novel without reserve, without trying to criticize it; it was enough for me to see and feel something different. And for me, everything was something different. Reading was like a drug, a dope. The novels created moods in which I lived for days. But I could not conquer my sense of guilt, my feeling that the white men around me knew that I was changing, that I had begun to regard them differently.

67   Whenever I brought a book to the job, I wrapped it in newspaper— a habit that was to persist for years in other cities and under other circumstances. But some of the white men pried into my packages when I was absent and they questioned me.

68   "Boy, what are you reading those books for?"

69   "Oh, I don't know, sir."

70   "That's deep stuff you're reading, boy."

71   "I'm just killing time, sir."

72   "You'll addle your brains if you don't watch out."

73   I read Dreiser's *Jennie Gerhardt* and *Sister Carrie* and they revived

in me a vivid sense of my mother's suffering; I was overwhelmed. I grew silent, wondering about the life around me. It would have been impossible for me to have told anyone what I derived from these novels, for it was nothing less than a sense of life itself. All my life had shaped me for the realism, the naturalism of the modern novel, and I could not read enough of them.

Steeped in new moods and ideas, I bought a ream of paper and tried   74
to write; but nothing would come, or what did come was flat beyond telling. I discovered that more than desire and feeling were necessary to write and I dropped the idea. Yet I still wondered how it was possible to know people sufficiently to write about them? Could I ever learn about life and people? To me, with my vast ignorance, my Jim Crow station in life, it seemed a task impossible of achievement. I now knew what being a Negro meant. I could endure the hunger. I had learned to live with hate. But to feel that there were feelings denied me, that the very breadth of life itself was beyond my reach, that more than anything else hurt, wounded me. I had a new hunger.

In buoying me up, reading also cast me down, made me see what   75
was possible, what I had missed. My tension returned, new, terrible, bitter, surging, almost too great to be contained. I no longer *felt* that the world about me was hostile, killing; I *knew* it. A million times I asked myself what I could do to save myself, and there were no answers. I seemed forever condemned, ringed by walls.

I did not discuss my reading with Mr. Falk, who had lent me his   76
library card; it would have meant talking about myself and that would have been too painful. I smiled each day, fighting desperately to maintain my old behavior, to keep my disposition seemingly sunny. But some of the white men discerned that I had begun to brood.

"Wake up there, boy!" Mr. Olin said one day.   77

"Sir!" I answered for the lack of a better word.   78

"You act like you've stolen something," he said.   79

I laughed in the way I knew he expected me to laugh, but I resolved   80
to be more conscious of myself, to watch my every act, to guard and hide the new knowledge that was dawning within me.

If I went north, would it be possible for me to build a new life then?   81
But how could a man build a life upon vague, unformed yearnings? I wanted to write and I did not even know the English language. I bought English grammars and found them dull. I felt that I was getting a better sense of the language from novels than from grammars. I read hard, discarding a writer as soon as I felt that I had grasped his point of view. At night the printed page stood before my eyes in sleep.

82   Mrs. Moss, my landlady, asked me one Sunday morning:

83   "Son, what is this you keep on reading?"

84   "Oh, nothing. Just novels."

85   "What you get out of 'em?"

86   "I'm just killing time," I said.

87   "I hope you know your own mind," she said in a tone which implied that she doubted if I had a mind.

88   I knew of no Negroes who read the books I liked and I wondered if any Negroes ever thought of them. I knew that there were Negro doctors, lawyers, newspapermen, but I never saw any of them. When I read a Negro newspaper I never caught the faintest echo of my preoccupation in its pages. I felt trapped and occasionally, for a few days, I would stop reading. But a vague hunger would come over me for books, books that opened up new avenues of feeling and seeing, and again I would forge another note to the white librarian. Again I would read and wonder as only the naïve and unlettered can read and wonder, feeling that I carried a secret, criminal burden about with me each day.

89   That winter my mother and brother came and we set up housekeeping, buying furniture on the installment plan, being cheated and yet knowing no way to avoid it. I began to eat warm food and to my surprise found that regular meals enabled me to read faster. I may have lived through many illnesses and survived them, never suspecting that I was ill. My brother obtained a job and we began to save toward the trip north, plotting our time, setting tentative dates for departure. I told none of the white men on the job that I was planning to go north; I knew that the moment they felt I was thinking of the North they would change toward me. It would have made them feel that I did not like the life I was living, and because my life was completely conditioned by what they said or did, it would have been tantamount to challenging them.

90   I could calculate my chances for life in the South as a Negro fairly clearly now.

91   I could fight the Southern whites by organizing with other Negroes, as my grandfather had done. But I knew that I could never win that way; there were many whites and there were but few blacks. They were strong and we were weak. Outright black rebellion could never win. If I fought openly I would die and I did not want to die. News of lynchings were frequent.

92   I could submit and live the life of a genial slave, but that was impossible. All my life had shaped me to live by my own feelings, and thoughts. I could make up to Bess and marry her and inherit the house.

But that, too, would be the life of a slave; if I did that, I would crush to death something within me, and I would hate myself as much as I knew the whites already hated those who had submitted. Neither could I ever willingly present myself to be kicked, as Shorty had done. I would rather have died than do that.

I could drain off my restlessness by fighting with Shorty and   93
Harrison. I had seen many Negroes solve the problem of being black by transferring their hatred of themselves to others with a black skin and fighting them. I would have to be cold to do that, and I was not cold and I could never be.

I could, of course, forget what I had read, thrust the whites out of   94
my mind, forget them; and find release from anxiety and longing in sex and alcohol. But the memory of how my father had conducted himself made that course repugnant. If I did not want others to violate my life, how could I voluntarily violate it myself?

I had no hope whatever of being a professional man. Not only had I   95
been so conditioned that I did not desire it, but the fulfillment of such an ambition was beyond my capabilities. Well-to-do Negroes lived in a world that was almost as alien to me as the world inhabited by whites.

What, then, was there? I held my life in my mind, in my con-   96
sciousness each day, feeling at times that I would stumble and drop it, spill it forever. My reading had created a vast sense of distance between me and the world in which I lived and tried to make a living, and that sense of distance was increasing each day. My days and nights were one long, quiet, continuously contained dream of terror, tension, and anxiety. I wondered how long I could bear it.

_____ CONSIDERATIONS _____

1. How do you heat a can of beans if you don't have a hot plate or a stove? How is Wright's answer to this question an autobiographical fact that might affect your appreciation of his essay?

2. In paragraph 65, Wright says of himself, "Reading grew into a passion." You don't have to look too far in the lives of other writers to find similar statements about reading. Reread the first paragraph of the Preface to this book, and think about the importance of reading to your prospects of improving as a writer. See also Ralph Ellison's "On Becoming a Writer."

3. Compare what Wright had to endure to use the public library with your own introduction to the same institution. How do you account for the motivation Wright needed to break the barriers between him and freedom to read?

4. The word Wright uses throughout to refer to his own race is no longer widely accepted. Why? What other words have been used at other times in American history? What difference does a name make?

5. Notice how Wright uses dialogue in this essay. How do you decide when to use dialogue? What are its purposes?

6. The authors mentioned by Wright in his essay would make a formidable reading program for anyone. If you were to lay out such a program for yourself, what titles would you include? Why?

A Rhetorical Index

The various writing patterns—argument and persuasion, description, exposition, and narration—are amply illustrated in the many essays, stories, journal entries, and poems in *A Writer's Reader.* If any classification of writing according to type is suspect—because good writers inevitably merge the types—this index offers one plausible arrangement. Anyone looking for models or examples for study and imitation may well begin here.

A word about subcategories: We index two sorts of argument—formal and implicit—because some selections are obvious attempts to defend a stated proposition, often in high style, whereas others argue indirectly, informally, or diffusely, but persuasively nonetheless. Under "Description" we index selections that primarily describe persons, places, or miscellaneous phenomena. We call "Expository" selections those that clearly show the various rhetorical patterns of development: example, classification, cause and effect, comparison and contrast, process analysis, and definition. "Narration" categorizes memoirs, essays, stories, and nonfiction nonautobiographical narratives.

At the end, we list the non-essay materials in the *Reader*—journal entries, short stories, poems, and drama.

EXPOSITION

*Analogy. See Comparison, Contrast,
Analogy*

A Thematic Index

EDUCATION, THE GETTING OF WISDOM

FAMILIES, PARENTS, AND OFFSPRING

FREEDOM AND RESTRAINT, OPPRESSORS AND OPPRESSED

HUMOR, WIT, SATIRE

NATURE, ENVIRONMENT, WONDERS OF CREATION

PLAY, GAMES, SPORTING LIFE

WORKING

WRITING, LANGUAGE, RHETORIC, AND STYLE